PERSPECTIVES ON PROMOTION AND DATABASE MARKETING

The Collected Works of Robert C Blattberg

PERSPECTIVES ON PROMOTION AND DATABASE MARKETING

The Collected Works of Robert C Blattberg

editor

Greg M Allenby

Ohio State University, USA

World Scientific

NEW JERSEY · LONDON · SINGAPORE · BEIJING · SHANGHAI · HONG KONG · TAIPEI · CHENNAI

Published by

World Scientific Publishing Co. Pte. Ltd.

5 Toh Tuck Link, Singapore 596224

USA office: 27 Warren Street, Suite 401-402, Hackensack, NJ 07601

UK office: 57 Shelton Street, Covent Garden, London WC2H 9HE

British Library Cataloguing-in-Publication Data
A catalogue record for this book is available from the British Library.

PERSPECTIVES ON PROMOTION AND DATABASE MARKETING
The Collected Works of Robert C Blattberg

ISBN-13 978-981-4287-05-0
ISBN-10 981-4287-05-9

Printed in Singapore by World Scientific Printers

Foreword

I am honored to call Robert Blattberg a great friend of mine. So, I am
delighted that I was asked to write a short foreword to this book showcasing
the research output of Robert Blattberg. He usually goes by Bob, but I
have always called him Robert, which I will continue to do. The collection
of articles in this book along with commentary by some of his doctoral
students is a magnificent testament to the genius of Robert Blattberg.

Robert Blattberg enrolled as an undergraduate at Northwestern University with the intention of majoring in business and subsequently becoming
a lawyer following his father's footsteps. Not enjoying the business school,
particularly the marketing course that he took, he switched to the College
of Arts and Sciences and graduated with a major in Mathematics. One of
the courses he did like in the business school was Operations taught by Professor Dirk Van Alysten. It was Professor Alysten who encouraged Robert
to get an advanced degree in a quantitative area of business. Taking the
advice to heart, Robert joined the Carnegie Institute of Technology, now
called Carnegie Mellon University, for his graduate work. He received his
Master's and Ph.D. degrees in Industrial Administration in 1966 and 1971
respectively. Two years prior in 1969, Robert joined the business school at
the University of Chicago as an Assistant Professor of Marketing. As Robert
describes it, the Dean of Carnegie called up the Dean of the Business School
at Chicago and recommended that Chicago take a look at him. He presented
a seminar at Chicago on his dissertation work which dealt with investigating the properties of the Durbin–Watson statistic. Actually, Robert was
given a choice between joining the Finance department or the Marketing
department. Looking at the heavyweights assembled in the Finance and
Economics departments at Chicago, Robert said, "Thank you very much, I
will take Marketing. That looks easy enough!" I may be embellishing this
story a bit, but Robert would have been just as successful in Finance as
he has been in Marketing. But then I probably would not have gotten to
know him. More importantly, the field of Marketing is fortunate that this
extraordinary individual decided to cast his die in Marketing.

The articles in this volume are organized in six parts. The first part, titled "Early Bob," traces research which he completed during the first decade after he joined Chicago. The impetus for this work is his training in econometrics and statistics at Carnegie. He published papers on the properties of the Durbin–Watson statistic, on allowing for non-normal errors in the regression model, as well as in the emerging field of stochastic brand choice models. This set concludes with the "Tracker" model, which is helpful in forecasting early sales of new products. An important feature of this model is in the use of less costly and more easily available data such as aggregate sales data and survey data to calibrate model parameters.

The second part is titled "Statistical Bob." This part comprises papers that Robert wrote in characterizing the response of consumers to dealing. The "deal-prone" segment as a term subsequently became common language in the marketing field. This body of work, almost twenty-five years old now, defined Robert's emerging interest in the area of sales promotions. Unlike earlier work in promotions which merely documented findings, Robert developed statistical models to explain and generalize consumer deal response.

The third part is titled "Promotional Bob," and covers roughly a ten year stretch from 1987 to 1996. This period was a defining time for Robert as it clearly cemented his leadership in the area of sales promotions. The publication of the book *Sales Promotions: Concepts, Methods, and Strategies*, with Scott Neslin in 1990 was a landmark event. The book, accessible to both academics and practitioners, laid out extant thinking in the area, described models to estimate the impact of consumer and trade promotions, and provided ideas for future research. Issues discussed in the book such as purchase acceleration, post-promotion dips, the importance of a good estimate of baseline sales to measure promotional impacts, short-term versus long-term effects, etc., led to burgeoning future work in the field by generation of young scholars. The marketing community as a whole profited immensely from this book.

The fourth part titled "Big Bob," describes Robert's contribution to and impact on marketing practice. Robert clearly saw the interaction between academic rigor and management practice. He was one of the earliest researchers to work with scanner panel data. He has been influential with data vendors such as Nielsen and IRI to make available scanner data sets for academic use. He started and managed the Center for Marketing Information Technology, while a professor at Chicago, and the Center for Retail Management at the Kellogg School at Northwestern University. Under his guidance, the Retail Management Center at Kellogg published a series of how-to guides for implementing category management in the grocery industry. He received the *Educator of the Year* award in 2004 from the Sales and Marketing Executives Council for his outstanding contribution to the practice of marketing.

The fifth part is titled "Direct Bob." Robert's strong empirical focus in his research naturally extended to questions such as what customer level data should be gathered, how they should be organized and linked, how they should be analyzed, and what metrics should be used to assess customer value. His first published articles in the area of database marketing and customer equity appeared almost twenty years ago, far ahead of its time. Since then, he has published several thought provoking articles on measuring customer lifetime value. Robert has carved out a clear leadership position in CRM and Database Marketing with the publication of two books, one titled *Customer Equity*, with Getz and Thomas, and a new, just released book, titled *Database Marketing*, with Kim and Neslin.

The sixth and final part titled "Micro-Macro Bob," is not genre or area specific as much as an illustration of Robert's overall research interests in marketing mix modeling. The advertising paper describes how to build an aggregate advertising-sales response model from a micro model of consumer response. The pricing paper incorporates consumer heterogeneity to generate optimal pricing decisions. Lastly, the market entry paper investigates the effect of entry by a Wal-Mart supercenter on the incumbent store.

Robert Blattberg is a remarkable individual. Quantitative marketing as a discipline started about the mid 60s with Professor Paul Green as one of the early contributors. So, the field is about 40 years old. There are only a handful of individuals who have dominated the field over this period, and Robert Blattberg is one of them. What makes him stand out is that he has been a leader in setting a research agenda. This is true of the sales promotion area, and customer equity, and database marketing. It is very rare for someone to dominate more than one area, so his impact is truly extraordinary. And, this impact cuts across the academic side as well as the practitioner side. So, how has he done this? One, he works very hard. Second, he is one of the smartest people I have met in my life. Third, he has uncompromising standards. And, he can multi-task very well so he can accomplish more in the same amount of time.

On a lighter note, in his younger days he has been mistaken for Chuck Norris. As he has gotten older, Al Pacino comes to mind. This identity confusion is mostly from Indian cab drivers who are easily confused!

Lakshman Krishnamurthi
Kellogg School of Management
Northwestern University

References

Blattberg, Robert C. and Scott A. Neslin (1990). *Sales Promotion — Concepts, Methods and Strategies*. Englewood Cliffs, New Jersey: Prentice-Hall.

Blattberg, Robert C., Gary Getz and Jacquelyn S. Thomas (2001). *Customer Equity: Building and Managing Relationships as Valuable Assets*. Boston, Mass.: Harvard Business School Press.

Blattberg, Robert C., Byung-Do Kim and Scott A. Neslin (2008). *Database Marketing — Analyzing and Managing Customers*. New York: Springer.

Contents

Part V: Direct Bob — Contributions to Customer Relationship Marketing, Direct Marketing and Database Marketing

Part VI: Micro-Macro Bob — Contributions Using Micro Consumer Models to Address Macro Marketing Problems

Part I: Early Bob — Contributions to Econometrics and Marketing

Bob graduated from Carnegie-Mellon University in June 1971, having already (September 1969) accepted a faculty position at the University of Chicago. As might be expected, his training at Carnegie emphasized the use of statistical tools to address business problems. Interestingly, his thesis work ("*Testing for Serial Correlation in Regression Models*") has very little to do with marketing. Bob's research in these early years can be viewed as a gradual transition from work grounded in econometrics to quantitative research with important implications for marketing.

This chapter reviews Bob's work from 1970, the year prior to his graduation from Carnegie, through 1978, the year that the TRACKER model appeared in print. Bob's early work showcases his training in statistical distribution theory, time series analysis, non-standard methods of model calibration, and Bayesian decision theory. Many of these tools proved useful in a marketing setting as he developed new methods of identifying consumer segments using household purchase panel data. This work is particularly interesting because it anticipates later research in marketing science investigating consumer heterogeneity with respect to marketing mix response (parameter heterogeneity) and type of decision rule (structural heterogeneity). The TRACKER model is a departure from all of Bob's previous research because it deals with the use of survey data to calibrate a macro-flow model of consumer behavior. Nevertheless, the work on TRACKER is illustrative of Bob's belief that marketing models must yield actionable insights for managers.

Econometric Methods

Bob's work in this area began with his thesis research on the Durbin Watson (DW) statistic. The setting for this problem is a regression model in which the errors are correlated over time. The DW statistic analyzes regression residuals to determine whether or not the errors are serially correlated. If errors are found to be correlated, the standard advice is to recalibrate the regression taking into account an AR(1) (first order autoregressive) error process. In one of his first articles, Bob shows that the DW test can attain statistical significance under a wide variety of serially correlated error models (Blattberg, 1973). For this reason, the standard advice — assume AR(1) and recalibrate the model — is wrong. Instead, the analyst must use time series procedures to identify the correct type of error process before recalibrating the model.

Bob's interest in the properties of regression model errors stimulated additional econometric work. This work is based on the idea that errors need not be normally distributed. Instead, the errors may be better represented by some type of symmetric-stable distribution (such as the Cauchy). Relative to the normal distribution, a symmetric-stable distribution has much fatter tails, and can generate extreme outcomes with considerable frequency. Symmetric-stable distributions have found applications in finance (modeling stock market returns) and in statistics (modeling outliers in regression analysis). Bob points out that symmetric-stable errors are probably more realistic if the error in the model represents omitted economic variables. It is interesting to note, however, that the Student t (another fat-tailed distribution) fits stock return data better than a symmetric-stable distribution (Blattberg and Gonedes, 1974).

Why are symmetric-stable distributions important to an applied researcher? One answer is that the methodology used to estimate the parameters of a regression model should depend upon the assumed error process. In two articles, Bob examines the properties of alternatives to ordinary least squares (OLS) in calibrating regression parameters (Blattberg and Sargent 1971, Blattberg and Stivers 1970). The key idea is that OLS is based upon a sum of squared errors loss function. In contrast, a sum of absolute errors (SAE) loss function works better as a model calibration criterion when the researcher expects to find occasional large residuals generated by a symmetric-stable error. Specialized programming, however, is required to implement the SAE algorithm.

These articles do not directly touch on research issues in marketing. However, they show an ability to implement non-standard models and a willingness to question conventional wisdom in analyzing data. Both of these qualities are evident in Bob's work on the use of panel data to undercover market segments. This work is discussed next.

Market Segmentation

Bob started his academic career in the age of stochastic brand choice (SBC) models in marketing. It is impossible here to provide a detailed discussion of this important stage in the development of marketing science. Briefly, SBC models permit the analysis of strings of binary purchase indicators (1 = purchase, 0 = no purchase) found in consumer panel data. The goal is to find statistical models that accurately describe consumer grocery shopping behavior. Although marketing mix variables are typically absent in a SBC model, impacts of marketing mix changes can be determined by using forecasts from a SBC model as a benchmark in a before-after study design.

The primary focus of most SBC models is the order of the choice process. The Zero Order model assumes that consumers make purchases in accordance with their long-run preferences, without taking into account what has been purchased on the previous occasion. The First Order model (known more commonly as a Markov model) generalizes the Zero Order model to allow the current purchase probability to depend on the brand that was purchased on the previous purchase occasion. Other models, such as the Linear Learning model, effectively assume an infinite order process in which purchase probabilities continually update as a function of the entire sequence of previous purchases. Against this background of models, Bob's work in the SBC area is based upon an elaborate typology of First Order models.

Bob's major contribution to the SBC area is the development of an approach to market segmentation based upon fitting SBC models to consumer panel data. The key elements of the approach are discussed in Blattberg and Sen (1974): (a) using exploratory data analysis, define a set of SBC models, each describing the purchase behavior of a segment of consumers, (b) allocate each consumer in a panel dataset into one SBC segment using statistical analysis of the consumer's purchase history, and (c) develop a profile for each segment by examining demographic and psychographic variables of the consumers known to be in the segment.

Although this general approach is often followed today, it was a major departure from the clustering approaches to segmentation popular in the 1960's and early 1970's. In modern terminology, the Blattberg Sen approach amounts to defining segments on the basis of structural heterogeneity: the idea that different consumers make choices using different types of decision rules. Moreover, because the parameters of each SBC model are tailored to the purchase data of a particular consumer, the Blattberg–Sen approach also allows for heterogeneity in the response parameters of consumers within each SBC group. These path-breaking ideas stimulated research by Greg Allenby and myself on (discrete) latent class and (continuous) Hierarchical Bayes representations of consumer heterogeneity in panel data.

Bob's continuing collaboration with Subrata Sen in the 1970s allowed the SBC segmentation approach to be further refined. Blattberg and Sen (1975) show how panel data purchase histories can be analyzed using Bayesian decision theory to decide the SBC segment membership of a particular consumer. Blattberg and Sen (1976) explain how different types of Markov models can be generated in order to create a wide variety of SBC segments for analysis. Taken together, these two papers effectively provide a blueprint for implementing the SBC segment approach.

The work by Blattberg, Peacock and Sen (1976) is particularly interesting because it uses the SBC segmentation approach to study whether consumer decision rules are consistent across different product categories. This project goes further than previous work by developing SBC models for both brand choice (within a category) and store choice. The general conclusion — that similarity in competitive structure and marketing mix activity yields similarity in decision rules — is intriguing and anticipates (by at least 20 years) the current research activity on multiple category choice.

The TRACKER Model

The work on the TRACKER new product model, reported in Blattberg and Golanty (1978), is the result of a collaboration between Bob and the Leo Burnett advertising agency. TRACKER is designed to forecast the long-run sales of frequently purchased consumer packaged goods (CPG) using two sources of information: consumer survey data and early results (usually three months) from an ongoing test market experiment.

The underlying approach is a type of macro-flow model. Consumers are assumed to move through different stages of the decision process (awareness, trial, repeat) based upon marketing mix activity (such as advertising and price) and product experience. The model, however, is completely aggregate in nature. As suggested by the name, TRACKER keeps track of the number of consumers in each stage of the decision process, altering the rate of flow between one state and another according to marketing mix activity and reactions to the product itself. By restricting the analysis to variables measurable in aggregate data, TRACKER yields excellent forecasts early in the test market without incurring the substantial costs of an ongoing consumer purchase panel.

In a historical sense, TRACKER is one of a number of new product forecasting models developed by marketers in the 1960s and 1970s using tools from operations research, statistics, and psychometrics. However, TRACKER is also a bridge between Bob's work on market segmentation and his later work on promotions and brand price competition. One of Bob's criticisms of the SBC approach — mentioned repeatedly in his articles — is the lack of an explicit role for marketing mix variables. In contrast, the TRACKER model allows marketing mix variables to alter the sales pattern both in the short run and in the long run. In later chapters, it will become clear that Bob's research after 1978 increasingly emphasized the role of price in the consumer purchase decision.

Some Personal Comments

The year 1979 marks my entrance to the Marketing doctoral program at the University of Chicago. I remember meeting with Bob early in my studies, and discussing the thesis process. He made two points, based upon his experiences both as doctoral student at Carnegie and later as a young Assistant Professor at Chicago. First, although the faculty can provide guidance, a doctoral student must learn to do research on his or her own. Self-sufficiency is particularly important for a young faculty member attempting to establish a research record. Second, each research project will be continually criticized — and often this criticism is either unfair or completely wrong. In fact, as the research becomes more innovative, the criticism becomes more intense. An academic must believe in the quality of his or her own research, and fight to convince the academic community of its value.

I cannot say that I welcomed this advice at the time. However, having been in academic marketing now for almost 25 years, Bob's advice has been repeatedly validated, both in my own career and in the careers of other marketing academics. In advising my own doctoral students, I often find myself making the same points.

I usually add one additional piece of advice in talking to my students. Bob's career shows adaptability, the ability to develop an interesting new idea and then to implement it using available data sources. Bob's training at Carnegie was largely in regression analyses of aggregate data. Nevertheless, after arriving at Chicago and obtaining access to the Chicago Tribune diary panel data, he was able to formulate a new approach to market segmentation and to quickly implement the methodology. This was only possible because he was open to new ideas and had strong statistical training while in graduate school. Bob has shown us all how to develop innovative research throughout a long and productive academic career. Thank you, Bob.

Gary Russell
Tippie College of Business
University of Iowa

References

Blattberg, R. and S. Stivers (1970). A Statistical Evaluation of Transit Promotions, *Journal of Marketing Research*, 7 (August), 293–299.

Blattberg, R. and T. Sargent (1971). Regression with Non-Gaussian Disturbances: Some Sampling Results, *Econometrica*, 39 (May), 501–510.

Blattberg, R. and S. Sen (1973). An Evaluation of the Application of Minimum Chi-Squared Procedures to Stochastic Models of Brand Choice, *Journal of Marketing Research*, 10 (November), 421–427.

Blattberg, R. (1973). Evaluation of the Power of the Durbin-Watson Statistic for Non-First Order Serial Correlation Alternatives, *Review of Economics and Statistics*, 55 (November), 508–515.

Blattberg, R. and S. Sen (1974). Market Segmentation Using Models of Multidimensional Purchasing Behavior, *Journal of Marketing*, 38 (October), 17–28.

Blattberg, R. and Nicholas J. Gonedes (1974). A Comparison of the Stable and Student Distributions as Statistical Models for Stock Prices, *The Journal of Business*, 47 (April), 244–280.

Blattberg, R. and S. Sen (1975). A Bayesian Technique to Discriminate Between Stochastic Models of Brand Choice, *Management Science*, 21 (February), 682–696.

Blattberg, R. and S. Sen (1976). Market Segments and Stochastic Brand Choice Models, *Journal of Marketing Research*, 13 (February), 34–45.

Blattberg, R., P. Peacock and S. Sen (1976). Purchase Strategies Across Product Categories, *Journal of Consumer Research*, 3 (December), 143–154.

Blattberg, R. and J. Golanty (1978). TRACKER: An Early Test Market Forecasting and Diagnostic Model for New Product Planning, *Journal of Marketing Research*, 40 (May), 192–202.

Econometrica, Vol. 39, No. 3 (May, 1971)

REGRESSION WITH NON-GAUSSIAN STABLE DISTURBANCES: SOME SAMPLING RESULTS[1]

BY ROBERT BLATTBERG AND THOMAS SARGENT

1. INTRODUCTION

ECONOMISTS OFTEN use the basic regression model

$$(1) \qquad y_j = BX_j + U_j \qquad\qquad (j = 1, \ldots, T),$$

where y_j is the dependent variable at j, X is a nonstochastic independent variable at j, B is a parameter, and the U_j's are independent, identically distributed random variables with mean zero. Economists usually estimate the parameter B by using the method of least squares. Aside from its computational simplicity, this method derives much of its popularity from the existence of the Gauss-Markov theorem and the central limit theorem.

The Gauss-Markov theorem states that if the U_j's in (1) follow a distribution with finite variance, then the least squares estimator has the minimum variance of all linear unbiased estimators of B. The central limit theorem is important because it establishes a foundation for hypothesis testing. It states that the sum of a large number of independently distributed variates, *each of which follows a distribution with finite variance*, will tend to be normally distributed. The relevance of this theorem is seen when it is recalled that the U_j's in (1) are usually said to represent the impact on the y_j's of the sum of a very large number of omitted independent variables, each of which is itself insufficiently important to include in the regression. If these omitted variables follow distributions with finite variances and if they enter additively, the U_j's will be normally distributed. This permits us to make the usual t and F tests. In addition, it means that least squares is the maximum likelihood estimator.

The assumption that the U_j's or the variates underlying them have a finite variance thus occupies an important role in justifying the use of least squares. In view of this fact, the accumulating body of evidence which suggests that many economic variables are best characterized as having infinite variances acquires special relevance.[2] If the omitted variables whose impacts are summarized by the U_j's have infinite variances, the assumptions of the central limit theorem fail to hold and the U_j's will not be normally distributed. Moreover, it is likely that the U_j's will be characterized by an infinite variance. Hence, that part of the Gauss-Markov theorem which demonstrates the minimum variance or efficiency property of least squares is no longer applicable. Thus in a world of infinite variances, both

[1] The authors thank John R. Meyer, Richard Roll, and the participants in seminars at the University of Toronto, University of Chicago, and the National Bureau of Economic Research for their helpful comments. A version of this paper was presented at the December, 1968 meetings of the Econometric Society.

[2] For example, see [2, 7, 8, and 11].

502   R. BLATTBERG AND T. SARGENT

the efficiency of least squares and the applicability of normal distribution theory for hypothesis testing are lost.

This paper investigates the performance of various estimators of B where the U_j's in (1) follow distributions which have fatter extreme tails than does the normal distribution. More precisely, we begin by investigating the consequences of the assumption that the U_j's follow a member of the class of symmetric stable Paretian distributions, a class which contains distributions with infinite variances.[3] The symmetric stable Paretian distributions are defined by the log characteristic function

$$(2) \qquad \log \phi_u(t) = i\delta t - |\sigma t|^\alpha$$

where t is a real number, α is the characteristic exponent, δ the location parameter, and $|\sigma|^\alpha$ a scale parameter. Inspection of (2) reveals that where $\alpha = 2$, the distribution is normal with mean δ and variance $2|\sigma|^\alpha$. If $\alpha = 1$, the distribution is Cauchy with central tendency δ and semi-interquartile range σ. Differentiation of (2) demonstrates that where α is less than two, only absolute moments of order less than α exist.[4] Hence, for α less than two, the variance is infinite, although the mean exists provided that α is strictly greater than one.

An important characteristic of this class of distributions is that they are stable or invariant under addition. That is, a sum of independent symmetric stable variates with characteristic exponent α will also be distributed according to a symmetric stable distribution with the same parameter α.[5] In addition, the stable Paretian distributions possess a domain-of-attraction property which generalizes the classical central limit theorem. In view of the body of evidence which suggests that many economic variables have infinite variances, the standard use of the central limit theorem to support the assumption that the U_j's in (1) are normally distributed thus actually suggests the weaker condition that the U_j's follow a stable distribution.

In this paper we investigate the performance of two types of estimators which have been suggested for use in the context of stable disturbances. The first type is the class of best (minimum dispersion) linear unbiased estimators which has been proposed by Wise [13]. The second is the estimator which minimizes the sum of absolute errors in (1). These estimators are discussed in Section 2. Section 3 then presents the results of some sampling experiments designed to assess the performances of these estimators. Our conclusions are stated in Section 4.

2. ALTERNATIVE ESTIMATORS

Wise [13] has suggested generalizing the concept of best linear unbiased estimator to include the case where disturbances are stable Paretian. As far as we

---

[3] For a description of the properties of stable distributions, see Feller [4].

[4] Recall that by differentiating the log characteristic function n times with respect to t and evaluating the result at $t = 0$, the nth cumulant of the distribution is obtained. The moments can then be obtained from the cumulants in the standard way.

[5] This can be proved easily by using the theorem that the log characteristic function of a sum of independently distributed variables is the sum of their log characteristic functions.

know, however, Wise has not written down an analytic expression for such estimators. For this reason, we present a derivation of the best linear unbiased estimator of B in equation (1) where the disturbances are distributed according to a symmetric stable distribution. Following Wise, we seek that estimator of B in (1) which is a linear function of the y_j's ($b(\alpha) = \Sigma_j\, C_j y_j$), which minimizes the dispersion parameter of $b(\alpha)$ (which is proportional to $\Sigma_j\, |C_j|^\alpha$), and which is unbiased, requiring that $\Sigma_j\, C_j X_j = 1$.

To see that the dispersion parameter of $b(\alpha)$ is proportional to $\Sigma_j\, |C_j|^\alpha$, recall that the U_j's have log characteristic functions given by $\log \phi_u(t) = -|\sigma t|^\alpha$. The estimator $b(\alpha)$ is given by the following linear combination of the U_j's:

$$b(\alpha) = B \sum_j C_j X_j + \sum_j C_j U_j$$

where $\Sigma_j\, C_j X_j = 1$. Then the log characteristic function of $b(\alpha)$ is given by

$$(3) \qquad \log \varphi_b(t) = iBt - |\sigma t|^\alpha \sum_j |C_j|^\alpha.$$

Since σ is a constant, by minimizing $\Sigma_j\, |C_j|^\alpha$ we minimize the scale parameter or dispersion of the distribution of $b(\alpha)$. Notice that for the normal distribution ($\alpha = 2$), this leads to minimizing the variance of the estimator.

Where $\alpha > 1$ the conditional minimization is performed by minimizing the Lagrangian expression

$$J = \sum_j |C_j|^\alpha - \lambda\!\left(\sum_j C_j X_j - 1\right)$$

where λ is the undetermined Lagrangian multiplier. The first order conditions are

$$(4) \qquad \frac{\partial J}{\partial C_j} = \alpha |C_j|^{\alpha-1}\, \text{sign}\, C_j - \lambda X_j = 0 \qquad\qquad (j = 1, \ldots, T),$$

$$\frac{\partial J}{\partial \lambda} = \sum_j C_j X_j - 1 = 0.$$

Rearranging (4) we have

$$(5) \qquad \alpha |C_j|^{\alpha-1}\, \text{sign}\, C_j = \lambda |X_j|\, \text{sign}\, X_j \qquad\qquad (j = 1, \ldots, T).$$

Notice that $\alpha |C_j|^{\alpha-1} > 0$ $(j = 1, \ldots, T)$, and that $\lambda |X_j|$ is either positive or negative for all j depending on the sign of λ. If it is negative, $\text{sign}\, C_j = -\text{sign}\, X_j$ for all j. But since $\Sigma_j\, C_j X_j = 1$, then $\text{sign}\, C_j$ must equal $\text{sign}\, X_j$ for all j. Thus, multiplying (5) by $\text{sign}\, X_j$, we have

$$\alpha |C_j|^{\alpha-1} = \lambda |X_j|,$$

$$(6) \qquad |C_j|^{\alpha-1} = \frac{\lambda}{\alpha}|X_j|,$$

$$|C_j| = \left(\frac{\lambda}{\alpha}\right)^{1/(\alpha-1)} |X_j|^{1/(\alpha-1)}.$$

504   R. BLATTBERG AND T. SARGENT

Hence

$$(7) \qquad C_j = \left(\frac{\lambda}{\alpha}\right)^{1/(\alpha-1)} |X_j|^{1/(\alpha-1)} \operatorname{sign} X_j.$$

We also have that

$$C_j X_j = C_j |X_j| \operatorname{sign} X_j = \left(\frac{\lambda}{\alpha}\right)^{1/(\alpha-1)} |X_j|^{\alpha/(\alpha-1)}.$$

Then

$$\sum C_j X_j = \left(\frac{\lambda}{\alpha}\right)^{1/(\alpha-1)} \sum_j |X_j|^{\alpha/(\alpha-1)} = 1$$

and

$$(8) \qquad \left(\frac{\lambda}{\alpha}\right)^{1/(\alpha-1)} = \frac{1}{\sum_j |X_j|^{\alpha/(\alpha-1)}}.$$

Substituting (8) into (7) we have

$$C_j = \frac{1}{\sum_j |X_j|^{\alpha/(\alpha-1)}} |X_j|^{1/(\alpha-1)} \operatorname{sign} X_j.$$

Thus for $\alpha > 1$, $b(\alpha)$ is given by

$$(9) \qquad b(\alpha) = \frac{\sum_j |X_j|^{1/(\alpha-1)} y_j \operatorname{sign} X_j}{\sum_j |X_j|^{\alpha/(\alpha-1)}}.$$

Notice that for $\alpha = 2$ we have

$$b(2) = \frac{\sum X_j y_j}{\sum X_j^2}$$

which is the familiar ordinary least squares estimator. For $\alpha = 1$, the Cauchy case, the best linear unbiased estimator has the form

$$b(1) = \frac{y_\tau}{X_\tau}$$

where τ corresponds to the observation which satisfies $X_\tau = \max_j X_j$.

In addition to several members of the class of best linear unbiased estimators (BLUE), we have included in this study the minimum sum of absolute errors (MSAE) estimator which Mandelbrot [8] and Fama [2], among others, have suggested might be used in the context of Paretian disturbances where α is less than two. The MSAE estimator was initially developed by Charnes, Cooper, and Ferguson [1] and was studied further by Wagner [12] and Fisher [5]. The estimator minimizes the criterion $\Sigma_j |u_j|$ where $u_j = y_j - \hat{b} x_j$, $j = 1, \ldots, T$, and where $\hat{b}$ is the MSAE estimate. The estimator is calculated using a linear programming algorithm. The solution has the form $\hat{b} = y_l/X_l$ where l is the observation in the optimal basis. Since it places less weight on extreme observations than does least squares, MSAE seems a natural estimator to apply in cases where extreme observations occur more frequently than where the disturbances are normally distributed. To make this a bit more precise, suppose that the U_j's in (1) are independently and identically distributed according to the second law of Laplace (two-tailed exponential distribution) with density function

$$f(U_j) = \frac{1}{2\lambda} \exp\left(-\frac{|U_j|}{\lambda}\right)$$

where the variance of U_j is given by $2\lambda^2$. This distribution is of some interest in the context of this paper, since it shares with the non-Gaussian stable distributions the property that, relative to the normal distribution, it is both more peaked and also denser in the extreme tails. If the U_j's follow this distribution, the likelihood function associated with (1) is given by

$$L = \left[\frac{1}{2\lambda}\right]^T \exp\left(-\frac{1}{\lambda} \sum_{j=1}^{T} |y_j - bX_j|\right).$$

The log of the likelihood function is then

$$\log L = T \log\left[\frac{1}{2\lambda}\right] - \frac{1}{\lambda} \sum_{j=1}^{T} |y_j - bX_j|,$$

which is maximized by minimizing $\Sigma_j |y_j - bX_j|$. This establishes that MSAE is the maximum likelihood estimator where the disturbances follow the second law of Laplace. The maximum likelihood property of the MSAE estimator in the context of such a fat-tailed distribution of disturbances suggests that it may be a good estimator in the context of other fat-tailed distributions like the non-Gaussian stable distributions.

To summarize, where the U_j's in (1) are assumed to be distributed according to a stable symmetric Paretian distribution with $\alpha > 1$ and mean zero, we propose to investigate the performance of the following estimators: (i) ordinary least squares (OLS); (ii) a class of best linear unbiased estimators which includes OLS as a special case; (iii) minimum sum of absolute errors (MSAE).

Under the assumed conditions, all three estimators are consistent, least squares and the best linear unbiased estimators also being known to be unbiased. Although we know of no proof of its lack of bias, the Monte Carlo studies summarized below convinced us that MSAE also is probably an unbiased estimator. Hence, our main interest centers on the relative efficiencies of the estimators. In the next section, we present the results of some sampling studies designed to assess this dimension of the estimators' performance.

3. SAMPLING RESULTS

Inclusion of MSAE among the estimators studied here introduces problems. Unlike the BLUE estimators, no analytic expression can be written down for the MSAE estimator. MSAE can only be calculated by applying a linear programming algorithm to the data at hand. This inability to write down a closed expression for the estimator makes it very difficult to determine its distribution. We are unaware of any analytic results on the sampling properties of the estimator, aside from the discussion of MSAE's consistency in Charnes, Cooper, and Ferguson [1]. In the face of the analytical intractability of MSAE, we propose to use sampling studies to throw some light on the properties of the various estimators.

In addition to OLS and MSAE, the performances of the $b(\alpha)$ estimators $b(1.1)$, $b(1.3)$, $b(1.5)$, $b(1.7)$, and $b(1.9)$ were studied in sampling or "Monte Carlo" experiments. For each experiment one hundred replications of fifty observations each were generated. The X_j's were generated according to the scheme $X_j = .3X_{j-1} + e_j$ where the e_j's were independent, identically distributed random variables distributed uniformly on the interval [40, 120]. The same X_j's were used throughout the study since this corresponds to the standard specification about the fixity of the independent variables used in regression analysis.[6] The U_j's, distributed according to a stable symmetric Paretian distribution with expected value zero, were produced by the method of Fama and Roll [3]. The y_j's were then generated from the model $y_j = BX_j + U_j (j = 1, \ldots, 50)$, for each replication. For each experiment, B equaled three.

Separate experiments were run for U_j's with the following six values of α: 1.1, 1.3, 1.5, 1.7, 1.9, and 2. Since one has to specify a value of α prior to calculating the $b(\alpha)$ estimator, the fact that we include such estimators for several α's for each experiment will thus provide us information on the loss associated with calculating the estimator $b(\alpha_1)$ when the value of α characterizing the disturbances is some $\alpha_2 \neq \alpha_1$.

For each estimator, equation (1) was estimated for the one hundred replications of each experiment. The resulting sample of one hundred estimates of B was viewed as an estimate of the population distribution of the estimator. Two measures of the dispersion of the estimates were calculated for each such sample distribution. The first is the mean absolute deviation (MAD) of the estimated values from the true value. The MAD associated with the estimator $\hat{b}$ is defined as

$$\text{MAD}(\hat{b}) = \sum_{i=1}^{100} \frac{|\hat{b}_i - B|}{100}$$

where i is an index running over replications.

The second measure is an estimate of the dispersion parameter σ of the characteristic function of the estimator. This seems an interesting measure since the BLUE estimators, being linear combinations of the U_j's, are distributed according to

---

[6] Sets of experiments were also carried out for X's generated by several other schemes. The results agreed in all important respects with those reported in the text.

symmetric stable Paretian distributions with characteristic parameter α equal to that of the U_j's. The estimator of σ was

$$S(\hat{b}) = \frac{\hat{b}_{.72} - \hat{b}_{.28}}{1.654}$$

where $\hat{b}_f$ is the f th fractile of the sample distribution of the estimates b. Fama and Roll [3] have shown that this estimator possesses an asymptotic bias of less than four-tenths of one per cent. However, its distribution in finite samples is not known. Of course, for the $b(\alpha)$ estimators, population values of the dispersion parameter can be calculated analytically using relation (3) given above. We report the population values below, but in addition it seems worthwhile to report $S(\hat{b})$ for the linear estimators both to serve as a rough check on the character of our sample and to make possible the comparison of MSAE and $b(\alpha)$ estimators on the basis of the same set of data.

The results of our experiments are recorded in Tables I and II. We refer first to Table I which reports $S(\hat{b})$ for each estimator and in parentheses the corresponding population value of the dispersion parameter for the linear estimators only. It is seen that $S(\hat{b})$ generally understates the population value, although the amount of the discrepancy varies both with α and $b(\alpha)$. Because of this bias in the empirical values of $S(\hat{b})$, it seems best to compare the estimated $S(\hat{b})$ for the linear estimators with the $S(\hat{b})$ associated with the MSAE estimator. Actually, however, the differences between the $S(\hat{b})$'s and their population values are quite small relative to the differences which exist betw·~n $S(\hat{b})$ for MSAE and the linear estimators, so that none of our conclusions would be altered by comparing $S(\hat{b})$ for MSAE with the population values of the dispersion parameter of the linear estimators.

Several features stand out in the empirical results in Table I. First, MSAE out-performs OLS for α less than 1.7 while OLS does better for α exceeding 1.7. The

TABLE I[a]

VALUES OF $S(\hat{b}) = (\hat{b}_{.72} - \hat{b}_{.28})/1.654$

α	MSAE	$b(1.1)$	$b(1.3)$	$b(1.5)$	$b(1.7)$	$b(1.9)$	OLS
1.1	.0132	.0466	.0521	.0533	.0559	.0575	.0587
		(.0550)	(.0578)	(.0596)	(.0607)	(.0613)	(.0616)
1.3	.0151	.0374	.0333	.0367	.0395	.0412	.0425
		(.0382)	(.0348)	(.0350)	(.0354)	(.0357)	(.0358)
1.5	.0151	.0276	.0241	.0211	.0218	.0223	.0223
		(.0299)	(.0241)	(.0238)	(.0239)	(.0240)	(.0240)
1.7	.0151	.0223	.0176	.0161	.0139	.0141	.0144
		(.0252)	(.0184)	(.0178)	(.0177)	(.0177)	(.0177)
1.9	.0137	.0201	.0147	.0137	.0132	.0115	.0115
		(.0222)	(.0149)	(.0141)	(.0140)	(.0140)	(.0140)
2.0	.0157	.0210	.0117	.0116	.0116	.0116	.0115
		(.0212)	(.0137)	(.0129)	(.0127)	(.0127)	(.0126)

[a] Based on one hundred replications for each experiment. Sample size was fifty for each replication. True values of σ are enclosed in parentheses beneath values of $S(\hat{b})$ for linear estimators.

                    R. BLATTBERG AND T. SARGENT

performance of OLS relative to MSAE diminishes steadily as α is decreased from two toward one. This outcome provides support for Mandelbrot's and Fama's proposal that MSAE be used where Paretian disturbances seem likely. For α less than 1.5, the relative superiority of MSAE is quite large, while for higher α's the relative margin in favor of OLS is much smaller. MSAE thus appears to be more robust than OLS over a range of α's.

Second, in both the empirical and theoretical data, the minimum dispersion BLUE estimator is always associated with the α actually characterizing the disturbances. In addition, the dispersion increases as the α assumed in calculating the estimator increasingly departs from the α characterizing the disturbances. However, the costs in efficiency of misspecifying α appear to be fairly small for all but very large mistakes, e.g., specifying α to be 1.1 when it is in fact 2.

Third, notice that for small α, MSAE out-performs even the best of the BLUE estimators by a sizable margin. Again, this outcome supports Mandelbrot's and Fama's advocacy of MSAE estimation. It suggests that in the face of Paretian disturbances, development of MSAE regression is a more promising path than developing the linear estimators proposed by Wise.

The results in Table II, which reports the MAD statistics, are very similar to those based on $S(\hat{b})$ and there is no need to comment on them in detail.

The pattern of these results seems entirely sensible. As α diminishes from two toward one, the tails of the distribution of disturbances become fatter and fatter and the performance of MSAE relative to OLS improves. What is perhaps more interesting is the relative robustness of MSAE across a variety of α's generating the U_j's.

On the basis of our results, a two-stage estimator may seem appropriate. Suppose we estimate equation (1), $y_j = BX_j + U_j$, by any of the estimators discussed above, say least squares. Each of these estimators is consistent, and hence $\hat{U}_j = y_j - \hat{B}X_j$, where $\hat{B}$ is the estimate of B, is a consistent estimator of U_j. By using these residuals, it is possible to estimate the α characterizing the disturbances. Then on the basis of Table I and this estimate of α, a more efficient estimator of B can be obtained, say by using MSAE, if the estimated α is less than 1.5. Preliminary experimentation with this procedure has convinced us that one can get quite a good estimate of α

TABLE II[a]

MEAN ABSOLUTE DEVIATION

α	MSAE	$b(1.1)$	$b(1.3)$	$b(1.5)$	$b(1.7)$	$b(1.9)$	OLS
1.1	.0162	.0996	.1249	.1436	.1537	.1601	.1623
1.3	.0169	.0534	.0527	.0572	.0600	.0618	.0625
1.5	.0172	.0355	.0299	.0307	.0317	.0324	.0326
1.7	.0174	.0270	.0199	.0199	.0202	.0204	.0205
1.9	.0174	.0226	.0151	.0146	.0147	.0148	.0148
2.0	.0174	.0213	.0136	.0131	.0131	.0132	.0132

[a] Based on one hundred replications for each experiment. Sample size equals fifty.

using the residuals as estimates of the disturbances. This suggests that such a two-stage procedure may be promising.

4. CONCLUSIONS

The results of previous sections suggest several conclusions. First, the MSAE estimator performs sufficiently well that it deserves further study and elaboration. In particular, the sampling theory of the estimator needs to be developed. In conjunction with the Monte Carlo results presented in Section 3, the large body of evidence suggesting that many economic variables are best described as being generated by non-Gaussian stable distributions makes the case in favor of MSAE estimation very strong. At the very least, the method deserves further study.

Second, the relative superiority of MSAE over OLS appears to be sufficiently large for small α (say less than 1.5) that it may be profitable for economists to begin to estimate the α's characterizing the residuals in their models. Then the application of a two-stage procedure such as that described in Section 3 may be useful.

Third, it seems fairly clear that the relative superiority of MSAE over OLS will hold for many fat-tailed distributions of disturbances that are not stable. For example, it is possible to show that MSAE out-performs OLS for various fat-tailed distributions of disturbances that are formed by blending normal and uniform distributions.[7] Although these distributions have finite variances, they are denser over portions of the extreme tails than is the normal distribution. These results suggest that one need not rely on acceptance of the stable Paretian model as a description of the disturbances in order to justify the use of the MSAE estimator. Of course, this point is also suggested by the maximum likelihood property of MSAE in the context of disturbances with a Laplace distribution.

Finally, it is interesting to speculate whether our results might provide an explanation of the rather remarkable outcome of an important experiment involving MSAE and several least-squares-based estimators recently reported by Meyer and Glauber [9]. Meyer and Glauber estimated a model of the determination of investment expenditures by several techniques including MSAE and OLS.[8] Then the estimates produced by each estimator were used to forecast investment for periods extending beyond the data employed in estimating the model. These forecast values were then compared with the actual values in order to assess the accuracy of the forecasts produced by the various estimators. On virtually every criterion (e.g., squared error, mean absolute deviation) MSAE out-performed the other estimators in the forecast period. Jorgenson [6] has cited these results as evidence that the equation employed to forecast was misspecified. However, while this is a possibility, it is not clear that MSAE is any less sensitive to specification errors than the other techniques used by Meyer and Glauber. An alternative explanation of the results is that they flow from the property of the MSAE estimator

---

[7] Demonstration of this proposition is contained in a manuscript by the authors which is available on request. Also, see Press [10] for a discussion of some related points.

[8] The others were a least squares estimator with a priori constraints imposed on some parameters and an estimator derived from a non-symmetrical error-cost function.

510 R. BLATTBERG AND T. SARGENT

established above, its relatively good performance in the presence of disturbances with very fat tails. Taken together with the evidence on the widespread existence of Paretian variables in economics, this provides a possible reason for the better performance of the MSAE predictor in Meyer and Glauber's study.

University of Chicago
and
University of Pennsylvania and NBER

Manuscript received February, 1969 ; revision received June, 1969.

REFERENCES

[1] CHARNES, A., W. W. COOPER, AND R. O. FERGUSON: "Optimal Estimation of Executive Compensation by Linear Programming," *Management Science* (1955).
[2] FAMA, E. F.: "The Behavior of Stock-Market Prices," *Journal of Business* (January, 1965).
[3] FAMA, E. F., AND R. ROLL: "Some Properties of Symmetric Stable Distributions," *Journal of the American Statistical Association* (September, 1968).
[4] FELLER, W.: *An Introduction to Probability Theory and Its Applications*, Vol. II. John Wiley and Sons, New York, 1966.
[5] FISHER, W. D.: "A Note on Curve Fitting with Minimum Deviations by Linear Programming," *Journal of the American Statistical Association* (June, 1961).
[6] JORGENSON, D.: Book Review in *Journal of Political Economy* (February, 1966), 99–100.
[7] MANDELBROT, B.: "New Methods in Statistical Economics," *Journal of Political Economy* (October, 1963).
[8] ———: "The Variation of Certain Speculative Prices," *Journal of Business* (1963).
[9] MEYER, J. R., AND R. R. GLAUBER: *Investment Decisions, Economic Forecasting, and Public Policy*. Harvard Business School, Boston, 1964.
[10] PRESS, S. J.: "A Compound Events Model for Security Prices," *Journal of Business* (1967).
[11] ROLL, R.: "The Efficient Market Model Applied to U.S. Treasury Bill Rates," Unpublished doctoral dissertation, Graduate School of Business, University of Chicago, 1967.
[12] WAGNER, H. M.: "Linear Programming Techniques for Regression Analysis," *Journal of the American Statistical Association* (March, 1959).
[13] WISE, J.: "Linear Estimators for Linear Regression Systems Having Infinite Residual Variances," manuscript, 1966.

EVALUATION OF THE POWER OF THE DURBIN-WATSON STATISTIC FOR NON-FIRST ORDER SERIAL CORRELATION ALTERNATIVES

Robert C. Blattberg *

Introduction

IN single equation regression analysis for economic time-series, many different error structures can be specified. The usual assumption made is that the errors are identically and independently distributed but quite often this assumption is violated. To test independence, Durbin-Watson (1950) devised a commonly used test. Their test (and others, see Blattberg (1971), Henshaw (1966) and Theil-Nagar (1961)) uses as the test statistic a modified von-Neumann ratio,

$$d = \frac{\Sigma(\hat{u}_t - \hat{u}_{t-1})^2}{\Sigma(\hat{u}_{t-1}^2)}$$

where $\hat{u}_t = Y_t - X_t\beta$ and β is the ordinary least squares estimator of β for the model $Y_t = X_t\beta + u_t, t = 1, \ldots, N$.

In the past, the alternative error structure to independence has been first-order serial correlation. Little is known about the power of d against non-first order serial correlation alternatives. This paper will show that the power of d for a second-order Markov process and a first-order moving average process can be greater than for a first-order serial correlation process. This implies that standard adjustment procedures, such as the Cochrane-Orcutt procedure (1949), which assume the error structure to be a first-order serial correlation process if independence is rejected, may often be inapplicable. Therefore, it is suggested that when independence is rejected, Box-Jenkins' procedures (1970) or other adjustment methods which try to determine the form of the error structures should be used instead.

I The Power Function for the Durbin-Watson Statistic

The development of the power function for the Durbin-Watson statistic is based on articles

Received for publication November 24, 1971. Revision accepted for publication May 18, 1973.

[508]

by Koerts and Abrahamse (1968) and Imhof (1961). The Durbin-Watson statistic defined earlier is

$$d = \frac{\Sigma(\hat{u}_t - \hat{u}_{t-1})^2}{\Sigma\hat{u}_t^2} = \frac{\hat{u}'A\hat{u}}{\hat{u}'\hat{u}} \tag{1}$$

where $\hat{u} = Y - X\beta$, Y is the $n \times 1$ vector of dependent variables, X is the $n \times k$ matrix of explanatory variables, β is the $k \times 1$ vector of ordinary least squares estimates of β and

$$A = \begin{bmatrix} 1 & -1 & 0 & . & . & . & 0 \\ -1 & 2 & -1 & 0 & . & . & . & 0 \\ 0 & -1 & 2 & -1 & . & . & . & . \\ . & . & . & . & . & . & . & . \\ . & . & . & . & . & 0 & -1 & 2 & -1 \\ 0 & . & . & . & . & . & 0 & -1 & 1 \end{bmatrix}$$

In developing the power function we will assume the variance-covariance matrix for the disturbances is $V_0 = E(uu')$ where u is the $n \times 1$ vector of the disturbances. By definition the power function is $Pr(\text{reject the null hypothesis})$. Using η_0 as the critical value chosen for the ath significance level and assuming we are testing independence against positive serial correlation, the power function evaluated at V_0 is

$$\phi(V_0) = Pr(d < \eta_0 | E(uu') = V_0) \tag{2}$$

Denoting $Pr(d < \eta_0 | E(uu') = V_0)$ by $Pr(d < \eta_0)$, we have

$$\begin{aligned} Pr(d < \eta_0) &= Pr\left(\frac{\hat{u}'A\hat{u}}{\hat{u}'\hat{u}} < \eta_0\right) \tag{3}\\ &= Pr(\hat{u}'A\hat{u} - (\hat{u}'\hat{u})\eta_0 < 0)\\ &= Pr(\hat{u}'(A - \eta_0 I)\hat{u} < 0)\\ &= Pr(u'(MAM - \eta_0 M)u < 0) \end{aligned}$$

since

$$\hat{u} = Mu \quad \text{and} \quad M = I - X(X'X)^{-1}X'.$$

Because V_0 is a symmetric positive definite matrix, we can write $V_0 = B'B$. Then letting $u = B\epsilon$, where $E(\epsilon\epsilon') = I$, we have

* Research financed in part by National Science Foundation Grant GS–2347. The author wishes to thank Professors Arnold Zellner, Timothy W. McGuire and Robert Lucas for their helpful comments.

$$Pr(\epsilon'B'(MAM - \eta_0 M)B\epsilon < 0) = P(\epsilon'H\epsilon < 0) \tag{4}$$

where

$$H = B'(MAM - \eta_0 M)B$$

H can be shown to be symmetric and can therefore be diagonalized into a real matrix. This is done by finding S such that

$$S'HS = \Lambda \text{ where } \Lambda \text{ is } \begin{bmatrix} \lambda_1 & 0 & & \vdots & \\ & \cdot & & \vdots & \\ & & \cdot & \vdots & \\ 0 & & \lambda_{n-k} & \vdots & 0 \\ \cdots & \cdots & \cdots & \cdots & \cdots \\ & 0 & & \vdots & 0_{k \cdot k} \end{bmatrix}$$

Making a final transformation $S\mu = \epsilon$ we have

$$Pr(d < \eta_0) = Pr(\epsilon'H\epsilon < 0) = Pr(\mu'S'HS\mu < 0)$$
$$= Pr\left(\sum_{i=1}^{n-k} \lambda_i \mu_i^2 < 0 \right) \tag{5}$$

where

$$\mu \sim N(0, I).$$

Thus

$$\phi(V_0) = Pr\left(\sum_{i=1}^{n-k} \lambda_i \mu_i^2 < 0 \,\big|\, E(uu') = V_0 \right), \tag{6}$$

where each $\mu_i^2 \sim \chi_1^2$, k equals the number of explanatory variables, and n equals the number of observations.

To evaluate $Pr\left(\sum_{i=1}^{n-k} \lambda_i \mu_i^2 < 0 \right)$ requires the distribution of $\sum_{i=1}^{n-k} \lambda_i \mu^2$, which is not known. Imhof (1961), however, developed a numerical procedure for evaluating $Pr\left(\sum_{i=1}^{n-k} \mu_i^2 \lambda_i < 0 \right)$.

Let $Q = \sum_{i=1}^{n-k} \mu_i^2 \lambda_i$. Then

$$Pr(Q < 0) = \frac{1}{2} - \frac{1}{\pi} \int_0^\infty \frac{\sin \theta(u)}{u\rho(u)}\, du \tag{7}$$

where

$$\theta(u) = \frac{1}{2} \sum_{i=1}^{n-k} (\tan^{-1}(\lambda_i u))$$

and

$$\rho(u) = \prod_{i=1}^{n-k} (1 + \lambda_i^2 u^2)^{1/4}$$

and

$$\lim_{u \to 0} \frac{\sin \theta(u)}{u\rho/(u)} = \frac{1}{2} \sum_{i=1}^{n-k} \lambda_i.$$

Through numerically integrating the right-hand side of equation (7) $Pr(Q < 0)$ can be calculated.

II The Variance-Covariance Matrix for a First-Order Moving Average Process and for a Second-Order Serial Correlation Process

The power function for the Durbin-Watson statistic for any covariance matrix, say V, was developed in section I. By specifying the covariance matrix for different alternative hypotheses, the value of the power function can be calculated.

To find the covariance matrix for a second-order serial correlation process, we begin by defining the process:

$$u_t = \rho_1 u_{t-1} + \rho_2 u_{t-2} + \epsilon_t \qquad \text{for } t = 1, \ldots, n \tag{8}$$

where

(a) $E(\epsilon_t) = 0$
(b) $E(\epsilon_t^2) = \sigma_\epsilon^2$
(c) $E(\epsilon_t \epsilon_{t-s}) = 0 \qquad \text{for } s \neq t.$ $\tag{9}$

It can be shown that

$$\sigma_u^2 = \frac{(1 - \rho_2)}{(1 + \rho_2)\{(1 - \rho_2)^2 - \rho_1^2\}} \cdot \sigma_\epsilon^2 \tag{10}$$

and

(a) $r(0) = 1$
(b) $r(1) = \dfrac{\rho_1}{1 - \rho_2}$
(c) $r(s) = \rho_1 r(s-1) + \rho_2 r(s-2) \qquad \text{for } s > 1$ $\tag{11}$

where

$$r(s) = \frac{\text{cov}(u_t u_{t-s})}{\text{var}(u_t)}.$$

Thus, the covariance matrix for second-order serial correlation process is

510   THE REVIEW OF ECONOMICS AND STATISTICS

$$V = \sigma_u^2 \begin{bmatrix} 1 & r(1) & r(2) & \ldots & r(n-1) \\ r(1) & 1 & r(1) & \ldots & r(n-2) \\ \cdot & \cdot & & & \cdot \\ \cdot & \cdot & & & \cdot \\ \cdot & \cdot & & & \cdot \\ r(n-1) & r(n-2) & \ldots\ldots & r(1) & 1 \end{bmatrix}$$

A first-order moving average process is defined by:

$$u_t = \zeta_1 \epsilon_t + \zeta_2 \epsilon_{t-1} \quad \text{for } t = 1, \ldots, n \qquad (12)$$

where ϵ_t follows the conditions in (2(a))–(2(c)) and $\zeta_1 + \zeta_2 = 1$.

It can be shown that

$$\sigma_u^2 = (\zeta_1^2 + \zeta_2^2) \cdot \sigma_\epsilon^2 \qquad (13)$$

and

(a) $r(0) = 1$

(b) $r(1) = \dfrac{\zeta_1 \zeta_2}{\zeta_1^2 \zeta_2^2}$

(c) $r(s) = 0 \quad s > 1$ \qquad (14)

Thus, the variance-covariance matrix for a first-order moving average process is

$$V = \sigma_u^2 \begin{bmatrix} 1 & r(1) & 0 & 0 & 0 & \ldots & 0 \\ r(1) & 1 & r(1) & 0 & 0 & \ldots & 0 \\ 0 & r(1) & 1 & r(1) & 0 & \ldots & 0 \\ \cdot & & & & & & \cdot \\ \cdot & & & & & & \cdot \\ \cdot & & & & & & \cdot \\ 0 & \ldots & 0 & r(1) & 1 & & r(1) \\ 0 & \ldots & 0 & 0 & r(1) & & 1 \end{bmatrix}$$

III Factors Affecting the Power Function of *d*

We begin by noting that the power of the Durbin-Watson statistic is $\phi(V) = Pr(Q < 0)$

$$= Pr\left(\sum_{i=1}^{n-k} \lambda_i \mu_i^2 < 0 \right)$$ where λ_i is the ith eigenvalue of $H - B'(MAM - \eta_0 M)B$ defined in (5) and the μ_i's are independent standard normal random variables. As the $E(Q)$ decreases, the probability that Q is less than zero increases, holding the other moments fixed. Be-

cause $E(\mu_i^2) = 1$ for all i, $E(Q) = \sum_{i=1}^{n-k} \lambda_i$. We know that the $tr\, H = \sum_{i=1}^{n-k} \lambda_i$ and, therefore, as the trace of H decreases, the $Pr(Q < 0)$ decreases, and the power increases.[1] By studying the factors affecting the trace of H, we can learn what conditions lead to increasing the power of d.

A) *Large Sample Properties of the Trace of H*

We can rewrite the trace of H.

$$\begin{aligned} tr(H) &= tr\{B'(MAM - \eta_0 M)B\} \\ &= tr\{V(MAM - \eta_0 M)\} \end{aligned}$$

where V is the covariance matrix for u defined just below (1).

For large samples, we can approximate $MAM - \eta_0 M$ as follows

$$MAM \doteq \begin{bmatrix} 1 & -1 & 0 & 0 & \ldots & 0 \\ -1 & 2 & -1 & 0 & \ldots & 0 \\ 0 & -1 & 2 & -1 & \ldots & 0 \\ & & & & \cdot & \cdot \\ & & & & -1 & 2 & -1 \\ 0 & 0 & 0 & 0 & & -1 & -1 \end{bmatrix}$$

and

$$\eta_0 M \doteq \begin{bmatrix} \eta_0 & & & 0 & \\ & \eta_0 & \cdot & & \\ 0 & & \cdot & \cdot & \\ & & & & \eta_0 \end{bmatrix} \qquad \cdot$$

[1] This statement is obviously conditional upon the behavior of higher moments. To study the behavior of the higher moments is extremely difficult. Since it appears the mean is more important in determining the power, we will concentrate our attention on it.

Then

$$MAM - \eta_0 M \doteq \begin{bmatrix} 1-\eta_0 & 1 & 0 & 0 & . & . & . & 0 \\ -1 & 2-\eta_0 & -1 & 0 & . & . & . & 0 \\ 0 & -1 & 2-\eta_0 & -1 & . & . & . & 0 \\ . & & & & & & & \\ . & & & & & & & \\ . & & & & & & & \\ 0 & & & & & -1 & & 1-\eta_0 \end{bmatrix}$$

Generally, $MAM - \eta_0 M$ is approximately a tri-diagonal matrix with the diagonal terms positive. (η_0 is usually between 1.0 and 1.9). The terms adjacent to the diagonal are negative and as large or larger than the diagonal terms.

Finally we can approximate

$$V(MAM - \eta_0 M) \doteq \begin{bmatrix} 1 & r(1) & r(2) & . & . & . & r(n-1) \\ r(1) & 1 & r(1) & . & . & . & r(n-2) \\ r(2) & r(1) & 1 & . & . & . & r(n-3) \\ . & & & & & & \\ . & & & & & & \\ . & & & & & & \\ r(n-1) & . & . & . & . & . & r(1) \end{bmatrix} \begin{bmatrix} 1-\eta_0 & 1 & 0 & 0 & . & . & . & 0 \\ -1 & 2-\eta_0 & -1 & 0 & . & . & . & 0 \\ 0 & -1 & 2-\eta_0 & -1 & . & . & . & 0 \\ . & & & & & & & \\ . & & & & & & & \\ . & & & & & & & \\ 0 & . & . & . & . & . & -1 & 1-\eta_0 \end{bmatrix}$$

where $r(i) = \dfrac{\mathrm{cov}(u_t, u_{t-i})}{\mathrm{var}(u_t)}$.

The diagonal terms $V(MAM - \eta_0 M)$ are approximately equal to $2 - \eta_0 - 2\,r(1)$ and therefore the $tr\ H \doteq n(2 - \eta_0 - 2\,r(1))$. Thus, the mean of Q depends primarily upon $r(1)$ and η_0. For fixed η_0, as $r(1)$ increases, the mean of Q decreases, and, therefore, the power of d increases.[2]

B) *A Large Sample Comparison of the Value of the Power Function of d for Frst-Order and Second-Order Serial Correlation Processes*

In section II the elements of V were derived for both a first and second order serial correlation process. For a first-order process, $u_t = \rho_1 u_{t-1} + \epsilon_t$, we have $r(1) = \rho_1$, whereas, for a second-order process, $u_t = \rho_1 u_{t-1} + \rho_2 u_{t-2} + \epsilon_t$, we have $r(1) = \rho_1/1 - \rho_2$. As we have just seen, *ceteris paribus*, the power function increases as $r(1)$ increases. Thus, for fixed ρ_1, if $\rho_2 > 0$, $r(1)$ is greater for a second-order process than for a first-order process. For ρ_2

< 0, $r(1)$ is greater for a first-order process. Therefore the value of the power function for d will be greater for a second-order serial correlation process if $\rho_2 > 0$ than for a first-order serial correlation process but if $\rho_2 < 0$ the value of the power function will be less for a second-order process.

C) *Comparison of the Value of the Power Function of d for First-Order Moving Average and First-Order Serial Correlation Processes*

Again in appendix A the elements of V are derived for a first-order moving average process, $u_t = \zeta_1 \epsilon_t + \zeta_2 \epsilon_{t-1}$ with $\zeta_1 + \zeta_2 = 1$ and $\zeta_1, \zeta_2 > 0$. We see that $r(1) = \dfrac{\zeta_1 \zeta_2}{\zeta_1 + \zeta_2}$ and, therefore, lies between 0 and 0.5 and is a maximum when $\zeta_1 = \zeta_2 = .5$. Thus, a first-order moving average process can be as powerful as a first-order serial correlation process with $0 < \rho_1 < .5$. However, in large samples a first-order serial correlation process is always more powerful than a first-order moving average process when $0.5 < \rho_1 < 1.0$.

IV Calculated Power Function Values for Specific Sets of Explanatory Variables

The last section results were approximations for large samples. For smaller samples the approximation for $MAM - \eta_0 M$ will not hold. This section studies the actual power function of d for small samples (15 to 20 observations with 2 to 5 independent variables).

The value of the power function is specific

to a set of explanatory variables. For this reason, more than one set of explanatory variables is used to study the power of the Durbin-Watson statistic against non-first-order serial correlation processes.

The goal of this section is to answer the following questions:

For small samples:

1. Does the Durbin-Watson statistic have any power against non-first order alternatives?

2. How does the power function for a first-order serial correlation process compare with that of (a) a second-order serial correlation process and (b) a first-order moving average process?

3. (a) How does the power function change for a second-order serial correlation process as a function of ρ_1 and ρ_2 where $u_t = \rho_1 u_{t-1} + \rho_2 u_{t-2} + \epsilon_t$?

(b) How does the power function change for a first-order moving average process as a function of $\zeta_1 \epsilon_t + \zeta_2 \epsilon_{t-1}$?

The results are divided into two sections. Section one discusses the results for the second-order serial correlation process; section two discusses the results for the first order moving average process.

For all studies the nominal significance level used is 5 per cent and the critical value used is calculated using the normal approximation described in Blattberg (1971). The significance level and critical value were chosen somewhat arbitrarily. In *comparing* power functions for first-order serial correlation and the other error processes, it is important that they have the *same* level of Type I error. The specific level of Type I error is unimportant. Because the same critical value is used for all error processes, the level of Type I error will be the same. Consequently, choosing Type I error arbitrarily should have no effect on the comparative results given in this section.

A) *The Data*

Two types of data sets are used to compare the power function: artificially generated data in which the lag structure of the independent variables is controlled, and actual economic time series data collected from different studies.

1) *The Artificial Data*: The model used to generate the explanatory variable is

$$X_t = \lambda X_{t-1} + \eta_t$$

where $|\lambda| < 1$ and $\eta_t \sim N(0,1)$.

Three data sets were generated: data set 1 with $\lambda = .95$, data set 2 with $\lambda = 0$, and data set 3 which is produced by multiplying every other observation in data set one by minus one. Data set 1 corresponds to a highly "smooth" economic time series, i.e., the first difference of the explanatory variables is small. Data set 2 represents uncorrelated explanatory variables. Data set 3 is an extremely oscillating time series. In generating data set 3, every other observation in data set 1 was multiplied by minus one rather than setting $\lambda = -.95$ so that the variance of X_t in data set 1 equals the variance of X_t in data set 3. Thus, it is easier to compare the results for the two data sets.

TABLE 1. — SUMMARY OF DATA SETS

Data Set Number	Description [a]
1	Artificial Data: $\lambda = .95$; $n = 20$, $k = 2$
2	Artificial Data: $\lambda = .0$, $n = 20$, $k = 2$
3	Artificial Data: Every other observation in data set 1 is multiplied by minus one; $n = 20$, $k = 2$
4	Economic Time Series Data: Klein (1950); $n = 21$, $k = 3$
5	Economic Time Series Data: Henshaw (1966); $n = 16$, $k = 5$
6	Economic Time Series Data: Theil-Nagar (1961); $n = 17$, $k = 3$
7	Economic Time Series Data: Durbin-Watson (1951); $n = 20$, $k = 3$

[a] All data sets include column of ones so that constant term is included.

2) *The Economic Time Series Data*: Four sources of data were used: [3]

    (4) Klein (1951, p. 135) — data on profits and wages for the United States 1921–1941. $n = 21$ and $k = 3$.

    (5) Henshaw (1966) — data on supply of California, Oregon and Washington pears and non-agricultural income for United States for 1925–1940. $n = 16$, $k = 5$.

[3] All data sets include column of ones so that constant term is included.

NON-FIRST ORDER SERIAL CORRELATION ALTERNATIVES   513

(6) Theil-Nagar (1961, table 4) — data on log real income per capita and log relative price for Netherlands, 1923–1939. $n = 17$, $k = 3$.

(7) Durbin-Watson (1951, table 1) data on log real income per capita and log relative price for United Kingdom for 1870–1889. $n = 20$, $k = 3$.

B) *Results for Second-Order Serial Correlation Process*

The error structure for the second-order serial correlation process is

$$u_t = \rho_1 u_{t-1} + \rho_2 u_{t-2} + \epsilon_t.$$

If $\rho_2 = 0$, this process becomes a first-order serial correlation process.

The values chosen for ρ_1 and ρ_2 are: set 1 — $\rho_1 = .3$, $\rho_2 = \begin{pmatrix} .5 \\ .0 \\ -.5 \end{pmatrix}$; set 2 — $\rho_1 = .6$, $\rho_2 = \begin{pmatrix} .3 \\ .0 \\ -.3 \end{pmatrix}$. These values allow us to compare the effects of positive versus negative ρ_2.

Table 2 gives the results for $\rho_2 = 0$ and $\rho_1 = (.3, .6, .9)$. The value of the power function for data sets 5 and 6 are considerably lower than for the other five data sets. Since these two data sets have $n = 16$ and $n = 17$, respectively, this indicates extreme sensitivity of the power function to small changes in the number of observations when n is relatively small. For the other five data sets $n = 20$ or 21.

TABLE 2. — POWER FUNCTION FOR FIRST ORDER SERIAL CORRELATION PROCESS

Data Set Number	$\rho = .3$	$\rho = .6$	$\rho = .9$
1	.29161[a]	.67208	.84462
2	.30816	.74786	.94235
3	.30554	.72911	.93000
4	.29038	.65858	.84711
5	.17643	.38790	.59256
6	.22932	.50336	.67831
7	.29061	.66403	.85026

[a] All values of the power function in tables 2–4 are computed numerically integrating equation (7).

Tables 3a and 3b give the comparative results between first-order and second-order serial correlation. The results indicate that for data sets 2 and 3 in tables 3a and 3b the power for $\rho_2 = .5$ is greater than for $\rho_2 = 0$ and the power for $\rho_2 = 0$ is greater than for $\rho_2 = -.5$. Data sets 2 and 3 are those with the least autocorrelation in the explanatory variables.

TABLE 3a. — COMPARISON OF THE POWER FUNCTIONS OF A FIRST-ORDER AND SECOND-ORDER SERIAL CORRELATION PROCESS

Data Set Number		$\rho_1 = .3$	
	$\rho_2 = .5$	$\rho_2 = 0$	$\rho_2 = -.5$
1	.27094	.29161	.22299
2	.45697	.30816	.13693
3	.43052	.30554	.17187
4	.25960	.29038	.27482
5	.16150	.17643	.16948
6	.15777	.22932	.27290
7	.27087	.29061	.24043

TABLE 3b. — COMPARISON OF THE POWER FUNCTIONS OF A FIRST-ORDER AND SECOND-ORDER SERIAL CORRELATION PROCESS (*continued*)

Data Set Number		$\rho_1 = .6$	
	$\rho_2 = .3$	$\rho_2 = 0$	$\rho_2 = -.3$
1	.61340	.67208	.69526
2	.80196	.74786	.66589
3	.77803	.72911	.67353
4	.61251	.65858	.70977
5	.40874	.38790	.41767
6	.43813	.50336	.60245
7	.61877	.66403	.68326

For the data sets with highly autocorrelated explanatory variables (data sets 1, 4, 5, 6, and 7) no conclusive comparative results exist though the second-order process often has greater power than the first-order process. The value of the power function appears to depend upon the characteristics of the data set and whether ρ_2 is plus or minus.

Results for First-Order Moving Average Process

The error structure for the first-order moving average process is

$$u_t = \zeta_1 \epsilon_t + \zeta_2 \epsilon_{t-1} \quad \text{where} \quad \zeta_1 + \zeta_2 = 1.$$

A first-order moving average process with $\zeta_1 = .25$ and $\zeta_2 = .75$ is comparable to a first-order serial correlation process with $\rho_1 = .3$ because both have a first-order correlation coefficient $(r(1))$ of .3. However, higher order correlation terms are non-zero for a serial correlation process whereas they are zero for a moving average process.

Table 4 gives the results. We see that for every case the moving average process results in greater power than the comparable first-order serial correlation process. We should note, however, that the maximum value for the first-order correlation coefficient of a moving average is .5 and occurs when $\zeta_1 = \zeta_2 = .5$. Thus the power for a first order moving average process will not greatly exceed that for a first-order serial correlation process with $\rho = .5$. However, a first-order serial correlation process can have $.5 < \rho < 1$.

TABLE 4. — COMPARISON OF THE POWER FUNCTIONS OF A FIRST-ORDER MOVING AVERAGE PROCESS AND A SECOND-ORDER MOVING AVERAGE PROCESS

Data Set Number	Serial Correlation Process $\rho = .3$	Moving Average Process $\zeta_1 = .25 \; \zeta_2 = .75$
1	.29161	.31253
2	.30816	.31068
3	.30554	.31446
4	.29038	.31064
5	.17643	.18741
7	.29061	.31287

V Limitations of the Standard Adjustment Procedure When Independence Is Rejected

The results of section 3 and 4 pose a problem in adjusting for serial correlation. When using the Durbin-Watson test, a common practice has been to assume first-order serial correlation if the null hypothesis of independence is rejected. The serial correlation coefficient, ρ, is often estimated by

$$\hat{\rho} = \hat{r}(1) = \frac{2 - d}{2}$$

where

$$d = \frac{\Sigma (u_t - u_{t-1})^2}{\Sigma u_{t-1}^2}.$$

The regression is then rerun using generalized least-squares with the covariance matrix estimated by

$$\hat{V} = \begin{bmatrix} 1 & \rho & \rho & . & . & . & \rho^{n-1} \\ \rho & 1 & \rho & . & . & . & \rho^{n-1} \\ . & & & & & & . \\ . & & & & & & . \\ . & & & & & & . \\ \rho^{n-1} & . & . & . & . & . & \rho\,1 \end{bmatrix}$$

The regression coefficients are estimated by

$$\beta = (X'\hat{V}^{-1}X)^{-1} X'\hat{V}^{-1}Y.$$

Only when first serial correlation is present is $\hat{V}$ consistently estimated.

For example, when a first-order moving average process is present, the estimate of the covariance matrix under the assumption of only first-order serial correlation will be approximated by V above.

The correct estimate should be

$$H = \begin{bmatrix} 1 & \hat{r}(1) & 0 & 0 & . & . & . & 0 \\ \hat{r}(1) & 1 & \hat{r}(1) & 0 & . & . & . & 0 \\ & & & & & & & . \\ & & & & & & & . \\ 0 & & & & & & & . \\ 0 & . & . & . & . & . & \hat{r}(1) & 1 \end{bmatrix} \cdot \hat{\sigma}_u^2.$$

where $\hat{r}(1) = \hat{\rho} = \dfrac{2 - d}{2}$ and $\hat{H}$ is an estimate of H, the true variance-covariance matrix for a first-order moving average process defined at the end of section 2.

The terms $\hat{r}(1)^2$, $\hat{r}(1)^3$, etc. should not appear. Since these higher order terms do appear in V, assuming first-order serial correlation will lead to inconsistent estimates of the covariance matrix. The inconsistent estimates of the variance-covariance matrix result in inefficient estimates of the regression coefficients and inconsistent estimates of the variance-covariance matrix for the estimated regression coefficients. Because of the biased hypothesis tests and inefficient coefficient estimates it is important to determine the exact form of the error specification and not merely assume first-order serial correlation when the null hypothesis of independence is rejected.

VI Conclusion

This paper has shown that tests using the Durbin-Watson statistic are powerful against non-first-order serial correlation alternatives. The implication of this result is that the standard assumption of first-order serial correlation when a test using the Durbin-Watson statistic rejects independence can no longer be made. If it is made and a non-first-order serial correlation process is generating the disturbances, then inefficient coefficient estimates and inconsistent hypothesis tests will result.

REFERENCES

Blattberg, R. C., "Testing for Serial Correlation in Regression Models," unpublished Ph.D. thesis, Carnegie-Mellon University, 1971.

Box, G. E. P., and G. M. Jenkins, *Time Series Analysis and Control* (San Francisco: Holden-Day, 1970).

Cochrane, D., and G. H. Orcutt, "Application of Least Squares Regressions to Relationships Containing Auto-correlated Error Terms," *Journal of the American Statistical Association*, 44 (1949), 32–61.

Durbin, J., and G. S. Watson, "Testing for Serial Correlation in Least-Squares Regression. I," *Biometrika*, 37 (1950), 409–428.

———, "Testing for Serial Correlation in Least-Squares Regression. II," *Biometrika*, 38 (1951), 159–178.

Henshaw, R. C., "Testing Single-Equation Least-Squares Regression Models for Autocorrelated Disturbances," *Econometrica*, 34 (1966), 646–660.

Imhof, J. P., "Computing the Distribution of Quadratic Forms in Normal Variables," *Biometrika*, 48 (1961), 419–426.

Klein, L. R., *Economic Fluctuations in the United States 1921–41* (New York: John Wiley and Sons, Inc., 1950).

Koerts, J., and A. P. J. Abrahamse, "On the Power of the BLUS Procedure," *Journal of the American Statistical Association*, 63 (1968), 1227–1236.

Theil, H., and A. L. Nagar, "Testing the Independence of Regression Disturbances," *Journal of the American Statistical Association*, 56 (1961), 793–806.

Robert C. Blattberg and
*Nicholas J. Gonedes**

A Comparison of the Stable and Student Distributions as Statistical Models for Stock Prices

I. INTRODUCTION

There has been a great deal of discussion about the statistical distribution of rates of return on common stocks. At an early stage the prevalent belief was that distributions of rates of return on common stocks were adequately characterized by the normal distribution. This belief seemed to be consistent with the pioneering work of Bachelier.[1] It was also observed, however, that empirical distributions of such returns had more kurtosis (i.e., "fatter tails") than that predicted by the normal distribution. The evidence provided by Mandelbrot and Fama suggested that one could explicitly account for the observed "fat tails" by using the symmetric-stable distribution.[2]

This article considers another family of symmetric distributions that can also account for the observed "fat tails" of returns distribution. This alternative is the Student (or t) distribution. It will be indicated that this alternative model has implications for empirical and theoretical work that are quite different from those of the symmetric-stable model. The descriptive validity of the Student model, relative to that of the symmetric-stable model, will be assessed using actual daily rates of return.

This article is organized as follows: Section II describes the prop-

* Graduate School of Business, University of Chicago. This research has been financed in part by National Science Foundation grant GS-2347. An earlier version of this paper was presented at the Annual Meetings of the Econometric Society, December 1971. We are indebted to Eugene Fama for supplying the daily rates of return used in this study. The comments of Eugene Fama, Arnold Zellner, Merton Miller, and Fischer Black are gratefully acknowledged. A special note of thanks is due to Harry Roberts for his many detailed and insightful remarks on substance and exposition. Results mentioned but not presented here are available from the authors or in Report No. 7242, issued (under the same title) by the Center for Mathematical Studies in Business and Economics, University of Chicago, 1972.

1. L. J. B. A. Bachelier, *Theorie de la speculation* (Paris: Gauthier-Villars, 1900), reprinted in *The Random Character of Stock Market*, ed. P. H. Cootner (Cambridge, Mass.: M.I.T. Press, 1964), pp. 17–78; *Le jeu, la chance, et le hasard* (Paris: E. Flammarion, 1914).

2. B. Mandelbrot, "The Variation of Certain Speculative Prices," *Journal of Business* 36 (October 1963): 394–419; "The Variation of Some Other Speculative Prices," *Journal of Business* 40 (October 1967): 393–413; "New Methods in Statistical Economics," *Journal of Political Economy* 71 (October 1963): 421–40; and E. F. Fama, "The Behavior of Stock Market Prices," *Journal of Business* 38 (January 1965): 34–105.

erties of the stable and Student distributions and then briefly discusses the importance of (1) explicitly recognizing that distributions of returns are "fat tailed" and (2) some important differences that result when the Student rather than the stable model is used to account for the "fat tails." Section III summarizes the derivations of both the Student and stable models using more basic stochastic processes. Details of the derivations appear in Appendix A. Also included in Section III is a discussion of empirical results for other models similar to the ones considered in this paper. Section IV discusses methods for empirically comparing the Student and stable models. Section V describes the specific estimation tools used for our comparative results. Finally, Section VI presents and discusses the empirical results.

II. PROPERTIES OF THE STUDENT AND SYMMETRIC-STABLE DISTRIBUTIONS

We begin this section by defining and stating some properties of the Student and symmetric-stable distributions. Then, we consider several implications of describing daily rates of return on common stocks with the Student and stable models.

A. Definitions and Properties of the Student and Stable Models

The Student distribution.[3]—The Student density function with location parameter m, scale parameter $H > 0$, and degrees of freedom parameter, $\nu > 0$, is:

$$f(x|m, H, \nu) = \frac{\nu^{(1/2)\nu}}{B\left(\dfrac{1}{2}, \dfrac{1}{2}\nu\right)} [\nu + H(x - m)^2]^{-1/2(\nu+1)}\sqrt{H},$$

where $B(\cdot, \cdot)$ is the "beta function," that is, $B(a, b) = \Gamma(a)\Gamma(b)/\Gamma(a + b)$, where $\Gamma(\cdot)$ is the "gamma function." The Student distribution has the following properties: (1) $E(\tilde{x}) = m$, for $\nu > 1$ and $\mathrm{Var}(\tilde{x}) = H^{-1}\nu/(\nu - 2)$, for $\nu > 2$; (2) in general, all moments of order $r < \nu$ are finite; and (3) when $\nu = 1$, the Student density function is the Cauchy density function. As $\nu \to \infty$, the Student distribution converges to the normal distribution.

When a Student random variable with $\nu > 2$, $\tilde{x}$, is standardized by dividing $\tilde{x} - E(\tilde{x})$ by $\sqrt{\mathrm{Var}(\tilde{x})}$, then the density function of the resulting standardized variable has the following properties: (1) it has fatter tails than the density function of a conventional standardized normal random variable (i.e., one with mean equal to zero and variance equal to unity), and (2) it is higher than the standard normal density in the

3. See H. Raiffa and R. Schlaifer, *Applied Statistical Decision Theory* (Cambridge, Mass.: Harvard University Press, 1961), chap. 7.

246   The Journal of Business

neighborhood of their common mean, zero. Note, however, that the above standardization scheme is not the one used in most tables and discussions of the density function of a "standardized" Student random variable. There, the scaling is by $\sqrt{H^{-1}}$ rather than $\sqrt{\text{Var}(\tilde{x})}$. The density function of $[\tilde{x} - E(\tilde{x})]/\sqrt{H^{-1}}$ exhibits the first property stated above, but it is not higher than the standard normal density in the neighborhood of their common mean, zero; in fact, the density function is lower in this neighborhood.

The differences induced by the different scaling procedures in the maximum ordinate of the scaled random variables' density functions are indicated in table 1 for selected values of ν. The effect on the ordinate

Table 1
Maximum Ordinates of Student Density Functions

ν	$f\left[y = 0 \mid m = 0, \text{Var}(\tilde{y}) = \dfrac{\nu}{\nu-2}, \nu\right]$	$f[y = 0 \mid m = 0, \text{Var}(\tilde{y}) = 1, \nu]$
3	.3676	.6367
4	.3750	.5305
5	.3796	.4900
6	.3827	.4687
7	.3850	.4555
8	.3867	.4465
9	.3880	.4399
10	.3891	.4350
11	.3900	.4311
12	.3907	.4279
13	.3914	.4254
14	.3919	.4233
15	.3924	.4215
16	.3928	.4199
17	.3931	.4184
18	.3934	.4172
19	.3937	.4162
20	.3940	.4153
75	.3976	.4030
∞	.3989	.3989

NOTE.—$\nu = \infty$ denotes normal distribution.

when the argument of the density function equals four is indicated in table 2.

The symmetric-stable distribution.[4]—This distribution is defined by its characteristic function because, in general, its density function is not known. The log characteristic function of a symmetric-stable distribution with location parameter δ, scale parameter $c > 0$, and characteristic exponent $\alpha \in (0, 2)$, is: $\ln \phi_{\tilde{x}}(t) = i\,\delta t - |ct|^{\alpha}$, where t is some real number and $i = \sqrt{-1}$.

4. See B. V. Gnedenko and A. N. Kolmogorov, *Limit Distributions for Sums of Independent Random Variables*, trans. K. L. Chung (Reading, Mass.: Addison-Wesley, 1954), chap. 7; and S. J. Press, *Applied Multivariate Analysis* (New York: Holt, Rinehart & Winston, 1972), chap. 6.

247   *Comparison of Distributions as Models*

Table 2
Ordinates of Student Density Functions When the
Argument Equals Four

ν	$f\left[4\|m=0,\ \mathrm{Var}(\tilde{y})=\dfrac{\nu}{\nu-2},\ \nu\right]$	$f[4\|m=0,\ \mathrm{Var}(\tilde{y})=1,\ \nu]$
3	.0092	.0023
4	.0067	.0022
5	.0051	.0019
6	.0041	.0017
7	.0033	.0015
8	.0028	.0013
9	.0023	.0011
10	.0020	.0011
11	.0018	.0009
12	.0016	.0009
13	.0014	.0008
14	.0013	.0007
15	.0012	.0006
16	.0011	.0006
17	.0010	.0006
18	.0009	.0005
19	.0009	.0005
20	.0008	.0005
75	.0003	.0002
∞	.0001	.0001

Note.—$\nu=\infty$ denotes normal distribution.

The symmetric-stable distribution has the following properties. (1) This distribution is the Cauchy distribution if $\alpha=1$. If $\alpha=2$, it is the normal distribution. (2) It is true that $E(\tilde{x})=m$, if $\alpha>1$. (3) In general, all moments of order $r<\alpha$ are finite except when $\alpha=2$, in which case moments of all orders are finite. (4) If a sum of independent identically distributed random variables has a limiting distribution, then it must be a stable distribution. Thus, the nonnormal stable distributions generalize the classical Central Limit Theorem (CLT) to cases where the second moments of the summed random variables are infinite. (5) A sum of independent stable random variables will be stable with characteristic exponent α^* if each summand is a stable random variable with characteristic exponent α^*.

When a symmetric-stable random variable is standardized by dividing $\tilde{x}-\delta$ by c, then the density function of the resulting standardized variable has the following properties. (1) If $\alpha<2$, its tails are fatter than the density function of a normal random variable that is standardized in the same way [i.e., by scaling with $c=\sqrt{1/2\ \mathrm{Var}(\tilde{x})}$ rather than $\sqrt{\mathrm{Var}(\tilde{x})}$, which is the conventional procedure]; and (2) if $\alpha<2$, it is higher than the density function of a similarly scaled normal random variable in the neighborhood of their location parameters' common value, zero. These properties are similar to those of the density function of a Student random variable that is scaled by its standard deviation.

The characteristic function given above only applies to symmetric-

248   **The Journal of Business**

stable distribution. The modifications needed to define asymmetric stable distributions are indicated in Appendix A, where an asymmetric stable distribution is used to derive the symmetric-stable model for rates of return.

Almost all of this paper focuses on the symmetric-stable model. Unless otherwise indicated, the label "stable model" will be used for the symmetric-stable model.

> B. *Some Implications of the Student and*
> *Stable Models for Empirical and*
> *Theoretical Work*

For our purposes, the most important parameters of the Student and symmetric-stable models are ν and α, respectively. Thus, throughout this section, we assume that all distributions are standardized so that $\delta = 0$ and $c = 1$ (for the stable model) and $m = 0$ and $H = 1$ (for the Student model).

The empirical evidence to which we referred in Section I suggests that empirical distributions of daily returns are approximately symmetric with "fatter tails" than the normal distribution. The discussion in the preceding subsection indicates that both the Student and stable models can account for such "tail behavior." Thus, there is a similarity between the Student and stable models when comparisons are made with the normal model. And this similarity suggests the potential descriptive validity of each model for daily rates of return.

While there are similarities between the Student and stable models, these two models have some very different implications for empirical and theoretical work. Several extremely important differences are due to differences in the properties associated with sums of random variables generated by each of the models.

Let $\tilde{x}_{it}$, $i = 1, 2, \ldots$, denote the rate of return, under continuous compounding, on security i for day t, $t = 1, 2, \ldots$ (throughout, tilde denotes a random variable). That is, $x_{it} = \ln[P_{it} + D_{it})/P_{it-1}]$, where P_{it} and D_{it} are the (ex-dividend) price and dividend, respectively, on security i for day t. Consider the cross-temporal sum for the ith security

$$\tilde{S}_i{}^T = \sum_{t=1}^{T} \tilde{x}_{it}.$$

Under continuous compounding, $\tilde{S}_i{}^T$ is the rate of return on security i over a period of T consecutive days. For example, if $t = 1$ and $t = T$ are, respectively, the first and last days of some month, then $\tilde{S}_i{}^T$ is the return on security i for that month. Now, suppose that $(\tilde{x}_{i1}, \tilde{x}_{i2}, \ldots, \tilde{x}_{iT})$ is a sequence of independent random variables. Under the Student model (for daily returns) with $\nu > 2$, the distribution of $\tilde{S}_i{}^T$ converges to a normal distribution as $T \to \infty$. This convergence result is a consequence of the classical CLT.[5] On the other hand, if $(\tilde{x}_{i1}, \tilde{x}_{i2}, \ldots, \tilde{x}_{jT})$ is a sequence from the stable model with $\alpha = \alpha^* < 2$, then the distribution of $\tilde{S}_i{}^T$ will not converge to a normal distribution because the classical CLT is not applicable to the stable model with $\alpha < 2$. Instead, the distribution of $\tilde{S}_i{}^T$ will be stable with $\alpha = \alpha^*$ for all T. Thus, the applicability of the Student model to daily returns implies that there is a time period (greater than 1 day) such that rates of return defined over this time period may be described by the normal distribution.

Our own empirical results (see Section VI) for the Student model indicate that estimates of ν for most securities examined are well in excess of 25 for sum sizes of 20, corresponding to monthly returns. Since a Student distribution with $\nu \approx 25$ is almost indistinguishable from a normal distribution, it seems reasonable to approximate distributions of monthly rates of return by normal distributions. Note that if the summed returns, $\tilde{S}_i{}^T$, on individual securities converge to normality as T increases, then the portfolio return,

$$\sum_j \theta_j \tilde{S}_j{}^T,$$

also converges to normality as T increases, where θ_j is the proportion of the portfolio invested in security j,

$$\sum_j \theta_j = 1.\text{[6]}$$

Whether distributions of summed daily returns converge to normality or to the stable model with $\alpha < 2$ has implications for the appropriateness of estimation tools. If, as a result of convergence, the normal model is applicable to returns defined over a period longer than 1 day (e.g., 1 month), then one may proceed as if these returns were generated from a finite variance process. Consequently, one may use, for example, "least-squares" estimation methods or spectral analysis. If, however, the nonnormal stable model is applicable to these returns, then one should proceed as if these returns were generated from an infinite variance process, for which sample variances (which are always finite) exhibit highly erratic behavior; see, for example, the results presented by Mandelbrot and Fama.[7] Thus, estimation tools relying upon sample second moments may induce misleading (and possibly meaningless) results.[8] In

5. The version of the Central Limit Theorem upon which we are relying assumes independent summands. As indicated in Section VI, rates of return on a given security defined over 1 day (or some longer period) conform reasonably well with this assumption.

6. That is, if the asymptotic distribution of $(\tilde{S}_1{}^T, \tilde{S}_2{}^T, \ldots, \tilde{S}_N{}^T)$ is N-variate normal, then the asymptotic distribution of a linear combination of $\tilde{S}_j{}^T, j = 1, 2, \ldots, N$ is univariate normal. Also note that, if the distribution of $(\tilde{S}_1{}^T, \tilde{S}_2{}^T, \ldots, \tilde{S}_N{}^T)$ is N-variate Student (stable) with $\nu = \nu^*$ ($\alpha = \alpha^*$), then the distribution of a linear combination of $\tilde{S}_j{}^T, j = 1, 2, \ldots, N$ is univariate Student (stable) with $\nu = \nu^*$ ($\alpha = \alpha^*$).

7. See n. 2 above.

8. The use of truncated sample second moments may not be a desirable

short, the suitability of measures of dispersion and estimation tools for returns defined over time intervals longer than 1 day depend upon the distributional model applicable to daily rates of returns.

The appropriateness of a distributional model is also important for theories of asset pricing under uncertainty, such as those based upon the mean-variance framework used in Markowitz, Tobin, Lintner, and Sharpe.[9] Suppose that individuals' preferences may be represented by continuous bounded utility functions and that individuals maximize expected utility.[10] Then, use of the mean-variance approach in describing maximum expected-utility strategies is easily justified when utility functions are defined on terminal wealth (or periodic consumption) and when the distributions of investment outcomes (i.e., rates of return) are normal.[11] If, using this approach, one also postulates nondecreasing strictly concave utility functions (i.e., "risk aversion"), then one can demonstrate that the expected utility of an investment varies directly (inversely) with the first (second) moment of that investment's outcome.

Now, for the same types of utility functions, consider the implications of limiting normal and nonnormal stable models for risk-taking behavior. For the stable model, one can show that the expected utility of all outcomes for which $\alpha < 2$ is strictly less than the expected utility of their normal counterparts, that is, outcomes with $\alpha = 2$. More generally, expected utility varies directly with α, $0 < \alpha \leqslant 2$.[12] Thus, if (as a

---

remedy for this problem, relative to the alternative of a more appropriate distributional model; see Mandelbrot (1967) (n. 2 above). This is particularly so if, for example, the appropriate value of α is not exceedingly close to 2.

9. H. Markowitz, *Portfolio Selection: Efficient Diversification of Investments* (New York: John Wiley & Sons, 1959); J. Tobin, "Liquidity Preference as Behavior Towards Risk," *Review of Economic Studies* 26 (February 1958): 65–86; J. Lintner, "Security Prices, Risk, and Maximal Gains from Diversification," *Journal of Finance* 20 (December 1965): 587–615; "The Valuation of Risk Assets and the Selection of Risky Investments in Stock Portfolios and Capital Budgets," *Review of Economics and Statistics* 47 (February 1965): 13–37; W. F. Sharpe, "A Simplified Model for Portfolio Analysis," *Management Science* 10 (January 1963): 277–93; "Capital Asset Prices: A Theory of Market Equilibrium Under Conditions of Risk," *Journal of Finance* 19 (September 1964): 425–42.

10. The boundedness property is needed to avoid violating utility-theory axioms when dealing with continuous random variables; see the discussion in K. J. Arrow, *Essays in the Theory of Risk Bearing* (Chicago: Markham Publishing Co., 1971), pp. 61–63, which is based upon the analyses of K. Menger, "Das Unsicherheitsmoment in der Wertlehre," *Zeitschrift für Nationalokonomie* 51 (1934): 459–85, reprinted in *Essays in Mathematical Economics in Honor of Oskar Morgenstern*, ed. M. Shubik (Princeton, N.J.: Princeton University Press, 1967). It is particularly important to note that the need for boundedness is not unique to the specific distributional models considered in this report.

11. The mean-variance framework can also be justified when utility functions are assumed to be quadratic in terminal wealth (or consumption). But this assumption has some well-known deficiencies within the context of asset-pricing models; see, for example, Arrow (*Essays*, pp. 96–97), or G. Hanoch and H. Levy, "The Efficiency of Choices Involving Risk," *Review of Economic Studies* 37 (July 1969): 342.

12. Consider two symmetric-stable Paretian distributions with parameters $(\delta_1, c_1, \alpha_1)$ and $(\delta_2, c_2, \alpha_2)$, respectively. In accordance with our assumptions, set

251   *Comparison of Distributions as Models*

result of convergence) the returns of interest (e.g., monthly rates of return) may be described by the normal model, then using the stable model with $\alpha < 2$ will induce an overstatement (understatement) of risk (expected utility). If this is the case, and if all securities' daily returns cannot be described by the same value of α, one may disprove theoretical propositions on asset pricing simply because those propositions do not provide rankings of assets consistent with optimality conditions. For the problem at hand, this inadequacy is due (once again) to inappropriate distributional assumptions.

Selecting either the Student or stable model (with $\alpha < 2$) for daily returns has implications for empirical work on daily returns as well as returns defined over longer time periods. The Student model allows the use of well-defined density functions. Well-defined density functions for the stable model exist in only two cases: $\alpha = 1$ and $\alpha = 2$. Thus, the likelihood function of the Student model can be expressed in closed form, and maximum-likelihood estimates for all parameters of the model may be obtained. This permits one to use the available statistical theory on

---

$\delta_1 = \delta_2 = 0$ and $c_1 = c_2 = 1$, and suppose $\alpha_1 > \alpha_2$. Let $F(x|\alpha_1)$ and $F(x|\alpha_2)$ denote the distribution functions conditional upon α_1 and α_2, respectively. Finally, let $U(\cdot)$ denote a bounded strictly concave nondecreasing utility function. Consider the change in expected utility given by:

$$E[U(\tilde{x})|\alpha_1] - E[U(\tilde{x})|\alpha_2] = \Delta E[U(\tilde{x})]. \tag{1.1}$$

Upon integrating (1.1) by parts, one gets:

$$E[U(\tilde{x})] = \int_{-\infty}^{\infty} [F(x|\alpha_2) - F(x|\alpha_1)]U'(x)dx,$$

$$= \int_{-\infty}^{0} [F(x|\alpha_2) - F(x|\alpha_1)]U'(x)dx \tag{1.2}$$

$$+ \int_{0}^{\infty} [F(x|\alpha_2) - F(x|\alpha_1)]U'(x)dx,$$

where $U'(x) \equiv \partial U/\partial x$. Since the distributions are symmetric about zero, $F(x|\alpha_1) = 1 - F(-x|\alpha_1)$ and $F(x|\alpha_2) = 1 - F(-x|\alpha_2)$. Thus (1.2) may be rewritten as:

$$\Delta E[U(\tilde{x})] = \int_{-\infty}^{0} [F(x|\alpha_2) - F(x|\alpha_1)]U'(x)dx \tag{2}$$

$$+ \int_{0}^{\infty} \left\{ [1 - F(-x|\alpha_2)] - [1 - F(-x|\alpha_1)] \right\} U'(x)dx.$$

Given that $\alpha_1 > \alpha_2$, we have: (1) $F(x|\alpha_2) > F(x|\alpha_1)$ for all $x \in (-\infty, 0)$, (2) $F(0|\alpha_1) = F(0|\alpha_2)$, and (3) $F(x|\alpha_2) < F(x|\alpha_1)$ for $x \in (0, \infty)$. This implies that the first integral in (2) is positive and the second is negative. But, by strict concavity, $U'(-x) > U'(x)$, for $x \in (0, \infty)$. Thus, the first integral in (2) has a value in excess of the absolute value of the second integral. Consequently, $\Delta E[U(\tilde{x})] = E[U(\tilde{x})|\alpha_1] - E[U(\tilde{x})|\alpha_2] > 0$. A more detailed statement of the reasoning used here can be had from Lemma 1 and Theorem 3 of Hanoch and Levy, "Efficiency of Choices Involving Risk." Related material appears in J. Hadar and W. Russell, "Rules for Ordering Uncertain Prospects," *American Economic Review* 59 (March 1969): 25–34.

252 The Journal of Business

optimum-likelihood estimators. For the stable model, maximum-likelihood estimators can be obtained, but the currently available methods for solving so involve approximations that appear to be quite costly (in terms of computer time).[13] The stable model's parameters may be estimated using other estimators, such as those proposed by Fama an Roll.[14] But there appears to be no statistical theory for the estimator of α proposed by the latter works.[15] And α is perhaps the most important parameter of the stable model. (Note that this entire paragraph says nothing about the costs incurred if one model is used when, in fact, the other is more descriptively valid. Thus, our remarks do not fully justify selection of other distributional model.)

C. Additional Remarks

Throughout, we have emphasized the implications of $\alpha < 2$ and $v > 2$ are not large) for empirical and theoretical work. We did not emphasize the "reasonableness" or "unreasonableness" of the implied nonexistence theoretical second moments when $\alpha < 2$ for the stable model, or the implied existence of the theoretical second moments when $v > 2$ for the Student model. It seems to us that emphasizing these factors really "misses the point." The nonnormal stable model's importance does not lie in its not having a finite theoretical second moment, even though this feature often attracts the most attention. The importance of this model does lie in its ability to account for the observed kurtosis of empirical distributions of daily rates of return; it accomplishes this by indicating a distribution whose theoretical second moment is infinite.

One additional comment is in order. In the preceding discussion, we used $\ln[(P_t + D_t)/P_{t-1}]$ to measure a rate of return. An often-used alternative measure is $[(P_t + D_t)/P_{t-1}] - 1$. The former measure was used by Fama, the latter was used by Blume, and both measures were used by Officer.[16] Empirically, these different measurement procedures do not appear to induce important differences in the kinds of estimation results to be considered here. The technical reason for this is that $\ln(1 + r) \approx r$ if r is not very large, such as $|r| \leqslant .15$. For daily returns on common stocks (particularly during the postwar period) this technical result

13. Of particular interest here are the estimation procedures discussed in W. DuMouchel, "Stable Distributions in Statistical Inference" (Ph.D. diss., Department of Statistics, Yale University, 1971).

14. E. F. Fama and R. Roll, "Some Properties of Symmetric Stable Distributions," *Journal of the American Statistical Association* 63 (September 1968): 017 36; "Parameter Estimates for Symmetric Stable Distributions," *Journal of the American Statistical Association* 66 (June 1971): 331–38.

15. The asymptotic distributions of the estimators proposed by Fama and Roll (ibid.) for δ and c are Gaussian because each estimator is a linear combination of estimated fractiles, which have asymptotic normal distributions. Truncated means are used to estimate δ when $\alpha < 2$.

16. Fama, "Behavior of Stock Market Prices"; M. E. Blume, "Portfolio Theory: A Step Toward Its Practical Application," *Journal of Business* 43 (April 1970): 152–73; R. R. Officer, "A Time Series Examination of the Market Factor of the New York Stock Exchange" (Ph.D. diss., University of Chicago, 1971).

253   *Comparison of Distributions as Models*

appears to have descriptive validity. All estimation results presented
this report are based on returns measured using: $[(P_t + D_t)/P_{t-1}]$ —
Given the experiences of others, we are confident that the use of $\ln[(P_t$
$D_t)/P_{t-1}]$ would not have altered our inferences.

III. MODELS FOR RATES OF RETURN

The Student and stable models can be derived as continuous mixture
of a normal distribution. In this derivation, the variance of the normal
distribution is a random variable. When the reciprocal of the variance
follows a gamma-2 distribution, then the unconditional distribution of
returns is Student. When the variance follows a strictly positive stable
distribution with $\alpha < 1$, then the unconditional distribution is symmetric
stable with $\alpha < 2$. Detailed derivations of the Student and stable models
are provided in Appendix A. Some brief remarks on our derivations are
provided in Subsection A. Several alternative models for rates of return
on common stocks are reviewed in Subsection B.

A. Derivation of the Student and Stable Models: Summary

Our derivation of the Student and stable models uses the notion of a
subordinated stochastic process. Here, the following definitions are
applicable. Let $[\tilde{X}(s); s \geqslant 0]$ and $[\tilde{h}(s); s \geqslant 0]$ denote stochastic processes. Define another stochastic process $\{\tilde{Z}(s) = \tilde{X}[\tilde{h}(s)]; s \geqslant 0\}$. The
process $[\tilde{Z}(s)]$ is said to be subordinate to the process $[\tilde{X}(s)]$; the process $[\tilde{h}(s)]$ is the directing process.

Let $\tilde{X}(s)$ denote the rate of return on a common stock over a time
interval of length s and suppose that $[\tilde{X}(s)]$ is a stationary Gaussian
stochastic process, with $\tilde{X}(s)$ independent of $\tilde{X}(s^*)$ for all $s \neq s^*$. We
assume that these returns are expressed as deviations about their mean;
hence, $E[\tilde{X}(s)] = 0$. The random variable $\tilde{h}(s)$ may be interpreted as
the change in the economic environment (or the change in available information) occurring during the time interval s. It is assumed that $\tilde{h}(s)$
is independent of $\tilde{h}(s^*)$, for all $s \neq s^*$. Before the realization of $\tilde{h}(s)$ is
available, the rate of return over the interval s may be written as $\tilde{Z}(s) =$
$\tilde{X}[\tilde{h}(s)]$. This formulation allows the distribution of rates of return,
$[\tilde{Z}(s)]$, to incorporate changes in the economic environment over intervals of length s. Specifically, this formulation allows the variance of
returns over the interval s to depend on the realization of $\tilde{h}(s)$.

All of the above is used in the derivation of both the Student and
stable models. The factor that distinguishes one model from the other is
the distribution function of $\tilde{h}(s)$, the directing process. If $\tilde{h}(s)$ follows a
strictly positive (asymmetric) stable distribution with $\alpha \in (0, 1)$, then
$\tilde{Z}(s)$ will follow a symmetric-stable distribution with $\alpha < 2$. On the
other hand, if $[\tilde{h}(s)]^{-1}$ follows a gamma-2 distribution (which is also

254　　　　　　　　The Journal of Business

asymmetric and strictly positive), then $\widetilde{Z}(s)$ will follow a Student distribution.

B.　Other Stock Price Models

A number of other models that use a mixture of a normal distribution and a distribution on the variance of a normal distribution have been proposed for rates of return on stocks. We will review three of these models in this section.

Press proposed the following model.[17] Let $\widetilde{Z}(t)$ denote the log of the price of a given security at time t and assume that $\widetilde{Z}(t)$ is a process with stationary and independent increments. Specifically,

$$\widetilde{Z}(t) = C + \sum_{k=1}^{N(t)} \widetilde{Y}_k + \widetilde{X}(t),$$

where $Z(0) = C$ is a known constant; $\widetilde{Y}_1, \ldots, \widetilde{Y}_k, \ldots$, is a sequence of mutually independent random variables following a normal distribution with mean θ and variance $\sigma_2{}^2$; $\widetilde{N}(t)$ is a Poisson counting process with parameter λt, which represents the number of random events occurring at time t; and $[\widetilde{X}(t), \ t \geqslant 0]$ is a Weiner process independent of $\widetilde{N}(t)$ and $(\widetilde{Y}_1, \widetilde{Y}_2, \ldots)$. The $\widetilde{X}(t)$ is normally distributed with mean 0 and variance $\sigma_1{}^2 t$.

To estimate his model, Press used monthly prices of 10 stocks in the Dow-Jones Industrials from 1926 to 1960. He split the data into three periods: (*a*) 1926–50, (*b*) 1926–55, and (*c*) 1926–60, for which his sample sizes were at most 300, 360, and 420 observations, respectively.

Press's method of estimating the model's parameters (θ, λ, $\sigma_1{}^2$, $\sigma_2{}^2$) was cumulant matching since, according to Press, "The method of maximum likelihood estimation does not yield explicit estimators in this problem" (p. 322.). His results showed negative signs for some estimated variances, which he set at zero. He suggests that these anomalous results were caused by insufficient sample sizes. Model inadequacy is another possible explanation.

It is apparent from Press's study that a major problem with his model is estimating the parameters. However, since Press's article appeared, the use of a mixture of a normal process and a distribution for the variance of the normal process has been found more frequently in the literature on distributions of returns on stocks.

Clark considered a mixture of a normal distribution and a lognormal distribution for the variance of the normal distribution.[18] Clark labels the unconditional distribution the "lognormal-normal distribution."

17. S. J. Press, "A Compound Events Model for Security Prices," *Journal of Business* 41 (July 1968): 317–35.

18. P. K. Clark, "A Subordinated Stochastic Process Model with Finite Variance for Speculative Prices" (Discussion Paper no. 1, Center for Economic Research, University of Minnesota, April 1971).

255   *Comparison of Distributions as Models*

This distribution has no closed-form expression and, thus, must be expressed in integral form. This presents some obvious difficulties for empirical work.

After defining the lognormal-normal distribution, Clark compares this distribution with the stable distribution (and others, though no results for the others are presented in his paper) using changes in the prices of cotton futures for two periods: 1947–50 and 1951–55.

The data series Clark uses makes it difficult to compare models. First, cotton contracts do not have 4-year lives. Thus, Clark had to splice series across contract lives. Consequently, additional noise may have been added to his series. Second, the time period from 1951 to 1955 was preceded by a suspension of trading due to existing price controls. This could have affected the amount of variation in the series at the beginning of the period, just as trading began. Finally, the open interest (similar to "shares outstanding") is not fixed. Volume and price fluctuations may be influenced by changes in open interest.

Another problem with Clark's results is that he uses the Kolmogorov-Smirnov test (K-S test) to test goodness-of-fit of the stable and lognormal-normal models. The critical values of the K-S test used by Clark assume the parameter values are known, but he estimated the parameters. Thus, the critical values he uses are inappropriate. Kendall and Stuart point out:[19] "Nothing is known in general about the behavior of the D_n statistic [D_n denotes the K-S statistic for a sample size of n] when parameters are to be estimated in testing a composite hypothesis of fit. . . . It will clearly not remain distribution free."[20] In light of the criticisms presented above, it seems that Clark's conclusions that the lognormal-normal model fits much better than the stable model must be viewed with caution.

Praetz studied a mixture of a normal distribution and a gamma-2 distribution for the variance of the normal distribution, which results in a Student distribution.[21] This is the same model that we are considering in this paper. However, the models Praetz compares, the data, his methods of estimation, and his method of comparison differ from ours.

The models Praetz compares are the: (1) Student distribution, (2)

19. M. G. Kendall and A. Stuart, *The Advanced Theory of Statistics*, 2d ed. (New York: Hafner Publishing Co., 1968), 3: 458.

20. A distributional hypothesis is a simple hypothesis if the type of distribution and all values of the distribution's parameters are specified in the test of fit. If estimates of the hypothesized type of distribution need to be used in a test of fit, then the distributional hypothesis is a composite hypothesis. Some simulation results on the K-S test of a composite hypothesis of normality are available; see H. W. Lilliefors, "On the Kolmogorov-Smirnov Test for Normality with Mean and Variance Unknown," *Journal of the American Statistical Association* 62 (June 1967): 399–402. However, these results do not directly apply to the composite hypotheses in Clark's paper, the lognormal-normal and nonnormal stable hypotheses.

21. P. D. Praetz, "The Distribution of Share Price Changes," *Journal of Business* 45 (January 1972): 49–55.

256   The Journal of Business

normal distribution, (3) compound events model (Press's model, described earlier), and (4) stable model. The compound events model is
not included in our study.

The data Praetz uses consist of weekly observations on 17 share-
price index series from the Sydney stock exchange from 1958 to 1966.
We use both daily and weekly observations for each of the 30 stocks in
the Dow-Jones Industrials. (It is well to note that such indices often
exhibit artificial serial correlation.)

To estimate the parameters in the models, Praetz first standardized
each data series by subtracting the sample mean and dividing by the
sample standard deviation. He then grouped the standardized data into
26 intervals and estimated the unknown parameters by selecting the
parameters values that minimized the χ^2 statistic, Σ [observed-expected]-/
expected. In contrast, we used maximum-likelihood estimation for the
Student model and the estimators proposed by Fama and Roll for the
stable model.

Praetz's method of comparing the models involves comparing the
minimum χ^2 statistics of the models. Our method is to test whether the
data converge to normality or are stable and to compute the likelihood
ratio for the two models.

In evaluating Praetz's study, we first note that his method of "stan-
dardizing" the data is inappropriate. Praetz standardizes by subtracting
the sample mean and dividing by the sample standard deviation. The
simulation results in Fama and Roll suggest the sample standard deviation is an extremely bad estimator of the scale parameter for stable data.[22]
This may explain why the stable distribution does not fit his data well.

Another point is based on the statement in Praetz's paper that "the
stable distribution always provides a better fit than the normal" (p. 54).
The stable model will never provide a worse "fit" than the normal model
because the normal distribution is a special case of the stable Paretian
distribution. To estimate α in the stable distribution, Praetz minimizes
the χ^2 statistic with respect to α, with α being constrained to lie within
the interval [1, 2]. The χ^2 statistic for the normal distribution assumes
$\alpha = 2$. Thus, the χ^2 statistic will never be less for the normal distribution
than for the stable distribution.

The above discussion casts serious doubts on Praetz's results. In
this paper, we hope to show, using more appropriate statistical procedures, that the Student model appears to describe rates of return data
better than the stable model.

IV. METHODS FOR MODEL
COMPARISON

This section discusses two methods for discriminating between the stable
and Student models. They are: (1) calculate the likelihood ratio, and

22. Fama and Roll, "Parameter Estimates," p. 332.

257   *Comparison of Distributions as Models*

(2) determine whether the distributions of rates of returns are stable under addition.

A.   The Likelihood Ratio

The likelihood function of n observations is their joint density function evaluated at the n observations using a given set of parameter values. Suppose the data are generated by one of two distributions but we are uncertain about which one. Each distribution has a different likelihood function. By evaluating each likelihood function at the n observations and the appropriate estimates, we can compute the ratio of the values of these two likelihood functions. The likelihood ratio can then be used to determine the distribution for which the odds are greater. The following proposition assures us that as the sample becomes large, the ratio of the values of the two likelihood functions will indicate which distribution has generated the data.

Let $w_1, \ldots, w_n$ be observations on a sequence of n independent random variables with common density function $f_1(\cdot)$. (In the following discussion we will omit the parameters when denoting the density function.) Then their joint density function will be

$$f_n(w_1, \ldots, w_n) = \prod_{i=1}^{n} f_1(w_i).$$

Consider any other (well-defined) density function $g_i(\cdot)$ and the corresponding joint density function

$$g_n(w_1, \ldots, w_n) = \prod_{i=1}^{n} g_1(w_i).$$

Finally, define the sequence of likelihood ratios

$$\Lambda_n = \frac{g_n(w_1, w_2, \ldots, w_n)}{f_n(w_1, w_2, \ldots, w_n)},$$

$$\Lambda_{n+1} = \frac{g_{n+1}(w_1, w_2, \ldots, w_n, w_{n+1})}{f_{n+1}(w_1, w_2, \ldots, w_n, w_{n+1})},$$

$$\cdots\cdots\cdots\cdots\cdots\cdots\cdots\cdots\cdots\cdots\cdots\cdots\cdots\cdots$$

$$\Lambda_{n+s} = \frac{g_{n+s}(w_1, w_2, \ldots, w_n, \ldots, w_{n+s})}{f_{n+s}(w_1, w_2, \ldots, w_n, \ldots, w_{n+s})}.$$

Doob proves that the

$$\lim_{k \to \infty} \Lambda_k = 0$$

with probability one, unless $f(\cdot)$ and $g(\cdot)$ are identical, in which case

$$\lim_{k \to \infty} \Lambda_k = 1$$

with probability one.[23]

    23. J. L. Doob, *Stochastic Processes* (New York: John Wiley & Sons, 1953), p. 349.

258   The Journal of Business

Given suitable regularity conditions for $g_1(\cdot)$ and $f_1(\cdot)$ and large samples, the ratio of likelihood functions evaluated at maximum-likelihood estimates may be given a useful Bayesian interpretation Specifically, assuming equal prior probabilities for models $g_1(\cdot)$ and $f_1(\cdot)$, this ratio represents the asymptotic posterior odds of model $g_1(\cdot)$ relative to $f_1(\cdot)$. Detailed discussions of this issue may be found in Jeffreys, Lindley, and Zellner.[24]

Parameter values are required to calculate the value of the likelihood function for each model. The true parameter values are unknown. A reasonable alternative is to use maximum-likelihood estimates because of their large-sample properties. The samples used in most of this paper are approximately 1,300 observations; consequently, we will assume we are in a "large-sample" situation. For the Student distribution, the maximum-likelihood estimates will be used. For the stable distribution maximum-likelihood estimates are very expensive to compute, particularly for a large number of securities. Fortunately, Fama and Roll have developed a low-cost method for finding parameter estimates for the stable distribution.[25] Their estimates are "fairly good" in large samples (see Fama and Roll), and, thus, for the stable distribution we will use the Fama-Roll estimators.[26]

Using parameter estimates which maximize the likelihood function for the Student distribution but not for the stable distribution causes problems when we are using the likelihood ratio to discriminate between models. Obviously, the likelihood ratio will favor the Student model more frequently than if both likelihood functions were evaluated using maximum-likelihood estimates. In Section VI we discuss simulation results that were used to assess the severity of this problem. For these results, the distribution of the data is known to be either stable or Student. The likelihood functions were evaluated using the same estimating techniques used for actual rates of return. The results for stable data with α equal to 1.65 or 1.80 (see table 11) indicate that for 1,300 observations, not using maximum-likelihood estimates for the parameters of the stable model does not cause incorrect classification (except in one case). For $\alpha = 1.50$ there are a number of incorrect classifications (seven out of 20). However, stock prices are generally found to have estimates of α between 1.65 and 1.80 and, therefore, the results for $\alpha = 1.65$ and $\alpha = 1.80$ are the most relevant for actual rates of return. For smaller sample sizes (260 or less), the results for stable data seem to indicate the likeli-

24. H. Jeffreys, *Theory of Probability,* 3d ed. (Oxford. Clarendon Press, 1961), pp. 193–94; D. V. Lindley, "The Use of Prior Probability Distributions in Statistical Inference and Decisions," in *Proceedings of the Fourth Berkeley Symposium on Mathematical Statistics and Probabilities,* ed. J. Newman (Berkeley: University of California Press, 1961), 1:453–68; A. Zellner, *An Introduction to Bayesian Inference in Econometrics* (New York: John Wiley & Sons, 1971), pp. 31–33.
25. Fama and Roll, "Properties."
26. Ibid., and Fama and Roll, "Parameter Values."

hood ratio frequently incorrectly classifies the data as coming from the Student model. (Incorrect classification does not happen nearly so often for small sample sizes when the data are Student.) For this reason, we will use the likelihood ratio to compare the two distributions for the original observations ("unsummed") so that the sample sizes will be sufficiently large to overcome the problem of not using maximum-likelihood estimates for the parameters of the stable model. A more detailed discussion of these results is provided in Section VI.

B. Stability

A theoretical property which differentiates the stable and Student distributions is stability. Stability simply means that if we have n identically and independently distributed random variables, the distribution of their sum will differ from the distribution of each random variable only by location and scale parameters. The Student distribution is not stable, but the symmetric-stable distribution is. For degrees of freedom greater than 2, the distribution of sums of independent identically distributed Student random variables will tend to a normal distribution. Consequently, we can use the property of stability to discriminate between the two models.

For rates of return, we can take sums of daily rates of return. If a daily series follows a stable distribution with a specific characteristic exponent, then so should the summed series. On the other hand, if a daily series follows a Student distribution with fixed degrees of freedom, the summed series will not follow a Student distribution (see Ruben).[27] The distribution for the summed series will have a smaller tail area and be less peaked than the distribution for the daily series. Therefore, if we estimate both the degrees-of-freedom parameter and the characteristic exponent for series with sum sizes of, say, 1, 5, 10, and 20 and observe that these parameter estimates increase as the sum size increases, then we can infer that the daily series is nonstable.

V.   ESTIMATION OF THE MODEL'S PARAMETERS

The likelihood function for both statistical models contains three unknown parameters. In order to calculate the value of the likelihood function, we must find estimates of these parameters. Obvious candidates are maximum-likelihood estimates (M.L.E.) since we are interested in the ratio of the likelihoods. We will use M.L.E. for the Student distribution. However, as has been discussed in the previous sections, getting M.L.E. for the stable distributions is both difficult and costly (in terms of computer time). The best method (to date) for finding M.L.E. for the stable distribution is given in Du Mouchel.[28] However, his method

27. H. Ruben, "On the Distribution of the Weighted Difference of Two Independent Student Variables," *Journal of the Royal Statistical Society*, ser. B., 22 (1960): 188–94.
28. DuMouchel, "Stable Distributions."

still takes considerable computer time. As an alternative, we will use estimators devised by Fama and Roll (see n. 14). This section outlines these two estimation procedures. The properties of these estimators are evaluated (in Section VI) using simulation results.

A. M.L.E. for the Student Distribution

The likelihood function for the Student distribution with location m, scale H, degrees of freedom ν, and sample size n is

$$L(m, H, \nu; x_1, \ldots, x_n) = \prod_{i=1}^{n} \frac{\nu^{(1/2)\nu}}{B\left(\dfrac{1}{2}, \dfrac{1}{2}\nu\right)} \cdot [\nu + H(x_i - m)^2]^{-(1/2)(\nu+1)} \sqrt{H}.$$

The usual method for finding the M.L.E. of m, H, and ν is to differentiate the likelihood function with respect to each parameter, set the resulting three equations equal to zero, and solve for m, H, and ν, the M.L.E. Unfortunately, finding analytical solutions to these three equations for m, H, and ν is extremely difficult. Therefore, we numerically searched for the parameter values which maximize the likelihood function. (Our numerical search routine uses a Fibonacci search on m and ν and a Newton search on H.)

B. Fama-Roll Estimates for the Stable Distribution

The finite-sample properties of several estimators for the characteristic exponent (α), the dispersion parameter (c), and the location parameter (δ) of a symmetric-stable distribution are described in Fama and Roll (see n. 14); these procedures are briefly described in this section.

Estimator for δ.—The estimator for δ is the .75 truncated mean computed by: (1) ordering the data from largest to smallest, (2) truncating the data so that 12.5 percent is discarded from each extreme, (3) calculating the mean for the remaining 75 percent of the ordered sample observations. Fama and Roll (see n. 14) indicate that for $\alpha \approx 1.70$, which is a common estimate of α for rates of return, the .75 truncated mean is a more efficient estimator than the sample mean, the median, the .25, or the .50 truncated means.

Estimator of c.—Let $\hat{x}_f$ and x_f denote the f sample and theoretical fractile, respectively, from a sample of N observations on $\tilde{Y}$. For the Cauchy distribution $(\alpha = 1)$ the dispersion parameter, c, equals the semi interquartile range, $1/2(x_{.75} - x_{.25})$. For $1 < \alpha \leqslant 2$, c is approximately equal to the semi interquartile range, suggesting that c might be estimated by $1/2(\hat{x}_{.75} - \hat{x}_{.25})$. Fama and Roll recommend an estimator that is similar to the estimator of the semi interquartile range but one that has a smaller asymptotic bias. This estimator, which we will use, is

$$\hat{c} = \frac{1}{2} \frac{\hat{x}_{.72} - \hat{x}_{.28}}{.827}.$$

Fama and Roll (see n. 14) indicate for $1 \leqslant \alpha \leqslant 2$, $\hat{c}$ has an asymptotic bias of less than .4 percent. Additional finite sample properties of $\hat{c}$ are given in Fama and Roll (see n. 14).

Estimator of α.—Consider a symmetric-stable random variable, $\tilde{x}$, with location δ, scale c, and characteristic exponent α. Let $\tilde{z} = (\tilde{x} - \delta)/c$. Then $\tilde{z}$ will be a standardized symmetric-stable random variable with location 0, scale 1, and characteristic exponent α.

The tail areas for the distribution of $\tilde{z}$ are sensitive to changes in α. We will exploit this to find an estimate for α by studying the f fractile of the distribution of $\tilde{z}$, z_f, with f chosen so that it is in the tail of the distribution. Tables of z_f for different values of α are available. By using estimates of z_f for different values of α and comparing them to actual values of z_f, we can find an estimate of α.

The estimate we will use for z_f is:

$$\hat{z}_f = \frac{\hat{x}_f - \hat{x}_{1-f}}{2\hat{c}},$$

where $\hat{c}$ is our estimate of c and $\hat{x}_f$ and $\hat{x}_{1-f}$ are sample fractiles computed from our observed data.

Our estimating procedure for α is then: (1) compute $\hat{z}_f$ from our rates-of-return series, (2) search for the value of α in the tables of the standardized symmetric-stable distributions which makes $\hat{z}_f$ closest to z_f. This value of α will be our estimate. Again, Fama and Roll (see n. 14) provide sampling results for the properties of α. Their results suggest that a suitable value of f for $\alpha \approx 1.7$, which is applicable to rates of return, is $f = .97$.

VI.   ESTIMATION RESULTS

The results discussed in this section consist of: (1) results from a Monte Carlo simulation study based upon simulated observations from the stable and Student distributions, and (2) results based upon actual daily rates of return. The simulation study was done to gain some insight into the finite-sample properties of the estimation and model-comparison methods that we used for the actual data.

A.   The Actual Data

The actual data used are consecutive daily rates of return for each of the 30 securities in the Dow-Jones Industrial Average over the period 1957–62. The daily rates of return were computed by deducting unity from daily price relatives adjusted for dividends and capitalization changes (e.g., stock splits). The time periods of the observations are not identical for all 30 securities. Typically, the time period is from about the end of 1957 to September 26, 1962. The actual date of the first observation for

262   The Journal of Business

a security varies from January 1956 to April 1958; the date of the last observation is the same for all 30 securities. These data are the same as those used by Fama (see n. 2).

Recent work on security returns has emphasized forms of cross-sectional dependence that results in cross-sectional correlation among securities' returns. We did not adjust the data in our sample for such correlation because it appears that, given our objectives, such an adjustment is not necessary.[29]

We will not present evidence regarding the serial independence of daily returns. Results on this topic, for the 30 securities in our sample, are provided by Fama (see n. 2). In general, it appears that daily returns, and returns defined over longer time intervals, do not strongly violate the assumption of serial independence. The most frequently observed inconsistency is the tendency for extreme values of daily returns (of unpredictable sign) to succeed extreme values of daily returns.

B.   The Design of the Monte Carlo Study

The design of our Monte Carlo Study is as follows: (1) 26,000 random numbers uniformly distributed over the interval (0, 1) were generated from a uniform random-number generator (see Appendix B for the properties of our uniform random numbers). (2) The random numbers from (1) were used to generate 26,000 random numbers from each of several stable distributions and Student distributions with prespecified parameter values. Each set of 26,000 values (in their original order of appearance) from the stable and Student distributions was partitioned into 20 non-overlapping samples of 1,300 observations. (3) The estimation proce-

---

29. The usual method of removing cross-sectional correlation is to base all estimation results on the residuals of the "market-model," $\tilde{R}_{it} = \alpha_i + \beta_i \tilde{I}_t + \tilde{\epsilon}_{it}$, where $\tilde{R}_{it}$ is the ith security's rate of return for period t, $\tilde{I}_t$ is the rate of return on the market index for period t, and $\tilde{\epsilon}_{it}$ is a serially independent disturbance term, with $E(\tilde{\epsilon}_{it}) = 0$. For the ith and jth securities cov$(\tilde{R}_{it} \cdot R_{jt}) \neq 0$ because both securities contain the same factor, $\tilde{I}_t$. Once this is removed, it is usually assumed that the residuals are uncorrelated, namely, $E(\tilde{\epsilon}_{it} \cdot \tilde{\epsilon}_{jt}) = 0$, for all i and j. The empirical results of Officer, "Time Series Examination," for the stable model showed that estimates of α based directly upon daily rates of return and estimates of α based upon the market model's residuals for these daily returns were essentially the same. The primary reason for this result appears to be that the cross-sectional correlation among daily return is close to zero. It is known, however, that the cross-sectional correlation for returns increases as the time interval over which returns are defined increases. When considering sums of 20 daily returns, Officer's estimates of α based directly upon sums of daily returns and those based upon sums of the market model's residuals for these returns were slightly different. However, this result showed that the direction in which $\hat{\alpha}$ moves as a function of the sum sizes was the same for sums of residuals and sums of daily returns. This suggests that our inferences about convergence to normality based upon estimates of α for increasing sum sizes will be unaffected by cross-sectional correlation. B. F. King, in "Market and Industry Factors in Stock Price Behavior," *Journal of Business* 39 (January 1966): 139–90, shows that there is also an industry factor along with the market factor. Thus, if the ith and jth security are in the same industry, then cov$(\tilde{\epsilon}_{it}, \tilde{\epsilon}_{jt}) \neq 0$. However, King found that the industry factor was small and, therefore, the cov$(\tilde{\epsilon}_{it}, \tilde{\epsilon}_{jt})$ will not be large.

263   *Comparison of Distributions as Models*

dures used for the actual price data were used on the random numbers from the stable and Student distributions for parameter estimates. It should be noted that the estimating procedure for the Student model was applied to the simulated stable data and vice versa. Thus, we have sampling distributions for estimators of the stable (Student) model's parameters based upon data actually generated from Student (stable) distributions as well as data actually generated from stable (Student) distributions. The purpose of applying the stable model to Student data, and vice versa, is to offer another means of comparing the models.

For each distributional model, part (2) requires prespecified parameter values. We decided to use values of the location and dispersion parameters that are consistent with values of estimated parameters observed for daily rates of return from a pilot study. Since estimates of ν (for the Student model) and α (for the stable model) are particularly important for our objectives, we decided to prespecify sets of parameter values for the Student and stable models that differed only with respect to their values of ν and α, respectively; that is, neither the values of location parameters (m and δ) nor those of dispersion parameters (H and c) were varied. The prespecified values of the location and dispersion parameters are: $\delta = m = .0003$, $c = .00725$, and $H = 6,000$. For the stable model, three values of α were specified: 1.5, 1.65, and 1.8. For the Student model, three values of ν were specified: 3, 5, and 8.

According to the procedure described in (2), the ith observation from each of the six distributions is associated with the same value of the uniform number, $\tilde{u}(0, 1)$. Thus, the simulated observations for different distributions are not independent. This lack of independence is consistent with our objectives, namely, evaluating results for (1) different values of ν and α for the Student and stable models, respectively, and (2) different distributional models, holding other things constant [such as the underlying values of $\tilde{u}(0, 1)$].

C.   Discussion of the Simulation Results

In this section, the Monte Carlo simulation results are discussed and then used to develop guidelines for interpreting the results for actual rates of return.

Results for estimating ν and α.—Our results for estimating ν are given in tables 3, 4, and 6. For a sample size of 1,300 and 20 replications, we see the following (table 3): (1) when $\nu = 3$ and $\nu = 8$, the estimates of ν deviate slightly from the true value, though the estimates are within 2 S.E. of the true value; (2) the sample standard deviation, and the mean squared relative deviation increase as ν increases.[30] A

30. We used the sample standard deviation (among other things) to measure the precision of our estimates of ν. We could just as easily have used the standard error of ν by dividing all the sample standard deviations by $\sqrt{20}$. The standard deviation and standard error are directly proportional and so either can be used without changing the results.

264   The Journal of Business

Table 3
Estimates of ν for Simulated Student Data
(Sample Size = 1,300)

Replication Number	True Value of ν		
	$\nu = 3$	$\nu = 5$	$\nu = 8$
1	2.80	4.84	7.66
2	3.06	5.61	10.21
3	3.05	5.61	10.71
4	3.31	6.62	13.01
5	3.05	5.34	9.43
6	2.54	4.33	6.37
7	3.30	6.37	12.75
8	2.80	4.85	7.90
9	2.80	4.84	7.65
10	3.05	5.09	7.90
11	3.05	5.34	8.93
12	3.31	6.12	10.97
13	3.06	5.35	8.66
14	2.53	3.83	5.60
15	2.53	3.83	5.60
16	2.80	4.84	7.66
17	2.79	4.58	7.14
18	2.29	3.82	5.35
19	2.79	4.33	6.38
20	2.54	4.33	6.38
Mean	2.87	4.99	8.31
Standard deviation	.28	.80	2.21
$\sqrt{\text{Mean squared relative deviation}}$*	.10	.16	.27

* $\sqrt{(1/N)\Sigma_i[(\hat{\nu}_i - \bar{\hat{\nu}}_i)/\bar{\hat{\nu}}]^2}$, where $\bar{\hat{\nu}}$ is the average estimate.

possible reason for this decrease in precision as ν increases is that the rate of change in the density function decreases as the degrees-of-freedom parameter increases. For example, a change from 2 to 3 df changes the shape of the density function quite perceptibly, whereas a change from 49 to 50 df results in an almost insignificant change in the shape of the density function. Thus, the likelihood function is much flatter for large values of ν than for small values, resulting in much less precise estimates of ν when the actual degrees-of-freedom parameter is large.

Table 5 shows how the properties of estimates of ν change as the sample size decreases. For "small" samples, $n = 65$, the estimates of ν for all three values of the degrees-of-freedom parameter appear to be extremely inaccurate. Our estimates for $\nu = 5$ and $\nu = 8$ also have large standard deviations and mean-squared relative deviations for sample sizes of 260. When using maximum-likelihood estimation for ν, very large sample sizes are needed. Even sample sizes as large as 260 appear to be too small to obtain accurate estimates. A reason for the need for large sample sizes is that the tail area offers much of the information for detecting differences in ν. For sample sizes of 260, there are still a small number of observations in the tails. Also, as ν increases it becomes more

265   *Comparison of Distributions as Models*

Table 4
Estimates of ν for Simulated Student Data
(Sample Size $= 260$)

Replication Number	True Value of ν		
	$\nu = 3$	$\nu = 5$	$\nu = 8$
1	4.08	7.65	14.03
2	2.54	4.34	6.89
3	2.79	4.84	8.66
4	4.58	11.23	55.14
5	5.34	14.03	60.00*
6	4.08	9.95	35.48
7	3.06	5.85	10.98
8	4.34	20.42	60.00*
9	3.31	5.86	9.95
10	2.54	4.08	5.86
11	3.56	6.62	13.27
12	3.31	7.65	23.99
13	2.28	3.57	5.10
14	2.28	3.56	4.85
15	2.79	4.85	7.90
16	2.03	3.05	3.83
17	2.28	3.31	4.59
18	3.05	5.34	10.20
19	2.53	4.07	5.87
20	3.06	5.34	9.43
Mean	3.19	6.78	18.00
Standard deviation	.87	4.18	18.52
$\sqrt{\text{Mean squared relative deviation}}$	.27	.62	1.04

* Upper bound established in estimation procedure used for simulated data.

difficult to notice changes in the tails of the density. Thus, even larger samples are needed.

Our results for estimating α are given in table 6. For sample sizes of 1,300 and 20 replications we observe a slight downward bias in our estimates of α. Similar results were found in Fama and Roll (see n. 14). For sample sizes of 260, we can study table 7 because sums of independent stable random variables each with characteristic α are also stable with characteristic exponent α. The results in table 7 indicate that for smaller samples, the downward bias is more pronounced. For a more extensive study of estimating α, see Fama and Roll (see n. 14).

Results for sums of stable and student random variables.—As indicated earlier, a method of discriminating between the stable and Student models is to test for convergence to normality. To decide whether the distribution of rates of return is converging, we must know how quickly sums of Student random variables converge to normality. To determine the rate of convergence, we generated Student random variables with known degrees of freedom and took sums of sizes 5, 10, and 20. We then computed an estimate of the degrees-of-freedom parameter for each sum size. Table 8 gives the results for 20 replications and a sum size of 5. We did not use the results for smaller sum sizes because the estimates of

266 The Journal of Business

Table 5
Comparisons of Estimates of ν for Simulated
Student Data for Different Sample Sizes*

Sample Size	True Value of ν		
	$\nu = 3$	$\nu = 5$	$\nu = 8$
1,300:			
Mean	2.87	5.00	8.31
Standard deviation	.28	.80	2.21
$\sqrt{\text{Mean}}$ squared relative deviation	.10	.16	.27
260:			
Mean	3.19	6.78	18.00
Standard deviation	.87	4.19	18.52
$\sqrt{\text{Mean}}$ squared relative deviation	.27	.62	1.04
65:			
Mean	9.74	17.28	26.04
Standard deviation	17.2	22.08	24.45
$\sqrt{\text{Mean}}$ squared relative deviation	1.77	1.28	.94

* The maximum-likelihood estimation program contained an upper bound of 60 on estimates of ν for the simulated data. The number of truncated estimates underlying the results summarized in this table is as follows:

Sample Size	True Value of ν	Number of Truncated Estimates of ν
260	8	3
65	5	2
65	8	6

ν appear to be extremely erratic; these results are available from the authors.

Before giving the simulation results, we should note that sums of independent identically distributed Student random variables do not follow a Student distribution. We shall use the estimates of ν only as a descriptive measure of convergence since ν can no longer be interpreted as a Student parameter.

For Student data with $\nu = 3$, and sums of size five, the average estimate of ν increases from 2.87 to 4.70. Unfortunately, the standard deviation and mean-squared relative deviation also increase quite noticeably (.281 to 1.52 and .098 to .322, respectively).[31] Faster convergence seems to result for $\nu = 5$ and $\nu = 8$ with the average value of ν changing from 5.00 to 16.87 and 8.31 to 34.36, respectively. Again, our estimates of ν are extremely inaccurate. From the results just given, we see that because of sampling error, it is difficult to determine the exact rate of convergence to normality.

Our alternative to the Student distribution—the stable distribution—

31. Our estimates for ν contain a number of values at 60.00. This is due to a truncating in our estimating procedure. The effect of this truncation is to bias our estimates of the standard deviation downward. For the actual daily returns, the upper bound on estimates of ν was usually set at 89.984 (see the nn. to the tables).

267   *Comparison of Distributions as Models*

Table 6
Estimates of α for Simulated Stable Data
(Sample Size = 1,300)

Replication Number	True Values of α		
	$\alpha = 1.50$	$\alpha = 1.65$	$\alpha = 1.80$
1	1.50	1.65	1.80
2	1.51	1.67	1.85
3	1.46	1.62	1.76
4	1.52	1.67	1.83
5	1.52	1.60	1.88
6	1.40	1.63	1.76
7	1.50	1.66	1.83
8	1.52	1.67	1.84
9	1.54	1.70	1.88
10	1.55	1.72	1.80
11	1.48	1.63	1.76
12	1.61	1.78	1.80
13	1.51	1.66	1.80
14	1.43	1.57	1.70
15	1.45	1.60	1.75
16	1.52	1.67	1.83
17	1.40	1.65	1.70
18	1.36	1.51	1.64
19	1.46	1.60	1.74
20	1.46	1.61	1.76
Mean	1.48	1.64	1.78
Standard deviation	.057	.055	.060
$\sqrt{\text{Mean squared relative deviation}}$	.04	.03	.03

implies lack of convergence to normality. To develop guidelines for applying the stable model to actual data, we generated stable numbers with known characteristic exponent. We then summed these random numbers and estimated the characteristic exponent for the sums. Table 8 gives the results for 20 replications on sums of size five. (Results for sums of sizes 10 and 20 are available from the authors.)

For stable data, our average estimate of α decreases when we take sum sizes of five (1.485 to 1.46, 1.64 to 1.62, and 1.79 to 1.73). The standard deviations do not increase as much as they did for the Student data. The decrease in the estimate of α is not due to sampling error, but it is probably a downward bias due to the smaller sample sizes used to estimate α for sum sizes of five. The downward bias in estimates of α was first found in the extensive simulations of Fama and Roll (see n. 14). For actual data and approximately 1,300 observations, if the estimate of α does not decrease when going from sum sizes of one to sum sizes of five, this suggests convergence.

Table 9 gives a summary comparison of the results from tables 7 and 8 as well as a cross comparison of estimates of ν for stable data and α for Student data. The results indicate that if we estimate α for the Student data using the Fama-Roll estimating technique, we observe an increase in the estimate of α as the sum sizes go from one to five. For

268 The Journal of Business

Table 7
Estimates of α for Sums of Size Five from
Simulated Stable Data
(Sample Size = 260 per Replication)

Replication Number	True Value of α		
	$\alpha = 1.50$	$\alpha = 1.65$	$\alpha = 1.80$
1	1.45	1.58	1.68
2	1.46	1.65	1.80
3	1.50	1.65	1.72
4	1.60	1.68	1.77
5	1.53	1.60	1.75
6	1.40	1.57	1.65
7	1.60	1.77	1.77
8	1.50	1.67	1.80
9	1.45	1.57	1.78
10	1.50	1.66	1.76
11	1.53	1.65	1.75
12	1.52	1.66	1.97
13	1.57	1.74	1.80
14	1.52	1.65	1.65
15	1.28	1.43	1.50
16	1.30	1.54	1.65
17	1.40	1.63	1.74
18	1.36	1.40	1.64
19	1.33	1.51	1.61
20	1.46	1.70	1.80
Mean	1.46	1.62	1.73
Standard deviation	.09	.09	.09
$\sqrt{\text{Mean squared relative deviation}}$	.06	.06	.06

stable data the estimates of α decrease, on average, as we go from sum sizes of one to five. On the other hand, the estimates of ν increase for both types of data as we go from sum sizes of one to five. This suggests that a more conservative approach in examining convergence to normality is to use estimates of α to indicate convergence. Thus, when studying actual rates of return, we will rely more heavily upon estimates of α to indicate convergence than estimates of ν.

The likelihood ratio.—In this section, we present results for the (natural) log-likelihood ratios. The log-likelihood ratios allow one to determine which model has the higher likelihood, given the data. For large samples these log-likelihood ratios provide measures of relative degrees of belief in each distributional model (see Section IV-A).

The results for the log-likelihood ratios are summarized in tables 10 and 11. The number computed is the log of: the value of the likelihood function for the Student distribution divided by the value of the likelihood function for the stable distribution.[32] The results are only given for sum sizes of one. For larger sum sizes, the fact that the number of times the value was in the wrong direction (i.e., was greater than zero when the

32. The approximation for the stable density function is given in H. Bergstrom, "On Some Expansions of Stable Distribution Functions," *Arkiv for Matematik* 2, no. 18 (1952): 375–78.

269   *Comparison of Distributions as Models*

Table 8
Estimates of ν for Sums of Size Five from
Simulated Student Data
(Sample Size = 260 per Replication)

Replication Number	True Value of ν		
	$\nu = 3$	$\nu = 5$	$\nu = 8$
1	3.82	7.14	10.21
2	4.85	14.80	60.00*
3	5.61	15.56	47.23
4	5.09	7.90	9.94
5	5.35:	9.43	12.24
6	3.56	7.90	26.81
7	5.35	14.55	41.36
8	6.12	34.72	60.00*
9	4.57	15.56	60.00*
10	3.06	5.35	8.42
11	6.38	60.00*	60.00*
12	9.44	60.00*	60.00*
13	5.86	20.67	60.00*
14	4.08	10.71	25.02
15	2.79	5.10	8.16
16	4.08	9.19	17.36
17	4.08	15.83	60.00*
18	3.06	6.11	12.51
19	3.31	8.92	27.31
20	3.56	7.90	20.67
Mean	4.70	16.87	34.36
Standard deviation	1.52	15.82	21.20
$\sqrt{\text{Mean}}$ squared relative deviation	.322	.938	.617

* Upper bound established in estimation program used for simulated data.

data came from a stable distribution) makes it difficult to use these results (which are available from the authors).

For sums of size one, when the actual data are Student, the log-likelihood ratios are greater than zero for every replication except one (when $\nu = 8$). For stable data, the ratio is less than zero for all replications when $\alpha = 1.65$ and $\alpha = 1.80$. For $\alpha = 1.50$, the ratio is greater than zero seven out of 20 times. Since estimates of α for daily returns are usually around 1.65, the inaccuracies that exist for $\alpha = 1.50$ should not interfere with our using this ratio to discriminate between the two distributions.

From our simulation results we see that the log-likelihood ratio is an exceptionally good discriminator between the Student and stable distributions when the samples contain 1,300 observations (approximately the number of observations available in each series of actual daily returns). For $\nu = 3, 5, 8$ and $\alpha = 1.65, 1.80$ we had only one incorrect classification from 100 trials.[33]

33. The simulation results for all the separate values of α (and ν) use the same uniform numbers to generate the Student and stable-random numbers. The results, therefore, reflect the influence of changes in ν and α, holding everything else constant.

270   The Journal of Business

Table 9

Estimates for ν and α for Sum Sizes of One and Five for Simulated Student and Stable Data

Data Type	Estimation Procedure	Sum Size	True Parameter Value		
			ν		
			$\nu = 3$	$\nu = 5$	$\nu = 8$
		1:			
		Mean	2.87	5.00	8.31
		Std. dev.	.281	.795	2.209
Student	Student	**5:**			
		Mean	4.70	16.87*	34.36†
		Std. dev.	1.52	15.82	21.20
			$\hat{\nu}$		
			$\nu = 3$	$\nu = 5$	$\nu = 8$
		1:			
		Mean	1.54	1.70	1.80
		Std. dev.	.046	.063	.083
Student	Stable	**5:**			
		Mean	1.68	1.80‡	1.86§
		Std. dev.	.088	.170	.104
			$\hat{\alpha}$		
			$\alpha = 1.50$	$\alpha = 1.65$	$\alpha = 1.80$
		1:			
		Mean	1.49	1.64	1.79
		Std. dev.	.057	.055	.060
Stable	Stable	**5:**			
		Mean	1.46	1.62	1.73
		Std. dev.	.090	.091	.095
			$\hat{\alpha}$		
			$\alpha = 1.50$	$\alpha = 1.65$	$\alpha = 1.80$
		1:			
		Mean	2.41	2.93	4.40
		Std. dev.	.803	.309	.740
Stable	Student	**5:**			
		Mean	2.40	3.10	4.97
		Std. dev.	.60	.63	1.94

* Two estimates of ν truncated at $\nu = 60$.
† Seven estimates of ν truncated at $\nu = 60$.
‡ Three estimates of α truncated at $\alpha = 2$.
§ Three estimates of α truncated at $\alpha = 2$.

Summary of the simulation results.—(*a*) The M.L.E. of ν for the Student model is not very good for sample sizes of 260 and 65 but is fairly accurate for sample sizes of 1,300. (*b*) As the degrees of freedom increase, the standard deviation and mean-squared relative deviation of the M.L.E. of ν increase. (*c*) To test for convergence, an increase in α appears to be a better measure of convergence than an increase in ν. (*d*)

271   *Comparison of Distributions as Models*

Table 10
Log-Likelihood Ratios for Simulated Student Data

Replication Number	True Value of ν		
	$\nu = 3$	$\nu = 5$	$\nu = 8$
1	18	16	10
2	19	13	7
3	32	18	21
4	21	21	10
5	8	11	8
6	8	9	13
7	21	18	12
8	7	15	6
9	19	11	5
10	9	3	−1
11	13	21	21
12	4	3	6
13	16	16	22
14	18	14	26
15	6	9	9
16	9	11	6
17	15	18	15
18	23	19	20
19	7	14	11
20	12	18	5

NOTE.—Log-likelihood ratio = Log_e [likelihood of Student model ÷ likelihood of stable model]. Digits to the right of the decimal point are omitted. The likelihood ratio for any entry, x, is $y = e^x$.

Table 11
Log-Likelihood Ratios for Simulated Stable Data

Replication Number	True Value of α		
	$\alpha = 1.5$	$\alpha = 1.65$	$\alpha = 1.80$
1	3	−5	−7
2	−19	−4	36
3	28	−1	−1
4	0.9	−1	−0.3
5	−9	−7	−2
6	−77	−11	−12
7	7	−1	−2
8	−4	−12	−8
9	−2	−10	−9
10	−41	−15	−18
11	2	−5	−2
12	−4	−9	−4
13	−11	−7	−8
14	8	−7	−5
15	−140	−10	−9
16	−11	−9	−9
17	−2	−8	−7
18	−957	−3	−2
19	−10	−14	−12
20	14	−14	−17

NOTE.—Log-likelihood ratio = Log_e [likelihood of Student model ÷ likelihood of stable model]. Digits to the right of the decimal point are omitted for log-likelihood ratios greater than one in absolute value. The likelihood ratio for any entry, x, is $y = e^x$.

The log-likelihood ratios will almost always indicate the true distribution when comparing the Student and stable distributions for sum sizes of one, 1,300 observations, and $\nu = 3,\ 5,\ 8$ or $\alpha = 1.65,\ 1.80$. In these cases, the (approximate) posterior odds in favor of the true distribution are usually quite high.

D. Results for Rates of Return

In the previous section, we saw that the best methods of discriminating between the Student and stable models were: (1) tests of convergence to normality using sum sizes of five, and (2) the value of the log-likelihood ratios for the daily rates of return. In this section, we present results from applying these two discriminators to actual rates of return for the 30 securities described in Section VI*A*. Our sample sizes range from 1,111 observations for Union Carbide to 1,693 observations for both Standard Oil of California and General Electric. Sample sizes for every security are listed in table 12.

Table 12
Sample Size for the Thirty Securities Used in the Study

	Sum Size	
	1	5
Union Carbide	1,111	223
Dupont	1,243	248
Proctor and Gamble	1,447	289
Sears	1,236	247
Standard Oil of California	1,693	338
Standard Oil of New Jersey	1,156	231
Swift	1,446	289
Texaco	1,159	231
Bethlehem Steel	1,200	240
Chrysler	1,692	338
Eastman Kodak	1,238	247
United Aircraft	1,200	240
U.S. Steel	1,200	240
Westinghouse	1,446	289
General Electric	1,693	338
General Foods	1,408	281
General Motors	1,446	289
Goodyear	1,162	232
International Harvester	1,200	240
International Nickel	1,243	248
International Paper	1,447	289
Johns Manville	1,205	241
Allied Chemical	1,223	244
Alcoa	1,190	238
American Can	1,219	243
American Telephone and Telegraph	1,219	243
American Tobacco	1,283	256
Anaconda	1,193	238
Woolworth	1,445	289
Owens Illinois	1,237	247

273   *Comparison of Distributions as Models*

The results from estimating the degrees-of-freedom parameter for daily observations are given in table 13. The estimates range from 2.53

Table 13
Estimation Results for Daily Rates of Return

	Estimates of Degrees of Freedom for Student Model		Estimates of the Characteristic Exponent for the Stable Model		Log-Likelihood Ratios for Sums of Size One*
	Sum Sizes		Sum Sizes		
	1	5	1	5	
Union Carbide	7.6562	23.315	1.71	1.80	14.46
Dupont	6.1215	8.267	1.67	1.76	12.81
Proctor and Gamble	3.3021	5.937	1.52	1.80	14.64
Sears	2.8021	4.089	1.55	1.62	9.61
Standard Oil of California	4.8368	.5.206	1.62	1.84	17.72
Standard Oil of New Jersey	3.5694	27.040	1.61	1.76	7.85
Swift	4.3281	14.417	1.60	1.78	17.03
Texaco	5.3455	9.657	1.65	1.83	15.48
Bethlehem Steel	4.7830	6.175	1.64	1.77	10.75
Chrysler	6.3715	9.666	1.73	1.77	10.04
Eastman Kodak	5.3542	3.598	1.72	1.47	7.88
United Aircraft	4.8455	10.394	1.66	1.89	8.71
U.S. Steel	13.2600	13.452	1.87	1.80	2.99
Westinghouse	6.1128	8.929	1.73	1.75	10.50
General Electric	4.8368	7.287	1.66	1.70	14.38
General Foods	5.0955	5.281	1.67	1.77	10.19
General Motors	5.0955	6.493	1.68	1.78	9.29
Goodyear	4.8368	11.162	1.65	1.77	8.24
International Harvester	5.1042	8.570	1.72	1.73	4.72
International Nickel	3.8194	6.044	1.58	1.65	11.30
International Paper	5.1042	8.096	1.68	1.60	10.78
Johns Manville	5.8542	8.783	1.77	1.72	6.54
Allied Chemical	5.0417	89.984†	1.73	1.94	7.43
Alcoa	4.8368	5.725	1.67	1.86	8.16
American Can	3.3198	4.735	1.65	1.61	7.89
American Telephone and Telegraph	2.5347	2.349	1.45	1.45	10.29
American Tobacco	2.8021	3.351	1.49	1.59	14.29
Anaconda	8.9323	6.731	1.76	1.61	11.27
Woolworth	3.3194	2.561	1.60	1.45	12.61
Owens Illinois	4.5781	9.182	1.60	1.66	14.10

* Log_e [likelihood of Student model ÷ likelihood of Stable model]. The odds ratio for any entry, x, is $y = e^x$.
† Upper bound established in the estimation procedure used for actual data.

for American Telephone and Telegraph to 13.26 for U.S. Steel with the average estimate 4.79. The estimates of α for the same daily observations are given in table 13. The estimates range from 1.45 for American Telephone and Telegraph to 1.87 for U.S. Steel. The mean estimate of α is 1.65, which is approximately the value of α found in other studies of daily returns using the stable model.

The results for estimates of ν and α for sum sizes of five are also given in table 13. The average estimated value of ν is 11.22, and the average estimated value of α is 1.72. Both show an increase. If we have simulated stable data with $\alpha = 1.65$ and we estimate ν for sum sizes of one and then for sum sizes of five, the results in table 9 show that these estimates of ν increase, on average, from 2.93 to 3.10, a very small increase. If we have Student data with $\nu = 5$, and we estimate ν for sum sizes of one and five, our estimate of ν increases, on average, from 5.00 to 16.87, a substantial increase. Our average estimate of ν for the actual data changes from 4.79 to 11.22; the magnitude of this increase is more consistent with the case of the Student model applied to Student data than the Student model applied to stable data.

Similar statements can be made about the changes in estimates of α for sums of sizes one and five. For simulated stable data with $\alpha = 1.65$, the average estimate of α for sum sizes of one is 1.64; for sum sizes of five, it is 1.62, a slight decrease which is consistent with the downward bias in our estimator of α as the sample size decreases. For simulated Student data with ν equal to 5.00, the average estimate of α for sum sizes of one is 1.70; for sum sizes of five it is 1.80. For actual rates of return, the average estimate of α changes from 1.65 to 1.72 as we go from sum sizes of one to five. This increase in the average estimate of α suggests a process that is not stable, but one which is much closer to a process converging to normality.

Our basic inference from the results about convergence is that the data appear to converge to normality. This conclusion is based upon how the estimates of α and ν change when we go from sum sizes of one to sum sizes of five.[34] (Results for sum sizes of 10 and 20 are available from the authors.)

Our second empirical comparison of the two models is based upon the log-likelihood ratios. The results for the daily returns on the 30 securities are given in table 13. In every case, the value of the log-likelihood ratio is greater than zero, indicating the Student model provides a better description of the data than the stable model. Our simulation results given in tables 10 and 11 show that this ratio almost always indicates the correct model. Only when $\alpha = 1.50$ were there any major misclassifications. Thus, observing that all values are greater than zero strongly indicates that the Student model provides a better empirical description of the data than the stable model.

For large sample sizes, log-likelihood ratios can be interpreted as log-odds (see Section VI); we shall use this interpretation for the results

---

34. Our results for estimates of α are consistent with those presented by Officer who applied the stable model to daily rates of return from the period July 2, 1962 through July 11, 1969 for a sample of 50 common stocks listed on the New York Stock Exchange. (Officer's sample does not include the 30 securities whose daily returns were used for our own results.) Officer secured estimation results for sum sizes of 1–5, 7, 10, 15, and 20. The upshot of his results is identical to that of our own; as the sum size increases, the estimates of α increase, on average, or remain almost unchanged. As indicated earlier, this result is inconsistent with the stable model, conditional on the procedures used to estimate α. (The procedures used by Officer to estimate the stable model's parameters are identical to those that we used.)

for sums of size 1. When we use table 13, it can be seen that the log-odds in favor of the Student model are quite high. The lowest log-odds is 2.99 (for U.S. Steel), which corresponds to odds of about 20 to one in favor of the Student model. Since we did not use maximum-likelihood estimates for the stable model, the reported log-odds are inflated. The adjustments needed to remove this inflation are unknown. Since, however, the odds are so strongly in favor of the Student model, any seemingly reasonable adjustment would not, we believe, alter our basic inference: the Student model appears to describe the data better than does the stable model. This inference is given additional support by the evidence indicating convergence to normality.

The log-odds reported in table 13 pertain to all observations available for each security. These results do not indicate which fractiles of the empirical distributions contribute most to the apparent superiority of the Student model, as reflected in the log-odds. In order to consider this issue, we applied the following procedure to the unsummed observations for three securities: (1) the observations were arranged in ascending order, (2) the value of the log-odds was then computed for each observation, and (3) the value of the log-odds was also computed for the first 2 percent of the observations (after the rearrangement in [1]), the second 2 percent, the third 2 percent, etc. The results for each security indicated that the superiority of the Student model is primarily due to the observations in the tails of the empirical distributions. A representative plot from step (3) is provided in figure 1. This plot is based upon the observed returns for Bethlehem Steel. The sample size for this security is 1,200. Thus, each plotted value of the log-odds is based upon $(.02)(1,200) = 24$ ordered observations. (The estimated median would fall between the twenty-fifth and twenty-sixth set of grouped observations.) The plot has a U-shape, indicating that the Student model is heavily favored in the tails of the empirical distribution, whereas the stable model is more heavily favored around the median of the distribution.

We inferred from our results that the Student model provides a better empirical description than the stable model. This does not mean that the rates of return do, in fact, follow a Student model. It only indicates that the latter provides a better empirical fit than the stable model. The Student model has fat tails as does the stable model, but converges to normality for large sum sizes. The stable model does not converge to normality. Some implications of this important difference for theoretical and empirical work were discussed in Section II.

Even though the Student model provides a good fit to actual rates of return, there are some empirical results that it does not describe adequately. First, it has been observed (in, for example, Fama [see n. 2]) that large rates of return tend to be succeeded by large returns of unpredictable sign. This suggests a dependency in rates-of-return series. The Student (and stable) model studied here assumes returns are independent, which is contrary to available empirical evidence. Second, when we

The Journal of Business

276

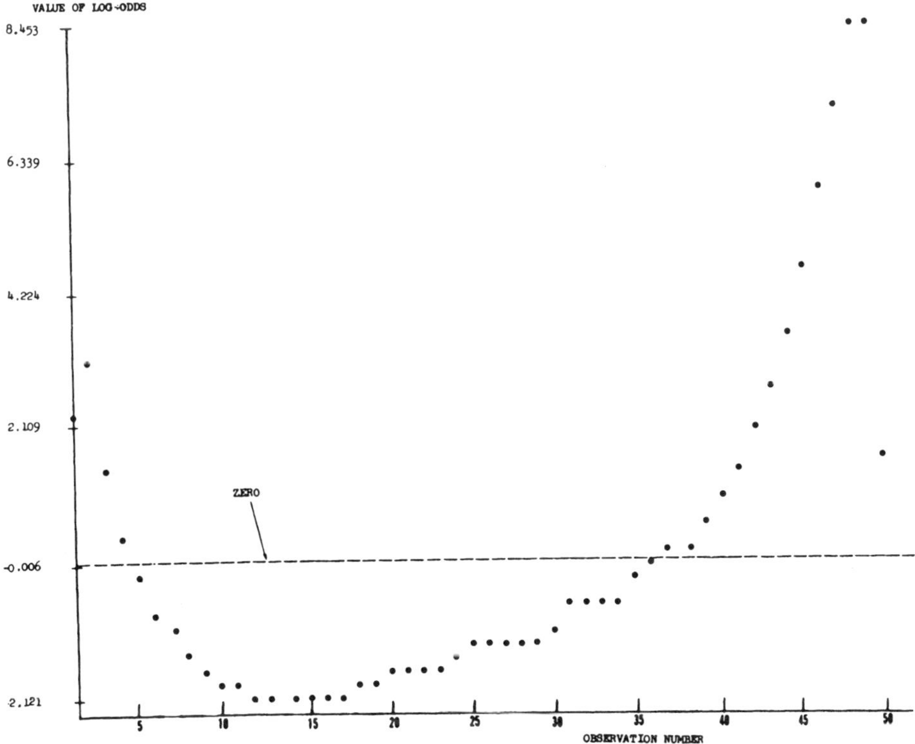

Fig. 1

went from sum sizes of one to sum sizes of five in our simulation study, the estimates of ν always increased. Using table 13, we observe a decrease in four of the 30 estimated values of ν when going to sum sizes of five (Eastman Kodak, American Telephone and Telegraph, Anaconda, Woolworth). This decrease may have occurred because large changes are, on average, followed by large changes. The dependency among large returns may cause the tail areas for sum sizes of five to be larger than if the returns were independent. However, in spite of these empirical deviations from theoretical expectations, we feel that the Student model offers a superior alternative to the stable model.

VII. SUMMARY

The Student and symmetric-stable distributions, as models for daily rates of return on common stocks, were discussed and empirically evaluated. Both models were derived using the framework of subordinated stochastic processes. Some important theoretical and empirical implications of these models were also discussed. The descriptive validity of each model, relative to the other, was assessed by applying each model to actual daily rates of return. Our interpretations of our empirical results were guided by results from a Monte Carlo investigation of the properties of our estimators and model-comparison methods. The major inference of this report is that, for daily rates of return, the Student model has greater descriptive validity than the symmetric-stable model.

APPENDIX A
DERIVATIONS OF THE STUDENT AND STABLE MODELS

Before beginning with the derivations, we state the definition of a subordinated stochastic process. Let $[\widetilde{X}(s); s \geqslant 0]$ and $[\widetilde{h}(s); s \geqslant 0]$ denote stochastic processes. Define another stochastic process $\{\widetilde{Z}(s) = \widetilde{X}[\widetilde{h}(s)]; s \geqslant 0\}$. The process $[\widetilde{Z}(s)]$ is said to be subordinate to the process $[\widetilde{X}(s)]$; the process $[\widetilde{h}(s)]$ is the directing process.[35] We shall present models below in which the Student and symmetric-stable distributions are subordinated stochastic processes with $[\widetilde{X}(s)]$ being a stationary Gaussian stochastic process.

Let $\widetilde{X}(\Delta t)$ denote the rate of return over an interval of time $[t, t + \delta]$ for $t \geqslant 0$ and fixed $\delta > 0$. We assume that the rates of return are expressed as deviations about their mean.

Assume that $[\widetilde{X}(\Delta t); t \geqslant 0]$ is a stationary Gaussian process with the following properties:[36]

$$E[\widetilde{X}(\Delta t)] = 0, \tag{A1}$$

$$\mathrm{Var}\,[\widetilde{X}(\Delta t)] = \sigma^2 \Delta t, \tag{A2}$$

$\widetilde{X}(\Delta t)$ is independent of $\widetilde{X}(\Delta t')$ for all $t' > t + \delta$, and any choice of t and δ. $\tag{A3}$

Next introduce another stochastic process $[\widetilde{h}(\Delta t); t \geqslant 0]$ with the properties:

$$\widetilde{h}(\Delta t) > 0, \tag{B1}$$

$\widetilde{h}(\Delta t)$ is independent of $\widetilde{h}(\Delta t')$ for all $t' > t + \delta$ and any choice of t and δ. $\tag{B2}$

Finally, consider the subordinated process $\{\widetilde{Z}(\Delta t) = \widetilde{X}[\widetilde{h}(\Delta t)]; t \geqslant 0\}$. Given the assumed properties of $[\widetilde{X}(\Delta t)]$ and $[\widetilde{h}(\Delta t)]$, the process $[\widetilde{Z}(\Delta t)]$ has the following properties:

$$E[\widetilde{Z}(\Delta t)] = 0, \tag{C1}$$

$$\mathrm{Var}\,[\widetilde{Z}(\Delta t)|h(\Delta t)] = \sigma^2 h(\Delta t), \tag{C2}$$

35. Subordinated stochastic processes are discussed in W. Feller, *An Introduction to Probability Theory and Its Applications*, 2d ed. (New York: John Wiley & Sons, 1971), 2: chap. 17, Sec. 7.

36. A stochastic process $Y(s)$ is (strictly) stationary if for every finite sequence of points, $s_1, s_2, \ldots, s_n$, the distribution function $F[Y(s_1), Y(s_2), \ldots, Y(s_n)]$ is identical to $F[Y(s_1 + k), Y(s_2 + k), \ldots, Y(s_n + k)]$ for all values of the translation parameter k. Additional details are given in Doob.

278   The Journal of Business

$$\widetilde{Z}(\Delta t) \text{ is independent of } \widetilde{Z}(\Delta t') \text{ for all } t' > t + \delta,$$
$$\text{and any choice of } t \text{ and } \delta, \tag{C3}$$

$$[\widetilde{Z}(\Delta t)] \text{ is a stationary stochastic process.} \tag{C4}$$

For a given realization, $h(\Delta t)$, of $\widetilde{h}(\Delta t)$, the probability density function of $Z(\Delta t)$ is a conditional normal density function with mean zero and variance $\sigma^2 h(\Delta t)$, denoted by $f_N[Z(\Delta t) \mid 0, \sigma^2 h(\Delta t)]$. To find the unconditional distribution of $Z(\Delta t)$ we need a distribution for $h(\Delta t)$.

Define $g(\Delta t) = [h(\Delta t)]^{-1}$. Suppose that $g(\Delta t)$ follows a gamma-2 distribution with parameters $s^2 \Delta t$ and ν denoted by $f_{\gamma 2}[g(\Delta t) \mid s^2 \Delta t, \nu]$.[37] Then the unconditional distribution for $Z(\Delta t)$ is:

$$D[Z(\Delta t) \mid 0, H(\Delta t), \nu] = \int_0^\infty f_N[Z \mid 0, g(\Delta t)\sigma^2] f_{\gamma 2}[g(\Delta t) \mid s^2 \Delta t, \nu] \, dg(\Delta t),$$
$$\tag{5}$$

where $H(\Delta t) = 1/s^2(\Delta t) \, 1/\sigma^2$. The distribution in (1) is a Student distribution with mean 0, scale $H(\Delta t)$, and degrees of freedom ν.

This derivation of the Student model allows the distribution of rates of returns, $[\widetilde{Z}(\Delta t)]$, to incorporate changes in the "states of nature" over the interval $[t, t + \delta]$. The state of nature at t is a complete description of the economic environment up to time t; $\widetilde{h}(\Delta t)$ may be interpreted as the change in state over $[t, t + \delta]$. The change in the "state of nature" may be viewed as a change in the stock of information available to the capital market transactors.

Observe that the kind of "state" dependency provided by the Student model is not the same as that considered by, for example, Radner, Arrow, and Hirshleifer.[38] In the latter works, all uncertainty attaches to the "state," or change thereof, and given the state, the value of the state-dependent random variable is known with certainty. In our scheme, only the distribution function of $\widetilde{Z}(\Delta t)$ is known with certainty when the change of state is known.

Prior to introducing the subordinated process $[\widetilde{Z}(\Delta t)]$, the variance of the process, $\sigma^2 \Delta t$, only depended upon the length of the interval of time, Δt, over which the rate of return was defined. It seems reasonable, however, to let the number and importance of events occurring within the fixed time interval cause changes in the level of variability in rates of returns. We accomplish this by introducing the directing process $[\widetilde{h}(\Delta t)]$.

37. Raiffa and Schlaifer (p. 227) give the mean and variance of the gamma-2 density, $f_{\gamma 2}[g(\Delta t) \mid s^2 \Delta t, \nu)$, as $E(\widetilde{g}(\Delta t)] = 1/s^2 \Delta t$ and

$$\mathrm{Var}\,[\widetilde{g}(\Delta t)] = \frac{1}{1/2\,\nu(s^2 \Delta t)^2}.$$

38. R. Radner, "Competitive Equilibrium Under Uncertainty," *Econometrica* 36 (January 1968): 31–58; K. J. Arrow, "The Role of Securities in the Optimal Allocation of Risk Bearing," *Review of Economic Studies* 32 (April 1964): 91–96; J. Hirshleifer, "Investment Decision under Uncertainty: Choice Theoretic Approaches," *Quarterly Journal of Economics* 79 (November 1965): 509–36; "Investment Decision under Uncertainty: Applications of the State Preference Approach," *Quarterly Journal of Economics* 80 (May 1966): 252–77.

279   *Comparison of Distributions as Models*

We derived the Student distribution by assuming that $\tilde{g}(\Delta t) = [\tilde{h}(\Delta t)]^{-1}$ followed a gamma-2 distribution. The stable model can be derived by assigning a particular asymmetric-stable distribution to $\tilde{h}(\Delta t)$. We have not yet defined the characteristic function of an asymmetric-stable distribution, so we tend to this task first.

The log characteristic function of a stable distribution (symmetric or asymmetric) is:

$$\ln \phi_{\tilde{x}}(t) = i\delta t - |ct|^{\alpha}[1 + i\beta \frac{t}{|t|} w(t, \alpha)],$$

where t is some real number; $i = \sqrt{-1}$; β is the skewness parameter, with $\beta \in [-1, 1]$; δ is the location parameter; $c > 0$ is the scale parameter; α is the characteristic exponent, with $\alpha \in [0, 2]$; and

$$w(t, \alpha) = \begin{cases} \tan(\pi \alpha/2), & \text{if} \quad \alpha \neq 1 \\ \dfrac{2 \ln(|t|)}{\pi}, & \text{if} \quad \alpha \neq 1. \end{cases}$$

If $\beta > 0$ and $\alpha < 2$, the distribution is skewed to the right; it is skewed to the left if $\beta < 0$ and $\alpha < 2$. A symmetric-stable distribution is defined by $\beta = 0$. A strictly positive stable random variable is defined by $\alpha < 1$ and $\beta = 1$.

Now, suppose $\tilde{h}(\Delta t)$ follows a strictly positive stable distribution with location parameter equal to zero, that is, $\beta = 1$ and $\alpha \in (0, 1)$. The characteristic function of this process is:

$$\phi_{\tilde{h}(\Delta t)}(u) = \exp\{-\gamma\Delta t|u|^{\alpha}[1 + i(u/|u|) \tan(\pi\alpha/2)]\}. \qquad (6)$$

Consider the subordinated process $[\tilde{Z}(t)]$ as defined above. If the characteristic function for $\tilde{h}(\Delta t)$ is defined by (6), then, as Mandelbrot and Taylor [1967] demonstrated, the unconditional distribution of $[\tilde{Z}(t)]$ is a symmetric-stable distribution with characteristic exponent $\alpha^* = 2\alpha < 2$, where α is the characteristic exponent of the distribution of $\tilde{h}(\Delta t)$.[39] This can be shown as follows.

$$\phi_{\tilde{Z}(\Delta t)}(u) = E_{\tilde{Z}}\left\{\exp[iu\tilde{Z}(\Delta t)]\right\},$$

$$= E_{\tilde{h}}\left[E_{\tilde{X}}\left(\exp\{iu\tilde{X}[h(\Delta t)]\}|\tilde{h}(\Delta t) = h(\Delta t)\right)\right], \qquad (7)$$

$$= E_{\tilde{h}}\left\{\text{Exp}[-1/2\, u^2\sigma^2\tilde{h}(\Delta t)]\right\},$$

since the characteristic function of $\tilde{X}[h(\Delta t)]$ is that of a normal distribution with mean 0 and variance $\sigma^2 h(\Delta t)$.

Now, let $w = i\, u\, \sigma^2/2$. Then (7) becomes

$$\phi_{\tilde{Z}(\Delta t)}(u) = E\left\{\exp[iw\tilde{h}(\Delta t)]\right\} = \phi_{\tilde{h}(\Delta t)}(w).$$

39. An alternative statement of this result appears in W. Feller, p. 348. The latter work, as well as B. Mandelbrot and H. M. Taylor, "On the Distribution of Stock Price Differences," *Operations Research* 15 (1967): 1057–62, considers processes with stationary independent increments. Such a framework can be used for rates of return under continuous compounding by considering increments of the log-price relative process.

 The Journal of Business

This becomes

$$\phi_{\tilde{z}(\Delta t)}(u) = \exp\{-\gamma\Delta t(\sigma^2/2)^\alpha|w|^{2\alpha}[1 - \tan(\pi\alpha/2)]\},$$

$$= \exp(-\hat{\gamma}\Delta t|w|^{2\alpha}), \qquad (8)$$

where $\hat{\gamma} = \gamma(\sigma^2/2)^\alpha[1 - \tan(\pi\alpha/2)]$. Equation (8) is simply the characteristic function for a symmetric-stable distribution with characteristic exponent $(2\alpha) < 2$.

Note that the methods used to derive the Student and stable models are identical. The difference between the two models is in the distributional assumptions for the directing process $\tilde{h}(\Delta t)$. In the Student model $[\tilde{h}(\Delta t)]^{-1}$ follows a gamma-2 distribution; in the stable model, $\tilde{h}(\Delta t)$ follows a strictly positive stable distribution with $\alpha \,\epsilon\, (0,1)$.

APPENDIX B
PROPERTIES OF THE UNIFORM RANDOM NUMBERS USED IN THE SIMULATIONS

The quality of our simulation results depends, of course, upon the properties of our sample drawn from the uniform distribution $\tilde{u}(0, 1)$, in particular: the consistency of our sample's properties with those of the theoretical distribution of $\tilde{u}(0, 1)$ and the randomness of our sample. In this regard, we note the following:

i. The first and second moments of $\tilde{u}(0, 1)$ are .5 and $(1/12) \approx .0833$, respectively. The first and second moments of our sample are .498 and .0835, respectively.

ii. For a serially independent series with $N = 26,000$ observations, the asymptotic distribution of the estimated first-order serial correlation coefficient, $\hat{\rho}$, has mean and standard deviation equal to: $-(1/N - 1)) = -.38 \times 10^{-4}$ and $\sqrt{1/(N-1)} = .0062$, respectively. For our sample, $\hat{\rho} = .00496$.

iii. For a χ^2 test of the sample cumulative probabilities against $\tilde{u}(0, 1)$, we had a χ^2 statistic of 13.514. This statistic is based upon 20 subintervals of $(0, 1)$, each of length .05. For a χ^2 random variable with 19 df, $\tilde{\chi}^2(19)$, $\Pr[\tilde{\chi}^2(19) \geq 13.7)] = .80$.

From these (and other) results, we infer that our samples properties are consistent with the distribution of $\tilde{u}(0, 1)$ and randomness.

ROBERT C. BLATTBERG and SUBRATA K. SEN*

The modeling of buyer behavior by stochastic brand choice models has typically involved the use of a *single* model to represent the behavior of all consumers though consumer heterogeneity is recognized by allowing the model's parameters to vary across the population. However, analysis of panel data for several frequently purchased products indicates the existence of several distinct consumer segments which are difficult to represent by a single model. It is shown, instead, that in order to describe adequately the behavior of these segments, it is necessary to use several *different* models while allowing consumers *within* a segment to have different model parameters. It is further shown that simple heterogeneous multinomial and Markov models appear to be adequate to represent the behavior of most of the segments.

Market Segments and Stochastic Brand Choice Models

INTRODUCTION

Stochastic models of consumer purchasing behavior have played an important role in recent efforts to model buyer behavior for frequently purchased products. The models are of two main types: (1) purchase incidence models, e.g. [10, 12], and (2) brand choice models, e.g. [1, 3, 14, 15, 18, 20, and 28, p. 51-253]. More recently, there have been attempts to integrate these approaches as evidenced in [13], [8], and [4]. This paper considers only stochastic brand choice (SBC) models. It evaluates current approaches to SBC modeling and suggests a different approach which appears to be more appropriate in the presence of market segments.

The earliest SBC models [21, 26] were based on the assumption that a *single* model using a *single set of parameters* could represent the buying behavior of *all* consumers. This assumption first was questioned by Frank [11], who showed that it is possible to arrive at erroneous conclusions by not considering consumer heterogeneity. Specifically, Frank demonstrated that the learning effects observed by Kuehn [21] could

be explained largely by assuming a Bernoulli model for each consumer but allowing the brand choice probabilities for different consumers to *differ* from one another. Frank's notion of consumer heterogeneity was formalized in subsequent models [1, 18, and 28, p. 51-253] which allowed one or more of the model's parameters to follow a probability distribution (e.g., a beta distribution) instead of having a fixed value which is the same for all consumers. More recently, Jones [19] suggested *two* types of heterogeneity. First, different *segments* of consumers might follow different *models*. Second, *within* a segment, consumers might have different model parameter values. Using these notions, Jones presented the Composite Heterogeneous model [19] which allows for three consumer segments represented by Bernoulli, Markov, and Linear Learning models.

Jones' notion of different consumer segments being represented by different models is a very useful one. However, his model captures only a small fraction of the heterogeneity that appears to be present in many consumer markets. Therefore, the writers address two main issues: (1) the number and nature of the market segments and (2) the types of SBC models that are required to represent the behavior of these segments. In other words, the primary objective is to advocate a *modeling strategy* which requires the development of *different* models for *different* market segments. The modeling strategy incorporates

*Robert C. Blattberg is Associate Professor of Marketing, University of Chicago, and Subrata K. Sen is Associate Professor of Business Administration, University of Rochester.

This research was financed in part by National Science Foundation Grant GS-40033.

Journal of Marketing Research
Vol. XIII (February 1976), 34-45

both types of heterogeneity discussed by Jones [19]. The principal goal in proposing this strategy is to provide a better model-based "description" of buying behavior for frequently purchased products. If the buying behavior of each segment can be modeled successfully, the segment models can be used to classify individual consumers into the various segments [6]. Once consumers have been classified into segments, the researcher can proceed to determine the sensitivity of the various segments to marketing variables and to identify the segments in terms of demographic and psychographic variables (see [6] for a more extended discussion).

To demonstrate the feasibility of the modeling strategy, a set of data on facial tissue purchases is used to describe the nine major segments that can be defined for a wide variety of frequently purchased products. Next several different SBC models are shown to be required to represent the behavior of these nine segments. Using the facial tissue data as well as data from two other product categories, waxed paper and aluminum foil, it is demonstrated that many of the segments can be well represented by existing SBC models such as Bernoulli and Markov models. For other segments, none of the currently available models is entirely appropriate. The concluding section of the paper indicates the nature of the new models that need to be developed to represent these segments.

PURCHASE SEGMENTS

Using panel data on five frequently purchased product categories, the writers [5, 6] have described a market segmentation approach based on several dimensions of a consumer's purchasing behavior: the brand purchased, the store shopped, and the price paid. Each person's purchase history in terms of these dimensions was analyzed separately to define several homogeneous market segments. The details of the procedure are described in [5] and [6].

Description of Data

A set of data on facial tissue purchases is used to illustrate the segments. Table 1 lists the purchase histories of individuals who represent nine of the segments found in [5]. The panel data were obtained from the *Chicago Tribune's* panel of women in the Greater Chicago area. The facial tissue data analyzed consisted of the panel's purchases between 1958 and the middle of 1961. There were 474 consumers in the panel with 10 or more purchases. However, the writers analyze in detail the purchase histories of the 179 consumers who had a record of 31 or more purchases, i.e., *only the "heavy" buyers*. For each consumer, information was available on the brand purchased, the store shopped, the size bought, and the price paid. Of the 16 brands coded 1 to 16, brands 1, 2, 6, 10, and 13 are national brands and the rest are private label brands. The stores are coded 1 to

10. Stores 1 to 4 represent major supermarket chains. Stores 5 to 7 represent independent food chains. Store 8 represents a major drug store chain, store 9 wholesale and discount stores, and store 10 all other stores. There are six possible sizes, boxes of 24, 100, 200, 300, 400, and 402 tissues. However, an overwhelming majority of the purchases (89.2 percent) were of the 400-tissue box.

Segment Descriptions

High National Brand Loyal Segment. Consumer 1731 represents a segment which is highly loyal to a single national brand. Table 1 indicates that consumer 1731 bought brand 1 on 29 out of the 32 purchase occasions. The proportion of purchases devoted to the favorite brand ranged from about 90 to 100 percent for this segment. It should be noted that this segment previously was called the "High Brand Loyal" segment [6]. The name was altered to make it more descriptive of the behavior of the segment members.

National Brand Loyal Segment. Consumer 1611 represents a segment which is also loyal to a single national brand. However, the degree of loyalty is not as strong as for the High National Brand Loyal consumer. As is evident from Table 1, the National Brand Loyal consumer switches occasionally from his favorite brand. However, he quickly returns to his favorite brand, usually after a single trial of the brand he had switched to. Earlier, this segment was called the "Brand Loyal" segment [6].

National Brand Switcher Segment. Consumer 1439 represents this segment. This consumer is not particularly loyal to any one brand, but 26 of his 32 purchases consist of two national brands, 1 and 2. Essentially, he appears to switch only between national brands and is willing to pay high prices for them. Only four of his 32 purchases are deal purchases. This segment previously was called the "National Brand Loyal" segment [6].

National/Private Switcher Segment. This segment is represented by consumer 1217 in Table 1. This consumer does not exhibit loyalty to any particular brand (brand 1, the most frequently purchased brand, is bought on only 31.4 percent of the purchase occasions), switches between both national and private brands (national brands are bought on 48.6 percent of the purchase occasions, private labels on the remaining 51.4 percent), and makes very few of his purchases on deal (only five of 35 are deal purchases).

Last Purchase Loyal Segment. Consumer 947 represents this segment. This consumer buys one brand on several successive occasions, switches to another brand, buys that several times, switches again, and so on. Though consumer 947 exhibits only a single switch and the switch is from one private label (brand 4) to another (brand 14), the Last Purchase Loyal consumer generally makes several switches. Further, the switching is not necessarily limited to either private

JOURNAL OF MARKETING RESEARCH, FEBRUARY 1976

36

Table 1
PURCHASE HISTORIES OF INDIVIDUAL CONSUMERS, FACIAL TISSUE

| | Consumer 1731 | | | | Consumer 1611 | | | | Consumer 1439 | | | |
| | High National Brand Loyal | | | | National Brand Loyal | | | | National Brand Switcher | | | |
Purchase number	Brand	Store	Size (# tissues)	Price (¢)	Brand	Store	Size (# tissues)	Price (¢)	Brand	Store	Size (# tissues)	Price (¢)
1	1	10	24	5	7	8	400	2/31*	8	3	400	19
2	1	2	400	27*	2	3	400	29	8	3	400	19
3	8	3	400	19	2	7	400	29	8	3	400	19
4	1	3	400	29	1	7	200	15	1	7	400	29
5	1	3	400	25*	1	3	400	25*	1	7	400	23*
6	1	3	400	29	2	3	400	25*	2	7	400	29
7	1	3	400	29	1	3	400	2/49*	14	9	402	29
8	1	3	400	29	7	8	300	9*	2	7	400	29
9	1	3	400	2/49*	13	5	400	31	1	9	400	25*
10	1	2	400	29	2	3	400	29	2	7	400	29
11	1	2	400	29	2	3	400	29	1	9	400	31
12	1	2	400	25*	2	7	400	29	16	9	400	27 N
13	1	2	400	29	2	3	400	29	2	7	400	29
14	1	3	400	29	8	3	400	19	2	7	400	29
15	8	3	400	2/39	2	3	400	29	2	1	400	29
16	1	3	400	25*	2	3	400	29	2	7	400	29
17	1	3	400	25*	2	3	400	29	1	7	400	29
18	1	2	400	29	2	3	400	29	2	7	400	29
19	1	3	400	29	2	3	400	29	2	10	400	29 N
20	1	3	200	15	2	3	400	29	2	7	400	29
21	1	2	400	29	8	3	400	22	1	7	400	2/49*
22	1	2	400	2/49*	2	3	400	25*	1	7	400	29
23	1	2	400	29	2	3	400	29	1	7	400	29
24	1	2	400	29	2	3	400	29	3	3	400	2/39
25	1	2	200	29	2	3	400	29	1	7	400	29
26	8	3	400	17*	2	3	400	29	2	3	400	29
27	1	6	400	29	2	3	400	25*	2	7	400	29
28	1	6	400	29	2	3	400	25*	1	7	400	29
29	1	6	400	29	1	3	400	29	2	7	400	29
30	1	6	200	2/39	2	3	400	29	1	7	400	3/98
31	1	6	400	29	2	3	400	23*	1	7	400	29
32	1	6	400	29	2	3	400	29	1	7	400	2/49*
33					2	3	400	23*				
34					2	3	400	23*				
35					2	7	400	29				
36					2	7	400	29				

*Deal price.
N: Not known whether or not this is a deal price.

labels or national brands but can cut across both national and private brands. Though the reasons for his switching are not entirely clear (switching might be triggered by receipt of an advertising message or a word-of-mouth recommendation), this consumer seems to exhibit loyalty to the brand last purchased.

Private Label Loyal Segment. This segment is represented by consumer 569. Essentially, this consumer is loyal to the private label of the store he usually visits. Thirty-three of the 35 purchases are made in store 3 and brand 3 is usually purchased. Brand 3 is store 3's private label. Because private label brand prices are generally lower than national brand prices, this consumer shows a certain amount of price sensi-

tivity. Previously, this segment was called the "Low Price Store Effect" segment [6].

Private Label Switcher Segment. This segment, represented by consumer 1135, is similar to the National Brand Switcher segment except that the consumer switches primarily between private label brands (84.8 percent of consumer 1135's purchases consist of private labels). This consumer does not exhibit any particular loyalty to a single private label, nor are most purchases made on deal (consumer 1135 makes only four deal purchases of a total of 33). However, because private labels are generally cheaper than national brands, this consumer also shows a certain amount of price sensitivity.

Table 1 (Continued)
PURCHASE HISTORIES OF INDIVIDUAL CONSUMERS, FACIAL TISSUE

| Purchase number | Consumer 1217 | | | | Consumer 947 | | | | Consumer 569 | | | |
| | *National/Private Switcher* | | | | *Last Purchase Loyal* | | | | *Private Label Loyal* | | | |
	Brand	Store	Size (# tissues)	Price (¢)	Brand	Store	Size (# tissues)	Price (¢)	Brand	Store	Size (# tissues)	Price (¢)
1	8	3	400	19	4	1	400	2/35*	8	3	400	19
2	8	3	400	19	4	1	400	2/35*	3	3	400	19
3	8	3	400	19	4	1	400	2/35*	3	3	400	19
4	1	2	400	29	4	1	400	2/35*	3	3	200	19 N
5	2	2	400	29	4	1	400	21	3	3	400	19
6	2	1	400	29	4	1	400	21	3	3	400	19
7	8	3	400	19	4	1	400	21	3	3	400	19
8	2	3	400	19*	4	1	400	21	3	3	400	19
9	11	7	400	2/45*	4	1	400	21	3	3	400	19
10	13	5	400	29	4	1	400	21	3	3	400	18*
11	1	1	400	29	4	1	400	21	3	3	400	18*
12	1	2	400	29	4	1	400	21	8	3	400	19
13	1	7	400	29	4	1	400	21	3	3	400	19
14	1	1	400	29	4	1	400	2/35*	3	3	400	2/35*
15	1	7	400	29	4	1	400	2/35*	3	3	400	19
16	3	1	400	2/35 N	4	1	400	2/35*	3	3	400	19
17	8	3	400	19	14	10	402	21	5	6	400	20
18	2	5	400	29	4	1	400	2/35*	3	3	400	19
19	11	5	400	6/125	14	10	402	21	5	2	200	20 N
20	4	1	400	2/39	14	10	402	28	3	3	400	20
21	1	1	400	29	14	10	402	19	3	3	200	19 N
22	5	2	400	2/39	14	10	402	2/39	3	3	400	20
23	8	3	400	19	14	10	402	2/39	3	3	400	2/37*
24	5	5	400	2/43	14	10	402	2/39	3	3	400	18*
25	8	3	400	19	14	10	402	2/39	3	3	400	2/39
26	1	1	400	29	14	10	402	2/39	3	3	400	2/39
27	8	3	400	19	14	10	402	2/39	3	3	400	17*
28	8	3	400	19	14	10	402	2/39	3	3	400	2/39
29	2	2	400	2/49*	15	10	400	18*	3	3	400	20
30	1	9	24	5	14	10	402	2/39	3	3	400	2/39
31	1	1	400	29	14	10	402	2/39	3	3	400	16*
32	8	3	400	2/39	14	10	402	2/39	3	3	400	2/35*
33	1	1	400	29	15	10	400	3/50*	3	3	400	2/39
34	14	5	402	9/190*	15	10	400	3/50*	3	3	400	2/39
35	4	1	400	2/35*	14	10	402	2/39	3	3	400	2/39

*Deal price.

N: Not known whether or not this is a deal price.

National Brand Switcher (Deal) Segment. Consumer 589 represents this segment, which is similar to the National Brand Switcher segment except that most of the purchases are made on deal. Consumer 589 buys a national brand on 32 of the 34 purchase occasions and 22 of the 34 purchases are on deal. In contrast, the National Brand Switcher (who also buys mostly national brands) is willing to pay high prices. This segment previously was called the "National Brand Deal-Oriented" segment [6].

Deal-Oriented Segment. This segment, represented by consumer 1440, buys almost exclusively on deal (26 out of 34 purchases are deal purchases for consumer 1440). Further, the Deal-Oriented consumer does not appear to have any brand preference *per se*, as the lowest-priced brand is purchased in general.

To obtain the lowest-priced brand, the Deal-Oriented consumer appears to be willing to shop around at many stores (note the store switching pattern for consumer 1440). The Deal-Oriented segment is distinguished from the National Brand Switcher (Deal) segment in terms of the brand assortment purchased. The Deal-Oriented consumer purchases either private labels on deal or a mixture of national and private brands as long as they are on deal. In contrast, the National Brand Switcher (Deal) consumer purchases only national brands on deal.

MODELING THE PURCHASE SEGMENTS

The next problem is to determine whether each of the segments described could be represented by mathematical models which are simple and easily tractable,

JOURNAL OF MARKETING RESEARCH, FEBRUARY 1976

Table 1 (Continued)
PURCHASE HISTORIES OF INDIVIDUAL CONSUMERS, FACIAL TISSUE

| | Consumer 1135 | | | | Consumer 589 | | | | Consumer 1440 | | | |
| | Private Label Switcher | | | | Nat'l Brand Switcher (Deal) | | | | Deal-Oriented | | | |
Purchase number	Brand	Store	Size (# tissues)	Price (¢)	Brand	Store	Size (# tissues)	Price (¢)	Brand	Store	Size (# tissues)	Price (¢)
1	1	6	400	31	2	7	400	24*	4	1	400	2/35*
2	2	6	400	25	1	7	400	19*	7	8	400	17*
3	11	6	400	25	2	7	400	23*	7	8	400	17*
4	8	3	400	19	1	7	200	19	4	1	400	2/45
5	4	1	400	21	1	7	400	29	11	5	400	2/49
6	4	1	400	19*	2	7	400	19*	7	8	400	17*
7	3	3	400	19	2	7	400	19*	11	5	400	2/49
8	4	1	400	20	1	7	400	19*	4	1	400	2/35*
9	16	3	400	19 N	2	7	400	29	4	1	400	2/35*
10	3	3	400	19	1	7	200	19	1	5	400	20*
11	8	3	400	19	1	7	200	19	4	1	400	2/35*
12	3	3	400	20	1	7	200	12*	4	1	400	2/35*
13	3	3	400	20	2	7	400	19*	7	8	400	17*
14	1	6	400	25*	1	7	400	19*	1	5	400	20*
15	5	2	400	20	1	7	400	29	11	6	400	2/49
16	3	3	400	18*	1	7	200	19	7	8	400	17*
17	5	6	400	20	1	7	200	12*	7	8	400	17*
18	4	7	400	20	1	7	400	29	1	5	400	20*
19	3	3	400	20	1	7	200	19	1	5	400	20*
20	5	2	400	20	2	7	400	19*	1	5	400	20*
21	16	6	400	20 N	1	7	400	19*	7	8	400	2/31*
22	3	3	400	20	1	7	200	19	4	1	400	2/45
23	4	7	400	20	1	7	200	19	1	8	400	2/37*
24	3	3	400	20	12	7	400	19*	7	8	400	17*
25	2	6	400	29	12	7	400	19*	1	10	400	2/25*
26	1	6	200	2/29	2	7	400	19*	7	8	400	2/29*
27	4	7	400	20	2	7	400	19*	7	8	400	2/31*
28	5	7	400	18*	2	7	400	19*	3	3	400	2/39
29	12	6	400	20	2	7	400	19*	1	6	400	23*
30	3	3	400	20	2	7	400	19*	7	8	400	17*
31	3	3	400	20	1	7	400	29	3	3	400	5/88*
32	3	3	400	20	2	7	400	19*	9	4	400	2/45
33	3	3	400	20	2	7	400	19*	15	10	400	3/47*
34					2	7	400	23*	3	3	400	2/39

*Deal price.
N: Not known whether or not this is a deal price.

such as simple SBC models. To simplify the discussion, the market was assumed to consist of two national brands, brands 1 and 2, and three private label brands, brands 3, 4, and 5. Given this market structure, the writers show that most of the segments can be represented by simple, five-state multinomial and Markov models. By using n-state (n = 5) models instead of the usual two-state models, the writers were able to represent a segment such as the National Brand Switcher segment and also were able to distinguish between the National Brand Loyal segment and the Private Label Loyal segment. Other advantages of using n states rather than two states are discussed in the Appendix.

High National Brand Loyal Segment. This segment can be described most simply by a multinomial model with a high probability of the consumer purchasing his favorite brand. As high brand loyalty appears to exist only for national brands, the transition matrix will appear as (1), where brand 1 is assumed to be the consumer's favorite brand.

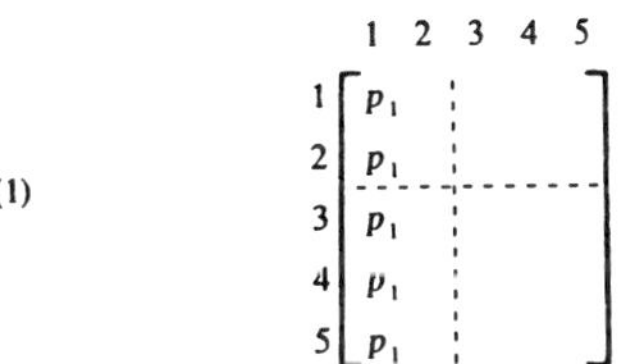

$$(1) \quad \begin{array}{c} \\ 1 \\ 2 \\ 3 \\ 4 \\ 5 \end{array} \begin{array}{ccccc} 1 & 2 & 3 & 4 & 5 \end{array} \left[\begin{array}{ccccc} p_1 & & & & \\ p_1 & & & & \\ p_1 & & & & \\ p_1 & & & & \\ p_1 & & & & \end{array} \right]$$

In (1), p_1 is close to 1.0. The blank cells in (1), and

in the transition matrices that follow, indicate that the probability of occurrence of those cells is close to 0.0. For example, the probability of buying brand 2 in (1) is always close to 0.0. If the five states described were collapsed into two states, state 1 to represent the consumer's favorite brand and state 0 to indicate all other brands, (1) would reduce to a Bernoulli model with a high probability of the consumer purchasing his favorite brand. It should be noted that heterogeneity is allowed in the parameters of this model. In other words, all High National Brand Loyal consumers are not required to have the same p_1. The exact method of incorporating this heterogeneity is indicated in [7, p. 686-91]. Parameter heterogeneity is incorporated similarly in the other models described hereafter.

National Brand Loyal Segment. This segment can be represented by an *n*-state (where $n > 2$) version of Morrison's Brand Loyal Markov model [28, p. 99]. In terms of the five-state market, the transition matrix of a National Brand Loyal consumer who is loyal to brand 1 is shown in (2).

$$
(2) \qquad
\begin{array}{c}
 \\ 1 \\ 2 \\ 3 \\ 4 \\ 5
\end{array}
\begin{array}{c}
1\;2\;3\;4\;5 \\
\left[\begin{array}{ccccc}
p_{11} & & & & \\
p_{21} & & & & \\
p_{31} & & & & \\
p_{41} & & & & \\
p_{51} & & & &
\end{array}\right]
\end{array}
$$

$p_{i1}\,(i = 2, ..., 5)$ will be very large to indicate that the probability of switching *back* to brand 1 is very high. Conversely, $p_{1j}\,(j = 2, ..., 5)$ will be very small to represent the very low probability of switching *away* from brand 1. p_{11} also will be large, but not as large as $p_{i1}\,(i = 2, ..., 5)$. However, most of the *transactions* will be concentrated in the (1, 1) cell. Other cell probabilities, such as p_{23}, are close to 0.0 as indicated by the blank in cell (2, 3) of (2).

National Brand Switcher Segment. This segment can be represented by a Markov model with the transition matrix shown in (3).

$$
(3) \qquad
\begin{array}{c}
1 \\ 2 \\ 3 \\ 4 \\ 5
\end{array}
\begin{array}{c}
1\;2\;3\;4\;5 \\
\left[\begin{array}{cc}
M_1 & M_2 \\
& \\
M_3 & M_4 \\
&
\end{array}\right]
\end{array}
$$

As indicated, (3) consists of four submatrices, M_1, M_2, M_3, and M_4. The entries of each of the M_i ($i = 1, ..., 4$) consist of the appropriate transition probabilities. For example, the entries of M_1 are as follows.

$$
M_1 =
\begin{array}{c}
 \\ 1 \\ 2
\end{array}
\begin{array}{c}
1\qquad\; 2 \\
\left[\begin{array}{cc}
p_{11} & p_{12} \\
p_{21} & p_{22}
\end{array}\right]
\end{array}
$$

Most of the *transactions* will be limited to the cells of matrix M_1 to represent the fact that the brand switching is confined to the two national brands, brands 1 and 2. In terms of the transition *probabilities*, the entries of M_1 will be large, the exact magnitudes of p_{11}, p_{12}, p_{21}, and p_{22} being dependent upon the sequence in which brands 1 and 2 are purchased. The entries of M_3 also will be large to indicate that there is a high probability of switching back to the two national brands if the consumer had previously bought a private-label brand. The entries of M_2 should be small to reflect the low probabilities of switching *away* from national brands, whereas the entries of M_4 should be close to 0.0 because consecutive purchases of private-label brands are unlikely for the National Brand Switcher consumer.

National/Private Switcher Segment. As this segment represents consumers who switch between both national and private brands, it can be represented best by a multinomial model with roughly equal probabilities of purchasing each brand. The transition matrix for this model can be represented as shown in (4).

$$
(4) \qquad
\begin{array}{c}
1 \\ 2 \\ 3 \\ 4 \\ 5
\end{array}
\begin{array}{c}
1\;\;2\;\;3\;\;4\;\;5 \\
\left[\begin{array}{ccccc}
p & p & p & p & p \\
p & p & p & p & p \\
p & p & p & p & p \\
p & p & p & p & p \\
p & p & p & p & p
\end{array}\right]
\end{array}
$$

p would be expected to equal 0.2 in the case of the five-brand market.

Last Purchase Loyal Segment. This segment can be represented by either Howard's Dynamic Inference model [16] or Morrison's Last Purchase Loyal Markov model [28, p. 99]. The transition matrix (for a five-state Last Purchase Loyal Markov Model) is shown in (5).

$$
(5) \qquad
\begin{array}{c}
1 \\ 2 \\ 3 \\ 4 \\ 5
\end{array}
\begin{array}{c}
1\quad 2\quad 3\quad 4\quad 5 \\
\left[\begin{array}{ccccc}
p_{11} & & & & \\
& p_{22} & & & \\
& & p_{33} & & \\
& & & p_{44} & \\
& & & & p_{55}
\end{array}\right]
\end{array}
$$

In this model, the probabilities for the diagonal cells all will be close to 1.0 to reflect the fact that the Last Purchase Loyal consumer continues to buy a particular brand on successive purchase occasions before suddenly switching to another brand, which he then buys on the next set of occasions before switching again. The probabilities of the nondiagonal cells are all close to 0.0. The *transactions* should be concentrated in cells (i, i) for $i = 1, 2, ..., 5$.

Private Label Loyal Segment. The Private Label Loyal consumer mostly purchases one particular store's private label brand. His transition matrix tends to be very similar to that of a National Brand Loyal consumer. Hence, this segment also can be represented by the Brand Loyal Markov model. However, the favorite brand for this consumer will be a private label brand. For example, the transition matrix for a consumer who primarily buys private label brand 4 can be represented as shown in (6).

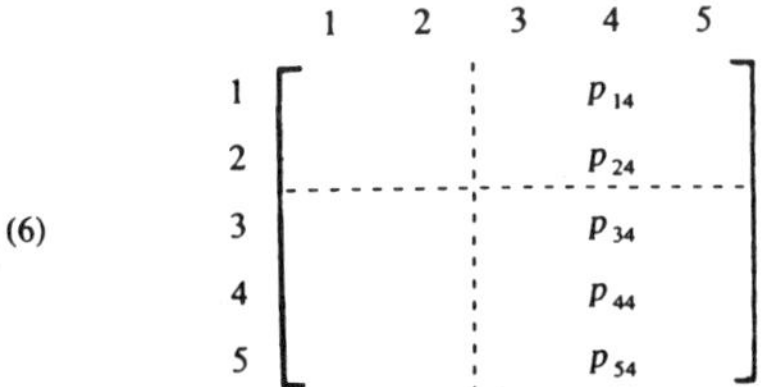

$$(6) \quad \begin{array}{c@{}c} & \begin{array}{ccccc} 1 & 2 & 3 & 4 & 5 \end{array} \\ \begin{array}{c} 1 \\ 2 \\ 3 \\ 4 \\ 5 \end{array} & \left[\begin{array}{ccc:cc} & & & p_{14} & \\ & & & p_{24} & \\ \hdashline & & & p_{34} & \\ & & & p_{44} & \\ & & & p_{54} & \end{array} \right] \end{array}$$

An examination of (6) indicates that the nonzero transitional probabilities are concentrated in cells $(i, 4)$ for $i = 1, ..., 5$, because the consumer's favorite brand is the private label brand, brand 4. In contrast, the nonzero transitional probabilities are concentrated in cells $(i, 1)$ in (2) for $i = 1, ..., 5$ because the consumer's favorite brand in (2) is national brand 1.

Private Label Switcher Segment. This segment can be represented by a Markov model with a transition matrix conceptually similar to (3). However, most of the *transactions* will be limited to the cells of matrix M_4 to represent the fact that brand switching is mainly confined to the three private labels, brands 3, 4, and 5. In terms of the transition *probabilities*, the entries of M_4 will be large, as will the entries of M_2, to indicate that there is a high probability of switching back to the three private labels if the consumer previously had bought a national brand. For reasons similar to those discussed for the National Brand Switchers, the entries of M_3 would be expected to be small and the entries of M_1 should be close to 0.0.

National Brand Switcher (Deal) Segment. This segment cannot be described adequately by existing SBC models as most of these models do not consider the effects of price and promotion directly. Those SBC models which do attempt to incorporate marketing variables (e.g. [27] and [30]) are evaluated in the final section of this paper.

Deal-Oriented Segment. For a similar reason, no models are yet available to represent this segment adequately.

EVALUATION OF SEGMENT MODELS

The empirical test of the modeling strategy involved the use of panel data on three product categories: facial tissue, waxed paper, and aluminum foil. Table 2 provides information on the sample sizes available for each product. Only "heavy" buyers, defined as consumers with 31 or more purchases, were included (the reasons for the choice of 31 as a cutoff criterion are discussed in [7, p. 693]). As indicated in Table 2, the numbers of "heavy" buyers were 179, 46, and 59 for facial tissue, waxed paper, and aluminum foil, respectively. The analysis was limited further to those heavy buyers with *stable* purchasing patterns, i.e., consumers whose purchasing pattern did not change over the time period of the data. The reason for this limitation is that it is very difficult to model the behavior of a consumer who changes his purchasing pattern from, say, High National Brand Loyal to Deal-Oriented to National Brand Switcher. Table 2 indicates that there were relatively few heavy buyers with *changing* patterns. Such consumers excluded, the final sample sizes were 150 for facial tissue, 43 for waxed paper, and 49 for aluminum foil.

Table 2
SAMPLE SIZES FOR THE THREE PRODUCTS

Minimum no. of purchases per consumer	Facial tissue	Waxed paper	Aluminum foil
10	474	297	240
31 (stable pattern)[a]	150	43	49
31 (changing pattern)	29	3	10
31 (total)	179	46	59
Time period of the data	1958–1961	1963–1966	1962–1966

[a]These consumers were used in the Bayesian Model Discrimination procedure.

The ability to model the segments described was evaluated by a two-stage procedure. First, each consumer was classified *visually* into one of the nine segments. Next, these classifications were compared with those produced by a Bayesian Model Discrimination (BDIS) procedure developed by Blattberg and Sen [7].

Bayesian Model Discrimination Procedure

The BDIS procedure analyzes each consumer's purchasing data separately to determine the *model* (out of a set of m pre-specified models) which best describes the purchasing behavior of the consumer. The technique begins with a prior distribution for the parameters of each of the m models. Next, the consumer's purchase history is substituted into each model to calculate the probability that the data were generated by the particular model. Finally, the consumer is classified into the model which had the highest probability of generating his purchase history. Additional details about the BDIS procedure are given in [7], where it is also demonstrated from an analysis of simulated data that the technique is accurate in classifying simple SBC models.

Application of Bayesian Model Discrimination Procedure to the Three Product Categories

In the following application of the BDIS procedure, four simple two-state models are used to represent the purchase segments: (1) a Brand Loyal Markov (BLM) model [28, p. 99], (2) a Last Purchases Loyal (LPM) Markov model [28, p. 99], (3) a Bernoulli model with a *high* probability of purchasing one's favorite brand (HLB), and (4) a Bernoulli model with a *low* probability of purchasing one's favorite brand (DNB). The DNB model attempts to represent a consumer who exhibits considerable brand switching. He does not really have any brand preference and his "favorite" brand is merely the brand bought most often. Hence, the probability of purchasing the "favorite" brand is very low. Two-state models are used to simplify the analysis even though the use of two-state models has certain disadvantages (see Appendix).

In terms of the purchase segments described heretofore, the BDIS procedure would be expected to classify members of the High National Brand Loyal segment (as determined by the visual classification scheme) into the HLB model, members of the National Brand Loyal segment into the BLM model, and members of the Last Purchase Loyal segment into the LPM model. Private Label Loyal consumers should be classified into either the HLB model or the BLM model, because some Private Label Loyal consumers buy their favorite brand nearly 100 percent of the time whereas others purchase their favorite private label only about 75 percent of the time. The remaining five segments, National Brand Switcher, National/Private Switcher, Private Label Switcher, National Brand Switcher (Deal), and Deal-Oriented, represent consumers who are brand switchers. Consequently, one would expect the BDIS procedure to classify members of these five segments into the DNB model which is the only model (of the four models considered in this analysis) that attempts to represent high brand switching.

Segment Modeling Results

Table 3 indicates the degree to which the classifications produced by the BDIS procedure matched the visual classifications. Overall, 79.3 percent of the facial tissue consumers, 74.4 percent of the waxed paper consumers, and 87.7 percent of the aluminum foil consumers are classified correctly. At a more disaggregate level, most members of the High National Brand Loyal, National Brand Loyal, Private Label Loyal, and Last Purchases Loyal segments are classified correctly (for all three products). For the other five segments, the "percent correctly classified" drops somewhat, particularly for facial tissue and waxed paper. In other words, the BDIS procedure is very accurate with members of the four segments that are well represented by the models being considered (the HLB, BLM, and LPM models) but it performs less efficiently for the segments that are only approximated by the DNB model.

For all three products, misclassified consumers usually are classified into the LPM model. Consumers never are misclassified into the DNB model and only rarely are misclassified into the HLB and BLM models. A major reason for the pattern of misclassifying, for example, a National/Private Switcher or a Private Label Switcher into the LPM model is the use of only two states (0 and 1) for the segment models. This issue is discussed in more detail in the Appendix.

It appears, therefore, that simple Bernoulli and Markov models can describe most of the purchase segments fairly well. This is an important point, because these simple models generally have been rejected in favor of more complex SBC models (see, for example, [28, p. 177–80]) when it is assumed that *all* consumers can be represented by a *single* model. As Bernoulli and Markov models are easier to estimate and easier to understand than some of the more complex SBC models, it would be undesirable to reject them too hastily.

However, present SBC models are really incapable of providing good descriptions of the behavior of the two deal-oriented segments. Consider, for example, the Deal-Oriented segment which is represented, as expected, by the DNB model (see Table 3). The assessment must be that the DNB model is not very useful in representing the behavior of this segment because the effects of price are considered by the model only in an *indirect* manner. In other words, the consumer's price sensitivity manifests itself in brand switching behavior, and it is this characteristic that is picked up by the DNB model. As price appears to be the principal determinant of brand choice for this segment, a model is needed which can link price with brand choice directly. For similar reasons, the National Brand Switcher (Deal) segment cannot be represented adequately by currently available SBC models.

If adequate models can be developed for each segment, the segment models can be used along with the BDIS procedure to classify individual consumers into the various segments. As discussed in [6], segment classification is a prerequisite for further segmentation analysis such as the determination of the sensitivity of each segment to marketing variables.

Incorporating Marketing Mix Variables into Stochastic Brand Choice Models

To adequately represent all segments, it appears necessary to develop models which deal explicitly with marketing mix variables. Several authors have tried

Table 3
REPRESENTATION OF PURCHASE SEGMENTS BY MARKOV AND BERNOULLI MODELS OF BRAND CHOICE

Segments	Facial tissue						Waxed paper						Aluminum foil					
	HLB	BLM	LPM	DNB	Total	Percent Correctly Classified	HLB	BLM	LPM	DNB	Total	Percent Correctly Classified	HLB	BLM	LPM	DNB	Total	Percent Correctly Classified
High National Brand Loyal	19	0	0	0	19	100.0	12	1	2	0	15	80.0	12	0	0	0	12	100.0
National Brand Loyal	3	17	2	0	22	77.2	0	10	1	0	11	91.0	1	8	1	0	10	80.0
Private Label Loyal	8	22	3	0	33	91.0	2	1	0	0	3	100.0	1	1	0	0	2	100.0
Last Purchase Loyal	0	2	15	0	17	88.3	0	1	2	0	3	66.7	0	1	4	0	5	80.0
National Brand Switcher	0	1	2	5	8	62.5	0	3	1	1	5	20.0	0	1	0	7	8	87.5
National/Private Switcher	0	1	4	10	15	66.7	0	0	1	2	3	66.7	0	0	0	3	3	100.0
Private Label Switcher	0	4	5	12	21	57.0	0	0	0	0	0	—	0	0	0	2	2	100.0
National Brand Switcher (Deal)	0	0	0	2	2	100.0	0	0	0	1	1	100.0	0	0	0	3	3	100.0
Deal Oriented	0	0	4	9	13	69.2	0	0	1	1	2	50.0	0	0	2	2	4	50.0
Total	30	47	35	38	150	79.3	14	16	8	5	43	74.4	14	11	7	17	49	87.7

to incorporate marketing mix variables into SBC models [2, 9, 22, 24, 25, 27, 29, 30]. Of these approaches, those of Telser [30] and MacLachlan [27] may be useful in representing the price-sensitive segments. Both authors use the framework of a Markov model in which the transition probabilities are functions of marketing variables such as price and promotion. A related approach which might also prove useful is Lee et al.'s method [23, p. 191-7] of estimating a modified Markov transition matrix. It should be noted that these models all analyze data at the aggregate level. It remains to be seen whether they also will be useful for individual level analysis. The writers now are investigating the feasibility of these and other approaches to the modeling of the price-sensitive segments.

CONCLUSIONS

Most current approaches to SBC modeling attempt to fit a *single* model to the purchasing data of *all* consumers though consumer heterogeneity is recognized by allowing one or more model parameters to vary across the population. Though such models, e.g. [3, 14], can be useful in predicting repeat purchasing and brand switching at the *aggregate* level, they typically do not provide an accurate picture of the degree of heterogeneity that may be present in the market. For example, using panel data on several frequently purchased products, the writers show the existence of nine major segments. Given the existence of such segments, it seems more sensible to represent *different* segments with *different* SBC models while allowing for parameter heterogeneity for each segment model. Simple SBC models appear to be adequate in describing many of the purchase segments. Other segments, however, cannot be described by existing models. To represent these segments adequately, it appears necessary to develop new models which directly incorporate the effects of marketing mix variables in the brand choice process.

APPENDIX

The facial tissue data also can be used to illustrate two other problems relating to SBC models. These problems have been mentioned elsewhere [17]. However, the following comments are illustrated by concrete examples drawn from the writers' data.

Number of States in Model

Most SBC models consider only two states. The consumer's "favorite" brand constitutes one state and *all* other brands constitute the other state. This arrangement greatly simplifies the analysis and requires fewer consumers and/or shorter purchase histories for parameter estimation. However, important information is lost by reducing the number of states to two. Consumer 349 can be used to illustrate this problem. This consumer's purchase history for facial tissue is provided in Table 4a. He purchased brand 1 fourteen times, brand 3 ten times, brand 2 seven times, brand 8 five times, brand 4 twice, and brand 16 once. His favorite brand is brand 1 because he purchased it on the largest number of occasions. If one represents a purchase of his favorite brand by "1," and a purchase of any other brand by "0," one obtains the following sequence of purchases (the actual purchase sequence also is provided for comparison).

0, 1   10100 00000 00001 10000 00000 11011 11100 1110

Actual   13138 33332 22821 12488 43223 11811 11133 111(16)

The (0, 1) purchase sequence can be summarized in

Table 4a
PURCHASE HISTORY OF CONSUMER 349, FACIAL TISSUE

Purchase number	Brand	Store	Size (# tissues)	Price (¢)
1	1	7	200	2/29
2	3	3	400	19
3	1	7	200	2/29
4	3	3	400	19
5	8	3	400	19
6	3	3	400	19
7	3	3	400	19
8	3	3	400	2/35*
9	3	3	400	19
10	2	7	400	29
11	2	7	400	29
12	2	3	400	29
13	8	3	400	19
14	2	7	400	29
15	1	7	400	29
16	1	7	400	29
17	2	7	400	28*
18	4	1	400	19*
19	8	3	400	20
20	8	3	400	20
21	4	1	400	20
22	3	3	400	2/35*
23	2	7	400	29
24	2	7	400	29
25	3	3	400	20
26	1	3	400	29
27	1	3	400	29
28	8	3	400	20*
29	1	3	400	29
30	1	3	200	15
31	1	3	200	15
32	1	3	400	29
33	1	8	400	21*
34	3	3	400	20
35	3	3	400	16*
36	1	3	400	23*
37	1	3	400	23*
38	1	3	400	29
39	16	3	400	29 N

*Deal Price.

N: Not known whether or not this is a deal price.

44

Table 4b
TWO-STATE TRANSITION MATRIX

	0	1
0	19	5
1	6	8

Table 4c
SIX-STATE TRANSITION MATRIX

	2	3	4	8	16	1
2	3	1	1	1	0	1
3	2	4	0	1	0	3
4	0	1	0	1	0	0
8	1	1	1	1	0	1
1	1	3	0	1	1	8

terms of the two-state transition matrix shown in Table 4b. The actual purchase sequence can be represented by the six-state (where each state refers to a particular brand purchased) transition matrix shown in Table 4c.

From the (0, 1) purchase sequence summarized in Table 4b, SBC models would assume that the consumer has a long string of purchases of a single brand, brand "O." Actually, the consumer has shifted brands several times (see Tables 4a and 4c). This pattern is lost if only two states are used. With the two-state transition matrix, consumer 349 is classified by the BDIS procedure into the Last Purchase Loyal Markov (LPM) model. However, a visual analysis of his purchasing patterns indicates that he is actually a National/Private Switcher. This example illustrates how it is possible to arrive at incorrect conclusions if only two states are used, as is done in most SBC models. It should be noted that some of the more recent SBC models, e.g. [3, 14], do use more than two states.

Sizes, Flavors, and End Uses

An unsolved problem in SBC models is the treatment of product size. Aluminum foil comes in 11-2/3, 23-1/3, and 37-1/2 foot rolls which are heavy duty foil. Is this a different product from the regular 25 or 75 foot size? A similar problem relates to the incorporation of different "flavors" of a product such as dog food. Is each flavor a different product? Finally, facial tissue can be bought in 24-tissue packages and headache remedies are available in 12-tablet boxes. These small packages clearly have different end uses (i.e., they are bought to be carried on the consumer's person) than the 400-tissue box of facial tissue and the 100-tablet bottle of headache remedy. Are the small packages essentially different "products" because of their different end uses? Nothing explicit

has been said in the SBC literature about these problems though one would guess that the different end uses and flavors in a product class would result in greater brand switching, *ceteris paribus*.

REFERENCES

1. Aaker, David A. "The New Trier Stochastic Model of Brand Choice," *Management Science*, 17 (April 1971), B435-50.
2. ______ . "A Measure of Brand Acceptance," *Journal of Marketing Research*, 9 (May 1972), 160-7.
3. Bass, Frank M. "The Theory of Stochastic Preference and Brand Switching," *Journal of Marketing Research*, 11 (February 1974), 1-20.
4. ______ , Abel Jeuland and Gordon P. Wright. "Equilibrium Stochastic Choice and Market Penetration Theories: Derivations and Comparisons," *Management Science* (forthcoming).
5. Blattberg, Robert C., Peter Peacock and Subrata K. Sen. "Purchase Segmentation: Beyond Aluminum Foil," Working Paper, University of Chicago (November 1975).
6. ______ and Subrata K. Sen. "Market Segmentation Using Models of Multidimensional Purchasing Behavior," *Journal of Marketing*, 38 (October 1974), 17-28.
7. ______ and ______ . "A Bayesian Technique to Discriminate Between Stochastic Models of Brand Choice," *Management Science*, 21 (February 1975), 682-96.
8. Chatfield, Christopher and Gerald Goodhardt. "Results Concerning Brand Choice," *Journal of Marketing Research*, 12 (February 1975), 110-3.
9. Cook, Victor J. and Jerome D. Herniter. "NOMMAD or How Consumers Behave," *Sloan Management Review*, 12 (Spring 1971), 77-97.
10. Ehrenberg, Andrew S. C. *Repeat Buying*. Amsterdam: North-Holland Publishing Company and New York: American Elsevier, 1972.
11. Frank, Ronald E. "Brand Choice as a Probability Process," *Journal of Business*, 35 (January 1962), 43-56.
12. Greene, Jerome D. and J. Stevens Stock. "A Rate-Frequency Model of Behavior," *Journal of Advertising Research*, 11 (August 1971), 9-19.
13. Herniter, Jerome D. "A Probabilistic Market Model of Purchase Timing and Brand Selection," *Management Science*, 18 (December 1971, Part II), P102-13.
14. ______ . "An Entropy Model of Brand Purchase Behavior," *Journal of Marketing Research*, 10 (November 1973), 361-75.
15. ______ . "A Comparison of the Entropy Model and the Hendry Model," *Journal of Marketing Research*, 11 (February 1974), 21-9.
16. Howard, Ronald A. "Dynamic Inference," *Operations Research*, 13 (October 1965), 712-33.
17. ______ . "Stochastic Models of Consumer Behavior," in Frank M. Bass, Charles W. King and Edgar A. Pessemier, eds., *Applications of the Sciences in Marketing Management*. New York: John Wiley and Sons, Inc., 1968, 69-83.
18. Jones, J. Morgan. "A Stochastic Model for Adaptive Behavior In a Dynamic Situation," *Management Science*, 17 (March 1971), 484-97.
19. ______ . "A Composite Heterogeneous Model for Brand

Choice Behavior," *Management Science*, 19 (January 1973), 499–509.

20. Kalwani, Manohar U. and Donald G. Morrison. "A Parsimonious Description of the Hendry System," Working Paper, Columbia University (1975).

21. Kuehn, Alfred A., "An Analysis of the Dynamics of Consumer Behavior and Its Implications for Marketing Management," unpublished Ph.D. dissertation, Graduate School of Industrial Administration, Carnegie Institute of Technology, 1958.

22. ______ and Albert C. Rohloff, "Evaluating Promotions Using a Brand Shifting Model," in Patrick J. Robinson, ed., *Promotional Decisions Using Mathematical Models*. Boston: Allyn and Bacon, 1967, 50–85.

23. Lee, T. C., G. G. Judge, and A. Zellner, *Estimating the Parameters of the Markov Probability Model from Aggregate Time Series Data*. Amsterdam: North-Holland Publishing Company, 1970.

24. Lilien, Gary L. "A Modified Linear Learning Model of Buyer Behavior," *Management Science*, 20 (March 1974), 1027–36.

25. ______ . "Application of a Modified Linear Learning Model of Buyer Behavior," *Journal of Marketing Research*, 11 (August 1974), 279–85.

26. Lipstein, Benjamin. "The Dynamics of Brand Loyalty and Brand Switching," in *Better Measurements of Advertising Effectiveness: The Challenge of the 1960's*, Proceedings of the Fifth Annual Conference of the Advertising Research Foundation, New York, 1959.

27. MacLachlan, Douglas L. "A Model of Intermediate Market Response," *Journal of Marketing Research*, 9 (November 1972), 378–84.

28. Massy, William F., David B. Montgomery and Donald G. Morrison. *Stochastic Models of Buying Behavior*. Cambridge: The M.I.T. Press, 1970.

29. Prasad, V. Kanti. "A Brand Choice Model with Store as an Intervening Variable," paper presented at the ORSA-TIMS-AIEE Joint National Meeting, Atlantic City, November 1972.

30. Telser, Lester G. "The Demand for Branded Goods as Estimated from Consumer Panel Data," *Review of Economics and Statistics*, 44 (August 1962), 300–24.

Part II: Statistical Bob — Contributions to Statistical Analysis in Marketing

Bob Blattberg's work in the late 1970s and early 1980s develops statistical applications in marketing that have both endured and have been developed by subsequent marketing researchers. His papers during this time period can be characterized as laying out underlying models that provide an *implicit* guide for analysis. Subject matter theory is used to develop an understanding of role played by model variables, which set the stage for later work by him and others to make an *explicit* link between marketing and/or economic theory, and the statistical specification of models.

Also remarkable is the breadth of problems examined, ranging over the marketing control variables to include pricing, promotion, advertising and product strategy in the form of market segmentation. Bob's work in this period develops marketing theories about consumer behavior, and provides a careful explanation of the implication of analysis.

His work is especially patient and careful, providing guidance to marketing practitioners and academics of the application of many undeveloped areas of marketing. These areas include Bayesian decision theory, and the use of economic theory to motivate model structures and variables. Both areas have since been developed into large bodies of literature in marketing, building on some of the basic examples and models proposed by Bob.

The goal of this chapter is to review Bob's contribution to early statistical research in marketing using major publications from 1978–1981, a period in which Bob had five publications in top-tier journals, plus two book chapters and a conference proceeding. Each of the major publications is discussed, followed by some concluding thoughts.

Bob's Work

Blattberg, Eppen and Lieberman (1981) is the most highly cited article during this period, and provides an early example of the development of demand and supply-side theories to understand the wide-spread existence of price deals across product categories. A household production function is developed that reflects consumer cost minimization while satisfying their demand for a product. A retailer model is offered that justifies the presence of dealing — the practice of offering short-term price reductions. Cost asymmetries between consumers, who can forward buy quantities and store them at low prices, and retailers is the driving force of the model. Both supply and demand models are used to explore implications for deal magnitude, deal frequency and deal quantity, providing guidance for the effect of variables such as home ownership and the presence of older children in the household.

The model implications are contrasted to a model of information asymmetries, where deals occur to teach consumers about the benefits of an offering. In the information model, trial drives dealing, and variables characterizing the household are expected to be different. The empirical analysis in the paper carefully works through the implications of the proposed cost model versus the information model, providing empirical support for a cost-based explanation for dealing by examining various marginal statistics such as the effects of deals on post-deal purchase timing. Recent researchers in marketing have extended this early work on demand and supply by explicitly relating model parameters to the data.

Bob's 1979 paper *"The Design of Advertising Experiments Using Statistical Decision Theory"* is a carefully conducted and extensive Bayesian analysis for advertising testing. As is common for Bob's papers during this period, the paper provides a detailed description of an actual marketing problem, and translates the issues faced by management to a set of research questions for analysis. The paper examines three aspects of decision analysis that has carried forward in present work: i) a quantitative specification of a profit function describing the decision problem; ii) a view of the decision problem in terms of the value of information; and iii) a detailed discussion of aspects of the prior distribution, in terms of some of the issues involved in obtaining the prior from managers and the sensitivity of results to the assumed form of the prior.

In addition to the breadth of issues examined in the paper, it provides a detailed and accessible discussion of each. The paper offers readers insight into the practical use of the model, making it a helpful tool to individuals who are new to decision theory.

Two papers during the "Statistical Bob" era examine issues in market segmentation. Blattberg *et al.* (1978) offer substantive findings regarding the identification of the "deal-prone" segment. Prior to this paper, the prevailing literature in marketing had come to the conclusion that the association between demographic and other socioeconomic variables and brand preference is weak, at best. This paper instead examines association with deal (i.e., price) sensitivity, a variable related to behavior across brands. A household decision problem of cost minimization subject to constraints on inventory and availability is used to suggest a set of demographic variables that are expected to be related to deal proneness. These variables are then examined in a series of cross-tabulations using a diary panel of purchase across five product categories. As with his other papers, a detailed discussion is offered about modeling assumptions needed to make the empirical predictions, and their strengths and their weaknesses.

The 1980 paper by Blattberg, Buesing and Sen examines segmentation strategies for new national brands. The analysis presented involves data from a natural experiment during the time that a new brand, Puffs bathroom tissue, was introduced in the market. The prevailing thinking at the time was that the target for new brands should be switchers currently in the market. The authors examine the validity of this approach using six segments derived from crossing national brand versus private label buyers with three categories of buyer price sensitivity (loyal, deal prone, and switcher). Through a thorough and explicit analysis, the empirical results indicate that shoppers who are loyal to existing national brands, and those that primarily purchase private label brands, are good targets. The paper contributes both to our empirical understanding of new product introduction, and our methodological understanding by providing a template for conducting thoughtful analysis.

The final major paper during this period is an assessment of the log-linear model in marketing research (Blattberg and Dolan, 1981). Simple and saturated log-linear models are compared to regression analysis with dummy variables, and an AID model that searches for interactions among variables. The paper starts out with a rich description of two problem settings, one involving the selection of target segments for a manufacturer selling through retail outlets, and the other involving the identification of demographics for list selection by a direct marketer. The response variables are discussed, and the results are compared in a manner that allows readers to thoroughly understand the benefits of the various approaches. The explicitness typically present in Bob's writing about assumptions is extended in this paper by a list of the lessons learned from the analysis, imploring researchers to keep models parsimonious while dealing with non-linear effects.

Some Personal Comments

Bob once said that there are two types of people in the world — thinkers and doers — and we need to decide what kind of person we are. Thinkers spend a lot of time carefully developing a set of plans that lead to a relatively short execution time. Doers are the opposite — they dive into problems first, and figure out the solution later. Bob was clearly a doer, and this orientation lead to a diverse and eclectic set of research publications both over his career, and in the short period of time covered by the papers discussed above.

His "doer" orientation spilled over into his role as an advisor. Bob was extremely flexible, and infectiously enthusiastic in guiding his students through their doctoral studies, allowing us to move off in directions that interested us and not necessarily him. We thank him for setting this example, and hope to continue this legacy with our own students.

Bob's work ethic has also had great influence on his students. His "stay focused" attitude has guided students in producing clear, logical, and relevant work. This attitude is especially beneficial to students in early stages of their learning curves. These people may often be overwhelmed by the vast amount of information in the literature and in the various possibilities of research questions that can be explored along the line of a decided topic. One can easily digress, or get off track, resulting in low efficiency and worse, resulting in unclear research goals and low quality work. Learning to stay focused is an important skill and it is much better learned when one can see a good example performing it in action. We learned from Bob.

The next section discusses "promotional Bob". With statistical methods as background, beginning in the 1980's and also in the 1990's, Bob explored the area of promotions as his major substantive area of interest. In this time period, he showcased his work in promotions, demonstrating, explaining, and applying managerial implications of how promotions affect trade, manufacturers, retailers, consumers, and product categories. Thank you, Bob!

Jennifer Chien-Wen Chang
Simon Fraser University

Greg M. Allenby
Fisher College of Business
Ohio State University

References

Blattberg, R., T. Buesing, P. Peacock and S. Sen (1978). Identifying the Deal Prone Segment, *Journal of Marketing Research*, **15**(3), 369–377.

Blattberg, R. (1979). The Design of Advertising Experiments Using Statistical Decision Theory, *Journal of Marketing Research*, **16**(2), 191–202.

Blattberg, R., T. Buesing and S. Sen (1980). Marketing Strategies for New National Brands, *Journal of Marketing*, **44**(4), 59–67.

Blattberg, R., G. Eppen and J. Lieberman (1981). A Theoretical and Empirical Evaluation of Price Deals for Consumer Non-durables, *Journal of Marketing*, **45**(1), 116–129.

Blattberg, R. and R. Dolan (1981). An Assessment of the Contribution of Log Linear Models to Marketing Research, *Journal of Marketing*, **45**(2), 89–97.

IV. Substantive Findings and Applications

ROBERT BLATTBERG, THOMAS BUESING, PETER PEACOCK, and SUBRATA SEN*

A model of consumer buying behavior is used to identify household characteristics that should affect deal proneness. The model treats household purchasing and inventory decisions like those of a firm. In other words, the household's purchasing decisions are assumed to be based on such factors as transaction costs, holding costs, and stockout costs in addition to product price. Household characteristics then are related to these cost parameters to identify households that are likely to be deal prone. The predictions are tested empirically by use of panel data for five frequently purchased products. The empirical results indicate that deal prone households can be identified and that the key variables affecting deal proneness are household resource variables such as home ownership and automobile ownership.

Identifying the Deal Prone Segment

Blattberg and Sen [4, 5] present a method of defining market segments based on purchase patterns. The usefulness of this approach is enhanced if segment membership can be identified on the basis of available demographic data. The purpose of this article is to show that deal prone consumers as defined by Blattberg and Sen [4, 5] are identifiable.

Marketing managers always have been interested in identifying the deal prone household on the basis of available demographic data. If such households can be identified precisely, specific marketing strategies designed to appeal to such households are likely to be more effective. For example, demographic information is available by zip codes or census tracts. If certain demographic groups are more deal prone, coupon distribution could be restricted to those areas where households with higher deal proneness reside. This approach would reduce couponing costs with a less than proportionate reduction in response. Similar-

ly, more accurate identification of deal prone households would increase the marketer's ability to match deal prone households and media audience characteristics, and thus increase the efficiency of media distribution of coupons and other promotional items.

Several researchers have tried to identify the deal prone household. Webster [13] and Montgomery [12] published two of the better known studies. The results of these and other studies are summarized by Frank et al. [6, p. 124], who state:

> The results of cross-sectional studies, almost without exception, indicate that there is, at best, only a modest degree of association between demographic, socioeconomic, and/or personality characteristics, and selected aspects of household purchasing behavior, such as total consumption, brand loyalty, and deal proneness.

One reason for this "modest degree of association" may lie in the methodological approach usually taken in these studies. Typically, a large number of potential explanatory variables is regressed against the proportion of purchases made on deal in a search for statistical significance. For example, Webster [13] ran 200 regressions with different combinations of 45 explanatory variables. This approach is open to serious question because one cannot always determine whether "significant" relationships reflect a valid relationship or a spurious one which has arisen by

*Robert Blattberg is Professor of Marketing and Thomas Buesing is a Ph.D. student in Marketing, University of Chicago; Peter Peacock is Associate Professor of Management, Wake Forest University; and Subrata Sen is Associate Professor of Business Administration, University of Rochester.

This research was funded in part by National Science Foundation Grant SOC73-05547.

Journal of Marketing Research
Vol. XV (August 1978), 369–77

chance alone. Without a theory to indicate which variables should affect deal proneness, the researcher risks accepting spurious results.

A related deficiency of prior studies of deal proneness arising from the absence of a clearly stated theory is improper specification of explanatory variables. For example, Montgomery [12] included "presence of children" as an independent variable in a regression model but was unable to predict *a priori* whether the presence of children should or should not increase deal proneness. However, if one hypothesizes that it is the *age* of the children that affects deal proneness (rather than their presence *per se*), it is possible to predict *a priori* the impact of "age of children" on deal proneness. If the children are below the age of six (and are consequently not yet in school), they require more of their parents' time, thus reducing the time the parents have available for shopping. Less time for shopping results in fewer shopping trips and fewer opportunities to take advantage of deals. Consequently, the household's deal proneness is reduced. Montgomery's results [12] led him to conclude that presence of children was not related to deal proneness. However, by considering the presence of children without determining how their presence should affect deal proneness, Montgomery may have arrived at an incorrect conclusion about a variable which, if properly specified, could well be related to deal proneness.

Like the researchers cited, the authors attempt to identify the deal prone household. However, the approach used here is different from that used in most of the earlier work. First a model of household purchasing behavior is formulated. The model then is used to predict how certain demographic variables should affect deal proneness. Finally, an empirical evaluation of the predictions is made. The empirical results show that it is possible to identify the deal prone household by using demographic variables and that the effect of these variables is substantial.

MODEL OF HOUSEHOLD PURCHASING BEHAVIOR

Model Assumptions

Development of a household inventory model is based on the assumption that the household is a producing unit which needs to stock inventory and meet demand. This assumption follows from the notion of the household as a production unit which Becker [1] and others used to model consumer behavior in the economics literature. This approach is used here because it has proved to be very fruitful in several applied studies in economics [11] and also because it appears to be a promising approach in marketing [10]. The inventory model proposed here also corresponds closely to models developed by management scientists to make better inventory decisions in more traditional production environments [8, p. 472–527].

The initial assumption in the model is that households make long-term decisions about whether to use a given product at all and the *average* number of units of the product to use per period. Decisions about product use and the average usage rate are determined exogenously by such factors as family size, family income, etc. Another assumption is that ratios of prices of the product in question and prices of substitutes and complements are constant during the period considered so that households need not evaluate their usage rate decision because of changes in relative price. The latter assumption is made in order to obtain a tractable model and because it permits concentration on the purchase timing decision which is the basic focus of this article.

The model is based on two additional assumptions: (1) all brands in the product class yield the same utility to the consumer and (2) the consumer purchases only one brand of the product class. Again, these assumptions are made only to obtain a tractable model. However, neither assumption is particularly restrictive.

Consider first the assumption that all brands in the product class provide the same utility to the consumer. For certain *multibrand* segments defined by Blattberg et al. [3, 4] (such as national brand switchers, national brand switcher deals, private label switchers, and private label switcher deals), it is clearly reasonable to assume that consumers are indifferent in terms of preference among a subset of brands. It is also reasonable to make a similar assumption about buyers of a *single* brand (e.g., members of the national brand loyal segment [3, 4]). If all brands provide the same utility to the consumer, it is sensible for him to restrict purchases to a single brand because such a purchasing strategy minimizes decision-making costs on each purchase occasion (see, for example, [14]). If, however, different brands provide different utilities to the consumer, a model which jointly considers utility maximization and purchase timing would have to be developed.

The assumption about the purchase of a single brand is even less restrictive. To extend the present model to households that purchase many brands that are about equally preferred, one only needs to recognize that such households have a larger array of prices to consider in the decision process. Slight differences in behavior would result because there are more deals available to, say, national brand switcher consumers (who are willing to buy two or three brands) than to, say, national brand loyal consumers (who are willing to buy only one brand). The result should be less stockpiling for national brand switcher households.

Cost Structure of the Household

Four categories of cost affect household inventory decisions: (1) transaction cost, (2) storage cost, (3) stockout cost, and (4) the actual price of the item.

Transaction cost is the opportunity cost of the time required to purchase an item once the consumer is actually in a store *plus* the opportunity cost of travel time required to get to and from the store where the purchase takes place. Transaction cost will vary across stores. And if a consumer has a "regular" or preferred store, one would expect the transaction cost of an item purchased there to be less than if a special trip were made to purchase the item at some other store. Storage cost represents interest on the capital required to maintain a given level of inventory plus the cost of the required space. Stockout cost relects the foregone utility of not consuming an item which is not in stock at the time it is demanded. If the household can easily substitute other items in the event of stockout, or if it derives little utility from consuming the item, stockout cost should be low. Observed price per unit is the final component of cost. For purposes of the analysis, the observed price in a store is assumed to be constant within any given period, e.g., a week. Prices may differ across stores and may change from period to period.

Mathematical Formulation of the Model

The household's purchase decision process is represented mathematically as:

$$(1) \qquad \min_{X_{i,t}} E\left\{ \sum_i \sum_t f_{i,t}[X_{i,t}] + h_t \bar{I}_{t-1} + u_t \bar{S}_t \right\}$$

subject to:

$$(2) \quad f_{i,t}[X_{i,t}] = \begin{cases} T_{i,t} + P_{i,t} X_{i,t} & \text{if } X_{i,t} > 0 \text{ for } i=1, \ldots, K \\ 0 & \text{if } X_{i,t} = 0 \end{cases}$$

$$(3) \quad \bar{I}_t = \begin{cases} I_{t-1} + \sum_i X_{i,t} - d_t & \text{if } d_t < I_{t-1} + \sum_i X_{i,t} \\ 0 & \text{if } d_t \geq I_{t-1} + \sum_i X_{i,t} \end{cases}$$

$$(4) \quad \bar{S}_t = \begin{cases} d_t - I_{t-1} - \sum_i X_{i,t} & \text{if } d_t > I_{t-1} + \sum_i X_{i,t} \\ 0 & \text{if } d_t \leq I_{t-1} + \sum_i X_{i,t} \end{cases}$$

$$(5) \qquad\qquad 0 \leq I_t \leq I \qquad\qquad \text{for all } t$$

where:

$T_{i,t}$ = transaction cost at store i at time t,
$P_{i,t}$ = price per unit of product at store i at time t,
$X_{i,t}$ = quantity purchased at store i at time t,
$\bar{I}_t$ = inventory on hand at beginning of time t,
d_t = quantity at time t,
h_t = unit holding cost at time t,
$\bar{S}_t$ = amount of stockout at time t,
u_t = unit stockout cost at time t,
I = the maximum inventory that can be stored each period, and
K = the number of stores.

The model described in equations 1–5 indicates that the household's objective is to purchase the product at a minimum "total cost." Given the assumption that all brands in the product class yield the same utility to the consumer, minimization of cost is the appropriate objective function. The costs being minimized are *expected costs* over a finite time horizon which includes present as well as future periods. Thus, expectations about future demand and future prices affect the present period's decision. Note that though the household's *average* demand per period is known, the exact quantity demanded in each period is unknown at the *start* of the period. Thus, this quantity, d_t, is represented as a random variable in the model. Future price expectations are generated by probability distributions of the time between deals and the length of time a given deal is in effect. These distributions are based on actual household experience with deal duration and time between deals in each store.

The model described is different from a one-period minimization problem. It incorporates the consumer's expectations about future prices. If consumers can anticipate accurately when deals occur as well as their duration, their current behavior should be affected. For example, if a store always deals a product for more than one period, a consumer's purchase timing behavior should be significantly different from his behavior when the deals last only a single period. By extending the decision horizon to more than one period, the model is able to incorporate consumer expectations.

Finally, equation 5 indicates that there is a storage constraint in the model. A consumer can have no more than a preset maximum number of units (I) in inventory in any period. This storage constraint is included in the model only because it simplifies the solution to the problem. The solution technique used is probabilistic dynamic programming [8, p. 269–74] and the storage constraint makes the number of states in the dynamic programming formulation finite.

VALUE OF THE INVENTORY MODEL

The inventory model described provides a *theoretical basis* for selecting demographic and household resource variables which should be associated with deal proneness. Consider Figure 1 which is a diagrammatic representation of the manner in which the inventory model links demographic and resource variables with household deal proneness. This diagram is used to indicate how the model enables the researcher to identify household variables that affect deal proneness.

Deal Proneness and Household Cost Parameters

The first link of interest in Figure 1 is the one that connects household cost parameters with deal proneness through the inventory model. This link indicates how the cost structure facing a household determines whether or not it will be deal prone. For

Figure 1
DEAL PRONENESS AND HOUSEHOLD DEMOGRAPHIC
AND RESOURCE VARIABLES

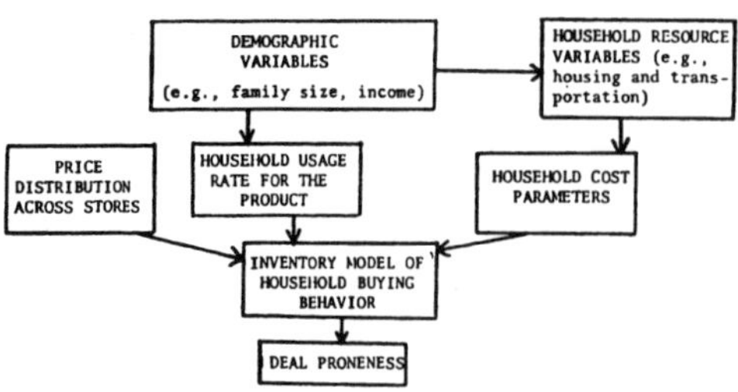

example, if a household's storage costs were low, one would expect it to stock up on a commodity when a deal is on. Similarly, if the household's transaction costs were low for all stores, one would expect it to buy primarily on deal because the household could easily take advantage of deals offered by any of the stores.

Cost Parameters and Household Demographics and Resources

Having seen how the household's cost structure affects deal proneness, one now must identify the factors that determine a household's cost structure. For this purpose, consider the link in Figure 1 which connects demographic variables (such as income) to household cost parameters through household resource variables (such as housing and transportation). Note first that income is an important determinant of household resources, i.e., households with higher income are more likely to own homes (as opposed to being renters) and are also more likely to own one or more cars. These household resources, in turn, affect the cost parameters of the model. For example, home owners typically have more storage space available than apartment dwellers and hence should incur lower storage costs. Similarly, car ownership makes transportation easier, thereby reducing the household's transaction costs.

It was noted that low storage costs and low transaction costs both lead to deal proneness. Because low storage costs are associated with home ownership and low transaction costs with car ownership, specific predictions can be made, such as: home owners and car owners will tend to be more deal prone than apartment dwellers and households without cars.

One can see, therefore, that the inventory model's links with deal proneness and with household cost parameters make it possible to (1) identify the relevant

variables that should affect deal proneness and (2) predict the direction of their effect.

EFFECT OF DEMOGRAPHIC AND HOUSEHOLD RESOURCE VARIABLES ON DEAL PRONENESS

In this section, the authors formally state predictions of how some specific household resource and demographic variables lead to deal proneness. Three types of variables are studied: (1) household resource variables such as car ownership and home ownership, (2) time-related variables such as the housewife's employment status and age of the youngest child, and (3) income.[1] Note that the data for these variables are available by zip codes or census tracts. Therefore, if these variables do affect deal proneness, the marketing manager can implement the results easily. In contrast, some of the variables found by Webster [13] and Montgomery [12] to affect deal proneness are less directly applicable. For example, both found that brand loyalty was associated negatively with deal proneness. However, one must first identify who the less brand loyal consumers are before one can use such a finding.

Household Resource Variables and Deal Proneness

A key component of the transaction cost of shopping is transportation cost. Households that do not have cars available are forced to shop at stores that are nearby. They are also more likely to shop at a single store [10, p. 376]. Because the ability to take advantage of deals depends on the freedom to shop often and at many stores, households without cars should be less deal prone.[2]

The second household resource variable is home ownership. This variable should be related to holding costs. Apartment dwellers usually have less storage space available than homeowners simply because apartments are smaller. Therefore, holding costs should be higher for apartment dwellers. Because lower holding costs should lead to greater deal proneness, homeowners should be more deal prone that apartment dwellers.

---

[1] Numerous other variables could have been considered but the inventory model concentrated on resource variables. Thus, these are the ones examined here.

[2] This heuristic argument and the ones that follow are consistent with the results of a simulation conducted to check the sensitivity of the model's solution (obtained by dynamic programming) to changes in the model's parameters. The parameters that were varied in the simulation were such items as transaction costs and storage costs, and the simulation allowed assessment of their quantitative impact on deal proneness. The simulation could not be published because of space constraints. However, interested readers can obtain a copy of the simulation results by writing to Subrata Sen, Graduate School of Management, University of Rochester, Rochester, New York 14627.

Effect of Income on Deal Proneness

The usual argument given in support of a negative relationship between deal proneness and income is that low income households have lower opportunity costs of time, and thus lower search and transaction costs. Furthermore, economic theory suggests that lower income households should be more price sensitive. Empirical research in marketing rarely has shown that income affects deal proneness (see [13] for example). If an effect is found at all, higher income seems to be associated with *greater* deal proneness rather than less.

The problem with studying the effects of income is that income effects are confounded by the effects of household resource variables. For example, higher income households are more likely to buy capital goods such as cars and homes, household resources which increase their ability to buy on deal. The interaction between the negative effects of income and the positive effects of household resources may result in the anomalous finding that high income households are more deal prone than low income households. If resources available were held constant, however, one should observe the opposite outcome.

Effect of Time on Deal Proneness

An important household decision is the amount of time to allocate to shopping. This decision will depend on other time demands facing the household. Two factors which should affect these time demands greatly are (1) the presence of children under six and (2) whether both the husband and wife work. A child below the age of six (who therefore does not attend school) requires large time inputs from his or her mother. Further, when the housewife does go shopping, she often may need to hire a babysitter, to use one of her other children to take care of the child, or to take the child with her. The result should be increased transaction costs of shopping. Specifically, the household will have higher transaction costs across all stores which result in less frequent shopping trips, more units purchased per trip, and purchasing on deal only if a deal is available during the trip. Once the child reaches the age of six, and begins school, the amount of time the housewife must spend with the child is decreased and a given shopping trip becomes less costly. Thus, households with at least one child below six should be less deal prone than households with no children below six.

The other factor affecting the amount of time available for shopping is whether both husband and wife are employed. Additional demands placed on a household's time because of the wife's employment should lead to a reduction in the time available for shopping. Thus, for such households, transaction costs should increase for all stores, and less deal proneness should be observed.

Summary

In summary, the households most likely to be deal prone are (1) homeowners, (2) car owners, (3) households with no children under six, and (4) households without working wives. In the next section consumer panel data are used to test these predictions.

EMPIRICAL RESULTS

The data used to analyze deal proneness were the Chicago Tribune Panel puchase data and associated demographic variables. Consumers classified into three segments defined by Blattberg et al. [3]—the national brand loyal deal, the national brand switcher deal, and deal-oriented—are defined here as being deal-oriented. All consumers classified into one of the other stable pattern categories (i.e., not including the changing pattern or last purchase loyal pattern) constituted the non-deal-prone population.[3] Five product categories were studied: aluminum foil, waxed paper, headache remedies, liquid detergent, and facial tissue. The data were gathered from 1958 to 1966, depending on the category.[4] The household variables studied are those described in the previous section.

Blattberg et al. [3] classified each household's purchase patterns into segments. Deal proneness was based on membership in one of the three segments and was a dichotomous variable: deal prone or not deal prone. Because the effect of the independent variables on deal proneness may be nonlinear, the authors decided to use cross-classification analysis instead of regression [see 6, p. 126–9]. A major problem in doing cross-classification analysis is that sample sizes may become small for certain cells when two or three sets of independent variables are analyzed simultaneously along with the dependent variable. This problem is particularly vexing here because most demographic and household resource variables are intercorrelated. For example, high income households that rented and did not own a car are a very small percentage of all high income households. Initially, the data are analyzed individually for each explanatory variable. Then certain combinations of variables are considered together. In future studies, if larger samples are available, interrelationships between more sets of explanatory variables should be studied.

Household Resource Variables

The first two variables analyzed are home ownership and car ownership. Tables 1 and 2 give the results for each of the five product categories. The table

---

[3] The nonstable buying patterns include some deal prone households which for certain periods of the data were deal prone and for other periods were not. They are excluded because they were difficult to categorize. The size of this group is never more than 20% of the total consumers and is usually much smaller.

[4] Aluminum foil (1962–66), waxed paper (1963–66), liquid detergent (1959–61), facial tissue (1958–61), and headache remedies (1959–61).

Table 1
HOME OWNERSHIP

Home ownership	Product category				
	Aluminum foil	*Waxed paper*	*Headache remedies*	*Liquid detergent*	*Facial tissue*
Rent	30.9%[a] (81)[b]	12.5% (88)	22.7% (97)	29.6% (98)	23.4% (137)
Own	37.5 (120)	29.5 (132)	29.8 (151)	38.9 (229)	28.7 (230)

[a]The table entry is the percentage of aluminum foil buyers who rent a home and are deal prone.
[b]Numbers in parentheses are total within-cell sample sizes on which each percentage is based.

Table 2
CAR OWNERSHIP

Car ownership	Product category				
	Aluminum foil	*Waxed paper*	*Headache remedies*	*Liquid detergent*	*Facial tissue*
No car	24.0%[a] (50)[b]	17.1% (70)	19.4% (67)	26.9% (67)	25.0% (88)
Car	38.4 (151)	25.3 (112)	3.0 (180)	38.8 (258)	27.3 (278)

[a]The table entry is the percentage of aluminum foil buyers who do not own a car and are deal prone.
[b]Numbers in parentheses are total within-cell sample sizes on which each percentage is based.

entries are the percentages deal prone. For example, in the case of waxed paper, 29.5% of the households that owned a home were deal prone and 12.5% of the households that did not own a home were deal prone.

The results in Tables 1 and 2 suggest that owning a car or a home makes a household much more deal prone. For every product category this result holds. These results are consistent with the predictions that home ownership and car ownership should be associated with greater deal proneness.

One problem with analyzing the variables separately is that if one owns a car, one is also more likely to own a home. Thus, the observed effect may be due to one of the two variables and not the other. Table 3 shows the effect of the two variables jointly. Except for facial tissue, owning both a home and a car results in the highest probability of being deal prone. The percentage deal prone is always higher when a household owned a car *and* a home than when it owned a car and rented. It is higher for four of the five products when a household owned both a car and a home than when the household owned a home, but not a car. Thus, the effect does not appear to be due to only one of the two variables.

To get some idea of the magnitude of the effect that owning both a car and a home had on deal proneness, the following model was estimated.

$$(6) \qquad D_{ij} = \alpha\beta_i\gamma_j\varepsilon_{ij} \qquad \begin{matrix} i=1,\dots,4 \\ j=1,\dots,5 \end{matrix}$$

where:

D_{ij} = percentage of deal-oriented consumers for product category j and consumer characteristic i,

α = average deal orientation,
β_i = the effect of consumer characteristic i on deal orientation,
γ_j = the effect of product category j on deal orientation, and
ε_{ij} = the disturbance term.

Because product categories with very low deal proneness may have a lower absolute difference in deal proneness for a given household characteristic than product categories with high deal proneness, a multiplicative model was used. If one takes logarithms of both sides of equation 6, the effects (β_i and γ_j) can be measured by using estimates calculated from standard analysis of variance formulas.[5] The constraints are that

$$\sum_i \ln(\beta_i) = \sum_j \ln(\gamma_j) = 0.^{[6]}$$

The model is similar to the log-linear models described by Green et al. [7] and Bishop et al. [2]. The exact estimates used are given in [9, p. 327–34].

Estimates of the model's β_i parameters are presented in Table 4. The results show that owning a car and a home yielded a β of 1.366, whereas not owning a car and renting yielded a β of 0.821. Averaging across all the products so that the grand mean represents average deal responsiveness, one sees that owning a car and a home increased deal responsiveness from 20.5 to 34.4%, a 67.9% increase. Owning either a car or a home, but not the other, increased deal

---

[5]Note that the data contain some households that are common to more than one product category.
[6]This constraint is the same as requiring $\prod_i \beta_i = \prod_j \gamma_j = 1$.

Table 3
CAR AND HOME OWNERSHIP

Home ownership and car ownership	Product category				
	Aluminum foil	*Waxed paper*	*Headache remedies*	*Liquid detergent*	*Facial tissue*
No car and rents	21.2%[a] (33)[b]	14.0 (43)	22.9% (48)	28.6% (35)	18.3% (60)
No car and owns home	29.4 (17)	22.2 (27)	10.5 (19)	25.0 (32)	39.3 (28)
Owns car and rents	37.5 (48)	11.1 (45)	22.4 (49)	30.2 (63)	27.3 (77)
Owns car and home	38.8 (103)	31.4 (103)	32.8 (131)	41.5 (195)	27.4 (201)

[a]The table entry is the percentage of aluminum foil buyers who do not own a car and who rent a home and are deal prone.
[b]Numbers in parentheses are total within-cell sample sizes on which each percentage is based.

Table 4
CAR AND HOME OWNERSHIP
(Grand Mean = 24.9%)

Category	Response
No car and rents	.821
No car and owns home	.932
Owns car and rents	.957
Owns car and home	1.366

responsiveness from 20.5 to 26.2%. It is clear, therefore, that owning both a car and a home greatly increases deal responsiveness, in comparison with not owning either or owning only a car or only a home.

Income

On theoretical grounds, household income level should be correlated negatively with deal proneness. Empirically, the opposite relationship may be observed because of the effects of confounding variables. Table 5 gives the results of income for three income levels—low ($0–5,999), medium ($6,000–8,999), and high ($9,000 or more). The income categories are based on roughly 33% groupings. The results indicate that, contrary to theoretical predictions, high income households are more deal prone than low income households. For every product category except facial tissue, a higher percentage of high income households are deal prone than low income households. The effect is not large in most categories, but it is persistent.

To isolate the effects of confounding variables, income was analyzed by adjusting first for home ownership and then for car ownership. (Because cell sizes became very small, it was impossible to analyze income simultaneously with home and car ownership). Table 6 and 7 present the results. Table 6 indicates that, except for liquid detergent, high income households are not generally more deal prone than low income households. If anything, low income households that own homes tend to be the most deal prone. Similar results are observed for car ownership. Table 7 indicates that if one considers car owners only, high income households are not uniformly more deal prone than low income households.

Thus, when suitable adjustments are made for car and home ownership, higher income is *not* associated with increased deal proneness. Without these adjustments, the opposite conclusion would have been reached. If the effects of car *and* home ownership could be *simultaneously* partialed out, one would expect to find even stronger evidence that lower income households are *more* deal prone than higher income households.

Time-Related Resources

The results for the two variables related to time are presented in Tables 8 and 9. Table 8 shows that

Table 5
INCOME

Income level	Product category				
	Aluminum foil	*Waxed paper*	*Headache remedies*	*Liquid detergent*	*Facial tissue*
$ 0–5,999	31.0%[a] (84)[b]	19.6% (97)	28.0% (100)	28.1% (114)	31.4% (137)
$6,000–8,999	39.1 (64)	23.9 (71)	23.0 (87)	36.8 (114)	19.2 (125)
$>9,000	35.8 (53)	26.9 (52)	31.1 (61)	44.4 (99)	29.5 (105)

[a]The table entry is the percentage of aluminum foil buyers whose income level is $0–5,999 and are deal prone.
[b]Numbers in parentheses are total within-cell sample sizes on which each percentage is based.

Table 6
HOME OWNERSHIP AND INCOME

Income level and home ownership[a]	Product category				
	Aluminum foil	Waxed paper	Headache remedies	Liquid detergent	Facial tissue
$0–5,999 and owns home	37.1%[b] (35)[c]	28.9% (38)	40.9% (44)	31.8% (66)	33.9% (62)
$0–5,999 and rents	26.5 (49)	13.6 (59)	17.9 (56)	22.9 (48)	29.3 (75)
$6,000–8,999 and owns home	45.0 (40)	30.2 (53)	22.0 (59)	36.1 (83)	23.5 (85)
$6,000–8,999 and rents	29.2 (24)	5.6 (18)	25.0 (28)	38.7 (31)	10.0 (40)
$9,000 or more and owns home	31.1 (45)	29.3 (41)	29.2 (48)	47.5 (80)	30.1 (83)

[a]Certain categories were omitted because the sample sizes were too small.
[b]The table entry is the percentage of aluminum foil buyers whose income level is $0–5,999 and who own a home and are deal prone.
[c]Numbers in parentheses are total within-cell sample sizes on which each percentage is based.

Table 7
CAR OWNERSHIP AND INCOME

Income level and car ownership[a]	Product category				
	Aluminum foil	Waxed paper	Headache remedies	Liquid detergent	Facial tissue
$0–5,999 and no car	21.6%[b] (37)[c]	17.6% (51)	20.0% (45)	21.1% (38)	25.9% (58)
$0–5,999 and owns car	38.3 (47)	21.7 (36)	35.2 (54)	32.0 (75)	35.4 (79)
$6,000–8,999 and owns car	37.5 (56)	23.3 (60)	25.0 (72)	37.5 (96)	19.0 (105)
$9,000 or more and owns car	39.6 (48)	27.3 (44)	31.5 (54)	46.0 (87)	29.8 (94)

[a]Certain categories were omitted because the sample sizes were too small.
[b]The table entry is the percentage of aluminum foil buyers whose income level is $0–5,999 and who do not own a car and are deal prone.
[c]Numbers in parentheses are total within-cell sample sizes on which each percentage is based.

Table 8
AGE OF CHILDREN

Age of children	Product category				
	Aluminum foil	Waxed paper	Headache remedies	Liquid detergent	Facial tissue
Children under six	41.5%[a] (41)[b]	21.7% (60)	26.6% (64)	39.8% (83)	24.0% (75)
No children under six	36.0 (89)	25.3 (95)	33.7 (98)	34.0 (141)	28.1 (160)

[a]The table entry is the percentage of aluminum foil buyers who have children under six and are deal prone.
[b]Numbers in parentheses are total within-call sample sizes on which each percentage is based.

there is a small increase in deal proneness when there are no children under six for three of the product categories, waxed paper, headache remedies, and facial tissue. For the other two categories, aluminum foil and liquid detergent, the predictions are not supported.

For the other time-related variable, housewife's employment status, the prediction was that working women should be less deal prone than nonworking women. The data in Table 9 show that for all five product categories, working women are less deal prone than nonworking women. A problem in analyzing the effect of working women on deal proneness is that income interacts with the housewife's employment status. For families in which the head has a low income, there is a higher likelihood of the housewife being

Table 9
HOUSEWIFE'S EMPLOYMENT STATUS

Employment status	Product category				
	Aluminum foil	*Waxed paper*	*Headache remedies*	*Liquid detergent*	*Facial tissue*
Employed	29.0%[a] (62)[b]	17.7% (62)	25.0% (76)	32.6% (92)	22.4% (116)
Unemployed	38.3% (128)	23.5% (153)	28.6% (161)	37.4% (214)	29.2% (226)

[a] The table entry is the percentage of aluminum foil buyers who are employed housewives and are deal prone.
[b] Numbers in parentheses are total within-cell sample sizes on which each percentage is based.

employed. Also, for larger families, the housewife may need to work. Unfortunately, the sample sizes were too small to analyze the effect of working women with income and family size held constant.

SUMMARY AND CONCLUSIONS

A specific model of household purchasing behavior is used to identify variables which should affect deal proneness. The essence of the model is that households and firms make the same kinds of inventory decisions. The variables that affect the household's purchasing behavior are holding costs, stockout costs, transaction costs, purchase price, and usage rates. Household characteristics were linked to these cost variables, and predictions were made about which types of households should be deal prone. The predictions then were tested empirically.

The empirical results showed that the household resource variables, car and home ownership, were strong predictors of deal proneness. Of the households that owned a car and home, 34.4% were deal prone. In contrast, only 20.5% of the households that did not own either a car or a home were deal prone. Time-related variables, age of youngest child and housewife's employment status, also affected deal proneness but not as strongly as household resource variables. The effects of income also were analyzed and the results showed that upper income households were more deal prone. However, when income was adjusted for household resources, this effect became negligible. The results are based on the analysis of purchasing data for five different frequently purchased products. Therefore, it seems reasonable to conclude that the results can be generalized to a wide variety of frequently purchased goods.

REFERENCES

1. Becker, Gary S. "A Theory of the Allocation of Time," *Economic Journal*, 75 (September 1965), 493–517.

2. Bishop, Yvonne M. M., Stephen E. Fienberg, and Paul W. Holland. *Discrete Multivariate Analysis: Theory and Practice.* Cambridge, Massachusetts: The M.I.T. Press, 1975.

3. Blattberg, Robert C., Peter Peacock, and Subrata K. Sen. "Purchase Segmentation: Beyond Aluminum Foil," working paper, April 1977.

4. —— and Subrata K. Sen. "Market Segments and Stochastic Brand Choice Models," *Journal of Marketing Research*, 13 (February 1976), 34–45.

5. —— and ——. "Market Segmentation Using Models of Multidimensional Purchasing Behavior," *Journal of Marketing*, 38 (October 1974), 17–28.

6. Frank, Ronald E., William F. Massy, and Yoram Wind. *Market Segmentation.* Englewood Cliffs, New Jersey: Prentice-Hall, Inc., 1972.

7. Green, Paul E., Frank J. Carmone, and David P. Wachspress. "On the Analysis of Qualitative Data in Marketing Research," *Journal of Marketing Research*, 14 (February 1977), 52–9.

8. Hillier, Frederick S. and Gerald J. Lieberman. *Operations Research*, 2nd ed. San Franciso: Holden-Day, Inc., 1974.

9. Hogg, Robert V. and Allen T. Craig. *Introduction to Mathematical Statistics*, 3rd ed. New York: The Macmillan Company, 1970.

10. Kunreuther, Howard. "Why the Poor May Pay More for Food: Theoretical and Empirical Evidence," *Journal of Business*, 46 (July 1973), 368–83.

11. Michael, Robert T. and Gary S. Becker. "On the New Theory of Consumer Behavior," *Swedish Journal of Economics*, 75 (December 1973), 378–96.

12. Montgomery, David B. "Consumer Characteristics Associated with Dealing: An Empirical Example," *Journal of Marketing Research*, 8 (February 1971), 118–20.

13. Webster, Frederick E. Jr., "The 'Deal-Prone' Consumer," *Journal of Marketing Research*, 2 (May 1965), 186–9.

14. Wright, Peter. "Consumer Choice Strategies: Simplifying vs. Optimizing," *Journal of Marketing Research*, 12 (February 1975), 60–7.

ROBERT C. BLATTBERG*

The author explains how decision theory can be applied to the design
and evaluation of advertising experiments and discusses its application to
marketing problems.

The Design of Advertising Experiments Using Statistical Decision Theory

A crucial marketing decision in most firms that sell directly to consumers is the size of the advertising budget. Sophisticated statistical methodology has been used in the design of experiments to determine the relationship between sales and advertising. Probably the most famous application of this methodology to advertising budgeting is the Anheuser-Busch experiment in which they attempted to determine how advertising spending affects the sales and profitability of Budweiser beer. (See Ackoff and Emshoff 1975 for the details of the experiment.)

At some point in their history most firms have designed some form of advertising experiment. Two of the most important questions that arise are: (1) How many markets should be used in the experiment? and (2) How do we make a decision based on the experimental results? The first question is important because it determines the cost of the experiment and how accurate the experimental results will be. Frequently, one experimental market in an advertising experiment costs $50,000 to $100,000. Therefore, the addition or removal of just one market has a major impact on the cost of the experiment. The second question affects how "good" the final decision will be. If the evaluation procedure leads to an incorrect decision too frequently, then the cost to the firm is potentially very high. Unfortunately, very little published literature directly addresses these issues. Most market researchers rely on classical statistical procedures to answer these questions. However, a better approach is available—statistical decision theory.

Other researchers have recommended using decision theory to design experiments (Banks 1965, Schlaifer 1961). There also have been several other applications of decision theory to marketing problems (e.g., Bass 1963, Green 1963, Roberts 1963). Some of the articles include illustrative examples, others actual applications of decision theory. After reading these articles one is left with the impression that it is straightforward

to apply decision theory to marketing problems. Yet when the theory is applied to an actual problem, many issues arise that are not discussed in the literature. In addition, though many researchers believe that they know the costs and benefits of decision theory in comparison with classical statistics, the lack of use of decision theory in marketing indicates that these issues should be studied in the context of an actual marketing problem to highlight the differences.

The purpose of this article is twofold: (1) to show how to apply decision theory to the design and evaluation of advertising experiments and (2) to discuss the application of decision theory to marketing problems. The following issues are discussed which are not considered in other marketing applications of decision theory:

1. How does the researcher determine the variance of the experimental markets before experimenting? (This step is important in computing the expected value of sample information.)
2. How do alternative distributional assumptions about the prior distribution (gamma vs. normal) affect the expected value of sample information?
3. What implicit prior distribution does the classical hypothesis testing procedure imply?

In addition, a case is presented in which the parameter value (states of nature) is continuous whereas Bass (1963) and Green (1963) and most other marketers use discrete parameter values.

The rest of the article includes a description of the problem and a model for the data, an outline of the decision theoretic approach for determining sample sizes and making decisions, an actual application of the theory to compute the "optimal" number of markets to be used in the experiment, and an evaluation of the experimental results. Finally, the use of a normal versus gamma prior distribution is considered.

THE BASIC DECISION PROBLEM

The problem to be studied is that of a firm trying to decide between two advertising spending levels for the next year. The first alternative is to spend γ fraction

---

* Robert C. Blattberg is Professor of Marketing, Graduate School of Business, University of Chicago.

Journal of Marketing Research
Vol. XVI (May 1979), 191–202

of sales on advertising which is the present spending level and the second alternative is to spend $\gamma + \delta$ fraction of sales on advertising.[1] To help make the decision, an experiment is designed to give information about the sales response to advertising.

The experimental design is a randomized design with two sets of markets.[2] Set one has advertising at the present level and is referred to as the control markets. Set two has advertising at the higher level ($\gamma + \delta$) and is referred to as the experimental markets.

Mathematical Description of the Decision Problem

The profit functions for the two alternatives can be defined mathematically as follows:

S = the expected dollar sales for the coming year,

c = the cost of goods sold per sales dollar,

K = the firm's fixed costs in dollars,

m = the marginal profit for each additional dollar of sales resulting from the advertising increase,

μ = the fraction change in dollar sales due to the increased advertising budget,

γ = the present fraction of dollar sales spent on advertising,

δ = the increased fraction of dollar sales spent on advertising, and

ρ = the cost of capital.

For alternative 1, spending γ fraction of sales on advertising, the profit function is:

$$(1) \qquad \pi_1 = S(m - \gamma) - K.$$

For alternative 2, spending $\gamma + \delta$ fraction of sales on advertising, the profit function is:

$$(2) \qquad \pi_2 = S(m - \gamma) - K + S(m\mu - \delta(1 + \rho)).$$

π_1 represents next year's profits if one does not increase advertising. π_2 is equal to π_1 plus a term which represents the incremental gain (decrease) in profits due to the additional advertising.[3] $S\delta\rho$ is included because it represents the return required on additional advertising spending which could have been invested elsewhere.

The breakeven point for μ occurs when $\pi_1 = \pi_2$.

Thus equating equations 1 and 2 gives the breakeven point $\mu_b = \delta(1 + \rho)/m$. If μ is greater than μ_b, one should take alternative 2, and if μ is less than μ_b one should take alternative 1.

A Statistical Model for Generation of Experimental Data

Suppose there are n experimental markets and n control markets. Let $\tilde{c}_1, \ldots, \tilde{c}_n$ denote the sales in the control markets and $\tilde{e}_1, \ldots, \tilde{e}_n$ the sales in the experimental markets for the experimental period (e.g., 1 year).[4] Let μ_e denote the mean sales for an experimental market and μ_c the mean sales for a control market. $\mu_e - \mu_c = \mu$ is the mean sales increase due to advertising.[5] Thus, one is assuming that $E(\tilde{e}_i) = \mu_e$ for all i and $E(\tilde{c}_i) = \mu_c$ for all i. Further, let $\bar{c}$ = the sample mean for the control markets and $\bar{e}$ = the sample mean for the experimental markets. Then $E(\bar{\tilde{e}}) = \mu_e$ and $E(\bar{\tilde{c}}) = \mu_c$.

Define $d = \bar{e} - \bar{c}$ where d is simply the difference between the mean sales responses in the experimental and control markets and is therefore an estimate of μ. The mean of $\tilde{d} = E(\bar{\tilde{e}} - \bar{\tilde{c}}) = \mu_e - \mu_c = \mu$.

To find the variance of d one must make some assumption about the variances of the individual $\tilde{e}_i$'s and $\tilde{c}_i$'s. Assume that the variances for all markets, both experimental and control, are equal, and denoted by σ^2. Thus $\text{Var}(\tilde{e}_i) = \text{Var}(\tilde{c}_i) = \sigma^2$ for all i. Further assume that all the markets' sales levels are statistically independent, and then, the $\text{Var}(\bar{\tilde{c}}) = \text{Var}(\bar{\tilde{e}}) = \sigma^2/n$ and $\text{Var}(\tilde{d}) = 2\sigma^2/n$.

The last assumption to be made is that each $\tilde{e}_i$ and $\tilde{c}_i$ follows a normal distribution. Because sales responses in each market depend on a large number of small factors, the Central Limit Theorem indicates that sales may be normally distributed. If the underlying data are normal, then d is normal. However, even if the underlying data are not normal, d may be approximately normal. This again is a consequence of the Central Limit Theorem.

Briefly, the major assumptions made in describing the model used for the experimental data are:

1. Normality of each observation in the experimental and control markets.
2. The same variance for all markets.
3. Statistical independence for all pairs of markets.
4. All control markets have mean sales μ_c and all experimental markets have mean sales μ_e.

THE DECISION THEORETIC APPROACH TO DESIGNING EXPERIMENTS

This section shows how statistical decision theory can be used to determine (1) how the firm should make decisions using experimental data and (2) if an

---

[1]Using a percentage of sales advertising rule is often criticized because it leads to decreases in advertising when sales are declining. One can easily do the analysis using a fixed level of advertising and increase it by some percentage. The analysis would not be any different. For the application considered in this article, a percentage of sales rule was used by the firm because of some practical considerations. Therefore, the analysis throughout the article is based on a percentage of sales rule.

[2]More than two alternatives could be considered but to do so would only add unnecessary complications.

[3]It is assumed that advertising has no carryover effect (or at least minimal carryover effect) and that its effects happen instantaneously. For the product being considered this is a reasonable assumption. If there are either carryover or noninstantaneous effects, a more elaborate time dependent model of profits is necessary. See McGuire (1972) for a discussion of how to model this carryover effect in experimental designs.

[4]A tilde is used to denote a random variable.

[5]An instantaneous effect of advertising is assumed.

experiment is conducted, how many markets should be used.

Using Prior Information to Make a Decision

For the decision problem defined heretofore, the marketing manager rarely knows the exact value of μ. However, he or she usually has some subjective judgments about the statistical distribution of μ.[6] Therefore begin by assuming μ is a random variable for which one has some statistical distribution, $f(\mu)$, that the manager can assess on the basis of subjective judgment about μ. This distribution then is used to make a decision about which alternative to select.

In the preceding section the profit functions for both alternatives are developed. The manager's goal should be to select that action which maximizes expected profits. Because the value of μ is unknown, one must maximize expected profits rather than profits.[7] By using the statistical distribution of μ one can find the expected profits for both alternatives.[8]

Let $E(\mu)$ be the expected value of μ for the distribution $f(\mu)$. Then, the expected profit for the profit function given in equations 1 and 2 is:

(3) $E(\bar{\pi}_1) = S(m - \gamma) - K$

(4) $E(\bar{\pi}_2) = S(m - \gamma) - K + S\,[mE(\mu) - \delta(1 + \rho)]$.

One chooses alternative 2 if $E(\bar{\pi}_2) > E(\bar{\pi}_1)$. This occurs when $S[mE(\mu) - \delta(1 + \rho)] > 0$ which simplifies to the following decision rule:

Choose alternative 1 if $E(\mu) < \dfrac{\delta(1 + \rho)}{m} = \mu_b$.

Choose alternative 2 if $E(\mu) > \mu_b$.
Remain indifferent if $E(\mu) = \mu_b$.

Thus, one chooses the alternative to increase the advertising budget if the expected value of μ is greater than the breakeven point. The equations formulate in mathematical terms the approach many managers already use to make decisions. They decide whether the profit for alternative 1 is greater or less than the profit for alternative 2 and select the alternative which maximizes profits. If they do not know μ, they substitute a subjective estimate of μ. It is suggested that they should use $E(\mu)$ as the estimate of μ because it has some optimal properties.[9] Therefore, the ap-

proach discussed in this section is an attempt to offer an economic framework for making decisions using subjective judgments about μ.

How to Incorporate Experimental Information into the Decision-Making Process

In a preceding section, sales in the control markets is denoted by $\bar{c}_1, \dots, \bar{c}_n$ and sales in the experimental markets by $\bar{e}_1, \dots, \bar{e}_n$. Then, $\bar{d} = \bar{e} - \bar{c}$ is an estimate of the increased sales due to increased advertising spending. $\bar{d}$ is shown to be normally distributed with mean $\mu = \mu_e - \mu_c$ and the variance $2\sigma^2/n$. What one now wants to do is use the sample information about μ contained in $\bar{d}$ and the prior distribution for μ to make a decision.

For computational convenience, suppose that the prior distribution for μ is a normal distribution with mean μ' and variance σ^2/n'[10] denoted by $N(\mu', \sigma^2/n')$. This prior distribution has two "free" parameters, n' and μ', which can be used to change its shape. μ' adjusts the mean and n' controls the variance. By using Bayes' theorem, one can combine the prior distribution and sample evidence to obtain a "posterior" distribution for μ. It is called a posterior distribution because it is the distribution of μ *after* sampling. As is shown by Winkler (1972, p. 171), using the assumptions about the distribution of $\bar{d}$ and the prior distribution for μ, the posterior distribution for μ is normal with mean $\mu'' = \mu'n' + d(n/2)/n''$ and variance σ^2/n'' where $n'' = (n' + n/2)$. One sees that $\mu'' = a\mu' + (1 - a)d$ where $a = (n'/n'')$. Thus the mean of the posterior distribution for μ is a weighted average of the prior mean μ' and the sample mean d. The weighting factor depends on n and n'.

To decide which alternative to select, one again chooses that alternative which maximizes expected profits. Taking the expected value of the two profit functions one has:

(5) $E(\bar{\pi}_1) = S(c - \gamma) - K$

(6) $E(\bar{\pi}_2) = S(c - \gamma) - K + S\,[mE(\mu) - \delta(1 + \rho)]$

$\qquad\quad = S(c - \gamma) - K + S\,[m\mu'' - \delta(1 + \rho)]$

where μ'' is the posterior mean of μ. The decision rule becomes:

(7) Choose alternative 1 if $\mu'' < \mu_b$
Choose alternative 2 if $\mu'' > \mu_b$
Remain indifferent if $\mu'' = \mu_b$

where $\mu_b = \delta(1 + \rho)/m$.

It is useful to study the decision rule for a few special cases. First, what happens as the sample becomes very large? As n increases, holding n' fixed, $(1 - a) \to 1$ and thus $\mu'' \to d$. Therefore, the decision

---

[6] Marketing managers may not refer to it in these terms but their prior feelings about the possible values of μ and the likelihood of these values constitute a prior statistical distribution for μ.

[7] In most discussions of decision theory, the criterion used is to maximize expected utility. Using utilities allows the decision-maker to be risk averse. It is very simple to redesign the profit functions to use utilities rather than profits. See Winkler (1972, p. 246–60) for a discussion of utility functions. Maximizing expected profits is used because the solutions require only the mean of the distribution to make decisions. It is therefore easier to discuss the solutions on an intuitive level.

[8] One is assuming that $E(\mu)$ exists.

[9] See footnote 8.

---

[10] Other priors can be used. In a following section the use of a gamma-1 prior for μ is described.

rule becomes: select alternative 1 if d is less than the breakeven point. Thus, as n becomes large, the firm makes its decision on the basis of the sample evidence only.

Next consider the case in which n' is very small. Here the prior distribution of $\bar{\mu}$ is very spread out, indicating a lack of knowledge about the value of $\bar{\mu}$. As n' decreases holding n fixed, $(1 - a) \to 1$ and thus $\mu'' \to d$. Hence, if one has very little prior information about $\bar{\mu}$, again the experimental evidence will dominate the decision.

From the foregoing, discussion, one sees that "knowing little" does not limit use of the decision approach. If one uses a large number of markets or knows little about μ, the experimental data become the major factor in making a decision.

Determining the Number of Experimental Markets to Use

To determine how many markets the firm should use, one computes the expected value of sample information (EVSI) for all feasible sample sizes.[11] Then one selects the "optimal" sample size by finding the sample size for which the incremental expected value of sample information equals the incremental cost of using an additional market.

The procedure for calculating the expected value of information is computed in Appendix A. The formulae are:

$$(8) \quad \text{EVSI}(n) = \begin{cases} \{S\,[mE(\bar{\mu}''|\mu'' > \mu_b) - \delta(1 + \rho)\} \\ \Pr(\bar{\mu}'' > \mu_b) - S\,[m\mu' - \delta(1 + \rho)] \\ \qquad\qquad\qquad \text{for} \quad \mu' > \mu_b \\ \{S\,[mE(\bar{\mu}''|\bar{\mu}'' > \mu_b) - \delta(1 + \rho)] \\ \Pr(\bar{\mu}'' > \mu_b) \qquad \text{for} \quad \mu' \le \mu_b \end{cases}$$

where:

$$E(\bar{\mu}''|\bar{\mu}'' > \mu_b) = \mu' + \frac{\sqrt{c'\sigma^2}\; f_N\left(\dfrac{\mu_b - \mu'}{\sqrt{c'\sigma^2}}\,\middle|\,0, 1\right)}{\Pr(\bar{\mu}'' > \mu_b)}$$

$f_N(\mu_b - \mu'/\sqrt{c'\sigma^2}\,|\,0, 1)$ is the standard normal density evaluated at $\mu_b - \mu'/\sqrt{c'\sigma^2}$, μ' is the prior mean, $\bar{\mu}''$ is the posterior mean prior to sampling, and $c' = (n/2n')(1/n/2 + n')$.

Because the variance of $\bar{\mu}''$ depends on n, the number of experimental markets, the EVSI depends on n. For different values of n one can compute the EVSI (n). Then one selects the value of n for which

$$(9) \quad \text{EVSI}(n + 1) - \text{EVSI}(n) < c(n + 1) - c(n)$$

and

$$\text{EVSI}(n) - \text{EVSI}(n - 1) > c(n) - c(n - 1)$$

where $c(n)$ is the cost of using n markets in the experiment.

The decision theoretic approach also allows the firm to determine the maximum amount the firm should be willing to pay for information, referred to as the expected value of perfect information (EVPI). This is

$$(10) \quad \text{EVPI} = \begin{cases} [S(mE(\bar{\mu}|\bar{\mu} > \mu_b) - \delta(1 + \rho)] \\ \Pr(\bar{\mu} > \mu_b) \\ -S\,[m\mu' - \delta(1 + \rho)] \qquad \text{for} \quad \mu' > \mu_b \\ [S(mE(\bar{\mu} > \mu_b) - \delta(1 + \rho)] \\ \Pr(\bar{\mu} > \mu_b) \qquad\qquad \text{for} \quad \mu' \le \mu_b \end{cases}$$

where $E(\bar{\mu}|\bar{\mu} > \mu_b) = \mu' + \sigma/\sqrt{n'}\, f_N(\mu_b - \mu'/\sigma/\sqrt{n'}\,|\,0, 1)/\Pr(\bar{\mu} > \mu_b)$ and $f_N(\cdot\,|\,0, 1)$ is defined as in equation 8.

From the analysis, one sees that the sample size is determined by computing the economic value of information. The value of information results from making the correct decision more frequently than if one did not sample. The EVSI will always be greater the larger n. However, at some point the cost of using an additional market is greater than the incremental value of information received. One then does not want to use any more markets in the experiment. If there are no sample sizes for which EVSI is greater than the cost of experimenting, one should not experiment. The next section gives an application of the theory just described in order to determine the sample size and decisions that should be made on the basis of the experimental evidence.

AN APPLICATION OF THE THEORY TO THE DESIGN OF AN ADVERTISING EXPERIMENT

This section begins with a description of the problem, the actual parameters of the profit function, and the data model. Next, a prior distribution is developed for $\bar{\mu}$, and then for different sample sizes the EVSI is computed and the sensitivity of the results studied for alternative prior distributions for $\bar{\mu}$. Finally, the actual experimental results are evaluated.

Description of the Experiment

The company was considering changing their advertising budget from 2 to 3% of sales. Before making this decision they wanted to use a controlled experiment to learn more about whether the 3% level paid out economically. The experimental design to be used was a simple randomized design with a control and experimental set of markets. In the experimental markets advertising would be set at 3% and in the control markets it would be set at 2%. The firm said that it was willing to commit 20 markets, 10 control and 10 experimental markets, if that many were neces-

---

[11] The company is often not willing to use more than some specified number of markets in the experiment. The sample size goes from one to this upper bound figure.

sary. However, they were hoping fewer markets could be used. They wanted to know: (1) How many markets should be used? (2) Would the experiment offer enough additional information to justify the costs of the experiment? To answer these questions the decision theory approach developed in the preceding section was used. The first step was to compute the parameters of the profit function.

For the profit function given in equations 1 and 2, the parameters needed to compute the EVSI are: S = dollar sales for the next year, m = the profit margin per dollar sale, γ = present percentage of sales spent on advertising, δ = the additional percentage to be spent on advertising, and ρ = the cost of capital.

Dollar sales for next year were estimated to be 300 million dollars. From the description of the problem, the present advertising level is .02 times sales and the additional level is .01 times sales. Thus S = 300,000,000, γ = .02, and δ = .01.

From the firm's accounting department estimates were obtained of the cost of capital and marginal profit per dollar of sales deriving from advertising. It is very important to use marginal profits which are computed by deleting "fixed" costs. If fixed costs are not removed from the estimate of marginal profit, then over some range of μ one will make an incorrect decision (forego potential profits). It is very common for firms to want to use a standard profit figure which includes fixed costs. However, using the incorrect measure of profits will result in an incorrect decision over some range of μ. Usually, this will cause μ_b to be higher than if marginal costs are used.

The values given were m = .20 and ρ = .10. Thus, $\mu^b = \delta(1 + \rho)/m = (.01) \cdot (1 + .10)/.20 = .055$. If μ, the additional sales due to the 1% increase in advertising, results in more than a 5.5% increase in sales, the increased advertising strategy should be followed.

All of the assumptions described heretofore about the data model were evaluated. The one key problem was knowing σ^2, the variance for each market. Not having experimented, one cannot go through the standard procedure of estimating σ^2 from the sample. In most cases an alternative is available. One can simply use past sales data for each of the firm's markets to estimate σ^2.[12] The estimate of σ^2 was computed as .012773.

The Prior Distribution for μ

In the analysis given in the preceding section a distribution for $\bar{\mu}$ is required. This raises the issue of whether one should use a distribution based on the subjective estimates of the manager to make a

decision. Before continuing with the analysis of the decision problem, it is useful to discuss this issue. First, it is important to realize that if one does use the manager's judgments about μ, there are costs. Suppose the manager is almost certain that advertising will pay out economically. Should the firm conduct a costly experiment which ties up markets and delays a potentially profitable decision when the manager has a fairly good idea of what the results of the experiment are going to be? The decision based on the experimental results will most likely be the same as that based on the manager's subjective distribution for $\bar{\mu}$. In this case the value of the additional information received from the experiment is most likely going to be less than the cost of experimentation. Therefore, if the firm disregards the manager's subjective judgments and conducts the experiment, it will incur unnecessary costs.

Second, using a subjective distribution does not mean misrepresenting the manager's state of knowledge about μ. By setting the parameters and form of $f(\mu)$ one can represent "knowing little" or knowing a great deal about μ. Care should be taken to guarantee that $f(\mu)$ represents the manager's belief about μ. Winkler (1967), von Staël (1970), and many others have worried about methods of assessing prior distributions so that they can represent subjective beliefs. With time-sharing computers, managers can assess their distribution, see the implications, reassess their distribution, etc., until they feel it represents their judgments. There are also well-prescribed mathematical requirements for the distribution of $\bar{\mu}$.[13] Time-sharing programs can be used to determine whether these are met.

Finally, assessing subjective distributions need not be quantification of ignorance. Most marketing managers have some idea about the effects of advertising. The manager's subjective distribution for $\bar{\mu}$ may come from previous studies of the relationship between advertising and sales, from experiences the manager has already had in setting the advertising budget and seeing the sales results, or from other sources. Jolson and Rossow (1971) discuss whether experts can assess parameters accurately. Their conclusion is that they can.

To assess the marketing manager's prior distribution for $\bar{\mu}$, two questions were asked. First, what is his expectation for the sales response to an increase of 1% in advertising? He felt that the mean increase would be 7%. This implies that $E(\bar{\mu}) = \mu' = .07$. Next, to determine n', what odds he would give that the sales increase was above the breakeven point of 5.5%? The manager's answer was 2 to 1. This translates

---

[12] Rather than assuming $\sigma^2 = \hat{\sigma}^2$, the past year's estimate, a full Bayesian analysis could be done using a prior distribution for σ^2 which would result in $\bar{\mu}$ following a student t distribution.

[13] Winkler (1972, p. 260 4) discusses axioms of coherence. These axioms are such that it is impossible to set up a series of bets against a person so that the person is sure to lose regardless of the outcome of the events.

into the probability statement $\Pr(\tilde{\mu} > \mu_b) = .67$. It is known that μ_b and $\mu' = .07$. The variance of $\tilde{\mu}$ is σ^2/n'. If σ^2 is known, n' can be determined by using a standardized normal table. From the estimate of σ^2 given previously, $\sigma^2 = .012773$, n' is computed to be 11. Thus the manager's prior was normal with $\mu' = .07$ and standard deviation $\sigma/\sqrt{n'} = .0341$.

A normal prior distribution is convenient to use because there are well-developed formulae for computing the expected value of sample information. Also the normal distribution offers a reasonably "rich" prior distribution in that it has two parameters and can represent many shapes. However, it has two major drawbacks. First, its range is $-\infty < \mu < \infty$, which allows μ to be less than zero, indicating that increased advertising may cause a decrease in sales. This does not seem reasonable. (For the prior used here, there is only a .02 probability that $\tilde{\mu} < 0$.) The second drawback is that the normal distribution is symmetric. It may be more reasonable to assume that the prior distribution is skewed to the right because the manager may believe there is some chance that advertising can have a very large effect. Therefore, a gamma-1 distribution may better represent the manager's prior beliefs about $\tilde{\mu}$. In a following section a gamma-1 prior distribution for $\tilde{\mu}$ is compared with the normal prior just described.

Computation of the EVSI

The EVSI can be computed with the foregoing parameters. Table 1 gives the EVSI for n going from 1 to 10 for $n' = 11$. As n increases, the incremental gain in the EVSI declines after $n = 2$.

To decide on the number of markets to be used in the experiment, it was necessary to estimate the cost of using a market for experimental purposes. The company believed that the cost of experimenting

was about \$15,000 per set of test and control markets. The costs were primarily due to foregone profits because of the firm's inability to introduce new products and react to competitors by using new promotions. The costs were not the same for each market. Larger markets were more costly. However, as an approximation \$15,000 was used. From Table 1 one sees that the EVSI(8) − EVSI(7) < 15,000 and EVSI(7) − EVSI(6) > 15,000. Therefore, n was set at 7.

To study the sensitivity of the EVSI to different parameters, other values of μ' and n' were used. Table 1 also lists the EVSI for different values of n'. One value of n' was chosen by requiring the $\Pr(\tilde{\mu} > \mu_b) = .6$ which corresponds to 3/2 odds the experiment will pay out. The other value was chosen by doubling the variance of the prior. The resulting values of n' were 3.6 and 5.5, respectively. Figure 1 shows the shapes of the three priors.

Figure 1

NORMAL PRIORS FOR DIFFERENT VARIANCES

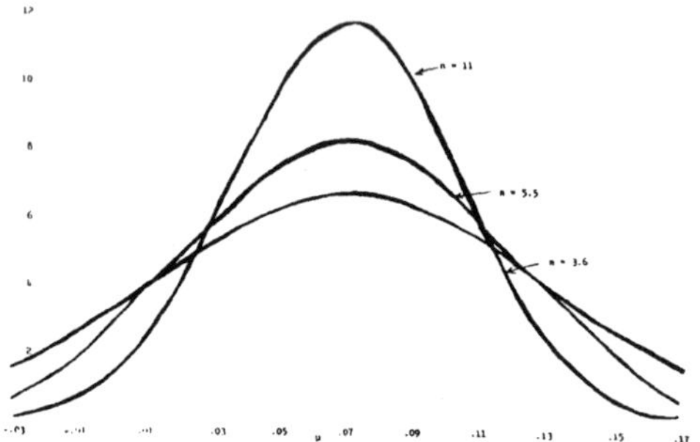

Table 1

EXPECTED VALUE OF SAMPLE INFORMATION FOR DIFFERENT SAMPLE SIZES

(prior mean = .07, σ^2 = .012773, breakeven point = .055)

N	1	2	3	4	5	6	7	8	9	10
					(000 omitted)					
$n' = 11$	\$ 3	16	34	52	70	86	101	116	128	140
$n' = 5.5$	60	137	200	251	292	327	357	383	406	426
$n' = 3.6$	172	310	405	477	533	578	615	646	673	696

Table 2

EXPECTED VALUE OF SAMPLE INFORMATION FOR DIFFERENT PRIOR MEANS

(σ^2 = .012773, breakeven point = .055, number of test and number of control markets = 7)

Prior mean	.00	.01	.02	.03	.04	.05	.055	.06	.07	.08	.09	.10	.11	.15
							(000 omitted)							
$n' = 11$	0	1	7	30	101	268	401	268	101	30	7	1	0	0
$n' = 5.5$	25	53	108	204	357	579	719	579	357	204	108	53	25	0

Table 3
EXPECTED VALUE OF PERFECT INFORMATION FOR DIFFERENT NORMALLY DISTRIBUTED PRIORS

	Prior value of n'		
	n' = 11	*n' = 5.5*	*n' = 3.6*
EVPI	$443,000	$760,000	$1,023,000

The results show that as n' becomes smaller, which makes the prior spread out, the EVSI increases. For example, for $n' = 11$ and $n = 7$, the EVSI is \$101,000 and for $n' = 3.6$ and $n = 7$, the EVSI is \$615,000. Therefore, the results definitely depend on the variance of the prior. With a tight prior (e.g., $n' = 11$), even if an incorrect decision is made, extreme outcomes away from μ_b are very unlikely.

In addition to changing the variance of the prior, the prior mean was changed holding n' fixed. Table 2 gives the results. As μ' becomes closer to $\mu_b = .055$, the EVSI increases to a maximum at $\mu' = \mu_b$. The EVSI is also symmetric around $\mu_b = .055$. (For example, EVSI for $\mu' = .05$ is the same as for $\mu' = .06$.) For $n' = 11$ the EVSI seems very sensitive to changes in μ'. The EVSI for $\mu' = .06$ and $n' = 11$ is approximately three and one-half times as large as for $\mu' = .07$. For $n' = 5.5$ and 3.6 the difference in the EVSI declines much less sharply for $\mu' = .06$ to $\mu' = .07$ than for $n' = 11$. This result makes sense intuitively because one chooses a tight prior when one has a good idea about the values of $\bar{\mu}$. As the prior mean moves away from the breakeven point when the prior is tight, the probability of making an error in the decision declines rapidly. Therefore, it becomes less valuable to sample.

From the foregoing analysis, one can make the following conclusions:

1. If there is uncertainty about $\bar{\mu}$, reflected by a small n', experimentation becomes valuable, particularly if the opportunity cost of an incorrect decision is large as it is in the problem discussed here.
2. If the prior for $\bar{\mu}$ is "tight" (large n'), the EVSI is sensitive to changes in μ'.
3. For μ' "far" from μ_b, the value of experimentation becomes small. Management should not incur the costs and risks of experimentation, but should make the decision on the basis of prior judgment.

These conclusions are obviously not rigid rules and depend on the problem and the prior used. However, the direction of the results will hold and only the relative values of μ' and n' for which they hold will vary from problem to problem.

Computation of the EVPI

Before studying the experimental results, it is useful to find an upper bound for the EVSI which is simply the EVPI. Equation 9 gives the formula for computing

the EVPI. Table 3 gives the values of EVPI for $n' = 11$, 5.5 and 3.6. The range is from \$443,000 to \$1,023,000. Therefore the maximum amount the information will be worth is known. The firm should never pay more for information than \$443,000 if its prior is normal with a mean of 7% and a standard deviation of 3.4%.

Evaluating the Experimental Results

In 1973 the experiment described heretofore was run with seven control and seven experimental markets ($n = 7$). The sales results are given in Table 4. The difference between the experimental and the control markets was 9.8% ($d = .098$). What decision should be made?

First,

$$(11) \qquad \mu'' = \frac{n'\mu' + (n/2)d}{n' + n/2}.$$

Next, the parameters for the prior distribution of $\bar{\mu}$ were $\mu' = .07$ and $n' = 11$ and $\sigma^2 = .012773$. With $n = 7$,

$$\mu'' = \frac{(.07)(11) + (7/2)(.098)}{11 + 7/2} = .077.$$

Using the decision rule given in equation 7 with the breakeven point being .055, alternative 2 is chosen—to increase advertising by 1%.

It is useful at this point to study the decision theory result in more detail. The sensitivity of μ'' to different values of d can be examined. In Table 5, μ'' is computed for different values of d. For $n' = 11$ and $\mu' = .07$, the parameters of the prior distribution given previously, the values of μ'' are not very sensitive to changes in d. The reason is that n' is 11 and $(n/2) = 3.5$. Therefore, the sample evidence is weighted by .24 and the prior mean by .76. If n' is changed, then the prior mean will be weighted less or more heavily depending on whether n' decreases or increases.

In Table 5, μ'' was also computed for $n' = 3.6$, another prior for $\bar{\mu}$ discussed previously. For this value of n' the results are much more sensitive to d. The

Table 4
EXPERIMENTAL RESULTS

Market	Control markets sales ratio	Experimental markets sales ratio
1	121.6	123.7
2	125.4	121.5
3	103.6	120.0
4	117.2	115.7
5	101.5	131.6
6	98.5	109.7
7	112.4	116.6
	$\bar{c} = 111.5$	$\bar{e} = 121.3$
	$d = 9.8$	$\mu'' = .077$

Table 5

THE POSTERIOR MEAN FOR DIFFERENT VALUES OF *d* AND *n'*

d	$n' = 11$ μ''	$n' = 3.6$ μ''
.098	.077	.084
.070	.070	.070
.055	.066	.062
.040	.063	.055
.025	.059	.048
.010	.056	.041
.000	.053	.035

weights are .49 for the sample evidence and .51 for the prior mean. For example, if $d = .098$, then $\mu'' = .084$ for $n' = 3.6$, whereas $d = .077$ for $n' = 11$. The choice of the prior parameter n', which determines the tightness of the distribution around the mean, affects the decision. Thus, the selection of the prior distribution for $\bar{\mu}$ is a very important part of the decision making.

Next, suppose d were equal to the breakeven point (5.5%). What alternative should one choose? Using equation 11 and assuming n', n, and μ' do not change,

$$\mu'' = \frac{(.07)(11) + (.055)(7/2)}{11 + 7/2} = .066.$$

Thus, one would still choose alternative 2 because the prior mean for $\bar{\mu}$ is greater than .055, making $\mu'' > .055$. If the prior distribution were not used to make a decision, one would discard the manager's judgment about $\bar{\mu}$. Suppose the sample evidence were "low quality," i.e., the variance is large and the number of markets is small. If the experimental results indicate that advertising resulted in a 4% increase in sales, should alternative 1 be selected? Because the sample evidence is "low quality," d is not a very precise estimate of μ. Suppose the manager, on the basis of past experience, believed that μ was greater than .055, the breakeven point. Which decision should he make? There is a reasonable chance that μ could be greater than .055 even though $d = .04$. Thus using his judgment and the sample evidence, he probably would select alternative 2. The decision rule and formula for μ'' merely offer a formal structure for doing this. Because the manager sets n', he can represent any state of knowledge. If n' is small, it represents less certainty about $\bar{\mu}$ and weights the sample evidence more heavily. Thus, by setting the prior parameters, the manager can incorporate his judgment as much or as little as he wishes.

The alternative to the decision rules derived from decision theory is classical statistical testing procedures. First, two hypotheses would be tested:[14]

$$(12) \qquad H_0: \mu \le .055 \text{ vs. } H_a: \mu > .055.$$

Using d as the test statistic, if one sets the probability of type I error equal to .10, the conventional level, then one would reject H_0 if $d > .20$.[15] *Given d = .098, the value observed from the experiment, H_0 would not be rejected and therefore alternative 1 would be selected.* Alternative 2 was selected by using decision theory. Why does this difference occur?

The prior distribution for $\bar{\mu}$ can be set so that there are equivalent decision rules for the classical test and the decision theory approach. Fix $n' = 11$, and only μ' will change. One wants a decision rule such that if $d > .20$ alternative 2 is selected for both approaches. For the decision theory approach one takes alternative 2 if $\mu'' > .055$. $\mu'' = n'\mu' + n/2(d)/n' + n/2$. Thus when $d > .20$, μ'' must be greater than .055. If $n' = 11$, $n = 7$, and $d = .20$, μ' can be determined so that $\mu'' = .055$. From the calculations, $\mu' = .009$. Thus, if the manager sets his prior mean equal to .009 and $n' = 11$, the two approaches result in identical decisions for any value of d observed. It is interesting to note that the *implicit prior mean is only .009*. In assessing the manager's prior he felt that $\mu' = .07$. However, if one uses the classical approach with the probability of type I error equal to .10, the implicit prior mean is much less than .07.

Because the implicit value of μ' depends on n', consider what happens if $n' = 3.6$. The value of μ' that would lead to identical decision rules is $-.086$. For $n' = 1.1$, $\mu' = -.41$. As n' becomes smaller, μ' becomes more negative. It is doubtful that a manager would have a prior mean for $\bar{\mu}$ equal to -41%. Yet, it is implicit in the classical test's decision rule that if the manager's prior is "loose" ($n' = 1.1$), his implicit prior mean is $\mu' = -.41$.

From this example, it is apparent that the classical approach gives strange results for the implicit prior mean of μ'. In the classical testing procedure, the prior distribution is not considered directly. However, the decision theory approach allows the manager to enter this directly into the analysis. He is advised as to the implications of his prior and then on the basis of his judgment he can set the parameters. He then combines past experience or intuitive judgment with the sample evidence. The weight that the two are given depends on his choice of the prior parameters. In contrast, the classical approach excludes prior judgment but uses *ad hoc* rules, e.g., the probability of type I error should be .10. No evaluation of the implication of choosing the probability of type I error equal to .10 is given. How informed the manager is about $\bar{\mu}$ does not affect the result. Some arbitrary cutoff point such as .20 is given and a decision is made. No economic framework is given for making

---

[14]The appropriate test is a one-tailed difference between means test discussed by Hays and Winkler (1971, p. 411).

[15]Assume $\sigma^2 = .012773$, and use the normal distribution to compute the critical points.

the choice of the cutoff point. No method is given for incorporating past judgment into the decision process. Yet, most managers would like to be able to approach the problem using past experience and economic rules for making decisions which the decision theoretic approach offers.

NONNORMAL PRIORS

In the preceding section a normal distribution was used to represent prior judgments about μ. The sensitivity of the results with respect to the parameters is discussed. One additional issue is whether a normal prior adequately represents one's feelings about μ. *A priori*, one would almost always expect additional advertising to increase and rarely (if ever) decrease sales.[16] Thus the prior for μ should always be positive. Second, the right-hand portion of the distribution of μ should be fairly long because it may be that additional advertising has a large effect. A reasonable shape

for a prior on μ is given by the gamma-1 distribution in Figure 2.

The density function for the gamma-1 distribution is

$$f_{\gamma 1}(\mu|r, \lambda) = \frac{e^{-\mu\lambda}\lambda^r\mu^{r-1}}{(r-1)!} \qquad 0 < \mu < \infty.$$

It is a two-parameter distribution with mean r/λ, variance r/λ^2, and range $(0, \infty)$.[17]

Figure 2 also compares a gamma-1 distribution with a normal distribution, both with mean .07 and $\Pr(\mu > \mu_b = .055) = .69$. The normal distribution has the parameters $\mu' = .07$ and $n' = 14$, and the gamma-1 distribution has parameters $r = 7$, $\lambda = 100$. From Figure 2 one sees that the gamma-1 distribution has a much longer right tail and cannot be less than zero by definition. Thus, it may represent the shape of a manager's prior beliefs about the effect additional advertising has on sales better than a normal distribution.[18]

Though computational convenience is important and should be weighed in the choice of priors, it may be that the EVSI changes drastically if a gamma-1 prior is used. To determine whether the EVSI changes much when a gamma-1 prior is used, the EVSI for this type of prior was computed.

The parameters for the gamma-1 distribution were chosen to require that the prior mean is .07 and $\Pr(\mu > \mu_b) = .67$. If $r = 7$ and $\lambda = 100$, then $E(\mu) = .07$, but $\Pr(\mu > \mu_b) = .69$. Because it is easier to work with integer values of r and λ, this prior was used rather than noninteger values but requiring $\Pr(\mu > \mu_b) = .67$.

The major limitation of a gamma-1 prior is computational. To compute the posterior mean of μ, which is the key parameter in making a decision if the framework of the preceding section is used, requires numerically integrating two functions. To compute the EVSI requires one additional numerical integration. Thus, the gamma-1 prior is not as easy to use as the normal prior when the likelihood function is also normal.

A corresponding normal prior was developed with $\mu' = .07$ and $\Pr(\mu > \mu_b) = .69$. The result was $n' = 14$. The EVSI was then computed using both priors and $n = 7$. The likelihood function was assumed normal with mean μ and variance $\sigma^2/n =$ with $\sigma^2 = .012773$.

The results are given in Table 6. The EVSI changes from $54,000 for a normal prior to $8,000 for a gamma-1 prior. The results indicate a substantial difference when a gamma-1 prior is used instead of a normal

Figure 2

NORMAL AND GAMMA-1 DISTRIBUTIONS

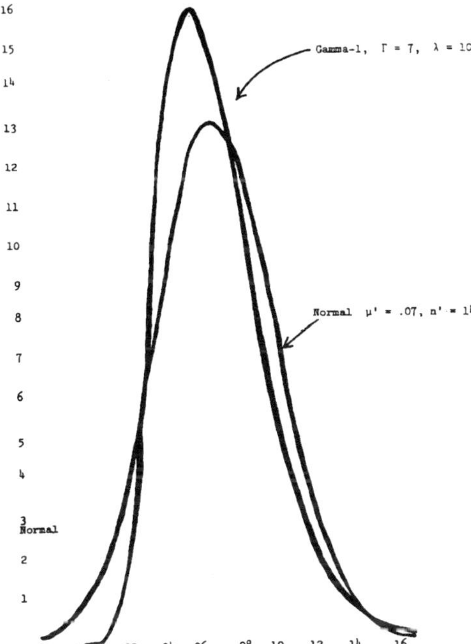

---

[16]Ackoff and Emshoff (1975) discuss an example for which they believe additional advertising actually decreases sales. In this case a gamma-1 prior may not be appropriate.

---

[17]See Raiffa and Schlaifer (1961, p. 225) for other facts about this distribution and how to compute its cumulative density function.

[18]Actually the gamma-1 distribution may have too low a density in the region of zero. Frequently managers feel there is some chance advertising has no effect on sales. In this case a spike or a truncated normal (at zero) may best represent their beliefs.

Table 6

THE EVSI FOR A NORMAL AND GAMMA-1 PRIOR DISTRIBUTION FOR μ

(000 omitted)	Parameters		EVSI
	$n' = 14$	$\mu' = .07$	54
Normal	$n' = 18.25$	$\mu' = .07$	23
	$n' = 23$	$\mu' = .07$	8
Gamma-1	$\Gamma = 7$	$\lambda = 100$	8

*To compute the EVSI, the likelihood function for d was assumed normal, $n = 7$, and $\sigma^2 = .012773$.

prior. The reason is the way in which the prior parameters were set. Though the mean and one value of the cumulative density of the two distributions are equal, they have very different shapes. Figure 2 shows that the gamma-1 distribution is more peaked and has a smaller tail area than the normal value when μ is less than .055. Thus, the probability of making an incorrect decision is very small.

For the normal distribution the distribution is higher from $\mu = 0$ to $\mu = .04$ than for the gamma-1 distribution. Over this range the cost of an error becomes large. Therefore, because the normal density has higher values over this range, the EVSI is larger.

To illustrate this issue in more detail, both the normal and gamma-1 distributions for μ'' were broken into discrete parts. Then, the EVSI was computed. Table 7 illustrates these calculations. The table entries for the discrete approximations show that the distribution of μ'' is much lower for the gamma-1 prior in the range of $\bar{\mu} = 0$ to $\bar{\mu} = .04$ than for the normal distribution. Because the losses are large in this range the EVSI will be much lower, as is shown.

Table 6 shows that for $\mu' = .07$ and $n' = 18.25$, the EVSI is 23,000 compared with 8,000 for the gamma-1. $n' = 18.25$ was chosen because the variances of the normal and gamma-1 priors are equal. Thus, equating the variance and mean of the priors still does not equate the EVSI. For $n' = 23$ and

$\mu' = .07$, the EVSI is the same for the normal and gamma-1 priors.

From the foregoing analysis one sees that priors with different shapes lead to different results. Therefore, practitioners applying decision theory must worry about the shape as well as the prior mean and variance.

CONCLUSIONS

The question of how to determine the sample size and evaluate the experimental results using decision theory is studied. The goal is to develop an economic framework in which these issues can be examined. An actual example is given to highlight some of the practical issues that must be considered in applying this approach.

Other issues not addressed in detail here may be useful to study in future research in this area. First, additional advertising should be viewed as a risky investment. What criterion should be used to decide whether to invest in additional advertising? Second, methods of computing the EVSI for other experimental designs should be studied. It is hoped that these issues and others raised in this article will serve as the basis for future studies and applications of decision theory in the design of advertising experiments.

APPENDIX A
PROCEDURE FOR CALCULATING EXPECTED VALUE OF SAMPLE INFORMATION

The purpose of this appendix is to derive the formulae for the expected value of sample information (EVSI). The variables, notations, and statistical distributions are defined in the article.

The profit functions given in equations 1 and 2 are:

$$\pi_1 = S(c - \gamma) - K$$

$$\pi_2 = S(c - \gamma) - K + S\left[\mu m - \delta(1 + \rho)\right].$$

The decision rule is to choose that alternative which maximizes expected profits. *Prior to sampling* one

Table 7

APPROXIMATE CALCULATION OF EVSI FOR NORMAL AND GAMMA-1 PRIOR DISTRIBUTIONS FOR μ

μ	(1) Loss<sup>	(2) Probability of μ for gamma-1 prior	(3) Col. (1) × Col. (2)	(4) Probability of μ for normal prior	(5) Col. (1) × Col. (4)
0–.03	—	.0000	0	0	0
.035	1350[a]	.0000	0	.0048	7
.040	1050	.0000	0	.0084	9
.045	750	.0002[b]	.2	.0190	14
.050	450	.0006	.3	.0372	17
.055	150	.0424	6.3	.0663	10
EVSI			6.8		57

*In thousands and is average for μ between .03 and .035.
^b$Pr(.040 < \bar{\mu} < .045)$.

DESIGN OF ADVERTISING EXPERIMENTS

chooses alternative 1 if $E(\tilde{\mu}) = \mu' \leq \mu_b$, and alternative 2 if $\mu' > \mu_b$ where μ_b is the breakeven value and μ' is the mean of the prior distribution of $\tilde{\mu}$. The expected profit *prior to sampling* is:

$$\text{(A1)} \quad E(\tilde{\pi}) = \begin{cases} S(c - \gamma) - K & \text{if } \mu' \leq \mu_b \\ S(c - \gamma) - K + S \\ [\mu'm - \delta(1 + \rho)] & \text{if } \mu' > \mu_b. \end{cases}$$

If one samples, the decision rule becomes: choose alternative 1 if $E(\tilde{\mu}) = \mu'' < \mu_b$ and alternative 2 if $\mu'' > \mu_b$ where μ'' is the mean of the posterior distribution for $\tilde{\mu}$ defined in the article. Then the profit function after sampling is:

$$\text{(A2)} \quad \pi = \begin{cases} S(c - \gamma) - K & \text{if } \mu'' \leq \mu_b \\ S(c - \gamma) - K + S \\ [m\mu'' - \delta(1 + \rho)] & \text{if } \mu'' > \mu_b. \end{cases}$$

Note that $\mu'' = a\mu' + (1 - a)d$. μ' and a are fixed but d is a random variable *prior to sampling*; therefore, $\tilde{\mu}''$ is a random variable *prior to sampling*. The expected profit, given a sample of size n prior to sampling, is:

$$\text{(A3)} \quad E(\tilde{\pi}\,|\,\text{sampling}) = \int_{-\infty}^{\mu_b} [S(c - \gamma) - K] f(\mu'')\,d\mu''$$
$$+ \int_{\mu_b}^{\infty} \{S(c - \gamma) - K$$
$$+ S[m\mu'' - \delta(1 + \rho)]\} f(\mu'')\,d\mu''$$
$$= [S(c - \gamma) - K]\Pr(\tilde{\mu}'' \leq \mu_b)$$
$$+ [S(c - \gamma) - K$$
$$+ S[mE(\tilde{\mu}''\,|\,\tilde{\mu}'' > \mu_b)$$
$$- \delta(1 + \rho)]\Pr(\tilde{\mu}'' > \mu_b).$$

Note that the expected profit function is separated into two parts because one takes alternative 1 if $\mu'' \leq \mu_b$ and alternative 2 if $\mu'' > \mu_b$.

To compute equation A3, the distribution of $\tilde{\mu}''$ is required. Once the distribution of $\tilde{d}$ is determined, the distribution of $\tilde{\mu}''$ is known. From the article one sees that $\tilde{d}$ is normally distributed with mean μ and variance $2\delta^2/n$. Therefore, the distribution of $\tilde{d}$ depends on μ. One does not know μ but does have a prior distribution for μ. Integrating over the distribution of μ gives the distribution of $\tilde{d}$ unconditional on μ. This is simply:

$$\text{(A4)} \quad f(d) = \int_{-\infty}^{\infty} f_N(d\,|\,\mu, 2\delta^2/n) f_N(\mu\,|\,\mu', \delta^2/n')\,d\mu$$
$$= f_N\left(d\,\middle|\,\mu', \delta^2\left(\frac{2}{n} + \frac{1}{n'}\right)\right).$$

Thus, the unconditional (on μ) distribution of $\tilde{d}$ is

normal with mean μ' and variance $\delta^2(2/n + 1/n')$. μ' is the mean of the prior distribution of $\tilde{\mu}$. Because $\tilde{d}$ is a normal random variable, $\tilde{\mu}''$ will be a normal random variable. The mean and variance of $\tilde{\mu}''$ are:

$$\text{(A5a)} \quad E(\tilde{\mu}'') = a\mu' + (a - a)E(\tilde{d}) = \mu'$$

$$\text{(A5b)} \quad \text{Var}(\tilde{\mu}'') = (1 - a)^2\,\text{Var}(d)$$
$$= \left(\frac{n/2}{n'}\right)\left(\frac{1}{n/2 + n'}\right)\sigma^2 = c'\sigma^2.$$

One now knows $f(\mu'')$, and therefore $\Pr(\tilde{\mu}'' \leq \mu_b)$, $\Pr(\tilde{\mu}'' > \mu_b)$, and $E(\tilde{\mu}''\,|\,\tilde{\mu}'' > \mu_b)$ from equation A3 can be computed. $\Pr(\tilde{\mu}'' \leq \mu_b)$ and $\Pr(\tilde{\mu}'' > \mu_b)$ are found from cumulative normal tables. $E(\tilde{\mu}''\,|\,\tilde{\mu}'' > \mu_b)$ is derived in Appendix B and is

$$\text{(A6)} \quad E(\tilde{\mu}''\,|\,\tilde{\mu}'' > \mu_b) = \mu' + \frac{\sqrt{c'\sigma^2} f_N\left(\frac{\mu_b - \mu'}{\sqrt{c'\sigma^2}}\,\middle|\,0, 1\right)}{\Pr(\tilde{\mu}'' > \mu_b)}$$

where:

$$f_N\left(\frac{\mu_b - \mu'}{\sqrt{c'\sigma^2}}\,\middle|\,0, 1\right)$$

is the standard normal density evaluated at $\mu_b - \mu'/\sqrt{c'\sigma^2}$.

To compute the EVSI, subtract the expected profit given no sampling from the expected profit if a sample of size n is used. This becomes:

$$\text{(A7)} \quad \text{EVSI}(n) = \{S[mE(\tilde{\mu}''\,|\,\tilde{\mu}'' > \mu_b) - \delta(1 + \rho)]\}$$
$$\Pr(\tilde{\mu}'' > \mu_b) - S[m\mu' - \delta(1 + \rho)]$$
$$\mu' > \mu_b$$
$$= \{S[mE(\tilde{\mu}''\,|\,\tilde{\mu}'' > \mu_b) - \delta(1 + \rho)]\}$$
$$\Pr(\tilde{\mu}'' > \mu_b) \qquad \mu' \leq \mu_b$$

where $E(\tilde{\mu}''\,|\,\tilde{\mu}'' > \mu_b)$ is defined in equation A6.

APPENDIX B
DERIVATION OF $E(\tilde{\mu}\,|\,\tilde{\mu} > \mu_b)$

To show:

$$E(\tilde{\mu}\,|\,\tilde{\mu} > \mu_b) = \mu' + \frac{\sigma f_N(u\,|\,0, 1)}{\Pr(\tilde{\mu} > \mu_b)}$$

where $u = \mu_b - \mu'/\sigma$, $\mu' = $ mean of $\tilde{\mu}$, $\sigma = $ standard deviation of $\tilde{\mu}$, $f_N(u\,|\,0, 1)$ is standardized normal density evaluated at u. From the article, $\tilde{\mu}$ is assumed normally distributed with mean μ' and standard deviation σ. By definition

$$\text{(B1)} \quad E(\tilde{\mu}\,|\,\tilde{\mu} > \mu_b) = \int_{\mu_b}^{\infty} \mu f(\mu\,|\,\tilde{\mu} > \mu_b)\,d\mu.$$

Because μ is normally distributed with mean μ' and standard deviation σ,

$$(B2) \qquad f(\mu \mid \mu > \mu_b) = \frac{f_N(\mu \mid \mu', \sigma)}{\Pr(\bar{\mu} > \mu_b)}, \qquad \mu > \mu_b.$$

Substituting equation B2 into B1,

$$(B3) \qquad E(\bar{\mu} \mid \bar{\mu} > \mu_b) = \frac{1}{\Pr(\bar{\mu} > \mu_b)}$$

$$\int_{\mu_b}^{\infty} \frac{\mu}{\sqrt{2\pi}\sigma} \exp\left\{ -\frac{1}{2}\left(\frac{\mu - \mu'}{\sigma} \right)^2 \right\} d\mu.$$

Making a change of variables to $u = \mu - \mu'/\sigma$ implying that $\sigma\, du = d\mu$,

$$(B4) \quad E(\bar{\mu} \mid \bar{\mu} > \mu_b) = \frac{1}{\Pr(\bar{\mu} > \mu_b)} \int_k^{\infty} \frac{u\sigma + \mu'}{\sqrt{2\pi}}$$

$$e^{-1/2u^2}\, du$$

$$= \frac{1}{\Pr(\bar{\mu} > \mu_b)} \left\{ \int_k^{\infty} \frac{\sigma u}{\sqrt{2\pi}} e^{-1/2u^2}\, du \right.$$

$$\left. + \int_k^{\infty} \frac{\mu'}{\sqrt{2\pi}} e^{-1/2u^2}\, du \right\}$$

$$= \frac{\sigma f_n(k \mid 0, 1)}{\Pr(\bar{\mu} > \mu_b)} + \mu'$$

where $k = \mu_b - \mu'/\sigma$.

REFERENCES

Ackoff, R. L. and Emshoff, J. R. (1975), "Advertising Research at Anheuser-Busch, Inc. (1963–1968)," *Sloan Management Review* (Winter).

Banks, S. (1965), *Experimentation in Marketing*. New York: McGraw-Hill, Inc.

Bass, F. M. (1963), "Marketing Research Expenditures: A Decision Model," *Journal of Business* (January), 77–90.

Blattberg, R. (1976), "A Decision Theory Approach for Determining Sample Sizes and Evaluating Results in Advertising Experiments," working paper, University of Chicago, July.

Green, P. E. (1963), "Bayesian Decision Theory in Pricing Strategy," *Journal of Marketing* (January), 5–14.

Hays, W. L. and Winkler, R. L. (1971), *Statistics, Probability, Inference and Decision*. New York: Holt, Rinehart, and Winston, Inc.

Hogarth, Robin M. (1973), "Cognitive Processes and the Assessment of Subjective Probability Institutions," IN-SEAD Research Paper Series, No. 97, October.

Jolson, M. A. and Rossow, G. L. (1971), "The Delphi Process in Marketing Decision Making," *Journal of Marketing Research*, 8 (November), 443–8.

McGuire, T. W. (1972), "Measuring and Testing Advertising Effectiveness with Split-Cable T.V. Panel Data," *Proceedings of the American Statistical Association* (Summer).

Raiffa, H. and Schlaifer, R. (1961), *Applied Statistical Decision Theory*. Cambridge, Massachusetts: The MIT Press.

Roberts, H. V. (1963), "Bayesian Statistics in Marketing," *Journal of Marketing* (January), 1–4.

Schlaifer, R. (1961), *Introduction to Statistics for Business Decisions*. New York: McGraw-Hill Book Company.

von Staël Holstein, C.-A. S. (1970), *Assessment and Evaluation of Subjective Probability Distributions*. Stockholm, Sweden: Economic Research Institute.

Winkler, R. L. (1972), *Introduction to Bayesian Inference and Decision*. New York: Holt, Rinehart and Winston.

———— (1967), "The Assessment of Prior Distributions in Bayesian Analysis," *Journal of the American Statistical Society* (September), 776–800.

ROBERT C. BLATTBERG, GARY D. EPPEN, & JOSHUA LIEBERMAN

Food retailers regularly offer products for less than normal market price in special sales or deals. This paper briefly examines several common explanations for this phenomenon and finds the analyses to be less than complete. It then presents an explanation for dealing of storable products based on the idea of transfering inventory carrying costs from the retailer to the consumer. An inventory control model is described in which both consumers and the retailer act so as to minimize their own costs. Results derived from this model are then presented. Data relevant to both the consumer and the retailer model are presented and analyzed. The conclusion is that the data are consistent with the predictions of the models. Finally, the strategic implications of the model for manufacturers and retailers are discussed.

A THEORETICAL AND EMPIRICAL EVALUATION OF PRICE DEALS FOR CONSUMER NONDURABLES

OVER the last half century, retailers, on a regular basis, have offered consumers periodic short term price cuts called deals.[1] Deals are one of the major forms of price competition used by retailers.

[1]Dealing will be defined as a short-term, usually a week or shorter, price cut to the consumer. After the deal is over, the price reverts back to its old level.

Robert C. Blattberg is Charles H. Kellstadt Professor of Marketing, and Gary D. Eppen is Associate Dean for Ph.D. Studies, both at the Graduate School of Business of the University of Chicago. Joshua Lieberman is Lecturer in Economics and Marketing, Bar-Ilan University, Ramat-Gan, Israel. The research for this paper has been funded in part by National Science Foundation Grant SOC73-05547

A natural question is, "Why do retailers prefer to offer substantial price reductions for a short period of time, and then raise the price to its normal level rather than permanently reduce price by less than the deal price?"

There are a number of alternative explanations though almost no published research exists on this topic. The most common explanation is that retailers deal to attract customers from other stores. We note that any given retailer would gain customers if he/she deals and his/her competitors do not retaliate also by dealing. However, it is very likely that other retailers also will respond by offering deals. A possible result is that all the retailers in the market offer deals but none of the retailers have increased their profits. Unless there were other

Journal of Marketing
Vol. 45 (Winter 1981), 116–129.

economic benefits to dealing, it would be unprofitable to the retailer.

The following analogy illustrates the point. Three gasoline dealers on the same corner engage in a price war. Dealer one reduces prices and gains customers. Quickly his/her competitors respond by reducing prices and their market shares return to their previous levels. The result is that the reduced prices do not increase volume enough so that total profits for the three stations are reduced below the pre-price war levels. It is almost always the case that after some relatively short period, the stations raise the price to pre-price war levels.

Food retailers price numerous items, and therefore, their environment is more complex than for a single-price retailer such as a gas dealer. The question remains, however, "If retailers can imitate one another, why do they continue to offer deals?" Eventually there should be an incentive to eliminate deals and simply charge lower prices. Other forms of promotion such as trading stamps, games and give-aways last a relatively short period of time,[2] yet dealing has persisted for 50 years. Another explanation for the persistence of dealing seems to be required.

Many researchers and store managers believe that retailers deal to attract customers. The previous discussion shows that dealing may lead to a zero-sum game. It is, of course, possible that retailers reach a non-optimal equilibrium in which each retailer cannot stop dealing because each retailer is worse off if he/she stops dealing and no one else does. Cases such as gas wars imply that these nonoptimal equilibria do not occur often. However, this proposition is very difficult to test with existing data sources. This article will propose an alternative explanation that future research may be able to contrast to the store traffic argument.

An alternative explanation of the cause of dealing is that manufacturers offer trade deals which require price reductions by the retailers. The manufacturers offer trade deals for two reasons: to increase market share, and to get nontriers of their products to learn about their form of attributes at a lower risk level (reduced price).

The first explanation is similar to the one just discussed for the retailer. Suppose the industry cannot increase category volume by dealing. Then if one firm offers a deal and its competitors follow, the overall price is reduced and profits are reduced. Thus, only if price reductions increase category volume enough to increase category profits, will dealing be economically viable. In most product categories it is unlikely that this will happen. Therefore, manufacturers will eventually stop offering trade deals. However, this has not happened.

The second explanation, offering consumers a reduced price to try their brand, will be analyzed in more detail in later sections of the paper discussing model implications and empirical results. It will be shown to be inconsistent with the empirical results.

The explanation studied in this paper is that dealing occurs because retailers have higher inventory holding costs than some consumers. The retailer is motivated to take a reduction in sales revenue if the consumer will hold some of the inventory. The consumer is willing to carry some inventory in return for a reduction in price. A deal is the condition needed to complete this exchange, since consumers cannot be persuaded to hold inventory by a constant price.

The inventory holding costs under consideration have two main components: the value of the capital tied up in inventory and the value of the space committed to holding the inventory. It seems clear that the second term is much greater for the retailer. Shelf space is a major concern for food retailers. Products and suppliers vie vigorously for shelf space. On the other hand, for a number of consumers the cost of some additional storage space is extremely low. Another dozen boxes of tissue in the bathroom closet or an additional case of pickles in the fruit cellar is of almost no concern. These costs alone seem sufficient to conclude that the opportunity for a mutually profitable exchange exists.

The idea that consumers buy and hold inventory when deals occur has appeared elsewhere in the literature. Frank and Massy (1967) used distributed lag models to measure the effect of past purchasing on a brand's sales and market share. Kunreuther (1973) and Blattberg et al. (1978) developed models of the household in which they traded off holding costs, transaction costs, and deal discounts to decide the quantity to buy each period. However, none of these papers tested an explicit inventory model. In addition, the retailer, i.e., the supply side of the model, was not considered. The purpose of this paper is to extend the holding cost theory to include the interaction between the consumer (demand) and retailer (supply), and thus be able to

---

[2]An example of retail promotions that are started and halted are games that retailers frequently offer to customers. These promotions initially attract customers to the first retailer who introduces the game. Quickly, other retailers adopt similar games and the profits due to the game for the first retailer are driven to zero. Soon all retailers drop the games and the market returns to its initial position. Games do not persist because they do not offer a sustained economic benefit to the retailer.

determine the magnitude and frequency of deals and the quantity sold on deal.

This paper is in the spirit of economic models in which the consumer and the firm (retailer) maximize their own objective function. This model is used to understand how deals work and to derive testable implications. Data are then used to test these implications.

Understanding and explaining dealing is complex. Economic reasoning was used to raise questions about several of the explanations of dealing commonly given. More detailed empirical tests are needed before any of these explanations can be accepted or rejected. In all likelihood, different explanations exist for the existence of dealing in different circumstances. The purpose of this paper is to offer an explanation as to why retailers deal in certain cases. It is shown that this explanation is consistent with consumer purchase data.

Section 2 of this article describes the model's structure, while Section 3 gives the testable implications. Section 4 tests these implications, and Section 5 gives a summary and our conclusions.

The Model's Structure

This section of the paper will outline two models, one for the consumer and one for the retailer. Each optimizes his/her own welfare in response to an action by the other. The equilibrium result is a dealing policy for the retailer. The retailer's model has implications regarding the quantity sold on deal and the frequency and magnitude of deals; the consumer model has implications regarding the quantity bought on deal and the time between purchases.

Before outlining the model, it is useful to list certain assumptions that will be used throughout this section. (Other assumptions that will be made are described in the appropriate section of the paper.) The first two are not restrictive but simplify the mathematics: time is a continuous variable, and all quantities sold and purchased are perfectly divisible.[3] The next four assumptions are more restrictive but are made to make the mathematics more tractable, so that a closed-form solution can be found for the optimal dealing price. These assumptions are: there is a single store in the market; deals are offered on a single brand only; the regular (nondeal) price of the deal brand, P, is fixed; and no trade allowances are offered to the retailer.

These assumptions do not perfectly mirror the real world. The first two assumptions are perhaps the worst offenders in this respect. However, they permit the construction of a relatively simple model that captures the essence of the inventory holding argument, yields analytically tractable results, and leads to conclusions that are empirically confirmed.

The assumption that the regular (nondeal) price is fixed, is not very restrictive because the relative prices in a category do not change substantially over short periods of time. The consumer's and store's behavior would not change dramatically if normal price fluctuations were included in the model.

The assumption of no trade allowances is consistent with the purpose of this paper. The goal is to demonstrate both with models and data analysis that deals by retailers are a reasonable economic activity with no additional outside motivation. It is not necessary or useful to include manufacturers in the model to establish this point. Other environments involving the three-way interaction between manufacturers, retailers, and consumers might also provide motivation for retailer dealing. This research does not claim to exclude all other reasons for dealing, but simply to establish the inventory explanation as a viable alternative. Other explanations and the associated research are left to other papers at another time.

The rest of this section includes an overview of the model, the consumer model, the retailer model, and testable implications.

An Overview of the Model

The model begins with the consumer. The consumer is assumed to respond to deals by "forward" buying additional items and holding inventory. The consumer decides his/her inventory level by trading off holding costs against the reduced price of the item. (See Blattberg et al. 1978 or Kunreuther 1973 for a discussion of this assumption.)

The model assumes that not all consumers have the same holding costs. For simplicity, there are two types of consumers: low-holding-cost consumers and high-holding-cost consumers.[4] Aggregation is done by weighting the two groups in the market by their relative size.

The retailer's objective is to maximize his/her profits. His/her main trade-off is that by dealing he/she can reduce his/her inventory but lose reve-

---

[3]Perfectly divisible means any amount of the product can be purchased.

[4]Splitting the market into two groups rather than having more segments or a distribution across the population to represent holding costs should have no effect on the results. The degree of response to deals will vary by segment but the general behavior should be similar.

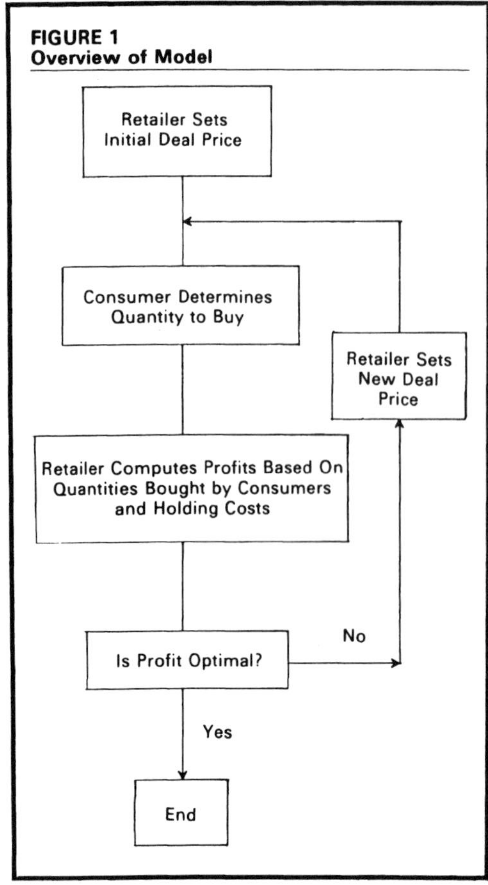

nue from the reduced deal price. The retailer controls the quantity bought on deal since the amount consumers will buy depends on the size of the deal. Figure 1 gives an overview of the model and shows that the retailer fixes his/her deal price as a function of the consumer's response to deals and his/her own cost of holding inventories.

Consumer Model

The consumer's objective function is to minimize his/her total costs subject to the constraint that he/she satisfy his/her demand at any point in time. It will be assumed that each consumer conducts regular shopping trips to the store, and on each trip he/she buys a bundle of items which may or may not include the deal brand. Each consumer, i, consumes the product category at a fixed rate

per unit of time, c_i, and has a fixed holding cost per unit of time, h_i, for the product category. (Note that h_i is the cost of holding one unit (e.g., a box or a can) of the product for one period of time. Thus, the holding cost for the same product (aluminun foil) will vary with the size of the box purchased.) In responding to deals the consumer never makes a special trip to the store, thus buying deal items during his/her regular trips, and responds to deals by changing purchase timing but not consumption of the product category.[5]

Based on these assumptions, the following model has been developed. In buying ahead on deal, the individual consumer, i, incurs a holding cost, h_i, on the quantity, q_i, which he/she stockpiles on deal but also gains a price reduction, D, for each unit bought on deal. The consumer wishes to minimize the total cost function, $TC(q_i)$, when he/she buys on deal subject to the constraint that he/she consumes c_i units per period and all consumption demand is satisfied. This leads to:

$$TC(q_i) = \int_0^{q_i/c_i} h_i(q_i - c_i t)dt - Dq_i$$
$$= \frac{h_i q_i^2}{2c_i} - Dq_i. \tag{1}$$

The time period of analysis is q_i/c_i which is the time required to consume q_i units. Equation (1) indicates that the cost of buying q_i units for the household is proportional to the holding costs (h_i) and the square of the quantity bought (q_i). It is inversely proportional to the consumption rate (c_i). As the deal (D) increases, costs also decrease.

From equation (1) one can determine the optimal quantity (q_i) to buy on deal. This yields

$$q_i^* = \frac{Dc_i}{h_i} \tag{2}$$

and the optimal purchase period is

$$t^* = \frac{D}{h_i} \tag{3}$$

Equation (2) shows that the optimal quantity to

---

[5]For products such as soft drinks and non-staple items, it is likely that dealing will increase the consumption rate. Therefore, c_i becomes a function of price, $c_i(p)$. The household will still forward buy, but the quantity bought will depend upon the effect of the deal on consumption as well as on the holding costs. The general results should not change, though it would be difficult to separate the two effects. The products studied in the empirical section are products whose consumption rates will not be greatly affected by dealing.

be bought increases as the deal magnitude (D) and consumption rate (c_i) increase, and it decreases as holding costs (h_i) increase. Equation (3) shows that the optimal purchase period increases as the deal magnitude (D) increases. The optimal purchase period decreases as the holding cost (h_i) increases.

To aggregate across consumers, it is assumed that all consumers have the same consumption rate, c.[6] Regarding holding costs, there are two segments in the market, one with a low per-unit holding cost, h_L, and the other with a high per-unit holding cost, h_H. Let there be N consumers in the market. α is a number lying between 0 and 1 so that there are αN consumers with low holding costs and $(1 - \alpha)$N consumers with high holding costs. It will be assumed that only consumers with low holding costs buy ahead on deal. The consumers with high holding costs just buy enough to meet their consumption per period.

From these assumptions, the aggregate quantity bought *on deal* is

$$Q_D = (\alpha N)q^* = \alpha Nc \frac{D}{h_L} \qquad (4)$$

Note that in (4) the term Nc is the accumulated rate of demand. Thus, if a deal occurs and another one is not offered for t^* or more weeks, the total amount bought on sale is $\alpha Q \frac{D}{h_L}$ or αQt^*, where Q is the cumulative rate of demand. In this derivation, it is assumed that the consumers with high holding costs do not buy any items on deal. In developing the model, it is assumed that the sale is instantaneous; i.e., that all items sold on deal are removed from the inventory instantaneously. It would be a simple matter to include some of the demand of high holding cost consumers in the quantity bought. However, it would add nothing new to the model except for some additional notation, and thus, this option was rejected. By the same token, other patterns for the demand of low holding cost during the deal could be assumed. These assumptions produce a model that is similar to the EOQ model, and thus, seemed worth exploring.

One generalization, however, is included in the model. At least in the early parts of the development, it is assumed that α is a function of D and α(D) is introduced as a nondecreasing function of D that

---

[6]This assumption avoids integrating TC(q_i) with respect to c which would greatly complicate the mathematics. The results would change, but the direction of the model's implications should not because each household will still forward buy. Only the quantity bought per household will vary.

represents the proportion of consumers who buy on deal.

The Retailer Model

To model the retailer, certain assumptions will also be made. The unit cost to the retailer, m, is fixed. He/she incurs a fixed set-up cost per order, K, and a fixed holding cost per unit, h_R. The retailer must satisfy all demand. Deliveries and sales are instantaneous. There is only one deal per inventory cycle, and deals are offered with a fixed time interval between them, k. Lastly, the same offer is made on each deal.

The purpose of dealing for the retailer is to be able to shift inventories to consumers, hence reducing his/her holding costs. The cost to the retailer is reduced profits per unit sold because the deal reduces his/her revenue on each unit sold at the deal price. The retailer will choose an inventory and dealing policy to maximize profits.

The optimal inventory policy will not be derived in this paper. Interested readers are referred to Lieberman (1978) and Eppen and Lieberman (1980). The main results with enough discussion to make them understandable follow.

It is shown that deals are offered at the beginning of the inventory cycle and that if $h_R > 2h_L$, the optimal value of the discount, D^*, is

$$D^* = kh_L$$

where k is the length of the inventory cycle. The retailer's cost as a function of the inventory cycle is

$$TC(k) = K + D\alpha(D)kQ + \frac{h_R Q}{2}[k^2 - \alpha(D)k^2] \qquad (5)$$

It is interesting to note that if $\alpha(D) \to 0$ as $D \to 0$, then TC(k) approaches the standard EOQ model as $D \to 0$. The objective is to minimize the cost per unit time (TC(k)/k). Using (5) and the fact that $D^* = kh_L$ yields

$$\frac{TC(k)}{k} = \frac{K}{k} + Kh_L\alpha(kh_L)kQ$$

$$+ \frac{h_R Q}{2}[k^2 - \alpha(kh_L)k^2] \qquad (6)$$

To proceed, one must assume a functional form for $\alpha(D)$. The results in this paper consider the case where $\alpha(D) = \alpha$. This is an abstraction of the notion that the proportion of deal buyers is not sensitive to the level of the discount. It also yields closed form expressions that can be conveniently compared to the EOQ model (see Eppen and Lieberman 1980). the next most simple assumption, $\alpha(D) = \alpha D$ yields a cubic during minimization, and thus, immediately turns one to a numerical investigation.

The retailer's inventory holding is shown in Figure 2. It shows that at the time of the deal, the retailer sells αkQ units on deal. Then the nondeal consumers buy at the rate of c units per unit of time.

The optimal deal magnitude can be shown to be

$$D^* = \left[\frac{Kh_L}{Q\left(\alpha + (1 - \alpha)\dfrac{h_R}{2h_L}\right)} \right]^{1/2} \tag{7}$$

The optimal reorder period is

$$k^* = \frac{D^*}{h_L} \tag{8}$$

and the minimum cost per unit of time is

$$TC_D^* = 2QKh_L\left[2 + (1 - \alpha)\frac{h_R}{h_L} \right]^{1/2}$$

Equation (7) shows that the deal magnitude increases with the set-up cost (K), and decreases with the quantity bought by consumers (Q) and the retailer's holding cost (h_R). If a product is purchased frequently, then the deal magnitude is less. The optimal reorder time is proportional to the deal magnitude. The minimum cost per unit of time increases with the cumulative demand rate

(Q), the set-up cost (K), and the retailer's holding cost (h_R).

Discussion

The model just described shows that the consumer and retailer decisions are interrelated. The consumer determines the optimal quantity to buy on deal given the optimal deal magnitude. The retailer sets an optimal deal magnitude given the quantity consumers buy on deal. The retailer increases his/her profits by dealing because he/she reduces the inventory carrying cost. A necessary condition for dealing to be profitable is that certain consumers have a holding cost for the product category that is less than one-half that of the retailer.

Implications from the Model

In the previous section a jointly optimal retailer-consumer dealing model was developed. The dealing and inventory policies as derived from the model result in a set of implications that will be used to test the model with consumer panel data. The purpose of this section is to determine and discuss these implications.

Optimal Deal Magnitude, Dealing Frequency, and Quantity Bought on Deal

There are three parameters that will be used in deriving the testable implications of the model: optimal deal magnitude, D^*; optimal dealing fre-

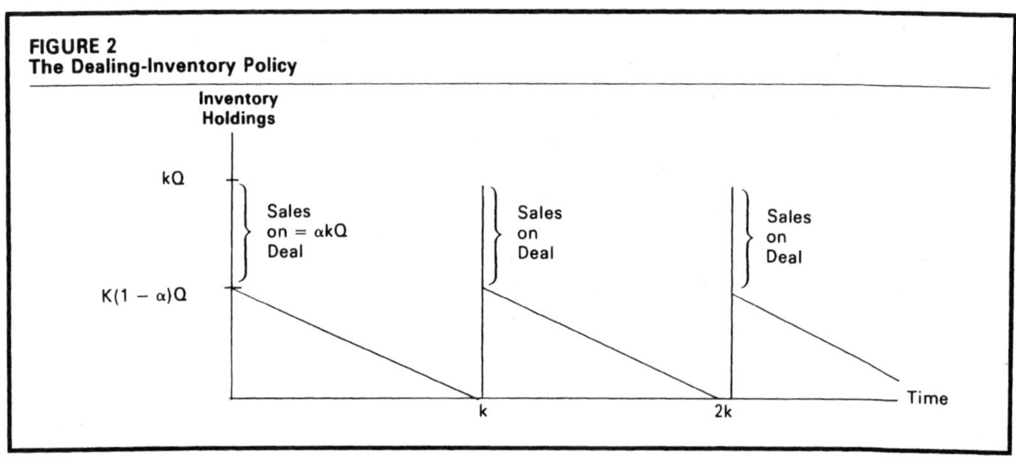

quency, F^*; and optimal quantity bought, q^{**}.[7] Equation (7) gives the optimal deal magnitude:

$$D^* = \left[\frac{Kh_L}{Q\left(\alpha + (1 - \alpha)\dfrac{h_R}{2h_L}\right)} \right]^{1/2}. \quad (7)$$

The dealing frequency is the number of deals offered during any given time interval, T. From the previous section, the jointly optimal time between deals is $t^{**} = D^*/h_L$. The optimal dealing frequency, therefore, is the reciprocal of t^{**} times T, or

$$F^* = T\frac{1}{t^{**}} = T\frac{h_L}{D^*}. \quad (9)$$

Substituting (7) for D^* gives

$$F^* = T\left[\frac{Q(2\alpha h_L + (1 - \alpha)h_R)}{2K} \right]^{1/2}. \quad (10)$$

To compute the optimal quantity bought on deal, the quantity bought by the low-holding-cost consumers is $q^* = Dc/h_L$. Replacing D by D^* gives the jointly optimal quantity to be bought on deal for each consumer responding to deals,

$$q^{**} = \frac{D^*c}{h_L} = c\left[\frac{2K}{Q(2\alpha h_L + (1 - \alpha)h_R)} \right]^{1/2}. \quad (11)$$

As can be seen from equations (7), (10), and (11), the dealing strategy parameters are strongly interrelated because F^* is inversely related and q^{**} is directly related to D^*. Therefore, factors influencing D^* also affect F^* and q^{**}. Thus, the effects of D^*, F^*, and q^{**} should be treated as interdependent when studying the implications of changing a given parameter. This approach is taken throughout the remainder of this section.

Implications

The equations derived in the previous section make it possible to trace the effects of the various parameters on the optimal dealing policy of the retailer. Consider K, the ordering cost. As K increases, the retailer is motivated to order less often and thus to offer deals often (F^* decreases). Then in order to persuade the consumer to buy enough on deal to carry him/her over to the next deal, the retailer must make a larger price reduction (D^* increases). This implies that the consumer will purchase more when the sale occurs (q^{**} increases).

As Q increases, it is clear from (7) and (10) that D^* increases and F^* decreases. Thus, a popular product, one with a large consumption rate, should be dealt often but with a small discount. Since Q = Nc and these two parameters have opposite effects on q^{**} [equation (11)], it is impossible to specify the effect that an increase in Q would have on q^{**}.

To see the effect of h_L, the consumer's holding cost, on the retailer's decisions, it is convenient to hold the ratio h_R/h_L constant. Let $\lambda = h_R/h_L$. Rewriting (7), (10), and (11) in terms of λ yields

$$D^* = \left\{ \frac{Kh_L}{Q[\alpha + (1 - \alpha)\lambda/2]} \right\}^{1/2}, \quad (12)$$

$$F^* = T\left[\frac{Q[2\alpha + (1 - \alpha)\lambda]h_L}{2K} \right]^{1/2}, \quad (13)$$

$$q^{**} = c\left[\frac{2K}{Q[2\alpha + (1 - \alpha)\lambda]h_L} \right]^{1/2}. \quad (14)$$

These three equations show that D^* and F^* increase when h_L increases, whereas q^{**} decreases. As h_L increases, the consumer is less anxious to hold inventory. The retailer responds to this reluctance by making the deals more attractive, (increasing D^*) and by enabling the consumer to carry inventory over a shorter interval (by increasing F^*). Since F^* increases, the consumer will buy less on deal at each sale, i.e., q^{**} decreases.

These three equations show the following. The deal magnitude increases when holding cost to the consumer (h_L) increases and the set-up cost (K) increases. As the rate of demand (Q) increases, more deals will occur, F^* increases, but the deal magnitude decreases.

The frequency of deals increases with higher holding costs (h_L) and rate of demand (Q) and decreases as the set-up cost increases.

Inventory vs. Information Explanation

The implications just derived for the retailer and consumer models can be contrasted to the following explanation. Manufacturers offer trade deals to force retailers to reduce price. For the manufacturers, the purpose of the reduced price is to increase trial among nonusers of their brands. Once new consumers have tried the brand, some percentage will repurchase. Thus, dealing is a mechanism for reducing the consumer's cost of experimenting with a brand they rarely use.

The above explanation fits consumer and manufacturers' behavior for a new product introduced into the market. The consumer is seeking informa-

---

[**]denotes jointly optimal for the retailer and consumer

FIGURE 3
Explanation

Holding Cost	Trial
Sizes with higher consumption rate will be dealt	Small sizes will be dealt
Consumers will stockpile dealt brand	Consumers will purchase only the unit on deal
High market share brands will be dealt more frequently	Low market share brands will be dealt more

tion and the manufacturer is trying to reduce the cost of trial. Manufacturers offer free samples, coupons, and smaller trial sizes. This explanation has also been given for the cause of dealing for existing brands.

The implications for the information explanation just given are different than for the holding cost explanation. First, the manufacturer should offer deals on smaller sizes to reduce the risk of trial to the consumer. For new products, manufacturers often introduce a "trial" size which is substantially smaller than the regular sizes. Second, consumers would not stockpile if they are sampling "new" brands. Instead they would try only one unit of the product and would not change their purchase timing. Third, brands which have lower consumption rates relative to other brands in the category (lower share brands) would have greater dealing activity because fewer consumers use these brands.[8]

The implications of the two theories are contrasted in Figure 3. In the empirical section, data are used to compare the two theories.

Empirical Findings

To test the model's implications, consumer panel data for four product categories will be used. The data do not give all the information (e.g., holding costs) that is needed to test the model's implications. However, these data do offer some evidence about the theory. It should be noted that trade dealing activity occurred in all the categories studied. The model given in Section 3 does not incorporate trade dealing. Some of the results may be due to the retailer receiving trade deals. However, if this sector

of the model were included, one could assume the manufacturer was responding to the retailer. How this would change the result is unknown.

Description of the Data

The consumer panel data are from the *Chicago Tribune* panel over the period 1958–1966. The advantage of this panel is that the data are from one city, and it is possible to identify deals much more accurately.

The purchase data contain number of units purchased, price paid, brand bought, size bought, store, and deal code. The key problem faced in using the deal code produced by the consumer is that it is not accurately recorded. This appears to be true across most panels. Therefore, a separate procedure was developed for coding deal purchases.

Private labels were not included in the study because it was impossible to compare them because of potential differences in quality across time. To keep the analysis consistent, only national brands were used. Casual observation of the data indicated that private labels were dealt and heavily stockpiled.

The Deal Code

For each store the price for a given brand and size combination was listed by day. It is possible to identify changes in the price of an item because most chains and voluntary chains have the same price for an item (size/brand combination) across stores. A statistical procedure was developed to identify the regular price in a given period. Once the regular price was determined, the deal price was found by defining the differential between the regular price and the reported price paid. If this differential exceeded a predetermined limit, the transaction was coded as a deal transaction.

While the procedure just described may result in some errors in coding deal purchases, it appears to be far more accurate than the consumer's recorded deal code. By looking at actual transaction data, one can quickly identify when a deal is occurring because of the heavy purchasing matching a price cut. Quite frequently consumers did not record these purchases as deals. Thus, any simple visual analysis of the transaction data shows the improved accuracy of the revised deal code.

Not all of the data were analyzed because certain stores did not deal certain items. This poses a problem because if A&P buyers have different consumption rates than Jewel buyers, and A&P does not deal, this may bias the results. Voluntary chains were not used in the analysis because the data are accumulated, and there is too much variability in

---

[8]Ehrenberg (1972) shows that brand penetration is highly correlated with market share.

TABLE 1
Consumers' Responses to Deals Through Stockpiling

Product Category	Package Size	Mean Number of Units Bought per Deal Transaction	Number of Deal Transactions	Mean Number of Units Bought per Nondeal Transaction	Number of Nondeal Transactions	Difference	P-value[g]
Aluminum foil[a]	25.0 ft.	1.21 (0.035)[e]	160	1.04 (0.01)	441	+0.17	less than .001
	37.5 ft.	1.01 (0.005)	102	1.03 (0.03)	97	−0.02	.07
	75.0 ft.	1.03 (0.015)	60	1.00 (0.00)	230	+0.03	.05
Facial tissue[b]	400 ts.	1.99 (0.03)	733	1.24 (0.01)	2,510	+0.75	less than .0001
Liquid detergent[c]	12 oz.	1.03 (0.006)	250	1.02 (0.005)	1,061	+0.01	.20
	22 oz.	1.03 (0.005)	602	1.01 (0.003)	891	+0.02	.001
	32 oz.	1.08 (0.0296)	165	1.02 (0.009)	572	+0.06	.05
Waxed paper[d]	100 ft.	1.68 (0.043)	69	1.25 (0.016)	789	+0.43	less than .0001
	125 ft.	1.29 (0.024)	106	1.02 (0.004)	1,409	+0.27	less than .0001

[a]Reynolds and Alcoa in Jewel.
[b]Kleenex and Scotties in A & P, National, Jewel, Kroger, and Walgreens.
[c]Ivory, Joy, and Lux (and 22 oz. Gentle Fels) in A & P, National, and Jewel.
[d]Rapinwax, Freshrap (100 ft.) and Cut Rite (125 ft.) in A & P, National, and Jewel.
[e]Number in parentheses is standard error.
[f]Some transactions were eliminated when it was uncertain whether they were deal or nondeal purchases.
[g]P-value is the significance level for which the null hypothesis is rejected.

dealing practice (price, amount of discount) within the voluntary chains.

Empirical Results

Stockpiling. To see if consumers were stockpiling, two analyses were done: number of units bought on deal, and average interval between purchases. If consumers stockpile, this is evidence that the inventory theory is influencing the purchasing strategy. The most direct way to measure stockpiling is to see if more units are bought on deal purchases than for non-deal purchases. However, for certain categories consumers rarely buy more than one unit because the rate of consumption is low. They may still stockpile by buying earlier than they would if no deal were offered. Thus, both measures are necessary in analyzing deal purchases.

The results in Table 1 show that consumers do stockpile on deal. In eight of nine cases, the quantity bought on deal is higher than for non-deal purchases.[9] Waxed paper and facial tissues show much greater quantities stockpiled. If consumers are stockpiling by buying earlier than they normally would if a deal occurs, then one would expect that the time before the next purchase would be greater after buying on deal than it would be if they did not buy on deal. To measure this effect, one must first put all purchases in standard units.[10] Next, the number of standard units bought is divided into the number of days in the interval following the purchase resulting in the number of days between purchase for a standard unit. This number is calculated for intervals following either a deal purchase

---

[9]A simple sign test reveals this is highly significant. The p-value is .02. Some of the differences are small (e.g., .02). These are categories in which purchase timing is usually affected.

[10]The standard units are: aluminum foil-25 ft. roll, waxed paper-100 ft. roll, liquid detergent-22 oz. size, facial tissue-400 tissue box.

Table 2
The Effect of Deals on Post-Deal Purchase Timing

Product Category	Mean Time Interval (in Days) between Deal and Nondeal Purchases	Number of Intervals	Mean Time Interval (in Days) between Deal and Nondeal Purchases	Number of Intervals	Difference (in Days)	P-value[b]
Aluminum foil	95.65 (5.55)[a]	374	71.65 (0.575)	1,198	24.00	less than .0001
Facial tissue	63.61 (2.4)	935	47.6 (1.2)	3,543	15.98	less than .0001
Liquid detergent	66.18 (3.39)	745	53.72 (1.58)	2,524	12.36	.0005
Waxed paper	135.88 (8.88)	255	100.25 (3.625)	1,005	35.63	.0002

[a] ( ) indicates standard error.
[b] P-value is the significance level for which the null hypothesis is rejected.

or a nondeal purchase in which the next purchase is a nondeal purchase.[11]

The inventory theory implies that the number of units bought per day will be less after a deal purchase than a non-deal purchase. To show this, suppose household 1 buys one unit on deal at time t_0. At the time of their purchase they had one unit in stock and they normally consume two units per month. They do not buy until they run out unless a deal occurs. Assuming no deals occur until after the next purchase, they will next buy one month after time t_0. If no deal occurred, they would have waited to purchase for two weeks, purchase one unit and repurchase again two weeks later. Thus, the interval to next purchase is longer after their deal purchase (one month) than after their non-deal purchase (two weeks). Stockpiling is occurring but not through more units per purchase occasion but through a higher on-hand inventory. A measure of this is the number of days between purchases.

The results are given in Table 2. They support the inventory dealing theory. For all four product categories the difference is quite large, and, no doubt, highly significant statistically. If one divides the difference by the interval following non-deal purchases, one sees that the time between purchases increases after a deal purchase between 23% and 36%, depending upon the category. It is apparent that there is stockpiling occurring even for categories (aluminum foil and liquid detergent) which had small quantity stockpiling.

Deal Magnitude and Deal Frequency. The first of these implications is the effect of consumption rate, c, and number of buyers, N, on the optimal values of deal magnitude and dealing frequency as set by the retailer. Since Nc = Q this implication will be analyzed in terms of Q, or the sales level of the retailer. The prediction is that within given product/size/chain combinations, brands with higher sales levels (higher values of Q) will be offered on deal more frequently and for lower deal magnitudes than brands with lower sales levels. These effects are directly observable from equations (7) and (10). The implication is analyzed at the brand level because this holds the holding cost of the product constant. Performing the analysis for given chains keeps constant chain variables (e.g., set-up cost, which may vary from chain to chain).

To account for possible dealing effects on sales (Q), weekly sales of each brand studied were regressed against their weekly prices to obtain an estimate of normal sales after adjusting for dealing effects. Substituting the normal (non-deal) price of the brand for the independent variable in the resulting regression equations and solving the equations, gives normal (deal controlled) weekly sales for each brand. The normal weekly sales were then multiplied

---

[11] Since the objective is to see whether dealing changes the purchase interval, one wants to hold fixed one end of the interval, i.e., the last purchase is nondeal. The prior purchase is then on deal or not. These two cases can then be compared. Adding deal to deal purchases does not allow us to hold fixed one end of the interval to make the comparisons required. It was therefore omitted from the analysis.

Table 3
The Effects of Normal Sales on Deal Magnitude and Dealing Frequency in the Aluminum Foil Product Category

Package Size	Chain	Brand	Normal Purchasing Rate (in units)	Mean Deal Magnitude (in cents)	Dealing Frequency
25.00 ft.	National	Reynolds	96	4.50	2
		Alcoa	78	6.00	1
		Kaiser	31	7.20	5
	Jewel	Reynolds	395	6.12	17
		Alcoa	143	9.08	6
		Kaiser	18	—	0
37.50 ft.	Jewel	Reynolds	177	15.63	19
		Alcoa	30	17.00	3

by the number of weeks included in the recorded history of each brand which resulted in normal (adjusting for deals) sales volumes. Brands are then compared in terms of their normal sales. Section 3 showed that it is expected that brands with higher normal sales will have a higher dealing frequency and be offered at a lower mean deal magnitude than brands with lower normal sales.

These predictions are tested only in terms of their directions, not magnitudes. Using Table 3 as an example, it is expected that for the 25 ft. aluminum foil in Jewel food chain, Reynolds (normal sales = 395) will be offered on deal at a higher frequency and for a lower mean deal magnitude than Alcoa (normal sales = 143). The results show that these predictions are confirmed. A summary

of the results for the aluminum foil category is given by Table 4.

To save space the detailed results for the other product categories are not presented here. However, summary results for all product categories are reported in Table 5. These results seem to support the inventory dealing model. The null model would imply correct prediction 50% of the time.[12]

The second implication concerns the effect of joint (to consumer and retailer) per unit holding cost on the parameters of deal magnitude and dealing frequency. This implication is tested at the package size level. By varying the package-size of an item (within given product/chain combinations), its holding cost varies. However, by varying the package-size variable the sales variables may change as well, which will have its own effects on both dealing parameters. Since it is impossible to hold

---

[12]A statistical test is very difficult to apply because predictions are not independent. Therefore, a standard binomial test of p = .5 cannot be used.

TABLE 4
Summary of Predictions for Aluminum Foil

Dealing Parameters	Deal Magnitude[c]	Dealing Frequency
Number of predictions	5	7
Number of correct predictions	5[a]	5[b]
Percentage of correct predictions	100.0	71.4

[a]25.00 ft. (Reynolds, Kaiser) and (Reynolds, Alcoa) in National and Jewel and (Reynolds, Alcoa) in Jewel; 37.50 ft. (Reynolds, Alcoa) in Jewel.
[b]25.00 ft. (Reynolds, Alcoa) in National and Jewel, (Reynolds, Alcoa) and (Alcoa, Kaiser) in Jewel; 37.50 ft. (Reynolds, Alcoa) in Jewel.
[c]Fewer deal magnitude predictions exist because no deals occurred for Kaiser at Jewel. Thus, the deal magnitude is unknown.

TABLE 5
Summary of Predictions for Brand Dealing Parameters: All Product Categories

Dealing Parameters	Deal Magnitude	Dealing Frequency
Number of predictions	46	49
Number of correct predictions	29	31
Percentage of correct predictions	59.2	63.3

TABLE 6
Summary of Predictions for Dealing Parameters at the Package-Size Level

Theory	Inventory	
Dealing Parameters	Deal Magnitude	Dealing Frequency
Number of predictions	3	12
Number of correct predictions	3	8
Percentage of correct predictions	100	66.7

TABLE 7
The Effect of Q and h_L on D^* and F^*

Q	h_L	D^*	F^*
+	−	−	
−	+	+	
+	+		+
−	−		−

sales constant, the analysis will focus on the combined effect of per-unit holding cost and sales on the two dealing parameters. This, however, requires some care since sales (Q) and holding cost (h_L) affect the deal magnitude (D^*) and the dealing frequency (F^*) differently. Consider equations (12) and (13). It is clear that we can determine the behavior of D^* and F^* in four cases. these cases are described in Table 7, where + stands for an increase and − stands for a decrease in the variable in question.

Predictions about the behavior of dealing parameters are generated from data by rank order-

TABLE 8
The Combined Effect of Holding Cost and Normal Sales on Deal Magnitude and Dealing Frequency at the Package-Size Level

Product Category	Chain	Package Size	Unit Holding Cost: Rank Ordering	Rank Ordering	Standardized Normal Purchasing Rate Units (in thousands)	Dealing Frequency	Mean Deal Magnitude (in cents)
Facial tissue[a]	A & P	200 ts.	2	2	15.4	0	
		400 ts.	1	1	126.0	9	
	National	200 ts.	2	2	77.6	0	
		400 ts.	1	1	420.0	23	
	Jewel	200 ts.	2	2	51.0	1	
		400 ts.	1	1	325.6	18	
Liquid detergent[b]	A & P	12 oz.	3	3	3.68	12	
		22 oz.	2	1	5.72	33	8.74
		32 oz.	1	2	5.25	8	13.43
	National	12 oz.	3	3	5.20	27	
		22 oz.	2	1	9.46	51	8.12
		32 oz.	1	2	8.58	17	12.05
	Jewel	12 oz.	3	3	7.2	27	
		22 oz.	2	1	18.85	67	8.06
		32 oz.	1	2	10.34	27	10.49
Waxed paper[c]	A & P	100 ft.	2	2	21.7	1	
		125 ft.	1	1	63.75	10	
	National	100 ft.	2	2	48.6	4	
		125 ft.	1	1	50.5	10	
	Jewel	100 ft.	2	2	39.2	11	
		125 ft.	1	1	70.75	11	

[a]Including the brands of Kleenex and Scotties.
[b]Including the brands of Ivory, Joy and Lux (and Gentle Fels for the 22 oz. package size category).
[c]Including the brands of Freshrap and Rapinwax for the 100 ft. size and Cut Rite for the 125 ft. size category.

ing different packages-sizes (within given product/chain combinations) by size and normal sales. The data are summarized in Table 8. The relationships in Table 7 are then used to make as many predictions as possible. Consider, for example, facial tissues at A&P. Since both h_L and Q are greater for the 400-tissue size, Table 7 suggests that it should be dealt more often, and that no prediction can be made regarding D^*. The prediction is correct. All of the results on facial tissue and waxed paper can be interpreted this way.

The situation with liquid detergent is somewhat more complicated. Again, consider the A&P data. The model suggests that the 32 oz. size should be dealt more often than the 12 oz. size. This prediction is incorrect. It is not possible to make a prediction about the relative frequency of deals for the 32 oz. and the 22 oz. sizes. However, the prediction that the 22 oz. size will be dealt more often than the 12 oz. size is correct.

It is also possible to use the data on liquid detergent to make predictions about deal magnitude. For example, compare the 32 oz. size to the 22 oz. size at A&P. Note that h_L is greater and Q is smaller. Table 7 predicts that the discount on the 32 oz. size will be greater, and the prediction is correct. Table 6 summarizes the results of the fifteen possible predictions.

Inventory vs. Information Explanation

Earlier, we stated several contrasting implications for the information and the inventory explanations. Using the data shown, the contrasting implications can be evaluated. The information explanation would imply that consumers would not stockpile products whereas the inventory explanation assumes consumers do stockpile products; the data given above show that consumers do stockpile all four products analyzed.

Next, the information explanation implies that lower volume items would be dealt more frequently, whereas the inventory explanation implies that higher volume items would be dealt more frequently. The results given above show that higher volume items deal more frequently. Again, the results favor the inventory explanation.

Finally the information explanation implies that smaller sizes should be dealt more frequently than larger sizes. The inventory explanation implies higher volume sizes would be dealt more frequently. In Table 1 for liquid detergent, it is shown that the smaller size (12 oz.) is dealt far less frequently than the 22 oz. which has slightly higher volume. Thus, volume, not size, appears to be a more important determinant of which item to deal.

The data presented appear to favor the inventory explanation in all three analyses. A more rigorous comparison is needed before one can reject the information explanation, but on the basis of the data presented in this study, it is less likely that dealing occurs as a form of information (for existing products) than as a form of shifting holding costs. It is also possible that a certain proportion of dealing is done to induce trial and the remainder related to transferring holding costs to low holding cost consumers.

Strategy Implications for Manufacturers and Retailers

The implications from the consumer and retailer model can be used to help design dealing strategies for both manufacturers and retailers.

Manufacturer's Dealing Strategy

The model and the empirical results suggest that consumer stockpiling is an important reaction to dealing for established, storable products. This fact has serious implications for the manufacturer who wishes to attract new customers to his/her product. Much of the cost of a retailer deal may not be at all related to new trials. A manufacturer thus may wish to devote increased attention to other devices such as home delivered samples and demonstrations in stores in attempting to attract new customers.

However, the manufacturer can use stockpiling behavior to his/her advantage. Trade deals can be timed to match production runs so that retailers and consumers stockpile the product, thus carrying inventory the manufacturer would otherwise be forced to carry. For products with high set-up costs and infrequent production runs, dealing can be an efficient mechanism for transfering inventory.

It is important to note the effect of the function $\alpha(D)$, the proportion of consumers who buy on deal, on the effectiveness of dealing. In equation (5) note that if $\alpha(D)$ is small, the retailers' costs are essentially the same as in the no deal case. Thus, the trade deal will have little effect. In these situations manufacturers should consider reducing trade dealing activity and attempting to offer retailers higher margins through lower case prices.

For products with low consumption rates, trade deals are very unlikely to be passed on to the consumer. Again, equation (4) shows that Q_D depends upon c. Retailers will take small ads in the Saturday paper ("obituary" ads) and reduce price on Monday-Wednesday (weak shopping days) to comply with the agreement. The manufacturer may be more successful using other forms of promotions or directly advertising to the consumer.

For sizes with low consumption rates, the retailer is unlikely to deal the product even with a trade deal. To increase the purchase of low volume sizes, manufacturers can consider alternative actions like special consumer promotions, tie in promotions with stronger sizes, and special consumer advertising.

Retailer's Dealing Strategy

The models discussed in this paper can be used by retailers to develop a more effective dealing strategy. An approach followed by Eppen and Lieberman (1980) is to derive and compare expressions for the cost per unit time with and without dealing. This approach leads to two main conclusions: (a) High-volume items, those with a large value of Q, yield greater profits to the retailer if he/she deals. We have already seen that for such products the optimal dealing policy involves frequent deals with relatively small discounts. (b) Items with widely different holding costs between the retailer and a segment of consumers are advantageous for the retailer to deal. This suggests that bulky items like paper products are good candidates for dealing.

Another strategy implication of the theory is dealing locally. This follows from the model because dealing is efficient when the proportion of low holding cost consumers is high. This may not be uniform over an SMSA. Obviously there are efficiencies in buying newspaper ads throughout an SMSA. However, through the use of flyers and store specials, retailers can also develop local deals which may be successful in one area but not another. Factors which influence the selections of items to deal are similar to those just discussed for the total market. However, consumption rates of products and storage costs may vary by region. For areas where households have freezers, retailers should deal items for the freezer. For areas with larger homes, bulkier products should be dealt. From scanning data it becomes possible for the retailer to analyze sales data by item by store so that more effective dealing can be done.

Within brands of a category it is rarely profitable for the retailer to deal low share items. Unless a strong performance contract exists, the retailer should run these items during low volume days such as Monday, Tuesday, and Wednesday so that he/she can perform on the trade deal requirements.

Conclusions

This paper began with the assumptions that the consumer purchases in order to minimize total cost (purchase cost and holding cost) and that the retailer sets price to maximize his profits. Based on these assumptions and other assumptions made throughout, the optimal deal price, frequency of dealing and quantity bought on deal were derived. Testable implications were then generated and using panel data, they were tested empirically. The empirical results showed that the inventory explanation for dealing is consistent with the data.

A major benefit of the view that consumers respond to deals by inventorying is that it leads to certain implications for the measurement of the consumer's response to deals. Instead of assuming that dealing increases sales through brand switching, the inventory theory explanation implies sales increase because consumers stockpile. This results in a trough in sales after a deal. Unless the dealing response model accounts for this trough, the effect of a deal will be greatly overstated.

This article offers a different explanation than the one most commonly held that dealing is used to attract customers to the store. Both explanations can be true and the cause of dealing. Theoretical and empirical work needs to be done comparing the inventory theory, proposed here, with other explanations for dealing. It is hoped that further work is developed to study these issues.

REFERENCES

Blattberg, Robert C., Thomas Buesing, Peter Peacock, and Subrata Sen (1978), "Identifying the Deal Prone Segment," *Journal of Marketing Research*, 15 (August), 369–377.

Ehrenberg, A. S. C. (1972), *Repeat Buying*, Amsterdam, Netherlands: North-Holland Publishing Company.

Eppen, Gary and Yehoshua Lieberman (1980), "Why Do Retailers Deal? An Inventory Explanation," working paper.

Frank, Ronald E. and William F. Massy (1967), "Effects of Short-Term Promotional Strategy in Selected Market Segments," in *Promotional Decisions Using Mathemati-*

cal Models, Patrick J. Robinson, ed., Boston: Allyn & Bacon, 147–225.

Kunreuther, Howard (1973), "Why the Poor May Pay More for Food: Theoretical and Empirical Evidence," *Journal of Business*, 46 (July), 368–383.

Lieberman, Joshua (1978), "A Theory of Price Deals in Supermarkets," Ph.D. dissertation, University of Chicago.

Wagrer, Harvey M. and Thomson M. Whitin (1958), "Dynamic Version of the Economic Lot Size Model," *Management Science*, 5, No. 1 (October), 89–96.

Part III: Promotional Bob — Contributions to Sales Promotions

Sales promotions are an important and expensive marketing expenditure, with Consumer Packaged Companies allocating more than 50% of their marketing budgets and 13% of their revenues to sales promotions (ACNielsen, 2002). In this context, sales promotions are defined more broadly than simply temporary price discounts to consumers. Sales promotions include trade promotions (manufacturer incentives to retailers), retail promotions (retailer incentives to consumers, including display and feature advertising activity) as well as consumer promotions (manufacturer incentives to consumers, including coupons).

Consistent with focus of this book, Robert Blattberg's contribution to and impact on the area of sales promotions is discussed in this chapter. Fourteen works published between 1987 and 1996 that address the general issue of sales promotions are considered. To get some indication of the impact of this body of research, Table 1 provides an informal citation count generated using Google Scholar of the seven most cited works.

One clear implication of this informal analysis is that it is difficult to overstate Blattberg's impact, as the top seven works collectively have more than 1,100 citations. To understand the reason for this impact, it is useful to define Blattberg's approach to research as combining behavioral research with behavioral science. "Behavioral research analyzes and models *actual* consumer behavior, in contrast to behavioral science that develops theories of *why* consumers follow certain behavior. Behavioral research therefore examines what consumers do whereas behavioral science examines why consumers behave in certain ways. Clearly, the two can and should be integrated." (Blattberg, 1991) Therefore, a common thread for all of his published work considered here is that he integrates behavioral research and behavioral science on theoretically and managerially important questions.

The remainder of this piece is organized as follows. The next section provides a framework to organize the fourteen published works by their primary contribution. Next, a brief summary of the key contributions of the works is

Table 1:   Citation count of top eight works

Work	Google Scholar Citations
Blattberg and Neslin (1990a)	449
Blattberg and Wisniewski (1989)	231
Blattberg *et al.* (1995)	189
Blattberg and Glazer (1994)[a]	96
Blattberg and George (1991)	98
Blattberg and Neslin (1990b)	39
Blattberg and Levin (1987)	36
Total	1,138

[a]This citation count includes all citations to the book, of which John DC Little was also an editor.

provided. Finally, the article concludes with a brief discussion of Blattberg's contribution and implications for future research.

Organizing Framework

Table 2 organizes the fourteen published works covered in this chapter based upon their primary contribution: summarizing the state of knowledge about sales promotions, extending the substantive knowledge about sales promotions, models and/or methods, or envisioning how technology and the environment is changing marketing and/or research into promotions.

Summarizing State of Knowledge about Sales Promotions

Blattberg and Neslin (1990a) is an insightful and comprehensive work about sales promotions. They brilliantly combined analytical and empirical models with behavioral science descriptions of why consumers, manufacturers, and retailers behave this way. For instance, a question posed in the first chapter is why do sales promotions exist? Why not just reduce price permanently if it increases sales? The remainder of the book then addresses this fundamental question in depth. Specifically, questions such as how do promotions affect the profitability of manufacturers and retailers (and how would one measure it), and how do promotions help managers meet strategic and tactical goals over the product life cycle are addressed. Therefore, one clear contribution is that it provides a comprehensive analysis of the triad involved the sales promotion phenomena.

Table 2:   Organization of published works

Primary Contribution	Papers
Summarizing State of Knowledge	Blattberg and Neslin (1990a)
	Blattberg and Neslin (1990b)
	Blattberg and Neslin (1993)
	Blattberg and Broderick (1993)
	Blattberg *et al.* (1994a)
	Blattberg *et al.* (1995)
Extending Knowledge	Blattberg and Levin (1987)
	Blattberg and Wisniewski (1989)
	Blattberg and George (1991)
	Blattberg and George (1992)
	Blattberg *et al.* (1996)
Envisioning	Blattberg (1991)
	Blattberg *et al.* (1994b)
	Blattberg and Glazer (1994)

Blattberg and Neslin (1990b) was the first in a sequence of seminal articles that summarized the state of knowledge about sales promotions. One common contribution of these articles was to lay out a research agenda for the field, which is why these articles (collectively) are highly cited. In this work, the authors focused on the phenomena of sales promotions and what was not understood. The authors separated the discussion into the short-term and long-term effects of sales promotions. Some of the key research questions posed and later addressed in the literature were:

(1) How do promotions affect repeat purchase?
(2) Why are promotional elasticities larger than price elasticities?
(3) How do promotions affect store traffic?
(4) What are the long term effects of sales promotions?
(5) Are promotions profitable?

Blattberg and Neslin (1993) takes a highly analytical approach to describing the models used in the sales promotions literature. It is focused on describing the prescriptive and descriptive models used in the sales promotions literature, so it updates the discussion found in the book by the same authors. This piece is targeted at academic researchers and has been recognized as an ideal complement to the book by the same authors (Pulsis Jr. and Stem Jr., 1994).

Blattberg *et al.* (1994a) and Blattberg *et al.* (1995) were companion articles that updated Blattberg and Neslin (1990b). Blattberg *et al.* (1994a) was organized five sets of issues that were still not well understood.

(1) Behavioral explanations for observed phenomena (e.g., why are there such large spikes for promotions?),
(2) Measurement of promotional response,
(3) Channel issues (e.g., how much of a deal is passed through to consumers? How does diverting affect retailer response?)
(4) Profitability of promotions (e.g., what is the long-term impact on brand and store image? How do promotions affect store volume?),
(5) Non-packaged goods issues (e.g., what is effect of promotions on lifetime value? How do promotions affect diffusion of innovations?).

Blattberg *et al.* (1995) was the last, and most cited of the summary articles. One reason for this result may have been that it was included in a set of articles describing empirical generalizations in marketing, and included the managerial implications of the questions and generalizations. As such, it summarized what was "known", i.e., consistent findings in the extant literature, what was "controversial", i.e., had conflicting findings. Some of the key questions raised were:

(1) Does the majority of volume comes from switchers, and what is the magnitude of acceleration vs. stockpiling effects?
(2) Is there a post-promotion dip?
(3) Are there negative long term effects to promotions?
(4) What is the shape of deal curve?
(5) What are the category volume effects of promotions?

Finally, Blattberg and Broderick (1993) is somewhat different than the above articles in that the intended audience is managers and curators of museums instead of marketing academics and practitioners. There is general agreement that museums have entered a difficult economic period and need a better understanding of how to market and promote their "product" to the public (Vine, 1993). This article addressed that need by providing a thoughtful and structured way for managers and curators to think about marketing and promoting museums. So the contribution was the application of marketing knowledge to the non-profit arena. One clear set of problems faced by museums is that they do not have a clear understanding of what they are trying to maximize. For instance, museums could have the preservation of art and artifacts as their primary objective, or they could have educating the public as their primary objective. The fundamental decision of the form of the objective function then allows managers to set their pricing (i.e., admission fees) and promotional (i.e., which exhibits) strategies within the constraints of their charters.

Extending Knowledge about Sales Promotions

Within this section, the papers are divided into those that are concerned with the profitability of promotions, and those that are concerned with the structure of competition within the category/industry.

Profitability of Promotions

The first of the articles directly related to profitability of sales promotions is Blattberg and Levin (1987). This original article focuses on understanding and measuring trade promotion effectiveness and profitability, i.e., promotions from the manufacturer to the retailer. The key applications of their model were: 1) evaluate individual trade promotions, 2) identify best trade promotions, 3) evaluate future promotional plans, and 4) evaluate future promotional plans. To evaluate the trade promotions, they combined data on market sales to consumers and data on trade shipments. Interestingly, they found that one key reason for a lack of profitability of trade promotions is heavy retailer forward buying (and stockpiling). One implication of this finding is that the retailers were not passing along most of the discount to the consumers, but using it to increase their own profitability. Therefore, they found great variability in trade deal effectiveness.

An important issue in determining the profitability of promotions (trade, consumer or retail) is determining what the sales would have been had the promotion not been run, i.e., baseline sales. Blattberg *et al.* (1996) tackles this issue and extends the extant literature to include competitive reactions to promotions. This article demonstrates that baselines are underestimated and, hence, the profitability of promotions is overestimated when competitive reactions to promotions are not considered.

Similar to empirical I/O literature, Blattberg and George (1992) uses the profit function of the retailer in the objective function to estimate price elasticities. Using this approach, they find that traditional estimation methods overestimate the price elasticity, suggesting that retailers should raise prices to increase their profitability. Interestingly, this article raises the question of why do retailers have lower than optimal prices in the store?

Structure of Competition

We start with the rigorous and relevant paper of Blattberg and Wisniewski (1989). The fundamental insight of this paper is that products within a category are differentiated goods, where they are grouped into tiers that have similar price and (real or perceived) quality levels. The behavioral model is that consumers always seek higher quality and lower prices. Competition within the tiers is symmetric, that is, after adjusting for their respective shares, the competitive effects of price and deals are similar between the brands. However, competition is asymmetric between price tiers. That is, price changes by higher quality brands have a much larger impact on lower quality brands than visa-versa. These tiers result from consumer heterogeneity, i.e., different relative weights placed on quality and price by different segments of consumers.

A fundamental principle of the price tiers is that they are empirical in nature. Therefore, good estimates of the cross-brand effects are required to understand which brands are in which tiers. However, most aggregate-level models would return either non-significant or nonsensical signed effects for the own and cross brand effects. Blattberg and George (1991) rigorously develop a shrinkage estimator that provides a method to get better estimates of the cross-brand and promotional effects. Not surprisingly, this estimator also has improved predictive ability over traditional methods.

Envisioning

The first of the envisioning articles, Blattberg (1991), tries to predict what areas of behavioral research will be addressed in the next 10 years. He uses the criteria of data availability, importance, new methodology, prior research funding and publishability to rank each of nine areas. More than 15 years later we can look back at this analysis to check his predictions. He was surprisingly accurate for several of the areas, predicting increased research into consumer models (e.g., panel data and pricing). However, he missed the mark in predicting lower levels of research into customer value (see Chapter 5 by Thomas and Lewis) due to lack of funding, lack of data and lack of prior research.

A provocative observation was that our "lack of understanding of how advertising affects sales has resulted in a lack of advertising spending" (p. 21). This prediction is consistent with the increase in spending on sales promotions versus advertising. Even with this prediction, there has been surprisingly little research into the direct relationship of advertising on sales, with the exception of the seminal articles by Lodish and his colleagues and Mela and his colleagues. One potential reason is the problem of finding statistically significant relationships. For instance, in a meta-analysis of advertising's effect on cigarette sales, Nelson (2006) argues that sales are inelastic to advertising and most advertising elasticities are not statistically significant.

Blattberg and Glazer (1994) is the introduction to the book (which also includes John D.C. Little as an editor) and lays out the basic framework and importance of the marketing information revolution. The main thesis of this chapter (and book) is that computers have created vast amounts of information about a firm's customers. This information can be leveraged into knowledge that can generate a competitive advantage by allowing the firm to customize their offerings to individual consumers.

Further, technologies are evolving that changes the communication between firms and consumers. Previously, communication was one-way, from the firm to the consumer. Technologies now exist that allow two-way communication between firms and their consumers which, in turn, allows firms to create and manage relationships with their customers and draw consumers into stronger association with the firm.

They define the five stages of the information value chain: data collection and transmission, data management, data interpretation, models, and decision support systems. This value chain is still valid today. Interestingly, we see much of their predictions put into practice with loyalty programs, customized offerings on the internet, one-to-one marketing, customer support (and management) systems. However, the current state of technology still has not reached some of the predictions in this piece.

Blattberg *et al.* (1994b) is one of the chapters in the above book and is focused on managerial support systems for pricing. It lays out the challenges of using panel and store data in managerial decision making. The first set of challenges relate to some of the substantive work above: getting correct coefficients to identify competing brands and offerings, understanding base-line sales, correctly modeling the consumer behavior for this category. However, getting coefficients and elasticities is not enough, as managerial support systems must then allow managers to interpret the profit and share impact of the estimates. Clearly, this interpretation is best done by providing simulations of the effect of different prices on category volume and market share. Interestingly, in several firms (e.g., KhiMetrics, DemandTec, Zilliant) entire business is focused on providing this exact type of managerial support system.

Some Personal Comments

This chapter presents a brief summary of Blattberg's body of work related to sales promotions. This body of work has been cited more than 1,100 times, demonstrating Bob's large impact on the field. His impact is all the more impressive considering that this chapter only covers one of his six different research areas. That said, just counting citations does not provide a true measure of Bob's impact on the field. It misses the support and guidance that he has given, and continues to give, to other academics, especially his students. In this role, he has had an even larger impact on the field. For all of this help, thank you, Bob!

Reflecting back on my experiences with Bob, this research stream reveals two important lessons he imparted to his students. The first lesson is to find interesting and managerially-relevant research questions. This chapter examines the simple but deceptively deep questions of "Why do consumers respond so strongly to temporary price promotions? And how does this response impact retailer and manufacturer behavior?" Even with all of the research on these questions, there are still unresolved issues. In fact, the next chapter on Industrial Bob discusses how his research has changed the way industries do business.

The second lesson is that in order to do good research, a deep understanding of the phenomenon is required. This lesson is linked to his integration of behavioral research with behavioral science. Behavioral science can provide a deep understanding of the phenomenon and ensures that the empirical models accurately reflect behavior. This link also allows the answers to become more comprehensive as research in other areas progresses. Thank you, Bob.

Richard A. Briesch
Edwin L. Cox School of Business
Southern Methodist University

References

ACNielsen (2002). ACNielsen 2002 Trade Promotion Practices Study, in *Consumer Insight Magazine*: ACNielsen.

Blattberg, Robert C. (1991). Behavioral Research in the 1990s, *Marketing Research* (September), 12–24.

Blattberg, Robert C., Richard A. Briesch and Edward J. Fox (1995). How Promotions Work, *Marketing Science*, **14**(3), G122–G32.

______ (1994a). Les Questions en Suspens Dans le Domaine de la Promotion des Ventes, *Recherche et Applications en Marketing*, IX, 109–123.

Blattberg, Robert C. and Cynthia Broderick (1993). Marketing of Art Museums, in *The Economics of Art Museums*, Martin Feldstein (Ed.) Chicago: University of Chicago Press.

Blattberg, Robert C. and Edward I. George (1992). Estimation under Profit-Driven Loss Functions, *Journal of Business & Economic Statistics*, **10**(4), 437–444.

______ (1991). Seemingly Unrelated Equations: Shrinkage Estimation of Price and Promotional Elasticities, *Journal of American Statistical Association*, **86**(414), 304–315.

Blattberg, Robert C. and Rashi Glazer (1994). Marketing in the Information Revolution, in *The Marketing Information Revolution*, Robert C. Blattberg and Rashi Glazer and John D. C. Little (Eds.). Cambridge, MA: Harvard Business School Press.

Blattberg, Robert C., Byung-Do Kim and Jianming Ye (1996). Defining Baseline Sales in a Competitive Environment, *Seoul Journal of Business*, **2**(1), 1–38.

______ (1994b). Large-Scale Databases: The New Marketing Challenge, in *The Marketing Information Revolution*, Robert C. Blattberg and Rashi Glazer and John D. C. Little (Eds.). Cambridge: Harvard Business School Press.

Blattberg, Robert C. and Alan Levin (1987). Modelling the Effectiveness and Profitability of Trade Promotions, *Marketing Science*, **6**(2), 124–146.

Blattberg, Robert C. and Scott A. Neslin (1993). Sales Promotion Models, in *Handbooks in Operations Research*, J. Eliashberg and G. L. Lilien, (Eds.) Vol. Marketing. Amsterdam, The Netherlands: Elsevier Science Publishers, B.V.

______ (1990a). *Sales Promotions: Concepts, Methods and Strategies*, Englewood Cliffs, N.J.: Prentice Hall.

______ (1990b). Sales Promotions: The Long and Short of It, *Marketing Letters*, **1**(1), 81–97.

Blattberg, Robert C. and Kenneth J. Wisniewski (1989). Price Induced Patterns of Competition, *Marketing Science*, **8**(4), 291–309.

Nelson, Jon P. (2006). Cigarette Advertising Regulation: A Meta-Analysis, *International Review of Law and Economics*, **26**(2), 195–226.

Putsis Jr., William P. and Donald E. Stem Jr. (1994). New Books in Review, *Journal of Marketing Research*, **31**(4), 571–575.

Vine, Naomi (1993), The Economics of Art Museums — Book Review, *Art in America* (June).

MARKETING SCIENCE
Vol. 8, No. 4, Fall 1989
Printed in U.S.A.

PRICE-INDUCED PATTERNS OF COMPETITION

ROBERT C. BLATTBERG AND KENNETH J. WISNIEWSKI
University of Chicago
A. C. Nielsen

This research focuses on how price changes influence the observed pattern of brand competition. The paper begins with a basic utility model formulation and examines the implications of three major classes of preference distributions on the expected patterns of competition. A price-tier model is proposed to operationalize the theory and to allow predictive testing. The price-tier model is estimated on 28 brands across four product categories.

The results show a specific asymmetric pattern of price competition. Higher-price, higher quality brands steal share from other brands in the same price-quality tier, as well as from brands in the tier below. However, lower-price, lower-quality brands take sales from their own tier and the tier below brands, but do *not* steal significant share from the tiers above. The results are consistent with a bimodal preference distribution, with the regular price indifference point being located toward the lower-quality end of the preference distribution for the categories analyzed.

(**Promotional Analyses; Market Structure Models; Price Competition**)

1. Introduction

How do brands within a retail category compete when one brand offers a price deal? What is the pattern of unit sales losses and gains? These issues have grown in practical and academic importance as temporary price reductions, or price deals, have become an important component of the manufacturer's and retailer's marketing strategy.

Promotional spending (including trade, sales force, and consumer) has grown dramatically since the mid-1970's, and currently accounts for over 65% of advertising/promotion expenditures in the U.S.[1] The 12% average yearly growth over the last decade is due in part to the fact that deals "work." Price deals can dramatically increase unit sales of the brand being promoted. However, exactly how and why price deals achieve the large promotional spikes typically seen in Universal Product Code (UPC) scanning data is not known. It is important for a retailer to understand how promotional prices affect brand competition, since brand switching affects the overall profitability of the retail category. In turn, the retailer's promotional profits affect the manufacturers' pass through of trade deals, and hence the overall profitability of their trade promotions.

This paper develops a basic framework for analyzing and explaining the pattern of deal price competition within a retail category. The primary focus is on the general characteristics of brand *price* competition within a product type and *not* on brand *attribute*

---

[1] Source: Donnelley Marketing (1986) based upon spending in retail channels by packaged goods manufacturers.

competition across product types. The theory deals with the short-run effects of price deals on demand, not on the long-run equilibria if such lower prices were maintained indefinitely. This article identifies how different promotional pricing structures affect the observed pattern of competition, given that brand attributes remain unchanged. The general shape of consumer preference distributions have important implications for which patterns of price competition will be observed. The concluding section comments on the implications of the research and on expanding the results to other types of product form competition.

2. Observations from the Literature

2.1. *The Literature on Price Promotions*

Few published studies are directly concerned with measuring the effects of price deals on unit sales, and still fewer examine how such price reductions affect the unit sales of other competitive brands in the retail line. Research on promotions tends to assume away competition (e.g. Sunoo and Lin 1978; Wilkinson, Mason, and Paksoy 1982), or assumes a specific pattern for the competitive effect (e.g. the implicit assumption of proportional share draw in the logit models of Guadagni and Little 1983 and McAlister 1984). There are several historical reasons for these limitations:

1. No theory exists to determine a priori which brands are likely to be highly price competitive within a product category.

2. The number of parameters in a series of brand level models increases significantly as competitive items are included, unless one assumes that all brands have the same price parameters.

3. Spurious correlations between one brand's prices and another brand's unit sales can occur when a large number of brands are simultaneously included in the estimation.

4. Historically, only limited (i.e. single brand) and/or poor quality sales and price data were readily available for nonproprietary research.

Assuming away competitive effects would not be serious if it could be shown that competitive dealing activities either did not significantly affect a given brand's sales or if competitive dealing activity affected all brands in some consistent way (e.g. the effect being proportional to market share). However, in at least three articles (Carpenter et al. 1988; Reibstein and Gatignon 1984; Batsell and Polking 1985), the effects seem to be asymmetric and unrelated to any specific summary statistic. Thus, the pattern of promotional price competition is not well understood.

2.2. *Other Approaches for Assessing Competitive Structure*

While much work exists on methodologies for identifying how brands may compete on the basis of product attributes and characteristics,[2] very little work exists on how *price* itself determines the observed pattern of competition. This is an important distinction. In hierarchial brand switching approaches, it may be that promotional prices or regular price changes, not simply "closeness" in terms of attributes, are causing the observed pattern of switching. For example, national brands and private label brands can have markedly different characteristics. If the national brands often price deal at substantial price discounts, a large amount of private label to national brand switching may result, implying a high degree of competitiveness between the classes of brands. If the national brands deal infrequently or deal at small discounts, little private label to national brand

---

[2] This substantial literature includes market structure approaches (see e.g. Kalwani and Morrison 1977; Urban, Johnson, and Hauser 1984; and Lilien and Kotler 1983 for examples and reviews); multidimensional scaling (e.g. Green and Wind 1973), and perceptual mapping and conjoint approaches (see e.g. Urban and Hauser 1980; Green and Srinivasan 1978; Johnson 1974; and Cattin and Wittink 1982).

PRICE-INDUCED PATTERNS OF COMPETITION   293

switching may be observed, implying a low degree of competitiveness. Thus, it can be the regular or promotional price structure of the category, and not just comparability in attributes, that *causes* the observed switching.

In multidimensional scaling, perceptual mapping, and conjoint approaches, brands "close" to one another are viewed as competitive substitutes, regardless of the absolute level of price. Even if price is included as a dimension (e.g. as a feature in conjoint analysis or as a dimension in a perceptual map), the implication is that price competition should be symmetric or bi-directional. A price decrease for Brand A should result in a unit sales decrease for a "close" Brand B, and a price decrease for Brand B should result in a unit sales decrease for Brand A. As shown below, this implied symmetry of competition may be an artifact of the estimation technique used unless the underlying consumer preferences for the attribute(s) is uniform or unimodal.[3]

One innovation in perceptual mapping that resolves some of the above problems is DEFENDER (Hauser and Shugan 1983; Hauser and Gaskin 1984; Shugan 1987). DEFENDER explicitly incorporates price into the perceptual map, scaling product attributes in a "quantity of the attribute-per-dollar" measure (Hauser and Simmie 1981). However, DEFENDER implies that there exist at most 2 (or n) competitors for a given brand in a 2 (or n) dimensional analysis (n typically being 2 to 4). As shown later, though, it is possible for a large number of brands to be price competitive with one another to varying degrees, and for one brand to take share from another brand when it lowers its price, but not vice versa.[4]

One major concern with many of the approaches to assessing competitive structure is that they try to empirically derive the "best" structure for the market either by trying a multitude of possible structures or by a priori selecting specific structures based upon a variety of heuristics and then testing to see which fits best. As Rao (1984) noted, promotional price research in general "has sought predictions of the phenomena rather than cogent explanations." (p. S49). This criticism is especially valid as applied to research on how price changes themselves influence market structure. The remainder of this paper derives a basis for how price deals affect the nature of competition and analyzes how various consumer preference distributions may affect inter-brand competition. This paper seeks to explain why certain competitive patterns occur when price changes.

3. Model of Price Tiers

3.1. *A Basic Utility Theory of Price Competition*

Let consumer c's overall utility U_i^c be:

$$U_i^c = \theta^c q_i^c - p_i \tag{3.1}$$

where q_i^c is consumer c's perceived quality of brand i, p_i is the actual price, and $\theta^c > 0$ is consumer c's willingness to pay for quality (i.e. θ^c is the importance weight on overall quality relative to an importance weight of 1 on price p_i).[5] Quality is defined here as a summary measure denoting the brand's overall attractiveness, exclusive of price. As such, quality is an overall preference for a particular usage occasion that summarizes

---

[3] It may be possible to extend some of these approaches to incorporate asymmetry by including interaction effects. Note too that the above approaches tend to use regular prices rather than deal prices.

[4] DEFENDER can handle different absolute amounts of sales loss depending on the underlying assumptions of the consumer preference distribution across product attributes. For an additional competitor to become efficient (significant) requires driving unit sales for one of the adjacent (close) competitors to zero unit sales. (See e.g. Hauser and Gaskin 1983.)

[5] This basic model is somewhat comparable to the approach taken in the self-selection literature in economics. See e.g. Mussa and Rosen (1978), Cooper (1984), Moorthy (1984), and Oren, Smith and Wilson (1984). However, equation (3.1) deals with quality as a perceived versus an objective dimension.

multidimensional consumer product perceptions or attributes, exclusive of price. Note that some consumers may place much greater importance on quality (have a higher θ) than others, and that this idiosyncratic desire for quality can have a significant effect on the price a given consumer is willing to pay for a specific level of quality.[6]

For the consumer comparing two brands i and k, the difference in utility is:

$$U_i^c - U_k^c = (\theta q_i^c - p_i) - (\theta q_k^c - p_k) = \theta^c(q_i^c - q_k^c) - (p_i - p_k). \qquad (3.2)$$

Thus, given that both prices are below the consumer's reservation price, the decision rule becomes:

Choose brand i if:

$$\theta^c(q_i^c - q_k^c) > (p_i - p_k), \qquad \text{or} \qquad (3.3a)$$

Choose brand k if:

$$\theta^c(q_i^c - q_k^c) < (p_i - p_k). \qquad (3.3b)$$

Suppose $(q_i^c - q_k^c) > 0$ and equation (3.3b) describes a particular consumer. Brand i is superior in quality to brand k, but this consumer is currently a buyer of brand k. As $p_i - p_k$, eventually the difference $(p_i - p_k)$ will become small enough for equation (3.3a) to hold since $\theta^c(q_i^c - q_k^c) > 0$, and this consumer will switch from brand k to brand i.

Suppose next that another consumer is currently described by equation (3.3a). At current prices, the consumer buys the higher quality brand i. As p_k declines, the consumer will buy brand k only if $\theta^c(q_i^c - q_k^c)$ is sufficiently small. In words, this means the consumer will switch down to the lower quality brand only if the perceived quality difference between the two brands is small and/or his strength of preference for quality relative to price is small. Even if $p_k = 0$, that is, brand k is free, it is still possible that the consumer will not shift to brand k if $\theta^c(q_i^c - q_k^c) > p_i$. Thus, depending on the distribution of preferences in the population and prices, some consumers (the higher θ's) may never be affected by price promotions of lower quality brands, while others may switch back and forth between products depending on the relative prices $(p_i - p_k)$ and their (lower) value of θ^c.

3.2 *Population Preference Distributions*

For ease of terminology, define R^c as consumer c's *relative preference* for brand i relative to brand k. Thus, let $R^c = \theta^c(q_i^c - q_k^c)$. If $q_i^c > q_k^c$, a consumer's relative preference for brand i increases as the perceived overall quality difference $(q_i^c - q_k^c)$ increases and/or as the importance consumer c places on quality θ^c increases. The pattern of brand competition in a market is thus a function of the shape of the distribution of relative preferences R^c over all consumers c. Little is known empirically about the shape of this relative preference distribution or its underlying components, the distributions of θ^c and $(q_i^c - q_k^c)$.

Three general distributions shown in Figures 1 and 2 can be examined to illustrate the range of the possible effects that the shape of the relative preference distribution R can have on the pattern of price competition. One assumption is a uniform distribution. A second is a normal distribution, assuming that an individual's relative preference is the result of many influences of the buyer's environment and thus is normally distributed because of the Central Limit Theorem. The normal distribution is an example of a

---

[6] As θ^c is larger, indicating a stronger desire for quality, price p_i can be larger for a given quality level q_i and still leave U_i^c unchanged. Thus, as the value of θ^c increases, the consumer is willing to pay more for the same absolute level of perceived quality.

PRICE-INDUCED PATTERNS OF COMPETITION   295

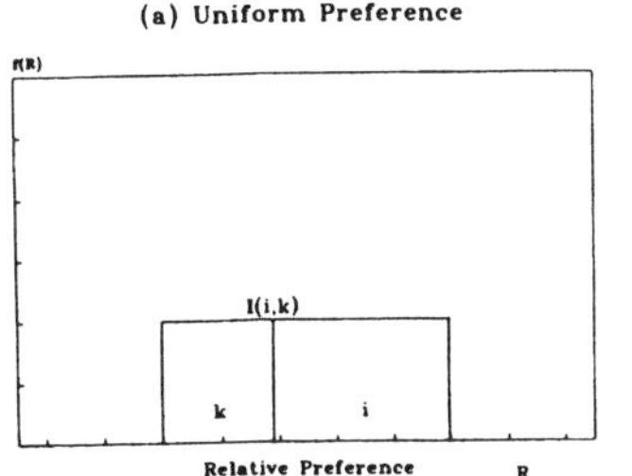

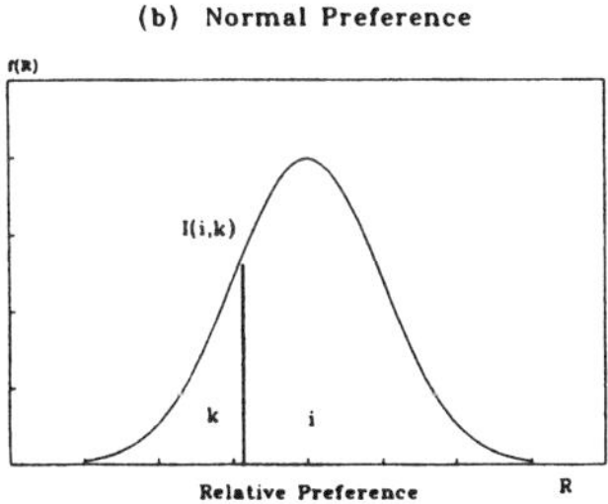

FIGURE 1.   Price Competition Symmetric in Direction.

unimodal distribution, while the uniform distribution is a constant. A third distribution is a "U-shaped" or a "J-shaped" distribution (such as a Beta distribution) as shown in Figure 2. Thus, the distributions in Figures 1 and 2 represent the proportion of consumers $f(R)$ with a specific value for the relative preference $R^c = \theta^c(q_i^c - q_k^c)$. For example, Figure 2a shows the relative preference distribution to be bimodal, with a large proportion of the population having low values of R (i.e. viewing the brands as having small quality differences and/or having a lower willingness to pay for quality) and a smaller proportion of the population with a large value R for their relative preference for brand i relative to brand k.

Equation (3.1) implies that a consumer will be indifferent between either of a pair of brands if:

$$\theta^c(q_i^c - q_k^c) = R^* = p_i - p_k = I_{ik}. \tag{3.4}$$

The vertical lines in Figures 1 and 2 represent the numerical value R^* at the point of indifference I_{ik}. At point I_{ik}, prices of brands i and k are such that a consumer receives the same level of overall utility if he/she buys either brand i or k. Consumers to the left of I_{ik} prefer brand k, since for them $\theta^c(q_i^c - q_k^c) < (p_i - p_k)$, while consumers to the right of I_{ik} prefer brand i. As brand i reduces its price, the point of indifference in Figure 1 and 2 moves to the left, and additional buyers of k are now willing to switch up to a purchase of i, even though $p_i > p_k$. The narrowing of the price difference is enough to cause some consumers to switch to the higher quality, yet still higher priced brand. This is caused by their willingness to pay for quality θ^c or the difference in perceived quality between the brands $(q_i^c - q_k^c)$ being high enough to cause the overall utility for brand i to become greater than the overall utility for brand k, given the reduction in price p_i [(i.e., $\theta^c(q_i^c - q_k^c) = R^* > p_i - p_k$)]. Thus, brand k loses customers, and brand i increases share.

In Figure 1, for the uniform and normal distributions, price competition operates in both directions in the sense that a price reduction in one of the brands results in significant numbers of consumer switching from the nondealt to the dealt brand. In other words,

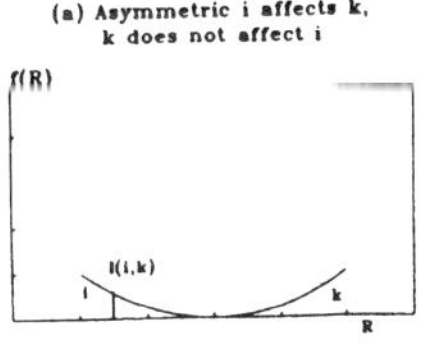

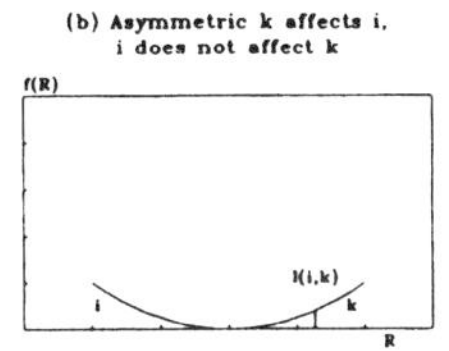

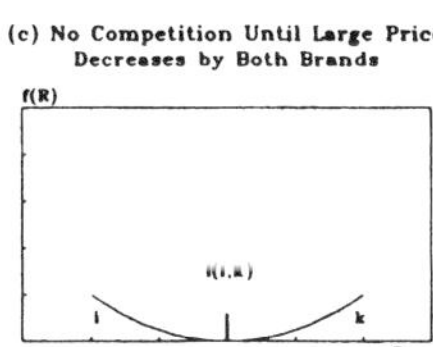

FIGURE 2.   Asymmetric and Independent Price Competition

cross-price elasticities can be expected to be positive and significant for both pairs of brands.[7]

Figure 2 helps explain a specific type of observed asymmetry in price competition. Figure 2a shows the case where price decreases by brand i take significant (nonzero) unit sales from brand k, but as brand k reduces its price, negligible sales loss occurs for brand i. Figure 2b reverses the order of this effect, and Figure 2c shows the case where the distribution of relative preferences is so polar between the brands that negligible sales loss occurs for either brand as the other price deals until large price cuts are in effect.

Note that the above discussion is based upon a paired comparison of those buyers who currently prefer either brand i or brand k to all other brands under "normal" or regular prices. There is no difficulty in extending the discussion to three brands or more, since the relevant comparison will *always* be between *two* brands. In equilibrium, the market consists of buyers of i, j, k, l, etc., each consumer purchasing the brand which generates the greatest utility according to equation (3.1). The above discussion is centered on what will happen to a given brand's baseline unit sales when a competitive brand reduces its price, and vice versa.

If brands i and j are high quality brands, and brand k is a low quality brand, it is possible that the $i - k$ and $j - k$ relative preference distributions may look like 2a, while the $i - j$ distribution may look like 1a or 1b. (Recall that while the willingness to pay for quality parameter θ^c is a constant for a given consumer across all brands, the quality of the brands q_i^c varies across the brands i, j, k, etc.) Thus, any given brand may compete with any number of competitive brands.[8]

3.3. *Theory of Price Tiers*

In many markets, one sees groups of brands with different prices and implied quality. For example, Sears offers their customers three grades at three price levels: good, better, best. In packaged goods there are national, private label and generic brands. Table 1 shows regular prices[9] offered for four grocery product categories over time for one grocery chain in the Chicagoland market. It shows national, moderate/private label and generic brands having significant price differentials. These separate distinct retail price groups will be called *price tiers*.

With a few relatively weak and plausible assumptions, it is possible to develop specific predictions about the structure of price competition between and within price tiers.

Assumption (1). In general, national brands (N) have higher perceived quality levels than moderate/private label brands (P); private labels (P) are higher quality than generics (G). Thus, $q_N^c > q_P^c > q_G^c$.

Based on this assumption, on average $\theta^c(q_i^c - q_k^c) > 0$ for i being a national brand and k a private label, or for i being a private label and k a generic brand. Different consumers

---

[7] Note that these cross-price elasticities need *not* be comparable in magnitude. In fact, if brands i and k are identically priced, Figures 1a and 1b imply the cross-price elasticity of i's effect on k is larger than the effect of k on i, simply because i's market share is greater. This is because for a fixed distance movement (fixed percentage change) of the indifference point I, brand k loses proportionately more of its base customers than does brand i, and hence its cross-price elasticity with k is greater than k's cross-price elasticity with i.

[8] Figure 2 can also be used to explain how DEFENDER can accomodate a form of asymmetric competition. In DEFENDER terminology (see e.g. Hauser and Shugan 1983, Shugan 1987), if the horizontal axis R in Figure 2 is viewed as the angle of the consumer's linear indifference curve with the vertical-axis attribute, then such a U-shaped distribution of preferences (angles) across attributes can generate asymmetric competitive effects of the type described above. A limitation, though, is that DEFENDER will only allow adjacent brands to compete with a given brand, limiting competition to at most n competitors in n-dimensional attribute space. In addition, such an approach requires a very complex pattern of indifference curves (preferences) in n-dimensional space (i.e. what do U-shaped preferences mean in 4-dimensional space) versus the simpler univariate overall relative preference approach described in the text.

[9] Regular prices are the nondeal regular shelf prices of the brands (i.e. the prices facing the consumer during nonpromoted weeks).

PRICE-INDUCED PATTERNS OF COMPETITION   297

TABLE 1

Price Tiers—Brands and Regular Price Ranges (Brands Ordered by Market Share Within Each Tier)

Flour (5 lb. All Purpose)		Margarine (1 lb. Sticks)		Bathroom Tissue (4-Roll Equivalent)		Tuna (6.5 Oz. in Oil)	
PREMIUM BRANDS							
Pillsbury	.98–1.23*	Imperial	.89	Charmin	1.39	Bumble Bee	1.09–1.19
Gold Medal	.98–1.19	Land O'Lakes	.75–.83	Northern	1.39	Chkn of Sea	1.09–1.37
Ceresota	.98–1.19	Parkay	.83	White Cloud	1.39	Starkist	1.09–1.37
		Bluebonnet	.85	Soft 'N Pretty	1.39		
		Chiffon	.59–.69				
MODERATE BRANDS							
Jewelmaid	.89–.99	Bluebrook	.49–.53	Scott Tissue	1.06[1]	Bluebook	.89–1.05
		Sunnyland	.49–.53	Coronet	.995[2]		
				Jewel	.99		
				Sable Soft	1.11		
GENERIC BRANDS							
Generic	.69	Generic	.35	Generic	.68–.69	Generic	.73

* Represents the actual regular price range observed throughout the data history.

[1] Scott Tissue is sold as 53¢/100-sheet roll; 2–3 rolls of Scott yield approximately 4 rolls of the premium brands on a volume basis.

[2] Coronet is sold in an 8-pack for $1.99, or .995 for 4 rolls.

may have different perceived quality for the brands, but for the purposes of the empirical analyses q_i^c is generally assumed to be greater than q_k.

Assumption (2). There is a positive correlation between price and quality. Thus $p_N > p_P > p_G$.

In general, retailers such as Sears, Roebuck and Co. and Jewel Food Stores and most manufacturers seem to set pricing policy based on the observation that increased levels of product quality for a particular type of product also produce increased costs and hence increased prices. Gabor and Granger (1966) find strong evidence that consumers do use price as an indicator of quality at the individual level.

If one accepts these assumptions, then predictions about brand price competition can be made. The predictions depend on the shape of the distribution of the consumers relative preferences R^c and on the location for the regular price indifference point I_{ik}.

Assuming *comparable* levels of quality q_i and q_k and comparable retail prices, competition *within* a price/quality tier should be bi-directional and resemble one of the situations shown in Figure 1. Thus, each brand significantly affects the other's unit sales when they price deal, although the absolute magnitude of sales loss need not be equal.

The most interesting predictions are those comparable to Figures 2a and 2b. What follows is a discussion of 2a, although the reverse argument can be made for case 2b. If Figure 2a describes the market's relative preferences, then when a brand i in a higher price tier reduces its price, it attracts buyers from the lower price tier brand k. Graphically, the indifference point moves to the left, and consumers who now find themselves to the right of the indifference point (i.e. R^c is now greater than I_{ik}) now buy brand i. However, when a brand in the lower tier reduces its price, brands in higher tiers lose little volume, since there are few consumers with relative preferences immediately to the right of the indifference point I_{ik}. (Reasons why this situation may occur are discussed in §7.) Within tiers, brands affect other same-tier brands as they price deal, since the perceived quality and retail price differences are assumed to be much smaller within than between tiers, and the shape of the distribution of relative preferences is more likely to look like Figures 1a or 1b.

How to distinguish between 1b and 2a using aggregate data is an empirical issue. Both result in a form of asymmetric or unidirectional competition. However, note that in general we would expect case 1b to show substantial percentage losses in brand i's market share, implying large sales losses for brand i during brand k's dealing periods relative to the usual fluctuation of brand i's baseline sales. Thus, we would expect to observe significant cross-price effects in case 1b. However, for case 2a, the loss in i's sales relative to its market share or baseline sales is minimal. Thus, sales loss relative to regular sales fluctuation should be minimal, and the cross-price coefficient will be small. The empirical statistical results reported later indicate that this is a logical way to distinguish between 1b and 2a.

§5 tests these predictions with the data described in the next section.

4. Description of the Data

To evaluate the theory described in the last section, data from four product categories were available at the time of this analysis: all-purpose flour, stick margarine, bathroom tissue, and chunk light tuna in oil. Forty-nine weeks of data were supplied by Jewel Food Stores, the leading market share grocery chain in Chicago. The data collected for this study include unit sales by item, price by item, newspaper feature advertising, and price deals by item. The dependent variable of interest is total unit sales across 26 stores in the sample. The 26 stores all have the same retail prices, and the timing of price changes and deals within these stores is identical.

Because this study's focus is on price and not on attribute effects, brands were selected to be comparable on the basic attributes. Thus, only regular stick margarine brands were studied in the margarine category. Omitted were tubs of margarine, corn oil margarine, and squeeze margarine. Similarly in tuna, only 6.5-oz. light chunk tuna in oil was studied. This reduced other nonprice effects by making the defined category more homogeneous.

Several issues arose in creating the data set. First, a hardware problem at the retailer resulted in the destruction of the data for week 17, reducing the usable sample to 48 weeks. Second, the original private label bathroom tissue was phased out during weeks 39–49. Estimations on this one brand use only the "stable" first 38 weeks of data. The third problem is common to many retailer scanning systems. Weekly data were collected Monday through Sunday and the price reported on the data tape was the Sunday price. In the Chicago SMSA, price deals are typically offered Thursday through Wednesday. If the price was higher (or lower) during the first part of the week (e.g. Monday–Wednesday), this was not recorded. Thus, it is necessary to modify some of the post-deal-period prices to reflect the actual price facing the consumer in a particular week. Because data on advertised price deals were collected, the deal length was known and the prices modified accordingly. Thus, if a deal was available during any part of the week, the price for that week was set to the deal price. This requires a variable in the model to adjust for the percentage of a given week in which the deal was offered, as noted in equation (5.1), §5.

5. Model Used for Testing Predictions

The structure of price competition is identified by examining the patterns of competitive brands' cross-price effects. The purpose of this section is to present a model that allows a test of the distributional assumptions and the price tier theory. The model used for estimation purposes is shown in equation (5.1).

The model is a modification of functional forms used by the authors in other promotional scanning research. It incorporates nonprice variables such as newspaper feature advertising, deal decay (which allows an exponential decay in a promotion's effectiveness), seasonality, and a data period adjustment to handle the fact that data are supplied on a Monday–Sunday scanning week while promotions in the Chicago market generally run Thursday through Wednesday. These nonprice variables which are not the focus of this

PRICE-INDUCED PATTERNS OF COMPETITION 299

paper allow more precise estimation of the price effects. The model incorporates three price variables to estimate own-brand regular price, own brand deal price, and competitive brand effects.

The own-price elasticity is $\beta_1 P_{it}$. The own-brand deal discount is modeled using a percentage discount from regular price, $[(P_{it} - d_{it})/P_{it}]$, and the elasticity is $\beta_2 d_{it}/P_{it}$. This implies consumers are evaluating percentage changes in deals, and is consistent with recent work which implies consumers frame the concept of a "good deal" on a relative instead of an absolute basis (e.g. Thaler 1985). Tests of other variable specifications (e.g. absolute penny discounts instead of the percentage discount used here) show that the percentage discount from regular price works as well or better (based on an R-squared measure of fit) than alternative specifications for over 80% of the brands analyzed, with the percentage decrease specification generally a close second (in R-Squared terms) in the other 20% of the cases (Wisniewski and Blattberg 1988).

The competitive price effects elasticities, which are the key focus of this study, are $(-\gamma_{ij}/d_{jt})$. The elasticities are point elasticities computed at the last regular price observed in the data history. Although using the mean regular price or some other measure of regular price changes the point estimates, the *pattern* of results is identical to that reported below.

The purpose of this research is to analyze the *pattern* of price competition in the market. Other functional forms can be specified, and several other forms were also estimated in this and other research (see e.g. Wisniewski and Blattberg 1988; Allenby 1988).

$$S_{it} = \exp(c_i - \beta_1 P_{it} + \beta_2(P_{it} - d_{it})/P_{it} - \sum_{j \neq i} \gamma_{ij}/d_{jt}$$

$$+ \alpha_1 A_{it} - \lambda_1 T_{it} + \alpha_2 W_{it} + \alpha_3 \phi_i) \quad (5.1)$$

where

S_{it} = total unit sales of brand i in period t (aggregated over the 26 stores in the price zone)

P_{it} = regular price of brand i at time t,

d_{it} = actual price of brand i at time t,

A_{it} = 1 if brand i advertised at time t, 0 otherwise,

$T_{it} = \begin{cases} \textit{deal decay variable:} \\ 0 \text{ during nondeal weeks,} \\ n - 1 \text{ during the } n\text{th week of a multi-week deal,} \end{cases}$

$W_{it} = \begin{cases} \textit{scanned versus deal week adjustment variable:} \\ 0 \text{ during nondeal weeks,} \\ -.43 \text{ during the first week of a deal (i.e. where the deal price is in effect from Thursday–Sunday),}^{10} \\ 0 \text{ during all "full-week" deal weeks (i.e. all deal weeks where the deal price is in effect all 7 days),} \\ -1.05 \text{ during the last week of a deal (i.e. all deal ending-period weeks where the deal price is in effect only Monday–Wednesday of the week),} \end{cases}$

ϕ_{it} = 1 during a "seasonal" period for the category, 0 otherwise (seasonal periods included Easter, Thanksgiving, and Christmas weeks),

c_i = constant for brand i,

α_i = feature advertising parameter,

---

[10] $e^{-0.43} = 0.65$ and $e^{-1.05} = 0.35$, the adjustments used for deals. In the current data base approximately 65% of the 1-week promotions effects occur during the Thursday–Sunday period, and some 35% occurs during the Monday–Wednesday period.

λ_i = exponential deal decay parameter,
β_1 = own brand price effect,
β_2 = own deal price effect,
γ_i = competitive brand price and deal effects.

However, the results in terms of the symmetric/asymmetric nature of promotional price competition are virtually identical. Thus, §6 presents the results of estimating equation (5.1) on the four product categories.

6. Analyses of Intra-Category, Interbrand Price Competition

The model shown in equation (5.1) was estimated for 28 brands: five 5-lb. all purpose flours, eight 1-lb. regular stick margarines, ten bathroom tissues, and five 6.5 oz. size tuna fish in oil brands. The estimation was performed over all 48 weeks of existing data. Since the objective of the estimation is to identify the structure of price competition, no holdout sample was used. This maximized the degrees of freedom available. The estimation technique used was OLS regression. Analysis of the residuals shows no significant correlations among the residuals between brands in the same category beyond the number expected by chance. Thus, use of SUR (seemingly unrelated regression) offers little additional information.

The summary of the estimation results for the relevant cross-price terms is presented in Table 2. The regular retail price at the end of the data history is used to compute the elasticities. Whether this last price or the average price is used makes no difference for the following discussion. Adjusted R^2 is in the range of 0.75 to 0.95, except for generics which are poorly modeled by any of the price and advertising variables in the data base. The margarine category, which did not have any special display activity associated with its deals at the time of this analysis, generally has the best fit, though bathroom tissue, having substantial display activity, is almost as high.

Figure 3 presents typical fitted versus actual sales histories for the largest-share premium brands in each category. For all brands except the generics the model given in equation (5.1) accurately fits the peaks and the decay patterns for price deals. This is an indication that the major competitive factors have been captured by the estimation model. Even in nondeal periods, the models do an adequate job of tracking the upward and downward movements in the data histories, indicating that competitive prices are affecting week-to-week unit sales.

6.1. *Summary of the Cross-Price Results*

There are 171 price coefficients estimated across these 28 brands, 135 being cross-price terms and hence particularly appropriate for this analysis. (Eight cross-price coefficients could not be estimated due to lack of price variation.) Since the generic brands did not often significantly reduce price, a separate 0/1 variable[11] was used to try to assess the effect of generic deals on other brands. Table 3 summarizes the significance of the coefficients based on a significance level of 0.05 ($t = 1.697$, $n = 30$), and also reports average price elasticities. Table 3 counts the effects as follows: For a given brand i, if any other brand's price within a tier affects the brand i, then the other brand's price-tier is said to affect the price tier of the brand i. For example, in margarine, there are 5 national brands, 2 private labels, and 1 generic. For a specific national brand, if any of the other 4 national brands' prices affects the specific brand, Table 3 says the national brand is affected by other national brands' prices. Since there are 5 national brands, there are 5 relevant national brand comparisons. Similarly, if *either* of the two private labels affects a given national brand's sales, then it would be counted as a moderate tier brand affecting a national brand's unit sales.

---

[11] A 0/1 generic-deal indicator variable was used to denote the absence/presence of a generic deal.

PRICE-INDUCED PATTERNS OF COMPETITION   301

TABLE 2
Cross-Price Elasticities

FLOUR — AFFECT UNIT SALES OF:

PRICES OF:	PIL	GDM	CER	JM	GNC
Pillsbury (PIL)	—	1.15	0.67	2.44	0.65
Gold Medal (GDM)	0.99	—	1.21	1.18[a]	0.01[a]
Ceresota (CER)-Deal	(0.06)*	0.03*		0.37*	0.03*
Jewel Maid (JM)	0.19[a]	1.74	0.08[a]	—	0.43[a]
Generic (GNC)-Deal	0.01*	0.03*	0.01*	0.15[a]	—
Market Share	0.37	0.09	0.11	0.08	0.34
Adjusted R^2	0.96	0.89	0.94	0.77	0.24

MARGARINE — AFFECT UNIT SALES OF:

PRICES OF:	IMP	LOL	PKY	BBT	CHF	BBK	SNY	GNC
Imperial (IMP)	—	0.84	0.71	0.27[a]	0.22*	0.00*	0.64	0.03*
Land O'Lakes (LOL)	0.16*	—	0.63	0.50	0.44	0.05*	0.75	0.06*
Parkay (PKY)	0.13*	0.34	—	0.32	0.23	0.15	0.20[a]	(0.04)*
Bluebonnet (BBT)	0.49	0.23	0.25	—	0.43	0.10*	(0.14)*	(0.08)*
Chiffon (CHF)	(0.14)*	0.19*	0.37*	0.43*	—	(0.24)*	0.85[a]	0.01*
BlueBrook (BBK)	(0.20)*	(0.13)*	0.05*	0.06*	(0.14)*	—	0.30[a]	0.19
Sunnyland (SNY)	0.03*	0.21[a]	0.19*	0.27[a]	0.02*	0.25	—	0.13
Generic (GNC)-Deal	0.01*	(0.16)	(0.06)*	(0.05)*	0.00*	0.01*	0.10*	—
Market Share	0.17	0.14	0.12	0.06	0.04	0.32	0.08	0.07
Adjusted R^2	0.91	0.95	0.96	0.95	0.88	0.93	0.88	0.66

BATHROOM TISSUE — AFFECT UNIT SALES OF:

PRICES OF:	CHM	NTH	WTC	SNP	SCT	COR	JWL	SBL	GNC
Charmin (CHM)	—	1.31	1.47	1.83	0.60*	(0.11)*	0.81*	1.33	(0.37)*
Northern (NTH)	0.80	—	0.72	1.58	0.18*	(0.24)*	0.80	1.56	0.39*
White Cloud (WTC)	1.14	0.90[a]	—	1.69	0.22*	0.44*	0.70*	0.98	(0.40)*
Soft 'N Pretty (SNP)	0.74	0.89	0.56		1.25	0.02*	0.71[a]	1.75	(0.90)
Scottissue (SCT)	0.27*	0.20*	0.26*	1.37[a]	—	1.50	1.99	1.30	0.92[a]
Coronet (COR)	0.24	0.02*	0.05*	0.22*	0.34[a]	—	1.04	0.39	0.64
Jewel (JWL)	0.19[a]	(0.40)*	0.00*	0.96[a]	0.24*	1.92	—	0.17	0.18
Sable Soft (SBL)	ND	ND	ND	ND	ND	ND	ND	ND	ND
Generic (GNC)	0.04*	(0.12)*	0.01*	(0.06)*	0.00*	(0.10)*	0.15[a]	0.03*	—
Market Share	0.15	0.10	0.07	0.05	0.12	0.03	0.03	0.03	0.42
Adjusted R^2	0.84	0.90	0.91	0.86	0.76	0.71	0.88	0.64	0.17

TUNA FISH — AFFECT UNIT SALES OF:

PRICES OF:	BBB	CKN	STK	*BBK	GNC
Bumble Bee (BBB)	—	0.64	0.37*	1.55	0.10*
Chicken/Sea (CKN)	1.05[a]	—	1.26	0.25*	0.20*
Starkist (STK)	0.85[a]	0.09[a]	—	0.54[a]	(0.27)[a]
Blue Brook (BBK)	0.36*	0.07*	0.17*	—	0.31*
Generic (GNC)	ND	ND	ND	ND	ND
Market Share	0.25	0.21	0.16	0.07	0.31
Adjusted R^3	0.84	0.90	0.88	0.69	0.04

All cross-elasticities significant at the 0.05 level unless otherwise noted.

[a] Significant at the 0.10 level.

* Insignificant at the 0.05 level.

( ) Indicates an incorrectly signed coefficient.

Deal—Some of these brands did not extensively price deal. The value reported is the coefficient of a 0/1 advertising variable for that brand's deal.

ND—No deals of any type for this brand.

PILLSBURY FLOUR: ACTUAL VERSUS PREDICTED
PILLSBURY'S SIZE: 5 POUNDS
SALES
ACTUAL
PREDICTED
WEEKS
IMPERIAL MARGARINE: ACTUAL VERSUS PREDICTED
IMPERIAL'S SIZE: 1LB STICK
SALES
ACTUAL
PREDICTED
WEEKS
CHARMIN BATH TISSUE: ACTUAL VERSUS PREDICTED
CHARMIN'S SIZE: 4 PACKS
SALES
ACTUAL
PREDICTED
WEEKS
BUMBLE BEE TUNA: ACTUAL VERSUS PREDICTED
BUMBLE BEE IN 6.5 OZ/OIL
SALES
ACTUAL
PREDICTED
WEEKS

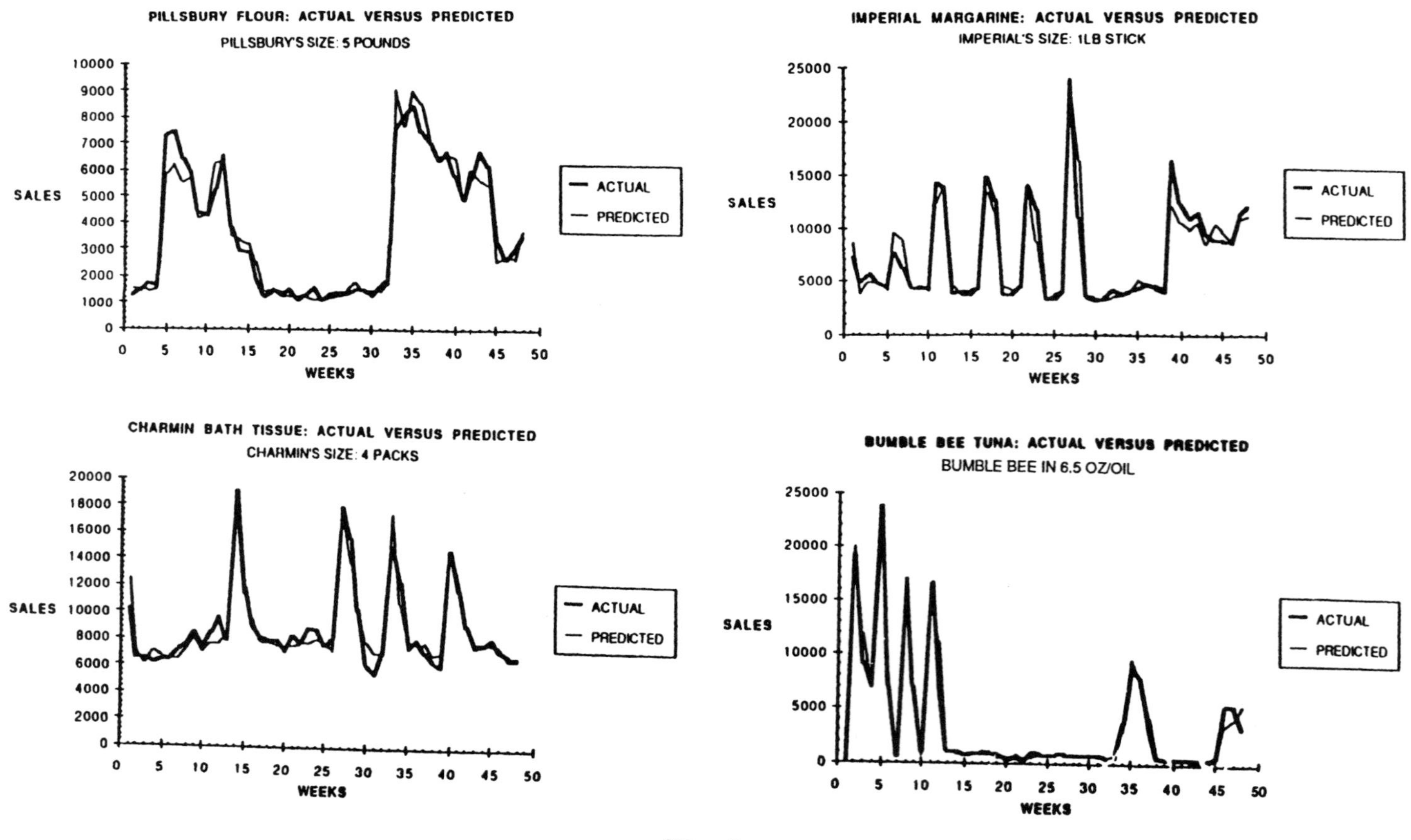

FIGURE 3.

PRICE-INDUCED PATTERNS OF COMPETITION   303

TABLE 3

Summary of Predictive Hypothesis Results and Average Cross-Price Elasticities

PRICE CHANGES OF:	AFFECT UNIT SALES OF:											
	PREMIUM				MODERATE				GENERIC			
				$\bar{\gamma}$				$\bar{\gamma}$				$\bar{\gamma}$
PREMIUM	FLOUR	3/3*		0.69	FLOUR	1/1		1.33	FLOUR	1/1		0.23
	MARG.	5/5	14/15	0.35	MARG.	2/2	7/8	0.24	MARG.	0/1	1/4	0.00
	TISSUE**	4/4		1.14	TISSUE	3/4		0.69	TISSUE	0/1		−0.32
	TUNA	2/3***		0.71	TUNA	1/1		0.78	TUNA	0/1		0.01
				$\bar{\gamma}$				$\bar{\gamma}$				$\bar{\gamma}$
MODERATE	FLOUR	1/3[a]		0.67	FLOUR	NA		—	FLOUR	0/1		0.43
	MARG.	0/5	2/15	0.04	MARG.	1/2[b]	4/6	0.28	MARG.	1/1	2/4	0.16
	TISSUE	1/4[c]		0.33	TISSUE	3/4		0.99	TISSUE	1/1		0.58
	TUNA	0/3		0.20	TUNA	NA		—	TUNA	0/1		0.31
				$\bar{\gamma}$				$\bar{\gamma}$				$\bar{\gamma}$
GENERIC	FLOUR	0/3		0.02	FLOUR	0/1		0.15	FLOUR	NA		—
	MARG.	1/5[d]	1/12	0.01	MARG.	0/2	0/7	0.06	MARG.	NA	NA	—
	TISSUE	0/4		−0.03	TISSUE	0/4		0.02	TISSUE	NA		—
	TUNA	NA		—	TUNA	NA		—	TUNA	NA		—

* Read as: "In 3 (numerator) out of 3 (denominator) cases, at least 1 of the premium brands (row type) prices affect at least 1 of the premium brands (column type) unit sales" ($\alpha = 0.05$, $t = 1.645$).

** Tissue category excludes Waldorf—see text.

*** 3/3 at the 0.10 level.

[a] Jewelmaid → Gold Medal.

[b] Bluebrook → Sunnyland (Bluebrook → Sunnyland at 0.10 level).

[c] Coronet → Charmin.

[d] Generic → Land O'Lakes (coefficient has wrong sign).

NA Not Applicable/Only 1 brand, no comparison possible.

$\bar{\gamma}$ Average cross-price elasticity or average deal cross-elasticity.

Thus, Table 3 presents a "worst-case" analysis which favors finding *symmetric* or bidirectional competitive price effects. Overall, the results strongly support *asymmetric* or unidirectional price tier competition of a very specific type.

We discuss first the diagonal and cells in the triangle above the diagonal. In 14 of 15 comparisons (15 of 15 at the 0.10 level), premium priced brands steal significant unit sales from other premium priced brands when they price deal. In 7 of 8 cases, premium priced brands take sales away from brands in the moderate or private label category when premium prices are reduced. In 1 of 4 cases (Pillsbury flour) a premium brand's price affects the generic brand. In 4 of 6 cases (5 of 6 at the .10 level), moderate/private label brand prices affect unit sales of other moderate/private label brands, the only exception (.10 level) being Scottissue, discussed below. In 2 of 4 cases, the moderate/private label brands also exhibit statistically significant unit sales effects on the generic brands. Thus when higher-price, higher-quality brands price deal, they steal sales from their own tier and the tier below.

In Table 3 the three cells below the diagonal provide the strongest evidence of asymmetry in the direction of competition. In only 3 of 32 comparisons do lower-tier brands statistically significantly affect upper-tier brand unit sales. The results are even stronger than they seem at first. In 2 of 4 categories, there are multiple moderate/private label brands (2 private label margarines, 4 moderate brand bathroom tissues). If any one of these moderate brands affects the premium brand, it is counted as a "violation" in Table 3. In fact, there are 45 moderate and lower tier coefficients summarized in the 3 cells below the diagonal. In only 3 of the 45 cases (6.7%) are the coefficients statistically significant.

Note that 2.25 (or 4.5) would be expected simply by chance at the 0.05 (0.10) level. One of the significant coefficients (the effect of a generic deal on Land 'O Lakes margarine) is actually positive (indicating that in the periods when the generic brand advertised, Land 'O Lakes unit sales were *up*), and is likely to be a statistical artifact.

The above results are also consistent with the absolute magnitudes of the cross-price elasticities. The average elasticities reported in Table 3 show strong own-tier effects, and premium/private label cross-elasticities that are greater than their private label/premium counterparts. The absolute magnitude of the private label's cross-price elasticities with the national brands is almost always much smaller than the national brand's cross-elasticities with the private labels. As Tables 2 and 3 indicate, moderate-affecting-premium brand cross-elasticities are typically smaller, often are insignificant, and sometimes are even negative.

The other two below-diagonal significant coefficients are instructive. Bimodal preference distributions do not rule out a lower-tier brand affecting an upper-tier brand. Such a result suggests that either the differences in quality are closer than for other across-tier pairs of brands, or the price of the lower-tier brand is being reduced sufficiently to offset the loss in utility from switching from the higher-tier brand to the lower-tier brand for some of the consumers in the market. In one of these cases, the moderate-tier private label flour Jewelmaid draws share from the upper-tier brand Gold Medal. Gold Medal flour is a national brand, priced at nearly the same price of the market leader Pillsbury. Yet, Pillsbury enjoys approximately a 37% share of the market, while Gold Medal languishes at 9%. Thus, there would seem to be some perceived differences in the mean level of quality offered by the two brands although prices are comparable. The results imply that the difference in perceived quality between Jewelmaid and Gold Medal is significantly less than the difference in the quality between Pillsbury and Jewelmaid.

This same argument cannot be made for the moderate brand Coronet bathroom tissue affecting the market share leader Charmin. All premium brands of bathroom tissue were regularly priced at $1.39 for four rolls. Of these 4 premium brands, Charmin was the market share leader. Coronet was the *only* 8-roll pack in our analysis (priced at $1.99, hence the highest *absolute* price). Coronet also is the only moderate brand *not* affected by other moderate brands' pricing. Thus, we are unable to determine if this effect is real, if it is due to a high absolute price causing consumers to perceive it to be in a higher price tier, or if it is simply a chance occurrence.

All of the other 25 brands are statistically consistent with price-tier theory of the type shown in Figure 2a or 2c. This means that "upper-tier" brands tend to affect own tier and tier below brands when they deal, but lower tier brands do not affect the upper-tier brands significantly. Occasionally, there may be no statistically observable effect between or within tiers.

Two brands, Scottissue and Chiffon, illustrate the value of price-tier theory in assessing competitive market structure. Based on square-footage, it was initially unclear whether Scottissue was a premium (3 rolls for $1.53) or a moderate (2 rolls for $1.06) brand. Scott's advertising strategy seems to focus on economy as its core benefit, implying it is positioned as a moderate brand. Its regular price is 53¢ per roll, the lowest absolute price in the category. The estimation results imply that consumers treat Scott as a moderate rather than a premium priced brand. It does *not* affect other national brands, although it is larger in market share than all national brands except Charmin. Scott is affected by one of the premium brands (Soft 'N Pretty), and is marginally affected by Coronet (0.10 level). Scott itself affects all of the other moderate brands and marginally affects generics (0.10 level). Thus, the market is behaviorally treating Scott as a moderate brand, although under some physical volume comparisons with other brands, Scott may actually be a high-priced brand.

Chiffon margarine provides another insightful example. Chiffon is the lowest-priced premium national brand, with a regular price starting at 69¢ and falling to 59¢ (versus the other national brands at 83¢–89¢, and the private labels at 49¢–53¢). Thus, Chiffon is borderline premium, borderline moderate. Table 2 shows that Chiffon's prices affect none of the other premium brands, while it is affected by the prices of 3 of the other 4 premium brands. Chiffon marginally affects the Sunnyland moderate brand. Thus, it acts like an inferior premium, or a superior moderate brand, and occupies an intermediate tier of its own.

6.2. *Analysis of the Causes of and Patterns in Asymmetry*

Table 3 provides strong evidence consistent with at least bimodal preference distributions in the population. However, if there is also asymmetry in the absolute amount of deal price discounts empirically observed, then it is possible that the results are an estimation artifact of the historical pattern of dealing in the market. Analysis of the depth of deals show that the margarine and bathroom tissue categories have comparable deal depth ranges for the various types of brands. In the tuna and flour categories, the private label brands tend to have smaller deal discounts (in absolute pennies off and percentage terms) than the national brands in those categories. For tuna, the maximum deal depth for the private label is 15.2%, versus an average maximum deal depth for the national brands of 19.2%. For flour, the maximum private label deal discount is 10.1%, versus a national brand average maximum of 15.6%. Thus, it may be that if the private labels or generics increased their depth of deal in the tuna and flour categories, significant cross-price effects with the national brands might be found. However, the conclusion is still valid that at this lower but significant level of discounting, the relative preference distribution is consistent with at least bimodal preferences in order to find significant national brand effects on the private labels but not vice versa.

The specific pattern of asymmetries observed in Table 2 shows primarily upper-tier brands affecting other brands in their own tier and in the tier below, while lower-tier brands rarely affect upper-tier brands. This is the result of both bimodal preference distributions *and* the location of the current regular price indifference point fitting the general pattern shown in Figure 2a.

Table 4 presents another way of looking at the data in order to infer the general location of the regular price indifference point. The table concentrates on those *between-tier* brand comparisons which have estimable cross-price terms for both brands, excluding the generic brand comparisons. The brand-level focus of Table 4, as opposed to Table 3's price tier focus, allows a more precise determination of the location of the regular price indifference point. Since Chiffon and Scottissue are distinct tiers as determined above, Table 4 separates out these brands from the other national brands.

Brand comparisons are classified based upon the elasticity reported in Table 2. For example, since Pillsbury flour affects the private label Jewelmaid flour when it deals, but not vice versa, this comparison is classified as a "$N \rightarrow PL$"—i.e., the national (upper tier) brand affects the private label (lower tier), but not vice versa.

Table 4 reveals that in 32 of 34 cases, the strength of preference for quality distribution is consistent with bimodal preference distributions. In 15 cases, the regular price indifference point is located to the left of the distribution as shown in Figure 2a. This conclusion holds since reductions in the upper-tier brand's price affects the lower-tier brand's unit sales, but reductions in the lower-tier brand's price has no significant effect on the upper-tier brand's sales.

An additional 15 cases imply an indifference point around the middle of the trough between peaks in the quality distribution, as shown in Figure 2c. The brands are not price competitive for price deal decreases of the magnitudes in the data base.

In only 2 cases is there evidence that the private label brand affects the national brand but not vice versa. Thus, in 30 of 34 cases, the regular price indifference point is either in the center or toward the left of the trough (Figures 2c and 2a respectively), while in

TABLE 4

Summary of Brand Competition-Paired Comparisons

	N ↔ PL[1]	N → PL[2]	N ← PL[3]	N ↮ PL[4]
FLOUR	1	1		1
MARGARINE				
N-Chiffon		3		1
N-PL		4	1	3
Chiffon-PL		1		1
BATHROOM TISSUE				
N-Scott		1		3
N-PL		2	1	5
SCOTT-PL	1	1		
TUNA FISH		2		1
TOTALS	2	15	2	15

[1] National and Private Label Affect One Another.
[2] National Affects Private Label, Not Vice Versa.
[3] Private Label Affects National, Not Vice Versa.
[4] Neither Affects the Other.

only 2 cases do the results indicate an indifference point to the right as shown in Figure 2b.

In the remaining 2 cases, both brands affect one another. This is consistent with Figure 1 or Figure 2, where in the latter case the modes are closer together due to perceived quality ($q_i - q_k$) differences being smaller than for the other national-private label comparisons.

7. Discussion, Implication and Conclusions

The preceding results allow several conclusions to be drawn about how price competition may influence observed market structure. Promotional price competition can logically result in asymmetric sales effects within a retail grocery category. For a majority of cases observed, higher-price-tier, higher-quality brands draw market share from their own price tier competitors, and typically from the tier below. However, the lower-quality, lower-price-tier brands take unit sales from own tier and tier below brands, but rarely take sales from higher-priced, higher-quality brands in the tier above. These results indicate that the preference distribution may be at least bimodal in the population, *and* that in this particular market the current regular price equilibrium is located either near the left side of the distribution as shown in Figure 2a or near the middle of the trough between modes as shown in Figure 2c. The fact that the structure of the asymmetry is so specific— lower tier brands generally do not significantly affect upper tier brands unless deal discounts are extreme—implies also that the market is treating the differing price tiers as significantly different in quality and hence the perceived quality difference ($q_i^c - q_k^c$) is substantial enough to preserve the separation in the peaks of the quality θ^c distribution. The markets analyzed are basically homogeneous in product features except for quality and only the price levels and implied quality levels vary. Thus, there is at least some support for the Mussa and Rosen (1978) proposition that multiple quality levels for an otherwise undifferentiated product do in fact exist, and that manufacturers and retailers price these differing quality levels in such a way as to create price-quality tiers in the marketplace.

The asymmetries raise questions about the existing techniques' ability to recover market structures. Since competitive effects may be asymmetric, one brand may be a strong competitor of a second brand when dealing, but the second brand may have no effect on the first. The majority of market structure, perceptual mapping and conjoint techniques thus have problems depicting asymmetric types of price competition.[12] DEFENDER (Hauser and Shugan 1983) is a notable exception because it can allow differential competitive responses. While useful as a proxy for quality, price may not be a perfect correlate of quality *as perceived* in the market. The above research, especially in its derivation of competition from the underlying quality preference distribution, assumes an objective measure of quality q_i for each brand. In reality, heterogeneity in individual perceptions of the relative quality of the brands is likely to influence brand choice in the market. Thus, it is perhaps surprising that the asymmetries found in this research appear to be so clearly defined.[13]

One major question is why the regular price indifference point should so often be found at the left instead of right side of the relative preference distribution. In many markets in the United States, private label brands command greater profit margins than national brands. Hence, to have the national brands cannibalizing the private labels within a retail line may not seem optimal. We might also question why the retailer does not simultaneously raise the prices of all the national brands, thus shifting the regular price indifference point right. The equilibrium would then resemble Figure 2b. (Note that if all national brands are raised in price by an equal absolute-penny amount, the relative prices $(p_i - p_k)$ remain the same for all national brand comparisons.) The major reason why this may not occur in the market is that such changes can raise the regular price of the brands above the reservation price of some of the consumers, causing them to switch not just to other brands but to other lower-priced retailers to purchase a particular brand. In the Chicagoland market, Jewel Food Stores faces a host of price-competitive retailers, including both discounters and warehouse operations as well as comparably-priced chains.[14] In markets that allow higher national brand prices relative to private label brands (e.g. markets with less price competition among retailers), or that have higher-quality private label brands, the indifference point may be shifted rightward and result in private label brands having a more-significant impact on the premium brands.

8. Summary and Future Areas of Research

This paper developed a model for analyzing and explaining price-induced patterns of competition. Three major classes of distributions of the population's preference distribution were proposed to examine how price might affect competition. Based upon the basic utility theory and the various preference distributions, it is possible to predict what the market's competitive structure should look like. The empirical evidence argues that the preference distribution across different quality brands in the population is consistent with at least bimodal relative preference distribution (i.e. there may be "quality" and "economy" seekers in the population). In addition, the current empirical application generally shows a regular price equilibrium located toward the lower peak of this distribution, i.e. closer to the "economy" seekers portion of the distribution. This causes a

---

[12] In fairness, these techniques are generally most interested in depicting attribute competition—which competitors are close attribute substitutes of one another—and not which brands are actually competitive in the real world when prices are included. Cooper and Nakanishi (1988) present one procedure for attempting to build asymmetries into perceptual maps.

[13] One outside influence not accounted for (except in the empirical estimates of the base levels of sales) is how brand image advertising affects consumers' perception of quality. The highly advertised national brands tend to have substantially larger market shares than the less advertised national brands within the same tier. If advertising reinforces or heightens the quality image of a national brand, it can shift the regular price indifference point leftward. Thus the brand captures a larger proportion of the consumer's relative preference distribution.

[14] Of course, one additional reason why such pricing behavior may occur is that buying and to a degree retail pricing decisions are made contemporaneously by factoring in the forward buy savings when brands are bought at reduced cost on price deals from manufacturers, and then are sold later at the regular (hence substantially higher margin) retail price.

very specific competitive structure to occur. When higher-price, higher-quality brands price deal, they steal unit sales away from other brands in their own price tier and from brands in the tier below (the moderate and private label brands). However, when lower-price, lower-quality brands deal, they draw sales from their own tier (other moderate and private label brands) and the tier below (generics), but in general do *not* take significant amounts of unit sales away from the tier above (national brands).

The specific results apply to the historical Chicagoland market. However, it is possible that the bimodal relative preference distribution holds across geographic regions. Thus, methods to determine market competition should take into account possible asymmetries in brand competition.[15] It is less clear that the regular price equilibria locations, hence the indifference points I_{ik}, will remain constant across markets. Local competitive circumstances may allow an upward shift in the price of the national brands, shifting the regular price indifference point to the right and making private labels less exposed to price promotion competition from the national brands. Future work on the supply side would also be of value in generating and equilibrium model. Further work is also required on the conditions necessary for profits to be optimized and the implication of these conditions for regular price equilibria in the market. This includes a better understanding of how to set retail and manufacturer regular and promotional price levels to maximize retailer and manufacturer profits.

Finally, this research concentrated on price-induced patterns of competition, and thus analyzed brands whose product forms, attributes, and sizes were comparable. There may also be significant own-brand size cannibalization when only one size of a given brand price deals. Thus, if the 12-ounce size deals, it may cannibalize sales of the 6-ounce and 18-ounce sizes of the same brand, due to cost-per-ounce factors for an identical (same brand formulation) product substitute. Additionally, size loyalties may exist in some markets, making switching between comparably sized brands much more likely than switching to other sizes of a competitive brand. Further work is needed to see what degree of form loyalties exist (e.g. tub versus stick margarine buyers, oil versus water tuna buyers, etc.), and/or if such loyalties can be related to price differentials caused by differing ingredients or production technologies.[16]

Acknowledgments.   This research was partially funded by the Center for Research in Marketing, by the Graduate School of Business of the University of Chicago, and by the National Science Foundation Grant SES 8421165. Our thanks are also extended to the Jewel Food Store Company and to Tom Richardson for the provision of the scanning data, to Linus Schrage, Chakravarthi Narasimhan, Ward Hanson, Steve Shugan, J. Brad Barbeau, Greg Allenby, and Sridhar Moorthy for helpful comments. The Area Editor and three anonymous reviewers also contributed valuable comments. Authors are listed alphabetically.

[15] Carpenter et al. (1988) in an article published subsequent to the research reported here propose an asymmetric attraction model for modeling asymmetric competition. Their empirical example from an Australia product category also exhibits competition of the form that lower-priced economy brands compete primarily with themselves, but have little influence on other higher-priced, higher-quality brands. Russell and Bolton (1988) also find a much greater tendency for private label brands to switch across subgroups versus national brands.

[16] This paper was received in December 1986 and has been with the authors 15 months for 3 revisions. Accepted by Subrata K. Sen.

Bibliography

Allenby, Gregory M. (1989), "A Unified Approach to Identifying, Estimating and Testing Demand Structures with Aggregate Scanner Data," Working Paper, College of Business, Ohio State University.

Batsell, Richard G. and John C. Polking (1985), "A New Class of Market Share Models," *Marketing Science*, 4, 3 (Summer), 177–188.

Blattberg, Robert C. and Kenneth J. Wisniewski (1987), "How Retail Price Promotions Work: Empirical Results," Center for Research in Marketing, Working Paper #42, University of Chicago, (December).

———— and ———— (1988), "Modeling Store Level Scanner Data," University of Chicago, Marketing Working Paper #43, (January).

Carpenter, Gregory S., Lee G. Cooper, Dominque M. Hanssens and David F. Midgley (1988), "Modeling Asymmetric Competition," *Marketing Science*, 7, 4 (Fall), 393–412.

PRICE-INDUCED PATTERNS OF COMPETITION 309

Cattin, Philippe and Dick R. Wittink (1982), "Commercial Use of Conjoint Analysis: A Survey," *Journal of Marketing*, 46, 3 (Summer), 44–53.

Cooper, Russel (1984), "On Allocative Distortions in Problems of Self-Selection," *Rand Journal of Economics*, 15, 4 (Winter), 568–577.

Cooper, Lee G. and Masao Nakanishi (1988), *Market Share Analysis*, Boston: Kluwer Academic Publishers.

Eskin, Gerald J. and Penny Baron (1977), "Effects of Price and Advertising in Test Market Experiments," *Journal of Marketing Research*, 14 (November), 499–508.

Gabor, Andre and C. W. J. Granger (1966), "Price as an Indicator of Quality: Report on an Enquiry," *Economica*, 33, 129 (February), 43–70.

Green, Paul E. (1973), *Multiattribute Decisions in Marketing*, Hindsdale, IL: The Dryden Press.

——— and Yoram Wind (1975), "New Way to Measure Consumer's Judgments," *Harvard Business Review*, (July–August), 107–117.

——— and V. Srinivasan (1978), "Conjoint Analysis in Consumer Research—Issues and Outlook," *Journal of Consumer Research*, 5, 2 (September), 103–123.

Guadagni, Peter M. and John D. C. Little (1983), "A Logit Model of Brand Choice Calibrated on Scanner Data," *Marketing Science*, 2, 3 (Summer), 203–238.

Hauser, John R. and Steven P. Gaskin (1983), "Application of the 'DEFENDER' Consumer-Model," *Marketing Science*.

——— and Steven M. Shugan (1983), "Defensive Marketing Strategies," *Marketing Science*, 2, 4 (Fall), 319–360.

——— and Patricia Simmie (1981), "Profit Maximizing Perceptual Positions," *Management Science*, 27, 1 (January), 33–56.

Johnson, Richard M. (1974), "Trade-Off Analysis of Consumer Values," *Journal of Marketing Research*, 11 (May), 121–127.

Jones, J. M. and Fred S. Zufryden (1980), "Adding Explanatory Variables to a Consumer Purchase Behavior Model: An Exploratory Study," *Journal of Marketing Research*, 17 (August), 323–334.

Kalwani, Manohar and Donald G. Morrison (1977), "A Parsimonious Description of the Hendry System," *Management Science*, 23, 467–477.

Kinberg, Yoram, Ambar G. Rao and Melvin F. Shakon (1974), "A Mathematical Model for Price Promotions," *Management Science*, 20, 6 (February), 948–959.

Lilien, Gary L. and Philip Kotler (1983), *Marketing Decision Making—A Model Building Approach*, New York: Harper and Row.

McAlister, Leigh (1985), "The Impact of Price Promotions on a Brand's Market Share, Sales Patterns, and Profitability," MIT Working Paper 1622-85, (February).

Moorthy, K. Sridhar (1984), "Market Segmentation, Self-Selection, and Product Line Design," *Marketing Science*, 3, 4 (Fall), 288–307.

Mussa, Michael and Sherwin Rosen (1978), "Monopoly and Product Quality," *Journal of Economic Theory*, 18, 301–317.

Oren, Shmuel, Stephen Smith and Robert Wilson (1984), "Product Line Pricing," *Journal of Business*, 57, 1, 2, S73–S99.

Rao, Vithala R. (1984), "Pricing Research in Marketing: The State of the Art," *Journal of Business*, 57, 1, 2 (January), S39–S64.

Reibstein, David J. and Hubert Gatignon (1984), "Optimal Product Line Pricing: The Influence of Elasticities and Cross-Elasticities," *Journal of Marketing Research*, 21 (August), 259–267.

Russell, Gary J. and Ruth N. Bolton (1988), "Implications of Market Structure for Elasticity Structure," *Journal of Marketing Research*, 25 (August), 229–241.

Shugan, Steven M. (1987), "Estimating Brand Positioning Maps Using Supermarket Scanning Data," *Journal of Marketing Research*, 24, 1 (February), 1–18.

Sunoo, Don and Y. S. Lin (1978), "Sales Effects of Promotion and Advertising," *Journal of Advertising Research*, 18, 5 (October), 37–40.

Thaler, Richard (1985), "Mental Accounting and Consumer Choice," *Marketing Science*, 4, 3 (Summer), 199–214.

Urban, Glen L. and John R. Hauser (1980), *Design and Marketing of New Products*, Englewood-Cliffs, NJ: Prentice-Hall Inc.

———, Philip L. Johnson and John R. Hauser (1984), "Testing Competitive Market Structures," *Marketing Science*, 3, 2 (Spring), 83–112.

Wilkinson, J. B., J. Barry Mason and C. H. Paksoy (1982), "Assessing the Impact of Short-Term Supermarket Strategy Variables," *Journal of Marketing Research*, 19 (February), 72–86.

Wisniewski, Kenneth J. and Robert C. Blattberg (1988), "Analysis of Consumer Response to Retail Price Dealing Strategies: A UPC-Based Approach For Modeling Deal Sales Response and Optimizing Deal Profitability," National Science Foundation Final Report Grant SES 8421165, (April).

Shrinkage Estimation of Price and Promotional Elasticities: Seemingly Unrelated Equations

ROBERT C. BLATTBERG and EDWARD I. GEORGE*

Consider the problem where a retailer or manufacturer wants to estimate product price and promotional elasticities based on supermarket scanner data. Classical linear modeling suffers from the following aggregation dilemma. Price and promotional elasticities appear to vary considerably among chains and brands so that one overall model is too restrictive. Alternatively, the use of a different model for each chain and brand leads to noisy and often nonsensical estimates of separate elasticities because of excessive data variation. To resolve this dilemma, shrinkage estimation procedures are proposed. By borrowing strength across chains and brands, these procedures reduce variability while providing flexibility that allows for separate elasticity estimates. Application of these procedures to a large data set yields not only more reasonable model estimates but also improved predictive power.

KEY WORDS: Gibbs sampler; Hierarchical Bayes; Scanner data.

1. INTRODUCTION

Both manufacturers and retailers need to be able to estimate price and promotional elasticities to make decisions about how to promote a given product and to determine the optimal price set. Prior to the last five years consumer nondurable manufacturers and grocery retailers relied on four-week warehouse withdrawal data [Sales Area Marketing Information (SAMI)] or bimonthly audit data to measure sales (Nielsen). These data masked the promotional and price effects because they were aggregated over time. With the advent of computerized point-of-sale data (scanner data) weekly sales for retail chains in local markets became available to manufacturers. Unfortunately, these more detailed data have led to numerous modeling problems.

Manufacturers would like to be able to develop models at the chain–brand level because they can send their sales force in to persuade the chain to promote their brand. (Chain refers to a chain of grocery stores and brand refers to a specific item in the store.) They want to ensure, however, that payments they make to entice the retailer to promote their brand pay out. By having a chain–brand model they can compute the incremental sales from a given promotion, allowing them to compute the profitability of the promotion. The problem is that modeling sales at the chain–brand level often leads to counterintuitive and theoretically unreasonable estimates of separate elasticities. Coefficient estimates fluctuate too much between different chain–brands, frequently having the wrong sign. For these models to have managerial relevance and to be used to aid decision makers, it is necessary to develop procedures that will improve the "reliability" of the coefficients.

The purpose of this article is to investigate the degree to which this coefficient instability can be resolved by using shrinkage estimation procedures based on hierarchical models. Such procedures offer the advantage of allowing elasticity estimates at the chain–brand level while reducing variability by exploiting coefficient similarity across equations. By application to a large data set, it is shown that such procedures can yield better model estimates than conventional ordinary least squares (OLS) estimates, with no sacrifice of forecasting power.

Hierarchical models for statistical inference were introduced in this context by Lindley and Smith (1972), although the statistical potential of such modeling was extolled as early as Good (1950). The literature in this area is now vast; an introductory survey and bibliography of hierarchical methods appears in Berger (1985). Another point of contact of this work is with the econometrics literature on pooled cross-sectional and time series data [see Dielman (1983) for an introductory survey and bibliography]. In addition to these references, a brief list of some articles that use related approaches for regression problems includes Berger and Robert (1990), Deely and Lindley (1981), DuMouchel and Harris (1983), Efron and Morris (1972), Garcia-Ferrer, Highfield, Palm, and Zellner (1987), Gelfand, Hills, Racine-Poon, and Smith (1990), Ghosh, Saleh, and Sen (1989), Highfield (1991), Hill, Cartwright, and Arbaugh (in press), Hui and Berger (1983), Morris (1983, 1986), Robert and Saleh (in press), Novick, Jackson, Thayer, and Cole (1972), Rubin (1980), Smith (1973), Swamy (1971, 1973), Tiao and Zellner (1964), Zellner (1986), Zellner and Hong (1988), and Zellner and Vandaele (1974).

This article is divided into eight parts: Section 2 describes a model of price and promotional effects; Section 3 describes the data used; Section 4 presents the results of OLS estimation and discusses some of the problems with these estimates; Section 5 describes a comprehensive hierarchical Bayes model; Section 6 motivates and develops shrinkage estimators based on the hierarchical model; Section 7 compares the performance of various estimators on actual scanner data; Section 8 concludes with a discussion of the methodology. [More elaborate and detailed support of the empirical analyses described in this article can be found in Blattberg and George (1990).]

* Robert C. Blattberg is Charles H. Kellstadt Professor of Marketing and Edward I. George is Associate Professor of Statistics, both at the Graduate School of Business, University of Chicago, Chicago, IL 60637. The authors thank Dean Foster, Yanxiu Li, Peter Rossi, George Tiao, Arnold Zellner, and anonymous referees for helpful suggestions, and Jayaram Muthuswamy for programming assistance. This research was supported by the Graduate School of Business at the University of Chicago.

2. A MODEL FOR PRICE AND PROMOTIONAL EFFECTS

In this section we describe and motivate the model for price and promotional effects that we used in our analyses. This model was specifically constructed to apply to data on supermarket sales of bathroom tissue. As will be seen, certain features of this product in this environment are relevant for our choice of model. The particular data that we used are described in more detail in Section 3.

There are many different models proposed in the marketing literature to measure price and promotional effects in this context (e.g., Blattberg and Wisniewski 1987, 1988, in press; Frank and Massy 1965; Guadagni and Little 1983; Kumar and Leone 1988). In any such reasonable model, certain variables must be included to capture these effects. A variable for the brand's price is needed. To capture promotional effects, variables that measure the following three aspects are needed: discount from regular price (deal discount), price-oriented newspaper advertising (feature advertising), and in-store display of the given brand (display). It is also necessary to model competitive effects for both price and promotions, and the trough after the deal caused by consumers delaying their next purchase because they have increased their household inventory of the product; see Blattberg, Eppen, and Lieberman (1981) and Neslin, Henderson, and Quelch (1985).

The chain–brand model used in this article is the following:

$$SL_t = \beta_1 + \beta_2 PR_t + \beta_3 DD_t + \beta_4 DD_{t-1} + \beta_5 AD_t$$

$$+ \beta_6 DP_t + \beta_7 FL_t + \beta_8 CD_t + \beta_9 SL_{t-1} + \epsilon_t, \quad (2.1)$$

where

SL_t = logarithm of sales in period t;

PR_t = relative price in period t (regular price divided by an average of competitive regular prices);

DD_t = deal discount in period t (normal shelf price minus actual divided by normal shelf price);

AD_t = feature advertising in period t (proportion of stores in chain using the ad);

DP_t = display in period t (proportion of stores in chain displaying the brand);

FL_t = 1 if period t is the final period of a multiweek deal, 0 otherwise;

CD_t = maximum deal discount for competing brands in chain in period t.   (2.2)

Specifically, price has been modeled using PR_t, a price index created by taking the price of the brand and dividing it by the prices of the competitive brands weighted by their market shares normalized so that they add to 100%. The price variable was designed to focus on the competitive effect of price. [This choice of the relative price variable was motivated by the AIDS demand model in Deaton and Muellbauer (1980).] Three variables are used to capture promotional effect: deal discount DD_t, feature advertising AD_t, and display DT_t. The competitive promotional effects were captured through the use of the variable CD_t, the maximum deal discount of the competing brands. This was a parsimonious way to model all of the competitive promotional effects. Lagged deal discount DD_{t-1} was used to model the trough after the deal. An indicator for the final week of the deal, FL_t, was incorporated into the model because retailers raise the price in the middle of the last week of the deal and so total sales for the week have both days in which a promotion was run and days in which no promotion was run. Finally, lagged sales SL_{t-1} was included to eliminate residual serial correlation.

Using various theories in marketing, it is possible to postulate the sign of the variables and their magnitudes. The coefficient of the price index PR_t should be negative (downward sloping demand curves). Deal discount DD_t, feature advertising AD_t, and display DP_t should all have a positive effect on sales. Lagged deal discount DD_{t-1} should have a negative sign because consumers stockpile when a promotion is offered, thereby reducing the next period's sales. Finally, the coefficient of competitive deals CD_t should be negative, implying that when a competitive brand promotes, the sales of the brand being analyzed should decrease.

The particular functional form of a semilog model was chosen based on prior research by Blattberg and Wisniewski (1988), which showed that a semilog model fit chain-level scanner data better than alternative models such as a log–log model or a linear model. In the discussion in Section 4, it will be seen that Model (2.1) fits the data quite well. Category price effects were not modeled because the category being studied is a low-priced stable household product with a low price elasticity. Based on other research it was felt that competitive price effects were far more important to capture.

In assessing the appropriateness of Model (2.1), one might argue that it does not directly mirror consumer demand models developed in economics. First, the semilog functional form violates the "adding up" constraint. [The adding up constraint means that the sum of all of the marginal propensities to consume (or the marginal budget shares) have to be equal to 1 at all income levels.] This is not apt to be important, however, because the model focuses on the demand for one product and is not trying to estimate the demand for multiple goods across categories. Second, the model does not control for income. However, the product being considered costs in the range of one dollar. Furthermore, since the time interval is weekly, income changes only minutely over each time interval. Even over the total period being considered, real income only changes in the range of 5%. Third, the model represents the "average" consumer and does not deal with aggregation across consumers. Most other consumer researchers have assumed away heterogeneity when aggregating. We have adopted the point of view of Houthakker and Taylor (1970, p. 200), who stated that ". . . of all the errors likely to be made in demand analysis, the aggregation error is the least troublesome."

3. THE DATA

The model given in Equation (2.1) was constructed to apply to sales, price, and promotional data on the four leading national brands of bathroom tissue from three grocery store chains in a large midwestern market, a total of 12

Journal of the American Statistical Association, June 1991

chain–brand combinations. Weekly measurements on each of the seven variables in (2.2) were obtained for 112 weeks in Chain 1, 126 weeks in Chain 2, and 110 weeks in Chain 3. The data are contemporaneous in that Week 1 of all 12 series coincides.

To get a sense of the nature of these data, Figure 1 displays time plots of the variables SL_t, PR_t, and DD_t for Chain 1, Brand 1. As is typical for each of the 12 chain–brand series, log sales SL_t exhibits high variation with many sharp peaks. Indeed, in this plot SL_t has a minimum of 6.72 [exp(6.72) $\approx$ 829 units] and a maximum of 9.80 [exp(9.80) $\approx$ 18,034 units]. Relative price PR_t is much more stable, reflecting a policy variable that is only occasionally changed. This behavior was typical of PR_t throughout Chain 1, although PR_t was varied much more throughout Chain 2 and much less throughout Chain 3. Deal discount DD_t, consists of many short-lasting spikes. As expected, these spikes seem to coincide with the peaks in the SL_t series. This was also true of the promotional series AD_t and DP_t. Unfortunately, the spikes in all three series DD_t, AD_t, and DP_t tended to occur together, making it difficult to measure the different types of promotional effects. This correlated behavior of DD_t, AD_t, and DP_t occurred in all 12 of the chain–brand data sets.

4.   OLS ESTIMATION

Most researchers working with these data bases treat each chain–brand combination as separate. Thus we set out to construct a single model to fit each of the 12 chain–brand data sets. Various functional forms in the variables in (2.2) were considered. Model (2.1) was selected because it gave the best overall results. For each of the 12 chain–brand data sets, Model (2.1) was then estimated by OLS. OLS was chosen as the benchmark because it is commonly used. Although variants such as seemingly unrelated regressions (SUR) and generalized least squares (GLS) are also used, these were not included because they added little with our data.

Table 1 gives a summary of the OLS model coefficients, their standard errors, the residual standard errors, and the adjusted R^2 values. The adjusted R^2 values are very high, ranging from .756 to .954 with a median value of .934. Such high values are attributable to the fact that promo-

tional effects, here captured by DD_t, AD_t, and DP_t, increase sales 5 to 15 times normal levels. Furthermore, the separate OLS model fits were extremely good. The linearity of Model (2.1) was supported by residual plots, and, apart from some mild "fatness in the tails" (the overall residual kurtosis was .85), the residuals appeared to be reasonably consistent with an iid normal assumption. Standard residual diagnostics showed no unusual behavior in the data. Finally, the robustness of the model fits were checked by comparing the OLS estimates against those obtained by rank regressions; see Hettmansperger (1984). For every chain–brand we found remarkable agreement between OLS estimates and rank regression estimates based on Wilcoxon scores.

The most striking drawback of the OLS coefficient estimates in Table 1 is the intermodel variability. Many of the coefficient estimates do not even have the correct signs. Indeed, of the price and promotion variables, only deal DD_t, display DP_t, and competitive deal CD_t always have the correct signs. As discussed in the introduction, price and promotion policy decisions based on these estimates would pose serious problems.

To shed some light on the sources of the extreme variation of the OLS coefficient estimates, consider the estimates of relative price PR_t. From Table 1 and the leftmost graph in Figure 2(a), one can see that the PR_t coefficients vary most in Chain 3 where their standard errors are largest and least in Chain 2 where their standard errors are smallest. Apparently, the disparity in standard errors results from the differential variation of PR_t across chains mentioned earlier. Note that, of the PR_t with the incorrect positive sign, only the one for Chain 1, Brand 1 is significantly different from 0, with a t ratio of $4.37/1.5 \approx 2.9$, which is not overwhelming.

5.   A HIERARCHICAL MODEL

A promising alternative to treating each of the chain–brand models as separate and unrelated, is to consider one large hierarchical model that links all of the parameters across chain–brands. As will be seen in the next section, estimators based on such an overall model can use ensemble information to "shrink" chain–brand estimators toward each other, thereby dampening some of the undesirable variation of the separate OLS estimates. In this section we describe such a hierarchical model that treats the parameters from the individual models of the form (2.1) as samples from a common prior distribution.

We use the following standard notation. The series of observations for chain–brand i ($i = 1, \ldots, p$) is denoted by

$$Y^i = (y^i_1, \ldots, y^i_{n_i})', \tag{5.1a}$$

where y^i_t equals log sales of chain–brand i at time t, and

$$X^i = (X^i_1, \ldots, X^i_j), \tag{5.1b}$$

$$X^i_j = (x^i_{j1}, \ldots, x^i_{jn_i})', \tag{5.1c}$$

where x^i_{jt} equals covariate j for chain–brand i at time t for $j = 1, \ldots, J$. The first covariate x^i_{1t} is set identical to 1, $x^i_{1t} \equiv 1$, to account for an intercept, and the other covariates

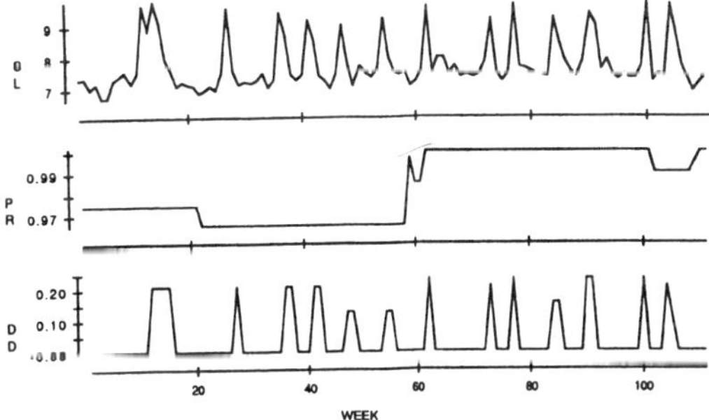

Figure 1. Raw Data for Chain 1, Brand 1.

Table 1. The 12 OLS Regressions

Chain–brand	Intercept	PR	DD	Lag DD	AD	DP	FL	CD	Lag SL	Residual standard error	Adjusted R^2
1-1	7.75	4.37	7.29	−.18	−.138	.93	−.567	−.92	.103	.203	.935
	(1.3)	(1.5)	(.67)	(.67)	(.11)	(.23)	(.13)	(.18)	(.08)		
1-2	8.28	.34	5.51	−1.47	.129	.87	.430	−.61	.139	.215	.924
	(1.4)	(1.3)	(.59)	(.71)	(.16)	(.19)	(.15)	(.19)	(.08)		
1-3	7.24	−2.57	6.20	−.47	.140	1.35	−.891	−.63	.127	.222	.933
	(.9)	(.7)	(.45)	(.60)	(.15)	(.20)	(.14)	(.20)	(.06)		
1-4	7.91	1.21	8.43	−4.38	.156	.10	−.648	−.98	.413	.216	.949
	(1.5)	(1.5)	(.76)	(.77)	(.14)	(.31)	(.24)	(.20)	(.07)		
2-1	6.04	−2.99	4.79	−1.29	.537	.77	−.40	−1.53	.264	.292	.817
	(1.0)	(.8)	(.46)	(.59)	(.14)	(.13)	(.16)	(.37)	(.08)		
2-2	7.35	−4.32	4.92	1.45	.369	.52	−.103	−.97	.102	.220	.860
	(.8)	(.4)	(.57)	(.82)	(.11)	(.11)	(.13)	(.27)	(.07)		
2-3	5.38	−3.24	2.87	−2.29	.452	1.07	.102	−.95	.413	.232	.756
	(1.0)	(.7)	(1.2)	(1.3)	(.18)	(.18)	(.19)	(.26)	(.07)		
2-4	6.89	−4.59	4.00	.90	.672	.70	.208	−.51	.149	.251	.862
	(.9)	(.6)	(.48)	(.53)	(.11)	(.11)	(.11)	(.31)	(.06)		
3-1	7.56	−17.5	6.49	−1.89	.163	.59	−.462	−1.01	.370	.186	.940
	(10.)	(10.)	(.75)	(.57)	(.16)	(.14)	(.14)	(.19)	(.07)		
3-2	7.78	8.33	2.37	−.98	.128	1.65	.023	−1.33	.206	.152	.943
	(9.1)	(9.2)	(.45)	(.43)	(.11)	(.11)	(.12)	(.16)	(.06)		
3-3	7.17	−13.7	7.19	−2.03	−.56	1.10	−.184	−1.10	.272	.199	.945
	(11.)	(11.)	(.69)	(.77)	(.12)	(.16)	(.11)	(.20)	(.07)		
3-4	8.15	−1.24	7.01	−.47	−.298	.98	−.638	−1.14	.082	.183	.954
	(3.6)	(3.5)	(.56)	(.54)	(.13)	(.14)	(.13)	(.20)	(.08)		

NOTE: Standard errors are given in parentheses.

are mean-centered (shifted to have mean 0) so that they will be uncorrelated with x^i_{1t}. For all p chain–brands, we consider the regression models

$$Y^i = X^i\beta^i + \epsilon^i, \qquad i = 1, \ldots, p; \qquad (5.2a)$$

$$\beta^i = (\beta^i_1, \ldots, \beta^i_j)' \quad \text{and} \quad \epsilon^i = (\epsilon^i_1, \ldots, \epsilon^i_{n_i})'; \qquad (5.2b)$$

$$[\epsilon^i \mid \sigma^2] \sim N_{n_i}(0, \sigma^2 I); \qquad (5.2c)$$

$$[\epsilon^1 \mid \sigma^2], \ldots, [\epsilon^p \mid \sigma^2] \quad \text{are all independent.} \qquad (5.2d)$$

The data discussed in Section 3 consist of $p = 12$ chain–brand time series each of lengths $n_i = 111$ for $i = 1, 2, 3, 4$, $n_i = 121$ for $i = 5, 6, 7, 8$, and $n_i = 109$ for $i = 9, 10,$

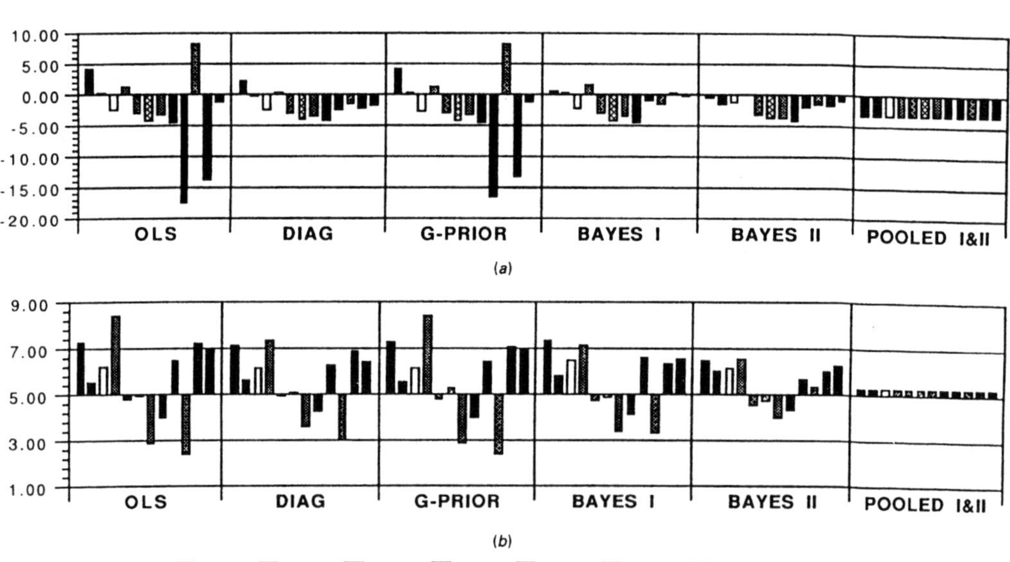

Figure 2. Shrinkage Toward the Grand Mean. (a) PR coefficient estimates. (b) DD coefficient estimates.

Journal of the American Statistical Association, June 1991

308

11, 12. Comparing (5.2) with the model in (2.1), y_t^i correspond to SL_t, and the covariates $x_{2t}^i, \ldots, x_{Jt}^i$ correspond to the eight $(J = 9)$ predictors in the model. Note that here the predictors have been mean-centered. Assumption (5.2c) was supported by a nonsignificant Bartlett's test (adjusted for kurtosis) for pooling variances; see Madansky (1988). Assumption (5.2d) was supported by low cross-correlations of the OLS residuals across the individual models. Apparently, this is an effect of including CD_t, competitive deal discount, in the models.

Reduction of (5.2) by sufficiency yields, in terms of the least squares estimators,

$$[\hat{\beta}^i \mid \beta^i, \sigma_i^2] \sim N_J(\beta^i, \sigma^2(X^{i\prime}X^i)^{-1}),$$

$$i = 1, \ldots, p \quad \text{independently}, \quad (5.3a)$$

where

$$\hat{\beta}^i = (X^{i\prime}X^i)^{-1}X^{i\prime}Y^i. \quad (5.3b)$$

If the p regression models are treated as separate and unrelated, as was done in the last section, then $\hat{\beta}^i$ carries all of the relevant information about β^i. Instead, we now consider the alternative approach of embedding the p separate models in one large hierarchical model. This model is obtained by imposing on the β^i a normal prior distribution of the form

$$[\beta^i \mid \theta^i, \Sigma] \sim N_J(\theta^i, \Sigma), \quad i = 1, \ldots, p \quad \text{independently}. \quad (5.4)$$

Combining (5.3) and (5.4), the posterior mean or Bayes rule for estimating β^i is

$$E[\beta^i \mid \hat{\beta}^i, \sigma^2, \theta^i, \Sigma] = D_i^{-1}(\sigma^{-2}X^{i\prime}X^i\hat{\beta}^i + \Sigma^{-1}\theta^i), \quad (5.5a)$$

where

$$D_i = \sigma^{-2}X^{i\prime}X^i + \Sigma^{-1}. \quad (5.5b)$$

This estimator shrinks each least squares estimate $\hat{\beta}^i$ toward the hyperparameter θ^i by a shrinkage factor $D_i^{-1}\sigma^{-2}X^{i\prime}X^i$. Note that, as the prior covariance Σ decreases, $\hat{\beta}^i$ is shrunk more toward θ^i.

Because the parameter σ^2 and the hyperparameters θ^i and Σ are not fully specified, the Bayes rule (5.5) is not an available estimator. One can consider, however, approximations of the Bayes rule that may themselves be useful estimators of β. The next section motivates several such approximations that exploit available information in the data. Such approximations are available here because the coefficient hypermeans θ^i may be meaningfully constrained. Because of the potential similarity of the β^i across chain–brands, simple constraints can be obtained by clustering the θ^i into homogenous groups, where they would plausibly be equal. As is discussed in Section 7.1, we considered three constraints: that the θ^i were equal overall, were equal across brands, and were equal across chains. Note that for such groupings to be meaningful, the variables in the model must be in comparable units across chain–brands. For example, the variables AD_t and DP_t were defined in units of proportion for just this reason. Furthermore, the choice of SL_t to be in units of log sales enables us to combine the overall effects in different chain–brands even when sales levels differ.

Stacking the vectors into one $pJ \times 1$ vector

$$\theta \equiv \text{vec}(\theta^1, \ldots, \theta^p), \quad (5.6)$$

these constraints can be written in the standard notation for a general linear model as

$$\theta = W\gamma, \quad (5.7)$$

where W is a $pJ \times K$ vector of 0s and 1s and γ is a $K \times 1$ vector of unknown coefficients. For example, the constraint of making the θ^i equal overall corresponds to the case $K = pJ$, with W consisting of stacked identity matrices. This case was considered by Lindley and Smith (1972) who referred to the situation as exchangeability between multiple regression equations. Note that by stacking the β^i's into one vector,

$$\beta \equiv \text{vec}(\beta^1, \ldots, \beta^p), \quad (5.8)$$

(5.4) combined with (5.7) can be summarized as

$$(\beta \mid \gamma, \Sigma) \sim N_{pJ}(W\gamma, \Sigma_*), \quad (5.9a)$$

where

$$\Sigma_* \equiv \text{diag}[\Sigma, \ldots, \Sigma]. \quad (5.9b)$$

6. SHRINKAGE ESTIMATORS

In this section the hierarchical model from the previous section is exploited to obtain estimators that are approximations of the Bayes rule (5.5). Four estimators are considered, two that are motivated by empirical Bayes considerations and two that are motivated by hierarchical Bayes considerations.

We begin by describing the empirical Bayes estimators. These use frequentist justifications to estimate the unknown σ^2, θ^i, and Σ in (5.5). Applying sufficiency considerations to the initial regression models in (5.2), the variance σ^2 may reasonably be estimated by

$$s^2 = \sum_{i=1}^{p} \|Y^i - X^i\hat{\beta}^i\|^2/(n - pJ + 2), \quad n = \sum_{1}^{p} n_i, \quad (6.1)$$

the best scale-invariant estimator of σ^2. This estimator has typically been used in shrinkage estimators to obtain desirable risk properties; see Ghosh, Saleh, and Sen (1989) and Stein (1966).

Estimates of θ^i and Σ can be based on the marginal or predictive distribution of the data, which are obtained by combining (5.3) and (5.9) and integrating out $\beta \equiv \text{vec}(\beta^1, \ldots, \beta^p)$. In terms of the stacked OLS estimates

$$\hat{\beta} = \text{vec}(\hat{\beta}^1, \ldots, \hat{\beta}^p), \quad (6.2a)$$

this marginal distribution is

$$[\hat{\beta} \mid \gamma, V] \sim N_{pJ}(W\gamma, V), \quad (6.2b)$$

where V is the $pJ \times pJ$ block diagonal matrix

$$V = \text{diag}[(\sigma^2(X^{1\prime}X^1)^{-1} + \Sigma), \ldots, (\sigma^2(X^{p\prime}X^p)^{-1} + \Sigma)]. \quad (6.2c)$$

For known V, based on (6.2), the GLS estimate as well as

the maximum likelihood estimate of $\theta\ (= W\gamma)$ is

$$\hat{\theta} = W(W'V^{-1}W)^{-1}W'V^{-1}\hat{\beta}. \qquad (6.3)$$

In conjunction with a reasonable estimator of V, (6.3) should yield useful empirical Bayes approximations of (5.5). Unfortunately, because $p = 12$ is not much larger than $J = 9$ in our problem, both the maximum likelihood and method-of-moments estimators for V are unreliable. Indeed, the resulting estimates we obtained were not even positive definite. Rather than abandon exploitation of the marginal distribution (6.2), we considered imposing constraints on Σ to reduce the number of hyperparameters that had to be estimated. Two such constraints were considered.

The first constraint was to assume that Σ was diagonal, $\Sigma \equiv \mathrm{diag}(a_1, \ldots, a_J)$, so that $a_1, \ldots, a_J$ become the unknown variance hyperparameters to be estimated. This constraint would correspond to the assumption of no prior "covariation" across the coefficients and would perform well if the "true" coefficients tended to be less correlated than OLS coefficients. For this case, we considered the truncated moment estimator

$$\hat{\Sigma}^D \equiv \mathrm{diag}(\hat{a}_1^+, \ldots, \hat{a}_J^+),$$

where $\hat{a}_j^+ = \max\{0, \hat{a}_j\}$,

$$\hat{a}_j = \sum_{i=1}^{p} [(\hat{\beta}_j^i - \theta_j^i)^2 - s^2(X^{i\prime}X^i)_{jj}^{-1}]/(p - q_j),$$
$$j = 1, \ldots, J, \qquad (6.4)$$

where $\hat{\beta}_j^i$ and θ_j^i are the jth components of $\hat{\beta}^i$ and θ^i, respectively, $(X^{i\prime}X^i)_{jj}^{-1}$ denotes the jth diagonal element of $(X^{i\prime}X^i)^{-1}$, and q_j is the number of groupings used to constrain the jth coefficient. A related empirical Bayes variance estimate is used in a shrinkage estimator proposed by Morris (1986).

Using $\hat{\Sigma}^D$ in conjunction with the GLS estimator for θ, we obtain

$$\hat{\theta}^D = W(W'(\hat{V}^D)^{-1}W)^{-1}W'(\hat{V}^D)^{-1}\hat{\beta}, \qquad (6.5)$$

where V^D is the $pJ \times pJ$ block-diagonal matrix with diagonal entries $[s^2(X^{i\prime}X^i)^{-1} + \hat{\Sigma}^D]$. Note that θ_j^i in (6.4) must be replaced by $(\hat{\theta}_j^D)^i$ in (6.5) so that $\hat{\theta}^D$ and $\hat{\Sigma}^D$ must be solved iteratively. (Starting with $\hat{\Sigma}^D = 0$, at most 10 iterations were required for convergence on our data.) Inserting the estimates s^2, $\hat{\theta}^D$, and $\hat{\Sigma}^D$ into (5.5), we obtain the empirical Bayes estimator $\hat{\beta}^D$, where

$$(\hat{\beta}^D)^i = (s^{-2}X^{i\prime}X^i + (\hat{\Sigma}^D)^{-1})^{-1}(s^{-2}X^{i\prime}X^i\hat{\beta}^i + (\hat{\Sigma}^D)^{-1}(\theta^D)^i).$$
$$(6.6)$$

This estimator bears a strong resemblance to a ridge regression estimator, where $\hat{\Sigma}^D$ would be replaced by a matrix proportional to I. $\hat{\beta}^D$ can be considered a "generalized" ridge estimator; see Vinod and Ullah (1981).

The second constraint on Σ we considered consisted of replacing the prior covariance in $[\beta^i \mid \theta^i, \Sigma] \sim N_J(\theta^i, \Sigma)$ in (5.4) by the distinct covariances $[\beta^i \mid \theta^i, \tau_i^2] \sim N_J(\theta^i, \tau_i^2(X^{i\prime}X^i)^{-1})$. Here $\tau_1^2, \ldots, \tau_p^2$ become the unknown variance hyperparameters to be estimated. This prior formulation, sometimes known as the g-prior, has been advocated in the literature because it is tractable and yields estimators with

some desirable sampling theory properties; see Zellner (1986), Ghosh et al. (1988), and Robert and Saleh (in press). This constraint would do well if the "true" coefficients tended to manifest the same correlation as the OLS estimates, quite the opposite of the previous diagonal case. In this case, each τ_i^2 can be estimated by the truncated moment estimator

$$\hat{\tau}_i^2 = \max\{0, [\|X^i\hat{\beta}^i - X^i(\theta^G)^i\|^2/(J - 1) - s^2]\}, \qquad (6.7a)$$

yielding

$$\hat{\theta}^G = W(W'(\hat{V}^G)^{-1}W)^{-1}W'(\hat{V}^G)^{-1}\hat{\beta}, \qquad (6.7b)$$

where V^G is the $pJ \times pJ$ block-diagonal matrix with diagonal entries $[(s^2 + \hat{\tau}_i^2)(X^{i\prime}X^i)^{-1}]$. Because $\hat{\theta}^G$ depends on the estimates $(s^2 + \hat{\tau}_i^2)$, (6.7) must be solved by iteration. (Starting with $\hat{\tau}_1^2 = \cdots = \hat{\tau}_p^2 = 0$, at most 10 iterations were required for convergence on our data.) By inserting the estimates s^2, $\hat{\theta}^G$, and $\hat{\tau}_i^2(X^{i\prime}X^i)^{-1}$ into (5.5), we obtain the empirical Bayes estimator $\hat{\beta}^G$, where

$$(\hat{\beta}^G)^i = (s^{-2} + \hat{\tau}_i^{-2})^{-1}(s^{-2}\hat{\beta}^i + \hat{\tau}_i^{-2}(\theta^G)^i). \qquad (6.8)$$

Alternatives to the empirical Bayes estimators are provided by the hierarchical Bayes estimators advocated by Lindley and Smith (1972) and Smith (1973). Rather than plug estimates for σ^2, θ^i, and Σ into (5.5), these can instead be integrated out using the following inverse gamma–normal–Wishart prior where σ^2, θ, Σ are independent,

$$\sigma^2 \sim IG(\nu/2, \nu\lambda/2),$$
$$\theta = W\gamma, \quad \text{with} \quad \gamma \sim N_K(\eta, Y),$$
$$\Sigma^{-1} \sim W_J((\rho R)^{-1}, \rho). \qquad (6.9)$$

$[\sigma^2 \sim IG(\nu/2, \nu\lambda/2)$ is equivalent to $\nu\lambda/\sigma^2 \sim \chi_\nu^2$, and $W_J((\rho R)^{-1}, \rho)$ is the J-dimensional Wishart distribution with mean $(\rho R)^{-1}$ and ρ df.] A hierarchical Bayes estimator of β^i can then be obtained as the posterior mean

$$(\hat{\beta}^B)^i = E(\beta^i \mid \hat{\beta}^i, \nu, \lambda, \eta, Y, \rho, R). \qquad (6.10)$$

We considered two special cases of (6.10), which we denote by $\hat{\beta}^{B1}$ and $\hat{\beta}^{B2}$. Letting

$$\nu = 0, \quad Y^{-1} = 0,$$
$$R = \mathrm{diag}[.0001, (.0001)v_2, \ldots, (.0001)v_J], \qquad (6.11)$$

where v_j is the variance of the covariate X_j^i in (5.1c), $\hat{\beta}^{B1}$ is obtained when $\rho = 2$, and $\hat{\beta}^{B2}$ is obtained when $\rho = 12$. [The terms v_j in R were included to remove dependence on scaling. The choice of λ and η in (6.10) is irrelevant under (6.11).] The prior for $\hat{\beta}^{B1}$ was chosen to be vague with respect to the information provided by the data; see Lindley and Smith (1972), Smith (1973), and Gelfand et al. (1990). The prior for $\hat{\beta}^{B2}$ is similar except that the prior information about Σ is increased to be as strong as the information provided by the data ($\rho = p = 12$). As will be seen in the next section, compared with $\hat{\beta}^{B1}$, $\hat{\beta}^{B2}$ puts more weight on the prior model, causing the estimator to "shrink" more. The added prior weight in $\hat{\beta}^{B2}$ would be appropriate if the OLS coefficient standard errors were understated, a typical consequence of overfitting where model error has not been accounted for. Although the estimators $\hat{\beta}^{B1}$ and $\hat{\beta}^{B2}$ require the precise input of a prior distribution, they have the advantage of not requiring a constraint on the form of Σ and so may do well over a wide variety of ensembles of the "true" coefficients.

Exact calculation of $\hat{\beta}^{B1}$ and $\hat{\beta}^{B2}$ is not feasible. For practical purposes, however, these can be successfully approximated using the Gibbs sampling approach advocated by Gelfand and Smith (1990) and Gelfand et al. (1989). Effectively, this procedure consists of repeated sampling from a close approximation to the distribution of $[\beta^i \mid \hat{\beta}^i, \nu, \lambda, \eta, Y, \rho, R]$ and then using the average of these samples. More precisely, the approximation of $(\hat{\beta}^B)^i$ in (6.10) is obtained as follows:

1. For $m = 1, \ldots, M$ repeat Steps 2–4.
2. Initialize the values of β and Σ.
3. Repeat Steps a–d in order K times.
   (a) Sample θ conditional on the most recent values of β and Σ using

   $$[\theta \mid \hat{\beta}, \beta, \sigma^2, \Sigma] \sim N_{pJ}[\bar{\theta}, W(W'\Sigma_*^{-1}W)^{-1}W'],$$

   $$\Sigma_* = \text{diag}[\Sigma, \ldots, \Sigma],$$

   $$\bar{\theta} = W(W'\Sigma_*^{-1}W)^{-1}W'\Sigma_*^{-1}\beta.$$

   (b) Sample σ^2 conditional on the most recent value of β using

   $$[\sigma^2 \mid \hat{\beta}, \beta, \theta, \Sigma] \sim IG[n/2, [\|Y^i - X^i\beta^i\|^2/2].$$

   (c) Sample Σ^{-1} conditional on the most recent values of β and θ using

   $$[\Sigma^{-1} \mid \hat{\beta}, \beta, \sigma^2, \theta]$$

   $$\sim W_J\left[\left[\sum_{i=1}^{p}(\beta^i - \theta^i)(\beta^i - \theta^i)' + \rho R\right]^{-1}, p + \rho\right].$$

   (d) Sample β conditional on the most recent values of σ^2, θ, and Σ using

   $$[\beta^i \mid \hat{\beta}, \sigma^2, \theta, \Sigma]$$

   $$\sim N_J[D_i^{-1}(\sigma^{-2}X^{i\prime}X^i\hat{\beta}^i + \Sigma^{-1}\theta^i), D_i^{-1}],$$

   $$D_i = \sigma^{-2}X^{i\prime}X^i + \Sigma^{-1}.$$

4. Let $\hat{\beta}_m^i$ be the most recent value of $D_i^{-1} \times (\sigma^{-2}X^{i\prime}X^i\hat{\beta}^i + \Sigma^{-1}\theta^i)$ in Step d.
5. Approximate $(\hat{\beta}^B)^i$ by $1/M \sum_{m=1}^{M}\hat{\beta}_m^i$.

Note that each sampled observation $\hat{\beta}_m^i$ in Step 4 is obtained as the final observation in a fixed number of iterations in Step 3 of a scheme of sampling from the full conditional distributions under (6.9) using (6.11). The essence of this approach is that the distribution of $\hat{\beta}_m^i$ converges to that of $[\beta^i \mid \hat{\beta}^i, \nu, \lambda, \eta, Y, \rho, R]$ as $K \to \infty$.

Using $K = 35$ iterations and $M = 50$ repetitions seemed to yield stable approximations of $\hat{\beta}^{B1}$ and $\hat{\beta}^{B2}$. This was also the experience of Gelfand et al. (1990) on a similar problem. For initial values in Step 2, we began with $\beta = \hat{\beta}$ and $\Sigma = I$ and thereafter used the last values of the previous iteration.

7. PERFORMANCE RESULTS

7.1 The Estimators Considered

This section reports the performance on the data described in Section 3 of the four shrinkage estimators $\hat{\beta}^B$,

$\hat{\beta}^G$, $\hat{\beta}^{B1}$, and $\hat{\beta}^{B2}$. Three constraints on the coefficient hypermeans θ^i were considered: (a) equal θ^i across all 12 chain–brand combinations, (b) equal θ^i within brands, and (c) equal θ^i within chains. The effect of these constraints is to cause the estimators to shrink the OLS estimates to a grand mean in Case (a), to their respective brand means in Case (b), and to their respective chain means in Case (c).

In selecting these constraints, our underlying goal was to partition the models into homogeneous groups where the coefficients would be most similar. For example, Chain 2 is an "everyday low price" chain, whereas Chains 1 and 3 price higher but offer more frequent price promotions. Thus, if consumers selected chains on the basis of their pricing policy (which seems likely), one would expect price and promotion coefficients to be similar within chains. This would support the choice of constraint (c). On the other hand, manufacturers set prices and offer promotions to retailers. Brands are advertised differently and in some cases have unique attributes. Most manufacturers would believe that there should be different price and promotional effects by brand and so would support the choice of constraint (b). The retail prices and deal discounts, however, are often similar within chains. Therefore, it is not clear whether brand differences would be as pronounced as chain differences. Finally, we included constraint (a) to allow for the possibility that overall similarity was unaffected by distinctions based on chain or brand.

An alternative to a priori selection of the constraints would be to base selection on the data. The simplest such approach might be to look for clusters of the OLS estimates. A casual inspection of the coefficients in Table 1 and low dimensional plots such as Figure 3 suggest that the OLS coefficients cluster into similar groups within chains. Such conclusions can be deceptive, however, because of the asymmetric covariance among all of the coefficients. Another approach we considered was to pool all of the data and use formal model-building criteria such as stepwise regression or Mallow's C_p to select the best constraints. Un-

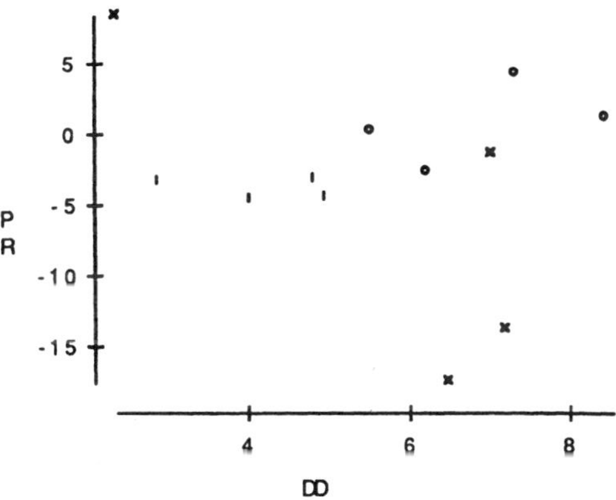

Figure 3. PR Versus DD OLS Coefficients. Chain 1 is denoted by O, Chain 2 is denoted by |, and Chain 3 is denoted by ×.

fortunately, every such criterion favored the saturated model with no constraints.

The performance of $\hat{\beta}^D$, $\hat{\beta}^G$, $\hat{\beta}^{B1}$, and $\hat{\beta}^{B2}$ is compared not only with that of the OLS estimator $\hat{\beta}$, but also with that of two classical pooled estimators

$$\beta^{P1} = W(W'(V^P)^{-1}W)^{-1}W'(V^P)^{-1}\hat{\beta} \qquad (7.1)$$

and

$$\beta^{P2} = U(U'(V^P)^{-1}U)^{-1}U'(V^P)^{-1}\hat{\beta}, \qquad (7.2)$$

where W is the matrix used to constrain the elements of θ in (5.7), U is the matrix that imposes exactly the same constraints as W except the intercept hypermeans are unconstrained, and V^P is the $pJ \times pJ$ block-diagonal matrix with diagonal entries $[(X^{i\prime}X^i)^{-1}]$. In contrast to the empirical Bayes estimators, the pooled estimators impose the constraints directly on the least squares estimates. $\hat{\beta}^{P1}$ forces all of the coefficients to be equal across the groupings. $\hat{\beta}^{P2}$ is identical to $\hat{\beta}^{P1}$ except for the intercept estimates, which are the same as the OLS estimates. Although $\hat{\beta}^{P1}$ corresponds to the same constraints used by the shrinkage estimators, $\hat{\beta}^{P2}$ is probably the more sensible pooled estimator for this problem because sales levels are apt to differ.

7.2 The Coefficient Estimates

The estimates obtained by the shrinkage estimators $\hat{\beta}^D$, $\hat{\beta}^G$, $\hat{\beta}^{B1}$, and $\hat{\beta}^{B2}$ are presented in Tables 2 and 3 for the coefficients of PR_t and DD_t. Similar results were obtained for the other coefficients, although the shrinkage effect was not always as pronounced. To illustrate an overall shrinkage effect on all of the coefficients, Table 4 presents the entire set of estimates obtained by $\hat{\beta}^{B2}$ shrinking toward the grand mean.

Compared with OLS, $\hat{\beta}^D$ and $\hat{\beta}^{B2}$ are providing substantial shrinkage with $\hat{\beta}^{B1}$ shrinking slightly less. By contrast, $\hat{\beta}^G$ is not providing very much shrinkage, yielding estimates similar to OLS. Examples of the different shrinkage patterns are illustrated in Figure 2, which compares some of the estimates that shrink to the grand mean under constraint (a). Note how the estimators adaptively apply more shrinkage to the less stable OLS estimates. An important consequence of this shrinkage is that it provides estimates that vary much less across chain–brands. In terms of the effect of the constraints, slightly less shrinkage was obtained by shrinking toward brand means under constraint

Table 2. PR_t Coefficients

Chain–brand	OLS	Diag	g-Prior	Bayes I	Bayes II	Pooled
			Target: Grand Mean			
1-1	4.37	2.36	4.22	.44	−.59	−3.29
1-2	.34	−.19	.32	.32	−1.45	−3.29
1-3	−2.57	−2.44	−2.64	−2.16	−1.32	−3.29
1-4	1.21	.29	1.16	1.46	−.13	−3.29
2-1	−2.99	−2.97	−2.99	−3.07	−3.30	−3.29
2-2	−4.32	−3.99	−4.20	−4.14	−3.67	−3.29
2-3	−3.24	−3.48	−3.24	−3.52	−3.66	−3.29
2-4	−4.59	−4.37	−4.58	−4.56	−4.20	−3.29
3-1	−17.45	−2.48	−16.54	−.92	−1.91	−3.29
3-2	8.33	−1.52	8.12	−1.41	−1.59	−3.29
3-3	−13.66	−2.29	−13.17	.18	−1.64	−3.29
3-4	−1.24	−1.81	−1.25	−.35	−.91	−3.29
			Target: Brand Means			
1-1	4.37	2.91	3.97	1.06	.97	−1.50
1-2	.34	−.06	.30	−.33	−1.44	−3.34
1-3	−2.57	−2.40	−2.57	−2.25	−1.53	−3.35
1-4	1.21	.56	1.02	.15	−.98	−3.78
2-1	−2.99	−2.91	−2.99	−2.99	−2.52	−1.50
2-2	−4.32	−4.13	−4.29	−3.81	−3.82	−3.34
2-3	−3.24	−3.49	−3.24	−4.23	−4.48	−3.35
2-4	−4.59	−4.42	−4.57	−4.19	−4.05	−3.78
3-1	−17.45	−1.48	−.16	−1.49	.53	−1.50
3-2	8.33	−1.16	−2.64	1.06	−2.75	−3.34
3-3	−13.66	−3.55	−2.59	−3.69	−1.07	−3.35
3-4	−1.24	−1.82	−1.15	−.56	−1.13	−3.78
			Target: Chain Means			
1-1	4.37	−.08	3.49	.63	−.25	−1.00
1-2	.34	−.42	.37	.27	−.18	−1.00
1-3	−2.57	−1.35	−2.51	−1.87	−.98	−1.00
1-4	1.21	−.35	1.41	1.52	−.09	−1.00
2-1	−2.99	−3.47	−3.00	−3.17	−3.48	−3.65
2-2	−4.32	−4.03	−4.31	−4.19	−4.16	−3.65
2-3	−3.24	−3.76	−3.24	−3.53	−3.59	−3.65
2-4	−4.59	−4.23	−4.58	−4.49	−4.17	−3.65
3-1	−17.45	−2.97	−14.64	−.12	−1.61	−2.16
3-2	8.33	−2.92	7.25	−2.35	−1.94	−2.16
3-3	−13.66	−2.96	−13.68	−.41	−1.38	−2.16
3-4	−1.24	−2.91	−1.37	−.90	−1.85	−2.16

Journal of the American Statistical Association, June 1991

Table 3. DD_t Coefficients

Chain—brand	OLS	Diag	g-Prior	Bayes I	Bayes II	Pooled
			Target: Grand Mean			
1-1	7.29	7.13	7.26	7.36	6.46	5.28
1-2	5.51	5.60	5.50	5.81	5.98	5.28
1-3	6.20	6.13	6.16	6.46	6.13	5.28
1-4	8.43	7.31	8.40	7.13	6.56	5.28
2-1	4.80	4.91	4.80	4.71	4.55	5.28
2-2	4.92	5.05	5.24	4.87	4.71	5.28
2-3	2.88	3.63	2.88	3.38	4.02	5.28
2-4	4.00	4.24	4.02	4.16	4.36	5.28
3-1	6.49	6.27	6.40	6.57	5.70	5.28
3-2	2.37	3.01	2.42	3.33	5.32	5.28
3-3	7.19	6.87	7.09	6.31	5.99	5.28
3-4	7.01	6.40	7.00	6.54	6.24	5.28
			Target: Brand Means			
1-1	7.29	7.32	7.27	7.20	7.69	5.82
1-2	5.51	5.44	5.47	5.47	5.80	4.49
1-3	6.20	6.11	6.28	6.37	6.36	6.12
1-4	8.43	7.52	8.02	7.33	6.57	5.40
2-1	4.80	4.91	4.80	4.78	4.47	5.82
2-2	4.92	4.89	4.89	4.63	4.03	4.49
2-3	2.88	3.68	2.88	3.78	3.05	6.12
2-4	4.00	4.24	4.01	4.35	4.33	5.40
3-1	6.49	6.46	7.07	7.19	7.36	5.82
3-2	2.37	2.77	2.45	2.88	4.10	4.49
3-3	7.19	6.81	6.87	6.98	6.76	6.12
3-4	7.01	6.66	7.05	6.54	6.60	5.40
			Target: Chain Means			
1-1	7.29	7.44	7.31	7.72	6.70	6.53
1-2	5.51	5.92	5.53	5.65	6.40	6.53
1-3	6.20	6.34	6.21	6.27	6.33	6.53
1-4	8.43	7.45	8.33	7.70	6.85	6.53
2-1	4.80	4.79	4.79	4.68	4.59	4.27
2-2	4.92	4.41	4.92	4.60	4.11	4.27
2-3	2.88	2.91	2.89	3.69	4.19	4.27
2-4	4.00	4.32	4.01	4.09	4.23	4.27
3-1	6.49	6.68	6.21	6.99	5.55	4.96
3-2	2.37	3.37	2.55	3.16	4.91	4.96
3-3	7.19	6.91	7.18	6.40	5.79	4.96
3-4	7.01	6.19	7.00	6.42	5.64	4.96

(b). Figure 4 highlights some of these comparisons on the PR_t coefficient estimates obtained by $\hat{\beta}^D$ and $\hat{\beta}^{B2}$.

It also appears that some of these shrinkage estimators are providing much more "reasonable" coefficient estimates than OLS. For example, in looking at the signs of the coefficients, when shrinking toward the grand mean $\hat{\beta}^{B2}$ yielded the correct sign most of the time, being incorrect only when the estimates were very close to 0. This is far more desirable than OLS. In the case of the relative price PR_t coefficients, OLS obtained only 8 out of 12 correct signs, and two of the negative OLS estimates were extremely large. If taken seriously, these estimates would lead to absurd pricing policies. In contrast, $\hat{\beta}^{B2}$ shrinking toward the grand mean yielded correct signs in all 12 models and

Table 4. Bayes II Coefficients

Chain brand	Intercept	PR	DD	Lag DD	AD	DP	FL	CD	Lag SL
				Target: Grand Mean					
1-1	7.75	−.59	6.46	−1.69	−.089	1.08	−.510	−.92	.236
1-2	8.20	−1.15	5.98	−.98	.010	.87	−.018	−.79	.147
1-3	7.24	−1.32	6.13	−1.81	.090	1.18	−.616	−.82	.260
1-4	7.91	−.13	6.56	−2.25	−.153	1.11	−.579	−.95	.228
2-1	6.05	−3.30	4.55	−1.27	.502	.87	−.089	−1.19	.296
2-2	7.36	−3.67	4.71	−.00	.352	.64	.052	−.96	.169
2-3	5.30	3.66	1.02	−1.54	.594	.98	.006	−1.08	.359
2-4	6.89	−4.20	4.36	.13	.555	.68	.213	−.86	.191
3-1	7.56	−1.91	5.70	−1.06	.111	.89	−.258	−.96	.213
3-2	7.78	−1.59	5.32	−1.24	.024	1.01	.316	1.02	.100
3-3	7.17	−1.64	5.99	−1.56	.145	1.05	−.114	−1.00	.256
3-4	8.15	−.91	6.24	−1.34	−.113	1.00	−.478	−.94	.187

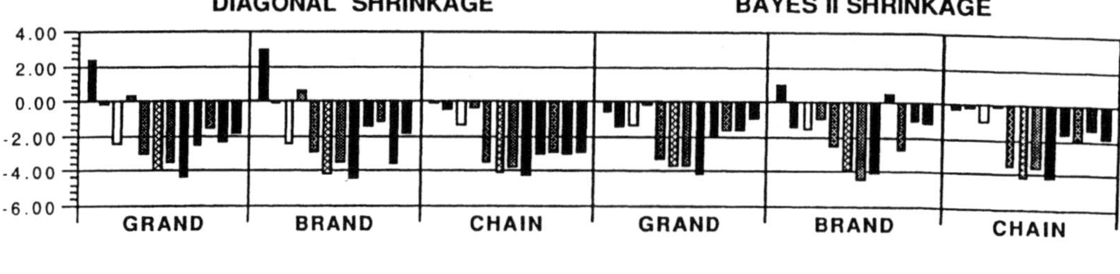

Figure 4. Target Comparisons on PR Coefficients.

greatly diminished the size of the extreme coefficients. For the deal discount DD_t coefficient, the problem is not wrong sign but deal magnitude. Here, too, the reduction in variation provided by $\hat{\beta}^{B2}$ shrinking toward the grand mean also led to better estimates. For example, by using the OLS estimate of 2.37 in Chain 3, Brand 2, a retailer would be offering very small discounts, much less than one usually sees in practice. Thus the OLS estimates would suggest actions that run counter to those used by most retailers. The estimates provided by $\hat{\beta}^{B2}$ shrinking toward the grand mean are much more in accord with typical managerial actions.

It is also useful to compare in Tables 2 and 3 the estimates obtained by $\hat{\beta}^D$, $\hat{\beta}^G$, $\hat{\beta}^{B1}$, $\hat{\beta}^{B2}$ with those obtained by the pooled estimator $\hat{\beta}^{P1}$(equals $\hat{\beta}^{P2}$ for PR_t and DD_t). It is interesting to note that all of the shrinkage estimators adaptively avoided shrinking the intercept coefficients and so behaved more like $\hat{\beta}^{P2}$ than $\hat{\beta}^{P1}$. By definition the pooled estimators yield more stable estimates than any of the other estimators, but what is impressive is that the correct sign was obtained most of the time, missing only when the estimate was very close to 0. Although the pooled estimator is not identical to the targets of any of our shrinkage estimators, it will probably be close. Good performance by pooled estimators signals strong potential for shrinkage estimation with a similar target. In some circumstances it may be better to use a standard Bayesian framework in which the mean of the prior distribution forces the estimators to have the correct signs and magnitudes. Unfortunately, no theory exists to tell us the appropriate magnitudes for the coefficients.

7.3   Mean Squared Error Comparisons

To evaluate the predictive performance of the various estimators, their predictive mean squared error (MSE) was calculated on a number of holdout samples. It was especially important to use holdout samples for comparison with OLS, since by definition OLS cannot be dominated in terms of in-sample MSE. For each of the holdout samples described subsequently, the nonholdout sample data were used to obtain estimates and the holdout sample was used to calculate MSE. It is important to emphasize that our main goal in using the shrinkage estimators was to obtain more reasonable coefficient estimates than those provided by OLS,

not to improve upon its predictive power, which is more than adequate. Our reason for predictive evaluation was to measure the cost of getting less variable estimates. Thus we viewed any predictive improvement obtained over OLS as a "windfall profit" for shrinkage estimation.

Three holdout samples of the data were considered: the final 10%, the middle 20%, and a randomly selected 20%. Because these models would be used to make policy decisions that would not be changed weekly, we were more interested in performance on the final 10% and middle 20% holdout samples, which contained long blocks of contiguous observations. Performance on these samples is a measure of long-range prediction. The random 20% holdout sample was considered for comparison because it is a natural alternative. Note that most points in this sample are adjacent to points that are not held out and used for estimation. Thus performance on this sample is more a measure of short-range prediction.

Table 5 presents the MSE performance of the six estimators, $\hat{\beta}^D$, $\hat{\beta}^G$, $\hat{\beta}^{B1}$, $\hat{\beta}^{B2}$, $\hat{\beta}^{P1}$, and $\hat{\beta}^{P2}$ relative to OLS on the holdout samples described previously and on the entire sample. Each entry is the ratio of estimator MSE to OLS MSE, so a value less than 1 indicates improvement over OLS. Note that the last row in every cell is at least 1 because OLS offers the smallest MSE over the entire sample.

In terms of long-range predictive performance (the final 10% and middle 20% holdout samples), $\hat{\beta}^{B2}$ provided the strongest improvement over OLS. This is impressive in view of the fact that $\hat{\beta}^{B2}$ also provided so much shrinkage and such reasonable estimates. Both $\hat{\beta}^D$ and $\hat{\beta}^{B1}$ also improved over OLS on these holdout samples, although the improvement was not as consistent as that of $\hat{\beta}^{B2}$. In terms of short-range prediction (the random 20% holdout sample), $\hat{\beta}^D$ provided the strongest improvement over OLS. Here, both $\hat{\beta}^{B1}$ and $\hat{\beta}^{B2}$ were worse than OLS, though not terribly so. Although the estimator $\hat{\beta}^G$ provided slight improvement over OLS, this was less interesting because the estimates were so close to OLS.

In terms of the pooled estimators, the performance of $\hat{\beta}^{P1}$ is terrible. The performance of $\hat{\beta}^{P2}$ is vastly better, illustrating how critical it is to leave the intercept coefficients unconstrained in this analysis, a feature that the shrinkage estimators provided automatically. However, $\hat{\beta}^{P2}$ was

Table 5. MSE Relative to OLS

	All	Brands	Chains
Diagonal	.966	.975	.994
	.959	.993	.925
	.977	.986	.970
	1.02	1.02	1.04
g-Prior	1.03	.987	.983
	.993	1.00	.986
	1.00	1.00	.994
	1.00	1.01	1.00
Bayes I	.962	1.00	.994
	.984	.945	.940
	1.03	1.04	1.01
	1.05	1.04	1.03
Bayes II	.962	.942	.968
	.945	.934	.932
	1.06	1.05	1.03
	1.05	1.08	1.09
Pooled I	10.7	6.86	4.97
	12.3	9.06	5.47
	14.6	9.49	6.28
	17.2	11.7	7.98
Pooled II	1.17	1.07	1.05
	1.02	1.04	.964
	1.20	1.16	1.11
	1.43	1.33	1.27

NOTE: Within each cell: Row 1 = final 10% holdout sample, OLS MSE = .0718; row 2 = middle 20% holdout sample, OLS MSE = .0608; row 3 = random 20% holdout sample, OLS MSE = .0610; row 4 = complete sample, OLS MSE = .0441.

dominated by OLS in terms of predictive performance, in every case but one, where it is dominated by $\hat{\beta}^D$, $\hat{\beta}^{B1}$, and $\hat{\beta}^{B2}$. Apparently, this is the cost of not allowing for any chain–brand coefficient variation.

7.4 Implications of This Analysis

For marketers, the results of the analysis just described raise a number of interesting issues. Consider the estimates in Table 4, obtained by $\hat{\beta}^{B2}$ shrinking toward the grand mean, one of the most successful estimators. First, it is clear that display is far more important than feature advertising. The marketing manager can use this information to design promotional activity and to focus the sales force on the importance of receiving displays. Second, the price effect and the deal effect are inversely correlated. Chain 2, which is an everyday low price chain, has higher price effects but lower deal responsiveness than the other two chains, which promote regularly. The reason is that the customers of Chain 2 are less deal-oriented but shop there because it gives better "everyday" prices. The model shows this effect clearly. Third, the competitive deal effect is almost identical for all of the brands. This implies that all brands lose about the same proportion of sales when a competitor promotes. This is an important finding for the retailer because they can then determine the optimal deal discount for a brand knowing that the sales loss due to cannibalization is approximately the same percentage of sales no matter which brand is promoted. Since margins are not identical for each brand, the retailer may be able to find certain brands to promote to intentionally steal sales from low margin brands in the category.

In summary, the results of these models indicate how price and promotion policy affects retail sales. The retailer can use this to set price and promotions. The manufacturer can use this to direct its promotional activity and sales force. The shrinkage estimators, by reducing variability, have provided far more believable estimates. Without "sensible" model results, managers will not use these models and will revert to making decisions based solely on their intuition.

8. CONCLUSION

The shrinkage estimation procedures described in this article have provided superior estimates to OLS by pooling brands that have different market shares and marketing strategies and chains that use different pricing philosophies. Some of these procedures yielded much more reasonable parameter estimates as well as improved prediction. This improvement was obtained by exploiting cross-equation similarities. We have used the phrase *seemingly unrelated equations* (SUE) in the title to emphasize the exploitation of cross-equation information to improve estimation. This contrasts with the seemingly unrelated regressions (SUR) methodology developed by Zellner (1962), which exploits the correlation of residuals from different models. Although for the data analyzed in this article, it was information across parameters rather than across residuals that was exploited, it is possible to combine both the SUE and SUR approaches; see Zellner and Vandaele (1974) and Srivastava and Giles (1987). We are hopeful that this general shrinkage methodology will provide a new approach for marketing researchers to pool information from many sources to obtain more useful model estimates.

[Received August 1989. Revised September 1990.]

REFERENCES

Berger, J. O. (1985), *Statistical Decision Theory and Bayesian Analysis* (2nd ed.), New York: Springer-Verlag.

Berger, J. O., and Robert, C. (1990), "Subjective Hierarchical Bayes Estimation of a Multivariate Normal Mean: On the Frequentist Interface," *The Annals of Statistics*, 18, 617–651.

Blattberg, R. C., Eppen, G. D., and Lieberman, J. D. (1981), "A Theoretical and Empricial Evaluation of Price Deals for Consumer Nondurables," *Journal of Marketing*, 45, 116–129.

Blattberg, R. C., and George, E. I. (1990), "Shrinkage Estimation of Price and Promotional Elasticities: Seemingly Unrelated Equations," Technical Report 79, University of Chicago, Statistics Research Center, Graduate School of Business.

Blattberg, R. C., and Wisniewski, K. J. (1987), "How Retail Price Promotions Work: Empirical Results," working paper, University of Chicago, Graduate School of Business.

——— (1988), "Issues in Modeling Store Level Scanner Data," working paper, University of Chicago, Graduate School of Business.

——— (1989), "Price-Induced Patterns of Competition," *Marketing Science*, 8, 291–309.

Deaton, A., and Muellbauer, J. (1980), *Economics and Consumer Behavior*, New York: Cambridge University Press.

Deely, J., and Lindley, D. V. (1981), "Bayes Empirical Bayes," *Journal of the American Statistical Association*, 76, 833–841.

Dielman, T. E. (1983), "Pooled Cross-Sectional and Time Series Data: A Survey of Current Statistical Methodology," *The American Statistician*, 37, 111–122.

DuMouchel, W. H., and Harris, J. E. (1983), "Bayes Methods for Combining the Results of Cancer Studies in Humans and Other Species," (with discussion), *Journal of the American Statistical Association*, 78, 293–315.

Efron, B., and Morris, C. (1972), "Empirical Bayes on Vector Observations: An Extension of Stein's Method," *Biometrika*, 59, 335–347.

Frank, R. E., and Massy, W. F. (1965), "Market Segmentation and the

Effectiveness of a Brand's Price and Dealing Policies," *Journal of Business*, 38, 186–200.

Garcia-Ferrer, A., Highfield, R. A., Palm, F., and Zellner, A. (1987), "Macroeconomic Forecasting Using Pooled International Data," *Journal of Business & Economic Statistics*, 5, 53–67.

Gelfand, A. E., Hills, S. E., Racine-Poon, A., and Smith, A. F. M. (1990), "Illustration of Bayesian Inference in Normal Data Models Using Gibbs Sampling," *Journal of the American Statistical Association*, 85, 972–985.

Gelfand, A. E., and Smith, A. F. M. (1990), "Sampling-Based Approaches to Calculating Marginal Densities," *Journal of the American Statistical Association*, 85, 398–409.

Ghosh, M., Saleh, A. K. Md. E., and Sen, P. K. (1989), "Empirical Bayes Subset Estimation in Regression Models," *Statistics and Decisions*, 7, 15–36.

Good, I. J. (1950), *Probability and the Weighting of Evidence*, London: Charles W. Griffin.

Guadagni, P. M., and Little J. D. C. (1983), "A LOGIT Model of Brand Choice Calibrated on Scanner Data," *Marketing Science*, 2, 327–351.

Hettmansperger, T. P. (1984), *Statistical Inference Based on Ranks*, New York: John Wiley.

Highfield, R. A. (1991), "Forecasting Similar Time Series With Bayesian Pooling Methods With Applications to Forecasting European Output Growth," in *Bayesian Inference in Statistics and Econometrics: Proceedings of the Indo-U.S. Workshop 1988*, eds. P. Goel and S. Iyengar, New York: Springer-Verlag.

Hill, R. C., Cartwright, P. A., and Arbaugh, J. F. (in press), "The Use of Biased Predictors in Marketing Research," *Journal of International Forecasting*.

Houthakker H., and Taylor, L. D. (1970), *Consumer Demand in the United States 1929–1970* (2nd ed.) Cambridge, MA: Harvard University Press.

Hui, S., and Berger, J. O. (1983), "Empirical Bayes Estimation of Rates in Longitudinal Studies," *Journal of the American Statistical Association*, 78, 753–760.

Kumar, V., and Leone, R. P. (1988), "Measuring the Effect of Retail Store Promotions on Brand and Store Substitutions," *Journal of Marketing Research*, 25 178–185.

Lindley, D., and Smith, A. F. M. (1972), "Bayes Estimates for the Linear Model" (with discussion), *Journal of the Royal Statistical Society*, Ser. B, 34, 1–41.

Madansky, A. (1988), *Prescriptions for Working Statisticians*, New York: Springer-Verlag.

Morris, C. (1983), "Parametric Empirical Bayes Inference: Theory and Applications," *Journal of the American Statistical Association*, 78, 47–65.

——— (1986), "Empirical Bayes: A Frequency-Bayes Compromise," in *Adaptive Statistical Procedures and Related Topics*, ed. J. Van Ryzin Hayward, CA: IMS, pp. 195–203.

Neslin, S. A., Henderson, C., and Quelch, J. (1985), "Consumer Promotions and the Acceleration of Product Purchases," *Marketing Science*, 4, 147–165.

Novick, M. R., Jackson, P. H., Thayer, D. T., and Cole, N. S. (1972), "Estimating Multiple Regressions in *m*-Groups; A Cross-validation Study," *The British Journal of Mathematical and Statistical Psychology*, 25, pp. 33–50.

Robert, C., and Saleh, A. K. Md. E. (in press), "Point Estimation and Confidence Set Estimation in a Parallelism Model: An Empirical Bayes Approach," *Annales d'Economie et de Statistique*.

Rubin, D. (1980), "Using Empirical Bayes Techniques in the Law School Validity Studies," *Journal of the American Statistical Association*, 75, 801–827.

Smith, A. F. M. (1973), "A General Bayesian Linear Model," *Journal of the Royal Statistical Society*, Ser. B, 35, 67–75.

Srivastava, V. K., and Giles, D. E. A. (1987), *SURE Models*, New York: Marcel Dekker.

Stein, C. (1966), "An Approach to the Recovery of Inter-block Information in Balanced Incomplete Block Designs," in *Festschrift for J. Neyman*, ed. F. N. David, New York: John Wiley, pp. 351–366.

Swamy, P. A. V. B. (1971), *Statistical Inference in Random Coefficient Regression Models*, New York: Springer-Verlag.

——— (1973), "Criteria, Constraints and Multicollinearity in Random Coefficient Regression Models," *Annals of Economic and Social Measurement*, 2, 429–450.

Tiao, G. C., and Zellner, A. (1964), "On the Bayesian Estimation of Multivariate Regression," *Journal of the Royal Statistical Society*, Ser. B, 26, 277–285.

Vinod, H. D., and Ullah, A. (1981), *Recent Advances in Regression Methods*, New York: Marcel Dekker.

Zellner, A. (1962), "An Efficient Method of Estimating Seemingly Unrelated Regressions and Tests for Aggregation Bias," *Journal of the American Statistical Association*, 57, 348–368.

——— (1986), "On Assessing Prior Distributions and Bayesian Regression Analysis With *g*-Prior Distributions," in *Bayesian Inference and Decision Techniques*, eds. P. Goel and A. Zellner, Amsterdam: Elsevier, pp. 233–243.

Zellner, A., and Hong, C. (1988), "Forecasting International Growth Rates Using Bayesian Shrinkage and Other Procedures," *Journal of Econometrics*, 40, 183–202.

Zellner, A., and Vandaele, W. (1974), "Bayes–Stein Estimators for *k*-Means, Regression and Simultaneous Equation Models," in *Studies in Bayesian Econometrics and Statistics*, eds. S. E. Fienberg and A. Zellner, Amsterdam: North-Holland, pp. 627–653.

MARKETING SCIENCE
Vol. 14, No. 3, Part 2 of 2, 1995
Printed in U.S.A.

HOW PROMOTIONS WORK

ROBERT C. BLATTBERG, RICHARD BRIESCH, AND EDWARD J. FOX
Northwestern University
New York University
Northwestern University

By synthesizing findings across the sales promotion literature, this article helps the reader understand how promotions work. We identify and explain empirical generalizations related to sales promotion; that is, effects that have been found consistently in multiple studies involving different researchers. We also identify issues which have generated conflicting findings in the research, as well as important sales promotion topics that have not yet been studied. This overview of the research and findings from the sales promotion literature is intended to offer direction for future research in the area.
(Sales Promotion; Retailer Promotions; Trade Promotion; Empirical Generalizations)

1. Introduction

In many industries, promotions represent a significant percentage of the marketing mix budget. Nondurable goods manufacturers now spend more money on promotions than on advertising. Airlines periodically offer discounts to generate incremental traffic. Financial institutions use promotions to induce customers to use their services or, as in the case of mortgages, often discount first-year rates to obtain a long-term income stream from the customer. Farm equipment manufacturers use price promotions to sell excess inventory. Across industries, then, price promotions are an important part of the marketing mix.

Consistent with the focus of this special issue, the purpose of this article is to describe the empirical generalizations that can be drawn from the published literature on price promotions. Actually, the price promotions literature is new relative to other research areas in marketing, having been developed primarily since the early 1980s.

Before proceeding, it is useful to describe the types of promotions that will be considered in this article. Generalizations will be drawn regarding both retail and trade promotions,[1] but not manufacturer couponing. Promotions will be considered in a broader context than simply price promotions and will include co-op advertising funds, display allowances to the trade (the intermediaries in the channel), as well as display and feature advertising activity direct to the consumer. While couponing represents a very important part of the promotional literature and a major expenditure for consumer packaged-goods firms, it will not be considered here due to space limitations.

---

[1] Price promotions are *temporary* price discounts offered to a customer. Retail promotions are promotions offered to consumers by retailers. Trade promotions are promotions offered to retailers by manufacturers. Definitions are paraphrased from Blattberg and Neslin (1990).

G122

In generalizing empirical findings, it is also important to recognize that most of the published literature is based on empirical research of packaged-good products. This is largely because of the availability of scanner (point-of-sale) data for consumer packaged goods from syndicated sources such as IRI and A. C. Nielsen.

The paper is organized as follows. Section 2 provides our definition of an empirical generalization; §3 offers the generalizations in the promotional literature; §4 selects the three most important generalizations to business practice and for academic research; §5 examines some topics for which it is difficult to develop an empirical generalization because of conflicting findings in the literature; §6 discusses important topics for which empirical studies have been limited; §7 discusses the managerial implications of selected generalizations; and §8 provides conclusions.

2. Definition of an Empirical Generalization

The definition of an empirical generalization used in this article is (1) the topic being analyzed is well-defined; (2) there are at least three articles by at least three different authors in which empirical research has been conducted in the specific area; and (3) the empirical evidence is consistent, i.e., the sign of the effect is the same in each of the articles.

Some research areas should and often do require more empirical evidence before an effect is considered an empirical generalization. It is not possible to make the criteria too stringent for promotions, however, because the area is relatively new. Other writers in this issue will use different definitions, and it will be interesting to compare the generalizations found. Lastly, the general direction of the generalizations will be reported, not the magnitudes. It is very difficult to conduct a meta-analysis or report the general magnitude of the effects because the articles do not report the results using a standardized mechanism. Economists, for example, report elasticities which are comparable across studies. No such standard reporting procedure has been used in the promotional literature, hence it is not possible to report the general magnitude of effects. This issue is discussed in more detail in the last section of the paper.

3. Empirical Generalizations

Before listing the specific generalizations, it is valuable to identify the types of topics that have received primary emphasis in the promotions literature. Table 1 provides a brief description of the topic areas and the number of articles devoted to each topic. Some articles cover multiple topics and are counted under several topics areas.

Listed below are the generalizations and the articles which support those generalizations.

1. *Temporary retail price reductions substantially increase sales.* The literature has found that temporary retail price promotions cause a significant short-term sales spike. This can be contrasted to consumer advertising (*not* retail feature advertising), where it is difficult to see a sales spike corresponding to increases in advertising spending. Sales increases due to temporary retail price promotions were documented by Woodside and Waddle (1975), Moriarty (1985), and Blattberg and Wisniewski (1987). This result is fundamental to virtually all research done in the area of promotions.

2. *Higher market share brands are less deal elastic.* This result implies that higher share brands have lower deal elasticities,[2] even though higher share brands may capture a large proportion of switchers. The result was found by Bolton (1989), Bemmaor and Mouchoux (1991), and Vilcassim and Jain (1991). These articles all use market share as the dependent variable.

---

[2] The term "deal elasticities" is difficult to define because the point elasticity may not be the best way to create a comparable measure across products. One may want to specify a "20% price reduction" to calculate the percentage change in sales so that comparison across products would be possible.

G124   ROBERT C. BLATTBERG, RICHARD BRIESCH, AND EDWARD J. FOX

TABLE 1
Number of Articles by Topic Area

Description of the Topic	Number of Articles
Variations in consumer responsiveness to deals—Differences in consumer response to promotions by product, category, market, and type of consumer	24
Sources of deal volume—Sources of incremental promotional sales as a result of changes in purchase behavior associated with the promotion, including brand- and store-switching, purchase acceleration, and stockpiling	17
Cross-deal effects—The impact of a particular brand's or category's promotion on other brands or categories	17
General magnitude of deal and price effects—Magnitudes of changes in purchase behavior and product sales as a result of promotions and associated temporary price reductions	14
Impact of deal depth and frequency of deals—Effect of variation in promotional discount levels and promotional frequency on product sales or consumer purchase behavior	14
Merchandising and advertising effects on promotion—Effect of merchandising and advertising conditions on promotional response	12
Long-term effects of deals—The effect of promotions over time on brand sales and profits	8
Pass-through of trade deal funds—The proportion of manufacturers' promotional funds offered to channel members which are, in turn, offered to consumers in the form of temporary price discounts	7
Troughs after deal—The reduction in product sales following a promotional period due to changes in consumer purchase behavior as a result of the promotion	6
Store switching effects—The impact of promotions on consumers' store choice (as opposed to the frequency of store visits)	6
Psychological pricing of deals—The effect of price points and multiple pricing, independent of the depth of discount	1

3. *The frequency of deals changes the consumer's reference price.* This finding is important because it offers an explanation for the loss of brand equity when brands are heavily promoted. A lower consumer reference price reduces the premium that can be charged for a brand in the marketplace, which results in less "equity." The effect of deal frequency on consumers' reference price was found by Lattin and Bucklin (1989), Kalwani et al. (1990), Kalwani and Yim (1992), and Mayhew and Winer (1992).

4. *The greater the frequency of deals, the lower the height of the deal spike.* This result is likely to be caused by (1) consumer expectations about the frequency of deals and (2) changes in the consumer's reference price. The empirical result was documented by Bolton (1989), Raju (1992), and indirectly through the preceding generalization (#3), which, in combination with Winer (1986)/Putler (1992), links reference price to purchase behavior. While some articles use cross-sectional models and some use time-series models, this generalization refers to time-series results.

5. *Cross-promotional effects are asymmetric, and promoting higher quality brands impacts weaker brands (and private label products) disproportionately.* Promoting certain brands causes customers to switch from a competing brand in greater numbers than promoting that competing brand will cause to switch from them. One possible explanation is that asymmetry in switching is due to differences in brand equity. Numerous other explanations have been offered in the literature, such as prospect theory (Kahneman and Tversky 1979 and Hardie et al. 1993). Asymmetric switching was documented by Blattberg and Wisniewski (1987) and (1989), Krishnamurthi and Raj (1988) and (1991), Cooper (1988), and Walters (1991). This result was also found by Allenby and Rossi (1991), Bemmaor and Mouchoux (1991), Grover and Srinivasan (1992), Kamakura and Russell (1989), Mulhern and Leone (1991), and Vilcassim and Jain (1991).

An extension of this finding focuses on asymmetries in brands' perceived type or tier and predicts the impact that promoting a brand in a given tier is likely to have on switching from brands in other tiers. Promoting higher tier brands generates more switching than does promoting lower tier brands. This result was found by Blattberg and Wisniewski (1989), Kamakura and Russell (1989), Mulhern and Leone (1991), and Allenby and Rossi (1991).

6. *Retailers pass-through less than 100% of trade deals.* Because retailers are the vehicle for pass-through of trade promotional money to consumers, it is important to recognize that most brands receive far less than 100% pass-through.[3] Curhan and Kopp (1986) found that brand characteristics result in different levels of pass-through. The finding that less than 100% of trade promotion funds are passed through was made by: Chevalier and Curhan (1976), Curhan and Kopp (1986), Walters (1989), and Blattberg and Neslin (1990).

7. *Display and feature advertising have strong effects on item sales.* Most practitioners already know this result—it is somewhat obvious. However, an important related issue is the *interaction* between feature advertising and display and the synergistic effect that is created. Few empirical results have been generated regarding the synergies between feature advertising, displays, and price discounts. The effect of display and feature advertising was found by Woodside and Waddle (1975), Blattberg and Wisniewski (1987), and Kumar and Leone (1988). Bemmaor and Mouchoux (1991), Bolton (1989), and Kumar and Leone (1988) also confirm this effect.

8. *Advertised promotions can result in increased store traffic.* There is surprisingly little empirical work devoted to this issue, given its practical importance. The weight of evidence (four studies versus one), however, is that advertised promotions of some products and categories do have an impact on store traffic.[4] A likely explanation for Vilcassim and Chintagunta's (1992) failure to find a significant store-switching effect for the cracker category is that the magnitude of this effect varies depending upon the category. Research should be done to identify which categories have more substantial impact on store switching. The positive effect of advertised promotions on store traffic was found by Walters and Rinne (1986), Kumar and Leone (1988), Walters and MacKenzie (1988), and Grover and Srinivasan (1992).

9. *Promotions affect sales in complementary and competitive categories.* This finding is also well understood by practitioners, though the magnitude of this effect is not. The sales impact of promoting one category on a complementary or competing category is very likely a function of the type and characteristics of the categories themselves. The effect of promotions on complementary and competitive categories was found by Walters and Rinne (1986), Walters and MacKenzie (1988), Mulhern (1989), Mulhern and Leone (1991), and Walters (1991).

4. Importance of the Generalizations

To highlight the most important generalizations, we have selected three generalizations which are particularly important to business practice and three which are particularly important to academic research. The selections are subjective and based on the authors' experiences, but they allow others to consider the impact of specific areas of research on both business practice and academic research. No inferences about relative importance are intended based on the order in which the key generalizations are presented.

The most important generalizations for business practice are (1) promotions significantly increase sales, (2) retailers pass-through less than 100% of trade deals, and (3)

---

[3] Pass-through is defined here as the percentage of funds, offered by a manufacturer to a retailer, which are reflected in promotional discounts to the consumer. Greater than 100% pass-through means the retailer offers discounts to the end user in excess of the funds which are received from the manufacturer.

[4] Store switching is viewed as a subset of increased store traffic, which also includes consumers visiting multiple stores.

advertised promotions can increase store traffic. That promotions significantly increase sales is vital to both packaged goods and durables in light of the dramatic growth of promotional spending in marketing budgets over the past decade. Retailers passing-through less than 100% of trade deals is a crucial issue which is fundamental to the success or failure of manufacturer programs to reduce promotional spending (e.g., Procter & Gamble's "value pricing"). That advertised promotions can increase store traffic is also critical to practitioners, because this must be true for a high-low, or promotional, retailer strategy to be viable.

Generalizations of particular importance for academic research are (1) the frequency of deals changes reference price, (2) greater deal frequency lowers the deal spike, and (3) cross-promotional effects are asymmetric. The generalization that deal frequency changes reference price has helped stimulate the development of an increasingly extensive literature on reference price. The generalization that deal frequency lowers the deal spike has contributed heavily to consumer behavior research regarding promotions. The empirical generalization that cross-promotional effects are asymmetric has had a large impact on the literature concerning how promotions work.

5. Key Issues with Conflicting Empirical Results

1. *The Majority of Promotional Volume Comes from Switchers*

Gupta (1988) and Totten and Block (1987) find that the majority of promotional volume comes from switchers.[5] Vilcassim and Chintagunta (1992) and Chintagunta (1993) find, however, that more promotional volume comes from category expansion than from switchers. This result is more consistent with observations that cross-price elasticities are much smaller than own-price elasticities (Bemmaor and Mouchoux 1991) which implies that most promotional volume is not gained at the expense of other brands.

One possible explanation of these conflicting results is that sources of promotional volume are dependent on the characteristics of the category (Blattberg and Wisniewski 1987). This explanation is supported by the understanding that categories have widely different potentials for increased consumption (e.g., toilet paper versus candy).[6] While increased consumption is only one component of category expansion (store switching, purchase acceleration, and stockpiling are others), it would nevertheless help explain category differences in sources of volume.

Totten and Block (1987), Gupta (1988), and Kumar and Leone (1988) found that switchers account for the majority of promotional volume. Vilcassim and Chintagunta (1992) and Chintagunta (1993) found that switchers did not account for the majority of promotional volume. Blattberg and Wisniewski (1987) found that the result varies by category.

2. *Promotional Elasticities Exceed Price Elasticities*

This is a critical issue and one that yields no conclusive results. Some argue that the price discount component of promotions works exactly like any price reduction (price elasticities are equal to promotional elasticities). Others argue that the temporary nature of promotional price reductions results in a higher sales spike because the consumer forward buys, purchase accelerates and increases category consumption in some situations. Still others argue that there is a "transaction" utility to promotions that does not exist

---

[5] The definition of a switcher is critical to the analysis. At one level, it is difficult to classify individuals into finite segments such as switchers. For a given consumer, the percentage of category requirements that a given brand represents can vary from 0% to 100%. Therefore, arguing the majority of volume comes from switchers means consumers increase the share of their category requirements to the brand because of the promotion.

[6] Increased consumption includes both new users due to the reservation price effect and increased usage by current consumers.

with longer-term price reductions, and therefore promotions increase sales more than simple price changes. The methodology for testing whether promotional elasticities are greater than price elasticities is to add an additional term to the model when a promotion is run. This term is then tested to see if it is positive and statistically significant.

Blattberg and Wisniewski (1987), Lattin and Bucklin (1989), and Mulhern and Leone (1991) found that promotional elasticities exceed price elasticities. Guadagni and Little (1983) found that the elasticities were the same.

3. *There is a Trough After the Deal*

This effect has been surprisingly difficult to find. The early literature (Blattberg et al. 1981 and Neslin et al. 1985) found evidence of purchase acceleration and stockpiling, but later studies do not seem to find these "post-deal troughs." Examination of store-level POS data for frequently purchased goods rarely reveals a trough after a promotion, but some researchers do find evidence of a trough in household panel data. This anomaly is surprising and needs to be better understood.

Blattberg et al. (1981), Neslin et al. (1985), and Jain and Vilcassim (1991) found a trough following the deal. Grover and Srinivasan (1992) and Vilcassim and Chintagunta (1992) found no trough.

4. *There is a Negative Long-term Effect to Promotions*

This is probably the most debated issue in the promotional literature and one for which the "jury is still out." Advocates of advertising (e.g., advertising agencies) often argue that promotions are detrimental to the long-term health of brands. Early research seemed to confirm this long-term negative effect (e.g., Dodson et al. 1978 and Strang 1975, but later studies began to question this result (e.g., Johnson 1984). This is still an open question that is critical to the effective use of promotions as part of the marketing mix.

Strang (1975), Shoemaker and Shoaf (1977), and Dodson et al. (1978) found empirical evidence that promotions have a negative long-term effect. Johnson (1984), Totten and Block (1987), and Neslin and Shoemaker (1989) did not find a negative impact long term. Boulding et al. (1994) found that the long-term impact of promotions may be negative or positive.

6. Key Issues with Limited Empirical Results

1. *What is the Shape of the Deal Effect Curve?*

Is the deal curve linear, concave, convex, or S-shaped? Little is known about the shape of the deal effect curve, though it determines the "optimal" dealing amounts. The importance of this topic relates to the "optimization" of promotional discounts. If the effect is convex (i.e., has increasing returns), then the firm will run deeper deals than if the effect is concave (i.e., has decreasing returns). Some argue that the curve has an S-shape, with increasing returns over some range and decreasing returns at higher deal discounts. The argument is based on the belief that consumers can stockpile only a certain amount, after which their storage and holding costs are too high.

2. *Is the Magnitude of the Purchase Acceleration Effect Larger than that of the Stockpiling Effect?*

The published literature indicates that the stockpiling effect is relatively small. Neslin et al. (1985) and Gupta (1988), for example, find limited stockpiling. Is the magnitude of stockpiling category-specific? Also, the distinction between purchase acceleration and stockpiling is not clear—both are forms of increasing the consumer's quantity of the good on hand. Are purchase acceleration and stockpiling distinctly different?

3. *What Are the Magnitudes and Signs of the Interaction Between Display, Feature Advertising, and Price Discount?*

This is very important for both retailers and manufacturers because (a) it will determine the trade spending strategy of manufacturers, and (b) it will impact the way that retailers allocate their display and feature advertising space. If there are synergies, then manufacturers must focus on obtaining joint merchandising with the retailer (Bemmaor and Mouchoux 1991 consider this issue), and retailers must focus on using these merchandising tools to maximize their return. Studies which consider interactive effects are Woodside and Waddle (1975), Popkowski-Leszczyc and Rao (1990), and Bemmaor and Mouchoux (1991).

4. *What Is the Category Expansion Effect of Deals?*

With increasing importance being placed on category management, this question becomes critical for practitioners to understand. Vilcassim and Chintagunta (1992) find that promotions in the cracker category expand category sales; however, there are no studies that evaluate the effect for other categories and conditions. Notwithstanding the lack of empirical results, manufacturers and retailers are very interested in the circumstances in which category expansion occurs and what causes it.[7]

5. *How Much Incremental Volume in Other Categories Do Deals Generate?*

Do deals bring in customers who generate incremental store sales? In what categories? Are these customers profitable to the retailer, given their acquisition cost? Walters and MacKenzie (1988), Walters (1988) and (1991), and Mulhern and Leone (1990) each studied the effect of promotions on store sales and/or sales of other categories.

6. *How Do Promotions Affect Price Image?*

Along with store-switching effects, this is one of the most important questions retailers face regarding promotions. Do promotions affect the price image of a retailer? How? Is an EDLP (everyday low price) strategy superior to a promotional strategy in creating or changing a price image? Which pricing strategy is better for attracting customers? An experimental study by Alba et al. (1994) provides the only findings on the topic.

7. Marketing Implications of the Empirical Generalizations

In identifying empirical generalizations, it is useful to understand the marketing implications. The purpose of this section is to select some of the aforementioned generalizations and consider how they affect marketing practices.

1. *Promotional Elasticities Exceed Price Elasticities*

Implication. While this is not actually a generalization, if true it has important implications for practitioners and academics. Promotions alter consumer behavior beyond the normal price/quantity trade-off. Promotions alter behavior by changing the time that the customer buys the product and how much the customer buys. There is also a belief that consumers will buy simply because the product is on promotion in order to be a "smart" shopper (see Schindler 1984a and 1984b, c.f. Blattberg and Neslin 1990 p. 286–287).

Managers should therefore consider a higher "shelf," or regular, price and then offer discounts from the regular price to increase total sales and profits. If promotional elasticities far exceed price elasticities, a retailer must question the effectiveness of an EDLP strategy.

---

[7] This subject is related to sources of promotional volume.

2. *Promotions Influence the Reference Price of the Product*

Implication. Products can be over-promoted. If a product is promoted heavily (meaning discounted deeply and promoted frequently) the consumer's reference price of the product decreases. The consumer will then buy less of the product at regular price because his or her reservation price has decreased correspondingly.[8]

3. *Cross-promotional Affects Are Asymmetric*

Implication. Because promotions are asymmetric, it becomes possible for firms to use promotions to gain an advantage. For example, suppose brand 1 attracts more of brand 2's customers than brand 2 attracts of brand 1's—hence the asymmetry. Brand 1 can then use promotions more effectively than brand 2. Under certain circumstances brand 1 should start a promotional war. By promoting heavily, brand 1 can capture significant share from brand 2. Brand 2 cannot easily retaliate because of the asymmetry in promotional response.

One caveat must be offered with this strategy. If brand 1 over-promotes, it is possible that the asymmetry may change. Based on some of the other empirical findings, as promotion frequency increases, consumers' reference prices change; hence, the asymmetry may decline. It is therefore critical to understand the dynamic behavior (if any) of the asymmetric cross-elasticities.

4. *Price-tiers Exist and Competition Across Tiers Is Asymmetric*

Implication. National brands can promote to capture share from private label brands and ultimately defend their position against private label brands. This is an argument that Lal (1990a) makes as a way for brands to dominate private label competition. His requirement is "tacit" collusion among the national brands and a rotation of national brand promotions so that the private label is constantly under attack by a national brand.

There are also other conditions under which private label brands can be attacked effectively by national brands. For example, if consumers in a category stockpile (or purchase accelerate), then a promotion by a national brand will influence price-sensitive consumers to stockpile. They will not buy the private label brand, then, until the next promotion. Less price-sensitive national brand customers will buy at regular price, so promotions serve as a price discrimination vehicle between private label and national brands, partly through stockpiling. Jeuland and Narasimhan (1985) make a similar argument, though not about private label versus national brands, that promotions are a mechanism to price discriminate.

The implication for a retailer who determines that national brands are attacking private label through promotional frequency is that the retailer must "shield" private label. Shielding can be accomplished by lowering the price of private label below the national brand price so that very price-sensitive consumers do not switch to the lower margin national brands. Retailers definitely follow this strategy and are aware of the problem.

5. *Retailer Pass-through Is Less than One Hundred Percent*

Implication. Some portion of funds spent by manufacturers to stimulate retailer promotions is pocketed by the retailer to enhance their profits. In fact, retailers manage promotional funds as if it is a profit center (and for some retailers it is). Thus, forward buying income is very important to the economic viability of many grocery retailers and wholesalers. However, this behavior can be detrimental to manufacturers, particularly weaker brand manufacturers, because they receive far less pass-through than leading brands. Their alternative is to employ pull strategies, which are designed to avoid the

---

[8] The reservation price is the price above which the consumer will not buy the product, but below which he or she will buy.

G130   ROBERT C. BLATTBERG, RICHARD BRIESCH, AND EDWARD J. FOX

pocketing of funds by the retailer. Pull strategies, however, are less effective in generating short-term sales per dollar invested. Hence, manufacturers are in a serious bind concerning how to avoid the lack of pass-through.

One solution that has been developed is to pay on "scan sales"—rather than paying allowances on cases shipped to the retailer, the manufacturer pays based on actual cases or units sold. The result is that forward buy is avoided, although the problem of less than 100% pass-through is not reduced. The question that remains unanswered is why the retailer would want to accept scan promotional payments. Also, how can the same concept be applied in nonpackaged goods retailing?

The focus on ECR (Efficient Consumer Response) in grocery retailing is also beginning to address the issue of efficiency of promotions, and this research will no doubt become focused on pass-through and forward buying issues.

8. Concluding Comments

The purpose of this paper is to identify the empirical generalizations in the promotional literature. While the literature is relatively new, we have identified a number of generalizations and topics that merit further research. Rather than reviewing these in the conclusions, we have chosen to make some comments about how to enhance researchers' ability to develop generalizations in the promotions area and, more generally, in the field of marketing.

(1) *We need a standard measure to compare results.* In economics, one can compute a price elasticity, and regardless of the product, results are comparable. In the promotions literature, no such simple common measure exists. The nature of promotions makes elasticities difficult to calculate. Two factors fundamentally influence promotional elasticity: (a) the presence or absence of a promotion, and (b) the depth of promotional discount. The conditions under which promotional elasticities are calculated varies among studies, making direct comparisons difficult if not impossible. This problem could be addressed by adopting a consistent approach to reporting promotional elasticities. If all effects were reported at a 20% discount (or some other fixed discount level), the ability to compare and generalize would be greatly improved. If journal editors or the Marketing Science Institute were able successfully to recommend a standard approach, it would be possible to estimate magnitudes of promotional effects, not simply direction of effects.

(2) *The importance of generalizations.* Without generalizations and the empirical foundations necessary to support them, the development of theories will be impeded. One of the reasons that areas such as economics and finance have spawned more theoretical results than marketing is their focus on empirical research. The early work in the 1960s on efficient markets was driven, in part, by empirical work and empirical generalizations. Without those empirical findings, many alternative research streams might not have developed. Marketing needs the same focus on empirical generalizations. Such a focus would result in more and richer theories.

References

Alba, J. W., S. M. Broniarczyk, T. A. Shimp, and J. E. Urbany (1994), "The Influence of Prior Beliefs, Frequency Cues, and Magnitude Cues on Consumers' Perceptions of Comparative Price Data," *Journal of Consumer Research*, 21 (September), 219–235.

Allenby, G. M. and P. E. Rossi (1991), "Quality Perceptions and Asymmetric Switching Between Brands," *Marketing Science*, 10 (3), 185–205.

Bemmaor, A. C. and D. Mouchoux (1991), "Measuring the Short-Term Effect of In-Store Promotion and Retail Advertising on Brand Sales: A Factorial Experiment," *Journal of Marketing Research*, 28 (May), 202–214.

Blattberg, R. C., G. D. Eppen, and J. Lieberman (1981), "A Theoretical and Empirical Evaluation of Price Deals for Consumer Nondurables," *Journal of Marketing*, 45 (1), 116–129.

———— and S. A. Neslin (1990). *Sales Promotion Concepts, Methods, and Strategies*, Englewood Cliffs, NJ: Prentice-Hall.

—— and K. J. Wisniewski (1989), "Price-Induced Patterns of Competition," *Marketing Science*, 8 (4), 291–309.

—— and —— (1987), "How Retail Price Promotions Work: Empirical Results," Working Paper 43, University of Chicago, Chicago IL.

Bolton, R. N. (1989), "The Relationship Between Market Characteristics and Promotional Price Elasticities," *Marketing Science*, 8 (2), 153–169.

Boulding, W., E. Lee, and R. Staelin (1989), "Mastering the Mix: Do Advertising, Promotion, and Sales Force Activities Lead to Differentiation," *Journal of Marketing Research*, 31 (May), 159–172.

Chevalier, M. and R. C. Curhan (1976), "Retail Promotions as a Function of Trade Promotions: A Descriptive Analysis," *Sloan Management Review* (Fall), 19–32.

Chintagunta, P. K. (1993), "Investigating Purchase Incidence, Brand Choice and Purchase Quantity Decisions of Households," *Marketing Science*, 12 (2), 184–208.

Cooper, L. G. (1988), "Competitive Maps: The Structure Underlying Asymmetric Cross Elasticities," *Management Science*, 34 (6), 707–723.

Curhan, R. C. and R. J. Kopp (1986), "Factors Influencing Grocery Retailers' Support of Trade Promotions," Report No. 86-114, Cambridge, MA: Marketing Science Institute, July.

Dodson, J. A., A. M. Tybout, and B. Sternthal (1978), "Impact of Deals and Deal Retraction on Brand Switching," *Journal of Marketing Research*, 15 (February), 72–81.

Dreze, X. (1994), "Loss Leaders, Store Traffic and Cherry Pickers," Working Paper, University of Chicago, Chicago, IL.

Grover, R. and V. Srinivasan (1992), "Evaluating the Multiple Effects of Retail Promotions on Brand Loyal and Brand Switching Segments," *Journal of Marketing Research*, 29 (February), 76–89.

Guadagni, P. M. and J. D. C. Little (1983), "A Logit Model of Brand Choice Calibrated on Scanner Data," *Marketing Science*, 2 (3), 203–238.

Gupta, S. (1988), "Impact of Sales Promotions on When, What, and How Much to Buy," *Journal of Marketing Research*, 25 (November), 342–355.

Hardie, B. G. S., E. J. Johnson, and P. S. Fader (1993), "Modeling Loss Aversion and Reference Dependence Effects on Brand Choice," *Marketing Science*, 12 (4), 378–394.

Jain, D. C. and N. J. Vilcassim (1991), "Investigating Household Purchase Timing Decisions: A Conditional Hazard Function Approach," *Marketing Science*, 10 (1), 1–23.

Jeuland, A. P. and C. Narasimhan (1985), "Dealing—Temporary Price Cuts—By Seller as a Buyer Discrimination Mechanism," *Journal of Business*, 58, 295–308.

Johnson, T. (1984), "The Myth of Declining Brand Loyalty," *Journal of Advertising Research*, 24 (1), 9–17.

Kahneman, D. and A. Tversky (1979), "Prospect Theory: An Analysis of Decision Under Risk," *Econometrica*, 47 (March), 263–291.

Kalwani, M. U., H. J. Rinne, Y. Sugita, and C. K. Yim (1990), "A Price Expectations Model of Customer Brand Choice," *Journal of Marketing Research*, 27 (August), 251–262.

—— and C. K. Yim (1992), "Consumer Price and Promotion Expectations: an Experimental Study," *Journal of Marketing Research*, 29 (February), 90–100.

Kamakura, W. A. and G. J. Russell (1989), "A Probabilistic Choice Model for Market Segmentation and Elasticity Structure," *Journal of Marketing Research*, 26 (November), 379–390.

Krishnamurthi, L. and S. P. Raj (1988), "A Model of Brand Choice and Purchase Quantity Price Sensitivities," *Marketing Science*, 7 (1), 1–20.

—— and —— (1991), "An Empirical Analysis of the Relationship Between Brand Loyalty and Consumer Price Elasticity," *Marketing Science*, 10 (2), 172–183.

Kumar, V. and R. P. Leone (1988), "Measuring the Effect of Retail Store Promotions on Brand and Store Substitution," *Journal of Marketing Research*, 25 (May), 178–185.

Lal, R. (1990a), "Price Promotions: Limiting Competitive Encroachment," *Marketing Science*, 9 (3), 247–262.

Lattin, J. M. and R. E. Bucklin (1989), "Reference Effects of Price and Promotion on Brand Choice Behavior," *Journal of Marketing Research*, 26 (August), 299–310.

Mayhew, G. E. and R. Winer (1992), "An Empirical Analysis of Internal and External Reference Prices Using Scanner Data," *Journal of Consumer Research*, 19 (June), 62–70.

Moriarty, M. M. (1985), "Retail Promotional Effects on Intra- and Interbrand Sales Performance," *Journal of Retailing*, 61 (3), 27–47.

Mulhern, F. J. (1989), "An Econometric Analysis of Consumer Response to Retail Price Promotions," unpublished doctoral dissertation, University of Texas, Austin, TX.

—— and R. P. Leone (1991), "Implicit Price Bundling of Retail Products: A Multiproduct Approach to Maximizing Store Profitability," *Journal of Marketing*, 55 (October), 63–76.

—— and —— (1990), "Retail Promotional Advertising: Do the Number of Deal Items and Size of Deal Discounts Affect Store Performance?" *Journal of Business Research*, 21 (November), 179–194.

Neslin, S. A., C. Henderson, and J. Quelch (1985), "Consumer Promotions and the Acceleration of Product Purchases," *Marketing Science*, 4 (2), 147–165.

G132   ROBERT C. BLATTBERG, RICHARD BRIESCH, AND EDWARD J. FOX

—— and R. W. Shoemaker (1989), "An Alternative Explanation for Lower Repeat Rates after Promotion Purchases," *Journal of Marketing Research*, 26 (May), 205–213.

Popkowski, L. and R. Rao (1990), "An Empirical Analysis of National and Local Advertising Effect on Price Elasticity," *Marketing Letters*, 1 (2), 149–160.

Putler, D. S. (1992), "Incorporating Reference Price Effects into a Theory of Consumer Choice," *Marketing Science*, 11 (3), 287–309.

Raju, J. S. (1992), "The Effect of Price Promotions on Variability in Product Category Sales," *Marketing Science*, 11 (3), 207–220.

Schindler, R. M. (1984a), "How Cents Off Coupons Motivate the Consumer," in *Research on Sales Promotion: Collected Papers*, in K. E. Jocz (Ed.), Report 84-104, Cambridge, MA: Marketing Science Institute, July, 84–104.

—— (1984b), "How Sales Promotions Stimulate Consumer Response: Implications for Designing More Effective Programs," Working Paper, University of Chicago, Chicago, IL, September.

Shoemaker, R. W. and F. R. Shoaf (1977), Repeat Rates of Deal Purchases," *Journal of Advertising Research*, 17 (2), 47–53.

Strang, R. A. (1975), *The Relationship Between Advertising and Promotion in Brand Strategy*, Cambridge, MA: Marketing Science Institute.

Totten, J. and M. Block (1987), *Analyzing Sales Promotion: Test and Cases*, Chicago, IL: Commerce Communications.

Vilcassim, N. J. and P. K. Chintagunta (1992), "Investigating Retailer Pricing Strategies from Household Scanner Panel Data," Working Paper, February.

—— and D. C. Jain (1991), "Modeling Purchase Timing and Brand-Switching Behavior Incorporating Explanatory Variables and Unobserved Heterogeneity," *Journal of Marketing Research*, 28 (February), 29–41.

Walters, R. G. (1991), "Assessing the Impact of Retail Price Promotions on Product Substitution, Complementary Purchase, and Interstore Sales Displacement," *Journal of Marketing*, 55 (April), 17–28.

—— (1988), "Retail Promotions and Retail Store Performance: A Test of Some Key Hypotheses," *Journal of Retailing*, 64 (Summer), 153–180.

—— and S. B. MacKenzie (1988), "A Structural Equations Analysis of the Impact of Price Promotions on Store Performance," *Journal of Marketing Research*, 25 (February), 51–63.

—— and H. J. Rinne (1986), "An Empirical Investigation into the Impact of Price Promotions on Retail Store Performance," *Journal of Retailing*, 62 (3), 237–266.

Winer, R. (1986), "A Reference Price Model of Brand Choice for Frequently Purchased Products," *Journal of Consumer Research*, 13 (September), 250–256.

Woodside, A. G. and G. L. Waddle (1975), "Sales Effects of In-Store Advertising," *Journal of Advertising Research*, 15 (3), 29–33.

Part IV: Big Bob — Contributions That Were Industry-Changing

Bob Blattberg wrote papers that changed how business is done across entire industries. These papers were sometimes published in academic journals, sometimes in monographs or books that were distributed more widely. Their impact is less evident in citation counts than by observing practices in the industries he studied.

Bob's industry-changing papers share three common characteristics. First and foremost he was a thought leader in whatever he did. As a result, his work led industries and developed new paradigms rather than making incremental contributions. He was a harbinger of important trends and issues whose work helped set the agenda for industries. Second, Bob focused on applying models to data to make better marketing decisions. In some cases, his work found new models to apply to existing data sources; in other cases, his work focused on applying models to new data sources. Either way, his objective was to improve the information available for marketing decisions. Third, Bob's papers made clear recommendations for implementation. He was never content just to describe the data and models; rather, he clearly intended that they be used.

The objective of this chapter is to highlight Bob's papers that changed industries. With one exception, the papers in this chapter relate to consumer packaged goods. Bob's work fundamentally changed the practices of both retailers and manufacturers in consumer packaged goods. The other paper in the chapter relates to the copper industry. Bob's work in direct marketing and customer loyalty also changed industries but is covered in another chapter of this volume and so is not included here.

The Copper Industry

Bob's first paper was published in *California Management Review* when he was still a doctoral student at the Carnegie Institute of Technology (Blattberg and McGuire, 1967). The paper used the copper industry as a case study to examine the effectiveness of wage-price guideposts. Wage-price guideposts were voluntary limits on prices that were tied to changes in industry productivity. They had been introduced in the copper industry as part of a broader government program in the 1960s to keep inflation under control.

Blattberg and McGuire carefully chronicled events in the copper industry over a five-year period, demonstrating large changes in supply and demand. The authors found that the firm-level price increases that had triggered US government intervention under the wage-price guideposts had been entirely justified by a reduction in copper supply worldwide. On the basis of the case study, Blattberg and McGuire concluded that wage-price guideposts interfered with, rather than supplemented, market competition which led to a misallocation of resources by both buyers and sellers.

As an explicit evaluation of government economic policy, this paper is perhaps Bob's most ambitious in scope. It was also an early response to increasingly interventionist US economic policies that culminated in 1974's wage-price freeze. This was to become a pattern in Bob's industry-level publications — early recognition of problems and opportunities with clear recommendations for decision-makers.

Consumer Packaged Goods

The remainder of Bob's industry-changing publications focused on consumer packaged goods and the application of technology. He studied issues that were of importance to both manufacturers and retailers. His applications for new product marketing impacted manufacturers; his scanner data studies primarily affected retailers; his category management publications impacted both.

New Product Marketing for Consumer Packaged Goods Manufacturers

With John Golanty of the advertising agency Leo Burnett, Bob developed TRACKER, a model for forecasting sales and diagnosing shortcomings of new products (Blattberg and Golanty, 1978). For a given new product introduction, the model follows consumers down the path from awareness to trial to repeat usage. The authors modeled each step in that path with a separate econometric specification that was applied to a time series dataset comprised of consumer surveys, media advertising weights and prices. Repeat usage was modeled with a long-term market share model in which consumers were segmented based on usage rates. The parameters of this long-term market share model could be used to diagnose problems with new product acceptance. Together, the awareness, trial and market share models could be used to forecast sales and market share for the new product.

TRACKER represents an effort to use test market data to make marketing decisions. The emphasis was on making those decisions quickly; in this case, forecasting year-end sales with only three months of data. Being able to determine quickly whether to roll out a new product and, if so, how to market it enabled consumer packaged goods companies to reduce the high costs of test markets and potentially gain a strategic advantage.

Bob took on another important issue related to new product introductions — who to target. Blattberg, Buesing and Sen (1980) addressed the targeting question with a segmentation approach. Using household panel data that the *Chicago Tribune* had recently begun to gather, households were segmented based on three dimensions: loyalty (loyal vs. switcher), brand preference (national vs. private label) and price sensitivity (deal prone vs. not). The authors used the introduction of Puffs facial tissue to test whether new products should target brand switchers, who conventional wisdom suggested were most open to buying new products. The data showed that switchers were the indeed more likely to buy Puffs but continued to switch between brands. On the other hand, households that were loyal to national brands were less likely to buy Puffs but *more likely* to become loyal Puffs purchasers if they had. The authors concluded that new product introductions of national brands should target national-brand loyals, as well as switchers. Buyers of more expensive private label products were also found to be attractive for targeting.

Bob's work with new products in the late 1970s and early 1980s focused on applying models to data from new sources to make better marketing decisions. Blattberg and Golanty (1978) emphasized the modeling; Blattberg, Buesing and Sen (1980) emphasized the data. Bob's interest in new data sources was piqued again as supermarkets began to use electronic scanners at checkout.

Scanner Data Applications for Consumer Packaged Goods Retailers

The use of scanning equipment in supermarkets began in 1974. Scanners were rapidly found to offer hard, or operational, benefits such as reduced labor costs and faster checkouts. Yet, scanners also held the promise of soft, or informational, benefits from data-based pricing, promotion, shelf and cost management applications. Supermarket companies found it difficult to quantify the soft benefits — the value of using scanner data to make better decisions — so they did not immediately implement these data-based applications.

In a study conducted for the Coca-Cola Retailing Research Council, Bob determined the costs and benefits from implementing a wide range of data-based applications at a hypothetical supermarket company (Blattberg, 1988). He found that the following applications would all return a positive payout within the first year of implementation:

- perishable management systems,
- direct product profitability (similar to more recent activity-based costing initiatives),
- display and ad analysis,
- localized marketing,
- price simulators,
- shelf management systems,
- promotional analysis and
- computer assisted ordering.

The highest overall benefits would be realized from direct marketing and perishable management applications. To help retailers prioritize potential applications, the study also considered implementation requirements including data quality, time and ease of implementation and technical sophistication.

This study was widely read by leaders and managers in the supermarket industry and helped many to understand and evaluate the soft benefits of scanning. Stimulating demand for scanning applications, the study helped create new markets for data-based applications and services that have grown during the past two decades.

The databases generated by supermarket scanners could include daily sales and pricing records for tens of thousands of individual items at hundreds of different stores. The sizes of such databases were measured in gigabytes or even terabytes. Estimating models to help retailers make pricing, promotion and inventory decisions using these vast databases is simply too large a task for manual modeling. In Bob's edited volume *Marketing Information Revolution*, Blattberg, Kim and Ye (1994) proposed automating or "mass-producing" models on which to build marketing decision support systems. Using item-level pricing models for illustration, the authors showed how models could be used to improve retailer decisions. In order to be used in decision support systems, the mass-produced models must have:

- predictive accuracy,
- correct parameter signs and magnitudes,

- adaptability to changes in the environment,
- little human intervention require,
- automatic recalibration and
- the right specification (i.e., automated variable selection).

The authors also suggested robust estimation techniques so that the mass-produced models would meet the above criteria. Robust regression, constrained regression and regression with time varying parameters were deemed superior to ordinary least squares regression for estimating the mass-produced models.

Bob was among the first to anticipate the value of scanner data in marketing decision making. His guidance about how retailers could use the data to help them make pricing, promotion and other marketing decisions has had an important influence on practice. His influence was also felt in his contributions to the practice of category management.

Category Management Consumer for Packaged Goods Retailers and Manufacturers

Category management represented a new paradigm in retail management — a shift in focus from the performance of individual items and brands to the performance of entire product categories. The new paradigm involved managing categories as separate business units with their own business plans, integrating the buying and merchandising functions under a single category manager, relying on data-based analysis and collaborating with suppliers to profitably deliver value to consumers. In 1995 and 1996, Bob published a series of practical guides to implementing category management for the entire grocery industry (Blattberg, Fox and Purk, 1995–1996).

The objective of the guide series was to give grocery retailers of any size the necessary information to implement category management. The guide series began with a ten-step process to implementation in the first guide, "Getting Started." This guide also spelled out the changes in organization, technology and business practices that would be required. The second guide, "A Blueprint for Implementation" offered case studies of retailers of different sizes that highlighted the obstacles and solutions to the implementation of category management. This guide also offered "how to" details, frameworks, and scorecards for each of the ten implementation steps. The third guide, "The Category Plan," focused on this important aspect of the process. It included a series of templates to make category planning consistent and efficient. The fourth guide, "Information Tools," addressed the technology requirements of category management. Its objective was to help retailers assess their data requirements, choose hardware and software solutions to meet those requirements, then integrate the technology into their business processes. The fifth and final guide, "The Role of Supplier Organizations," focused on establishing and maintaining the collaborative relationships that were important to the success of category management. Category captains, as collaborating suppliers were known, offered retailers category expertise, insights into consumer behavior and analytical sophistication. Yet, category captains were understandably more interested in the success of their own products than in the success of their competitors' products on the retail shelf. The final guide addressed this issue and discussed the roles of other potential collaborators: wholesalers, brokers, merchandisers and data vendors.

The category management guide series helped bring about a paradigm shift among retailers of consumer packaged goods. Retailers changed how they viewed their business, relying on different categories for specific contributions (to margin, to store traffic, etc.). Retailers also came to rely on their suppliers for information and recommendations. Equally important, retailer decision-making became more fact based as retailers began to harness the power of their data for marketing decisions.

Some Personal Comments

This chapter highlighted Bob Blattberg's industry-changing work. In particular, that work has had an important impact on consumer packaged goods retailers and manufacturers. Bob was among the first to recognize the potential of scanner data and statistical modeling techniques for marketing decision-making; his work paved the way for their widespread use. One can see evidence of his contribution today — the applications and techniques that he championed are now in common practice.

Perhaps it is fitting that I have had the opportunity to focus on Bob's industry-changing work because he was heavily engaged in this work during the early years of our association. As a student and research associate, I watched Bob define category management for packaged goods retailers and suppliers. At the same time, he was helping to usher in the era of database marketing. However, watching Bob at work provided only limited insight into "Big Bob." A review of his industry-changing work has offered a little more perspective. I have come to believe that foresight may be Bob's greatest gift. Not that he saw changes before they happened; rather, he saw the potential for positive changes before they were realized and had the wherewithal to make them happen. We would all be well served to follow his lead and try to see the world not just as it is, but as it could be if we helped to change it for the better. Thank you, Bob.

Edward Fox

Edwin L. Cox School of Business

Southern Methodist University

References

Blattberg, Robert C. (1988). *Assessing and Capturing the Soft Benefits of Scanning,* Atlanta, Georgia: Coca-Cola Retailing Research Council.

Blattberg, Robert C., Edward J. Fox and Mary E. Purk (1995–1996). *Category Management a Series of Implementation Guides 1-5,* Washington, DC: Food Marketing Institute.

Blattberg, Robert and John Golanty (1978). Tracker: An Early Test Market Forecasting and Diagnostic Model for New Product Planning, *Journal of Marketing Research,* 15(May), 192–202.

Blattberg, Robert C., Byung-Do Kim and Jianming Le (1994). in *The Marketing Information Revolution,* Robert C. Blattberg, Rashi Glazer and John D.C. Little (Eds.). Boston Massachusetts: Harvard Business School Press.

Blattberg, Robert C. and Thomas Buesing and Subrata K. Sen (1980). "Segmentation Strategies for New National Brands," *Journal of Marketing,* 44(Fall), 59–67.

ROBERT BLATTBERG and JOHN GOLANTY*

A new product forecasting model is described which uses survey data (not panel data) to predict year-end test market sales from early test market results (usually three months). In addition to offering a sales forecast, the model is designed to provide diagnostic information about a new product's strengths and weaknesses. By relating advertising expenditures, price, and perceptions of performance/acceptability of the product to sales, the model indicates how an unsuccessful product can be redesigned or the marketing mix changed to make possible a successful introduction. The model also can be used for new product planning. Given a media plan, price, sampling level, couponing, and some estimate of repeat usage, a pre-test market forecast of year-end sales can be made which allows management to evaluate different marketing plans to see which best meets profit or sales goals.

Tracker: An Early Test Market Forecasting and Diagnostic Model for New Product Planning

INTRODUCTION

A new product forecasting model is described that predicts year-end test market sales from early test market results (usually three months). In addition to offering a sales forecast, the model is designed to provide diagnostic information about the product's performance. By relating actual sales to advertising expenditures, price, product quality, and consumer data, the model indicates how a marginal or unsuccessful product can be redesigned or the marketing mix changed to increase its success.

The model also can be used for new product planning. Given a media plan, price, sampling level, couponing, and some estimate of repeat usage, a pre-test market forecast of year-end sales can be made which allows management to alternate different marketing plans to see which best meets profit or sales goals. Obviously, the pre-test market forecasts are based solely on "norms" and not actual test market results. When the product is introduced results may fall below (or above) norms, but before test market the model will indicate "average" responses to different media and pricing strategies.

Many other new product forecasting models are available [see 2, 5, 7–14]. The model presented here has several distinct features. First, it requires only three months of test market data whereas many other models require longer time periods (commonly six months or longer). Second, it uses survey data. Almost all other models require panel data which are much more expensive and take longer to recover and process from the marketplace. Third, the model is inexpensive to use. The total cost of using the model, including data collection, is roughly $15,000. Many other new product models offering comparable forecasts cost $50,000 to $100,000. Fourth, the model is very easy to understand and to use.[1] Many of the other new product forecasting models are not applied because very few people understand them. Since the primary

*Robert Blattberg is Professor of Marketing and Statistics, Graduate School of Business, University of Chicago. John Golanty is an Account Executive, Leo Burnett Co., Inc. The authors thank James Livingston, David Olson, and Subrata Sen for their helpful comments. This research was funded in part by National Science Foundation grant GS-40033.

[1] To aid users, a time sharing version is available.

purpose was to develop a model that would be used, the authors believed that the model should be kept as simple as possible. Therefore, the model uses only one or two variables at each stage, all easily understandable, and the relationships involved can be explained to any potential user. Fifth, the model is very accurate. TRACKER has been applied to 11 new product introductions since it was developed.[2] The forecasts have been made with three months of test marketing in most cases. Table 1 lists the results. It should be noted that the forecasts given in Table 1 are not merely fitted values from a model, but are actual forecasts. Finally, the model offers its users diagnostic information about problems with respect to awareness, trial and repeat rates, and can indicate causes of these problems, e.g., low spending, high price, poor product quality. All of this diagnostic information is based on the standard data collected. Other models, particularly models using panel data, often require additional studies to identify the causes of a new product's failure. The model forecasts and simultaneously diagnoses product problems.

OVERVIEW OF THE MODEL

The basic theory underlying the model is similar to that outlined in [6]. The process begins with advertising of the new product. Advertising results in a fraction of potential users becoming aware of the product and the rest entering the nonaware class. The aware consumers then become triers or they enter the nontrier class. The members of the trier class develop attitudes about product quality and product satisfaction from their initial trial experience. These attitudes determine whether they become repeat users or move into the nonrepeat user class. Finally, repeat users can either continue to repeat purchase or move into the nonrepeat users class. Figure 1 is a flow chart of the model.

---

[2]The forecasting and planning models are being used by Leo Burnett Co. The results given are for forecasts that they have made by using the model.

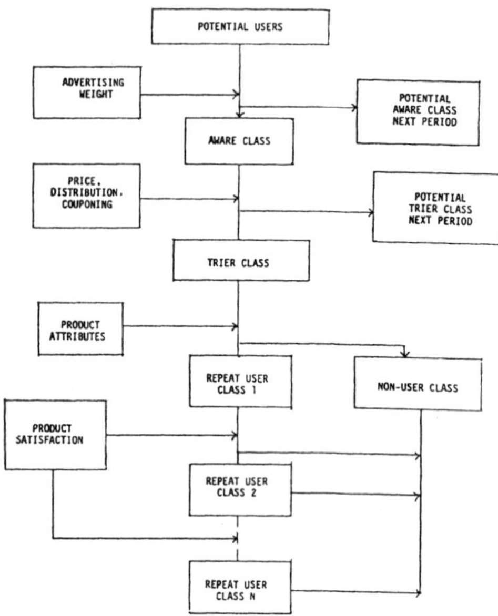

Figure 1
FLOW CHART OF THE MODEL

The data inputs for the model are obtained from questionnaires administered to potential users of the product. Table 2 lists the information available from the questionnaire. Three waves of 500 to 1,000 questionnaires are collected for each new product introduction. The waves are sequenced every four weeks after introduction.[3] Also collected for each product

---

[3]Deviations in the timing of these waves occur when the purchase cycle of a product is exceptionally long or short.

Table 1
VALIDATION OF PROJECTIONS

Case	Forecast made after	Forecast	Actual results
1	4 months	1.6% share	2.0% share
2	2 months	0.9% share	1.0% share
3	2 months	0.3% share	Withdrawn after 3 months with 0.3 share
4	7 months	$36mm annual rate	$39mm annual rate at 15 months
5	3 months	Early product failure	Withdrawn—6 months
6	3 months	2.1% share	2.3% share
7	2 months	Early product failure	Withdrawn—3 months
8	3 months	5.8% share	5.2% share after 8 months
9	7 months	$25mm rate	$23mm annual rate at 15 months
10	4 months	$7.5mm 1st year	Withdrawn at 5 months
11	6 months	30% share	26% share

Table 2
INFORMATION AVAILABLE FROM QUESTIONNAIRE

1. Product usage	7. Other brands used
2. Frequency of product usage	8. Frequency of purchase for
3. Unaided awareness of brand	each brand used
1st mentioned	9. Rating of each brand
2nd mentioned	10. Receipt of free sample
Others	11. Use of coupon
4. Aided awareness of brand	12. Repurchase intentions
5. Length of time since last	1st choice
purchase	2nd choice
6. Brand bought last	Others

are media weight, price, special distribution problems, and other data which may be applicable to a specific introduction.

In estimating parameters for each model, separate estimates are computed when possible for each product category (e.g., dog food, cereal, etc.).[4] This step is very important for making predictions and using the model for planning. There is large variation in parameter estimates across product categories. For example, some product categories (not brands) are very responsive to advertising, others are not; some have high trial among aware consumers, others do not. Therefore, separate parameter estimates are needed for each product category. An example is given in the following section.

THE AWARENESS MODEL

The Model

In developing the advertising-awareness model, several prior ideas about how advertising affects awareness were considered. The goal was to develop a model consistent with both the limitations of the data and prior ideas about the relationship between awareness and advertising.

The first consideration was data. The intention was to keep the data costs low and to collect only a minimal amount of data. The authors planned to measure two variables, total brand awareness and advertising weight defined in gross rating points (GRP's).[5] Total brand awareness was the dependent variable and GRP's the independent variable.

Total brand awareness was measured by aggregating the positive responses to two questions among product category users: "What brands of (product category) can you think of?" (a positive response is the mention of the new brand) and, among those who did not respond positively to the first question, "Have you

ever heard of (new brand)?" (a positive response would be "yes"). Total brand awareness is the sum of the positive responses to these two questions divided by the total number of product category users.

Many other variables also affect awareness, such as word-of-mouth communications. In theory these variables should be included in the model. If they are omitted and the variables are correlated with the advertising levels, the estimated coefficients will be biased. However, the costs of measuring these other variables would be prohibitive. If, for a given new product, the percentage change of these omitted variables does not greatly vary from period to period, then by using the ratio of this period's awareness to last period's awareness (A_t / A_{t-1}) as the dependent variable, one would not have to worry as much about excluding these other variables from the model. Their effect could be absorbed into the error term without greatly biasing the estimates. Therefore, a function of (A_t / A_{t-1}) was chosen as the dependent variable.

A second consideration in determining the functional form was to design the model to permit diminishing returns to advertising (GRP's). As awareness increases it becomes harder and harder to reach nonaware consumers with media. Further, most of the literature on the effects of advertising seems to indicate that there are diminishing returns to advertising. The mathematical form of the dependent variable in equation 1 shows diminishing returns to advertising.

A third consideration is that the model should have the capability to allow awareness to decline if the advertising weight is below some level in a period. In most new product introductions consumers begin losing their awareness of the product unless advertising continually repeats the new brand's name. Thus, if advertising weight is below a threshold frequency, awareness may decline from the previous period's level. Through a parameter of the model, either decreasing or increasing awareness can result for low advertising spending levels, depending on the sign of the parameter.

The mathematical relationship decided upon which meets the foregoing requirements is:

$$(1) \qquad \ln\left(\frac{1 - A_t}{1 - A_{t-1}}\right) = \alpha - \beta\, GRP_t$$

where A_t is the brand's total awareness in period t, GRP_t is the number of GRP's delivered for the brand in period t, and α and β are parameters of the model.

An alternative dependent variable that could have been used is ($1 - A_{t-1} / 1 - A_t$). This ratio also results in diminishing returns to advertising. However, there are some advantages to using the logarithmic form. If awareness is very high, say .9, to increase it any further would require a very high level of media weight. The logarithmic form of the dependent variable makes

---

[4] For product categories for which available data are not sufficient for estimation, general norms are used or in certain situations norms for similar products are used (e.g., cat food for dog food).

[5] GRP's are equal to the percentage of TV households reached at least once with the advertised message multiplied by the average number of times the household is exposed to the message.

it relatively harder to increase awareness by 1% at 90% than does the nonlogarithmic form.[6] For low awareness, say .1, it is relatively easier for the logarithmic form to increase awareness than the nonlogarithmic form. It is very difficult to increase awareness when awareness is high because some people have media habits which make it difficult to reach them given limited media funds. Using the logarithmic form of the dependent variable more adequately models this concept.

There are two parameters in equation 2. α represents the effect no advertising has on awareness. If α is positive, then awareness declines when there is no advertising. If α is negative, awareness increases when there is no advertising. For any given product category, it may be possible to specify the direction of α before estimation. However, in general, it is assumed that $-: < \alpha < \infty$.

β represents the responsiveness of awareness to advertising. It is assumed that $\beta > 0$ indicating that advertising increases awareness. The larger the value of β, the greater is the effect of advertising on awareness.

A third parameter also must be set, initial awareness. Equation 2 is undefined for period 1 unless A_0, initial awareness, is available. Through the use of the econometric methods A_0 can be estimated and it therefore is considered a parameter of the model.

The next step is to fit data to the model described in equation 2.

Estimation Results

The estimation results are given for two considerably different product categories.[7] Product category 1 primarily contains new introductions for a well-known company. Consequently, initial awareness was expected to be high due to a bias from consumers stating they are aware of a new product for brands of this company when they are not. Some decay of awareness also was expected if advertising were not very high. However, it was difficult to assess whether the decay rate would be very large. Finally, the category was expected not to be very responsive to advertising. Thus, β would not be very large.

For product category 2, many brands are sold (more than 50), none of which has a very large market share. Initial awareness was expected to be low because there were no dominant brands nor is the company name used in the brand's name (e.g., Del Monte X). For the decay rate parameter a positive increase in awareness was believed possible if advertising levels were

Table 3
PARAMETER ESTIMATES FOR ADVERTISING-AWARENESS MODEL

Product category	A_0	α	β	$\bar{R}^2$
1	.38	.0154 (.00905)[a]	.0003995 (.0000665)	.732
2	.16	.0031 (.00930)	.0007543 (.000270)	.654

[a]The standard errors are the values given in parentheses.

low because the product is purchased frequently and therefore consumers could become aware through in-store exposure rather than advertising. However, the authors were not very certain about this outcome, or about the effect advertising would have on awareness. Thus, the prior estimates of the parameter's distribution were fairly diffuse.

The results of estimating the parameters are listed in Table 3. The actual and fitted observations along with the residuals are given in Table 4.

The data given in Table 4 are for eight introductions for product category 1 and 10 introductions for product category 2. No more than three periods of data are available because the surveying process ends after three waves. In some cases, there is an omitted observation. For example, for product category 1, product 1, period 2 is missing because no survey was taken in that period. Some of the data used for a product category were collected prior to the development of the model. In these cases missing periods were common. However, these data can also be used in estimating the parameters.[8]

For product category 1 initial awareness is very high, .38, and α is positive. $\beta = .0004$, which is very low. From the values of α and β one can find the number of GRP's required before awareness does not decline; 385 GRP's per month are needed.[9] This is a fairly high level. Thus, the decay rate is large.

For product category 2, the results are very different. First, initial awareness is low, .16. Next $\beta = .0007543$ which is twice as large as for product category 1. α is also positive but very small. By computing the number of GRP's before awareness declines, one finds that only 4 GRP's are required. Thus, there is very little decay. However, as there are only three periods of data, the decay rate may only represent what happens over the first three

---

[6]"Relatively harder" means that the ratio of GRP's required to increase awareness 1% at 90% is higher than for the nonlogarithmic model. Of course, one must make the model equivalent at some other point to make this comparison.

[7]The procedures used to estimate the model are available from R. Blattberg.

[8]Some econometric adjustments were necessary to estimate parameters for categories missing observations. For example, weighted least squares was used to adjust for the change in the variances of the errors. Because of the complexity of the adjustment procedure and because new data do not contain missing observations, the exact estimation steps are not given.

[9]The high number of GRP's to maintain awareness is due to the nature of the product category. There are a large number of brands and heavy advertising.

Table 4
AWARENESS MODEL'S PREDICTIONS

Brand number	Period	Actual	Predicted	Absolute error
Product category 1				
1	1	65	64	1
1*	3	91	91	0
2	1	32	48	16
2	2	43	42	1
2	3	48	55	7
3	1	40	38	2
3	2	46	40	6
3	3	38	48	10
4	1	69	60	9
4	2	85	78	7
4	3	84	86	2
5	1	23	42	19
5	3	53	36	17
6	1	49	57	8
6	2	56	57	1
7	1	53	44	9
7	2	53	51	2
7	3	53	70	17
8	1	55	43	12
8	2	69	58	11
8	3	58	65	7
			Average absolute error 7.8	
Product category 2				
1	2	23	7	16
1	3	32	31	1
2	1	30	20	10
2	2	45	45	0
3	2	45	50	5
4	3	58	56	2
5	3	30	38	8
6	2	69	56	13
6	3	76	68	8
7	1	29	47	18
7	2	43	41	2
7	3	32	41	9
8	2	14	41	27
9	3	64	56	8
10	1	24	26	2
10	2	23	34	11
10	3	22	27	5
			Average absolute error 8.5	

*Missing observations are due to no awareness data available for a product in a given period.

periods. In later periods awareness may increase or decline if the GRP level is low, but the change cannot be determined from the available data.

Looking at Table 4, one sees that the model seems to predict actual awareness fairly well. There are a few cases in which the errors are large. The adjusted R^2's are reasonably high for a time-series cross-sectional model. The average absolute error for product 1 is 7.8 and for product 2 is 8.5. On the basis of both the fits and the reasonableness of the parameter estimates, the model appears to represent the advertising-awareness process fairly well.

From the values given in Table 3, it seems that the parameter estimates are very different for the two product categories. If the parameters are not estimated separately but instead the two data sets are pooled and a single set of parameters is estimated, the fitted predictions would be much poorer. This conclusion is based upon a casual study of the parameters. However, given the different magnitudes of the parameters (initial awareness is .38 versus .10, decay rate 385 versus 4 GRP's, etc.), it seems necessary to estimate parameters separately for individual product categories. This result is somewhat counter to that of other authors [e.g., see 3]. More theoretical work, beyond the scope of this study, is necessary to explain why product categories should differ in their response to advertising.

Predicting awareness was accomplished by use of only one variable and thus the data costs were low. Because the models seem to fit the data fairly well, the cost of collecting information on additional variables to improve the fit did not seem justified. Therefore the fairly simple model described was used to represent the advertising-awareness relationship.

THE TRIAL MODEL

The Model

After consumers become aware of the new product, they decide whether or not they should try it. Trial theoretically follows awareness, and therefore triers should be a percentage of the customers who are aware of the new product. However, there are different groups of consumers who are aware and have not tried the brand. One consists of consumers who become aware in the present period $(A_t - A_{t-1})$. The other group consists of those who were aware in the previous periods but have not yet tried the product $(A_{t-1} - T_{t-1})$. The two potential trier groups presumably have different probabilities of trial. In most cases, the newly aware potential triers should have a higher probability of trial than those who have been aware in the past and have not yet tried the new product. These two groups form the pool of individuals available for trial. Thus the model is

$$(2) \qquad T_t = T_{t-1} + \alpha (A_t - A_{t-1}) + \beta (A_{t-1} - T_{t-1})$$

where T_t is the cumulative percentage of triers of the new product in period t, A_t is the cumulative percentage of potential triers of the new product who are aware of the new product in period t, and α and β represent the fraction of potential triers who actually become triers in a given period.

The parameters are expected to be constrained by $0 < \beta < \alpha < 1$.

Other factors also should be considered in the model. One is price. Price does not affect awareness, but it does affect trial. Consumers may be interested in trying a new product on the basis of attitudes developed from the advertising, but may not actually try once they learn that the product is twice as expensive as their present brand. Consequently, awareness may be high but trial low because the price is too high. The opposite effect also may occur; that is, low price may induce trial. Couponing is an example of creating high trial by reducing the price of the initial purchase.

Price can be included in the model in several ways. First, one can simply make it an additive term, i.e., $T_t = T_{t-1} + \delta P_t + \dots$. Another approach, which is the one used, is to adjust incremental trial, ΔT_t, by a relative price term. The advantage of this form of the dependent variable of the model is that it adjusts trial by a percentage rather than simply reducing trial by some fixed amount as the additive approach does. Using a multiplicative approach also precludes a negative prediction for the change in trial which can happen for the additive model. The trial model now becomes

$$(2a) \qquad \Delta T_t^* = \alpha(A_t - A_{t-1}) + \beta(A_{t-1} - T_{t-1})$$

$$(2b) \qquad \Delta T_t^* = \Delta T_t \cdot \bar{P}_t^\gamma$$

$$(2c) \qquad \Delta T_t^* = T_t^* - T_{t-1}^*$$

$$\Delta T_t = T_t - T_{t-1}$$

where $\bar{P}_t$ is the relative price of the brand at time t and is defined by $\bar{P}_t = P_{b,t} / P_{a,t}$, with $P_{a,t}$ = average price of the product category at time t and $P_{b,t}$ = price of the new brand at time t. If $\bar{P}_t$ is greater than one, then $P_{b,t} > P_{a,t}$ and expected trial is reduced. If $\bar{P}_t$ is less than one, expected trial is increased. $\bar{P}_t$ is raised to the γ power to allow greater or less effect of the price ratio than the simple form $\bar{P}_t$. If $\gamma > 1$, the effect of price differences across products will be accentuated. If $\gamma < 1$, the difference will be less pronounced.

Another factor that affects trial is distribution. Unfortunately, the available distribution data were extremely poor. [10] Because the model is estimated for each product category and because many of the new products in a specific category are marketed by the same firm, distribution will be approximately the same for many of the brands in a specific product category. Therefore, it may not cause serious estimation problems if distribution is not included in the model. [11]

Certain other factors also affect trial but cannot be included explicitly in the model because of the costs of measuring them. Examples of these factors are word-of-mouth communication, package design, and quality of the advertising message. These factors can be included in the error term of the model, but to do so may cause the error terms for a given brand to be correlated over time. Thus, the error term for period t is $u_t = \rho u_{t-1} + \varepsilon_t$ where u_{t-1} is the previous period's error term and ε_t is an error unique to period t. Assume the ε_t's are uncorrelated over time and across products. The u_t's will be correlated over time.

Assume $0 < \rho < 1$, which implies that if last period's error is positive, this period's error will have a higher chance of being positive, and similarly if last period's error is negative, this period's has a higher chance of being negative. The effect of designing the error term in this manner is to adjust implicitly for factors that are not measured but belong in the model.

The magnitude of the error term also should be affected by the price adjustment. Therefore, the variance of the error will be a function of $\bar{P}_t^\gamma$. By simply letting $u_t^* = u_t \bar{P}_t^\gamma$, this problem can be overcome.

The final model becomes

$$(3a) \qquad \Delta T_{i,t}^* = \alpha(A_{i,t} - A_{i,t-1}) + \beta(A_{i,t-1} - T_{i,t-1}) + u_{i,t}^*$$

$$(3b) \qquad \Delta T_{i,t}^* = \Delta T_{i,t} \cdot \bar{P}_t^\gamma \qquad\qquad t = 1, \dots, n_i$$

$$i = 1, \dots, k$$

$$(3c) \qquad u_{i,t} = \rho u_{i,t-1} + \varepsilon_{i,t} \qquad\qquad t = 2, 3, \dots, n_i$$

$$(3d) \qquad u_{i,t}^* = u_{i,t} \cdot \bar{P}_t^\gamma \qquad\qquad t = 1, \dots, n_i$$

where $\Delta T_{i,t}^*$ = price adjusted incremental trial for the ith product in period t, $\Delta T_{i,t}$ = incremental trial for the ith period, $A_{i,t}$ = cumulative awareness for the ith product in period t, $P_{i,t}$ = the relative price in period t for brand i, and $u_{i,t}$ is the disturbance term which follows the process given in equation 3c, $\varepsilon_{i,t}$ is assumed to have zero mean and to be uncorrelated across time and products, i is the brand subscript, t is the time subscript, n_i is the number of periods of data available for brand i, and k is the total number of brands for the category.

Estimation Results

Estimates were computed for the same two products as were used with the awareness model. Table 5 gives the parameter estimates and Table 6 the fitted predictions and average absolute errors. [12]

Table 5
PARAMETER ESTIMATES FOR AWARENESS-TRIAL MODEL

Product category	Parameters*			
	$\hat{\alpha}$	$\hat{\beta}$	$\hat{\gamma}$	$\hat{\rho}$
1	.274	.048	.2	.1
2	.277	.074	—[b]	—[c]

*Standard errors are not reported because nonlinear estimation was used and therefore the standard errors are only large sample approximations.

[b] The prices for all products in category 2 were the same.

[c] Because there were very few products in category 2 for which time series observations were available, the serial correlation coefficient was not calculated.

---

[10] The problem with distribution estimates is that they vary depending on the data source. The source of the distribution data varied within a category and therefore these data were not used.

[11] Distribution statistics are still used for diagnostic purposes.

---

[12] The estimation procedure used for the awareness to trial model is available from R. Blattberg.

Table 6
TRIAL MODEL'S PREDICTIONS

Brand number	Period	Actual	Predicted	Absolute error
Product category 1				
1	1	21	15	6
1[a]	3	29	31	2
2	1	9	8	1
2	2	7	13	6
2	3	9	10	1
3	1	7	10	3
3	2	8	10	2
3	3	9	10	1
4	3	28	27	1
5	1	5	6	1
5	3	23	14	9
6	1	7	12	5
6	2	10	10	0
7	1	15	15	0
7	2	17	17	0
7	3	22	19	3
8	1	11	14	3
8	3	16	16	0
			Average absolute error	2.4
Product category 2				
1	2	11	10	1
2	1	12	10	2
2	2	20	17	3
3	2	15	14	1
4	3	27	19	8
5	3	8	11	3
6	2	16	22	6
6	3	23	23	0
7	1	2	8	6
7	2	5	8	3
7	3	−3	2	5
			Average absolute error	3.5

[a]Missing observations are due to no trial or no awareness data for a product in a given period.

The parameter estimates seem to make sense intuitively. First, α and β meet the assumed restrictions that $\alpha > \beta > 0$. For product category 1, $\alpha = .274$ and $\beta = .048$; that is, 27.4% of consumers who became aware in the recent period will purchase in that period and 4.8% of those who were previously aware but did not try the product will try the brand in the present period. For product category 2, $\alpha = .277$ and $\beta = .074$ which indicates a higher percentage of previously aware consumers who did not try will try the brand in the present period than for product category 1.

For category 1 it was possible to calculate γ and ρ, but for category 2 the price was the same for all brands. Therefore γ could not be calculated. Also because of data limitations, very few time series observations were available which meant ρ could not be estimated accurately. Only for category 1 are ρ and γ estimated.

The estimate of γ for product category 1 was .23 which indicates the effect of price for this category is less than if the relative price had been used. The brands in category 1 are heavily advertised and there

is substantial product differentiation which may explain the lack of price sensitivity as indicated by $\hat{\gamma} = .23$.

The estimate of ρ is .1 which indicates a low correlation between the period-to-period error for a specific brand. In fact, setting $\rho = 0$ does not greatly affect the results.

The prediction accuracy of the model seems satisfactory. In only a few cases were the errors large for either product category. The average error was very low, 2.4 and 3.5 for categories 1 and 2, respectively. When the prediction accuracy and the signs and magnitudes of the coefficient estimates are combined, this model appears to be very good.

One last point deserves discussion. Because only three months of data are used, all past aware but nontriers were aggregated into a single variable, $A_{t-1} - T_{t-1}$. However, the longer the time that a consumer is aware and does not try, the less likely he is to try eventually. In use of the model as a planning tool, it may be sensible to adjust β downward after some time period.[13]

THE PROJECTION MODEL

The final stage is the projection model, the goal of which is to forecast year-end market shares (or sales) of the new product using as inputs forecasts of trial rates made from the trial model, repeat usage rates, repeat purchase proportions, and trial usage rates.

The idea underlying the projection model is simple. The consumer begins as a trier. He can then either use the product again, becoming a repeat user, or enter the nonuser class. He then either continues to use the product or enters the nonuser class.[14] This process continues each period after initial trial with the consumer either staying in the user class or moving into the nonuser class. The model does the tracking of the percentage of consumers in each stage of repeat usage. To compute each period's sales, the model simply aggregates the percentage of users in each repeat class and the period's new triers. Figure 2 is a flow chart of the projection model.

As seen from Figure 2, to make year-end market projections one needs trial rates, the percentage of repeat users, consumption rates for triers and repeat users, and a decay rate for repeat users. The next section shows how these inputs were combined to project year-end market share or sales.

Projection Model Equations

The basic mathematical relationships used to make projections are:

---

[13]Parfitt and Collins [11, p. 136] state that late triers have lower average repeat purchasing rates.

[14]Aaker [1, p. 448] in his new trier model found that consumers replace their old brand with the new brand or they discard the new brand if they do not like its attributes.

Figure 2
FLOW CHART OF THE PROJECTION MODEL

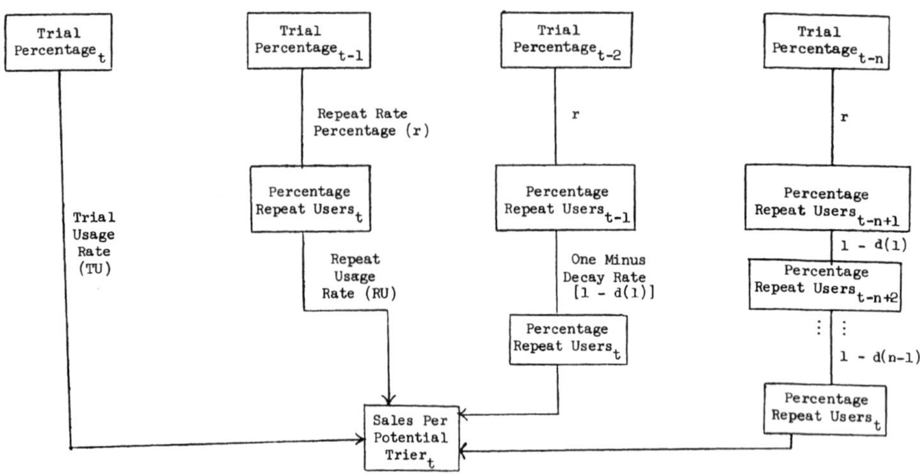

(4a)
$$UC_{t-1}(t) = r\Delta T(t - 1) \qquad t = 2, \ldots$$

(4b)
$$UC_{t-i}(t) = [1 - d(i - 1)]\, UC_{t-i}(t - 1)$$
$$i = 1, \ldots, t - 1$$

where:

$\Delta T(t) =$ the percentage of new triers for period t,

$r =$ the percentage of triers in period t who remain users in period $t + 1$,

$UC_{t-i}(t) =$ the percentage of new triers in period $t - i$ who are still in the user class at time t,

$d(i - 1) =$ the percentage of new triers in period t who purchased in period $t + i - 1$ and stop purchasing in period $t + i$,

$t =$ the time period which is usually in months.

Equation 4a says that r proportion of new triers in period t will repeat purchase in period $t + 1$. Equation 4b says that $[1 - d(i - 1)]$ proportion of users who purchased in period $(t + i - 1)$, will repeat purchase in period $(t + i)$. Thus, equations 4a and 4b compute the proportion of new triers in period t who repeat purchased in period $t + 1, t + 2, \ldots$

To compute total sales in a given period, one multiplies the proportion in each user class by their usage rate. Then total sales per potential trier[15] in period t, $TS(t)$, is simply

(5)
$$TS(t) = TU \cdot \Delta T(t) + \sum_{i=1}^{t-1} UC_i(t) \cdot RU,$$
$$t = 2, 3, \ldots$$
$$TS(t) = TU \cdot \Delta T(t) \qquad t = 1$$

where:

$TU =$ the quantity purchased by a trier, and
$RU =$ the quantity purchased by members of the user class.

In equations 4a, 4b, and 5 there are several unknown parameters, $d(1), \ldots, d(12)$, r, TU, and RU, that must be estimated. To estimate these parameters some simplifying assumptions are made. To begin, it is assumed that the repeat usage percentage r is not dependent on time. This is obviously not true. However, if r is time dependent, one must estimate 12 parameters. A simplifying assumption is that the repeat usage percentage is constant. Evidence about early adopters versus late adopters contradicts this assumption. However, the authors have found accurate predictions assuming a constant repeat rate, and therefore as an approximation it may not be too costly, in a prediction sense, to assume the same value of r for all periods.[16]

To estimate the other parameters of the projection model it is also assumed that they are not dependent on time. Note that $d(i)$ still depends on the length

---

[15] To compute total sales, the number of potential triers (users) of the product class is multiplied by $TS(t)$.

[16] Note that in many models parameters probably vary from period to period. As an approximation they are often assumed to be fixed.

200   JOURNAL OF MARKETING RESEARCH, MAY 1978

of time from the first period the consumer tried the product, but it does not depend on the length of time since the new product was introduced.

To compute year-end sales one can sum the sales for each month, $\Sigma_{t=1}^{12} TS(t)$, and obtain a forecast. Usually firms are interested in longer term sales in addition to first year sales. To forecast future sales, sales for the last few months of the first year are used to make projections. The reason is that new product sales usually spurt in the early months of the introduction and then dampen after four or five months. By months nine or ten, sales have usually reached "steady state." Thus, the last few months of the first year are more representative of future sales than are the total first year sales.[17]

Parameter Estimation

The parameters that need to be estimated are TU, RU, $d(1)$, ..., $d(12)$, and r. Two of these parameters, r and RU, were estimated by using telephone surveys done monthly for the first three months of the introduction.[18] The $d(i)$'s were estimated subjectively by using repeat rates and product satisfaction information received from the questionnaire. (The reasons for using subjective estimates are explained hereafter.) TU was set equal to one because triers automatically use one unit in the period they become triers.

Two procedures were used to estimate r. In the first period after the introduction, most triers have not had time to repurchase. Consequently, questions about purchase intentions and product satisfaction measures were used to estimate a repeat purchase probability. If the customer seems to have had a positive experience with the product and intends to purchase, he is classified as being a repeat user. If he says he intends to repurchase but then expresses negative opinions about the product, he is classified as a nonrepeat user. The percentage of triers classified as users gives an estimate of r.

For periods two and three, actual repeat rates can be used. Customers who first bought more than one period ago and have repurchased in the last period are classified as repeat users. The percentage of customers who repurchase divided by the total number who have tried the new product more than one period ago gives an estimate of r.

The three estimates of r (one for each wave) are averaged to give a final estimate of r. Even though the first period's estimate is subjective, it seems to be close to the last two in almost all of the new product introductions that have been studied. This averaged estimate of r is used as an input to the projection model.

To estimate the repeat purchaser's usage rate, RU, data collected from the telephone survey were used. A repeat user is not required to be "brand loyal" to the product. He is only required to have used the new product in the last period. The repeat usage rate measures the consumption rate for the new brand by repeat users.

The final parameters to be estimated are the decay percentages for each user class, $d(1)$, ..., $d(12)$. Estimating the $d(i)$'s requires data about when the product has been first purchased and the repurchase rates for users who tried one, two, three, ... periods ago. In the first three months of the introduction one usually gets information about trial and one repurchase. Occasionally there are two or three repurchases. However, only a few, if any, triers have repurchased often enough for estimation of $d(1)$. Almost never can one estimate $d(2)$, ..., $d(12)$. Therefore, the authors decided to use subjective estimates of the $d(i)$'s.

To obtain subjective estimates for $d(1)$, assume that the probability of repurchasing given trial and one repurchase is higher than that of simply repurchasing after initial trial. Thus $r < [1 - d(1)]$. Using a similar argument, assume that $[1 - d(1)] \leq [1 - d(2)] \leq$, ..., $\leq [1 - d(12)]$. From information about purchase intentions and product satisfaction among repeat users, one can also determine whether repeat customers seem satisfied. If they are, it is assumed that the $[1 - d(i)]$'s will be high. If there seems to be dissatisfaction, then the estimates of the $[1 - d(i)]$'s are lowered.

Because subjective estimates of the $d(i)$'s were used, a sensitivity analysis of the $d(i)$'s was applied to show whether the resulting forecasts change drastically. An example of the sensitivity analysis is given in Table 7. To show the effect of different values of $d(i)$'s, the same values of r, RU, and $\Delta T(t)$ were used for all three runs, r was set at .4, RU was set at 1.4 units per period, and the trial figures are listed in Table 7. The output of the projection model represents units purchased per potential customer. For example, in Table 7, for all three sets of $d(i)$'s, .08 units per potential trier were consumed in period 1. In other words, each potential consumer used eight hundredths of a unit in period one. The total number of potential consumers for this product category would be multiplied by .08 to obtain a sales estimate for period one.

The results show that year-end sales for the first set of (low decay) $d(i)$'s are approximately 33% larger than those for the third set of $d(i)$'s (high decay). This finding indicates that the sales results are somewhat sensitive to the values of the $d(i)$'s used. However, it is important to note that even though each $d(i)$ may not look very different between set one and set three, their aggregate effects are very different. For a trier with $d(1) = .2$ and $d(2) = .1$, there is a 29% chance of his using the product three

---

[17] If the product is seasonal, then a seasonal adjustment needs to be made before using the last three months.

[18] Occasionally shorter or longer time periods are used because of the length of the purchase cycle of the product.

Table 7
SALES PER POTENTIAL TRIER FOR DIFFERENT DECAY PERCENTAGES

Repeat rate percentage = .4, repeat usage rate = 1.4												
Period	*1*	*2*	*3*	*4*	*5*	*6*	*7*	*8*	*9*	*10*	*11*	*12*
Trial percentage	8	5	4	2	2	1	1	1	1	.5	.5	.5

Decay percentage $[d(i)]$													
Period		*1*	*2*	*3*	*4*	*5*	*6*	*7*	*8*	*9*	*10*	*11*	*12*
Decay rate	Low	20%	10	5	4	3	2	2	2	2	2	2	2
	Medium	25	15	8	5	3	2	2	2	2	2	2	2
	High	30	20	10	5	3	3	2	2	2	2	2	2

Sales per potential trier													
Period		*1*	*2*	*3*	*4*	*5*	*6*	*7*	*8*	*9*	*10*	*11*	*12*
Decay rate	Low	.0800	.0948	.1038	.0971	.0999	.0948	.0948	.0963	.0983	.0954	.0946	.0947
	Medium	.0800	.0948	.1016	.0920	.0921	.0853	.0841	.0849	.0864	.0831	.0822	.0819
	High	.0800	.0948	.0994	.0871	.0851	.0771	.0752	.0753	.0764	.0729	.0716	.0712

periods later $(.4 \times .8 \times .9)$. With $d(1) = .3$ and $d(2) = .2$, he has a 22% chance of using the product three periods later. Therefore, there is a considerable difference in the two sets of $d(i)$'s used.

To use the projection model one must input one more parameter, the trial usage rate, TU. This parameter was set equal to one, because a trier, by definition, must purchase one unit in the period in which he initially tries the product.

From the description just given one sees that two parameters of the projection model are estimated from each period's telephone survey, RU and r, one set of parameters is estimated subjectively, $d(1)$, ..., $d(12)$, and TU is set equal to one. As one obtains more experience with the model, it becomes easier to estimate the $d(i)$'s. If consumer diary panel data were used, more accurate estimates of these parameters could be obtained. However, on the basis of the forecasting accuracy of the model with the estimation procedures described, the additional cost of panel data does not seem justified.

Using the Projection Model When the New Product Is Sampled Heavily

When a new product is sampled (free samples are given to potential users), the awareness-trial-repeat usage chain is broken. Trial occurs simultaneously with awareness. The trial rates may be different for consumers given samples than for consumers who must pay for the product in order to try it. If a consumer has tried the product but did not purchase it, the reason may be that it is more expensive than he had expected. Therefore, a sampled customer's repeat rate will probably be different from that of a nonsampled customer. Other factors also may intervene which will make his repeat rates different from those of nonsampled customers. Therefore, in estimating the parameters of the projection model, the sampled and nonsampled triers are separated. Usually sampled customers have both higher trial rates (more like initial repeat usage rate for nonsampled consumers) and higher repeat usage rates. By knowing the initial percentage sampled one can easily combine the sampled and nonsampled groups to make year-end sales projections.

Diagnostic Information from the Projection Model

The projection model is also used to diagnose problems with the introduction. Because the main factor in the ultimate success of a new product is repeat purchasing, it is useful to determine why a product has a low or high repeat rate. This is done by asking questions about product satisfaction and repeat purchase intentions. From these questions one often can learn why a new product is failing or why it is successful. The latter is important because if a product has a high repeat user percentage but appears to have relatively low product satisfaction, repeat rates may soon begin to decline. Thus the decay percentage will be higher than normal.

If a product has a low repeat usage percentage, one can often identify the causes. Perhaps there are unexpected design problems, or the product is too similar to other products on the market. From the diagnostic information, advice can be given about how to redesign the product so that it can be introduced in other test markets and retested.

Obviously, the diagnostic feature is an essential component of the projection model. Models using panel data such as Parfitt-Collins model [11] would require additional research because diagnostic information is not a natural byproduct of the model. One can be more confident in making projections when repeat usage percentages correspond to consumer statements about product satisfaction and purchase intentions.

THE PLANNING MODEL

The model described in the preceding sections also can be used as a planning model prior to test marketing. In many cases firms are interested in evaluating how several marketing strategies affect sales. By specifying a media spending strategy, price, and sampling level plus some estimate of usage and repeat rates, the model can make pre-test market sales forecasts. These forecasts are based on "norms" for the product category. Often products exceed or fall below the norms.[19] However, using the planning model gives the firm some indication of the effects of alternative strategies.

The most difficult inputs to obtain for the planning model are the repeat usage percentage and trial and repeat usage rates. Because these parameters are extremely important, usually a number of alternative rates are used. The normal repeat usage percentage is about 40%. Successful products often have values around the 50% level and unsuccessful products around 30%. One can make projections using all three rates to see their effect on sales.[20] In addition results from concept tests and in-home use tests are often helpful in making pre-test market estimates.

Using the planning model has helped firms determine the potential magnitude of sales expected from the test market. In one study, the firm's prior sales estimate was 6 million case sales for the first year. Use of the planning model with optimistic repeat usage percentages and high trial rates generated only 2 million case sales. Therefore, the firm was able to revise its initial production requirements downward to a more appropriate level.

In another case a firm evaluated different advertising budgeting strategies to see what effect they had on sales. Given the cost of goods sold, the firm could do a profitability analysis to determine which strategy led to maximum profits.

CONCLUSION

A new product forecasting model that is fairly accurate and inexpensive to use is presented. The model uses survey data rather than panel data. It also uses marketing inputs such as advertising and price. The model can forecast year-end sales after only three months of test marketing so that a quick decision about the success of the product can be reached. The model also gives diagnostic information about the reason for low awareness, trial, or repeat purchasing. It thus helps firms to redesign the product or the introduction strategy. Finally, the model also can be used for evaluating alternative marketing strategies. The next step is to develop accurate inputs to the model before test marketing so that the model can be used to predict success or failure of products without requiring test marketing. Thus the high cost of test marketing can be avoided.

REFERENCES

1. Aaker, D. A. "The New Trier Stochastic Model of Brand Choice," *Management Science*, 17 (April 1971), B435–50.
2. Ahl, D. H. "New Product Forecasting Using Consumer Panels," *Journal of Marketing Research*, 7 (May 1970), 160–7.
3. Claycamp, H. J. and L. E. Liddy. "Prediction of New Product Performance: An Analytical Approach," *Journal of Marketing Research*, 6 (November 1969), 414–20.
4. Eskin, G. J. "Dynamic Forecasts of New Product Demand Using a Depth Repeat Model," *Journal of Marketing Research*, 10 (May 1973), 115–29.
5. Fourt, L. A. and J. W. Woodlock. "Early Prediction of Market Success for New Grocery Products," *Journal of Marketing*, 24 (October 1960), 31–8.
6. Johnston, J. *Econometric Methods*. New York: McGraw-Hill Book Company, Inc., 1972.
7. Learner, D. B. "Profit Maximization through New Product Marketing Planning and Control," *in* F. M. Bass, C. W. King, and E. A. Pessemier, eds., *Applications of the Sciences in Marketing Management*. New York: John Wiley and Sons, Inc., 1968, 151–67.
8. Massy, W. F. "Stochastic Models for Monitoring New Product Introduction," *in* F. M. Bass, C. W. King, and E. A. Pessemier, eds., *Application of the Sciences in Marketing Management*. New York: John Wiley and Sons, Inc., 1968.
9. NEWS. *New Early Warning System*. Technical Report, Management Science Department, BBDO (no data given).
10. NEWS. The NEWS Model, A Technical Description, Technical Report, Management Science Department, BBDO.
11. Parfitt, J. H. and B. J. K. Collins. "Use of Consumer Panels for Brand-Share Prediction," *Journal of Marketing Research*, 5 (May 1968), 131–45.
12. Silk, A. J. and G. L. Urban. "Pre-Test Market Evaluation of New Packaged Goods: A Model and Measurement Methodology." MIT working paper, 834–76, January 1976.
13. Urban, G. L. "Sprinter Mod III: A Model for the Analysis of New Frequently Purchased Consumer Products," *Operations Research*, 17 (September–October 1969), 805–54.
14. ———— and Richard Karash. "Evolutionary Model Building," *Journal of Marketing Research*, 8 (February 1971), 62–71.

---

[19] Forecast accuracy for the model will be less than that given in Table 1 when the planning model is used because test market data are not used for the first three periods.

[20] To facilitate these calculations, a time-sharing version of the model has been developed which allows the model's users to test alternative strategies very rapidly.

ROBERT C. BLATTBERG, THOMAS BUESING, & SUBRATA K. SEN

The authors examine the issue of determining the market segments to which a new national brand should be targeted. The usual recommendation is that the new brand should be targeted toward those segments that exhibit considerable brand switching. However, a new national brand should also attempt to attract segments that are loyal to existing national brands as well as segments that primarily purchase private labels. These implications follow from an explicit consideration of the changes in pricing and distribution patterns which occur when a new national brand is introduced. The results are illustrated with a set of diary panel data for facial tissue.

SEGMENTATION STRATEGIES FOR NEW NATIONAL BRANDS

AN important managerial issue in new product introduction is the determination of the target segments for the new brand. However, most new product models (see, for example, Blattberg and Golanty 1978; Eskin 1973; Mahajan and Muller 1979; Parfitt and Collins 1968; Shocker and Srinivasan 1979, Silk and Urban 1978) have concentrated primarily on predicting the sales of the new product. In fact, other than some work in conjoint analysis (see Green and Srinivasan 1978), the only attempt at determining the target segments for a new brand consists of the Hendry model (Butler 1976) which predicts that a new brand will obtain most of its consumers from segments that are not loyal to any single brand.[1]

Is it indeed true that brand switchers are the only relevant target segments for a new brand? We address this question by providing a detailed analysis of the sources of a new brand's sales. In particular, we examine the impact of the introduction of Puffs in the facial tissue market. The principal managerial implication of our analysis is the determination of the market segments to which a new brand should be targeted.

Description of the Segmentation Scheme

We employ a segmentation approach (see Blattberg and Sen 1974, 1976) that has proved to be useful in other applications. The approach is limited to inexpensive frequently purchased products and requires the availability of consumer panel data. The analysis is done at the individual household level and each household is classified (by a Bayesian model discrimination procedure described by Blattberg and Sen 1975) into one of a set of segments defined a priori. The segment definitions are based on three purchasing dimensions: (1) the degree of household brand loyalty, (2) the type of brand

Robert C. Blattberg is Professor of Marketing and Statistics, Graduate School of Business, University of Chicago, Thomas Buesing is with Peat, Marwick and Mitchell, and Subrata K. Sen is Associate Professor of Business Administration, Graduate School of Management, University of Rochester. The authors would like to thank Jerry Wind for his very valuable comments.

[1]The full details of the Hendry approach have not been published. Hence, our knowledge of the Hendry model is limited to the information contained in publications such as Butler's (1976) and Kalwani and Morrison's (1977).

preferred (national or private label), and (3) the household's price sensitivity (see Blattberg and Sen 1974 for a justification of this approach). The six most important segments thus defined are used in the analysis. They are briefly described below.

- *National Brand Loyal.* Members of this segment primarily buy a single national brand at its regular price.

- *National Brand Deal.* This segment is similar to the National Brand Loyal segment except that most of the purchases are made on deal. To buy the preferred national brand on deal, the consumer engages in considerable store switching.

- *Private Label Loyal.* Households in this segment primarily buy the private label offered by the store at which they usually shop.

- *Private Label Deal.* This segment shops at many stores and buys the private label of each store, usually on deal.

- *National Brand Switcher.* Members of this segment tend not to buy private labels. Instead, they switch regularly among the various national brands on the market.

- *Private Label Switcher.* This segment is similar to the Private Label Deal segment except that the members are not very deal prone and purchase the private labels at their regular prices.

Purchase histories of households typical of these segments are given by Blattberg and Sen for aluminum foil (1974) and for facial tissue (1976).

This segmentation method has been applied to five frequently purchased products: aluminum foil, waxed paper, facial tissue, liquid detergent, and headache remedies. Comparability of results across products is discussed by Blattberg, Peacock, and Sen (1976), who show that consumers frequently use identical or similar purchasing strategies across product categories.

Market Share Predictions for the Hendry Model

Description of the Hendry New Product Analysis

The Hendry model states that a new brand's market share depends on the "consumer preference profile" of the market (Butler 1976, p. 53). The consumer preference profile consists of the distribution of consumer "preferences and buying habits" (Butler 1976, p. 53). A typical consumer preference profile is reproduced in Figure 1. Further, a new product will obtain most of its customers from the "middle section of the preference

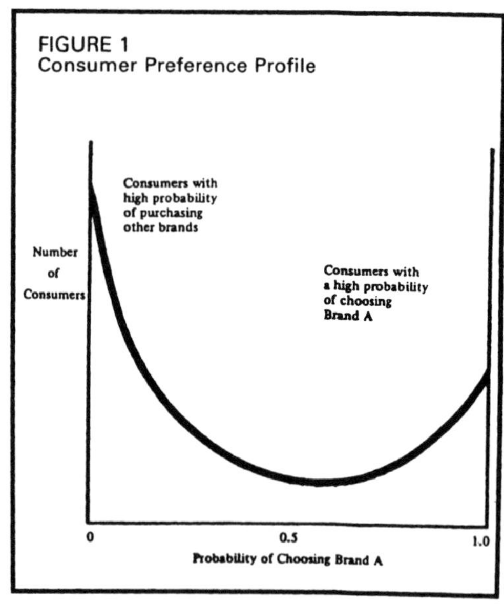

profile" (Butler 1976, p. 56). In other words, a new brand's market share will come primarily from those consumers who do not have a high probability of buying any particular brand, i.e., brand switchers. If brand switchers are the primary source of a new brand's sales, we can predict the degree to which the new brand will obtain market share in each of the six segments described in the preceding section.

Market Share Predictions by Segment

Clearly, the new brand should achieve its largest market share in the two segments that consist primarily of brand switchers: the National Brand Switcher segment and the Private Label Switcher segment. The new brand's market share should be second largest in the National Brand Deal segment and the Private Label Deal segment. Members of these two segments are sensitive to deals and, hence, are willing to switch brands if the deal is sufficiently attractive. The new brand should do least well in the two segments that are loyal to a single brand: the National Brand Loyal segment and the Private Label Loyal segment.

We now examine the degree to which these predictions are supported in the case of Puffs, a national brand of facial tissue that was introduced in the Chicago market in August 1961.

TABLE 1
Market Share and Penetration of Puffs in the Six Segments

Segment	Period	Market Share	Penetration	Number of Households in Segment[a]
National Brand Loyal	47-56[b]	17.4%	.514	74
	57-66	12.4	.446	65
National Brand Deal	47-56	15.6	.571	28
	57-66	16.1	.556	27
Private Label Loyal	47-56	13.1	.560	50
	57-66	11.2	.438	48
Private Label Deal	47-56	20.2	.531	64
	57-66	13.8	.377	61
National Brand Switcher	47-56	20.1	.681	72
	57-66	16.6	.531	64
Private Label Switcher	47-56	16.6	.673	52
	57-66	13.8	.500	46

[a]The number of households in each segment decreases in periods 57-66 in relation to periods 47-56 because some of the households either drop out of the panel in the latter period or do not make any purchases of facial tissue.
[b]Puffs was introduced in period 47.

Description of the Data

A set of diary panel data on facial tissue purchases was obtained from the *Chicago Tribune*'s panel of women in the Greater Chicago area. The data analyzed consist of purchases for 260 weeks starting in 1958. Of the 16 brands coded 1 to 16, brands 1 (Kleenex), 2 (Scotties), 6 (Puffs), 10 (Vanity Fair), and 13 (Doeskin) are national brands and the rest are private labels. The stores are coded 1 to 10. Stores 1 to 4 are major supermarket chains (Store 1 is A&P, Store 2 is National, Store 3 is Jewel, Store 4 is Kroger). Stores 5 to 7 are independent food chains (e.g., Store 6 is Certified). Store 8 is Walgreen's, a major drug store chain, Store 9 represents other drug stores, and Store 10 represents all other stores.

For the first 46 four-week periods of the data, Puffs was not available in the market. This section of the data was used to classify individual households into the six segments.[2] The behavior of these segments in relation to Puffs was then analyzed for the remaining 20 four-week periods (47-66) when Puffs was introduced into the Greater Chicago market.

Results

Market Share

Puffs' market share figures for the six segments are listed in Table 1. The results are presented separately for two subperiods after the introduction of Puffs: periods 47-56 (which can be viewed as an initial period) and periods 57-66 (a longer run repeat buying period).[3] The market share of Puffs is larger in the earlier time period (periods 47-56) than in periods 57-66,[4] as expected, for all segments except the National Brand Deal segment.

If the market shares for the latter period are converted into a rank order, the rank ordering is reasonably consistent with the rank ordering predicted in the preceding section. For example, Puffs achieves its largest market share in the National Brand Switcher segment and its two smallest shares in the National Brand Loyal and Private Label Loyal segments.

---

[2]The classification was applied to the 474 households that had made at least 10 purchases of facial tissue prior to the introduction of Puffs. The cutoff figure of 10 was chosen because it is very difficult to interpret the purchasing patterns of consumers making less than 10 purchases. The 474 households that qualified for the analysis accounted for 91.8% of the panel's facial tissue purchases. Note, however, that the results reported exclude 17.3% of the 474 households. The omitted households changed their purchasing patterns in the pre-Puffs period.

[3]Table 1 also provides penetration figures for the six segments, where penetration has the usual definition of the proportion of households in the segment that have tried Puffs at least once.

[4]It would be desirable to report whether these differences are statistically significant. However, appropriate statistical tests for diary panel data are very complex. The test must incorporate the fact that the observations are correlated between periods (because the data are being obtained from the same households). It is also necessary to consider other factors such as seasonal buying differences and the number of panel members who drop out of the panel and need to be replaced. The exact formula for the variance of the appropriate test statistic is complicated and beyond the scope of this article. Hence, the results are presented without significance tests.

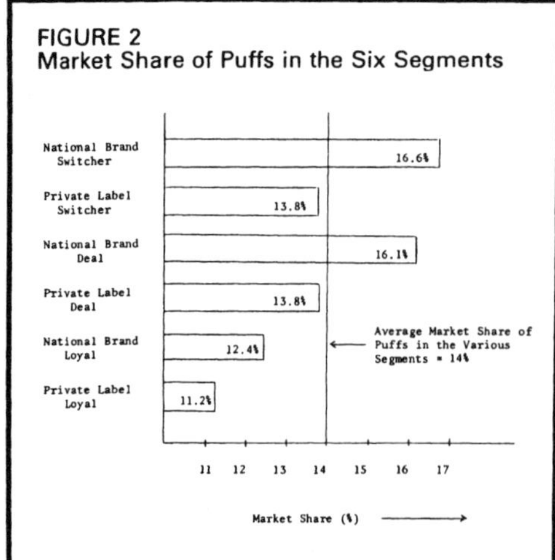

consumers across the board. This point is highlighted in Figure 2 which is a plot of Puffs' market share for periods 57–66 for the six segments. We observe that Puffs' share in each segment deviates very little from its average market share of roughly 14%.

We conclude, therefore, that a new national brand obtains its sales not only from brand switchers but from all consumers. This finding has important marketing implications which we explore in the next section. First, however, we examine the brands from which Puffs obtained most of its share.

Sources of Puffs' Market Share

Table 2 lists the market shares of eight of the leading brands in the facial tissue market for the two periods before and after the introduction of Puffs. We can examine this table to make rough estimates of the brands from which Puffs has obtained most of its share.

For the National Brand Loyal and National Brand Deal segments, Puffs' share has come mainly at the expense of Scotties. For the Private Label Loyal, Private Label Deal, and Private Label Switcher segments, Puffs' share has come mainly from brands 4 and 5 (Angel Soft and Swanee Color Soft, respectively), two relatively high-priced "limited distribution" private labels. In addition, brand 7 (Walgreen's private label) lost market share to Puffs in the Private Label Deal segment, and in the Private Label Switcher segment some of Puffs' share came from the "other" brands. Finally, for the National Brand Switcher segment, Puffs' share

Though there is a reasonable match between the actual and predicted *rank orders*, the dominant feature of Table 1 is that the range of the *actual market share figures* in the various segments is very small. The market shares all are between 11.2% and 16.6% for periods 57–66. This finding indicates that Puffs obtains its sales not just from the two switching segments but from

TABLE 2
Market Shares of Leading Brands in the Six Segments

| Segment | Period | National Brands | | | Limited Distribution Brands | | Private Labels | | | |
| | | 1 | 2 | 6 | 4 | 5 | 3[a] | 7[b] | 8[a] | |
		Kleenex	Scotties	Puffs	Angel Soft	Swanee Color Soft	Jewel	Walgreen	Jewel	Others
National Brand Loyal	1-46	.466	.427	.000	.007	.015	.017	.004	.004	.033
	47-66	.414	.321	.150	.003	.014	.032	.000	.000	.045
National Brand Deal	1-46	.640	.189	.000	.018	.013	.019	.022	.005	.053
	47-66	.580	.124	.159	.013	.006	.052	.016	.000	.032
Private Label Loyal	1-46	.053	.020	.000	.319	.154	.278	.014	.080	.031
	47-66	.089	.057	.122	.239	.093	.279	.008	.025	.051
Private Label Deal	1-46	.181	.040	.000	.212	.069	.097	.196	.031	.121
	47-66	.172	.091	.174	.079	.031	.158	.124	.006	.081
National Brand Switcher	1-46	.262	.178	.000	.059	.103	.108	.014	.023	.126
	47-66	.257	.193	.184	.020	.052	.140	.015	.006	.081
Private Label Switcher	1-46	.069	.028	.000	.206	.200	.204	.039	.055	.092
	47-66	.102	.096	.154	.088	.161	.262	.028	.008	.064

[a]Brands 3 and 8 are both private labels of the Jewel food chain.
[b]Brand 7 is the private label of the Walgreen's drug chain.

TABLE 3
Segment Membership Before and After Introduction of Puffs

Segments Before Introduction of Puffs	Segments After Introduction of Puffs						
	National Brand Loyal	National Brand Deal	Private Label Loyal	Private Label Deal	National Brand Switcher	Private Label Switcher	Row Totals
National Brand Loyal	64.1%[a]	15.4	2.6	0.0	17.9	0.0	39
National Brand Deal	11.8	70.6	0.0	0.0	17.6	0.0	17
Private Label Loyal	5.7	8.6	40.0	20.0	17.1	8.6	35
Private Label Deal	0.0	8.0	0.0	68.0	12.0	12.0	25
National Brand Switcher	13.5	24.3	5.4	10.8	37.8	8.1	37
Private Label Switcher	0.0	13.3	3.3	43.3	13.3	26.7	30
Column Totals	34	36	18	41	37	17	183

[a]The entry in cell (i,j) represents the percentage of members of row segment i in column segment j.

appears to have been achieved mainly at the expense of Swanee Color Soft and the "other" brands.

Marketing Implications

Strategies Followed After the Introduction of Puffs

Before discussing specific marketing implications, we examine whether households continued to use the same purchasing strategy after the introduction of Puffs. For example, did Private Label Loyal households continue the strategy of buying private labels or did they start to buy Puffs or some other national brand? Also, did members of the National Brand Loyal segment continue to purchase the national brand they had purchased before the introduction of Puffs or did a significant number of them switch their loyalty to Puffs? The purchasing strategy changes discussed below have a bearing on certain marketing implications discussed later in this section.

Table 3 is a cross-tabulation of the purchasing strategies used by families before and after the introduction of Puffs.[5] The diagonal entries of the table indicate

the degree to which households continued to use the purchasing strategy they had used prior to the availability of Puffs.[6]

Table 3 indicates that members of two of the three national brand segments (National Brand Loyal and National Brand Deal) tend to follow the *same* purchasing strategy before and after the introduction of Puffs (see the relatively large diagonal entries for these two segments). When a national brand segment's purchasing strategy does change after Puffs' introduction (see the relatively low 37.8% diagonal entry for the National Brand Switcher segment), it changes to a relatively similar strategy. For example, most of the National Brand Switchers who change strategies change to similar strategies such as those followed by members of the National Brand Deal and National Brand Loyal segments. Specifically, Table 3 indicates that 24.3% of National Brand Switchers change to a National Brand Deal strategy and 13.5% switch to a National Brand Loyal strategy. In contrast, members of the three private label segments tend to switch strategies after the

---

[5]Table 3 is based on the 183 households that had made at least 10 purchases in *both* pre-Puffs and post-Puffs periods and which did not change their purchasing patterns in either of the two periods.

[6]To better evaluate the figures in Table 3, it would be desirable to use as a benchmark the degree to which households switch purchasing strategies *in the absence* of the introduction of a new brand such as Puffs. Though the figure is not exactly analogous to the data in Table 3, note that 17.3% of the households switched purchasing strategies in the pre-Puffs period. This level is considerably lower than the switching indicated in Table 3.

introduction of Puffs (see, in particular, the relatively low diagonal entries for the Private Label Loyal and Private Label Switcher segments). Further, relatively large proportions of the switchers become members of the national brand segments, particularly the National Brand Switcher and National Brand Deal segments.

To illustrate the impact of Puffs on purchasing strategies at the *individual* household level, consider the purchasing histories of three different households. Household 952 made 49 purchases prior to the introduction of Puffs. Kleenex accounted for 84% of these 49 purchases. After the introduction of Puffs, this household made 21 additional purchases. Puffs was purchased on every one of these 21 purchase occasions. Thus, household 952 illustrates a household that continued to use a National Brand Loyal purchasing strategy after the introduction of Puffs. However, the household's loyalty switched dramatically from Kleenex to Puffs.

Household 297 purchased Kleenex in 98% of the 98 purchases it made before the introduction of Puffs. However, after Puffs was introduced, this household switched among several national brands, including Puffs. For example, Puffs accounted for 33% of the 46 purchases made by the household after it was introduced and Kleenex's share dropped from the 98% pre-Puffs figure to 48%. Thus, household 297 represents a household that switched its purchasing strategy from National Brand Loyal to National Brand Switcher.

Finally, household 1210 made 10 purchases before the introduction of Puffs. Brand 8 (one of Jewel's private labels) was bought on all 10 purchase occasions. After the introduction of Puffs, this household made 15 additional purchases. Puffs was bought on every one of these 15 purchase occasions. Thus, household 1210 represents a household that switched from a Private Label Loyal strategy (loyal to brand 8) to a National Brand Loyal strategy (loyal to Puffs).

Targeting to the National Brand Loyal Segment

The analysis reported in Table 3 indicates that households purchasing national brands tend to use the same or similar buying strategies even after a major perturbation of the market as caused by the introduction of a successful new national brand such as Puffs. Let us concentrate in particular on the National Brand Loyal segment. Table 3 indicates that most households in this segment continue to follow the strategy of buying a single national brand. Some of these households continue to purchase the brand they had purchased before the introduction of Puffs (e.g., Kleenex). However, other households (e.g., household 952 described earlier) switch to Puffs and continue to buy Puffs almost exclusively. Clearly, it would be extremely profitable to persuade National Brand Loyal households to switch their

loyalty to Puffs. Convincing them to switch might be difficult, but if one succeeds the household becomes a steady buyer of Puffs and hence a very profitable customer.

It is also clear from Table 3 (and household 297) that a National Brand Loyal household can be changed to a National Brand Switcher household that will purchase Puffs along with other national brands. This group would be another important source of sales for a new national brand such as Puffs. The fairly large size of the National Brand Loyal segment (Table 1) further highlights the advantages of attempting to persuade such households to switch to Puffs either completely or partially.

Thus, an important implication of our analysis is that a new national brand should target its appeals to the National Brand Loyal segment. [7] This implication is not obtained from a more aggregate analysis of panel data for new product introductions, e.g., the Parfitt and Collins (1968) and Eskin (1973) brand share prediction models. Nor is this implication suggested by models such as the Hendry model (Butler 1976) which implicitly recommends that brand switchers are the only appropriate target segment for a new national brand.

Targeting to Private Label Segments

The Effects of Price Changes. Table 1 indicates that Puffs' market share was very high in two of the *private label* segments, Private Label Switcher and Private Label Deal. This finding may be somewhat surprising for a *national* brand such as Puffs. The explanation lies in certain price and distribution changes.

Because of Puffs' introduction, the price differential between national brands and private labels became narrower in general, as indicated in Table 4 which lists average prices for the eight leading brands before and after the introduction of Puffs. The prices of the two national brands, Kleenex and Scotties, drop by a cent or two after the advent of Puffs whereas the prices of the "limited distribution" brands and the private labels either remain unchanged or increase slightly. Brand 3 (one of Jewel's two private labels) is the only non-national brand that decreases in price. [8]

Because the price difference between national brands and private labels narrowed after the introduction of Puffs, many purchasers of private labels (particularly the relatively more expensive "limited distribution" private labels such as Angel Soft and Swanee Color Soft) switched to national brands (including Puffs). Thus,

---

[7] Of course, to implement this strategy effectively, one must *reach* this segment through the appropriate media.

[8] Note, however, that none of these price changes is very significant in a statistical sense (see the standard deviations reported in Table 4).

TABLE 4
Prices of Leading Brands Before and After Introduction of Puffs

Brand	Period[a]	
	1-46	47-66
National Brands		
1 Kleenex	26.40 (1.28)[b]	25.42 (1.80)
2 Scotties	26.85 (1.18)	25.02 (1.44)
6 Puffs		25.27 (1.11)
Limited Distribution Brands		
4 Angel Soft	20.01 (1.64)	20.16 (1.04)
5 Swanee Color Soft	20.02 (0.87)	20.09 (1.50)
Private Labels		
3 Jewel[c]	18.88 (0.72)	17.72 (1.59)
7 Walgreens[d]	16.51 (1.78)	17.74 (2.31)
8 Jewel[c]	19.99 (1.50)	20.38 (2.06)

[a]Puffs was introduced in period 47.
[b]The prices are average prices (in cents) for each brand for a 400-tissue box. The numbers in parentheses are the standard deviations of the prices.
[c]Brands 3 and 8 are both private labels of the Jewel Food Chain.
[d]Brand 7 is the private label of the Walgreens Drug Chain.

the market shares of all three national brands (Kleenex, Scotties, and Puffs) increased for the three private label segments (see Table 2). The lone exception is Kleenex whose market share decreased slightly in the Private Label Deal segment.

Targeting to Private Label Segments

The Effects of Distribution Changes. We also examined the impact of Puffs' introduction on the distribution patterns of existing brands. For instance, Store 3 (Jewel) had two private labels, brands 3 and 8. Brand 8 was relatively more expensive (see Table 4) and was dropped by Jewel some time after the introduction of Puffs. Many of the smaller brands in the "other" category were dropped by retailers and the "limited distribution" brands were given less shelf space.[9]

The result of Jewel dropping brand 8, its relatively expensive private label, was that some of the customers of brand 8 shifted to Jewel's other private label (brand 3). This shift is indicated in the first two columns of Table 5 which show that brand 3's market share in Jewel increased in each of the segments whereas brand 8's share in Jewel decreased in each segment. Other customers of brand 8 undoubtedly shifted to the now relatively cheaper national brands.

National brands also gained share at the expense of many of the smaller brands in the "other" category that were dropped by retailers. Finally, the "limited distribution" brands such as Angel Soft and Swanee Color Soft also declined in share because of more limited shelf space (and relatively higher prices). Table 5 indicates that Angel Soft lost share in all six segments in A&P whereas its share in Independent Food Stores decreased in two of the segments and increased marginally in two others. The other major "limited distribution brand," Swanee Color Soft, lost market share in all six segments in both the National and Certified chains (see Table 5). These share losses for Angel Soft and Swanee Color Soft were picked up by the national brands.

The implication of the preceding analyses is that private label buyers are also good prospects for a new national brand, *particularly buyers of the relatively expensive private labels.* Again, this is an implication that is not obtained from the more aggregate analyses of new product introductions such as the Parfitt and Collins (1968) and Hendry models (Butler 1976). Our more disaggregate analysis of panel data shows that such data are a rich source of information that can provide important insights if properly analyzed.[10]

---

[9]The scenario described in terms of changes in distribution and price spreads between national and private label brands is a fairly accurate description of what happens to the market when a new national brand is introduced. More recently, the scenario was repeated in an almost identical manner in the coffee market in Pittsburgh when Procter and Gamble decided to introduce Folgers into that market (Hendrickson 1977).

[10]Note that other disaggregate methods of analysis, e.g., multiattribute models at the individual consumer level (see Johnson 1974, for example), do not provide these insights either. Such methods are based mainly on survey data on perceptions and preferences and do not typically consider the impact of price changes and distribution changes in analyzing the effect of introducing a new brand.

TABLE 5
Brand/Store Market Shares in the Six Segments

Segment	Period	Brand/Store					
		3/3 Brand 3/ Jewel	8/3 Brand 8/ Jewel	4/1 Angel Soft/ A&P	4/5 Angel Soft/ Independent Food Stores	5/2 Swanee Color Soft/National	5/6 Swanee Color Soft/Certified
National Brand Loyal	1-46	.086[a]	.022	.149	.000	.064	.023
	47-66	.144	.000	.055	.000	.055	.008
National Brand Deal	1-46	.204	.053	.420	.021	.032	.044
	47-66	.394	.000	.190	.039	.021	.000
Private Label Loyal	1-46	.743	.213	.974	.090	.846	.557
	47-66	.761	.068	.842	.036	.421	.390
Private Label Deal	1-46	.648	.206	.931	.037	.358	.520
	47-66	.816	.033	.718	.000	.268	.110
National Brand Switcher	1-46	.587	.124	.726	.000	.305	.125
	47-66	.657	.029	.350	.000	.115	.080
Private Label Switcher	1-46	.753	.202	.973	.015	.820	.407
	47-66	.833	.026	.690	.024	.492	.340

[a]The figure 0.086 is interpreted as: the average market share of brand 3 in Jewel in time periods 1-46 among members of the National Brand Loyal Segment.

Limitations

The value of the analysis we describe would be enhanced if data on perceptions and preferences were also available. For example, the analysis of the sources of Puffs' market share (see the discussion related to Table 2) would be even more revealing if, in addition to the panel data, data had been available on the perceptions and preferences of the households in the panel. In that case, we could have constructed joint-space maps (see Carroll 1972, for example) for each segment and predicted which brands were likely to be most vulnerable to Puffs in each segment.

Finally, we emphasize that our results are extremely tentative because we have analyzed only *one* brand in only *one* product category. Before our results can be generalized, similar analyses must be performed for other brands in other product categories.

Summary

We describe a method of analyzing the effect of introducing a new national brand of a frequently purchased product. The analysis is performed at the level of individual households by means of diary panel data and a market segmentation scheme developed by Blattberg and Sen. The main managerial implication of the analysis is that marketing efforts for a new national brand could be targeted toward brand switchers *as well as* toward households that are loyal to existing national brands and toward purchasers of private label brands. This implication is somewhat unexpected because the usual recommendation (by the Hendry model, for example) is that a new brand should be targeted only toward brand-switching households. However, we point out that models such as the Hendry model and the multiattribute model focus mainly on consumer brand preferences and tend to de-emphasize the effect of other factors such as changing prices and distribution patterns which are very common when new brands are introduced. The method of analysis we describe takes such factors into account (along with brand preference) and suggests that we should re-examine the commonly accepted recommendations about strategies for new product introduction.

REFERENCES

Blattberg, Robert C. and John Golanty (1978), "TRACKER: An Early Test-Market Forecasting and Diagnostic Model for New Product Planning," *Journal of Marketing Research*, 15 (May), 192–202.

———, Peter Peacock, and Subrata K. Sen (1976), "Purchasing Strategies Across Product Categories," *Journal of Consumer Research*, 3 (December), 143–54.

——— and Subrata K. Sen (1974), "Market Segmentation Using Models of Multidimensional Purchasing Behavior," *Journal of Marketing*, 38 (October), 17–28.

——————— and ——————— (1975), "A Bayesian Technique to Discriminate Between Stochastic Models of Brand Choice," *Management Science*, 21 (February), 682–96.

——————— and ——————— (1976), "Market Segments and Stochastic Brand Choice Models," *Journal of Marketing Research*, 13 (February), 34–45.

Butler, Jr., B. F. (1976), "The Next Brand Into the Market," *Speaking of Hendry*, Croton-on-Hudson, New York: The Hendry Corporation, 50–61.

Carroll, J. Douglas (1972), "Individual Differences in Multidimensional Scaling," in *Multidimensional Scaling*, Vol. I, Roger N. Shepard et al., eds., New York: Seminar Press, 105–55.

Eskin, Gerald J. (1973), "Dynamic Forecasts of New Product Demand Using a Depth of Repeat Model," *Journal of Marketing Research*, 10 (May), 115–29.

Green, Paul E. and V. Srinivasan (1978), "Conjoint Analysis in Consumer Research: Issues and Outlook," *Journal of Consumer Research*, 5 (September), 103–23.

Hendrickson, Bill (1977), "Tiny Firms Are Losers in Coffee War Fought by Two Big Marketers," *The Wall Street Journal* (November 3).

Johnson, Richard M. (1974), "Trade-Off Analysis of Consumer Values," *Journal of Marketing Research*, 11 (May), 121–7.

Kalwani, Manohar U. and Donald G. Morrison (1977), "A Parsimonious Description of the Hendry System," *Management Science*, 23 (January), 467–77.

Mahajan, Vijay and Eitan Muller (1979), "Innovation Diffusion and New Product Growth Models in Marketing," *Journal of Marketing*, 43 (Fall), 55–68.

Parfitt, J. H. and B. J. K. Collins (1968), "Use of Consumer Panels for Brand Share Prediction," *Journal of Marketing Research*, 5 (May), 131–45.

Shocker, Allan D. and V. Srinivasan (1979), "Multi-Attribute Approaches for Product Concept Evaluation and Generation: A Critical Review," *Journal of Marketing Research*, 16 (May), 159–80.

Silk, Alvin J. and Glen L. Urban (1978), "Pre-Test-Market Evaluation of New Packaged Goods: A Model and Measurement Methodology," *Journal of Marketing Research*, 15 (May), 171–91.

Part V: Direct Bob — Contributions to Customer Relationship Marketing, Direct Marketing and Database Marketing

Few people can claim to be thought leaders in *any* domain. Far fewer can claim to be thought leaders in more than one. Bob Blattberg is one of those rare few who can claim such an honor. As an academic and a consultant he has impacted both the thought and practice of marketing in several areas. The focus of this synopsis is on the important and lasting impact of Bob Blattberg's work in the areas of customer relationship management (CRM), direct marketing, and database marketing.

Anyone who knows or has worked with Bob can attest to his forward and "out-of-the-box" thinking. It is hard to truly know when he began pondering topics in CRM, database and direct marketing. However, we do know that Bob's published work in this area dates back to 1986. It was in this year that he published, *"Research Opportunities in Direct Marketing."* The fact that Bob took the time to write an article of this nature, exemplifies his character as a person and a professional. Instead of trying to establish his own authority in this emerging area, he writes a piece that will spur and motivate others to do pioneering research in the direct marketing research domain. Thus, Bob was and still is not only interested in developing himself he is also interested in building the careers of others.

Over the last 20 years of his career Bob Blattberg has left a legacy in the area of CRM, database, and direct marketing. He has left it via the people that he worked with, mentored, advised as well as through his writings. There are four consistent themes that have permeated through this phase of his career. These themes are what are discussed in the remainder of this synopsis.

Creating New Marketing Paradigms

There is great risk that comes with 'out-of-the box' thinking. There is no guarantee that those fresh ideas will be validated, accepted, or even published. *The Marketing Information Revolution* which Bob co-authored with Rashi Glazer and John Little is an example of such forward thinking for its time. Published in 1994, this work brought data and customer databases to the forefront of the minds of marketers. More importantly, it suggested that data was a critical tool for marketers but not an end in and of itself. Blattberg and his colleagues argued that the value of data comes from its use and management. Specifically, this book introduces the idea of an 'information value chain.' This chain starts with data collection and transmission, and is followed by data management, interpretation, models and decision support systems. Thinking about marketing as being data driven persists today, over 20 years later, and is the foundation of many modern marketing programs.

Likely evolving out of his interest in databases, Bob introduced a new term to the field of marketing, *customer equity*. In a seminal piece, Bob Blattberg and John Deighton introduced business to a new way of thinking about marketing and a new way or measuring marketing performance. *"Managing Marketing by the Customer Equity Test,"* was published in the Harvard Business Review and resonated with both academics and practitioners. The core premise of this piece was that the customer is a financial asset of the firm that can and should be managed. Moreover, they introduced the field to an analytic approach that could be used to place a financial value on customers and customer databases. This type of thinking rattled a marketing field that had historically been so dominated by a brand and product orientation. Since then critical questions have been raised about how brand equity reconciles with customer equity. A leading authority on brand equity, Kevin Keller, has now been noted for writing about customer-centered brand equity.

The profound impact of the customer equity concept has shaped, influenced, and given birth to numerous academic careers. In addition, the lifetime value of a customer is now a metric that practitioners are increasingly using across the world to assess their business' performance.

Challenging Conventional Wisdom

As the impetus behind new marketing paradigms, it is not surprising that Bob Blattberg's work can also be characterized as challenging conventional wisdom. However, Bob did not just tackle big ideas, he also knew how to examine problems at a very detailed level. Bob can be linked to a series of publications in the database marketing domain in which he elaborates on the intricacies of the collection and management of data. Examples would be his chapter called "Database Marketing" in the *Handbook of Marketing* or his chapter entitled "The Design and Application of Databases to

Enhance Customer Equity," co-authored with Jacquelyn Thomas and published in the German publication called *The Handbook of Customer Bonding: Basics, Concepts, and Experiences.* Through these works, Bob introduced ideas which made practitioners reexamine how they went about collecting and organizing their customer data. In particular this research advocated developing a functional database system that could be leveraged to manage customers as financial assets. For some, this database approach would require the collection of new types of customer interaction data that had never previously been integrated into a customer file.

Just as the field began to catch hold of the concept of customer lifetime value, once again Bob is linked to a controversial assertion. "Can We Predict Customer Lifetime Value?" was the title of a paper with Edward Malthouse which challenged the status quo. It had been presumed by many that we can accurately predict the future profitability of customers. Counter to this wisdom, in this research Blattberg and Malthouse argue and demonstrate that this is not always the case. They find that frequently customers will be misclassified as either valuable when they truly are not or not highly valuable when they truly are. As a result, management practices are not always appropriately discriminating treatment levels to their customers based on their value to the firm.

Deepening Our Understanding

Bob's prowess at being able to conceptualize big ideas and provide the depth of analysis to advance the knowledge in the field is a notable characteristic of his career. Prior to 2001, both the practitioner and academic communities had overwhelmingly focused on customer retention as the main tenant of CRM. Little attention had been given to other strategic aspects of managing customer relationships. Taking a slightly different approach than his contemporaries, in 2001 he co-authored a book with Gary Getz and Jacquelyn Thomas called *Customer Equity.* This book developed a conceptual model called the A-R-A (Acquisition-Retention-Add-On Selling) model. This model expanded conventional thinking and raised the awareness of other strategic aspects of customer relationships. This book argued for a balanced approach to managing relationships and provided additional metrics for assessing the quality and financial value of customer-firm relationships.

Continuing in this trend of expanding thought, in 2004 Bob again teamed up with his colleagues and raised the awareness of another aspect of customer-firm relationships. In a paper titled "Recapturing Lost Customer," Thomas, Blattberg, and Fox address the issue of how firms should price to recapture lapsed or defected customers. They developed a statistical model that measured the *second lifetime value of a customer.* Not only had the idea of a second lifetime value been under researched and overlooked by many in the literature, it had never been explored empirically.

Unlike some, Bob never felt constrained or limited about how disseminate new knowledge. Whether via books, book chapters, or peer reviewed articles, all were viable outlets to Bob's work. While it is not publically available yet, we are sure Bob's most recent book entitled *Database Marketing* co-authored with Scott Neslin and Byung-Do Kim will have an impact similar to his prior work and expand the knowledge in the CRM and database marketing fields.

Practical and Actionable Research

As academics we are trained to be critical and seek to enhance and advance past research. At times this can lead one to investigate topics that have little managerial relevance or develop complex methods whose incremental value is questionable. Avoiding these research pitfalls was a position that Bob not only preached to others but lived by himself. To that end, his legacy of research is one that can be appreciated by not only academics but also those who practice marketing. Several of Bob's papers reflect this type of thinking. For example, Bob and Steve Hoch published a paper entitled "Database Models and Managerial Intuition: 50% Model +50% Manager." While this paper was published in a top academic journal, *Management Science,* it embodies Bob's insistence for managerial relevance. Similarly, Greg Allenby and Bob teamed up in 1987 and published a paper that focused on direct market testing.

Another example of the actionability of Bob's research is his paper with John Deighton, "Interactive Marketing: Exploiting the age of Addressability." This paper gives practical advice on designing a marketing database and staffing an interactive marketing department. In addition, this paper addresses the public debate over marketing and privacy. Published in 1991, this paper was clearly ahead of its time as these issues persist to be highly relevant and important over 15 years later.

Some Personal Comments

It is no trivial task to impact an audience such that it results in a change in their conventional thoughts and behaviors. This is even more challenging if one attempts to influence multiple audiences that are at times as distinct and diverse as marketing academics and marketing practitioners. Bob Blattberg is a unique individual who has had such an impact in numerous domains. He is a charismatic and prolific researcher, teacher, and consultant. His legacy continues to live via the multiple lives he has touched and careers he has supported. Thank you, Bob.

Jacquelyn Thomas
Cox School of Business
Southern Methodist University

Mike Lewis
Olin School of Business
Washington University

References

Allenby, Greg and Robert Blattberg (1987). A New Theory of Direct Market Testing, or Why Your Rollout Results Do Not Match Your Test Results, *Journal of Direct Marketing*, **1**(4), 24–37.

Blattberg, Robert (1986). Research Opportunities in Direct Marketing, *Journal of Direct Marketing*, **1**(1), 7–14.

Blattberg, Robert and Stephen Hoch (1990). Database Models and Managerial Intuition: 50% Model + 50% Manager, *Management Science*, **36**(8), 887–899.

Blattberg, Robert and John Deighton (1991). Interactive Marketing: Exploiting the Age of Addressability, *Sloan Management Review*, **33**(1), 5–14.

Blattberg, Robert, Rashi Glazer and John D.C. Little (1994). *The Marketing Information Revolution*, Boston, MA: Harvard Business School Press.

Blattberg, Robert and John Deighton (1996). Manage Marketing by the Customer Equity, *Harvard Business Review*, July-August, pp 136–144

Blattberg, Robert and Jacquelyn Thomas (1999). The Design and Application of Databases to Enhance Customer Equity, in *The Handbook of Customer Bonding: Basics, Concepts, and Experiences*, M. Bruhn and C. Homburg (eds.), Wiesbaden, Germany: Gabler Publishing.

Blattberg, Robert, Gary Getz and Jacquelyn Thomas (2001). *Customer Equity: Building and Managing Relationships as Valuable Assets*, Boston, MA: Harvard Business School Press.

Blattberg, Robert, Byung-do Kim and Scott Neslin (2008). *Database Marketing*, Springer Verlag.

Malthouse, Edward and Robert Blattberg (2005). Can We Predict Customer Lifetime Value, *Journal of Interactive Marketing*, **19**(1), 2–16.

Thomas, Jacquelyn, Robert Blattberg and Edward Fox (2004). Recapturing Lost Customers, *Journal of Marketing Research*, **41**(1), 31–45.

Attracting and keeping the highest-value customers is the cornerstone of a successful marketing program.

Manage Marketing by

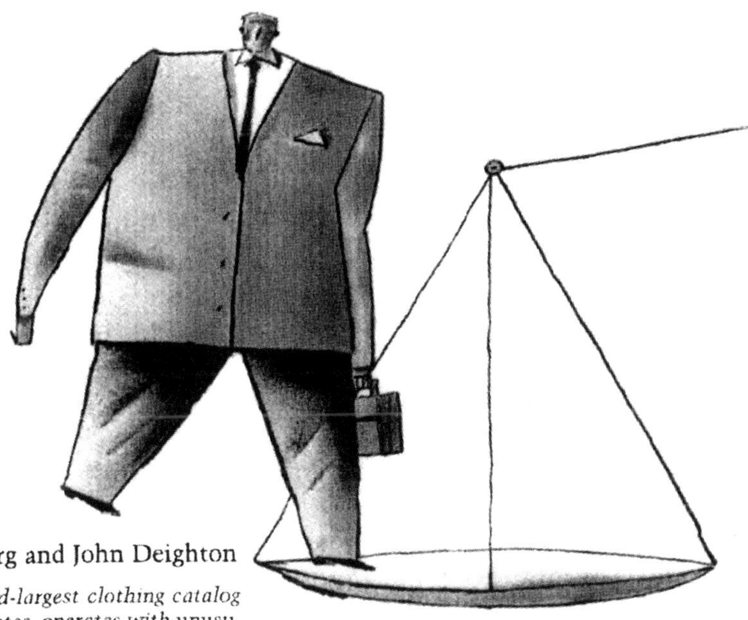

by Robert C. Blattberg and John Deighton

☐ *Lands' End, the second-largest clothing catalog retailer in the United States, operates with unusually high inventory levels. Its managers would rather inflate inventory than fail to fill an order and risk losing a customer. "If we don't keep the customer for several years, we don't make money," said the company's CEO at the time, William End, in 1994. "We need a long-term payback for the expense of coming up with a buyer."*

☐ *The main goal of McDonald's Corporation's 1995 marketing plan was to get its current customers to eat at its restaurants more often. The corporation's managers noted the value of what they call "super-heavy" users – typically males aged 18 to 34 who eat at McDonald's an average of three to five times a week and account for 77% of its sales – and they planned their marketing efforts accordingly. A senior executive offers the general rule that it is "easier to get a current customer to use you more often than it is to get a new customer."*

There is a curious similarity in the way managers at Lands' End and McDonald's articulate marketing goals. They each talk not about selling products but about keeping customers. The traditional rhetoric of customer orientation has taken on a sharper definition, in which growing the business is a matter of spending to capture the attention of high-value prospective customers and then staying with them until they are converted and retained in committed – and therefore relatively low-maintenance – relationships. For Lands' End, this style of talk is not unexpected; it is the language of direct mail. But it is also becoming increasingly common at businesses whose methods of going to market are by no means limited to the mail.

At a time when marketing methods are becoming more interactive, from frequent-user-club services to ID-card-operated kiosks to Web pages, it is not surprising that marketing talk is beginning to sound like direct-marketing talk. When most marketing communication primarily involved broad-

the Customer Equity Test

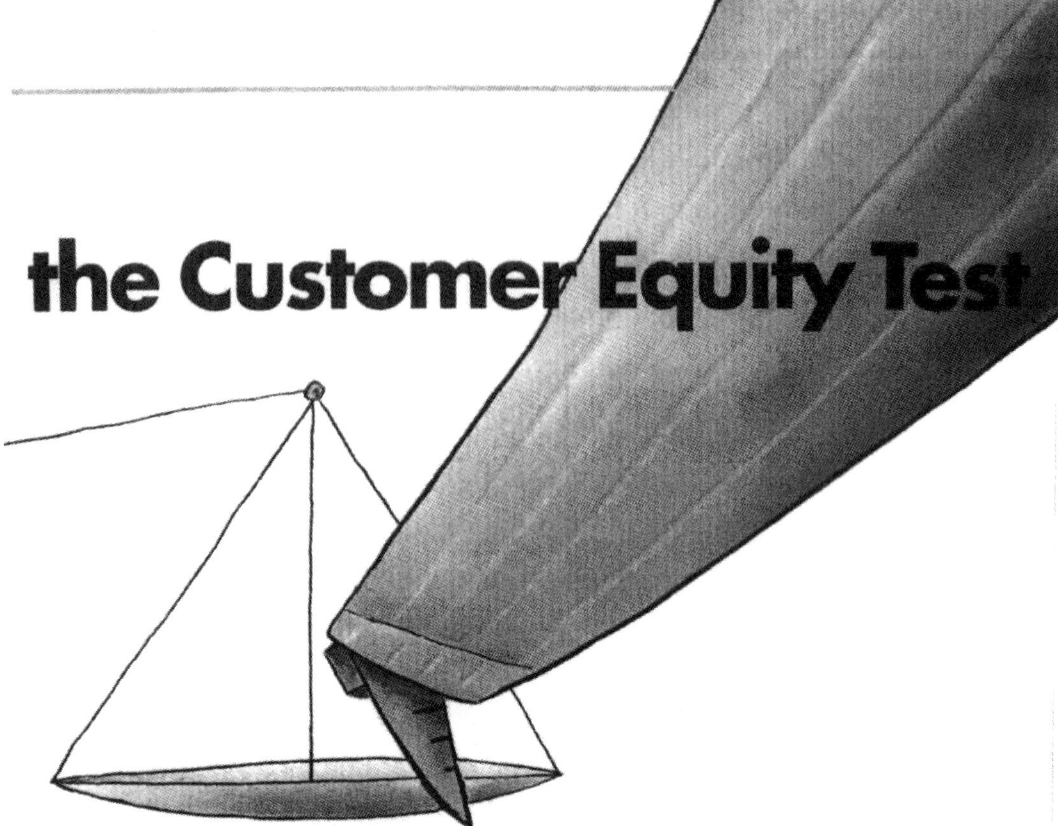

cast technologies, marketers set goals that broadcast marketing could achieve: increased share of voice or market and higher awareness and recall of products by consumers. As communication tools become interactive, marketing managers talk more about goals that pertain to individual relationships, such as share of customer requirements, customer-contact outcomes, and customer satisfaction measures. Managers have begun to think of good marketing as good conversation, as a process of drawing potential customers into progressively more satisfying back-and-forth relationships with the company. Just as the art of conversation follows two separate steps – first striking up a conversation with a likely partner and then maintaining the flow – so the new marketing naturally divides itself into the work of acquiring customers and the work of retaining them.

Growing a business can therefore be framed as a matter of getting customers and keeping them so as to grow the value of the customer base – the sum of all the conversations – to its fullest potential. In these terms, setting a marketing budget becomes the task of balancing what is spent on customer acquisition with what is spent on retention.

Clearly, not every company wants to balance acquisition and retention at the same point. In some industries, such as low-end, used-car retailing, to take an extreme example, retention strategies have no leverage, because the intrinsic "retainability" of customers is simply too low. In others, the relative importance of retention changes as the industry evolves. How can managers determine the optimal balance between acquisition and retention for their particular companies?

The criterion we propose for determining the optimal balance is the company's customer equity. The balance is optimal when customer equity is at its maximum amount. To measure that equity, we first measure each customer's expected contribution toward offsetting the company's fixed costs

Robert C. Blattberg is the Polk Brothers Distinguished Professor of Retailing at Northwestern University's J.L. Kellogg Graduate School of Management in Evanston, Illinois. John Deighton is an associate professor of marketing at the Harvard Business School in Boston, Massachusetts.

CUSTOMER EQUITY

over the expected life of that customer. Then we discount the expected contributions to a net present value at the company's target rate of return for marketing investments. Finally, we add together the discounted, expected contributions of all current customers.

Appraising customer equity is conceptually similar to appraising the value of a portfolio of income-producing real estate. Two of its main determinants

The appropriate question for judging new products and customer service initiatives is, Will it grow our customer equity?

are the cost of acquiring customers and the future profit stream from retained customers. But a host of other factors, including remarketing costs and brand strategy, can also have significant influence.

Ultimately, we contend that the appropriate question for judging new products, new programs, and new customer-service initiatives should not be, Will it attract new customers? or, Will it increase our retention rates? but rather, Will it grow our customer equity? The goal of maximizing customer equity by balancing acquisition and retention efforts properly should serve as the star by which a company steers its entire marketing program.

Finding the Balance

To use customer equity as the criterion that balances spending on getting and keeping customers, we need to express it as the sum of two net present values: the returns from acquisition spending and the returns from retention spending. We use a tool called *decision calculus* to build a model of this relationship by creating two curves. The first curve relates acquisition spending to the resulting acquisition rate, and the second curve relates retention spending to the resulting retention rate. These curves characterize the company and its industry.

What is decision calculus? It is an approach to decision making in which a manager breaks down a complex problem into smaller, simpler elements, forms judgments about each element separately, and then uses a formal model to turn those small judgments into an answer to the larger question. Studies have shown that people can predict simple events better than complex ones, and models are

better than people at combining simple predictions to address a larger issue. The result of using decision calculus is only as good as the managers involved in the process, but the tool allows managers and models to do what they do best in the face of a complex dilemma.

In this case, we approach the larger question – What is the optimal balance between customer acquisition and customer retention at my company? – by asking several smaller questions about acquisition and retention. The curves we will create reveal the points at which a company is spending more than a customer is worth to acquire or retain. Those points, along with consideration of several other factors, show managers how their acquisition and retention efforts should be balanced.

Let's look at a practical example, using, for ease of description, a case in which a company markets a single product that customers buy once or twice a year. By keeping the case simple, complications – such as the problem of accounting for ancillary sales or of allocating the effect of one marketing investment to more than one product – will not distract from the essence of the process. Amending the method later to accommodate refinements will be a straightforward task.

We have chosen to work with a product that is purchased at least once a year to make it practical to express retention rates on a per-year basis. If customers' purchase cycles are longer than a year, as they are with automobiles and other durables, it is better for managers to estimate retention rates on a per-cycle basis.

Finally, and again simplifying for the sake of exposition, we gloss over the question of the lapsed customer. If a customer is not retained, we will assume that the cost of reactivating that customer will be the same as the cost of acquiring a prospect. In practice, it usually costs less.

We begin by estimating the shape of the company's acquisition curve. To do this, we ask the manager to provide two points on the curve: first, the company's current level of acquisition and second, the ceiling – the highest possible number of customers the company could reasonably acquire in a given time period. (Acquisition and retention do not increase without limit as spending increases. There is a ceiling, which will vary from industry to industry. For example, the ceiling is much lower for a property and casualty insurance company using direct mail to acquire new customers than it is for the average catalog retailer. Similarly, the retention ceiling for banks is generally high because the relationship between the customer and the bank becomes more complex over time with the addition of direct deposit, loans, and so forth. On the other hand, in the automotive industry, even the strongest brands have low retention ceilings. On average, manufacturers seldom induce more than 40% of buyers to purchase the same brand of automobile on two successive occasions.)

We first ask the manager, What did you spend last year to attract prospects? To figure out what was spent per prospect, estimate how many prospects were converted into customers. What proportion of the prospect pool was converted?

The manager answers, We spent $5 per prospect to attempt to induce a first transaction, and we succeeded 20% of the time.

Then we ask, If for all practical purposes there had been no limit to spending, what proportion of the prospects that you targeted over the course of the last year could have been converted?

The manager answers, I don't think we could ever induce more than 40% of our prospect pool to become first-time customers.

Those answers are all that is needed to decide on the optimum amount to spend to acquire a customer. (For an explanation of the calculations involved, see the insert "Calculating the Optimal Level of Acquisition Spending.") First, we use the answers to generate a curve showing how the acquisition rate varies with spending on acquisition. The curve has a characteristic "diminishing returns" shape. (See the graph "How First-Year Value Depends on Acquisition Spending.") Second, we use that curve, with no further information except the margin generated by a customer in a year, to compute the U-shaped curve in the upper half of the graph. That second curve depicts how the average value of acquired customers in the first year varies with spending on acquisition, first growing as the company attracts eager buyers and then declining as it goes after more reluctant prospects who require more expensive wooing. The peak of that curve tells us at what point to stop acquiring.

We now need a second dialogue to elicit the manager's insight into the shape of the retention curve. We begin by asking the manager, What did you spend last year on retention activities? Divide that amount by the number of customers you had at the start of that year to get the retention expenditure per customer. What proportion of your customers did you succeed in keeping for the year?

The manager answers, Last year, we spent at the rate of $10 per customer and retained 40% of the customer base.

Then we ask, If your budget had been unlimited, what proportion of customers in one year would have remained customers in the following year?

The manager answers, At best, we might retain 70% of our customers from one year to the next.

Those answers give us the other side of the balance point between acquisition and retention. (See

---

Calculating the Optimal Level of Acquisition Spending

Here we describe how to compute an organization's optimal level of acquisition spending, using the manager's answers to the acquisition questions: How much did you spend, and what is the limit to your attraction of new customers? The answer to the first question gives us $A, the acquisition expenditure per prospect, and a, the acquisition rate obtained as a result of that expenditure. The answer to the second question gives us the ceiling rate on the acquisition curve. If we assume that the curve is exponential (an assumption that is supported by our experience), then the curve of the actual acquisition probability as pictured in the lower half of the graph "How First-Year Value Depends on Acquisition Spending" is described by the equation

$$a = \text{ceiling rate} \times [1 - \exp(-k_1 \times \$A)]$$

where k is a constant that controls the steepness of the curve. Thus, knowing the two points on this curve and the ceiling rate—as given to us by the manager—we can solve the equation to find k.

Next, we compute the contribution from an acquired customer in the first year after acquisition (see the upper curve in the graph). If the margin on a transaction is $m, then

the net contribution from acquiring a prospect in the first year = $a\$m - \$A$.

Note that this quantity need not be positive; it may be that the optimum amount to spend to acquire a customer is more than the contribution generated by that customer in the first year. Whether a marketer should acquire a customer at a loss can be judged only when the retention returns have been calculated.

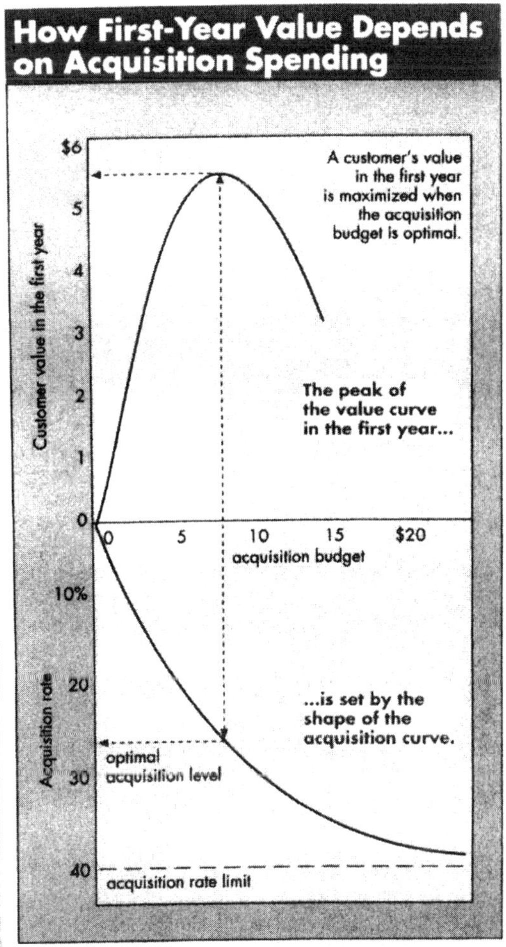

the insert "Calculating the Optimal Level of Retention Spending.") We use the answers first to generate a curve that relates retention spending to success at retention. (See the graph "How Customer Equity Depends on Retention Spending.") Again, the curve reflects the diminishing returns in efforts to retain customers. Next, we generate the curve in the upper half of the graph, a curve that grows as retention spending gives the customer more reasons to remain loyal, and then declines as customers no longer value the retention service enough to cover its cost.

Despite the simplicity of this example, it illustrates how the decision-calculus process – in this case, using four small, explicit decisions and a model to solve one large, messy problem – can pay off. Do this manager's actions coincide with his or her intui-

tions? Are the current spending levels consistent with the curves he or she believes apply in this market? Here, as we find in many of our real-world applications, breaking down the problem into components has helped, and either intuition or current practice needs to be updated if the manager is to be consistent. The actual expenditures of $5 per prospect and $10 per convert are, given the manager's own opinions about the market's responsiveness, both too low. The acquisition budget should be increased to $7.50 per prospect; the retention budget would be optimal at $15 per customer. At these levels of spending, the company's customer equity would reach its peak.

Maximizing Customer Equity

The balance between acquisition and retention spending is never static. Managers must constantly reassess the spending points determined by the decision-calculus model, keeping in mind a host of considerations. The following guidelines should help frame the issue.

Invest in highest-value customers first. In the model just described, we showed how to allocate marketing investments between only two groups, prospects and customers, and we used averages to characterize the responsiveness of each group. This logic should be applied to much finer distinctions among the company's customer base and prospect list. Instead of using averages drawn across the entire customer base, for example, a more subtle analysis would partition the base into behaviorally and attitudinally homogeneous groups that spend at different levels, and it would estimate the shape of acquisition and retention curves for each group. The analysis would then proceed to evaluate the customer equity of each group, starting with the most valuable and proceeding to the least. For each group, the analysis first would determine the optimal investment required to retain members of that group and then how much to spend to acquire more people who fit that group's profile.

Targets with particularly high equity might justify major investments. Airlines, for example, know that a large investment in retention incentives pays off. One result is the progressive structure of airline frequent-flier incentives: The more a customer flies, the easier it becomes for that customer to earn more generous benefits. Similarly, long-distance phone companies in the United States recognize that one of their highest-value customer groups is recent immigrants, who maintain phone contact with relatives and friends in their countries of origin. The phone companies work hard at retaining

CUSTOMER EQUITY

that segment, serving it with native-language phone operators and offering special promotions.

Transform product management into customer management. The customer-equity perspective favors customer management over product or brand management as an organizing principle. When evaluating new products and services, keep in mind that small changes can have a big impact. Indeed, the value of improvements in customer equity is often not fully appreciated until it is expressed as a capitalized amount. Consider what happened when a major manufacturer of durable goods discovered that a component of one of its products was failing at a rate of 35% within one year of purchase. The operations manager determined that it was less costly to replace the component in the 35% of products that failed in customers' homes than it was to replace it in 100% of the products in inventory. His calculation accurately assessed the single-period cost to the company of each course of action but took no account of the impact on customer satisfaction or the probability of repeat purchases. When the problem was reframed from the perspective of the potential for losing customers, the managers saw immediately that replacing the component in the warehouse was the better alternative.

American Airlines' introduction of the frequent-flier program in 1981 inspired an astonishing range of industries to create membership clubs, including car rental agencies, restaurants, cosmetics companies, ski lodges, photofinishing shops, and overnight package shippers. Some critics argue that competition has negated the influence of the benefits. We would argue, on the contrary, that retention programs, if skillfully designed, can be much more than volume-discount programs. They can inspire loyalty from the market's biggest spenders. The key is to deliver benefits that appeal more to heavy users than to light users, that draw attention to a brand's claimed distinction, and that enliven the buying experience so that the heavy user becomes an even heavier user. For example, Nintendo and Lego designed clubs that showed members new ways for kids to enjoy their games and toys. Through the clubs, children also came into contact with other heavy users. For adults, Harley-Davidson and Corvette have designed clubs with a similar impact on users. And hotels have made club membership a source of customer recognition and a way to ease the strains of the traveling life.

Consider how add-on sales and cross-selling can increase customer equity. The value of a customer is reflected not only in the revenue earned from the initial purchase but also in the present value of future revenues contingent upon that purchase. In other words, if the customer buys product A, will he or she buy products that supplement or complement product A? A customer who purchases a laser printer may well buy additional memory, toner cartridges, special paper-handling devices, and supplemental fonts in the future. Someone who buys a new car will later need service visits, body repairs, and new parts. An accounting partnership can be confident that if it wins the contract to perform audits for a client, it will probably be able to sell other accounting services to that same client. Additional sales enhance the value of the customer relationship over time.

In the terminology used by direct marketers, the cost of marketing additional products and services to the installed, or existing, customer base is called *remarketing cost*. Customers who like a company's

How Customer Equity Depends on Retention Spending

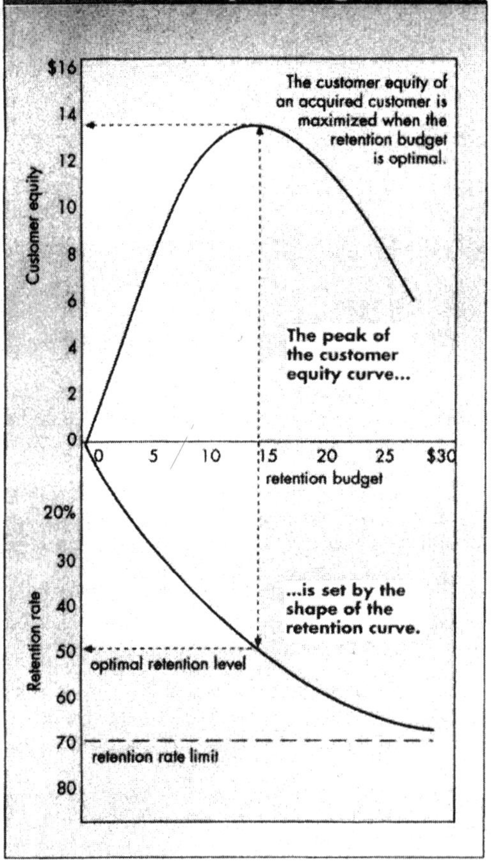

Calculating the Optimal Level of Retention Spending

Here we describe how to compute an organization's optimal level of retention spending, using the manager's responses to the retention questions: How much did you spend last year, and what is the maximum percentage of customers you could hope to retain? The answer to the first question gives us $R, the acquisition expenditure per prospect, and r, the retention rate obtained as a result of that expenditure. The answer to the second question gives us the ceiling rate on the retention curve. Again assuming that the curve is exponential, the curve of the retention probability rate as pictured in the lower half of the graph "How Customer Equity Depends on Retention Spending" is described by the equation

$$r = \text{ceiling rate} \times [1 - \exp(-k_2 \times \$R)].$$

As before, k is a parameter controlling the shape of the exponential curve. Knowing the margin on a transaction, we can compute the value of a customer in any year after acquisition. To keep this illustration simple, assume that we earn the same margin in each year as the $m we earned in the year in which we acquired the customer. (The basic method is the same when modeling situations in which customers become more valuable over time.) Then the value of the customer in any given year (y) is simply $m, less the retention budget and discounted by the probability that the customer will still be around in that year. That is, the value of the customer in any given year is the retention rate raised to the yth power:

year y contribution from retention $= r^y (\$m - \$R/r)$.

($R gets divided by r to allow for the fact that retention investment is spent on the number of customers we attempt to keep, not on the number we succeed in keeping. The number we succeed in keeping is one r^{th} of the number that we had attempted to keep.)

We then sum up the annual values for each year of the customer's projected life, add the value of a first-year customer, discount to a present value at a rate of return appropriate for marketing investments, $d\%$, and so obtain the amount of customer equity attributable to that customer.

The top half of the graph plots this customer equity against the retention budget for the retention curve illustrated in the graph's lower half. It is a simple matter to read the value of $R, which takes the retention rate r to its optimum level.

Alternatively, the relationship between retention spending and return can be expressed algebraically. If we define $r' = r/(1 + d)$, then the customer equity generated from investments of $A in acquisition and $R in retention is given by

$$\text{customer equity} = a\$m - \$A + a(\$m - \$R/r)[r'/(1 - r')].$$

We can find the value of $R that, when substituted into this expression, yields the greatest value for customer equity. The result is the expected customer equity of an average customer acquired by spending $A and retained by spending $R each year.

---

products and services are less expensive to serve with new products and services. In this way, reduced costs of remarketing are one of the less visible rewards of investment in customer satisfaction.

Look for ways to reduce acquisition costs. Acquisition costs have a strong impact on customer equity. With high acquisition costs, retention rates and add-on sales must be high to make the product or service viable. Therefore, if the company can acquire customers at a lower cost, the long-term payoff improves significantly. Despite this potential benefit, many companies do not know what percentage of their marketing budget is being used to acquire new customers and what percentage is being spent on existing customers. Is the company's general advertising building loyalty, acquiring customers, or both?

For example, a life insurance company, noticing that its customer acquisition costs were higher than normal for the industry, introduced prequalification procedures in order to discourage agents from pursuing prospects when the likelihood of writing a policy was low. Although the procedures reduced the company's rate of sales, they reduced the cost of acquiring customers by even more and boosted both the company's profits and its customer equity.

Track customer equity gains and losses against marketing programs. A customer-value flow statement – much like an organization's cash flow statement – can highlight problems that the income statement conceals. A company that churns its customer base (acquires customers just as fast as it loses them) can report good sales and profits even as its customer equity is evaporating. As it churns, the company has an increasingly difficult time acquiring new customers cost-effectively, and, finally, when it has churned all prospects through the sys-

CUSTOMER EQUITY

tem, acquisition costs become impossibly high. Whereas an income statement gives no indication of churning, a customer-value statement reports whether the company's marketing programs are building or eroding the customer base.

When American Express Company acquired IDS Financial Services, a company that markets insurance and mutual fund products through a 5,000-member sales force, it found that behind IDS's attractive rate of sales and profit growth lurked a high rate of churning. IDS was losing a client almost every time it gained one. And marketing programs implemented at headquarters were fueling the churning. IDS was spending $16 on marketing programs to generate leads for the sales force for every $1 that it spent on programs to strengthen the relationship between the company and existing clients. When an American Express study found that IDS was managing only 15% of a typical client's financial assets, the company immediately shifted its focus from acquisition marketing to retention marketing. The key was to encourage sales representatives to open up a relationship with a customer by selling a personal financial plan as the first transaction, rather than an insurance policy or a single investment. By promoting personal financial plans, IDS made it easier for reps to make additional sales to existing customers than it had been. The result was not seen in annual sales, which continued at their steady clip, but rather in much more rapid growth in the lifetime value of the customer base, which promised a more secure future for IDS.

Relate branding to customer equity. Brands don't create wealth; customers do. Despite the fashionable concern with brand power, few would dispute that highly visible brands are just one instrument among many with which to build customer equity; they are a magnet to attract new customers and an anchor to hold existing customers. Brands are never more important than the customers they reach. Once Sears reanalyzed its transaction records – asking not, What are our most valuable brands? but rather, Who are our most valuable customers? – the company began to seek shoppers for new clothing much more vigorously than ever before.

Managers should watch for signs that brand management is impeding customer management. Consider a Canadian manufacturer that makes products in three distinct markets under the same brand name. One product is strong; the other two are weak. Several years ago, each was managed by a different brand manager bent on maximizing share in his or her market, and the manager of the strong brand resisted allowing the weaker siblings to ride on its coattails. But research showed that the strong brand had as much to gain from cooperation as the other two. When experiments were conducted to measure the response to coupons for one product delivered only to users of the other two, all three brands showed impressive results. It was easier to persuade a user of two of the products to try the third than to persuade a nonuser of any of the products to try one. Brand-management myopia had been preventing the company from discovering that it could be good at customer management; it could cross-sell to increase a customer's equity more efficiently than it could acquire a customer three times over – once in each market.

Monitor the intrinsic retainability of your customers. Intrinsic retainability is determined by the way the customer uses a product or service. When that use changes, retainability changes at the same time, and companies must scramble to adjust their allocation of marketing funds.

For years, marketers in the air freight industry required expertise in customer acquisition. An efficient acquirer earned a higher return than a skilled retention marketer because customer satisfaction was out of the hands of the shipper and in the control of the airlines that carried the freight. Federal Express's innovation, the creation of an airline dedicated to nothing but freight, gave shippers more control over customer satisfaction and sharply increased the returns that could be earned through retention marketing. Suddenly, the successful companies were successful retainers.

> # A customer-value statement reports whether a company's marketing programs are building or eroding the customer base.

Traditionally, IBM ran its mainframe computer business as a retention business, training its sales force to follow the initial sale with attempts to sell peripheral equipment, software, a contract with its service bureau, and so on. Customers were prized because they became lifetime IBM users. But as microcomputers displaced mainframes for many applications, the company was compelled to deploy more of its marketing funds for acquisition. The

CUSTOMER EQUITY

pace of technological evolution weakened brand loyalty, and a new consumer emerged who ascribed much less value to relationships. For a time, IBM tried to exploit past loyalties by endorsing selected software and attaching its brand name to peripherals, but the game had changed. Today the company has cut back on its famed sales force in favor of less expensive retention tools such as database technology and catalog-based direct sales.

When managers strive to grow customer equity, they put the customer at the forefront of their strategic thinking.

When the time is ripe to change direction, the signal usually comes from the environment, not from the organization. The winner is the company that reads the signal first.

Consider writing separate marketing plans – or even building two marketing organizations – for acquisition and retention efforts. Locating customers, attracting them, and then managing the ongoing relationships are very different tasks. They require different kinds of market research, different cost analyses to calculate the return on investment, and different measures to monitor compliance. Therefore, we recommend that once managers have determined the most appropriate ratio of acquisition and retention spending, they plan for each task separately. In direct-marketing organizations and in industries with a large customer-service component, such as airlines, it may in fact be advantageous to place acquisition activities under separate control from retention activities.

Separate marketing teams to manage customer acquisition projects and retention projects have proved effective in many companies, especially when the projects can be sharply defined by the needs of particular customer groups. British Airways, for example, identified U.S. residents who used the airline to fly *within* Europe but did not use it to fly from the United States *to* Europe. The company then formed a team to address acquisition efforts for that customer segment. Next, it charged a retention team with the task of finding what it would take to keep those customers. The team came up with a fast track for arriving transatlantic passengers that included accelerated processing of customs and immigration documents, private suites, and valet services.

An organizational structure built around getting and keeping customers, not simply selling products, has some significant benefits. It allows the marketing organizations to use tactics that are appropriate for different customer segments. Marketing research can be used to understand the needs of existing customers as distinct from the needs of prospective customers. And the performance and compensation of marketing managers can be linked to increases in the customer equity between these two groups.

When managers strive to grow customer equity rather than a brand's sales or profit, they put the customer and the quality of customer relationships at the forefront of their strategic thinking. Product sales, brand strength, and short-term financial performance are mere secondary indicators of success.

Furthermore, when managers ask how much a marketing investment will increase a company's customer equity, the interests of the marketer and the company's shareholders are precisely aligned. Just as an investment firm's interests are served if its investment managers are judged by the change in portfolio value from one period to the next, so a company is well served if its marketers are judged by the increase in the company's customer equity over time. If a marketing organization backs away from the challenge to link its fortunes to the customer-equity criterion, it either misunderstands the purpose of the marketing function or lacks the authority to carry out that purpose. ⊟

Reprint 96402   To order reprints, see the last page of this issue.

MANAGEMENT SCIENCE
Vol. 36, No. 8, August 1990
Printed in U.S.A.

DATABASE MODELS AND MANAGERIAL INTUITION: 50% MODEL + 50% MANAGER*

ROBERT C. BLATTBERG AND STEPHEN J. HOCH

University of Chicago, Graduate School of Business,
1101 E. 58th Street, Chicago, Illinois 60637

We focus on ways of combining simple database models with managerial intuition. We present a model and method for isolating managerial intuition. For five different business forecasting situations, our results indicate that a combination of model and manager always outperforms either of these decision inputs in isolation, an average R^2 increase of 0.09 (16%) above the best single decision input in cross-validated model analyses. We assess the validity of an equal weighting heuristic, 50% model + 50% manager, and then discuss why our results might differ from previous research on expert judgment.
(FORECASTING; DECISION MAKING; EXPERTISE; DECISION SUPPORT SYSTEMS)

1. Introduction

Everybody's got so much information all day long that they lose their common sense. (Gertrude Stein)

A very important problem in sales forecasting is combining the wisdom of experienced businessmen with statistical analysis. (Lorie 1957)

With the availability of more and better sources of data, decision makers must begin to systematically incorporate such information into the decision process. At present, however, we know much more about building and processing databases than about how experts might use such data to improve decision quality. We show how firms can take advantage of the data explosion by combining simple database models with managerial intuition, viewing the two decision inputs in combination rather than in competition. We identify differences between models and intuition, and develop a way to isolate and evaluate intuition. We analyze several on-line business forecasting situations and show that decision quality could have been improved dramatically by relying on both models *and* intuition. We find that a 50% Model + 50% Manager heuristic improves forecast quality. The essential message is that both statistical and human inputs should guide final decisions, at least given the current state of model building and the difficulty in quantifying expert intuition.

The paper is applicable to a large constituency in the business community. Forecasters can use "econometric" models effectively only if they have a built-in adjustment mechanism to capture the changing environment. We argue that managerial forecasts can fill this role and improve predictive accuracy. Thus we will not simply conclude that combination rules are best. This is of course the overwhelming conclusion reached in the forecasting literature (Clemen 1989), though most of the empirical work in that literature has focused on a model-model (Granger and Ramanathan 1984) or expert-expert (Ashton and Ashton 1985) combinations. Because the model-expert case is arguably the most common, it deserves special attention. In previous judgment research, experts often have provided little predictive power beyond that contained in models (Camerer 1981), so it was not obvious a priori that model-expert combinations would actually work. Our psychological view highlights how the dynamic interplay between model and expert improves

---

* Accepted by Robert L. Winkler, former Departmental Editor; received September 8, 1988. This paper has been with the authors 4 months for 2 revisions.

888   ROBERT C. BLATTBERG AND STEPHEN J. HOCH

forecast accuracy. Models and experts have shared but also unique forecasting aptitudes; models are *too* consistent and experts are *too* flexible. By integrating these decision inputs, we can exploit strengths and compensate for weaknesses.

2. A Comparison of Model Predictions and Expert Judgment

How do forecasts based on statistical models and expert judgment differ? Both methods operate on target information, but while models do so in a consistent, mechanical fashion, experts rely on intuition. Dictionaries define intuition as the act or process of coming to direct knowledge or certainty without reasoning or inferring, a keen and quick insight. Opinions about intuition have varied greatly over time, glorified as the only certain form of knowledge (the view of Descartes and Spinoza) and castigated for its unreliability (Noddings and Shore 1984). But despite disagreement over its value, there is consensus that purely intuitive judgments represent global decisions about which the decision maker is usually not able to offer a clear and complete justification. The expert has difficulty articulating the bases for intuition beyond a reliance on "gut-feel." The illusiveness of intuition is problematic for managers who have to rationalize their decisions, but (valid) "tacit" knowledge may result from the automatization of decision processes.

Evidence on the validity of intuition is equivocal. We briefly review the literatures on (a) comparisons of experts and novices and (b) comparisons of experts to simple quantitative models in order to highlight the relative strengths and weaknesses of models and expert judgment.

Experts versus Novices versus Simple Models

Research in cognitive science (Larkin et al. 1980; Lesgold et al. 1988) suggests that experts have highly organized, domain-specific knowledge that allows them to encode complex information; this knowledge results in faster and more accurate performance (Chi, Glaser, and Rees 1981). The judgment and decision making literature presents a less flattering picture of the expert. Experts often have performed no better than novices (Einhorn 1974; Goldberg 1959; Hoch 1988). These results are puzzling since, by definition, experts should be more skillful. Research suggests that experts are better at knowing what questions to ask (diagnosis) than at predicting the future.

Research comparing experts to simple actuarial models is much clearer. In studies of medical diagnosis, psychological assessment, financial forecasting, student admissions, and security analysis, actuarial models always produce more accurate forecasts than the experts (Dawes, Faust, and Meehl 1989; Sawyer 1966). The most common paradigm has been to present multiattribute profiles of a target stimulus to the expert and then ask for relevant judgments about some criterion. The models typically have been built using multiple regression, regressing the criterion onto the various predictor variables that make up the multiattribute description. In an early influential study, Meehl (1959) had 29 clinical psychologists rate the mental health of 861 patients described by profiles consisting of 11 scores from a commonly used psychological test (MMPI). The actuarial model ($r = 0.46$) fit better than the average ($r = 0.28$) and the best clinician ($r = 0.39$).

Another body of research, known as judgment bootstrapping, has demonstrated an even more interesting finding. A model of the expert's judgment policy is constructed regressing the expert's forecasts onto the multiattribute profiles. Multiple studies (Camerer 1981) have shown that the predictions from the model of the expert (fitted values from the regression) are more highly correlated with the criterion than are the original judgments on which the expert's model is based. Bootstrapping works when the residuals from the model of the expert consist mainly of random variance in judgment; use of the fitted values from the expert's model eliminates a source of variance not predictive of outcomes.

Bootstrapping systematizes judgment, but also discards any intuition the expert may have that is not compatible with the model. The robustness of the bootstrapping result has led some to conclude that model consistency more than compensates for any valid intuition experts might have not captured by the simple model (Dawes et al. 1989).

Some valid aspects of judgment, however, are not easily captured by a linear model. Meehl (1954) coined the term "broken leg" cue to describe highly diagnostic cues that occur so infrequently that they are difficult to incorporate into a statistical model. He gave the example of a sociologist predicting whether a professor would go to the movies on a particular night. A sociometric model could be built containing a variety of relevant variables (tenure, children). If, however, the sociologist found out that the professor had just broken his leg, then he could confidently ignore the model and still make an accurate forecast based on a single fact. Models have difficulty incorporating broken leg cues. There may not be enough historical evidence showing the effect of these rare cues; moreover, the modeler could exhaust the available degrees of freedom by attempting to incorporate all the potential candidates, a problem not faced by experts. Johnson (1988) found that without broken leg cues experts and novices performed at comparable levels and were outperformed by both an actuarial and bootstrapping model. With access to broken leg cues, however, experts improved dramatically, outperforming the bootstrapping model (which ignores broken leg cues) though not the actuarial model (which also ignores broken leg cues).

Combining Models and Experts

Over the last 20 years an extensive literature on combining forecasts has accumulated (Clemen 1989). In searching for the single "best" combining method (Granger and Ramanathan 1984), the lasting conclusion is that almost any combination of forecasts proves more accurate than the single inputs. Most research has focused on combinations of multiple models or multiple experts, but not model and expert (cf. Conroy and Harris 1987; Lawrence, Edmundson, and O'Connor 1986; Pankoff and Roberts 1967). Models from different sources (e.g., competing econometric forecasting firms) often will have different predictor variables and be calibrated on databases that are only partially redundant (so sample size effectively increases). In the face of random error, averaging these different model specifications can improve accuracy. Combining models can also work because of difficulties in consolidating all exogenous variables into a single comprehensive model (Bunn 1988). If such a model is estimated on an unstable covariance matrix, then a combination of submodels which ignore intercorrelations and treat forecast errors as independent can do better. Combinations of experts, on the other hand, increase accuracy because the inconsistencies of one judge tend to cancel out the inconsistencies of another (Hogarth 1978). Studies (Goldberg 1970) have found that an average of experts' forecasts performs comparable to bootstrapping models; both methods eliminate random variance.

But what about model-expert combinations? One might argue that combining experts with models is simply another form of combining forecasts. However, in light of the bootstrapping literature, it is not clear that experts would add anything to the model forecasts, since their residual expertise (above that captured by a model) typically has been very small. Alternatively, experts and models have quite different strengths and weaknesses, which might be beneficial for combining purposes; these respective strengths and weaknesses are summarized below.

Where Experts Are Weak and Models Are Strong:
> Experts display decision biases of perception and evaluation. Models are unbiased.
> Experts suffer from overconfidence and are influenced by organizational politics. Models take base-rates into account and are immune to social pressures for consensus

> Experts get tired, bored, and emotional. Models do not.
> Experts do not consistently integrate evidence. Models optimally weight the evidence.

Where Models Are Weak and Experts Are Strong:
> Models know only what the expert has told the model-builder. Experts know what questions to ask and can identify new variables. Experts diagnose *and* predict, models only predict.

> Experts are proficient at attribute valuation, providing subjective evaluations of variables that are difficult to measure objectively (Einhorn 1974).

> Models are consistent, but as a consequence are also rigid. Experts are inconsistent but are flexible in adapting to changing conditions.

> Experts have highly organized, domain-specific knowledge. They may be able to recognize and then interpret abnormal cases containing "broken leg" cues, cues that are very diagnostic but so rare that they are difficult to anticipate and therefore include in a model.

Experts and models are both substitutes and complements; *substitutes* because both take into account much of the same decision relevant information; *complements* because where one decision input is weak the other is stronger and vice versa. In the next section we offer a method for taking advantage of the consistency offered by a model and the intuition that only can come from an expert.

3. Quantifying Managerial Intuition

From the perspective of engineering higher quality decisions, it is not necessary to completely understand intuition in order to use it to good advantage. In fact, if experts could tell us the information on which they base their intuition, we would include it in our models if quantifiable. In situations where experts do have valid intuition, all that is necessary is that we can isolate that part of subjective judgment that contains the intuition. Our approach shares similarities with the Lens Model analysis developed by Brunswik (1952) used in judgment bootstrapping (Goldberg 1970). We start with a target event (Y) that is a probabilistic function of multiple correlated cues or environmental information (X_i's). The X_i's are observable predictor variables available to both decision maker and modeler. The expert also makes a prediction (P) of Y, the target event.

We begin by building the best fitting model of Y given the X_i cues using multiple regression,

$$Y = X\beta + \epsilon. \tag{1}$$

Let $\hat{M} = X\hat{\beta}$ be the vector of model predictions. We consider only linear models, though our approach could be adapted to any estimable nonlinear form. On the estimation data, the decision maker cannot integrate (linearly) the same information in a more efficient manner; the model predictions ($\hat{M}$) represent an upper bound on the linear information extractable from these environmental cues. The question is whether the expert adds any predictive power above and beyond that of the model.

Operationally, we define intuition as the residual portion of an expert's prediction controlling for the predictor variables (the X_i's). Intuition can be isolated by regressing the expert's predictions (P) onto the model's predictions (M),

$$P = \gamma\hat{M} + U, \tag{2}$$

with all variables in standardized form (including the residuals), equation (2) can be rewritten as

$$p = \alpha\hat{m} + \sqrt{1 - \alpha^2}\,u, \tag{3}$$

DATABASE MODELS AND MANAGERIAL INTUITION   891

where α equals the correlation between p and $\hat{m}$, and u represents the standardized residuals (Hoch 1987). The residuals, u, contain the "unique" part of the expert's forecast composed of both valid intuition and random error. The valid intuition could result from the expert's ability to pick up omitted variables or nonlinearities and interactions not in the model. Because u and $\hat{m}$ are orthogonal, the expert's predictive accuracy, the correlation between y and p $[r(y, p)]$, can be expressed as,

$$r(y, p) = \alpha r(y, \hat{m}) + \sqrt{1 - \alpha^2} r(y, u), \tag{4}$$

where the correlation $r(y, \hat{m})$ represents the accuracy of the model and the correlation $r(y, u)$ represents the validity of intuition (Hoch 1987).[1]

With a means of isolating intuition, the question becomes whether we can put u to better use than the experts have in their raw predictions; in other words, can we combine the model ($\hat{m}$) and intuition (u) together in a better manner? On the estimation data, the answer is obviously yes. An optimal combination of model and intuition can be no less accurate than the best of the inputs in isolation. Adding any new variable would increase the overall fit, though this may not hold true when moving on to out-of-sample forecasting. Consider first the optimal combination ($\hat{y}$) of model predictions with expert predictions that is obtained from regressing y onto $\hat{m}$ and p,

$$\hat{y} = b_1 \hat{m} + b_2 p. \tag{5}$$

The overall fit of the optimal combination of model and expert can be written as

$$R^2(y, \hat{y}) = b_1 r(y, \hat{m}) + b_2 r(y, p), \tag{6}$$

where b_1 and b_2 are the relative weights for model and expert. The trade-off between model and intuition is revealed by substituting equation (4) into equation (6),

$$R^2(y, \hat{y}) = (b_1 + b_2 \alpha) r(y, \hat{m}) + b_2 \sqrt{1 - \alpha^2} r(y, u). \tag{7}$$

Because the orthogonality of $\hat{m}$ and u allows for a unique variance partitioning between model and intuition, equation (7) further simplifies to

$$R^2(y, \hat{y}) = R^2(y, \hat{m}) + R^2(y, u). \tag{8}$$

Whenever experts have valid intuition $[r(y, u) \neq 0]$, model-expert combinations will be more accurate than either of the single inputs. Two useful statistics fall out of this analysis. The first is $r(y, u)$, the validity of expert intuition, which is equivalent to the semipartial correlation between y and p after partialling the model ($\hat{m}$) out of p (Cohen and Cohen 1975). Regular partial correlations, where the model is controlled for in both y and p, can also be calculated [equivalent to the correlation between the residuals in equations (1) and (3), $r(\epsilon, u)$]. When squared, the regular partial correlation represents the percent of outcome variance unexplained by the model that can be explained by expert intuition.

4. Database Models and Managerial Intuition

Forecasting Situations

Two different forecasting situations were studied: (a) buyers' predictions of catalog sales of fashion merchandise, and (b) brand managers' predictions of coupon redemption rates. Statistical models were built and then contrasted against managerial forecasts and

---

[1] The residuals here are estimated by controlling for the actuarial model ($\hat{y}_e$ in Lens Model terms). The Lens Model residuals, z_s, are estimated by controlling for the model of the judge (y_s). We use this formulation because in combining models and intuition, we wish to use the best available model and the actuarial model always will be at least as good as the model of the judge.

a model-expert combination. Models were developed during various consulting projects, and as such represented good faith efforts to identify the "best" model given time and money considerations.

Catalog Fashion Sales. In two different firms selling apparel through direct mail catalogs, buyers were responsible for estimating demand for an item at the SKU (stock keeping unit) level. Predicting fashion is extremely difficult—fashions are constantly changing and buying decisions need to be made anywhere from 3 to 6 months in advance of the catalog drop in order to ensure adequate inventory. These catalog companies were interested in improving the ordering process.

There were two types of predictor variables (X_i's): (a) characteristics of the item and the way it was merchandised in the catalog; and (b) information about each item from a consumer survey. Variables in the first category included: percent of page devoted to the item; location in the catalog; department (e.g. lingerie); price and percent markup; and other variables like the number of colors. These variables were identified both through discussions with buyers, management, and previous catalog research. Also, a sample of target consumers were shown mocked-up versions of the catalogs. After browsing through the catalog, consumers answered a series of questions about each item such as "Is the item a good value for the money?" and also could purchase any of the items at a 10% discount, allowing us to calculate sample response rates.

Buyers made sales forecasts for each of the items in the context of normal decision making about item purchasing and inventory. Buyer forecasts were made after all other decision parameters (price, etc.) had been set. In each firm, multiple buyers were involved in forecasting, though for each item only one buyer made a forecast. The criterion variable (Y) was the number of orders for each item received by each firm, more appropriate than actual sales because it is unaffected by item stock-outs due to inaccurate forecasts. Models were built using OLS regression, regressing the logarithm of orders onto the predictors. Buyer forecasts were also logged.

Coupon Redemption Rates. In three other firms, brand managers routinely made predictions about the redemption rates for price-off coupons on frequently purchased consumer packaged goods. Such forecasts are a common aspect of managing promotional activities; accurate forecasts are important because managers need to anticipate the product's financial liability, and for purposes of choosing among different promotional activities depending on tactical goals (e.g., inducing trial).

Predictor variables for these models were identified through interviews with product management and from related published research in the area (Blattberg and Neslin 1990). Predictors included: coupon face value, percent discount, brand, duration of the offer, a product category development index, and media type (FSIs, in-packs). Managers made forecasts at the time of the coupon issue date so all decision parameters had been set. Models were built using weighted least squares regression; the observations were weighted to reflect the number of coupons dropped during the promotion. The criterion and manager forecasts were logged before estimation.

Results

The final fashion buying models for Company 1 (CO1) and Company 2 (CO2) each contained 11 predictors. The coupon redemption models for Companies 3–5 each contained over 30 predictors, most of which were dummy variables for media type and brand. To control for shrinkage, cross-validated models were tested, where the model was fit on half the data and then used to predict the remaining data. To ensure robustness of the results, 10 separate cross-validation analyses, randomly splitting the samples 10 different ways, were conducted for each data set; the reported results represent the average of the 10 analyses. The cross-validation results appear in Table 1.

Model, Manager, and Model + Manager. In all cases, the statistical models fit quite well. Though some shrinkage was observed in the cross-validation analyses, the model fits were still quite good, an average R^2 of over 0.55. Managers also displayed substantial expertise, predictive accuracy comparable to that of the models except for CO1, $t(105) = 2.4, p < 0.01$.

Hierarchical regression analyses were conducted to assess whether the combination of the model and manager provided a significant incremental increase in accuracy over either decision input in isolation. The overall fit of "model + manager" was assessed by regressing the criterion onto the predictions of the model $(\hat{M})$ and the expert (P). The statistical tests are F tests of the differences between the fit (R^2) of the full model (model + manager) and the two reduced models (database model or manager alone). In all cases a combination of the model *and* the manager led to a significant increase in predictive accuracy over the model or the manager alone, all p's < 0.0001. The fourth column labled Δ shows the increase in R^2 that accompanies relying on a combination of model + manager compared to using the best single decision input. Δ averages 0.09 in the cross-validation results, increasing from 0.05 in the complete data sets. This suggests that manager forecasts assume an even more important role when model shrinkage occurs (whether due to overfitting or structural changes in the environment). Model shrinkage averaged almost 13% in the cross-validation analyses. When manager forecasts were combined with model predictions, however, shrinkage was reduced to only 5.5%, resulting in almost 60% less shrinkage in the model + manager combination forecasts. The two decision inputs are complementary. *When misspecified models break down during implementation, expert judgment can significantly improve predictive accuracy.*

Several other analyses are of interest. First, there was a significant degree of overlap between manager forecasts and model predictions, average $r(\hat{M}, P) > 0.7$ for the five firms. At the same time, however, managers displayed a significant amount of intuition about fashion buying and coupon redemptions. To examine intuition, we calculated semipartial and regular partial correlations between actual sales (Y) and manager forecasts (P) *controlling for model predictions.* These statistics allow us to assess the incremental contribution of the manager adjusting for the correlation between the manager and the database model. The results appear in the last two columns of Table 1. One thing is very clear: in all five data sets, managers demonstrate a substantial degree of intuition about the nonlinear aspects of their forecasting tasks. On average the validity of intuition is over 0.31 in the hold-out samples. These results differ markedly from almost all previous studies of expert judgment, where typically intuition is quite low. A reanalysis of 15 bootstrapping studies by Camerer (1981) found much lower nonlinear intuition, an average validity of less than 0.06 (comparable to the fifth column in Table 1).[2] Managers

TABLE 1

Regression Results Comparing the Predictive Accuracy of the Model, the Manager, and a Combination of the Model + the Manager

Cross-validation Hold-out Sample	R^2 of Model	R^2 of Manager	R^2 of Model + Manager	Δ	Validity of Intuition $r(y, u)$	Unexplained Variance Picked Up by the Manager $[r(y, p.\hat{m})]^2$
Company 1 ($n = 108$)	0.47	0.30	0.53	0.06	0.25	12%
Company 2 ($n = 100$)	0.63	0.67	0.74	0.07	0.33	29%
Company 3 ($n = 203$)	0.56	0.52	0.66	0.10	0.31	22%
Company 4 ($n = 173$)	0.71	0.74	0.83	0.11	0.34	40%
Company 5 ($n = 1008$)	0.39	0.39	0.50	0.11	0.32	17%

[2] Bootstrapping residuals $(z_s - y_s - \hat{y}_s)$ always are more highly correlated with the criterion than the residuals $(u = y_s - y_e)$ used here because $r_z = r(y_e, z_s) = r(y, u)/r(z_s, u)$.

also were able to pick up a substantial amount of the variance not explained by the model, 24% in the hold-out samples, corroborating the significant improvements in accuracy due to combination of model and manager. These results provide a much more flattering picture of expert judgment than most previous studies.

Stabilizing Models with Manager Forecasts. The cross-validation results for both the catalog and coupon redemption data suggest that managerial forecasts can play an important role in the decision making process by providing a stabilizing influence on model forecasts which serves to reduce model shrinkage. Managers may be able to take into account structural changes in the decision environment that models cannot detect. Although models can be reparameterized periodically, sudden changes in the data generating process (possibly signalled by broken leg cues) will be difficult to detect without the extended history required for recalibration.

To examine whether managers can indeed anticipate structural changes not detected by the statistical models, temporally-based analyses of CO4 and CO5 were conducted using information about coupon issue date. The data sets covered 20 months. Models were initially fit to the first 10 months of data, and then these models were used to forecast coupon redemptions in the succeeding months. The results appear in Table 2. During the "fitted" period the models fit very well; however, in the forecast period, model fits decreased significantly, CO4, $z = 4.04$, $p < 0.001$, and, for CO5, $z = 2.32$, $p < 0.01$. This suggests nonstationarity (or trend) in the data and that the model is unable to account for whatever structural changes occurred. In contrast, manager forecasts were robust across time periods. Managers successfully picked up environmental changes, and so in the forecast period manager's forecasts explained almost 38% of the variance in redemptions not captured by the model $[r(y, p.\hat{m})]^2$. By spending 10 months collecting data (and then building a model), the two firms could have increased forecast accuracy by 12% (R^2 increase of 0.06) above manager forecasts. Alternatively, by combining manager forecasts with existing database models calibrated on past data, accuracy could have been increased by 38% (R^2 increase of 0.17). Discussions with managers indicated that they believed that over time there had been a general decline in coupon redemption rates, whether due to increased use as a promotional tool by competitors or changes in buying patterns. Even if redemptions were declining (something not obvious in the data), it is not clear how this fact could have been incorporated into our models.

Optimal and Heuristic Weighting of Model and Manager. The optimal trade-off between model and manager can be expressed in percentage terms (the percentages represent a ratio of the standardized beta weights), where the percents would reflect the relative weights applied to a linear combination of the standardized forecasts of model and manager. On average the optimal trade-off in the hold-out samples is 50:50, ranging from 64:36 for CO1 to 44:56 for CO2 and CO4. These model/manager tradeoffs can be trans-

TABLE 2

Time-Based Redemption Rate Analyses Comparing Model, Manager, and Model + Manager

Time Period	R^2 of Model	R^2 of Manager	R^2 of Model + Manager	Δ	Validity of Intuition $r(y, u)$	Unexplained Variance Picked Up by the Manager $[r(y, p.\hat{m})]^2$
Model Estimation:						
Company 4 ($n = 174$)	0.87	0.74	0.90	0.03	0.24	28%
Company 5 ($n = 1048$)	0.42	0.41	0.51	0.09	0.31	17%
Future Forecast:						
Company 4 ($n = 172$)	0.61	0.74	0.80	0.06	0.44	49%
Company 5 ($n = 968$)	0.36	0.45	0.52	0.07	0.41	26%

DATABASE MODELS AND MANAGERIAL INTUITION   895

lated into unique model/intuition tradeoffs using equation (7). Part of the valid variance in manager forecasts is already contained in model predictions. The 50:50 split between model and manager translates into a 70:30 split between model and intuition.

The robustness of the 50:50 heuristic was tested through a simulation where the relative weights given to model and manager were systematically varied in increments of 10% from 100% model to 100% manager. The cross-validation results are shown for each firm in Figure 1. The simulation demonstrates that the utility of combining the two decision inputs is relatively insensitive to the exact weights applied to each. Substantial drop-offs in fit occurred only at the extremes, where most or all of the emphasis was given to one of the decision inputs. Robustness with respect to the exact weighting of model and manager is expected in this case given the relatively high correlation between the two inputs. Using a 50:50 rule for each of the five firms, in lieu of the optimal weights (indicated by the dots), resulted in only about a 1% decrease in R^2 on average.

The Value of Less Sophisticated Models.   Our analyses show that model and manager forecasts are complementary sources of information that increase in predictive accuracy when considered in tandem. Managerial judgments are more adaptable to new circumstances and therefore can help to stabilize the performance of models in changing decision environments. Models provide a consistent information source that compensates for the inconsistency inherent in human judgment. The final set of analyses examines potential benefits from combining less sophisticated models with managerial judgment. The basic analytic strategy involved building of systematically "degraded" models.

The data were reanalyzed using degraded models containing 50% of the variables contained in the full models. For each firm the "$\frac{1}{2}$" models represent the average fit of 10 models each constructed from random subsets of variables in the full model. The $\frac{1}{2}$-models explain only 63% of the variance captured by the full models. However, a combination of manager + $\frac{1}{2}$-model still results in significant improvements in accuracy over the best single decision input—an average increase in R^2 of 8.8% ($\Delta = 0.07$). Degraded models containing less than 20% of the variables in the full model were also constructed. Because 20%-models were more likely not to contain one of the key predictors, their fit

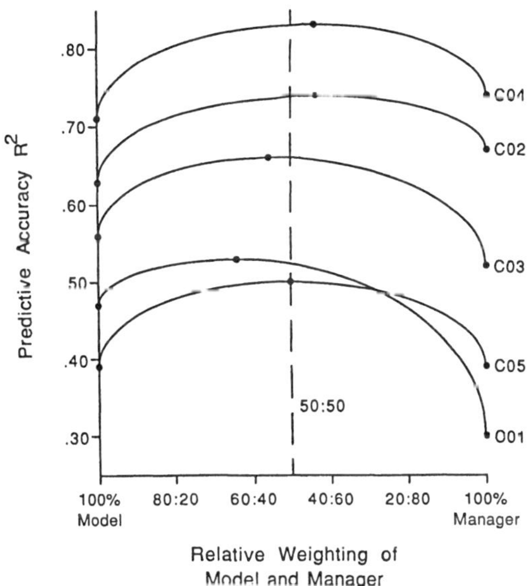

FIGURE 1.   Predictive Accuracy for Different Weighting Combinations of Model and Manager.

was poor, an average R^2 of 0.18 (28% of the variance explained by the full models). These weak models still improved the accuracy of manager forecasts in isolation, increasing R^2 by over 3%, and suggest that model-expert combinations may be worthwhile even in the early stages of model building. Despite an obviously naive model, the consistency inherent in such a model may improve the accuracy of forecasts based solely on intuition.

5. Discussion

Our findings suggest an encouraging view of the complementarity of database models and managerial intuition. Managers displayed quite high levels of intuition; they picked up almost 25% of the variance left unexplained by our models. We still do not know where the intuition comes from, but it is clear that it would be foolish to disregard it and rely solely on a statistical model for future forecasting.

Although the optimal combination of model and manager will always be more accurate on the estimation data, this need not be the case on hold-out samples or if a heuristic weighting rule is employed. The combination of model + manager increased predictive accuracy by a substantial degree (average $\Delta > 0.09$ in the hold-out samples). The inclusion of the manager provided the added benefit of dramatically decreasing model shrinkage in hold-out samples. Across the five firms, the goodness of fit of the models and managers varied substantially, a range in R^2 for the model of 0.24 and for managers of 0.44. But in each case the 50:50 heuristic improved predictive accuracy.

Why did our experts display substantial intuition? We will discuss four possible reasons: (a) building of "naive" models; (b) use of realistic tasks where performance matters; (c) presence of certain artificial factors inflated expert performance; and (d) existence of valid intuition in business forecasting. Although our remarks are speculative, we hope that a discussion of each will put into perspective when and where one might find similar improvements in decision making quality by relying on models *and* intuition.

Naive Models?

It is possible that we built overly simplistic models that make the experts look better on a relative basis and inflate the validity of intuition. Although what constitutes a "good" model depends on the phenomenon being predicted, our models fit quite well ($R^2 = 0.55$ on cross-validated samples), much better than most actuarial models reported in the bootstrapping research previously demonstrating the superiority of models over expert judgment. Moreover, extensive discussions with the buyers and managers did not reveal any omitted factors that could be easily incorporated into the models, only qualitative considerations ("fashion orientation"). Nonlinear transformations possibly could have improved model fits, but without prior theory, the possibilities are infinite. Better models could have been built, but given time, money, and potential payout, we feel reasonably confident that the results are not due to obviously naive modeling efforts.

Realistic Task Where the Performance Matters?

Our results were obtained in the context of everyday decision making, offering a "veridical" task (Johnson 1983) where experts could tap into domain-specific knowledge. In the typical experimental study, experts are asked to make judgments about artificial stimuli, usually depicted in multiattribute rather than holistic form (cf. Phelps and Shanteau 1978). Experts have available to them exactly the same information as does the model—they cannot take advantage of any skill they may have at identifying other information not incorporated in the model. Therefore, the only way that experts can perform better than the model is if they can execute a better information integration policy. By definition, we know that experts cannot execute a better "linear" policy on the estimation sample; therefore, they must apprehend the nonlinear aspects of the *given* attributes. Previous research clearly has demonstrated that experts are not proficient at this. Whereas

DATABASE MODELS AND MANAGERIAL INTUITION 897

previous studies have tended to place the burden on the expert to figure out the exact weighting of all the pre-specified cues, our study, in contrast, probably placed more of the burden on the modeler to specify *all* the appropriate cues available in naturally occurring decision environments. But since the burden will usually be on the modeler in most on-line forecasting situations, our results may be fairly representative. One additional point—bootstrapping of the experts did not work except for CO1; the benefits of consistency (linearization) could not compensate for the loss of a substantial amount of valid intuition.

Our experts also understood the incentives for performing well, so motivation was high. In experimental situations, this may not always be the case. More importantly, fatigue, boredom, and temporary distractions were less likely to influence performance. In laboratory studies multiple judgments are required in short time spans (1–2 hours), whereas our experts could elect to deliberate extensively over each prediction. Also, managers in the coupon redemption studies may have learned from experience, as they did receive some outcome feedback over time.

Artificial Factors Inflate Decision Maker Accuracy?

In discussing why the earnings forecasts of management are consistently superior to those of analysts and extrapolation methods (Armstrong 1983), Brown (1988) identifies three factors: self-selection of events to be predicted; inside information; and control over the phenomenon being forecast. Although our study required experts and models to make forecasts for all events, some self-selection may be at work—fashion items and coupon offers characterized by high uncertainty or low expectations of success could have been censored early in the process. Experts also had inside information, not the Machiavellian variety available to corporate officers, but they clearly had more information available to them than did the models. We have elected to label this inside information as intuition and see it as a valuable decision input. Finally, although expert and model forecasts were made after all decision parameters (price, media type) were established, experts probably exerted some control because expectations may have guided their setting of some of decision parameters. Expectations may produce outcomes that are at least partly self-fulfilling. These factors would be inoperative in a randomized experiment, but in most on-line forecasting situations decision makers do exert some control and as a consequence will display higher predictive accuracy. Whether one chooses to label the reasons for this improved performance as artificial or real is irrelevant to the decision to rely on a model-expert combination. We see this as another reason why model builders cannot ignore expert forecasts.

Truly Valid Intuition?

If we assume that our models are adequate and that our experts had only minimal control over future outcomes, then one is left with the fact that our buyers and product managers demonstrated valid intuition. Our experts explained almost 10% incremental variance in the target events which represents almost 25% of the outcome variance not captured by the statistical models. At the same time, experts and models were highly correlated, indicating that a substantial part of judgment was linear in form and also fairly consistent. So the question becomes why do decision makers display so much valid intuition about these two forecasting situations? It could be that our experts were capable of the categorical thinking not easily simulated by a linear statistical model, possibly taking account of interactions and nonlinear predictors. They may have had access to cues that either could not be quantified or were perceived at a less conscious, pattern-recognition level. Also, experts may have been able to interpret abnormal cases ("broken leg"-like omitted variables) when encountered even though they could not anticipate them a priori.

898   ROBERT C. BLATTBERG AND STEPHEN J. HOCH

Weather forecasters also have consistently demonstrated forecasting prowess, and in a situation where the forecaster has no control over the target event. Although not forecasting a physical system, our task had characteristics similar to those that Murphy and Brown (1984) believe make weather forecasting amenable to the development of expertise. The tasks were circumscribed, each target event being characterized by similar background information. Experts had substantial experience with the forecasting domain, were comfortable with the response scales, and had access to a variety of general industry analyses and other experts' forecasts.

Conclusions

In two forecasting situations where managers made real-time forecasts, we found that statistical models and managerial judgment achieved about the same level of predictive accuracy. We also found that a combination of model + manager outperformed either decision input in isolation. Models and managers have complementary skills. Models combine complex data in a consistent and unbiased manner. Managers have additional insight that the model cannot incorporate, such as the state of the economy, fashion trends, idiosyncratic features of an item, and shifting coupon redemption patterns. Managers may pick up a "broken leg" cue, so rare, that it would never be anticipated by a model. The trick is to incorporate model consistency and managerial insight into one forecast. Models are inflexible, making them less accurate as environments change. Managers, on the other hand, may tend to be too adaptive and overreact to current developments. Model-manager combinations can increase adaptivity while placing a regressive, but needed, upper bound on that adaptivity. Thus, model and manager may stabilize each other.

Given the well-recognized limits to human information processing capacity and the explosion of new data sources, managers need to move away from intuition as the sole basis for decision making. Intuition needs to be made "less intuitive." Until more is known about how to build better models, the 50% Model + 50% Manager decision heuristic is a nonoptimal but pragmatic solution offering three key advantages: (a) simplicity—managers do not need to understand or develop models, so the natural organizational separation of modelers and managers can continue; (b) palatability—managers retain a considerable amount of control over the decision making process; and (c) accuracy—a combination of model + manager will be more accurate than the individual decision inputs.

Model-manager combinations are easily incorporated into existing decision support systems. If managers (possibly working with modelers) can identify the informational basis for exceptions to the model, the model refinement process could be improved. Future research might investigate the efficacy of a procedure where, like weather forecasters who modify model predictions on the fly when not jibing with subjective assessments (Murphy and Brown 1984), managers make adjustments to model predictions rather than making independent forecasts. Whether or not an interactive procedure such as this would lead to an improvement (or decrement) over a mechanical combination rule is an open question, but the opportunity for training managers to use the system is intriguing given the success of weather forecasters.[3]

[3] Order of authorship is alphabetical. The authors thank Ken Hammond, Scott Hawkins, Robin Hogarth, Josh Klayman, George Loewenstein, and Jay Russo for comments.

References

ARMSTRONG, J. S., "Relative Accuracy of Judgmental and Extrapolative Methods in Forecasting Annual Earnings," *J. Forecasting*, 2 (1983), 437–447.
ASHTON, A. H. AND R. H. ASHTON, "Aggregating Subjective Forecasts: Some Empirical Results," *Management Sci.*, 31 (1985), 1499–1508.

BLATTBERG, R. C. AND S. NESLIN, *Sales Promotions*, Prentice-Hall, Englewood Cliffs, NJ, 1990.

BROWN, L. D., "Comparing Judgmental to Extrapolative Forecasts: It's Time to Ask Why and When," *Internat. J. Forecasting*, 4 (1988), 171–173.

BRUNSWIK, E., "The Conceptual Framework of Psychology," in *International Encyclopedia of Unified Science*, Vol. 1, No. 10, University of Chicago Press, Chicago, 1952.

BUNN, D. W., "Combining Forecasts," *European J. Oper. Res.*, 33 (1988), 223–229.

CAMERER, C., "General Conditions for the Success of Bootstrapping Models," *Organizational Behavior and Human Performance*, 27 (1981), 411–422.

CHI, M. T. H., R. GLASER AND E. REES, "Expertise in Problem Solving," in R. J. Sternberg (Ed.), *Advances in the Psychology of Intelligence*, Erlbaum, Hilldale, NJ, 1981.

CLEMEN, R. T., "Combining Forecasts: A Review and Annotated Bibliography," *Internat. J. Forecasting*, 4 (1989), 559–584.

COHEN, J. AND P. COHEN, *Applied Multiple Regression/Correlation Analysis of the Behavioral Sciences*, Erlbaum, Hillsdale, NJ, 1975.

CONROY, R. AND R. HARRIS, "Consensus Forecasts of Corporate Earnings: Analysts' Forecasts and Time Series Methods," *Management Sci.*, 33 (1987), 725–738.

DAWES, R. M., D. FAUST AND P. E. MEEHL, "Clinical Versus Actuarial Judgment," *Science*, 243 (1989), 1668–1674.

EINHORN, H. J., "Cue Definition and Residual Judgment," *Organizational Behavior and Human Performance*, 12 (1974), 30–49.

GOLDBERG, L., "The Effectiveness of Clinician's Judgments: The Diagnosis of Organic Brain Damage from the Bender-Gestalt Test," *J. Consulting Psychology*, 23 (1959), 25–33.

————, "Man vs. Model of Man: A Rationale, Plus Some Evidence, for a Method of Improving on Clinical Inferences," *Psychological Bulletin*, 73 (1970), 422–432.

GRANGER, C. W. J. AND R. RAMANATHAN, "Improved Methods of Forecasting," *J. Forecasting*, 3 (1984), 197–204.

HOCH, S. J., "Perceived Consensus and Predictive Accuracy: The Pros and Cons of Projection," *J. Personality and Social Psychology*, 53 (1987), 221–234.

————, "Who Do We Know: Predicting the Interests and Opinions of the American Consumer," *J. Consumer Res.*, 15 (1988), 315–324.

HOGARTH, R. M., "A Note on Aggregating Opinions," *Organizational Behavior and Human Performance*, 21 (1978), 40–46.

JOHNSON, E. J., "Expertise and Decision Under Uncertainty: Performance and Process," in M. T. H. Chi, R. Glaser, and M. J. Farr (Eds.), *The Nature of Expertise*, Erlbaum, Hillsdale, NJ, 1988.

JOHNSON, P. E., "What Kind of Expert Should a System Be?," *J. Medicine and Philosophy*, 8 (1983), 77–97.

LARKIN, J., J. McDERMOTT, D. P. SIMON AND H. A. SIMON, "Expert and Novice Performance in Solving Physics Problems," *Science*, 208 (June 1980), 1335–1342.

LAWRENCE, M. J., R. H. EDMUNDSON, AND M. J. O'CONNOR, "The Accuracy of Combining Judgmental and Statistical Forecasts," *Management Sci.*, 32 (1986), 1521–1532.

LESGOLD, A., H. RUBINSON, P. FELTOVICH, R. GLASER AND D. KLOPFER, "Expertise in Complex Skills: Diagnosing X-Ray Pictures," in M. T. H. Chi, R. Glaser, and M. J. Farr (Eds.), *The Nature of Expertise*, Erlbaum, Hillsdale, NJ, 1988.

LORIE, J. H., "Two Important Problems in Sales Forecasting," *J. Business*, 30 (1957), 172–179.

MEEHL, P. E., *Clinical Versus Statistical Prediction*, University of Minnesota Press, Minneapolis, 1954.

————, "A Comparison of Clinicians with Five Statistical Methods of Identifying Psychotic MMPI Profiles," *J. Consulting Psychology*, 6 (1959), 102–109.

MURPHY, A. H. AND B. G. BROWN, "A Comparative Evaluation of Objective and Subjective Weather Forecasts in the United States," *J. Forecasting*, 3 (1984), 369–393.

NODDINGS, N. AND P. J. SHORE, *Awakening the Inner Eye: Intuition in Education*, Teacher's College Press, New York, 1984.

PANKOFF, L. D. AND H. V. ROBERTS, "Bayesian Synthesis of Clinical and Statistical Prediction," *Psychological Bulletin*, 80 (1968), 762–773.

PHELPS, R. H. AND J. SHANTEAU, "Livestock Judges: How Much Information Can An Expert Use?," *Organizational Behavior and Human Performance*, 21 (1978), 209–219.

SAWYER, J., "Measurements *and* Prediction, Clinical *and* Statistical," *Psychological Bulletin*, 66 (1966), 178–200.

JACQUELYN S. THOMAS, ROBERT C. BLATTBERG, and EDWARD J. FOX*

For both academics and practitioners, the dominant focus of customer relationship management has been customer retention. The authors assert that customer winback should also be an important part of a customer relationship management strategy. Customer winback focuses on the reinitiation and management of relationships with customers who have lapsed or defected from a firm. In some cases, firms engage in extensive efforts to reacquire lapsed customers or defectors, and a common tactic is lowering the price to reacquire a customer. This investigation goes beyond the reacquisition pricing strategy and also examines the optimal pricing strategy when the customer has decided to reinitiate the relationship. By simultaneously modeling reacquisition and duration of the second tenure with the firm, the authors determine that the optimal pricing strategy for their application involves a low reacquisition price and higher prices when customers have been reacquired. In addition to pricing strategy, they also discuss the implications of their findings for targeting lapsed customers for reacquisition.

Recapturing Lost Customers

Loyalty and retention have been the dominant themes among scholars interested in customer relationship management (CRM). Books and articles have been written and businesses have been developed around the central theme of the management and maintenance of customer relationships (see, e.g., Reichheld 1996). Although progress has been made in the management of customer relationships, there are still high defection rates. Table 1, which we have adapted from the work of Griffin and Lowenstein (2001), shows customer defection rates across various industries.

Although all aspects of CRM need to be assessed and strategies and tactics developed, an area that has been largely neglected in the marketing literature is customer "winback" strategies. *Customer winback* is the process of firms' revitalizing relationships with customers who have defected. The importance and impact of customer winback as a key element in a firm's CRM strategy cannot be underestimated. Research has shown that a firm has a 60% to 70% chance of successfully repeat-selling to an "active" customer, a 20% to 40% chance of successfully repeat-selling to a lost customer, and only a 5% to 20% chance of successfully closing the sale on a brand new customer (Griffin and Lowenstein 2001). These statistics suggest that a key

*Jacquelyn S. Thomas is an associate professor, Integrated Marketing Communications Department, Medill School of Journalism (e-mail: jakki@northwestern.edu), and Robert C. Blattberg is the Polk Bros. Professor of Retailing, J.L. Kellogg Graduate School of Management (e-mail: r-blattberg@kellogg.northwestern.edu), Northwestern University. Edward J. Fox is W.R. Howell Director of the JCPenney Center for Retail Excellence and Assistant Professor of Marketing, Edwin Cox School of Business, Southern Methodist University (e-mail: efox@mail.cox.smu.edu).

Table 1
ANNUAL CUSTOMER DEFECTION RATES

Industry	Defection Rate
Internet service providers	22%
U.S. long distance (telephone)	30%
German mobile telephone market	25%
Clothing catalogs	25%
Residential tree and lawn care	32%
Newspaper subscriptions	66%

Adapted from Griffin and Lowenstein (2001).

opportunity for firms to increase or maintain a customer base is the mining and evaluation of the firm's database of defected customers. Stauss and Friege (1999) make this argument even more convincing in a case study in which they find that the net return on investment from a new customer obtained from an external list is 23% compared with a 214% return on investment from the reinstatement of a customer who has defected.

A critical element in the process of firms' recapturing of lost customers is the assessment of customer profitability. Customer lifetime value (LTV) is a central profitability metric in analysis of customer relationships; it is typically defined as the net present value (NPV) of the customer's profitability throughout the customer–firm relationship (Dwyer 1989). However, when it comes to the recapturing of lost customers, the second lifetime value (SLTV) of the customer (Stauss and Friege 1999) is the metric of interest. This metric focuses only on the NPV generated after a customer has been reacquired. Specifically, Stauss and Friege

(1999) define SLTV as the future value of a recaptured customer. They assert that when it comes to development and implementation of a customer recapture program, expectations about the potential future value of a recaptured customer should be the guiding factor. Logically, the SLTV should guide the decisions with respect to which customers should be recaptured and how much should be spent to reacquire them.

Some firms engage in extensive efforts to recapture defected customers or to reactivate lapsed customers. For example, during the long-distance telephone wars, one segment of customers frequently switched providers. Some customers switched to benefit from the introductory offer of a competing provider, whereas others simply wanted to solicit a better offer from the original provider (Marple and Zimmerman 1999). To recapture lost customers, telecommunications firms engaged in aggressive "come-back" campaigns. When the original provider approached customers to come back, they typically presented them with offers that were better than the original offer. Thus, the consumer usually benefited. However, reacquisition costs (e.g., reactivation fees, telemarketing efforts, come-back cash incentives) often caused the SLTV for the reacquired customers to be negative, thereby representing a net loss to the provider firms. This example illustrates the importance of SLTV to the strategy and tactics of customer reacquisition.

The focus of our article is on determining how firms should price customers when reacquiring them and how they should price them when they have been reacquired. In practice, the favored approach is to offer restarts lower prices for the same product. To stimulate purchase activity, Amazon.com offers lapsed customers discounts on their next purchases. Similarly, HoneyBaked, the ham company, offers a $10 gift certificate to reactivate customers (Schmid 1998), and Self Care, a health care products marketer, offers discounts of up to 25% to customers who have not ordered from the company in 18 to 24 months (Kiley 1996). Determining the optimal price for recapturing a customer is only part of the challenge in firms' customer winback strategy. An equally important decision is how to price when the customer has been reacquired.

The objective of this research is to assess optimal pricing strategies for the recapture of lost customers and the management of the SLTV of the recaptured customer (i.e., a restart customer). Specifically, we examine the relationship between the price used to recapture the customer and the subsequent price when the customer has been reacquired.

Prior research has shown that the acquisition of a customer affects the future relationship that a firm has with that customer (Thomas 2001). In this context, we examine how the reacquisition of a customer correlates and influences the reinstated customer–firm relationship. A key consideration in this analysis is the influence of the customer's relationship with the firm before reactivation. Using observable characteristics about the prior relationship (e.g., tenure, pricing, duration of lapse), we also draw conclusions about which lapsed customers are the most profitable targets for reacquisition.

We explore these questions in the context of services such as newspapers and magazine subscriptions and organizational memberships (e.g., health clubs). A common characteristic of these services is that the quantity purchased is typically one unit of the service. Thus, demand is typically determined by the duration of the customer–firm relationship. This context also offers the additional benefit that relationship durations and lapses are clearly identified. Although these relationships tend to involve contracts, the service we analyze allows customers to defect at any time without a penalty. This service also may change its prices over time. Thus, the context of our research offers the benefit of explicitly identifying relationship duration, but it is not limited by the pricing and duration constraints that often characterize contracted services.

In the next section, we review the relevant literature on pricing and CRM. In subsequent sections, we present a theory of restart customer behavior, detail the modeling framework used to test our theory, describe the data and variables used to estimate the model, present the empirical results, and examine the financial implications of our analysis. Finally, we conclude with a general discussion of our analysis and our study's limitations.

SLTV AND WINBACK LITERATURE REVIEW

On the surface, research on dynamic pricing seems an appropriate foundation on which to base our research. However, this research domain provides limited insight into the use of pricing to reacquire and retain lapsed customers. Traditional pricing research does not focus on the long-term relationship between the customer and the firm. This is evidenced by the fact that demand models typically used in pricing research do not monitor the churn or retention behavior of individual customers (for a review, see Mahajan, Mueller, and Bass 1993). Kalyanam (1996) shows that different ways of specifying demand can lead to different profit-maximizing prices.

In contrast, the CRM literature focuses on the individual customer and emphasizes LTV, which is a relatively new area and has been the subject of little empirical research, particularly research that addresses customer reacquisition and SLTV. For example, the research that is most similar to ours in that it explicitly addresses customer winback is that of Stauss and Friege (1999). They explore a concept that they term "regain management," which they define as the process of winning back customers who either give notice to terminate or have already ended the relationship. Stauss and Friege present a conceptual framework for customer winback that entails regain analysis (i.e., determining which customers have defected and why), regain actions (i.e., engaging in dialogue with the customer to determine the appropriate regain offer), and regain controls (i.e., the profit/loss analysis of the regain actions).

Our research addresses the three areas of Stauss and Friege's (1999) framework in a more rigorous context. Unlike Stauss and Friege, we perform a statistical analysis of defected and restart customers to determine drivers of reacquisition, we model both the reacquisition and the retention of a lapsed customers, and we focus explicitly on pricing as a means to recapture customers. Although our data do not enable us to determine why the lapse occurred, prior research has shown that unfavorable price perceptions have a direct effect on a customer's intention to switch providers (Keaveny 1995).

Building on the framework introduced by Stauss and Friege (1999), Griffin and Lowenstein (2001) introduce a general outline for winning back lost customers. Citing best practices from industry, they highlight the importance of highly trained winback teams and customer information systems. However, counter to the mantra of "zero defections," they assert that not all customers should be won back. According to Griffin and Lowenstein, firms should calculate SLTV, segment customers on the basis of SLTV, and evaluate customers in those segments to determine why they defected. Assessments of SLTV and rationale for defection guide the targeting and offers made in the regain process. Using case analyses, Griffin and Lowenstein find that the duration of a customer's lapse and the way that customer was acquired affect SLTV estimates. Our research incorporates and extends their insights into the domain of pricing strategies for customer winback.

Unlike the research we have mentioned, the majority of other CRM research does not address customer winback directly. However, a few researchers have addressed pricing issues related to CRM. Bolton and Lemon (1999) show that customers' use of two continuously provided services partly depends on prices. Bolton, Kannan, and Bramlett (2000) find that a price gain (i.e., a decrease in price) has a significant impact on repatronage, but a price loss (i.e., a price increase) does not. This finding is consistent with that of Krishnamurthi, Mazumdar, and Raj (1992), who show that for customers who switch often among consumer packaged-goods brands, price gains have a larger impact on brand choice than do price losses.

Another common theme in the CRM literature is the degree of price sensitivity among loyal customers. Previous researchers have asserted that loyal customers are willing to pay higher prices (Reichheld and Sasser 1990). Reinartz and Kumar (2000) test this assertion empirically. Using a median split, they segment customers into long- versus short-life customers and then examine the mean price paid by the two segments. They determine that long-life customers actually pay a lower mean price than do short-life customers.[1] Although Reinartz and Kumar never actually estimate price sensitivity, they draw inferences about the price sensitivity of customers who have longer relationships with the firm compared with that of customers whose tenures are shorter. Our research is distinct in that we model customer reacquisition and duration as a function of price. Thus, we actually estimate price sensitivity. In addition, our focus is not on long- versus short-life customers but on the pricing strategy for restart customers who may have either long or short prior relationships with the firm.

TOWARD A THEORY OF RESTART CUSTOMER BEHAVIOR

There are two basic issues that we address in our theory about restart customer behavior: (1) the nature and influence of the prior relationship on customer reacquisition and the subsequent relationship that evolves and (2) the responsiveness of restart customers to price. These two issues are par-

ticularly relevant. The first is critical for targeting; that is, which lapsed customers should the firm target for reacquisition? The second issue is critical for making offer decisions; that is, what are the optimal reacquisition and follow-up (after reacquisition) prices?

Targeting Decision

A popular approach for making targeting decisions in direct marketing firms is recency, frequency, and monetary value analysis. Although weaknesses in this approach have been identified, a widely held belief among direct marketers is that customers who have bought most recently and more often and have the highest monetary value are more likely to respond favorably to subsequent offers (Hughes 1996). This belief is consistent with other research findings. For example, Schmittlein and Peterson (1994) find that in a brokerage context, customers who make fewer transactions (i.e., purchase less frequently) are most likely to terminate their relationship with the firm. Boulding, Kalra, and Staelin (1999) find that, more generally, consumers' prior experience with a service affects their subsequent attitudes and assessments of that service.

Bolton, Kannan, and Bramlett (2000) find that experience with a product, measured by the number of prior transactions, is positively associated with a higher likelihood of repatronage. It is noteworthy that this result holds regardless of whether repatronage is measured either in terms of the decision to stay or to terminate the relationship or in terms of how much to use the service. They explain this finding by relating a customer's prior experience to repatronage intentions and to the customer's desire to maintain the status quo. Specifically, they assert that prior experience drives customer expectations and intentions. They argue that intentions are strongly related to the actual decision because customers strive to maintain the status quo; however, they also find that a customer's level of satisfaction can moderate this result.

Although the preceding articles are unique, the consistent theme in the results is that previous experience affects customer behavior. For lapsed or defected customers, experience can be measured by their prior tenure (which we refer to as Tenure 1 or first tenure) with the firm. Consistent with prior research, we assert the following:

> H_1: For restart customers, the length of their first tenure with a firm is positively related to (a) the reacquisition probability and (b) their subsequent tenure in a reinitiated relationship.

Although the normative beliefs of direct marketers about which customers to target for repurchasing may hold in many cases, in the context of this research, it is important to acknowledge that the relationship was terminated. The finality of this termination is not known at the time when the firm evaluates potential reacquisition candidates. This raises the question, How does the amount of time elapsed since the last purchase (or the length of the lapse) affect the chances of reacquisition and the nature of the relationship that may ensue?

Prior research has asserted that with the passage of time, customers adapt to the new level of service provided by the switched-to firm (Ganesh, Arnold, and Reynolds 2000). In addition, customers who have switched to a new firm after

---

[1] An inquiry with Reinartz and Kumar revealed that this result held even when they accounted for basic differences in product categories.

having experienced another firm's service exhibit higher levels of loyalty and repeat patronage to the switched-to firm than do patrons of the firm who had never experienced another provider (Ganesh, Arnold, and Reynolds 2000). Logically, the longer the time since the last purchase, the more likely a lapsed customer is to have engaged a new service or simply to have developed new behaviors. On the basis of this reasoning, we believe that the prior research suggests the following hypothesis:

H_2: The greater the time since last purchase, the lower is the likelihood of customer recapture.

Note that this hypothesis is still well founded even if the customer has not switched to a new provider, because it is consistent with status quo bias, that is, an exaggerated preference for the current state or inaction (Samuelson and Zeckhauser 1988).

To gain insight into the relationship between lapse duration and the duration of the reinitiated relationship (which we refer to as Tenure 2 or second tenure), we reference the theory of cognitive dissonance (Festinger 1957). A key premise of dissonance theory is that dissonance, or lack of fit between two elements (e.g., attitudes and behaviors, behavioral decisions and commitments), gives rise to pressures to eliminate or reduce the dissonance. This can be conceptualized as a drive to obtain consistency.

For any lapsed customer, the decision to reinitiate a relationship with the firm creates dissonance relative to the customer's prior state (i.e., inactivity) with the firm. Dissonance can vary in magnitude and is moderated by the importance or intensity with which attitudes are held (Eagly and Chaiken 1993; Festinger 1957). Applying this idea to our research, we argue that longer lapses may represent more extreme attitudes. Therefore, the decision to reinitiate a relationship after a long lapse results in a greater amount of dissonance relative to the decision to reinitiate a relationship after a shorter lapse. Cohen (1960) asserts that the greater the amount of dissonance, the stronger are the attempts to reduce it. This implies that customers who have had longer lapses make stronger attempts to reduce the dissonance between their prior behavior (i.e., the lapse) and their decision to reengage in a relationship with the firm.

To reduce or resolve the dissonance that occurs after a decision, a person attempts to engage in postdecision processing that reinforces the new decision that has been made (Festinger 1957, 1964). In the case of reacquired customers, the current decision is the choice to reengage in a relationship with the firm. In this context, the second tenure can be evidence of the reacquired customer's degree of reinforcement processing. Thus, because customers with longer lapses make stronger attempts to reinforce the reacquisition decision, they will have longer subsequent relationships than customers with shorter lapses.

H_3: Longer lapse durations are positively associated with longer second tenures.

Offer Decision

The most basic question about the price offer decision is, How will restart consumers respond to price? General laws of supply and demand assert that higher prices lead to lower demand (e.g., Einhorn 1994). This general principle can be directly applied to the reacquisition price offer.

H_4: The reacquisition rate is higher if the price offered is lower.

Consistent with economic theory, Reinartz and Kumar (2000) show that long-life customers pay lower mean prices than do short-life customers; theirs was one of the first CRM articles to demonstrate this unique result. However, it is worth acknowledging that this conclusion is not based on a statistical estimate of price sensitivity but on a median split of customers based on relationship duration.

We use caution in applying traditional economic theory to the price response of reacquired customers, because economics typically focuses on price responsiveness in discrete transactions. In contrast, CRM considers the long-term effects of price on customer relationships. Because of the long-term perspective, responsiveness to price may be more complex. For example, Bolton and Lemon (1999) use the concept of payment equity (i.e., the customer's perception of fairness with respect to the exchange of payment for service usage) to discuss consumers' use of services. Their research shows that consumers seek to maintain payment equity in a service relationship and adjust usage levels in response to price changes. Specifically, Bolton and Lemon find that service usage levels may increase as price increases in order to maintain equity in the relationship. However, the implied positive relationship between price and usage contradicts both the long history in economics of the negative effect of price on demand and the compelling empirical evidence across many disciplines. Thus, on the basis of weight of evidence, we hypothesize the following:

H_5: The second tenure is longer if the retention prices are lower.

Although we derive H_5 from the history of pricing research, we believe that it is important to test this hypothesis and either to reinforce the similarity between CRM and a transaction-oriented business perspective or to highlight the unique perspective of CRM.

To understand further how price affects reacquisition and repatronage, we revisit the issue of prior experience. Boulding, Kalra, and Staelin (1999) show that customers give different weights to prior experience and current experience. They find that as customers gain confidence or experience with a product, they weight their prior assessment of a given service more heavily than they do new information about the service. Thus, it might be expected that when restart customers assess their reinitiated relationship with the firm, they reflect on their prior relationship with the firm and give significant consideration to that assessment. This behavior is consistent with the existence of reference prices in consumer decision making.

The reference price literature enables us to generalize that consumers use prior prices in the formation of reference prices and that reference prices have a significant impact on demand (Kalyanaram and Winer 1995). The specific combination of prior prices and process by which internal reference prices are formed remains an open issue (for a review, see Kalyanaram and Winer 1995). For customer winback, the logical reference point is the customer's prior relationship with the firm. Consistent with these arguments and with H_4, we propose the following:

> H_6: The difference between the reacquisition price offering and the last price paid before lapse (i.e., reacquisition price minus last price in prior relationship) negatively affects the probability of reacquisition.

It is notable that this hypothesis allows for the price difference to be either positive or negative.

Further drawing on reference price literature, we assert that differences between the new price and prior prices can influence how restart customers assess their experience. This assertion is supported by arguments that customers' assessments of value, which directly affect relationship continuity, are based on differences relative to a reference point (e.g., Bolton 1998; Thaler 1985). More specifically, Varki and Colgate (2001) show that price perceptions significantly affect customer retention. Consistent with the cited research, we assert the following hypothesis:

> H_7: The difference between the current price offering and the last price paid before lapse (i.e., current price minus last price in prior relationship) negatively affects the duration of the second tenure.

H_6 and H_7 can have significant implications for the offer and targeting decisions. If supported, these hypotheses suggest that the price paid in the prior relationship anchors customers' perceptions and guides their subsequent behavior in the reinitiated relationship. This implies that firms should target customers for reacquisition and make the offer based on prices paid before the lapse.

The assertion that customers respond to differences in price raises the question of whether their response is the same for gains (e.g., price decreases) as it is for losses (e.g., price increases). Consistent with prospect theory (Einhorn and Hogarth 1981; Kahneman and Tversky 1979; Thaler 1985), another finding of the reference price literature is that customers respond more to losses than gains (Kalyanaram and Winer 1995). However, CRM researchers have observed a different effect with respect to price. Bolton and Lemon (1999) find that gains in price (i.e., decreases) have a larger impact on usage amount than do losses in price (i.e., increases). Similarly, Bolton, Kannan, and Bramlett (2000) find that gains in price have a larger effect than do losses on both the decision to stay in a relationship and the usage level. Given the solid support for both sides of the issue, we refrain from making predictions about the impact of gains versus losses with respect to prices, and we defer to the empirical results.

MODEL DEVELOPMENT

Modeling Customer Relationships

The growing CRM literature includes several modeling approaches (for a review, see Jain and Singh 2002). Some of these articles model SLTV within the broader context of LTV. This implicitly assumes that the firm can regain lapsed customers ("always a share") instead of customers being "lost for good." The most commonly used models are discrete Markov chains, so called because (1) time periods are discrete and (2) the probability of entering a particular state in the subsequent period depends only on the current state.

Dwyer (1989) outlines alternative discrete Markov models for customer migration, assuming an always-a-share scenario, and for customer retention, assuming a lost-for-good scenario. When the initial share of the customer is zero (i.e., customers are identified before having developed a relationship with the firm), the models can be interpreted as incorporating customer acquisition.

Pfeifer and Carraway (2000) and Rust, Zeithaml, and Lemon (2000) generalize Dwyer's (1989) approach by incorporating both migration and retention. Of particular interest, Rust, Lemon, and Zeithaml (2001) allow for the investigation of other decision variables, such as price, by modeling transition probabilities as a function of covariates.

Using alternative approaches such as selection models or decision calculus, researchers have explicitly modeled both acquisition and retention simultaneously (Berger and Nasr-Bechwati 2001; Blattberg and Deighton 1996; Thomas 2001). Such approaches are drawing increasing interest from researchers in the modeling of customer relationships.

Another CRM literature stream assumes that customers' probability of purchasing again (given that they do not explicitly terminate their relationships with the firm) depends not only on their current state but also on their purchase history. Schmittlein, Morrison, and Columbo (1987) and Schmittlein and Peterson (1994) use a stochastic modeling framework, the Pareto/NBD, for this purpose. Reinartz and Kumar (2000) dichotomize the continuous probability predictions of the Pareto/NBD model and, using individual customer cost information, are able to estimate LTV. The Pareto/NPD allows for continuous rather than discrete time, but it does not explicitly model price or other decision variables as covariates.

Given this history, we focus on five important characteristics of our investigation in making our modeling choices. First, we focus exclusively on the second lifetime (we term this "single spell," in line with the statistics literature). Although we may lose some generality by not adapting an always-a-share model, our focused approach is necessary to address the four remaining characteristics, thereby enabling us to provide managerially useful insights about the second lifetime. Second, because our hypotheses relate to the effects of price, we model price explicitly using covariates. Third, because many of our hypotheses relate to second tenure duration and because the data set we analyze lacks consistent decision intervals, we select a continuous-time specification. Fourth, our hypotheses for customer reacquisition and duration differ, which requires us to model the two as distinct processes. Fifth, the data set includes many customers whose relationship with the firm exceeds the period we observe, so we must allow for censoring.

Given these requirements, we specify a hazard model. Bolton (1998) uses a hazard model in a CRM context to examine the relationship between customer satisfaction and customer duration. Hazard models are well established in statistics, can incorporate covariates, and are adaptable to all types of censoring. Furthermore, hazard models have been shown to be well suited for analysis of duration data and superior to other common methods, such as logistic and least squares regressions, in terms of stability, face validity, and predictive accuracy (Helsen and Schmittlein 1993). To distinguish our approach from the more common proportional hazards model (Cox 1972), we refer to it as a "split hazard model" (it may also be termed a "censored duration model").

Model Specification

As we stated previously, we focus on a single spell that starts when the customer is reacquired by the firm and ends when the customer terminates the subsequent relationship. Our split hazard specification comprises separate reacquisition and duration components. The reacquisition component measures the probability of recapturing a lapsed customer, and the duration component predicts the length of the second tenure, given that the firm successfully recaptures the customer. This approach to linking acquisition and retention explicitly incorporates left censoring (Thomas 2001).

For customer i (i = 1, ..., C), we specify the reacquisition component as a latent variable probit with observation equation

$$(1) \qquad z_i = \begin{cases} 1 & \text{if } z_i^* \geq 0 \\ 0 & \text{otherwise} \end{cases}.$$

We model the latent dependent variable z_i^* with the linear model

$$(2) \qquad z_i^* = \mathbf{w}_i'\gamma + \eta_i,$$

where $\mathbf{w}_i'\gamma$ is the deterministic component, η_i is the stochastic component, $\mathbf{w}_i$ is the customer's vector of predictors, and γ is the associated parameter vector. Probit specifications have been used previously to model customer acquisition (Hansotia and Wang 1997; Thomas 2001).

Modeling of the second tenure is somewhat complicated by the firm's propensity to change the offer price during the relationship. Although this occurs relatively infrequently (see the data description in the following section), we must nevertheless allow for price changes to affect the customer's probability of terminating the relationship. We note that Amemiya (1985, pp. 433–35) shows that a split hazard model of the form that we specify is simply a generalization of a single spell of a continuous Markov model. Recognizing this relationship, we adopt the continuous Markov process assumption that the probability of the customer terminating the relationship at any point in time is independent of the current duration (i.e., it is stationary). Using this assumption of stationarity, we partition the second tenure so that each period during which a given price is offered to the customer is a "subspell." Thus, each customer's second tenure consists of one or more subspells that differ only in the offer price. Moreover, the stationarity assumption implies that the duration of a subspell does not depend on the length of prior subspells.[2] To illustrate, consider a hypothetical customer who is reacquired by the firm at time t as a result of a reacquisition price offer, is offered a second price at time t + δ_1, and then terminates the second tenure at time t + δ_1 + δ_2. This customer's duration consists of two subspells: one of length δ_1 (which is right censored) that is associated with the reacquisition price and one of length δ_2 that is associated with the second price. This approach enables us to capture parsimoniously the effect of price on second tenure duration.[3]

We model the duration component for customer i during subspell s_i ($s_i = 1, ..., S_i$) as a conditional regression with the following observation equation:

$$(3) \qquad y_{is_i} = \begin{cases} y_{is_i}^* & \text{if } y_{is_i} < c_{is_i}, \\ c_{is_i} & \text{otherwise} \end{cases},$$

where $y_{is_i}^*$ is the latent duration of the relationship and c_{is_i} is the censoring value, or length of time that a given price was offered. If the customer terminates the relationship before the price changes, then $y_{is_i}^* = y_{is_i}$ (i.e., it is observed). Otherwise, the duration of the subspell is right censored. The observed duration may also be limited by the observation horizon, in which case it is also right censored. Note that the censoring value is known; it is a necessary condition to estimate this model (Amemiya 1985, p. 363). We specify the latent duration of subspell s_i of customer i as

$$(4) \qquad \ln(y_{is_i}^*) = \mathbf{x}_{is_i}'\beta + \varepsilon_{is_i},$$

where $\mathbf{x}_{is_i}'\beta$ is the deterministic component, ε_{is_i} is the stochastic component, $\mathbf{x}_{is_i}$ is the customer's vector of predictors during subspell s_i, and β is the associated parameter vector. The dependent variable is log-transformed to approximate more closely the normality assumption about the residuals.[4]

Given the likely relationship between the customer's acquisition and retention behavior (Thomas 2001), it is important that these components be linked. We explicitly model this linkage, along with customer heterogeneity, by specifying variance components. We specify errors of the reacquisition and duration components, respectively, as follows:

$$(5) \qquad \eta_i = \iota_i + \psi_i, \text{ and}$$

$$(6) \qquad \varepsilon_{is_i} = \alpha_i + \xi_{is_i},$$

where $\psi_i \sim N(0,\sigma_\psi^2)$ and $\xi_{is_i} \sim N(0,\sigma_\xi^2)$.

For the reacquisition and duration components, respectively, ι_i and α_i represent customer-specific preferences, and ψ_i and ξ_{is_i} are random errors. As the subscripts of ι and α indicate, customer-specific preferences for reacquisition and duration are not fixed; they are distributed across households. In this way, we allow for heterogeneity across customers. Moreover, we allow the distributions of customer-specific preferences to be correlated so that $\theta_i \sim BVN(\overline{\theta},\Sigma_\theta)$, where

$$\theta_i = \begin{bmatrix} \iota_i \\ \alpha_i \end{bmatrix}, \overline{\theta} = \begin{bmatrix} \overline{\iota} \\ \overline{\alpha} \end{bmatrix}, \text{ and } \Sigma_\theta = \begin{bmatrix} \sigma_\iota^2 & \sigma_{\iota\alpha} \\ \sigma_{\iota\alpha} & \sigma_\alpha^2 \end{bmatrix}.$$

---

[2]We tested whether there were systematic differences between customers with a single subspell and customers with multiple subspells by estimating a more general specification of our model with a dummy variable that captured single versus multiple subspell customers as a predictor of duration. The CAIC and BIC for this specification are 1289 and 1282, respectively. For the specification without the dummy variable, CAIC and BIC are 1285 and 1279, respectively. We conclude that there is no evidence of systematic differences between the durations of customers with single and multiple subspells.

[3]We empirically validated the assumption of stationarity for our application. We estimated an alternative specification of our model that included a dummy variable for subspells beyond the first, and we found no difference in duration between the first (or only) subspell and subsequent subspells.

[4]Details of normality tests and alternative transformations are available from the authors.

In this way, we allow a customer's preference to reenter a relationship with the firm to be correlated with the customer's preference for the duration of that resumed relationship. Allowing for correlation between customer preferences for the discrete and continuous components of our split hazard specification is similar in spirit to a selection model, in which single stochastic error terms for the two components are correlated. In summary, the error variances of Equations 2 and 4 are

$$(7) \qquad \mathrm{Var}(\eta_i) = \sigma_\psi^2 + \sigma_\iota^2 + \sigma_{\iota\alpha}, \text{ and}$$

$$(8) \qquad \mathrm{Var}(\varepsilon_{is}) = \sigma_\xi^2 + \sigma_\alpha^2 + \sigma_{\iota\alpha}.$$

We follow Ainslie and Rossi (1998) in estimating our variance components specification in a Bayesian framework by using Markov chain Monte Carlo methods. The simulation-based methods of estimating posterior distributions of parameters in censored and missing data problems have only recently become available (Casella and George 1992; Gelfand and Smith 1990; for application to censored regressions, see Chib 1993). (A complete discussion of our estimation procedure is available as a technical report on request.)

DATA AND MODEL VARIABLES

Data

The data we used to estimate the model come from a newspaper subscription database and comprise 566 lapsed customers targeted for reacquisition (i.e., C = 566).[5] Of the customers, 416 were successfully reacquired. The reacquisition component of the data includes a single observation for each lapsed customer that consists of the reacquisition price offered, the result of that offer (i.e., successful or failed reacquisition), the number of periods elapsed since the customer's most recent purchase (each period as defined by the company is roughly one month), the price of the last purchase, and the length of the first tenure. Note that the firm made only one reacquisition offer per customer during our observation period (i.e., customers who did not respond did not receive multiple offers). Moreover, each customer in the data set lapsed only once, so none had received reacquisition

offers from the firm at any time before our observation period. Thus, our application does not include sequential offers to lapsed customers, and we conjecture about their response to such a sequence of offers.

Observations for the duration component differ from reacquisition observations in two ways. First, some customers have multiple subspells. More specifically, of the 416 customers that were reacquired, 140 received multiple price offers during the observation period (an average of 2.19 price offers for customers who received multiple prices), for a total of 582 subspells. Recall that each subspell represents a different price offer from the firm during a given customer's second tenure. Thus:

$$(9) \qquad N_1 = \sum_{i=1}^{C} S_i = 582.$$

The second difference is that the price in each observation is characteristic of that subspell and so may differ from the reacquisition price. Thus, although most reacquired customers paid a single price (the reacquisition price) throughout their relationship with the firm, more than one-third received multiple price offers.

All the customers examined in this analysis receive the newspaper seven days a week. When customers agree to receive the newspaper, they commit to a weekly price that remains fixed for a given period (roughly one month). We were unable to determine from the data whether a customer precommits to buy for several consecutive periods. Regardless, the firm does not engage in price discounting for purchase commitments of more than one period. Furthermore, unlike some other contractual selling agreements, subscriptions are nonbinding; therefore, customers can decide to continue or terminate the subscription at any point during a period. The average length of the second tenure is 177.4 days (see Table 2). Of the customers who reinitiated relationships with the firm, 66.8% terminated the relationship during the two-year observation horizon. The remaining customer durations are right censored. Descriptive statistics are provided in Table 2.

Model Variables

The first and most obvious variable included in the estimation is price, that is, the current price offered/paid in the reinitiated relationship (recall that customers are offered a single price for reacquisition but may be offered multiple

---

[5]We removed customers who lapsed or defected as a result of relocation or vacation from the data.

Table 2
DESCRIPTIVE STATISTICS

	Total Sample			Successfully Reacquired Sample		
	Mean	*Standard Deviation*	*Range*	*Mean*	*Standard Deviation*	*Range*
Reacquisition price offer	$2.22	$.44	$3.00–$1.75	$2.28	$.44	$3.00–$1.75
Average retention price offer[a]				$2.43	$.46	$3.00–$1.75
Last price paid in prior relationship	$2.32	$.47	$3.00–$1.75	$2.38	$.47	$3.00–$1.75
Reacquisition price difference	$.10	$.41	$1.15–($1.25)	$.10	$.48	$1.15–($1.25)
Average retention price decrease[a]				$.12	$.30	$1.15–$.00
Average retention price increase[a]				$.17	$.32	$1.25–$.00
Duration of lapse (in periods)	10.31	11.05	34–1	5.03	4.62	30–1
Prior tenure (in days)	179.75	279.97	684–1	229.00	282.05	684–7
Observed restart relationship tenure (in days)				177.42	217.92	684–2

[a]Because the price is time varying, we present the averages over the duration of the reinitiated relationship.

prices over the duration of the second tenure). The Tenure 1 variable measures the total duration of the customer's relationship with the firm before lapsing. Lapse duration measures the number of periods elapsed since the customer's last purchase.

A fourth variable measures the difference in price with respect to the last price paid before the relationship lapsed, which we suggest is a logical reference for the customer. We considered two alternative approaches to modeling price differences, and we specified the preferred approach on the basis of model selection tests. The first approach is to have a single variable, price difference, which is the difference between the last price in the prior relationship and the current price paid or offered (i.e., price difference = current price – reference price). A positive value for price difference means that the current offer price is higher than the last price observed by the customer. The second approach to modeling price differences enables us to assess asymmetric response to gains and losses by defining price decrease (i.e., a gain) and price increase (i.e., a loss) variables. Specifically, we define *price decrease* as the dollar amount of price decrease relative to the last price the customer was offered by the firm before the relationship lapsed; *price increase* is the dollar amount of the price increase relative to the last price the firm offered the customer. In interpreting the results, note that both variables are coded as positive values. The data show that 26.6% of the prices paid or offered in the restart relationship were decreases relative to the last price paid in the prior relationship, and 34.7% of the prices paid or offered were increases relative to the last price paid in the prior relationship.

RESULTS

Covariate Effects on the Reacquisition Probability

Consistent with H_{1a} and H_2, the reacquisition model shows that the probability of a firm reacquiring a customer is higher if the lapse duration is shorter and/or if the first tenure is longer. Consistent with economic theory and H_4, the results also show that customers are more likely to be reacquired if the reacquisition price is lower.

As we noted previously, we estimated alternative specifications, one with the price difference variable only and one which separated gains and losses. Comparing the corrected Akaike information criterion (CAIC) and the Bayesian information criterion (BIC) for the two specifications, we find that the model specification with price difference was preferred to the specification with separate price increase and price decrease variables.[6] Thus, we report parameter estimates from the former specification. The results support H_6: The likelihood of a customer being reacquired decreases with the difference between the reacquisition price and the last price offered in the prior relationship. This result implies that pricing in the prior relationship anchors response to the reacquisition offer. More generally, this supports the assertion that customers make decisions about reinitiating the relationship based on comparisons with the lapsed relationship. Table 3 reports posterior means of parameter estimates

---

[6]For the model specification with price decrease and price increase variables, CAIC and BIC are 1288 and 1281, respectively. For the specification with only price difference, CAIC and BIC are 1285 and 1279, respectively. Thus, the second specification represents a better balance of fit and parsimony.

Table 3
COVARIATE IMPACT

Variable	β (Posterior Probability)[a]	Elasticity
Impact on Customer Reacquisition		
Price	−.900	−.9000
	(.97)	
Lapse duration	−.686	−.6860
	(1)	
Tenure 1	.784	.7843
	(1)	
Price difference	−.526	−.0526
	(.91)	
Impact on Relationship Duration		
Price	1.194	1.1936
	(1)	
Lapse duration	−.047	−.0473
	(.78)	
Tenure 1	.454	.4539
	(1)	
Price decrease	1.556	.1802
	(1)	
Price increase	−.312	−.0523
	(.76)	

[a]β is less than or greater than zero.

for the reacquisition model as well as posterior probabilities (in parentheses) that the parameter is less than or greater than zero, depending on the sign of the posterior mean.

In terms of relative impact, the elasticities indicate that the offer price has the largest effect on reacquisition likelihood. Tenure 1 and lapse duration also have a material influence on the reacquisition outcome. Notably, price difference has a much smaller effect. Thus, the absolute effect of price is much more important than the effect of price relative to the last price paid in the prior relationship. This is an important insight for managers because it suggests that reacquisition strategies that emphasize decreasing price relative to the prior relationship are not likely to be effective. A more fruitful approach to winning back lapsed customers is simply to offer a low price, regardless of the price that the customer was accustomed to paying before the lapse. This also implies that customers who previously paid low prices should not be enticed with significantly lower prices.

Covariate Effects on Length of the Second Tenure

Table 3 also reports posterior means for parameters (and associated posterior probabilities that parameters are less than or greater than zero) for the duration equation. As in the reacquisition decision, the duration elasticity of price has a higher magnitude than other predictors. However, there are several notable differences between the factors that affect reacquisition and the length of the second tenure. An important difference is the sign of the price effect. Consistent with Bolton and Lemon (1999) and contrary to economic theory, we find that higher retention prices lead to longer relationship durations. Comparing this to the other relevant CRM literature, we find that it is consistent with the assertion that loyal customers are willing to pay higher prices (Reichheld 1996) but contradicts Reinartz and Kumar's (2000) finding that long-life customers pay lower average prices than do short-life customers (in a catalog retailing context). However, Reinartz and Kumar (2000, p. 28) state, "we expect these factors to have differential impacts in different industries."

Bolton and Lemon (1999) explain this effect in terms of payment equity. An alternative explanation is heterogeneity in reservation prices. However, our modeling approach allows for different reference prices across households. Because we replicate Bolton and Lemon's (1999) finding in the presence of heterogeneous reference prices, we can reject this alternative explanation. It is also possible in some contexts that price sensitivity decreases with use because of product familiarity, knowledge about how to use the product efficiently, or bias in favor of the status quo, which leads to repeat purchases. Both payment equity and decreased price sensitivity are plausible explanations in our application.

Although customers did not distinguish between price increases and price decreases in the reacquisition decision, they made this distinction after the relationship had been reinitiated, which is in support of H_7. This result further highlights the importance of the prior relationship price to the reinitiated relationship. Consistent with other CRM research (Bolton, Kannan, and Bramlett 2000; Bolton and Lemon 1999), the positive impact of gains (i.e., price decreases) on second tenure duration has a greater magnitude than does the negative impact of losses (i.e., price increases). Furthermore, we find that the effect of price decreases on the second tenure is statistically significant, but the effect of price increases is not. This asymmetric response to gains and losses points to a notable behavioral insight. Specifically, the results suggest that when price deviations (i.e., price increases or price decreases) are consistent with the customer's decision to reestablish a relationship, they have a noticeable effect. However, the customer is unaffected by deviations that do not support the decision to reestablish the relationship. This behavior is consistent with Festinger's (1957, 1964) assertion that people engage in postdecision processing that reinforces the decisions they have made.

Although Festinger's (1957, 1964) theory about postdecision processing can explain the effect of price comparisons, it does not explain our results about the effect of lapse duration on the second tenure. Specifically, the results do not support H_3, suggesting that there is no relationship between the length of the lapse and the customer's second tenure. It is possible that this null result is due to the relationship between lapse duration and the incorporation of customers' preference heterogeneity. If unmodeled individual characteristics, such as a propensity toward variety seeking or inertial behavior (Bawa 1990) in newspaper subscription, were correlated with the lengths of both the lapse and the second tenure, any relationship between the lapse and the second tenure would be obscured by the specification of preference heterogeneity.[7] In summary, although firms are less likely to reacquire customers who have had longer lapses, when they have been reacquired, the length of the second tenure appears to be unaffected.

Link Between Reacquisition and Length of the Second Tenure

Another issue in our investigation is the link between reacquisition and duration of the second tenure. Using a variance components approach, we allow for customer heterogeneity and correlation between customers' intrinsic preference to be reacquired and for their intrinsic preference to maintain the relationship after reacquisition. The estimates reveal that customers have a negative bias toward reacquisition (posterior mean of $\bar{\iota} = -1.592$, 95% posterior probability that $-2.789 \leq \bar{\iota} \leq -.094$), but when they have been reacquired, they are positively inclined to continue the relationship (posterior mean of $\bar{\alpha} = 1.743$, 95% posterior probability that $1.116 \leq \bar{\alpha} \leq 2.309$). This positive intercept parameter estimate for the duration model is consistent with our previous conjecture that a customer's price sensitivity may be lower in the reinitiated relationship.

The posterior mean of the correlation between the two preferences (estimated using $\sigma_{\iota\alpha}$) is $-.09$, which suggests that the likelihood of the customer being reacquired is inversely related to the likelihood of the customer remaining in the relationship. In other words, customers who may be more inclined to restart a relationship (i.e., customers who are easiest to win back) may not always be the best customers in terms of retention.

The descriptive data in Table 2 reveal some short first and second tenure observations. To assess the robustness of our results, we estimated our model with three reduced data sets: elimination of (1) all first tenures less than ten days, (2) all second tenures less than ten days, and (3) all first and second tenures less than ten days. Compared with our parameter estimates from using the full data set, we found no sign changes in any parameter estimate in the three reduced data sets. In addition, in none of the three reduced data sets did any parameter estimate that had been statistically significant at $\alpha = .05$ in the full data set become nonsignificant, and in only one case did a parameter that had not been significant become significant.[8] Thus, we suggest that our inferences are robust to the inclusion or exclusion of unusually short tenures.

FORECASTING SLTV

The asymmetric impact of price increases and decreases in conjunction with the current price effect suggests that pricing decisions for restart customers is complex. Specifically, the parameter estimates suggest that the last price in the prior relationship affects a customer's price sensitivity and behavior in both reacquisition and retention. In this section, we explore how the prior price affects the profitability of restart customers and the optimal pricing strategy of the firm.

Ultimately, a firm's targeting decision and offer decision should be based on the expected profitability of a reacquired customer. We used estimates from the reacquisition and duration models to predict the likelihood of a firm reacquiring and retaining a customer with certain characteristics. By assuming specific marketing costs, we determined the expected SLTV of a potentially reacquired customer.[9]

---

[7]We thank an anonymous reviewer for pointing out the possibility that our heterogeneity specification might mask this relationship.

[8]The price difference parameter for the reacquisition equation, which was significant at $\alpha = .10$ in the full data set, was significant at $\alpha = .05$ (actual *p*-value = .041) in the second reduced data set (i.e., eliminating all second tenures of less than ten days).

[9]It is important to note that we computed expected SLTV and not the NPV of the profits generated after a customer is reacquired. The difference is that the expected SLTV takes into account the reacquisition profit or loss and discounts the post-reacquisition LTV by the probability of reacquiring the customer.

Targeting Decision

We assumed that before reacquisition, the firm knew three characteristics of lapsed customers: (1) the duration of their lapse, (2) the length of their first tenure with the firm, and (3) the last price they paid. Logically, these are variables that the firm can use to distinguish customer reacquisition targets who are likely to be profitable from targets who are not. Fixing all other predictors at their median values except the three factors that are known before reacquisition, we predicted the expected SLTV for various customer types, as is shown in Table 4. The analysis shows that the expected SLTV of a customer whose profile reflects the tenth percentile (from the data) of each of the three factors is $.01. In theory, this is a profitable customer and one the firm should attempt to reacquire. However, this customer's expected profit is sensitive to reacquisition costs. If the reacquisition costs increase even slightly, the customer becomes unprofitable for the firm to pursue. Firms that target this type of customer must carefully manage their reacquisition investment. This is important because it suggests that customer winback should be a selective process and that not all lapsed customers should be pursued.

Table 4 also shows the expected SLTV of the average and modal customers of the firm. For the average and modal customers, we fixed all covariates at their averages and modes, respectively. The predictions reveal that, on average, the firm targets attractive prospects among its lapsed customers and implements a profitable reacquisition strategy.

Offer Decision

To assess how the offer decision affects expected SLTV, we provide highlights of a numerical simulation in Table 5. The values reported in Table 5 are the expected SLTVs of customers for different reacquisition prices and the average retention prices. In our numerical analysis, we fixed all variables that characterize the prior relationship at their median values and assumed that the costs are fixed over time.[10] This analysis addresses several important issues about pricing strategies for the reacquisition and retention of lapsed customers. When conducting this type of analysis, it is important to acknowledge that firms may not focus on price optimization but rather employ heuristics to set their prices. In this section, we assess optimal pricing strategies in terms of SLTV and evaluate heuristics that may be observed in practice.

Optimal pricing strategy. If the optimal strategy is explored within the range of prices that the firm typically offers ($1.75 to $3.00), the result is that the firm should offer a reacquisition price of $1.75 and then raise the retention price to $3.00. This strategy results in an acquisition likelihood of approximately .677. Note that this strategy does not maximize the length of the second tenure and thus does not maximize the firm's long-term market share. However, the increased margin from the retention price compensates for the reduced duration of the second tenure.

Note that whereas this strategy is theoretically "optimal," it is uncertain whether the anticipated customer response and associated profit will actually occur. The theoretically optimal reacquisition price is $.45 less than the last price in the prior relationship, and the optimal retention price is $.80 greater than the last price. Price changes of this magnitude rarely occurred in the data, in which the average reacquisition price was $.10 less than the last price paid before lapse, and if the retention price was increased, the average increase was $.17.

Pricing relative to costs. A class of heuristic approaches that the firm can use is cost based: pricing at cost ($1.00) or below cost (we used $.50) for reacquisition. At the extreme, the firm may price low enough so that the probability of reacquisition is nearly one. To generate a reacquisition probability that is virtually one, we fixed the covariates at their median levels and found that the model suggests a reacquisition price of $.30. As the firm lowers the reacquisition price through these three levels, respectively, the likelihood of reacquiring a customer increases from .890 to .985 to .998. Given that our estimation results reveal that the second tenure duration is negatively correlated with the likelihood of reacquiring a customer, the logic of considering these reacquisition pricing strategies might be questioned. However, it is important to acknowledge that duration and profits are not always strongly, or even positively, correlated (Reinartz and Kumar 2000). Our analysis shows that lowering the reacquisition price to $.30 and then increasing the price above the last price in the first tenure results in the highest SLTV. Table 6 highlights some of the calculations at a reacquisition price of $.30. Again, note that the second tenure duration and market share are not maximized with this pricing strategy. As with the pure optimization approach, we find that implementing a heuristic approach in which prices increase over time maximizes profits, even though second tenure duration is not maximized.

Pricing relative to the last price paid before lapse. Another class of heuristics that can guide pricing strategies for restart customers is pricing above, below, or equal to the last price paid before lapse. In our data, the median value of the last price paid before lapse is $2.20. Firms may be tempted to choose $2.20 as the reacquisition price, because the likelihood of reacquiring a customer is .56. Our analysis shows that reinstating a customer at the same price as the last price paid before lapse ($2.20) and maintaining this price is suboptimal from a profitability perspective. Profits can be improved if the firm follows one of two pricing strategies.

First, if the firm's tendency is to offer restart customers prices that are lower than the last price paid before lapse, the most profitable approach is to offer a low reacquisition price and a low retention price. If we limit the price decrease to be within two standard deviations of the mean price decrease, the most profitable offer is a reacquisition price and a retention price of $1.80. This price is two standard deviations below the mean of the last price before lapse. Region A in Table 5 shows some of the possible pricing combinations that are consistent with this strategy. At a fixed price of $1.80, for a prospective target, the reacquisition likelihood is .66 and the expected SLTV is $27.49.

---

[10]Relaxation of the time-invariant costs assumption is a trivial exercise because our demand functions are not a function of costs. If we had individual-level cost information, we could make demand a function of costs, and the results might vary.

Table 4
TARGETING CUSTOMER PROFILES

Profiles	10th Percentile Value of All Observable Covariates	25th Percentile Value of All Observable Covariates	50th Percentile Value of All Observable Covariates	75th Percentile Value of All Observable Covariates	90th Percentile Value of All Observable Covariates	Average Reacquired Customer	Modal Reacquired Customer
Reacquisition							
Reacquisition price	$ 2.22	$ 2.22	$ 2.22	$ 2.22	$2.22	$2.28	$1.75
Last price in prior relationship	$ 2.90	$ 2.75	$ 2.20	$ 1.75	$1.75	$2.38	$1.75
Lapse duration (periods)	35	17	6	2	1	5	1
Tenure 1 (days)	5	50	117	192	365	229	91
Probability of reacquisition	.001	.146	.553	.847	.968	.774	.869
Reacquisition costs	$ 1.00	$ 1.00	$ 1.00	$ 1.00	$1.00	$1.00	$1.00
Expected reacquisition margin	$ .00	$ 1.15	$ 4.35	$ 6.67	$7.62	$.99	$.65
Retention							
Average retention price per period	$ 2.43	$ 2.43	$ 2.43	$ 2.43	$2.43	$2.43	$2.43
Price change	$ (.47)	$ (.32)	$ .23	$ .68	$.68	$.05	$.68
Predicted Tenure 2 (days)	38	102	127	155	213	178	113
Predicted Tenure 2 (periods)	1	2	4	5	7	6	4
Period retention costs	$ 1.00	$ 1.00	$ 1.00	$ 1.00	$1.00	$1.00	$1.00
Expected retention margin given reacquisition	$11.07	$29.97	$36.96	$45.09	$61.83	$51.75	$32.89
Expected retention margin	$ .01	$ 4.38	$20.43	$38.19	$59.83	$40.08	$28.59
Expected Reacquisition Value	$ .01	$ 5.53	$24.79	$44.86	$67.45	$41.07	$29.24

Notes: For reacquisition and retention profiles, all numbers are per customer. With the exception of the characteristics that are observable before reacquisition, all covariates are fixed at their median values.

Table 5
EXPECTED SLTV

Reacquisition Price	Average Retention Price														
	$1.75	$1.85	$1.95	$2.05	$2.15	$2.20	$2.25	$2.35	$2.45	$2.55	$2.65	$2.75	$2.85	$2.95	$3.05	$3.15
$ .30	$35.81	$34.94	$33.84	$32.56	$31.15	$30.41	$31.53	$33.79	$36.04	$38.30	$40.55	$42.78	$44.99	$47.19	$49.35	$51.48
.50	36.15	35.29	34.21	32.94	31.55	30.81	31.92	34.15	36.38	38.61	40.82	43.03	45.22	47.38	49.51	51.62
1.00	34.44	33.67	32.69	31.55	30.28	29.62	30.62	32.63	34.65	36.66	38.67	40.66	42.64	44.59	46.52	48.42
Region A																
1.75	28.21	27.62	26.88	26.01	25.05	24.54	25.31	26.84	28.37	29.90	31.42	32.94	34.44	35.92	37.39	38.83
1.85	27.31	26.74	26.03	25.20	24.28	23.79	24.52	25.99	27.46	28.92	30.39	31.84	33.28	34.70	36.11	37.49
1.95	26.41	25.87	25.18	24.39	23.51	23.04	23.74	25.15	26.55	27.96	29.36	30.75	32.13	33.49	34.84	36.17
2.05	25.53	25.01	24.35	23.59	22.75	22.30	22.97	24.32	25.66	27.01	28.35	29.68	31.00	32.31	33.60	34.87
2.15	24.66	24.16	23.53	22.80	22.00	21.57	22.21	23.50	24.79	26.08	27.36	28.63	29.90	31.15	32.38	33.60
2.20	24.23	23.74	23.13	22.42	21.63	21.21	21.84	23.10	24.36	25.62	26.87	28.12	29.36	30.58	31.79	32.98
Region B																
2.25	23.81	23.33	22.73	22.03	21.26	20.85	21.47	22.70	23.93	25.16	26.39	27.61	28.82	30.02	31.20	32.36
2.35	22.98	22.52	21.95	21.28	20.54	20.15	20.74	21.92	23.10	24.28	25.45	26.61	27.77	28.91	30.04	31.16
2.45	22.17	21.73	21.18	20.55	19.84	19.47	20.03	21.16	22.28	23.41	24.53	25.65	26.75	27.85	28.93	29.99
2.55	21.38	20.97	20.44	19.83	19.16	18.80	19.34	20.41	21.49	22.57	23.64	24.71	25.76	26.81	27.84	28.86
2.65	20.62	20.22	19.72	19.14	18.49	18.15	18.67	19.69	20.73	21.75	22.78	23.80	24.81	25.81	26.80	27.77
2.75	19.88	19.50	19.02	18.47	17.85	17.52	18.01	19.00	19.98	20.97	21.95	22.92	23.89	24.84	25.78	26.71
2.85	19.17	18.81	18.35	17.81	17.23	16.91	17.38	18.32	19.27	20.21	21.14	22.07	23.00	23.91	24.81	25.70
2.95	18.48	18.13	17.69	17.19	16.62	16.33	16.77	17.67	18.57	19.47	20.37	21.25	22.14	23.01	23.87	24.72
3.05	17.81	17.48	17.06	16.58	16.04	15.76	16.18	17.04	17.90	18.76	19.62	20.47	21.31	22.14	22.97	23.78
3.15	17.17	16.86	16.46	15.99	15.48	15.20	15.61	16.44	17.26	18.08	18.90	19.71	20.51	21.31	22.10	22.87

Table 6
EXAMPLE OF SLTV CALCULATION

Profiles	*Variations in Retention Price*						
Reacquisition							
Reacquisition price	$ .30	$ .30	$ .30	$ .30	$ .30	$ .30	$ .30
Last price in prior relationship	$ 2.20	$ 2.20	$ 2.20	$ 2.20	$ 2.20	$ 2.20	$ 2.20
Lapse duration (periods)	6	6	6	6	6	6	6
Tenure 1 (days)	117	117	117	117	117	117	117
Probability of reacquisition	.998	.998	.998	.998	.998	.998	.998
Reacquisition costs	$ 1.00	$ 1.00	$ 1.00	$ 1.00	$ 1.00	$ 1.00	$ 1.00
Expected reacquisition margin	$ .20	$ .20	$ .20	$ .20	$ .20	$ .20	$ .20
Retention							
Average retention price per period	$ 1.75	$ 2.00	$2.25	$ 2.50	$ 2.75	$ 3.00	$ 3.25
Absolute price change	$ (.45)	$ (.20)	$ .05	$ .30	$ .55	$ .80	$ 1.05
Predicted Tenure 2 (days)	178	142	118	123	128	131	134
Retention costs	$ 1.00	$ 1.00	$1.00	$ 1.00	$ 1.00	$ 1.00	$ 1.00
Expected retention margin given reacquisition	$35.68	$33.09	$31.39	$37.05	$42.66	$48.16	$53.48
Expected retention margin	$35.61	$33.02	$31.33	$36.97	$42.58	$48.07	$53.37
Expected Reacquisition Value	$35.81	$33.22	$31.53	$37.17	$42.78	$48.27	$53.57

There are two key factors that increase the expected SLTV with the low-price strategy. The first is the significantly higher reacquisition rate, relative to a price of $2.20. Table 7 shows how the reacquisition rates vary with the reacquisition prices. The second factor is the impact of the price decrease on length of the second tenure. Specifically, the length of Tenure 2 increases when the reacquisition price is less than $2.20. The increased duration compensates for the lower retention margin that is received when the retention price is less than $2.20.

Table 7
CUSTOMER REACQUISITION RATES

Reacquisition Price	Reacquisition Probability
$1.75	.677
1.80	.663
1.85	.649
1.90	.635
1.95	.622
2.00	.608
2.05	.595
2.10	.582
2.15	.570
2.20	.557
2.25	.545
2.30	.533
2.35	.521
2.40	.510
2.45	.498
2.50	.487
2.55	.476
2.60	.466
2.65	.455
2.70	.445
2.75	.435
2.80	.425
2.85	.416
2.90	.407
2.95	.398
3.00	.389

Notes: We calculated all probabilities at the median values of the prior tenure, lapse duration, and last prior price variables.

Second, to hedge against the risk and potential costs of a restart customer lapsing again, firms may opt to increase prices above their prior levels. Our analysis shows that the firm can moderately reduce the reacquisition rate (see Table 7) and still increase expected profits.[11] To increase profits by using this strategy, the firm must increase both the reacquisition and the retention prices above the last price before lapse. Region B of Table 5 shows some of the price combinations for which expected SLTV exceeds the SLTV obtainable when reacquisition and retention prices are both $2.20.

The key to a firm's successful implementation of a price increase strategy is managing the trade-off between a lower acquisition rate (due to higher reacquisition prices) and increased margins (due to higher retention prices). Because of this trade-off, there are limits on how high the firm can set the reacquisition price relative to the retention price and generate profits beyond those of a $2.20 fixed price. A reacquisition price that is greater than $2.20 and significantly higher than the retention price will result in an expected SLTV below the expected SLTV attainable at a fixed price of $2.20.

Summary of Numerical Simulation

From these results, it might be concluded that the key to managing customer winback most profitably is successful customer reacquisition. However, our targeting discussion has revealed that the firm may not want to price so as to reacquire all lapsed customers and instead may want to focus on customers with attractive profiles. Note that we performed our simulation analysis by assuming a moderately attractive profile (i.e., at the median value of the prior relationship characteristics). When attractive customers have been recaptured, their behavior is such that the firm can recoup the losses from reacquisition by charging higher prices. This approach maximizes margins but not long-term

---

[11]It is notable that when we computed expected profits for price increase strategies, the effect of price increase relative to prior price on relationship duration was small (the effect of price decrease was irrelevant).

market share. To maximize share, firms must be concerned with second tenure duration. A better strategy for maximizing share is to implement the heuristic of lowering prices relative to the last price before the lapse.

DISCUSSION AND LIMITATIONS

Early CRM advocates touted the benefits of having mature or long-life customers and consequently emphasized retention. However, a 100% retention rate is seldom feasible. Our analysis provides the additional insight that 100% retention (or other high retention rates) is not always desirable or profitable, particularly when it requires setting a low retention price. It is not worth it for firms to try to reestablish relationships with customers who are likely to lapse or to defect rapidly. Furthermore, our research suggests that lapsed customers who are more likely to be reacquired have a shorter second tenure with the firm after they have been reacquired.

For the relationships that are attractive to reestablish, firms need to employ profitable winback strategies that maximize customers' SLTV. Our analysis shows that reacquisition is the critical phase in the winback initiative. Firms' significant lowering of reacquisition prices to increase the likelihood of reacquisition is an optimal strategy. To maximize profits, firms should increase prices when the relationship has been reestablished. If market share is the metric of interest, the firm should focus on maximizing duration of the second tenure. To do this, our analysis shows that both reacquisition and retention prices should be low.

In addition, this research shows that lapsed consumers' response to price varies at different phases of the relationship. Throughout the relationship, the customer is sensitive to the absolute price. At the point of reacquisition, customers respond negatively to price. However, customers who are reacquired at higher prices have longer second tenures. Consistent with this outcome, our research shows that there is a negative correlation between a customer's preference for reacquisition and their intrinsic "retainability."

Customers also demonstrate a dynamic response to relative prices. At the time of reacquisition, customers respond to deviations in price relative to the last price paid before lapse. However, after the relationship is reestablished, customers respond in a way that reinforces their decision to reenter the relationship. In other words, price increases have no affect on second tenure duration, and price decreases relative to the prior price result in longer second tenures. This is an important insight for firms because it shows that the last price paid during the first tenure plays a role throughout the winback process.

Although this research highlights the importance of dynamic pricing and the customer's prior history with the firm to a winback strategy, there are some limitations and areas that need further exploration. In particular, individual-level remarketing efforts and marketing cost data might affect our conclusions. A paucity of cost data prevents us from exploring this; however, our findings apply to firms that have relatively standard costs across customers in their winback programs. A firm that sends fixed-value coupons to all lapsed customers, such as HoneyBaked (as we mentioned in the first section), is an example of this. Ideally, winback spending levels should vary on the basis of the customer's prior history and/or current response. In this context, demand becomes a function of marketing expenditures, and thus actual profit-maximizing pricing strategies may vary. Also related to individual-level remarketing efforts, it would be useful to address price endogeneity (Villas-Boas and Winer 1999), particularly for reacquisition pricing. Many firms make reacquisition offers conditional on customers' responses to prior offers; however, in our application, only a single reacquisition offer is made. Price endogeneity might be explored using a game theoretic analysis. In addition, given a data set in which the firm makes many price changes over time, dynamics of the baseline hazard could be studied. Such an investigation would improve our understanding of the dynamics of customer winback and foster insights into dynamic pricing strategies.

REFERENCES

Ainslie, Andrew and Peter E. Rossi (1998), "Similarities in Choice Behavior Across Product Categories," *Marketing Science*, 17 (2), 91–106.

Amemiya, Takeshi (1985), *Advanced Econometrics*. Cambridge, MA: Harvard University Press.

Bawa, Kapil (1990), "Modeling Inertia and Variety Seeking Tendencies in Brand Choice Behavior," *Marketing Science*, 9 (3), 263–78.

Berger, Paul D. and Nada I. Nasr-Bechwati (2001), "The Allocation of Promotion Budget to Maximize Customer Equity," *OMEGA: The International Journal of Management Science*, 29 (1), 49–61.

Blattberg, Robert C. and John Deighton (1996), "Manage Marketing by the Customer Equity Test," *Harvard Business Review*, 74 (July–August), 136–44.

———, Gary Getz, and Jacquelyn S. Thomas (2001), *Customer Equity: Building and Managing Relationships as Valuable Assets*. Boston: Harvard Business School Press.

Bolton, Ruth N. (1998), "A Dynamic Model of the Duration of the Customer's Relationship with a Continuous Service Provider: The Role of Satisfaction," *Marketing Science*, 17 (1), 45–67.

———, P.K. Kannan, and Matthew D. Bramlett (2000), "Implications of Loyalty Program Membership and Service Experiences for Customer Retention and Value," *Journal of the Academy of Marketing Science*, 28 (1), 95–108.

——— and Katherine N. Lemon (1999), "A Dynamic Model of Customers' Usage of Services: Usage as an Antecedent and Consequence of Satisfaction," *Journal of Marketing Research*, 37 (May), 171–86.

Boulding, William, Ajay Kalra, and Richard Staelin (1999), "The Quality Double Whammy," *Marketing Science*, 18 (4), 463–84.

Casella, George and Edward I. George (1992), "Explaining the Gibbs Sampler," *The American Statistician*, 46 (August), 167–74.

Chib, Siddhartha (1993), "Bayes Inference in the Tobit Censored Regression Model," *Journal of Econometrics*, 51 (1–2), 79–99.

Cohen, Arthur R. (1960), "Attitudinal Consequences of Induced Discrepancies Between Cognitions and Behavior," *Public Opinion Quarterly*, 24 (2), 297–318.

Cox, David R. (1972), "Regression Models and Life Tables," *Journal of the Royal Statistical Society*, Series B (34), 187–200.

Dwyer, F. Robert (1989), "Customer Lifetime Valuation to Support Marketing Decision Making," *Journal of Direct Marketing*, 11 (4), 6–13.

Eagly, Alice H. and Shelly Chaiken (1993), *The Psychology of Attitudes*. Orlando, FL: Harcourt Brace Jovanovich.

Einhorn, Michael A. (1994), "Optimal Nonuniform Pricing with Generalized Consumer Choice," *Journal of Industrial Economics*, 42 (March), 105–112.

———— and Robin M. Hogarth (1981), "Behavioral Decision Theory: Process of Judgment and Choice," *Annual Review of Psychology*, 32, 53–88.

Festinger, L. (1957), *A Theory of Cognitive Dissonance*. Evanston, IL: Row, Peterson.

———— (1964), *Conflict, Decision, and Dissonance*. Stanford, CA: Stanford University Press.

Ganesh, Jaishankar, Mark J. Arnold, and Kristy E. Reynolds (2000), "Understanding the Customer Base of Service Providers: An Examination of the Differences Between Switchers and Stayers," *Journal of Marketing*, 64 (July), 65–87.

Gelfand, Alan E. and Adrian F.M. Smith (1990), "Sampling-Based Approaches to Calculating Marginal Densities," *Journal of the American Statistical Association*, 85 (410), 398–409.

Griffin, Jill and Michael W. Lowenstein (2001), *Customer Winback: How to Recapture Lost Customers—And Keep Them Loyal*. San Francisco: Jossey-Bass.

Hansotia, Behram J. and Paul Wang (1997), "Analytical Challenges in Customer Acquisition," *Journal of Direct Marketing*, 11 (2), 7–19.

Heckman, James (1979), "Sample Selection Bias as a Specification Error," *Econometrica*, 47 (January), 153–61.

Helsen, Kristiaan and David Schmittlein (1993), "Analyzing Duration Times in Marketing: Evidence for the Effectiveness of Hazard Rate Models," *Marketing Science*, 11 (4), 395–414.

Hughes, Arthur M. (1996), *The Complete Database Marketer*, Rev. ed. Chicago: Irwin Professional Publishing.

Jain, Dipak and Siddhartha S. Singh (2002), "Customer Lifetime Value Research in Marketing: A Review and Future Directions," *Journal of Interactive Marketing*, 16 (2), 34–46.

Kahneman, Daniel and Amos Tversky (1979), "Prospect Theory: An Analysis of Decision Under Risk," *Econometrica*, 47 (March), 263–91.

Kalyanam, Kirthi (1996), "Pricing Decisions Under Demand Uncertainty: A Bayesian Mixture Model Approach," *Marketing Science*, 15 (3), 207–221.

Kalyanaram, Gurumurthy and Russell S. Winer (1995), "Empirical Generalizations from Reference Price Research," *Marketing Science*, 14 (3), G161–G169.

Keaveney, Susan M. (1995), "Customer Switching Behavior in Service Industries: An Exploratory Study," *Journal of Marketing*, 59 (2), 71–82.

Kiley, Kathleen (1996), "Back to Life," *Catalog Age*, 13 (2), 37–38.

Krishnamurthi, Lakshman, Tridib Mazumdar, and S.P. Raj (1992), "Asymmetric Response to Price in Consumer Brand Choice and Purchase Quantity Decisions," *Journal of Consumer Research*, 19 (3), 387–400.

Mahajan, Vijay, Eitan Muller, and Frank M. Bass (1993), "New Product Diffusion Models," in *Marketing*, Vol. 5, Handbooks in Operations Research and Management Science, Jehoshua Eliashberg and G.L. Lilien, eds. Amsterdam: North-Holland, 349–408.

Marple, Mark and Michael Zimmerman (1999), "A Customer Retention Strategy," *Mortgage Banking*, 59 (11), 45–49.

Pfeifer, Phillip E. and Robert L. Carraway (2000), "Modeling Customer Relationships as Markov Chains," *Journal of Interactive Marketing*, 14 (2), 43–55.

Reichheld, Frederick F. (1996), *The Loyalty Effect*. Boston: Harvard Business School Press.

———— and W. Earl Sasser Jr. (1990), "Zero Defections: Quality Comes to Services," *Harvard Business Review*, 68 (September–October), 105–111.

Reinartz, Werner and V. Kumar (2000), "On the Profitability of Long-Life Customers in a Noncontractual Setting: An Empirical Investigation and Implications for Marketing," *Journal of Marketing*, 64 (October), 17–35.

Rust, Roland T., Katherine N. Lemon, and Valarie A. Zeithaml (2001), "Driving Customer Equity: Linking Customer Lifetime Value to Strategic Marketing Decisions," working paper, Department of Marketing, University of Maryland.

————, Valarie A. Zeithaml, and Katherine N. Lemon (2000), *Driving Customer Equity: How Customer Lifetime Value Is Reshaping Corporate Strategy*. New York: The Free Press.

Samuelson, William and Richard Zeckhauser (1988), "Status Quo Bias in Decision Making," *Journal of Risk and Uncertainty*, 1 (1), 7–59.

Schmid, Jack (1998), "The 8 Commandments … of Design," *Catalog Age*, 15 (1), 57–64.

Schmittlein, David C., Donald G. Morrison, and Richard Colombo (1987), "Counting Your Customers: Who Are They and What Will They Do Next?" *Management Science*, 33 (1), 1–24.

———— and Robert Peterson (1994), "Customer Base Analysis: An Industrial Purchase Process Application," *Marketing Science*, 13 (Winter), 41–67.

Stauss, Bernd and Christian Friege (1999), "Regaining Service Customers," *Journal of Service Research*, 1 (4), 347–61.

Thaler, Richard (1985), "Mental Accounting and Consumer Choice," *Marketing Science*, 4 (Summer), 199–214.

Thomas, Jacquelyn S. (2001), "A Methodology for Linking Customer Acquisition to Customer Retention," *Journal of Marketing Research*, 38 (May), 262–68.

Varki, Sajeev and Mark Colgate (2001), "The Role of Price Perceptions in an Integrated Model of Behavioral Intentions," *Journal of Service Research*, 3 (3), 232–40.

Villas-Boas, J. Miguel and Russell S. Winer (1999), "Endogeneity in Brand Choice Models," *Management Science*, 45 (October), 1324–38.

CAN WE PREDICT CUSTOMER LIFETIME VALUE?

EDWARD C. MALTHOUSE AND ROBERT C. BLATTBERG

EDWARD C. MALTHOUSE

is an Associate Professor, Integrated Marketing Communications, Medill School of Journalism, Northwestern University, Evanston, IL; e-mail: ecm@northwestern.edu

• •

ROBERT C. BLATTBERG

is Polk Bros. Distinguished Professor of Retailing, Kellogg School of Management, Northwestern University

• •

The authors are grateful to Karsten Hansen and Kay Peters for helpful discussions, and several anonymous reviewers for helpful comments. They also thank Experian for the Z-24 data set.

Relationship marketing assumes that firms can be more profitable if they identify the most profitable customers and invest disproportionate marketing resources in them. While intuitive, such strategies presume that a firm can accurately predict the *future* profitability of customers. In particular, we argue that the feasibility of such strategies depends on the *probabilities* and *costs* of misclassifying customers. This paper presents a detailed empirical evaluation of how accurately the future profitability of customers can be estimated. We evaluate a firm's ability to estimate the future value of customers using four data sets from different industries. Out-of-sample estimates of predictive accuracy are provided. We examine (1) the accuracy of predictions, (2) how accuracy depends on the length of time over which estimates are made, and (3) the predictors of the firm's best customers. We propose the 20–55 and 80–15 rules. Of the top 20%, approximately 55% will be misclassified (and not receive special treatment). Of the future bottom 80%, approximately 15% will be misclassified (and receive special treatment). Thus, a firm cannot assume that high-profit customers in the past will be profitable in the future nor can they assume that historically low-profit will be low-profit customers in the future.

JOURNAL OF INTERACTIVE MARKETING VOLUME 19 / NUMBER 1 / WINTER 2005

Published online in Wiley InterScience (www.interscience.wiley.com). DOI: 10.1002/dir.20027

INTRODUCTION

The long-term value (CLV) of a customer "represents the present value of the expected benefits (e.g., gross margin) less the burdens (e.g., direct costs of servicing and communicating) from customers" (Dwyer, 1997, p. 7). CLV has become central to relationship marketing (e.g., Sheth, Mittal, & Newman, 1999) and customer equity approaches to marketing (e.g., Blattberg, Getz, & Thomas, 2001; Rust, Zeithaml, & Lemon, 2000). "In relationship marketing, relationships with single customers are interpreted as capital assets requiring appropriate management and investment (e.g., Hennig-Thurau & Hansen, 2000, p. 16)." Such approaches to marketing contend that a firm can ultimately be more profitable by evaluating the profitability of customers and then designing marketing programs for its best customers. Disproportionate marketing resources should be allocated to retaining best customers and keeping them loyal. This strategy would seem to make obvious sense, since it is common for a small percentage of customers to account for a large percentage of revenues and profits (Mulhern, 1999).

Using CLV or predictors of CLV (e.g., historical purchasing behavior) to allocate marketing resources assumes that the *future* value of a customer can be estimated accurately. This assumption is rarely discussed and there is little empirical evidence evaluating it. The accuracy with which the future value of a customer can be predicted falls along a continuum. One extreme is where future behavior can be predicted perfectly given the customer's past behavior and the firm's marketing actions (in regression terms this would correspond to $R^2 = 1$). The other extreme is where the future behavior of customers is independent of their past behavior and the firm's marketing actions (in regression this would correspond to $R^2 = 0$). As Mulhern (1999, p. 28) notes, "models incorporating predicted future purchases are subject to a great deal of forecasting error," but he does not quantify how much forecasting error.

The firm considering whether or not to practice such relationship marketing and customer equity strategies must understand where it falls along this continuum. Investing disproportionate resources in specific customers makes unquestionable sense when their future behavior can be predicted perfectly, but no sense when future behavior is unpredictable ($R^2 = 0$).

In the latter case, an egalitarian strategy where all customers are treated equally or the quid-pro-quo incentives discussed below should be used.

Suppose a firm offers two levels of treatment: "best-customer" treatment and "normal" treatment. Assuming the firm cannot predict the future behavior of customers perfectly, the firm can misclassify customers in two possible ways. It could misclassify a future normal customer as a future best customer—a false positive using the language of hypothesis testing—or misclassify a future best customer as future normal customer—a false negative. There are costs associated with both types of misclassifications. When a firm makes a false positive misclassification it is spending scarce marketing resources to deliver best-customer treatment to a future "normal" customer whose behavior does not justify such treatment. It is more difficult to quantify the costs of a false negative. The customer who deserves best-customer treatment but receives normal treatment could switch part or all of its future expenditures to a competitor, spread negative word of mouth, etc. Whether or not a firm should make disproportionate marketing investments across customers depends on the probabilities and costs of misclassifying customers. The costs of misclassification have not be quantified in either the literature or by business practitioners, to our knowledge.

Some examples illustrate our point. An executive who has been using a credit card to spend a large amount of money on expensive clothing, airline tickets, car rentals, hotel rooms, cellular phone service, etc. may retire and spend far less in these categories. This executive goes from being a "best customer" of the companies that provide these products or services to a non-best customer. Showering this executive with discretionary marketing investments after retirement may not be an optimal strategy. This is an example of a false positive. Alternatively, someone who is not so valuable today can, for example, take a new job and become a star customer tomorrow—a false negative.

In using historical information to allocate marketing investments a firm may be relying on chance purchases. There will always be a certain level of randomness in a customer's purchases. Are the customers who receive special treatment really better customers? Or, are they customers who just happened to be "better" during some recent period and will "regress" back to their true, non-best-customer behavior in the future? For example, a consultant who is normally an occasional flyer on some airline may be assigned to a job in the airline's hub city. The consultant may fly on the airline every week during the job, but resume the occasional-flyer status when the job is completed. Giving this consultant special perks will not be a good strategy.

This paper provides a direct evaluation of how accurately the future behavior of customers can be estimated. The focus of this paper is on companies that maintain databases of customer/end-user information on a substantial percentage of customers and that can customize marketing "investments," at least to some extent, across customers. Such companies include hotels, airlines, credit card companies, banks and financial service providers, companies that sell over the internet, telecommunications companies, catalogers, retail stores with "loyalty/frequent-shopper" programs, publishers, computer companies that sell direct to consumers, and many more. We shall refer to such companies as *database marketing companies.* The discussion here is not as applicable to organizations that do not know their specific end-users, e.g., most producers of consumer package goods.

TYPES OF MARKETING INVESTMENTS

Day (2000) discusses different types of exchanges between customers and companies. Value-adding exchanges involve "giving continuing incentives for the customer to concentrate most of their purchases with them . . . Some customers are more equal than others when it comes to deciding how close a relationship will be formed (p. 25)." In some industries, this is accomplished through a loyalty program, which is "designed to build customer loyalty by providing incentives to profitable customers (Yi & Jeon, 2003, p. 230)." We introduce a distinction between types of value-adding exchanges.

Our thesis, that disproportionate marketing investments should depend on the firm's ability to forecast future profits and the costs of misclassification, has varying levels of relevance for different types of marketing investments. Our thesis is most applicable to marketing investments *without* quid-pro-quo terms. The firm has discretion over which customers will receive these investments and how much it invests in individual customers. We call these *discretionary marketing investments.* There are numerous examples. Direct communication with customers is usually discretionary. Catalog companies decide how many catalogs each customer receives over some period of time. More generally, any organization using direct mail decides the number of contacts to make with each customer, and thus the level of investment. Firms can also customize investments for in-bound communication. Day (2000, p. 25) describes how Hertz has a dedicated phone line for preferred customers so that they do not have to wait so long to make reservations. Likewise, some credit card companies use caller ID to route incoming calls from best customers to shorter phone queues.

Communication is not the only form of discretionary marketing investment. Collinger (2002, p. 32) defines *surprises and delights* as "the unexpected and unpromised benefits that enhance the product or service." Credit card companies waive late-payment fees of certain customers and banks waive checking overdraft fees of some customers. Hotels might unexpectedly leave a bouquet of flowers, bottle of wine, or some other gift in the room of a best customer. Hotels will occasionally upgrade best customers to a larger room. Airlines might give best customers priority for upgrades and have even delayed a flight so that some very important passenger could make a connection. Airlines offer shorter check-in queues for their very best customers. Some catalog companies send an unexpected holiday gift to their best customers. The concept of *customer delight* (Rust & Oliver, 2000), which refers to "a profoundly positive emotional state generally resulting from having one's expectations exceeded to a surprising degree (p. 86)," is closely related. A company that spends resources to customize the product itself without full compensation from the buyer is also making a discretionary investment.

Discretionary investments are often extras or perks, intended to cause the recipient to have positive affect towards the company. In a different context, Geyskens, Steenkamp, Scheer, and Kumar (1996) discusses *affective* commitment. "An affectively committed channel member *desires* to continue its relationship because it likes the partner and enjoys the partnership . . . It experiences a sense of loyalty and belongingness (p. 304)."

Our thesis is less relevant to marketing investments having explicit quid-pro-quo terms. The company and buyer explicitly agree on the terms of such "investments" at the time of purchase, although they are not part of the product/service being purchases. To a large extent, loyalty/reward programs fall into this category. For these programs, many, if not all, benefits that end-users receive and investments that firms make are on explicit quid-pro-quo terms. For example, most frequent flyer programs offer explicit rewards/incentives such as "if I fly X miles/trips, I get a free flight." Hotel programs usually have explicit terms such as "if I stay X nights, I get Y." Credit card programs typically offer explicit rewards such as miles or cash-back bonuses for usage; "for every dollar I spend on this card I get X." Promotions such as "buy two get one free" and negotiated price breaks to high-volume customers are of the same ilk. Such programs, at one level, attempt to increase share of wallet and/or consumption. The firm *rewards* the buyer for behaving in a certain way, usually involving multiple purchases over time. The free flight is an explicit *incentive* for the buyer to fly often with a particular airline. Loyalty programs that offer proportionally larger rewards to best customers such as an airline that awards best customers with 1.5 times the actual mileage flown is practicing a hybrid between discretionary and quid-pro-quo.

Our thesis is less central to quid-pro-quo investments because (1) the investments are available to all customers and (2) the firm is not directly choosing to "invest" more in one customer than another. Any customer can join the program, get the two-for-one special, or the free flight—customers self-select into the programs. The customer's behavior directly determines the level of awards; e.g., a customer who flies more will get more free tickets. The important question with these investments is whether the customer would consume at the same level without the reward/incentive.

METHODOLOGY

As stated above our objective here is to estimate the *future* CLV for individuals or households using past purchase behavior and other available information. For a review of CLV models see Jain and Singh (2002). To evaluate the accuracy of estimates of future CLV, we use a study design that "turns back the clock." The process is illustrated in Figure 1. Assume a long time series of contributions and expenses are available for a sample of customers. For example, we might have data from January 1, 1994 until December 31, 2000. Pretend that "now" is some moment in the past such as the beginning of January 1, 1997. The universe of customers will be those who were on file as of "now," January 1, 1997. The objective of our analysis is to predict the discounted value of a customer from January 1, 1997 through 2000, hereafter called the *target period*, using information from the period 1994–1996, hereafter called the *base period*. The length of the target and base periods will be denoted by T and B, respectively. It will be convenient to think of having $T + B$ discrete time periods. Similar designs are commonly used for direct marketing scoring models, where the target is some measure of response to an offer.

The central empirical question addressed here is whether a customer's value can be estimated over some long period of time rather than a customer's entire lifetime. Firms periodically evaluate a customer's value and adjust marketing investments accordingly. Hotels and airlines, for example, evaluate customer tier membership every calendar year. Since these adjustments occur periodically, the firm should be primarily interested in estimating *long-term*, rather than *lifetime* value. The approach used here does exactly this in a direct way.

Statistical Modeling

Assume a sample of n customers on file as of "now" and measurements of the contributions each

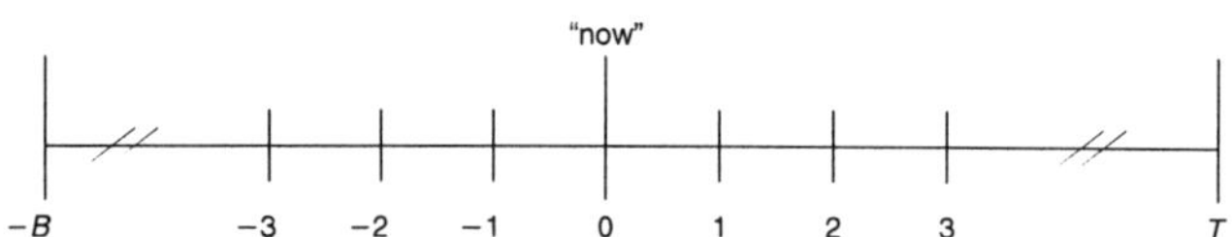

FIGURE 1

Illustration of Target and Base Periods for CLV Estimation

customer makes during the target period. Let c_{it} denote the net contribution of customer i during time period t. By net contribution we mean some appropriate measure of profit attributable to a transaction without consideration of fixed costs, e.g., gross sales less cost of goods sold, direct marketing costs, order processing, return processing, etc. We also have p measurements, $\mathbf{x}_i$, on customer i that are known as of "now," time 0, aggregated from base-period information. Denote the discount rate by d. The CLV of customer i is $y_i = \sum_{t=1}^{T} c_{it}(1 + d)^{-t}$.

CLV is related to the predictor variables with some "regression" function f

$$g(y_i) = f(\mathbf{x}_i) + e_i,$$

where e_i are independent random variables with mean 0 and (ideally) homoscedastic error variance $V(e_i) = \sigma^2$. Because the dependent variable (y_i) is an amount, its variance often increases with its mean, violating the assumption of homoscedasticity. Invertible function g is a variance stabilizing transformation (e.g., Carroll & Ruppert, 1988) such as the logarithm or square root, usually assumed to be known prior to the estimation of f.

We consider three regression methods for f in this paper. The first is a linear regression with variance stabilizing transformations estimated with ordinary least squares. Residual plots inform our selection of a variance stabilizing transformation (Cook & Weisberg, 1982), which we select from the Box-Cox family (Neter, Kutner, Nachtsheim, & Wasserman, 1996, p. 132). Further discussion of the variance stabilizing transformation is given in the empirical results section. To address possible nonlinearities (e.g., diminishing marginal returns to scale) with predictor variables that are amounts or counts, we compute square root and logarithm "first-aid" transformations (Mosteller & Tukey, 1977, p. 109). The influence of outliers of untransformed count and amount variables is reduced with 1% Winsorization, i.e., values greater than the 99th percentile are set equal to the 99th percentile.

The second regression method is linear regression estimated with iteratively re-weighted least squares (IRLS), as described in Neter et al. (1996, pp. 403–405). IRLS is another way of addressing the problem of heteroscedasticity. We use the same predictor variables

as in the OLS model. When the dependent variable (CLV) is highly right skewed, we apply the logarithm transformation to symmetrize its distribution, increase the density of observations in the right tail, and reduce the influence of outliers. We implement IRLS by initially estimating the model with OLS. Next, we estimate the absolute value of the residuals (following the recommendation of Neter et al. after equation 10.15) using the same predictor variables. We then re-estimate the original regression equation using weighted least squares, with the reciprocal of the squared residual estimates as weights (equation 10.16a in Neter et al., 1996). We iterate between estimating residuals (and thus weights) and CLV.

The estimates from the IRLS regression model are also estimates of the following random coefficient model, which accounts for unobserved heterogeneity:

$$y_i = (\alpha + a_i) + \sum_j (\beta_j + b_{ij})x_{ij} + e_i$$
$$= \alpha + \sum_j \beta_j x_{ij} + \left(a_i + \sum_j b_{ij}x_{ij} + e_i \right),$$

where a_i is a random variable with mean 0 and standard deviation σ_a, b_{ij} is a random variable with mean 0 and standard deviation σ_b, and e_i is a random variable with mean 0 and standard deviation σ. We assume that a_i and b_{ij} are independent of e_i. We group all of the random components into a single error term. We do not give separate estimates of the variance components, because comparing the variance components is not relevant to the thesis of this paper.

The third method is a feedforward neural network (Venables & Ripley, 1999, section 9.4), estimated using S-Plus Version 6.0.2. The conclusions we make in this paper depend on the predictive accuracy of the regression model. Neural networks are universal approximators and thus provide a bound for predictive accuracy. They can uniformly approximate any continuous function over compact sets (Ripley, 1996, section 5.7).

Estimating Predictive Accuracy

All examples give out-of-sample estimates of predictive accuracy. Evaluating predictive accuracy using the same data that were used to estimate f is problematic because the estimated model could capture sampling idiosyncrasies of the data set. The problem of making "honest" estimates (e.g., ones that are not subject to overfitting) has been thoroughly studied (e.g., see Efron & Tibshirani, 1993, Ch. 17; Ripley, 1996, sections 2.6–7). Two common ways of making out-of-sample estimates of predictive accuracy are to use holdout samples and k-fold cross validation. When data are plentiful, a good solution is to use an independent data set to evaluate f. Prior to estimation we partition the available data into *estimation* and *holdout* samples of roughly equal size. The estimation sample is used to estimate the free parameters of the model while the holdout sample is "kept in a locked safe where it has rested untouched and unscanned during all the choices and optimizations" (Mosteller & Tukey, 1977, p. 38) involved in estimating f. The estimated model is then applied to the holdout sample and summaries of predictive accuracy are computed.

When data are scarce, k-fold cross validation is a good way to get an "honest" estimate of prediction accuracy (Efron & Tibshirani, 1993, p. 240). For the smaller data sets we use 10-fold cross validation. We assign each observation randomly to one of 10 groups and estimate the model 10 times. First, we estimate the model using all but the first group, and then apply the estimated model to the first group. Second, we estimate the model using all but the second group and apply the estimated model to this group, etc. Estimates of predictive accuracy are computed on the left-out groups.

EMPIRICAL RESULTS

We examine how accurately CLV can be predicted with four case studies from organizations. None of the companies offered "special treatment" to any of its customers during the study periods. The objective here is to evaluate the best tools that companies currently have to predict CLV. Two of the data sets are available to other researchers; SAS code related to these examples is available from the first author's Web site. To calculate CLV we used an annual discount rate of 15% ($d = .15$). We also have data from 131 catalog companies, which though less extensive, will be used to confirm some of the results from this study. To compute CLV we use a discount rate of $d = 15\%$, consistent with Reinartz and Kumar (2000, p. 23).

Description of Organizations

Service Company. We have a simple random sample of 150,000 customers from a company that offers its members a single service. Customers enroll in the service by signing a one-, six-, or 12-month contract, where cancellation is not allowed. Lapsed customers sometimes re-enroll in the service during a later time period. We have five years of membership history and the date of the first purchase (for those who were customers prior to the five-year period). For each customer and month, we have the following information. First, we have the length of the current contract (0, 1, 6, or 12 months), where 0 indicates that the customer was not a member during a particular month. Second, we have a measure of the quantity of involvement during the month, defined as the number of times that a customer uses the service varies. A customer who likes and enjoys the service will use it more often. The monthly charge is the same, regardless of the level of usage. Third, we have a measure of quality of involvement. Think of the service as providing a lesson. The quality measure indicates how well the customer is learning the lesson. This data set is interesting because of its simplicity; it offers only a single product line and price and has no outliers. We expect it to provide an upper bound for predictive accuracy.

The first two years of data constitute the base period and the last three years the target period. The universe consists of the 71,381 customers who were active at least one month during the base period. The 71,381 observations were randomly split into estimation and holdout samples of roughly equal size. The predictor variables were recency, frequency, the involvement quantity measure averaged over all months during the base period, the involvement quality measure averaged over the base period, dummies for different contract types, and longevity (months on file). All variables were examined for outliers and high skewness.

Not-for-Profit Organization. Each year the Knowledge Discovery and Data mining Special Interest Group (SIG-KDD) of the Association for Computing Machinery (ACM) sponsors a data mining competition. SIG-KDD provides contestants with a data set and a data-mining task. In 1998, the data set was from a not-for-profit organization and the task was to determine which "one-year lapsed donors" should be sent a solicitation during 6/1997.[1] A one-year lapsed donor was one who had not responded to any solicitations since 6/1996.

---

[1] See http://kdd.ics.uci.edu.

KDD98 contains the promotion and donation history for the two years prior to the lapsed period (6/1994–6/1996). KDD98 contains all 191,779 one-year lapsed donors.

There are several features of this data set that make it interesting. First, the data have extensive overlays at both the household and five-digit zip code level. These overlay variables are often the only information a company or organization has on prospective donors/customers. This data set will allow us to evaluate the predictive power of various levels of overlay variables vis-à-vis behavioral variables (e.g., RFM). Second, this data set is available to the general public so that it can be used for benchmarking and comparing methods. If other researchers develop alternative methods to the one proposed here, the performances can be compared directly on this data set. Third, there are very large, defined estimation and holdout samples (the documentation calls them "learning" and "validation" sets) of 95,412 and 96,367 donors, respectively. In total there are 481 variables.

We use this data set in a different way than it was used for the data-mining contest. Details of our analysis and SAS code for preparing the data are available from the first author's Web site. Define "now" as June 1, 1994. Our universe of donors is all who were on file before this date, reducing the sizes of the estimation and holdout samples to 68,026 and 68,804, respectively. The organization sent out 22 "card promotions" during 6/94–6/96; the data set contains the date each solicitation was mailed, the date a donation in response to a particular solicitation was received, and the dollar amount. The (discounted) sum of these 22 amounts is the revenue during the target period. The mean is $37.43, the minimum $0, the 99th percentile $141, and the maximum $8,137. The estimation sample has a 99th percentile of $142 and a maximum of $1,686 while the holdout sample has a 99th percentile of $140 and a maximum of $8,137. The difference in the maximum values emphasizes the importance of paying close attention to outliers. The dependent variable of our analysis is the square root of revenues less costs. The square root variance stabilizing transformation ($g(y) = y^{1/2}$) is used to reduce heteroscedasticity, make the distribution more symmetric, and reduce the influence of observations in the right tail.

We constructed predictor variables following the examples given in the Direct Marketing Educational Foundation (DMEF) data sets. These data sets have a large number of variables capturing interactions between RFM, product category, and purchase channel. Interactions between recency and the frequency and monetary variables are captured with variables such as orders (or dollars) within the most recent year, orders (dollars) last year, orders (dollars) two years ago, orders (dollars) three years ago. Interactions between frequency and monetary are captured by dividing monetary by frequency giving "average order amounts." Interactions between purchase channel and the frequency and monetary variables are captured with variable such as orders (or dollars) from category A, orders (dollars) from category B, etc. Likewise for purchase channel.

Business-to-Business Company. We have a simple random sample of 100,000 "small-business" customers of a large company. For each of these customers we have the transaction history over a seven-year period and Dunn and Bradstreet overlays. The transaction file gives the customer ID, date, price, quantity, and SKU of every transaction. SKUs are categorized into five main product lines, and several other small ones accounting for a very small percentage of transactions and dollars.

This data set is interesting for several reasons. First, it is a very complicated data set, with many SKUs, multiple product lines, strong seasonal buying patterns, a large number of extreme outliers, and multiple delivery channels. This empirical study thus spans a wide range of CLV situations from simple (service company) to complex (this company). Second, many, but not all, of the products have long inter-purchase times. If a customer buys one of these products today, the customer will not need to buy the product again for several years, unless the business expands. Between purchases of one of these products, a customer may buy from other product lines, or complementary SKUs from the same product line. Third, prior to acquiring a customer, often companies know only the information contained in the Dunn and Bradstreet overlays about prospects. This data set will allow us to evaluate the predictive power of such overlays, compared with behavioral data such as RFM. Fourth, this is an unusually long time series. Many companies would not be able assemble information at this level of detail from seven years ago.

For this evaluation we use the first two years as the base period and the last five years as the target period. We have tried other splits and found similar conclusions, e.g., three-year base and four-year target, four-year base and three-year target, etc. The universe for the analysis described here is all customers "on file" as of the beginning of year 3, giving a sample of size 24,047. Using the transaction file, we computed 61 variables from base-period transactions including RFM variable overall and by product category. We computed frequency in terms of items and orders (one order can contain multiple items), and monetary value during the most recent year and the most recent two years. We also computed square root and logarithm transformations for variables where we expected diminishing marginal returns.

Catalog Company. The Direct Marketing Educational Foundation (DMEF) has made available four real data sets for academic research and teaching. We use the "DMEF3" data set here, which is from a long-time specialty catalog company that mails both full-line and seasonal catalogs to its customer base. The data set is a random sample 106,284 customers who have bought before from the company and were being considered for a mailing in Fall, 1995. The data set has 12 years of purchase history through July 31, 1995.

The DMEF3 data set is interesting for several reasons. First, it is from a retail consumer catalog company, an industry not represented by the other detailed data sets in this paper. Second, it contains an exceptionally long time series: 12 years. Third, it is available to all researchers from the DMEF.

For this analysis, we define "now" as August 1, 1990 and select as our universe all customers who were on file before this date. This gives a sample of 41,669 customers, with six-year base and target periods. These observations are randomly assigned to estimation and holdout samples of approximately equal size. We are able to construct RFM variables, time on file, first purchase amount, and indicators of product classes and sub-classes. We Winsorized (1%) and applied the square root transformation to all amount and count variables.

Experian Z-24 Catalog Data. The Z-24 database, which is owned by Experian, allows catalog companies to exchange mailing lists. Hundreds of catalog companies periodically provide their mailing lists to Experian along with RFM in exchange for names from other lists to be used in prospecting for new customers. We have a random sample of 1 million households from this database with RFM information as of January 1, 2001, 2002, and 2003. For this analysis, we take "now" to be 1/1/2001, the target period to be the two years 1/1/2001–1/1/2003, and the base period to be the time prior through 1/1/2001. We analyze companies for which we have at least 3,000 households in our sample; using this criterion we have 131 companies. Sample sizes range from 3,005 to 94,523 for individual companies. We model the logarithm of CLV as a linear function of the logarithms of RFM.

This data set is interesting because it allows us to study the variation *across* catalog companies in how the RFM variables affect CLV and how accurately CLV can be predicted from RFM. By having data from 131 distinct catalog companies, which we consider representative of all catalogs, we can make strong statements concerning the generalizability of our conclusions.

Marketing Cost Data. We do not have variables measuring the level of marketing investment for three of the four organizations or for the Z-24 catalog companies. The service organization gives all of its customers the same contacts, so marketing investment is irrelevant for this company. While it is desirable to have such information, our impression is that very few companies currently keep it. The goal of this paper is to evaluate what companies are doing today and we can achieve this goal with the present data. If companies tracked marketing contacts and they could be included in the model, perhaps our conclusions would change, but our conclusions apply to what companies are currently doing.

Accuracy of Predictions

We developed regression and neural network models for each of the data sets. We also estimate IRLS for the business-to-business company. The final model was the one that gave the best fit, measured by R^2 computed on the holdout sample. Fit is the criterion suggested in the data-mining literature (e.g., Breiman, 2001, p. 204, 205, 229; Breiman, 1996; Hastie, et al., 2001, section 2.9, ch. 7) for problems where the primary objective is making predictions that are as accurate as possible, as it is here.

Once a final model has been selected, we evaluate its predictive accuracy in two ways. The first is the familiar coefficient of determination (R^2). The second comes from a classification table. Part of the goal of CLV is to separate "best" customers from others. For simplicity, we assume that the top 20% based on *actual* CLV values in the *target period* are "best" customers. We use the estimated regression models to rank customers from best to worst. The 20% with the largest predicted values are assigned "best-customer" status and would receive perks. The classification table is a cross tabulation of actual group versus predicted group.

Table 1 gives an example cross-tabulation for the Service Company. The false positive and false negative rates give us more details about the accuracy of the predictions. These terms are usually applied to hypothesis tests. Define the null hypothesis H_0 to be that a customer is part of the (actual) bottom 80% and does not deserve special treatment. The alternative hypothesis, H_1 is that a customer is in the top 20% and "deserves special treatment." The *false positive rate* is $P(\text{Reject } H_0 \mid H_0 \text{ True}) = 3{,}832/28{,}615 = 13.4\%$. Of the customers who do not deserve special treatment, 13.4% would receive it if this model were used. The *false negative rate* is $P(\text{Do not reject } H_0 \mid H_1) = 3{,}891/7{,}154 = 54.4\%$. Of the (actual) best customers in the future, 54.4% would not be identified by this model. The *power* of the model is $P(\text{Reject } H_0 \mid H_1) = 45.6\%$.

We estimated models for each of the data sets and also varied the length of the future time horizon. The false positive and negative rates for the estimation and holdout samples are summarized in Table 2.

TABLE 1 — Classification Tables for the Service Company Predicting 20–80 Group for 3-Year CLV

| | ACTUAL | | |
PREDICTED	BOTTOM 80	TOP 20	TOTAL
Bottom 80	24,783	3,891	28,674
Col Pct	86.6%	54.4%	80.2%
Top 20	3,832	3,263	7,095
Col Pct	13.4%	45.6%	19.8%
Total	28,615	7,154	35,769
Row Pct	80.0%	20.0%	100.0%

TABLE 2 — Measures of Predictive Accuracy

| | LENGTH | FALSE NEGATIVE | | FALSE POSITIVE | | R-SQUARED | |
COMPANY	FUTURE (T)	ESTIMATION	HOLDOUT	ESTIMATION	HOLDOUT	ESTIMATION	HOLDOUT
Service	1 year	0.2482	0.2466	0.3021	0.3063	0.4800	0.4850
Service	2 years	0.1632	0.1625	0.4641	0.4678	0.3861	0.3870
Service	3 years	0.1339	0.1366	0.5439	0.5448	0.3362	0.3374
Nonprofit	2 years	0.1431	0.1443	0.5722	0.5774	0.1303	0.1332
B2B	1 year	0.1326	0.1345	0.5305	0.5379	0.2812	0.2868
B2B	2 years	0.1261	0.1288	0.5050	0.5151	0.3135	0.3104
B2B	3 years	0.1252	0.1281	0.5008	0.5126	0.3200	0.3126
B2B	4 years	0.1233	0.1254	0.4933	0.5019	0.3538	0.3375
B2B	5 years	0.1213	0.1268	0.4854	0.5073	0.3617	0.3442
Catalog	1 year	0.1386	0.1394	0.5545	0.5574	0.2077	0.1983
Catalog	2 years	0.1339	0.1349	0.5356	0.5395	0.2326	0.2205
Catalog	3 years	0.1322	0.1366	0.5289	0.5442	0.2452	0.2249
Catalog	4 years	0.1310	0.1345	0.5244	0.538	0.2465	0.2198
Catalog	5 years	0.1306	0.135	0.5226	0.5401	0.2423	0.2175
Catalog	6 years	0.1336	0.1366	0.5345	0.5465	0.2402	0.2152

The third row of the table summarizes the service company example discussed above from Table 1. The fifth row, "B2B 1 year," gives summarizes the misclassifications for the one-year predictions of the business-to-business company.

20–55 and 80–15 Rules

It is striking how similar the results are across the data sets. With the exception of the one- and two-year estimates for the service company, the false negative rates are all approximately 51–55% and the false positive rates are all approximately 13–15%. We posit two new empirical rules of thumb based on these results.

The 20–55 Rule. Of the *actual* best customers (top 20%), approximately 55% will be misclassified (and not receive special treatment).

The 80–15 Rule. Of the actual normal customers (bottom 80%), 15% will be misclassified (and receive special treatment).

We evaluate whether these rules generalize across catalog companies with the Z-24 data. Figure 2 shows the predictive accuracy of 131 regression models with boxplots. We estimated separate multiple regression models for each of the companies. The distribution of R^2 values is concentrated among small values, with $R^2 < 17.5\%$ for three-fourths of the catalogs. There

are outliers in R^2 values, indicating that a few companies can predict the future values of customers with greater accuracy, but these are exceptions. We conclude that most companies will not be able to predict the future behavior of customers accurately, as measured by high R^2 values.

The top boxplot shows the distribution of Type I error rates across the catalogs. The median Type I error rate (dot in middle of box) is 16.1%, which is approximately equal to the 15% posited by our rule. The lower quartile is 15.0% (left end of box) and the upper quartile is 17.5% (right end of box), so half of these catalog companies have Type I error rates between 15% and 17.5%. The range extends from 11.1% to 20.0%. The 80–15 rules thus holds fairly consistently across catalog companies.

There is more variation in Type II error rates across companies. The mean is 57%, the median is 62%, and the quartiles are 54% and 66%. There are several outliers in the left tail, indicating that some exceptional companies have substantially lower Type II error rates. Thus, the 20–55 rule appears to hold "on average" for catalogs, although there is more variation across companies and some exceptions.

SENSITIVITY TO VARIANCE STABILIZING TRANSFORMATION AND METHOD OF ESTIMATION

Using the Business-to-Business data set, we evaluate whether our conclusions change when different variance stabilizing transformations are used or when the model is estimated with IRLS. Box-Cox transformations have the form $g(y) = (y + a)^p$. When $p = 0$, the logarithm transformation is used. Constant a is added to every value to avoid, for example, taking the logarithm or inverse ($p = -1$) of 0. Table 3 gives the results using a $T = 1$ year future period and $T = 9$ year future period. We estimate the same model with the following transformations: none ($p = 1$, $a = 0$), square root ($p = 1/2, a = 0$), cube root ($p = 1/3, a = 0$), fourth root ($p = 1/4$, $a = 0$), and logarithm ($p = 0, a = 1$). The "For 6" row gives the results when forward selection is used and only the first six variables are allowed to enter. The IRLS row gives the results when iteratively re-weighted least squares is used to estimate the model parameters, as described

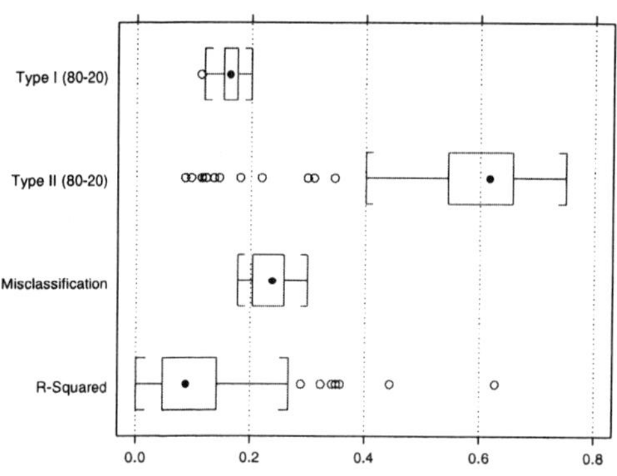

FIGURE 2

Boxplots Showing Predictive Accuracy for 131 Catalog Companies From Z24 Database

TABLE 3 — Performance and Fit Measures for the Business-to-Business Company Using Different Variance Stabilizing Transformations and Estimation Methods

TRANS	EST	x	FALSE NEGATIVE		FALSE POSITIVE		R-SQUARE	
			TRAIN	TEST	TRAIN	TEST	TRAIN	TEST
			$T = 1$ Year Future Period					
None	OLS	All	0.1341	0.1327	0.5363	0.5309	0.6714	0.5973
$\sqrt{}$	OLS	All	0.1274	0.1301	0.5096	0.5205	0.5371	0.5193
$3\sqrt{}$	OLS	All	0.1299	0.1336	0.5196	0.5346	0.3659	0.3668
$4\sqrt{}$	OLS	All	0.1326	0.1345	0.5305	0.5379	0.2812	0.2868
Log	OLS	All	0.1346	0.1364	0.5384	0.5458	0.1971	0.2052
Log	OLS	For 6	0.1361	0.1358	0.5442	0.5433	0.1837	0.1983
Log	IRLS	All	0.1349	0.1377	0.5396	0.5508	0.1946	0.2022
			$T = 5$ Year Future Period					
None	OLS	All	0.1219	0.1267	0.4875	0.5068	0.7583	0.6692
$\sqrt{}$	OLS	All	0.1172	0.1221	0.5313	0.4886	0.6281	0.5866
$3\sqrt{}$	OLS	All	0.1189	0.1244	0.4758	0.4977	0.4704	0.4452
$4\sqrt{}$	OLS	All	0.1213	0.1268	0.4854	0.5073	0.3617	0.3442
Log	OLS	All	0.1335	0.1389	0.5338	0.5557	0.2401	0.247
Log	OLS	For 6	0.1404	0.1423	0.5618	0.5694	0.2193	0.2366
Log	IRLS	All	0.1340	0.1403	0.5359	0.5611	0.2384	0.2450

above. Table 4 gives the parameter estimates for the six-variable model. The variables were selected using stepwise selection. There is a healthy mixture of RFM variables in the models.

First, note the similarity between the false negative rates, which are all within less than a percent of each other. For a $T = 1$ year future, the test-set values vary between 13.01% with a square-root transformation to 13.77% with the IRLS estimate. Our rounding to the "80–15" rule introduces more error than the variance stabilizing transformation or method of estimation. The same is true for the false positive rates, in that they range from 52.05% to 55.08%. Predictive accuracy does not change much across these models. The R-squared values are not comparable across these models because the variance stabilizing transformation changes the denominator SST $= \sum(y_i - \bar{y})^2$ (e.g., see Scott & Wild, 1991). We report their values to highlight the importance of paying close attention to outliers. There is a large difference between the training and test set values when no

transformation is used (0.6714 versus 0.5973). The differences are smaller when the influence of outliers is reduced. Outliers and the long right tail inflate the value of SST for the identity and other weak transformations, but the influence of these values are reduced for, e.g., the logarithm. Extreme outliers can exert a strong influence on the estimation even when the sample sizes are large.

It is not surprising that the method of addressing heteroscedasticity does not matter. Having heteroscedastic error variance implies that the OLS estimates are no longer the best linear unbiased estimates (BLUE). Estimates from heteroscedastic data are still unbiased, but do not have the lowest variance across all unbiased estimates. The variance of a slope estimate, however, is also a function of the sample size used to estimate the model. Finding the transformation that gets closest to homoscedasticity will have more effect on the variance of the slope estimates when the sample size is small, but when the sample size is very large—as it is here—the variance

TABLE 4   Parameter Estimates for the 6-Variable Forward-Selection Models ("For 6") Using the Business-to-Business Data ($n = 11,979$)

VARIABLE	ESTIMATE	STD ERR	T VALUE
$T = 1$ Year Future Period			
Intercept	−0.1946	0.1639	−1.19
$\sqrt{}$(number orders)	0.9236	0.0580	15.95
$\sqrt{}$(dollars most recent year)	0.0397	0.0030	13.43
log(dollars product line 2)	−0.1802	0.0093	−19.33
log(total dollars)	0.3148	0.0366	8.61
$\sqrt{}$(total dollars product line 3)	−0.0332	0.0041	−8.04
Dollars most recent year	−0.0001	0.00001	−8.25
$T = 5$ Year Future Period			
Intercept	2.8419	0.04262	66.66
$\sqrt{}$(number items purchased)	0.1970	0.0012	19.75
$\sqrt{}$(dollars most recent year)	0.0233	0.0012	19.75
Indicator first order product line 3	−0.3651	0.0535	−6.82
log(total number orders)	0.7543	0.0638	11.82
$\sqrt{}$(total dollars product line 2)	−0.0284	0.0027	−10.68
$\sqrt{}$(total dollars product line 3)	−0.0148	0.0021	−6.95

of the estimate will be small regardless of whether the square root or logarithm (or even identity) was used.[2]

MANAGERIAL IMPLICATIONS

The managerial implications of the empirical rules are important. If a company were to start offering special treatment for its best 20% of customers, it would have to reward customers based on their past behavior, since that is all that would be known. The 20–55 rule suggests that such a company would be wrong about 55% of the time in deciding who deserves the perks. It would give perks to the wrong customers. The customer who deserves best-customer treatment but receives normal treatment could switch part or all of its future expenditures to a competitor or spread negative word of mouth.

A false negative can also be a missed opportunity to develop a best customer if the customer were responsive to best-customer interventions. This raises several questions requiring further research. How does a customer being misclassified affect that customer's attitude and commitment towards the company? Is the customer who deserves perks but does not receive them more likely to defect? We conjecture that these issues are particularly problematic when the perks are visible. Duncan and Moriarty (1998, p. 8) note that "everything a company does (and sometimes does not do) sends a message that can strengthen or weaken relationships." When customers know what perks other customers are receiving, we conjecture the misclassified best customer will be more likely to defect and have a more negative attitude towards the company. If there is an

---

[2] Some justification for these claims can be easily seen from the simple linear regression formulas. Suppose that $y_i = \alpha + \beta x_i + e_i$, where e_i is normal with mean 0 and standard deviation σ_i. Assume also that e_i is independent of e_j for $i \neq j$. Let $S_{xx} = \sum(x_i - \bar{x})^2$. The OLS estimate of β is $b = \sum(x_i - \bar{x})(y_i - \bar{y})/S_{xx}$. It is easy to show that

$$V(b) = \frac{\sum \sigma_i^2 (x_i - \bar{x})^2}{S_{xx}^2}.$$

Note that under homoscedasticity there is cancellation and $V(b) = \sigma^2/S_{xx}$, which is the formula given in textbooks. As the sample size grows, the denominator should become larger and the variance of the slope estimate decreases. As we get more data our estimates become more precise.

interaction between the perk and customer status (e.g., the perk works better on best customers), the firm also loses the additional revenue due to the interaction.

The managerial implications of the 80–15 rule include the fact that the company is spending scarce marketing resources on the wrong customers. It also highlights that best customers do not remain best customers forever. Reinartz and Kumar (2002) hint at something similar when they recommend "let butterflies fly." When a company discovers that a former best customer is no longer deserving of perks and stops giving them, does this customer become more likely to defect? Does revoking a perk cause a declining customer to decline faster? We have anecdotal evidence that this is true in the airline industry, where former frequent fliers avoid an airline after their "executive status" has been taken away. If this is true, the lost revenue due to an accelerated decline must be taken into consideration when deciding whether to offer perks. Companies should have a plan in place to keep the loyalty of customers who have had their level of perks lowered.

These ideas can be incorporated into a profit function. Let P_B be the baseline profit from a best customer, i.e., the profit that a best customer would produce without any additional perks. Let P_N be the baseline profit from a normal customer. Let C be the cost of a perk, I_B be the incremental profit generated by giving an actual best customer perks, and I_N be the incremental profit generated by giving an actual normal customer perks. When $I_B \neq I_N$, the perks have a different effect on a best customer than on a normal customer; we conjecture that for most companies $I_B > I_N$. Let C_{II} be the cost of a type II error, i.e., not giving perks to someone who deserves them. Then profit is

$$P = .2 \times .45(P_B + I_B - C) + .2 \times .55(P_B - C_{II})$$

$$+ .8 \times .85P_N + .8 \times .15(P_N + I_N - C)$$

$$= .2P_B + .09I_B - .21C + .8P_N + .12I_N - .11C_{II}$$

Giving perks is thus sensible when $.09I_B + .12I_N > .21C + .11C_{II}$. Companies will want to evaluate this function based on their specific costs, benefits, and misclassification probabilities.

DISCUSSION

Neils Bohr wrote "prediction is very difficult, especially about the future." This quote applies to making CLV estimates for the four organizations examined here. Historical value is not a very accurate predictor of future value. In situations where the future cannot be predicted accurately, an organization that invests a disproportionate amount of marketing resources in historically valuable customers may be investing in the wrong customers.

Relationship marketing and customer equity strategies suggest that firms should determine the value of customers and invest disproportionately in better customers. These approaches to marketing should emphasize the importance of the accuracy of value estimates. Our empirical work suggests that if a firm offers its alleged best 20% of customers special treatment, it will frequently misclassify customers. Of the actual top 20%, approximately 55% will be misclassified (and not receive special treatment). Of the actual bottom 80%, 15% will be misclassified (and receive special treatment). Misclassifying customers has potential costs. The best customer who is misclassified as normal could defect to a competitor, develop a negative attitude towards the firm, or not consume as much as it would if given best-customer treatment. The now-normal customer who receives perks is not as deserving as others.

Should organizations invest *discretionary marketing resources* in alleged best customers? The answer depends on the probabilities and costs of misclassifying customers, the additional revenue generated as a result of the special treatment, and the cost of the special treatment itself. In some cases this accuracy could be adequate, while in others it could be inadequate. Our point is that these misclassification rates and costs must be considered. This thought process is not currently emphasized—or even mentioned—by writers and speakers on the subject. Offering premium treatment to a select group of customers may improve that group's CLV, but could it have a negative effect on other customer groups? Does the percentage of true positives increase substantially by offering special treatment? Rust and Oliver (2002, p. 92) ask "What happens if a firm delights the customer in one period and then reverts to the former level of quality?" They label this "hit-and-run delight." If a customer stops receiving discretionary marketing investments, is the customer more likely to defect to a competitor than if the customer had never received any such investments? These are important research questions that need to be addressed in future research. Future research should also examine how including information about contacts affects predictive accuracy. Management judgment, absent empirical research, may not provide adequate intuition to answer this question.

We have provided evidence that firms will have difficulty predicting future behavior of their customers with much accuracy. One might ask why customers' future behavior is not very predictable? Some reasons have been hypothesized in the relationship marketing literature. As Day (2000, p. 24) notes "a strategy of investing in or building close relationships is neither appropriate nor necessary for every market, customer, or company. Some customers want nothing more than the timely exchange of the product or service with a minimum of hassles. And because close relations are resource intensive, not every customer is worth the effort." Diller (2000, pp. 39–43) suggests classes of "demotivators of loyalty." *Opportunism* means that customers are willing to "take any opportunity to get more value for the money, to be fully flexible when shopping and to only be interested in their own personal benefit (p. 40)." *Variety seeking* is a second reason. *Autonomy* "means freedom from others and decision-making independence (p. 42)." Clearly there are many potential explanations.

Our discussion so far has focused on discretionary marketing investments. Our position on quid-pro-quo investments is different because the amount of a quid-pro-quo investment depends on *actual future behavior*, whereas the discretionary investments are made based on *predicted future behavior*. For example, the customer who actually flies more miles in the future will receive more free flights—the number of free flights is roughly in proportion to future miles flown. The free flight is offered as a carrot to reward desirable future behavior. The important question when deciding to offer carrots is whether the customer would behave in the same way without the carrot. See Humby, Hunt, and Phillips (2003, especially pp. 29 and 215–216) for excellent discussion on this topic and hybrid approaches where better customers are offered proportionally larger carrots than less profitable customers.

Based on reading this paper, we expect that firms would be highly circumspect about their targeting and CRM strategies based on predicted customer value. The 20–55 rule means that treating lower valued customers poorly may cause defectors of potentially future high valued customers.

REFERENCES

Blattberg, R.C., Getz, G., & Thomas, J.S. (2001). Customer Equity: Building and Managing Relationships As Valuable Assets. Boston: Harvard Business School Press.

Breiman, L. (1996). Heuristics of Instability and Stabilization in Model Selection. Annals of Statistics, 24(6), 2350–2383.

Breiman, L. (2001). Statistical Modeling: The Two Cultures. Statistical Science, 16(3), 199–231.

Carroll, R.J., & Ruppert, D. (1988). Transformation and Weighting in Regression. New York: Chapman and Hall.

Collinger, T. (2002). The Tao of Customer Loyalty: Getting to "My Brand, My Way." In D. Iacobucci & B.J. Calder (Eds.), Kellogg on Integrated Marketing (pp. 16–38). Hoboken, NJ: Wiley.

Cook, R.D., & Weisberg, S. (1982). Residuals and Influence in Regression. New York: Chapman and Hall.

Day, G. (2000). Managing Market Relationships. Journal of the Academy of Marketing Science, 28(1), 24–30.

Diller, H. (2000). Customer Loyalty: Fata Morgana or Realistic Goal? Managing Relationships With Customers. In T. Hennig-Thurau & U. Hansen (Eds.), Relationship Marketing: Gaining Competitive Advantage Through Customer Satisfaction and Customer Retention (pp. 29–48). New York: Springer.

Duncan, T., & Moriarty, S. (1998). A Communication-Based Marketing Model for Managing Relationships. Journal of Marketing, 62, 1–13.

Dwyer, F.R. (1997). Customer Lifetime Valuation to Support Marketing Decision Making. Journal of Direct Marketing, 11(4), 6–13.

Efron, B., & Tibshirani, R.J. (1993). An Introduction to the Bootstrap. New York: Chapman and Hall.

Geyskens, J.-B., Steenkamp, E.M., Scheer, L.K., & Kumar, N. (1996). The Effects of Trust and Interdependence on Relationship Commitment: A Trans-Atlantic Study. International Journal of Research in Marketing, 13(4), 303–317.

Hastie, T., Tibshirani, R.J., & Friedman, J.F. (2001). The Elements of Statistical Learning: Data Mining, Inference, and Prediction. New York: Springer.

Hennig-Thurau, T., & Hansen, U. (2000). Relationship Marketing—Some Reflections on the State-of-the-Art of the Relational Concept. In T. Hennig-Thurau and

U. Hansen (Eds.), Relationship Marketing: Gaining Competitive Advantage Through Customer Satisfaction and Customer Retention (pp. 3–27). New York: Springer.

Humby, C., Hunt, T., & Phillips, T. (2003). Scoring Points: How Tesco is Winning Customer Loyalty. London: Kogan Press.

Jain, D., & Singh, S.S. (2002). Customer Lifetime Values Research in Marketing: A Review and Future Directions. Journal of Interactive Marketing, 16(2), 34–46.

Mosteller, F., & Tukey, J. (1977). Data Analysis and Regression. New York: Addison-Wesley.

Mulhern, F. (1999). Customer Profitability Analysis: Measurement, Concentration, and Research Directions. Journal of Interactive Marketing, 13(1), 25–40.

Neter, J., Kutner, M., Nachtsheim, C., & Wasserman, W. (1996). Applied Linear Statistical Models (4th ed.). Chicago: Irwin.

Reinartz, W., & Kumar, V. (2000). On the Profitability of Long-Life Customers in a Noncontractual Setting: An Empirical Investigation and Implications for Marketing. Journal of Marketing, 64, 17–35.

Reinartz, W., & Kumar, V. (2002). The Mismanagement of Customer Loyalty. Harvard Business Review, 86–94.

Ripley, B. (1996). Pattern Recognition and Neural Networks. Cambridge: Cambridge University Press.

Rust, R.T., & Oliver, R.L. (2000). Should We Delight the Customer? Journal of the Academy of Marketing Science, 28(1), 86–94.

Rust, R.T., Zeithaml, V.A., & Lemon, K.N. (2000). Driving Customer Equity: How Customer Lifetime Value Is Reshaping Corporate Strategy. New York: Free Press.

Scott, A., & Wild, C. (1991). Transformations and R^2. The American Statistician, 45(2), 127–129.

Sheth, J., Mittal, B., & Newman, B.I. (1999). Customer Behavior: Consumer Behavior and Beyond. Forth Worth: Dryden.

Venables, W., & Ripley, B. (1999). Modern Applied Statistics with S-PLUS. New York: Springer.

Yi, Y., & Jeon, H. (2003). Effects of Loyalty Programs on Value Perception, Program Loyalty, and Brand Loyalty. Journal of the Academy of Marketing Science, 31(3), 229–240.

Part VI: Micro-Macro Bob — Contributions Using Micro Consumer Models to Address Macro Marketing Problems

Unlike other chapters in the volume that focus on Bob's work in a specific area or time period, this note discusses three papers that represent different areas and were published over three decades. Blattberg and Jeuland (1981) develop an advertising-sales response model, Kim, Blattberg, and Rossi (1995) provide an application of random coefficient model for optimal pricing decision, and Singh, Hansen, and Blattberg (2006) analyze retail completion in the context of entry by a dominant discount store. Despite these apparent differences, a common theme across all these papers is use of rigorous modeling approach, meticulous execution, attention to minor details, and the choice of problems with importance to academics and practitioners alike. In many ways, these three papers encapsulate the attributes found in all of Bob's research discussed in earlier chapters.

Advertising-Sales Mode

Understanding the sales-advertising relationship constitutes an important goal of marketing academics and managers. As is well known, the effects of advertising are generally enduring and may not completely dissipate in the period in which advertising investments are made. In empirical applications, a typical approach to capture the carryover effects of advertising involves using some distributed lag formulation. At the time Blattberg and Jeuland (1981) appeared, there had been a growing debate in the literature on the reliability of lagged dependent variables in measuring the impact of advertising. This was in part stemming from the murky interpretation of the carryover advertising effects that seemed to depend on the time interval used in measuring sales. In particular, findings from the empirical studies at the time indicated that the implied duration of advertising's impact depended on the length of the data interval used.

Blattberg and Jeuland was an important paper in this era as it provided a novel "bottoms-up" approach of building advertising-sales models. The key insight in the paper was to specify the impact of advertising on purchase behavior at the individual consumer level that incorporated two key factors: reach of the ads and the rate of decay over time. The individual level model is then aggregated over time and across individuals to develop firm's advertising-sales relationship. This was a departure from the convention at the time of relaying on aggregate formulations. Blattberg and Jeuland show that aggregating infinitesimal individual behavior produces an aggregate sales-advertising relationship that provides a clear guidance on the specification of the advertising lag structure and functional forms. Importantly, the model was applicable regardless of the time interval thereby providing a cleaner interpretation of the estimated coefficients.

Optimal Pricing

Marketing researchers have long recognized the prevalence of consumer taste heterogeneity and the role it plays in guiding aspects of firm's marketing strategies. Not surprisingly, methods to incorporate variation in consumer preferences have generated tremendous interest in the marketing literature. In the context of consumer choice models, this involves using a random coefficient model to allow the parameters of brand preference and sensitivity to marketing mix to vary across consumers. Kim, Blattberg, and Rossi (1995) represent one such effort in this literature but with an important distinction. As is typical of all Bob's work, the paper takes an important leap forward in not just modeling and measuring consumer heterogeneity, but testing the implications of differences in consumer taste parameters in guiding optimal pricing decisions.

The consumer demand model used in the paper, while not novel, is carefully formulated for the problem at hand. For example, given the focus of the paper in deriving optimal pricing strategies, the distribution of price sensitivity coefficient is assumed to be lognormal (instead of normal) to ensure correct parameter signs at household level. Similarly, since costs figures are typically not observed in panel data, the paper combines two different sources to obtain those numbers. While these issues seem relatively minor in the context of the overall goals of the paper, the rigor of the empirical application and the attention to minor details such as product aggregation is typical of Bob's research. The paper convincingly demonstrates that the proposed model outperforms other benchmarks, and that incorporating consumer heterogeneity has a significant impact on category pricing decisions.

Market Entry

The role of supermarkets in the grocery retailing industry has undergone dramatic changes over the last decade. Rapid growth of alternative retail formats, in the form of mass discounters, price clubs, and supercenters, has transformed not only the competitive structure of the industry, but also the way in which consumers shop. The biggest threat to the supermarket industry comes from none other than the world's largest retailer: Wal-Mart. Singh, Hansen and Blattberg (2006) provide the first empirical study that analyzes the impact of entry by a Wal-Mart supercenter into a local market. Using a unique frequent shopper database that records transactions for over 10,000 customers, the authors study the impact of Wal-Mart's entry on two key household decisions: store visits and in-store expenditures. The authors develop a joint model of inter-purchase time and basket size to study the impact of competitor entry on consumer purchase behavior. The model allows for consumer heterogeneity due to observed (such as demographics and distance to stores) and unobserved factors. Results show that the incumbent store lost 17% volume — amounting to a quarter million dollar in monthly revenue — following Wal-Mart's entry. Decomposing the lost sales into components attributed to store visits and in-store expenditures, the authors find that the majority of these losses were due to fewer store visits with a much smaller impact attributed to basket size. Analyzing individual households the authors find that Wal-Mart cannibalizes some of the incumbent's best customers, and retention of a small number of households can significantly reduce losses at the focal store. The paper discusses several strategies for supermarket managers to compete with Wal-Mart.

The findings reported in the paper have implications for marketing academics and practitioners. Previous academic research had primarily focused on competition between supermarkets with little attention given to alternative formats. Furthermore, this research focused on retail competition and store choice a static environment, whereas this study considered the short- and long-run impact of entry in a changing competitive environment. The research is also related to the literature focusing on customer management as discussed in the chapter on "Direct Bob". For instance, the findings that a small proportion of customers account for a large proportion of store losses give credence to the general recommendation in the CRM literature on the importance of customer retention. Similarly, the empirical analysis demonstrates how a retailer can exploit the information contained in its frequent-shopper database to understand and respond to its most valuable customers. This is significant because, although the information contained in frequent-shopper databases is commonly assumed to be valuable, many retailers are struggling to convert data into actionable marketing strategies.

Some Personal Comments

As reflected in the writings in the previous chapters, Bob has had a significant impact on the careers of his students and we all owe him a debt of gratitude. As an advisor, Bob was always a constant source of encouragement and guidance. He identified the strengths and weaknesses of his students and related them in an honest but friendly tone.[1] He provided just the right balance between a hands-off approach and spoon-feeding and was extremely generous in supporting his students financially (a nontrivial matter as a graduate student). Interactions with Bob always ranged from very broad research topics to specific details, and despite all his knowledge there was always room for independent thinking.[2] In my experience, the most important aspect of Bob as an advisor was his willingness and ability to relate to his students as individuals, colleagues, and friends. I have always enjoyed uncensored conversations with Bob about a variety of topics. Many of these conversations have turned into questions that continue to influence my professional and personal life.[3] Thank you, Bob.

Vishal Singh
Stern School of Business
New York University

References

Blattberg, Robert and Abel Jeuland (1981). A Micro-modeling Approach to Determine the Advertising-Sales Relationship, *Management Science*, **27**(9), 988–1005.

Kim, Byung-Do, Robert Blattberg and Peter Rossi (1995). Modeling the Distribution of Price Sensitivity and Implications for Optimal Retail Pricing, *Journal of Business & Economic Statistics*, **13**(3), 291–303.

Singh, Vishal, Karsten Hansen and Robert Blattberg (2006). Market Entry and Consumer Behavior: An Investigation of the Wal-Mart Supercenter, *Marketing Science*, **25**(5), 457–476.

---

[1] For the most part.

[2] The only downside to the meetings: they were always scheduled at 8 am.

[3] One such conversation involved a business plan. It was a great idea but unfortunately (for me) Bob was already too rich.

MANAGEMENT SCIENCE
Vol. 27, No. 9, September 1981
Printed in U.S.A.

A MICROMODELING APPROACH TO INVESTIGATE THE ADVERTISING-SALES RELATIONSHIP*

ROBERT C. BLATTBERG† AND ABEL P. JEULAND†

The purpose of this paper is to derive a model of advertising effects on the firm's sales. A micromodel is postulated and aggregated across individuals and over time to produce a macromodel of the aggregate sales-advertising relationship for a single product. The micromodel postulated is very simple. It incorporates two factors: reach of the ads and rate of decay of their effectiveness over time.

This approach to modeling advertising effects is shown to be fruitful in several respects: (1) the coefficients of the aggregate equation are easily interpretable—in terms of the reach and decay parameters; (2) the model derived is nonlinear yet estimable; (3) a special case of the model is very similar to lag models that have been in use; (4) the model can be used whatever the unit of time is; (5) the carryover effect of advertising (as commonly defined) is not constant, but depends upon the previous spending levels; and (6) the model helps illustrate that the duration of advertising may be greatly overstated if aggregate lagged dependent variable models are simplistically interpreted.
(MARKETING: MARKETING—ADVERTISING/PROMOTION)

1. Introduction

Marketing researchers' interest in the sales-advertising relationship stems from the important goal of marketing research to develop more optimal advertising budgets than simple rules of thumb such as percentage of sales. If the relationship is known, the appropriate procedure can be chosen to find the profit maximization spending level.

The "standard" approach to find the relationship between advertising and sales has been to apply an econometric model to the firm's sales and advertising data. The models have ranged from simple two-variable regression models to simultaneous equation models. (See for example Palda [7], Bass [1], and Bass and Clarke [2], Schmalensee [8], and Lambin [5].) Because researchers realized that the effects of advertising may not totally dissipate in the period in which the advertisement is seen, most of the models have used a distributed lag formulation. After twenty years of research using distributed lag models, the results have not been very satisfactory. Clarke [4] evaluated most of the advertising-sales studies that used distributed lag models and found that distributed lag models do not provide good measures of the duration of advertising, in part because the measured duration seems to depend on the time interval used to measure sales. Even though these lagged dependent variable models have passed standard diagnostic tests, they have not proven reliable in measuring the effects of advertising. The main conclusion that one may draw from Clarke's survey is that, at least in the case of advertising, a serious problem of interpretation of distributed lag models exists. However, realizing that distributed lag

---

* Accepted by Donald R. Lehmann, former Departmental Editor; received March 27, 1979. This paper has been with the authors 12 months for 2 revisions.
† University of Chicago.

models leave a lot to be desired does not in itself provide alternative model specifications.

The purpose of this article is to offer a different strategy for building advertising-sales models. The modeling process begins with a "micromodel" of specific advertising influences on purchase behavior at the individual level for a given purchase occasion and then aggregates over time and across individuals to develop the firm's advertising-sales equation. This approach should help researchers determine how these influences affect the specification of the lag structure, identify more appropriate functional forms, and enhance the meaning of the estimated coefficients.

As a starting point, the authors have elected to focus on two aspects of how advertising is expected to affect behavior: (1) the percentage of the population of potential buyers *reached* by a given ad, and, (2) the effectiveness of a given insertion on future behavior of the individual over time. The simple micromodel will be aggregated to derive the aggregate advertising-sales relationship. This approach will make it clear that it is not obvious a priori what properties of the aggregate sales-advertising equation result from some given micro assumptions. The macromodel will be compared with existing econometric models theoretically, through simulations and with an actual application.

The paper is organized as follows: §2 describes the micromodel, derives the aggregate macromodel and compares it to existing econometric models and shows how the model can be estimated on real data; §3 uses the model to study distributed lags and lagged dependent variable models; and §4 gives our conclusions.

2. The Model

2A. *Introduction*

In this section, an aggregate sales-advertising equation for the firm is derived. This derivation begins with a micromodel which incorporates two aspects of how advertising influences purchasing behavior. Obviously, many other factors influence sales and hence should be built into the model. Consequently, this model should be viewed as a first step in the process of developing aggregate models based on individual level/short time interval micromodels.

2B. *The Consumer Model*

The model of how advertising affects consumers makes the following assumptions:

Assumption 1:   Any given consumer has a probability, q, of being exposed to any given ad; q is called the reach of an insertion. It is assumed that the exposure process is Bernoulli with probability q; in other words, given n insertions, the probability that a consumer will be exposed x times is $[n!/(x!(n - x)!)]q^x(1 - q)^{n - x}$ for $x \leqslant n$. For reasons of simplicity, the authors have elected to assume that the population is homogeneous with respect to the probability of reach, q. One could relax that assumption by using the compound Beta-Bernoulli process.

Assumption 2:   Because the consumer will gradually forget the advertisement, we will assume an exponentially decaying effectiveness function. If the effectiveness of the ad just after it is seen is taken as a reference, the effectiveness at time $t \geqslant t_i$ (t_i denotes the time of the ith ad, that is the last one seen by the individual) is:

$$p(t) = e^{-\alpha(t - t_i)} \tag{1}$$

990 ROBERT C. BLATTBERG AND ABEL P. JEULAND

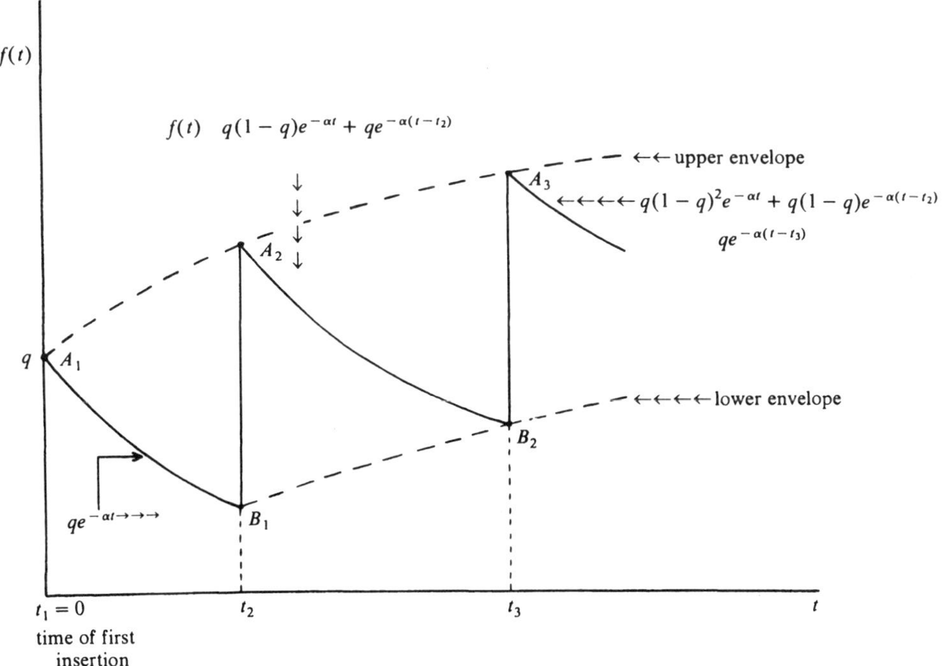

FIGURE 1. Aggregate Effectiveness Function.

where α is the decay factor. Given the formulation of equation (1), one may define the duration of advertising effects as the time it takes for an ad to lose, say, 90% of its effects.[1]

Combining the assumptions (1) and (2), one obtains an aggregate function of relative effectiveness over time, $f(t)$. The derivations are discussed in the next section. The graph of the function is given in Figure 1.

The function is clearly very similar to the pattern of the data reported by Zielske [1959] and the function used later by Lodish [1971] on the same data. The function has a saw-toothed representation due to the decaying that takes place during the time between exposures. Between time $t_1 = 0$ and t_2, q per cent of the population has been exposed to the first ad (at $t_1 = 0$) so that $f(t) = qe^{-\alpha t}$. A proportion, $1 - q$, of this first group will not see the second ad (at time t_2). The contribution of this group of size $q(1 - q)$ to $f(t)$ for $t > t_2$ is $q(1 - q)e^{-\alpha t}$. The group exposed to the second ad contributes for $qe^{-\alpha(t-t_2)}$. Consequently, $f(t) = q(1 - q)e^{-\alpha t} + qe^{-\alpha(t-t_2)}$. If the insertions are placed at regular intervals $t = 0, 1, 2, \ldots$, the A-curve (cf. Figure 1) would have an asymptote at

$$q + q(1-q)e^{-\alpha} + q(1-q)^2 e^{-2\alpha} + \cdots = \frac{q}{1 - (1-q)e^{-\alpha}}$$

[1] The duration $t_{90\%}$ is given by the equation $1 - 0.9 = 0.1 = e^{-\alpha t_{90\%}}$, i.e.,

$$t_{90\%} = \frac{1}{\alpha}\ln(10) = \frac{2.30}{\alpha}.$$

MICROMODELING APPROACH TO ADVERTISING-SALES RELATIONSHIP   991

(upper envelope), The B-curve (lower envelope) would have an asymptote at $qe^{-\alpha}/[1 - (1 - q)e^{-\alpha}]$.

Additional Assumptions: The function $f(t)$ defined earlier corresponds to effectiveness of advertising at one instant in time. In order to compute sales over an interval, one integrates $f(t)$ over that interval. This gives:

$$s(k) = c_1\tau + c_2\int_{(k-1)\tau}^{k\tau} f(t)\,dt. \tag{2}$$

Assuming the data are available for period of length τ (monthly, quarterly or yearly data, for example), the kth period starts at time $(k-1)\tau$ and ends at $k\tau$. The intercept c_1 is a sales rate and depends upon the number of the potential buyers, the average rate of purchase of the product class and the market share of the brand studied under stable conditions of no advertising. The other parameter, c_2, is also a function of the number of buyers of the product class, the average rate of purchase and the market share under stable conditions. The reason for including the latter is that a brand that has a higher market share does not have as much potential for growth as a small brand. Parameter c_2 would also include a factor of effectiveness of the ads since $f(t)$ only incorporates the number and timing of insertions.[2] Because of the above assumptions, it is believed that the model is expected to apply to frequently purchased consumer products like detergents, paper towels, etc. Finally, because the sales curve includes only $f(t)$ and not any functions of competitive effects, it is implicitly assumed that the competitive environment is stable.[3]

It should be pointed out that the function $f(t)$ represented in Figure 1 does not assume that the rate of decay α varies over time. It would indeed be desirable to make α a decreasing function of the number of past exposures: individuals obviously learn and in particular would forget less quickly as they are exposed repeatedly to the same

---

[2] One specific example of equation (2) is as follows. Assume that there are N buyers of the product class whose average choice probability of the brand under study is θ at equilibrium. They make an average of r purchases of the product in a period of unit length. Equilibrium sales in a period of length τ are $Nr\theta\tau = c_1\tau$ where $c_1 = Nr\theta$. Let us also assume that because of exposure to advertising at time t the market share θ becomes $\theta(t) = \theta + h(1 - \theta)$ where $0 < h < 1$. h measures the effectiveness of the ad in changing choice probabilities. If no further exposure to advertising takes place after t, then market share for the consumers exposed once at t is $\theta(t') = \theta + h(1 - \theta)e^{-\alpha(t'-t)}$ $t' > t$. However, not all individuals are exposed to any given insertion. Consequently, for the population as a whole and any insertion pattern, $\theta(t) = \theta + h(1 - \theta)$ $f(t)$ where $f(t)$ is the aggregate effectiveness function. Next, one needs to translate this dynamic choice probability equation into a sales equation: $dS = Nr[\theta + h(1 - \theta)f(t)]\,dt$ denotes sales in a short interval of length dt. Through integration, one gets:

$$S(k) = \int_{(k-1)\tau}^{k\tau} dS = Nr\theta\tau + Nrh(1 - \theta)\int_{(k-1)\tau}^{k\tau} f(t)\,dt.$$

One should emphasize that the above illustration is only one of the ways of obtaining equation (2).

[3] Some competitive effects could be incorporated as an error term in equation (2):

$$s(k) = c_1\tau + c_2\int_{(k-1)\tau}^{k\tau} f(t)\,dt + \epsilon_k.$$

A more appropriate model of competitive effects of advertising would be as follows:

$$s_i(k) = c_{1i}\tau + c_2\int_{(k-1)\tau}^{k\tau} E\left(\frac{a_i + f_i(t)}{b + \sum_j f_j(t)}\right) dt$$

where $f_j(t)$ denotes the exposure function of a given individual with respect to brand j. The symbol E denotes the expected value operator (taking expected value over the population). This model is obviously considerably more complex. Future research will address the important question of competitive effects.

992   ROBERT C. BLATTBERG AND ABEL P. JEULAND

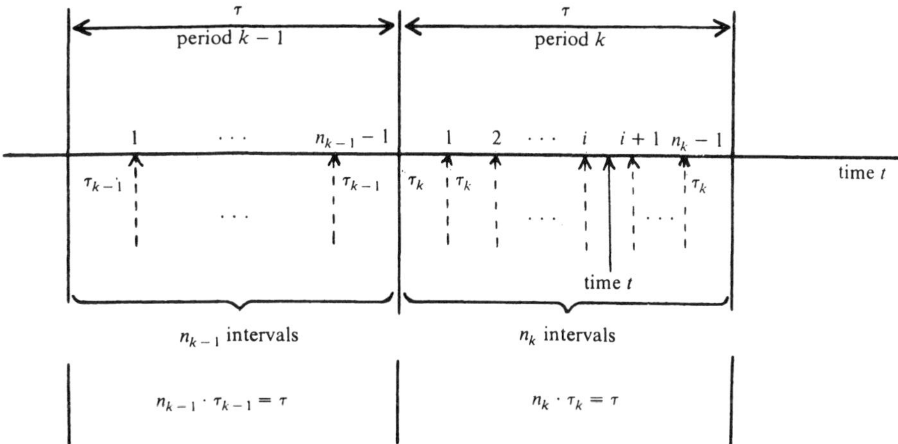

FIGURE 2.   Insertion Pattern.

ad. However, this mathematical extension is not straightforward. The basic model would have to be very different than the present $f(t)$ function so as to be tractable.[4]

2C. *Mathematical Derivations of the Rationship between Sales and Advertising*

We will now derive the function $f(t)$ which depends upon parameters q and α. Given assumption (1), the probability that a consumer was exposed to the most recent insertion is q (group I), to the insertion just preceding this last one $(1 - q)q$ (group II), etc. If one denotes by t_i the time of the most recent insertion (ith insertion in period k) and t_{i-1} the time of the insertion just preceding it (cf. Figure 2), the relative effectiveness functions for groups I and II is $e^{-\alpha(t-t_i)}$ and $e^{-\alpha(t-t_{i-1})}$ respectively. In general, the function $f(t)$ of expected relative effectiveness for the entire population (all groups included) then becomes:

$$f(t) = qe^{-\alpha(t-t_i)} + q(1 - q)e^{-\alpha(t-t_{i-1})} + q(1 - q)^2 e^{-\alpha(t-t_{i-2})} + \ldots . \tag{3}$$

To make the model more tractable, the following insertion pattern will be assumed. Let τ be the length of each time period; within each period of length τ, insertions of the advertising campaign occur at a constant rate: if in period k there are n_k insertions, then an insertion occurs each $\tau_k = \tau/n_k$ time interval (cf. Figure 2).

Using equations (2) and (3) and the insertion pattern just described, the sales function is derived in Appendix A. The sales-advertising equation is:

$$s_k(\tau) = c_1\tau + \frac{c_2 q}{\alpha}\frac{(1 - e^{-\alpha\tau_k})}{1 - \lambda_k}\left\{ n_k\ \frac{\lambda_k(1 - \lambda_k^{n_k})}{1 - \lambda_k} + (1 - \lambda_k^{n_k})\gamma_{k-1}\right\} \tag{4}$$

---

[4]There is another aspect concerning learning. Making α a function of past exposures recognizes that the rate of decay may diminish with repeated exposures but does not recognize that a second or third exposure may not affect the consumer the same way as a first exposure. In the terminology of footnote 2, this means that h itself is not constant. However, this issue is complex. On the one hand, an ad seen for the first time may have more impact because of newness. On the other hand, reinforcement because of multiple exposure may help. Which effect is dominant is certainly an important question.

where $s_k(\tau)$ are the sales in period k of length τ, n_k being the number of insertions in period k, q the probability of exposure to an ad, α the decay rate, and c_1, c_2 the constants described in equation (2), $\tau_k = \tau/n_k$, $\lambda_k = (1 - q)e^{-\alpha}$ and

$$\gamma_{k-1} = \lambda_{k-1}^{n_k-1}\gamma_{k-2} + \frac{\lambda_{k-1}(1 - \lambda_{k-1}^{n_k-1})}{1 - \lambda_{k-1}} \tag{5}$$

with $\gamma_0 = 0$ if the advertising campaign starts at the beginning of period 1.

It is an approximation to assume that the insertions are equally spaced in a given period. If they are not (which is the case in practice), then obviously the number of insertions alone does not describe advertising in the period. Besides the average inter-insertion interval $\bar{\tau}_k = \tau/n_k$, one can define the standard deviation $\sigma_k = \sqrt{E(\tau_k - \bar{\tau}_k)^2}$. Sales in period k depend not only on $n_k = \tau/\bar{\tau}_k$ but also on σ_k and in fact higher moments. Thus, we have a case of implicitly omitted explanatory variables. Further research is needed to satisfactorily address this question.

2D.   *A Special Case of the Model*

Before analyzing in detail what equations (4) and (5) imply about the effects of reach and decay on the advertising-sales relationship, let us derive a special case of the model. It seems reasonable to expect that in a significant number of situations, the reach parameter q would be small: a single insertion can only reach a small fraction of the potential market.

For very small q, the model given in equations (4) and (5) can be approximated.[5] Appendix B gives the steps followed to derive the approximation. The resulting equation is:

$$S_K(\tau) = c_1\tau + \beta'\left[k_1 n_k + k_2 \sum_{j=0}^{\infty} \gamma^j n_{k-j-1}\right] \tag{6}$$

where

$$\beta' = \frac{\beta}{\alpha} = \frac{c_2 q}{\alpha}, \quad k_1 = 1 - \frac{1 - e^{-\alpha\tau}}{\alpha\tau}, \quad k_2 = \frac{(1 - e^{-\alpha\tau})^2}{\alpha\tau}, \quad \text{and} \quad \gamma = e^{-\alpha\tau}$$

so that $k_1 + k_2\sum_{j=0}^{\infty}\gamma^j = 1$. Thus, if q is small, equations (4) and (5) can be approximated by a distributed lag model.

In model (4) and (5) α is directly related to the duration of an ad. In equation (6) k_1, k_2 and γ are all functions of $\alpha\tau$. As parameters of an aggregate equation they are thus related to the duration interval of a given ad. According to the definition of duration given in §2B, advertising duration, t, and γ are related through the equation:[6]

$$\frac{t}{\tau} = \frac{\ln 0.1}{\ln \gamma} \ .$$

---

[5]The idea of letting $q \to 0$ resulted from trying to find the conditions for which equation (4) becomes linear.

[6]There is no closed form expression of t as a function of k_1 or k_2. The two relationships are respectively

$$k_1 = 1 - \left(\frac{1 - (0.1)^{\tau/t}}{\ln 10}\right)\frac{t}{\tau} \quad \text{and} \quad k_2 = \frac{(1 - (0.1)^{\tau/t})^2}{\ln 10}\frac{t}{\tau} \ .$$

994   ROBERT C. BLATTBERG AND ABEL P. JEULAND

2E. *Estimation*

For the simpler model of equation (6), a single search on α combined with OLS is sufficient. Rewrite equation (6) as:

$$ s_k = c_1\tau + \beta'\left[k_1 n_k + k_2\left(n_{k-1} + \gamma n_{k-2} + \cdots + \gamma^{k-2} n_1 + \gamma^{k-1}\{ n_0 + \gamma n_{-1} + \cdots \}\right)\right] $$

where the advertising series n is split into the subseries posterior to n_0 for which data are available and the subseries that include n_0 and all previous periods and for which no data are available or used in the analysis. Consequently, $s_k = c_1\tau + \beta'X_k + \beta''Y_k$ where $X_k = k_1 n_k + k_2(n_{k-1} + \gamma n_{k-2} + \cdots + \gamma^{k-2} n_1)$, $Y_k = \gamma^{k-1}$ and $\beta'' = \beta'(n_0 + \gamma n_{-1} + \cdots)$. A single search on α is needed. Given α, one can compute the explanatory variables X_k and Y_k; $c_1\tau$ and β' are then determined by OLS estimation of $s_k = c_1\tau + \beta'X_k + \beta''Y_k$. The search proceeds until the sum of squared errors is minimized. This procedure was first described by Zellner and Geisel [11] and gives the maximum likelihood estimate if one assumes normally distributed error terms.

It is easy to generalize the above procedure for the estimation of the general model of equations (4) and (5). The estimation of α, q, c_1 and c_2 can be performed as a combination of search on the parameters α and q and ordinary least squares. One can use the information matrix to compute large sample standard errors for the parameters α, q, c_1, c_2 (see for example, Theil [9, Chapter 8]). Hypothesis tests can be performed using likelihood ratio tests.

3. Evaluation of the Model

We will now use the model to investigate: (1) the nature of the effect of advertising on sales, (2) the carryover effects of advertising, (3) the behavior of the coefficient of the lagged dependent variable in econometric models, and (4) the size of the coefficients of lagged advertising variables as a function of whether it is the first, second, or subsequent lag.

3A. *The Effect of Advertising on Sales*

The sales equation given by (4) and (5) indicates that the effect of advertising on sales is nonlinear. Figure 3a plots sales, s_k, as a function of the number of insertions, n_k. It is important to note that this nonlinear effect is not simply of the form $s_k = \ln(n_k)$ or $\ln(s_k) = \ln(n_k)$. Further implications of this will be discussed in §3C.

The effects on sales of the decay rate, α, and the probability of seeing an ad, q, are shown in Figures 3b and 3c. As the decay rate increases, sales decline but at a decreasing rate. As the probability of seeing an ad increases, sales increase but again at a decreasing rate.

It is interesting to note that the model separates reach (q) and frequency (n_k) and makes advertising effects a function of both, whereas most models concentrate on advertising dollars.

3B. *The Carryover Effect*

The carryover effect is given by equations (4) and (5) and is

$$ \frac{c_2}{\alpha}q\left(\frac{1 - e^{-\alpha\tau_k}}{1 - \lambda_k} \right) \cdot (1 - \lambda_k^{n_k})\gamma_{k-1} $$

MICROMODELING APPROACH TO ADVERTISING-SALES RELATIONSHIP   995

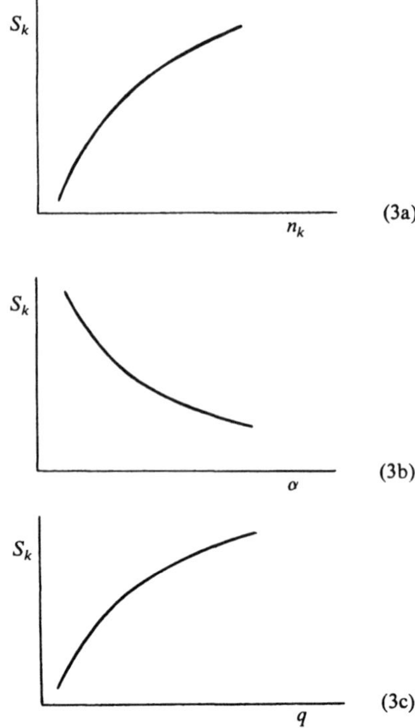

FIGURE 3.   Plots of Sales as a Function of n_k, α, q.

where

$$\gamma_{k-1} = \lambda_{k-1}^{n_k-1}\gamma_{k-2} + \frac{\lambda_{k-1}(1 - \lambda_{k-1}^{n_k-1})}{1 - \lambda_{k-1}}$$

and $\lambda_k = (1 - q)e^{-\alpha\tau/n_k}$.

Thus, the carryover effect depends upon: (1) n_k and (2) past advertising levels through $\gamma_{k-1}, \gamma_{k-2}, \cdots$.

To study it in detail, it is necessary to define the carryover effect precisely. Here we define the one-period carryover effect as the effect of the present period's advertising on next period's sales divided by the effect of the present period's advertising on this period's sales. Using this definition, the one-period carryover effect is defined mathematically[7] as:

$$CE(1) = \frac{\partial s_{k+1}}{\partial n_k} \Big/ \frac{\partial s_k}{\partial n_k} \tag{7a}$$

and in general,

$$CE(j) = \frac{\partial s_{k+j}}{\partial n_k} \Big/ \frac{\partial s_k}{\partial n_k}. \tag{7b}$$

[7]For the linear distributed lag model, $S_t = \alpha + \beta\sum_i\lambda^iA_{t-i}$, $CE(1) = \lambda$, and $CE(j) = \lambda^j$.

996   ROBERT C. BLATTBERG AND ABEL P. JEULAND

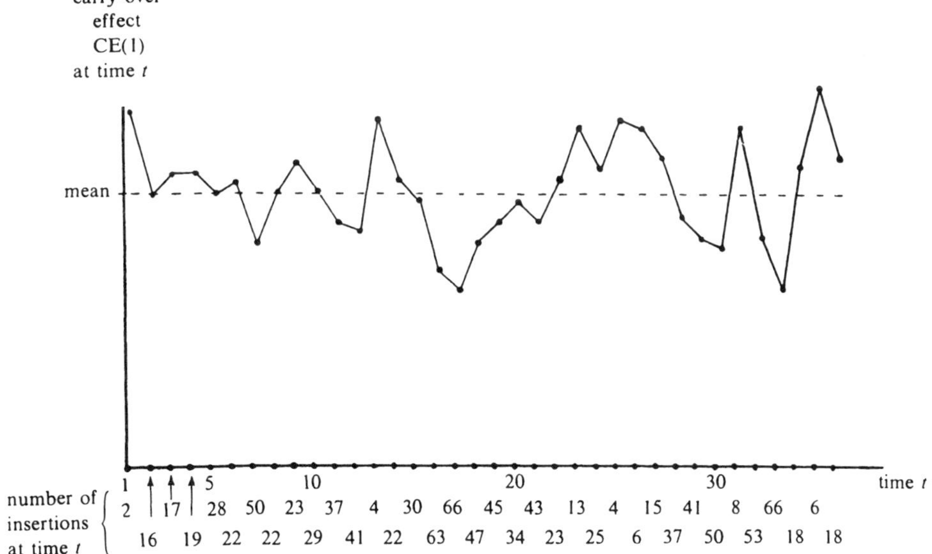

FIGURE 4.   Sequence Plot of Standardized Values of One-Period Carryover Effect.

Returning to the model given in equations (4) and (5), the carryover $CE(1)$ effect depends upon q, α, and n_{k+1}. The specific effects are: (1) As the decay rate, α, or the reach, q, increase, the carryover effect declines; (2) As the frequency of ads, n_{k+1}, increases, the carryover effect declines. The reason n_{k+1} and q influence the carryover effect due to n_k in period $k+1$ is that as the number of consumers seeing an ad in period $k+1$ increases, the number affected by ads in previous period declines.

A further implication of equations (4) and (5) is that the carryover effect is not constant over time. Figure 4 gives a time series plot of the one period carryover effect, $CE(1)$, as a function of the number of insertions. This is obviously different from the linear distributed lag model for which $CE(1) = \lambda$ and is therefore constant.

In conclusion, the reach and constant decay model implies a particular carryover effect that (1) depends upon past spending levels and is thus not constant over time, (2) depends upon reach q and frequency n_k in the present period, (3) is nonlinear in frequency n_k. It is easy to say after the analysis has been performed that these effects are obvious, but they seem to prove the usefulness of the modeling strategy employed in this paper.

3C.   *Analysis of the Lagged Dependent Variable Effect in Econometric Models*

Models of the form $S_k = a + bA_k + \lambda S_{k-1}$ or with logarithms ($\log S_t$, $\log A_t$) have been extensively used in econometric analysis of advertising effects on sales. Yet, as is reported by Clarke [4], no consensus seems to emerge from the many analyses concerning the implications of these models with regard to the effects of advertising on sales. We will focus on parameter λ which has been viewed as an indicator of carryover effects of advertising.

i. *Sensitivity of λ to Insertion Patterns.*   We will first study the effect of the pattern of insertions on λ. Two cases will be studied: (1) the insertions increase by one each month (high auto-correlated insertion pattern); (2) the same insertions as used in (1)

TABLE 1

OLS *Parameter Estimates for Koyck Model*
Model: $S_t = a + \lambda S_{t-1} + bA_t$
High vs. Low Autocorrelation in Spending Pattern

	a	λ	b	Average Carryover Effect $CE(1)$
High Autocorrelation	12,127	0.97778	1.94	0.1032
Low Autocorrelation	375,240	0.19339	476.75	0.1692

but randomized so that they are not auto-correlated. Thus, for data set 1, $n_k = k$, $k = 1, 2, \ldots, 361$ and for data set 2, each integer between 1 and 361 is randomly assigned to a period. Sales data were generated using equations (4) and (5) with the parameters set as follows: $\alpha = 1$, $q = 0.1$, $c_1 = 50,000$ and $c_2 = 532,000$. To control for the effect of initial starting conditions, the first 96 observations were excluded. Then the linear model was applied to the next 96 observations.

The results are given in Table 1. They show that $\lambda = 0.97778$ for the highly auto-correlated insertion pattern (Set 1) and $\lambda = 0.19339$ for the randomized (non-auto-correlated) insertion pattern (Set 2). This is a striking difference. One explanation might be that the two spending patterns could result in different carryover effects and λ is measuring this difference. To determine whether this is true, the average of the carryover effect, $CE(1)$, based on equation (7a) was computed for both insertion patterns. The results are also given in Table 1. They show that the average marginal carryover effect is actually higher for the randomized spending pattern than for the highly auto-correlated spending pattern. Thus, the values of λ are not due to differences in the carryover effect since λ is larger when the true carryover effect is smaller.

The effect just described is not accidental but has a theoretical explanation. The effect is due to a combination of nonlinearity in response to the number of insertions and auto-correlated spending patterns. The nonlinearity causes the residuals to be negative for low and high spending levels and positive for moderate spending levels. To remove the nonlinearity, a common adjustment procedure is to use a log transformation on the explanatory variables. However, large lagged sales coefficients can remain in the Koyck model even after the log transformation is made.

If the spending pattern is also auto-correlated, the residuals will be serially correlated, i.e., $u_k = \rho u_{k-1} + \varepsilon_k$. The value of λ is thus directly affected by ρ. If the spending pattern is random, the small spending levels will not be close to one another in the data series, nor will the large spending levels be close to one another. Therefore, the residuals will not be auto-correlated and thus, λ is small. Hence, the value of λ depends on a combination of nonlinear responses to advertising and an auto-correlated insertion pattern. By controlling how auto-correlated the insertion pattern is, one can create almost any value of λ desired.

One might also argue that we have not used the appropriate estimation procedure for models of the type $S_k = a + bA_k + \lambda S_{k-1}$. For models of this type, the errors are likely to be serially correlated resulting in inconsistent OLS estimates. For this reason, additional analyses were run. The estimation procedure employed was devised by Zellner and Geisel [11]. One hundred ninety-two observations were generated with the number of insertions increasing from 1 to 192. For the auto-correlated pattern, simulated observations 97 through 192 were used. For the random pattern, the 192 observations of number of insertions were first randomized. Observations 97 through

TABLE 2

Maximum Likelihood Estimates of λ Model

| | Form of Variables | | | |
Spending Pattern	S_t, A_t	$S_t, \ln A_t$	$\ln S_t, \ln A_t$	Average $CE(1)$
High Auto-Correlation	λOLS = 0.98 λMLE = 0.99	λOLS = 0.97 λMLE = 0.99	λOLS = 0.97 λMLE = 0.99	0.332
Random Spending Pattern	λOLS = 0.37 λMLE = 0.17	λOLS = 0.45 λMLE = 0.25	λOLS = 0.44 λMLE = 0.21	0.455

192 of the randomized pattern were then used. Table 2 gives the maximum likelihood estimates of λ using the Zellner and Geisel procedure for three different models:

$$S_k = a + bA_k + \lambda S_{k-1}, \tag{1}$$

$$S_k = a + b \ln A_k + \lambda S_{k-1}, \quad \text{and} \tag{2}$$

$$\ln S_k = a + b \ln A_k + \lambda \ln S_{k-1}. \tag{3}$$

Again, the result is that λ reflects the nature of the spending pattern and not the carryover effect. λOLS and λMLE are both very close to 1 for the highly auto-correlated spending pattern; for the random pattern, λMLE is about 0.2 and λOLS about 0.4. The average carryover effect is 0.33 for the correlated spending pattern and 0.45 for the random spending pattern.

ii. *Implications for Time Aggregation.* Marketers generally use monthly, quarterly, or annual advertising spending and corresponding sales data. Clarke [1976] found that the coefficient for lagged sales, λ, increased as the length of the measurement period was increased. Suppose firms budget advertising spending levels on a quarterly basis. If there is a sales trend or a seasonal pattern expected for the sales data, then the advertising spending usually follows the same pattern. Monthly data, however, are often quite random for two reasons; (1) advertising agencies' media departments usually use some type of flighting or waving strategy when the advertising budget is small, and (2) "make good" and other institutional buying problems result in more random monthly patterns.[8] Thus, in some months there are very small spending levels and in others high levels. This would imply low auto-correlations of spending on a monthly level and relatively higher auto-correlations of spending on a quarterly basis. If this is the case, λ would actually increase when the data interval goes from monthly to quarterly.

To support the above supposition, equations (4) and (5) again were used to generate data. The parameter values were $c_1 = 50,000$, $c_2 = 532,000$, $\alpha = 1$, $q = 0.1$. The insertion pattern for the first year is given in Table 3. For each year after the first, the monthly insertions were equal to $n_{k+12} = n_k + 4$, $k = 1, \ldots, 84$; 96 months of data were generated. The first two observations were discarded to eliminate effects from initial conditions. The quarterly data were computed by simply adding each three months of the monthly data.

---

[8]Because the media insertions are not always aired at the time they were planned, the stations "make good" the insertion at another time. This results in a more random insertion pattern over short time intervals.

MICROMODELING APPROACH TO ADVERTISING-SALES RELATIONSHIP   999

TABLE 3
Monthly Spending Pattern

Month	1	2	3	4	5	6	7	8	9	10	11	12
Number of Insertions	5	12	13	19	5	9	7	21	8	16	13	10

The results given in Table 4 show that $\lambda = 0.182$ for the monthly data and $\lambda = 0.807$ for the quarterly data. This is quite an extreme jump. If one were to interpret λ as the carryover effect of advertising and to calculate the effect of quarter t spending on quarter $t + 2$ sales, it would be approximately $0.65\beta A_t$, which is quite high. The effect one year after the spending is $0.42\beta A_t$. Thus, it would seem advertising has a very long duration. The true duration can be computed from the fact that $\alpha = 1$. The 90 percent duration interval is 2.3 months.[9] Thus, the seemingly long duration found for quarterly data is simply due to some misinterpretation of what λ actually measures.

TABLE 4
OLS *Monthly vs. Quarterly Estimates of*
$$S_k = a + bA_k + \lambda S_{k-1}$$

	a	λ	b
Monthly Data	181,750	0.182	2,974.6
Quarterly Data	214,050	0.807	603.57

3D.   *Bass-Clarke Result*

As a last use of the model, we will analyze observations made by Bass and Clarke [2] concerning the size of the coefficients of lagged advertising variables. The results of Table 5 were obtained using the approximated model of equation (6).

TABLE 5
Lag Structures
$$S_k = a + \beta_1 n_k + \beta_2 n_{k-1} + \beta_3 n_{k-2} + \beta_4 n_{k-3} + \cdots$$

Duration Parameter, α	Coefficient			
	β_1	β_2	β_3	β_4
0.10	0.048	0.091	0.082	0.074
0.42	0.184	0.281	0.184	0.121
0.50	0.213	0.309	0.188	0.113
1.00	0.368	0.400	0.147	0.054
5.00	0.801	0.197	0.001	0.000

The lag structure can have the first lag the largest ($\alpha = 5$), the second lag larger than the first ($\alpha = 0.5$), the second and third lags larger than the first ($\alpha = 0.1$), or the first and third lags equal ($\alpha = 0.42$). Still, each insertion effect decays and has its maximum impact immediately after being seen.

The different lag structures just described are due to temporal aggregation. The

---

[9] $1 - e^{-\alpha t} = 0.90$; if $\alpha = 1$, then $t = 2.3$.

1000 ROBERT C. BLATTBERG AND ABEL P. JEULAND

TABLE 6
Bass-Clarke Data

Month k	1	2	3	4	5	6	7	8	9	10	11	12
S_k-Sales	12.0	20.5	21.0	15.5	15.3	23.5	24.5	21.3	23.5	28.0	24.0	15.5
A_k Advertising	15.0	16.0	18.0	27.0	21.0	49.0	21.0	22.0	28.0	36.0	40.0	3.0

Month k	13	14	15	16	17	18	19	20	21	22	23	24
S_k-Sales	17.3	25.3	25.0	36.5	36.5	29.6	30.5	28.0	26.0	21.5	19.7	19.0
A_k Advertising	2.10	29.0	62.0	65.0	46.0	44.0	33.0	62.0	22.0	12.0	24.0	3.0

Month k	25	26	27	28	29	30	31	32	33	34	35	36
S_k-Sales	16.0	20.7	26.5	30.6	32.3	29.5	28.3	31.3	32.2	26.4	23.4	16.4
A_k Advertising	5.0	14.0	36.0	40.0	49.0	7.0	52.0	65.0	17.0	5.0	17.0	1.0

effect of an ad seen at the end of a period will last for some time in the future if α is small enough. Even though it is decaying, it is decaying very slowly. With low α, an ad seen early in the period will still have a sizeable effect next period, and an insertion seen at the end of the period will have almost all of its effect next period. For example, if an insertion occurs January 31, most of its impact will be in February, but its expenditure is attributed to January. Also, relatively low reach (small q) would seem to be required for the observed phenomena of Table 5. High reach would eliminate the carryover effect of previous insertions. For this reason, the simplified model of equation (6) was estimated on Bass-Clarke data.

The data were derived from Figure 2 in their article [2, p. 300] using a scale graduated in millimeters. (Each series is thus determined up to a linear transformation. The linear formulation of equation (6) is unaffected by a linear transformation on the dependent and the independent variables). The 36 monthly observations are shown in Table 6. Bass and Clarke provided a description of the data. The three year history of sales and advertising is for a dietary weight control product. Sales are measured in multiples of "equivalent serving units" (to account for the different sizes in which the product was distributed) and the advertising is given in dollar expenditures. Advertising expenditure is recognized in the month in which the advertising occurred, rather than the month in which it is billed to the company.

Table 7 summarizes the estimation results. Its first and third rows correspond to the maximum likelihood estimates of the derived model (using the procedure outlined in section 2E[10]) for the 36 monthly series shown in Table 6 and the 18 bi-monthly series respectively that are obtained by aggregating the former. The derived model explains more variance and is less sensitive to time aggregation since a 3.07 month duration is not as far away relatively from 2.30 month as 6.08 is from 3.66. The duration of about 2 or 3 months implied by the micromodels is consistent with the lagged advertising models (rows 5 through 7 in Table 7).

[10] A step of 0.05 was used in the search for α.

TABLE 7

Estimation Results

		Derived Model vs. Koyck Model	R^2	90% Implied Duration (months)
Monthly Data	I Derived Model	$S_k = 13.5 + 0.389 X_k - 2.599 Y_k \quad \alpha = 1$ $\qquad\qquad (0.046) \qquad (3.405)$	0.73	$\dfrac{\ln 10}{\alpha} = 2.30$
	II Koyck	$S_k = 7.053 + 0.533 S_{k-1} + 0.157 A_k$ $\qquad\qquad (0.099) \qquad (0.033)$	0.69	$\dfrac{\ln 0.1}{\ln 0.533} = 3.66$
Bi-Monthly Data	III Derived Model	$S_k = 26.42 + 0.400 X_k - 1.139 Y_k \quad \alpha = 1.50$ $\qquad\qquad (0.066) \qquad (6.44)$	0.77	$\dfrac{\ln 10}{\alpha} = 3.07$
	IV Koyck	$S_k = 15.3 + 0.469 S_{k-1} + 0.193 A_k$ $\qquad\qquad (0.148) \qquad (0.049)$	0.66	$\dfrac{2\ln 0.1}{\alpha} = 6.08$
		Lagged Advertising Models		
Monthly Data	V	$S_k = 18.3 + 0.208 A_k$ $\qquad\qquad (0.044)$	0.40	
	VI	$S_k = 15.6 + 0.142 A_k + 0.167 A_{k-1}$ $\qquad\qquad (0.035) \qquad (0.035)$	0.64	More than one month (A_k and A_{k-1} significant)
	VII	$S_k = 14.3 + 0.146 A_k + 0.147 A_{k-1} + 0.058 A_{k-2}$ $\qquad\qquad (0.035) \qquad (0.038) \qquad (0.036)$	0.66	More than two months kA_k, A_{k-1} significant, A_{k-2} almost significant for 5%; one-tail test)

4. Conclusions

This paper has attempted to offer a different approach to constructing models of the relationship between advertising and sales. We have begun with a micromodel of some effects an insertion may have on consumers. We have then aggregated temporally and cross-sectionally. Aggregation was done analytically. Most articles studying the effects of advertising on sales have usually included a description of the micro-process but then simply used the same ideas on the aggregate model itself. Only under very stringent conditions will the aggregate model be the same as the micromodel.

A main advantage of this approach is to be able to interpret precisely the parameters of the sales function. It is much more difficult to interpret the parameters of a global or aggregate equation when its form has not been derived from micro assumptions. This aspect of interpretation of aggregate models has also been recognized by Bass and Pilon [1979].

By beginning with a micromodel which postulated two basic processes, the reach process and a decay process, assumptions frequently used, an aggregate advertising-sales model was generated. The form of the model is similar to but different from the models presently being used by researchers. The model is nonlinear in spending levels and has diminishing returns to advertising. The carryover effect is not constant but

1002   ROBERT C. BLATTBERG AND ABEL P. JEULAND

depends upon the present and past levels of spending. Thus, while some common assumptions were used, the aggregation process results in a different representation of the advertising-sales relationship.

After developing the model, it was then used to generate sales data. Distributed lag models were used to estimate the effect of advertising on sales. Many of the observations that researchers have made when using distributed lag models were produced. These included: (1) abnormally long lags (large coefficient on the lagged sales term); (2) the lagged sales coefficient increasing when going from monthly to quarterly data; (3) a higher coefficient for A_{k-1} than A_k. The causes of observations (1) and (2) seem to be a combination of a nonlinear response to advertising and a highly autocorrelated spending pattern. Observation (3) is explained by a combination of time aggregation, the reach process, and the decay process.

Bass [1] has also recently investigated some of the problems plaguing aggregate econometric sales-advertising models. If one knows that a micromodel applies at the weekly or monthly level, then even when only annual data are available, it may still be possible to recover the micro-parameters. Windal and Weiss [10] have devised a systematic procedure that precisely does this. Obviously, the difficulty is in knowing the level of aggregation, 52 if the basic micromodel applies to weekly data or 12 if it applies to monthly data. The best procedure may be to assume a continuous process as here and perform the aggregation so as to use available data for estimation purposes.

It is hoped that this research has shown how important the aggregation process is. Frequently, aggregation is done simply by assuming that the micromodel is the same as the aggregate model. This paper has tried to show that this is not true. A specific simple micromodel has focused on a limited number of aspects of the effects of an ad. There is a need to find better micromodels than the one used here. In particular, competition and learning effects need to be incorporated.

Appendix A—Derivation of Model

The model assumes that only q percent of the population is exposed to any given insertion. The probability of seeing any given ad is assumed independent from previous behavior and constant over time. Therefore, the exposure process follows a Bernoulli process. Consider the effect of an insertion at time t. The relative effectiveness of the ads is assumed to be represented by the equation $p(t) = e^{-(t-t_i)}$ with t_i being the time of the last exposure, $t > t_i$, $\alpha > 0$. Then, q percent of the population see the most recent ad and the relative effectiveness at time t of this ad on this segment is $e^{-\alpha(t-t_i)}$. Of those not exposed, q percent saw the previous insertion and since there are $(1 - q)$ percent not exposed to the ith insertion, $q(1 - q)$ percent are characterized by the relative effectiveness $e^{-\alpha(t-t_{i-1})}$ where t_{i-1} is the time of the $i - 1$th insertion. This process continues back to the beginning of the product's introduction though the effect will be negligible as $(t - t_j)$ becomes large.

Expected sales generated between insertions i and $i + 1$ in period k are:

$$S(t_i, t_{i+1}) = c_1 \tau_k + c_2 \int_{t_i}^{t_i + \tau_k} f(t)\, dt \tag{A.1}$$

where $\tau_k = \tau/n_k$ (the measurement periods all have length τ, e.g., month, quarter, year and n_k denotes the number of insertions in period k) and $f(t)$ is the aggregate

MICROMODELING APPROACH TO ADVERTISING-SALES RELATIONSHIP   1003

effectiveness function given by:

$$f(t) = qe^{-\alpha(t-t_i)} + q(1-q)e^{-\alpha(t-t_{i-1})} + q(1-q)^2 e^{-\alpha(t-t_{i-2})} + \cdots$$

$$= qe^{-\alpha(t-t_i)}\left[\sum_{j=0}^{i} (1-q)^j e^{-\alpha j\tau_k} + \sum_{j=1}^{n_{k-1}} (1-q)^{i+j} e^{-(i\alpha\tau_k + j\alpha\tau_k)} + \cdots \right]. \quad (A.2)$$

Noting that the first term of $f(t)$ depends upon t and the rest do not. We have:

$$S(t_i, t_{i+1}) = c_1\tau_k + \frac{c_2 q}{\alpha}(1 - e^{-\alpha\tau_k})F_{i+1} \quad (A.3)$$

where

$$F_{i+1} = \sum_{j=0}^{i} (1-q)^j e^{-j\alpha\tau_k} + (1-q)^i e^{-\alpha i\tau_k}\left[\sum_{j=1}^{n_{k-1}} (1-q)^j e^{-j\alpha\tau_{k-1}} + \cdots \right]. \quad (A.4)$$

If we let $\lambda_k = (1-q)e^{-\alpha\tau_k}$, then

$$F_{i+1} = \sum_{j=0}^{i} \lambda_k^j + \lambda_k^i \sum_{j=1}^{n_{k-1}} \lambda_{k-1}^j + \lambda_k^i \lambda_{k-1}^{n_{k-1}} \sum_{j=1}^{n_{k-2}} \lambda_{k-2}^j + \cdots$$

$$= \frac{1 - \lambda_k^{i+1}}{1 - \lambda_k} + \lambda_k^i \frac{\lambda_{k-1}(1 - \lambda_{k-1}^{n_{k-1}})}{1 - \lambda_{k-1}} + \lambda_k^i \frac{\lambda_{k-1}^{n_{k-1}}\lambda_{k-2}(1 - \lambda_{k-2}^{n_{k-2}})}{1 - \lambda_{k-2}} + \cdots. \quad (A.5)$$

To compute total sales in period k we have

$$S_k(\tau) = \sum_{i=0}^{n_k-1} S(t_i, t_{i+1}) = c_1\tau + \frac{c_2 q}{\alpha}(1 - e^{-\alpha\tau_k}) \sum_{i=0}^{n_k-1} F_{i+1}. \quad (A.6)$$

$$\sum_{i=0}^{n_k-1} F_{i+1} = \sum_{i=0}^{n_k-1}\left(\frac{1 - \lambda_k^{i+1}}{1 - \lambda_k} \right) + \lambda_k^i\left[\frac{\lambda_{k-1}(1 - \lambda_{k-1}^{n_{k-1}})}{1 - \lambda_{k-1}} + \frac{\lambda_{k-1}^{n_{k-1}}\lambda_{k-2}(1 - \lambda_{k-2}^{n_{k-2}})}{1 - \lambda_{k-2}} + \cdots \right]$$

$$= \frac{1}{1 - \lambda_k}\left[n_k - \frac{\lambda_k(1 - \lambda_k^{n_k})}{1 - \lambda_k} + (1 - \lambda_k^{n_k})\gamma_{k-1} \right]$$

where

$$\gamma_{k-1} = \frac{\lambda_{k-1}(1 - \lambda_{k-1}^{n_{k-1}})}{1 - \lambda_{k-1}} + \lambda_{k-1}^{n_{k-1}}\gamma_{k-2}, \qquad k = 1, 2, \ldots. \quad (A.7)$$

Thus, the final sales equation is:

$$S_k(\tau) = c_1\tau + \frac{c_2 q}{\alpha}\frac{(1 - e^{-\alpha\tau_k})}{1 - \lambda_k}\left[n_k - \frac{\lambda_k(1 - \lambda_k^{n_k})}{1 - \lambda_k} + (1 - \lambda_k^{n_k})\gamma_{k-1} \right] \quad (A.8)$$

where $\lambda_k = (1-q)e^{-\alpha\tau_k}$, $\tau_k = \tau/n_k$ and γ_{k-1} is defined in equation (A.7).

Appendix B—Approximation to Model When q Is Small

The sales equation is

$$S_k(\tau) = c_1\tau + \frac{c_2 q}{\alpha}\frac{(1 - e^{-\alpha\tau_k})}{1 - \lambda_k}\left[n_k - \frac{\lambda_k(1 - \lambda_k^{n_k})}{1 - \lambda_k} + (1 - \lambda_k^{n_k})\gamma_{k-1} \right] \quad (B.1)$$

1004   ROBERT C. BLATTBERG AND ABEL P. JEULAND

where

$$\gamma_{k-1} = \lambda_{k-1}^{n_{k-1}}\gamma_{k-2} + \frac{\lambda_{k-1}(1 - \lambda_{k-1}^{n_{k-1}})}{1 - \lambda_{k-1}} .$$

If q is small, we can approximate $S_k(\tau)$ as follows.

First, let $c_2 q = \beta$ and assume when q is small, β is still nonzero. Because c_2 is expected to be large, even if q is small, $c_2 q$ is still going to be large. Next, note that $\lambda_k = (1 - q)e^{-\alpha\tau/n_k} \doteq e^{-\alpha\tau/n_k}$ when q is small. If $\alpha\tau/n_k$ is close to zero (large number of insertions per measurement period) then

$$\lambda_k \doteq (1 - \alpha\tau/n_k). \tag{B.2}$$

Also,

$$1 - \frac{e^{-\alpha\tau/n_k}}{1 - \lambda_k} \doteq 1.$$

When q is small,

$$1 - \lambda_k^{n_k} = 1 - \left((1 - q)e^{-\alpha\tau/n_k}\right)^{n_k} = 1 - a^{-\alpha\tau}. \tag{B.3}$$

Finally, using (B.2)

$$\frac{\lambda_k}{1 - \lambda_k} \doteq \frac{1 - \alpha\tau/n_k}{\alpha\tau/n_k} = \frac{n_k}{\alpha\tau} . \tag{B.4}$$

Substituting (B.2), (B.3) and (B.4) into (B.1) we have

$$S_k(\tau) = c_1\tau + \frac{\beta}{\alpha}\left[n_k - \left[\frac{n_k}{\alpha\tau}(1 - e^{-\alpha\tau}) \right] + \frac{(1 - e^{-\alpha\tau})^2}{\alpha\tau} n_{k-1} \right.$$
$$\left. + \frac{(1 - e^{-\alpha\tau})^2}{\alpha\tau} \sum_{j=1}^{\infty} (n_{k-1-j})e^{-\alpha j\tau} \right].[11] \tag{B.5}$$

[11] This research has been funded in part by National Science Foundation Grant SOC73-05547. The authors would like to thank Robert Dolan, Darral Clarke and Subrata Sen for their comments.

References

1. Bass, F. M., "The Data Interval Bias, Simultaneous Causality, and the Estimation of Advertising-Sales Relationships from Annual Data," Working Paper, Purdue University, 1980.
2. —— and Clarke, D. G., "Testing Distributed Lag Models of Advertising Effect," *J. Marketing Res.*, Vol. 9 (1972), pp. 298–308.
3. —— and Pilon, T. L., "A Stochastic Brand Choice Framework for Econometric Modelling of Time Series Market Share Behavior," Working Paper, Purdue University, 1979.
4. Clarke, D. G., "Econometric Measurement of the Duration of Advertising Effects on Sales," *J. Marketing Res.*, Vol. 13 (1976), pp. 345–357.
5. Lambin, Jean-Jacques, *Advertising, Competition and Market Conduct: A Statistical Investigation of Western European Countries*, North-Holland, Amsterdam, 1975.
6. Ludish, L. M., "Empirical Studies on Individual Responses to Exposure Patterns," *J. Marketing Res.*, Vol. 8 (1971), pp. 212–218.
7. Palda, K., *The Measurement of Cumulative Advertising Effects*, Prentice-Hall, Englewood Cliffs, N.J., 1964.

8. SCHMALENSEE, R., *The Economics of Advertising*, North-Holland, Amsterdam, 1972.
9. THEIL, H., *Principles of Econometrics*, Wiley, 1971, pp. 392–396.
10. WINDAL, P. M. AND WEISS, D. L., "An Iterative GLS Procedure for Estimating the Parameters of Models with Autocorrelated Errors Using Data Aggregated Over Time," *J. Business*, Vol. 53 (1980). pp. 415–424.
11. ZELLNER, A. AND GEISEL, M. S., "Analysis of Distributed Lag Models, with Applications to Consumption Function Estimation," Paper presented to European Meeting of the Econometric Society, 1968, pp. 415–424.
12. ZIELSKE, H. A., "The Remembering and Forgetting of Advertising," *J. Marketing*, Vol. 23 (1959), pp. 239–243.

INSTITUTIONAL MEMBERS

Ⓒ 1995 American Statistical Association   Journal of Business & Economic Statistics, July 1995, Vol. 13, No. 3

Modeling the Distribution of Price Sensitivity and Implications for Optimal Retail Pricing

Byung-Do Kim
Graduate School of Industrial Administration, Carnegie Mellon University, Pittsburgh, PA   15213

Robert C. Blattberg
Kellogg Graduate School of Management, Northwestern University, Evanston, IL   60201

Peter E. Rossi
Graduate School of Business, University of Chicago, Chicago, IL   60637

This article focuses on the distribution of price sensitivity across consumers. We employ a random-coefficient logit model in which brand-specific intercepts and price-slope coefficients are allowed to vary across households. The model is estimated with panel data for two product categories. The implications of the estimated model are deduced through an optimal retail pricing analysis that combines the panel data with chain-level cost figures. We test parametric distributional assumptions using semiparametric density estimates based on series expansions.

KEY WORDS: Heterogeneity; Optimal pricing; Random-coefficient logit.

Marketing researchers have long recognized that differences among consumers play an important role in the development of pricing policy and the positioning of consumer products. Consumer preferences or perceived quality of different brands within a product category are critical in determining the pricing of existing brands as well as in planning the introduction of new brands. In addition to quality perceptions, the distribution of reservation prices for a given level of perceived quality, or the *price sensitivity* of consumers, is also fundamental to the pricing decision. Traditional *category-management* models do not incorporate consumer heterogeneity [see Blattberg and Neslin (1990) for a brief discussion of category-management models]. The goal of this article is to demonstrate the importance of proper modeling of consumer heterogeneity in the context of the pricing problem.

The availability of detailed household panel data combined with the application of econometric methods for handling unobserved heterogeneity has fostered a rapidly growing literature in marketing. Table 1 summarizes the models for heterogeneity and estimation methods used in the choice literature. In the choice-model context, Guadagni and Little (G&L) (1983) were among the first to recognize that traditional demographic variables were not sufficient to explain the different patterns of product loyalty observed in household panel data. Their solution is to introduce a "loyalty" variable, which has the effect of making the intercepts of a logit model vary according to the past purchase history of the household. The G&L approach has been adopted by many in the choice field. Kamakura and Russell (1989) used a finite-mixture random-coefficient approach to modeling heterogeneity that has also attracted a large following in the choice literature. Chintagunta, Jain, and Vilcassim (1991) reviewed

many parametric approaches to intercept heterogeneity and compared these to a nonparametric approach. Recently, researchers are experimenting with models in which the slopes of the price variable, as well as the intercepts, are household specific. Allenby and Lenk (1994), McCulloch and Rossi (1994), and Gonul and Srinivasan (1993) implemented choice models in which both the intercepts and the slopes vary according to some joint distribution over households. Table 1 summarizes some of the key works in the heterogeneity literature.

Although the recent literature focuses on methods for estimation of random-coefficient choice models, there has not been a careful assessment of the importance of heterogeneity and, in particular, slope heterogeneity, for actual marketing decisions. Allenby and Rossi (1991) were among the first to use a retailer pricing problem as a means of comparison of alternative choice models, but they did not consider the impact of incorporating heterogeneity. Vilcassim and Chintagunta (1992) discussed the problem of optimal retail pricing in a model with intercept heterogeneity but made no assessment of the importance of heterogeneity in terms of profits or optimal prices. Gupta (1993) extended the model of Vilcassim and Chintagunta to include slope heterogeneity and concentrated on deriving optimal dynamic price discount schedules. Again, he did not evaluate the substantive importance of incorporating heterogeneity in the model in terms of its effects on the dynamic schedule of optimal prices. While he emphasized the dynamic problem of choosing a promotional or discounting schedule over time, our work focused on the problem of choosing the regular price level against which a schedule of discounts of the sort derived by Gupta can be applied.

292   Journal of Business & Economic Statistics, July 1995

Table 1. *Heterogeneity in Choice Modeling:*
Summary of the Literature

Study	Heterogeneity type	Distributional model
Guadagni and Little (1983)	Intercept	None. Weighted average past purchases
Kamakura and Russell (1989)	Intercept/slope	Discrete mixture
Chintagunta et al. (1991)	Intercept	Discrete mixture
Rossi and Allenby (1993)	Intercept/slope	Bayesian fixed effect
Allenby and Lenk (1994)	Intercept/slope	Bayesian random coefficient logistic regression
McCulloch and Rossi (1994)	Intercept/slope	Bayesian random coefficient multinominal probit
Gonul and Srinivasan (1993)	Intercept/slope	Random-coefficient logit

A point of departure for our analysis is the use of the model to solve an optimal-retail-pricing problem. We use cost data obtained from a large Chicago grocery chain to solve for profit-maximizing regular (shelf) retail prices. In addition to providing insights into the optimality of the existing retail pricing system, the optimal-pricing analysis provides a useful model-evaluation tool.

We also make several methodological contributions. In the application of random-coefficient models in marketing, it is common to assume a specific parametric form for the distribution of coefficients across households. We employ a seminonparametric density estimator due to Gallant and Nychka (1987) to check our assumption of a lognormal slope distribution of the price coefficient. It is also common to restrict analysis to a small subset of the total number of households in the panel. Frequently, the sample of households is restricted to households who have made over a certain number of purchases in the product category (particularly for studies that employ a G&L loyalty measure). Kim and Rossi (1994) demonstrated a strong bias from including only households with high volume or frequency of purchase. In our continuous random-coefficient approach, it is not necessary to restrict the sample to households with long purchase histories, and we use the full sample of over 3,000 households.

The organization of the article is as follows: Section 1 introduces the model and lays out the statistical specification, Section 2 discusses the data and parameter estimates, Section 3 discusses optimal retail pricing, Section 4 discusses methodological issues, and Section 5 provides some conclusions.

1. MODEL AND STATISTICAL SPECIFICATION

To formulate pricing and positioning strategies, we must first develop and estimate a demand system for the items under consideration. At the lowest level of Universal Product Code (UPC) aggregation, the average supermarket contains some 25,000 to 40,000 items. It is common, therefore, to limit analysis to groups of similar or highly substitutable brands. There is an implicit assumption that groups of similar products are weakly separable in the household utility function; this reduces the size of the demand-system parameterization. In addition, the panel data commonly available to marketing researchers are only available for a few product categories.

The demand for a category or group of brands of a given product (e.g., different sizes and brands of canned tunafish) can be broken into two components. The substitutability between brands in this given category and other products will determine the overall category demand (sometimes termed "category expansion" in the marketing literature) and the substitutability among brands in the category. The substitutability of brands in the category is modeled by brand-choice or market-share models. In this article, we will focus on modeling heterogeneity in the brand-choice portion of the category-demand model. In many categories, such as the ketchup category considered later, the quantity-choice decision is not critical because most consumers buy only one unit; it is the brand-choice and category-purchase decisions that are most important. Even for the categories in which multiple units are purchased, price plays much more of a role in the brand-choice decision than in the category-purchase decision (see Chiang 1991).

We follow the standard random-utility framework introduced by McFadden (1973) to formulate a household-level choice model. To fix the notation and clarify the sources of randomness, we will briefly review this approach. If we assume that the household subutility function over the brands in the product category is linear with marginal utility of brand j $\exp(\psi_j)$, then the choice model is derived from the first-order conditions, and we choose brand j iff $\exp(\psi_j)/p_j \geq \exp(\psi_m)/p_m$ for $m = 1, 2, \ldots, J$ (J brands in the category); p_j is the price of brand j.

To develop an econometric specification, an error term is introduced into the marginal utility of brand j. We write the marginal utility of consumer i $(i = 1, \ldots, I)$ for brand j $(j = 1, \ldots, J)$ on purchase occasion k $(k = 1, \ldots, K_i)$ as $u_{ijk} = \exp(\psi_{ij})\exp(\varepsilon_{ijk})$. The marginal utility constant ψ_{ij} varies across consumers as well as brands, reflecting different levels of intrinsic brand preference for different households. It is important to differentiate between randomness induced by differences between households that are unobservable to the data analyst and randomness across purchase occasions for the same household. The error term, ε_{ijk}, should be viewed as representing factors affecting purchase behavior beyond the included price variable *conditional* on the values of household-specific parameters. Later we will introduce a random-coefficient specification that will capture variation across households in ψ and other key parameters.

As is well known, the distribution of the error terms will determine the functional form of these probabilities. With the errors assumed to be iid as the Type I extreme value, we obtain a standard logit specification with slopes and intercepts that vary across households:

$$P_{ik}(j) = \frac{\exp(\psi'_{ij} - 1/\sigma_i \ln p_{ijk})}{\Sigma_m \exp(\psi'_{im} - 1/\sigma_i \ln p_{imk})}.$$

Note that the ψ' are normalized intercepts, $\psi'_{ij} = \psi_{ij}/\sigma_i$; σ_i is the scale parameter for the error term for household i; σ_i represents the relative size of the unobservable component of the ith household's behavior to that determined by the intercept parameters, ψ'_{ij}, and prices. We can interpret this term by writing the price coefficients as $\beta = -1/\sigma_i$. Households that are influenced primarily by price and not by other considerations will have a low value of σ_i and a very large (negative) price coefficient, which will make them very sensitive to price changes.

To summarize, we have now specified and interpreted the parameters of a logit model with intercepts and a price coefficient that vary across households:

$$P_{ik}(j) = \frac{\exp(\psi'_{ij} + \beta_i \ln p_{ijk})}{\Sigma_m \exp(\psi'_{im} + \beta_i \ln p_{imk})}. \tag{1}$$

The role of ψ' parameters is to allow for different patterns of brand preference across consumers, whereas the price coefficients allow for differences in price sensitivity.

To model the heterogeneity in the parameters of the household logit model given by (1), we adopt a random-coefficient framework (e.g., see Heckman 1982). In this approach, each household is viewed as obtaining its parameter vector $(\psi_{ij}, j = 1, \ldots, J, \beta_i)$ as a draw from some superpopulation distribution. The form of the heterogeneity distribution is the key modeling decision in random-coefficient models. For any reasonable number of brands, this J-dimensional distribution ($J - 1$ intercepts and one slope coefficient) can be quite complex and highly parameterized. It is common, therefore, to restrict the dimensionality of the problem by either eliminating heterogeneity in some of the parameters or simplifying the structure of the multivariate distribution.

Our approach is to build a parsimonious random-coefficient model that captures the essential features of household behavior without the introduction of many potentially poorly identified parameters. We will justify the exact choice of our model specification by examination of the purchase patterns in our data and by comparison to less restricted models. Three key assumptions are made in the development of our random-coefficient model: (1) The slope and intercepts are assumed to be independent, (2) the negative of the price-sensitivity parameter is assumed to be lognormally distributed [i.e., the price-sensitivity parameter, β, is parameterized as $\beta = -\exp(\gamma), \gamma \sim N(\mu, \sigma)$], and (3) heterogeneity in the intercept is restricted to a one-dimensional discrete random variable. Each of the intercepts ψ_{ij} is parameterized in terms of the loyalty-shifter variable. We assume that loyalty patterns are of two "types," A and B; for example, A is oil and B is water:

$$\psi'_{ij} = \psi'_j + \tau_i D_j, \tag{2}$$

where D_j is an indicator variable that switches on if brand j is of the certain key loyalty type and τ_i is the random draw for household i from the loyalty heterogeneity distribution $\tau_i \sim$ iid f.

Before making these assumptions, we experimented extensively with fixed-effects or individual logit models fit to households with relatively long purchase histories. We found

evidence from these individual logit coefficient estimates to support the first assumption of independence. From both scatterplots and correlation analysis, we could detect no relationship at all between the slope and intercepts. (We constructed a sample of households with 10 or more purchases and for which the individual-level estimates exist. This leaves a sample of 225 households. The correlation between the intercepts and slope for these estimates is .00091.) For a sample of 100 households, Allenby and Lenk (1992) found only weak evidence of correlation. [Allenby and Lenk (1994) allowed for price, display, and feature effects to be correlated with three intercept terms. Of a total of nine covariance terms, only one has any appreciable mass away from 0. Allenby and Lenk did not, however, compute the posterior distribution of the correlation coefficient so that it is difficult to gauge the strength of their evidence against the assumption of zero correlation.]

Allenby and Lenk (1994), McCulloch and Rossi (1994), and Gonul and Srinivasan (1993) assumed that the price coefficient is normally distributed. Given the overwhelming demand theoretic arguments and empirical evidence that price coefficient must be negative, we decided instead to employ a reflected lognormal distribution that is only defined over negative values. Our assumption of lognormality is strongly supported by nonparametric density estimation methods applied to our data as shown in Section 4.1.

Our third assumption concerning the nature of heterogeneity in the intercept or quality perception terms deserves further discussion. We exploit certain observed patterns of loyalty that characterize the data. For example, in the tuna category, there is strong loyalty to form [e.g., households are loyal to the form in which canned tuna is packed (in oil or water) not to brands]. In the ketchup category, only one national brand earns any appreciable degree of loyalty. Thus, there is only one major dimension in quality perceptions along which households differ. We model this by including a "type"-shifter variable into the logit model and by allowing this variable to be random across households. We believe that this approach captures the salient features of intercept heterogeneity without the introduction of many parameters. In addition, the form of intercept heterogeneity we adopt is easily interpretable from the marketing perspective. Section 4.2 provides a comparison to an unrestricted model of intercept heterogeneity that supports these views.

Under these assumptions, the likelihood for a sample of households given in the following equation involves averaging each household likelihood over the joint distribution of τ and γ. In the equation, ψ' is the vector of the $J - 1$ identified intercepts:

$$L(\psi', q_A, q_B, \mu, \sigma)$$
$$= \sum_{i=1}^{I} \log l_i(\psi', q_A, q_B, \mu, \sigma)$$
$$= \sum_{i=1}^{I} \log \left[\int_{-\infty}^{\infty} \int_{-\infty}^{\infty} \prod_{k=1}^{n_i} \prod_{j=1}^{J} P_{ik}(j \mid \psi', \tau, \gamma)^{y_{ijk}} f \right.$$
$$\left. \times (\tau \mid q_A, q_B)\phi(\gamma \mid \mu, \sigma) d\tau d\gamma \right].$$

Here P_{ik} is defined in (1), $Y_{ijk} = 1$ if brand j is purchased on occasion k, and $\phi(\ )$ is the normal density function; n_i is the number of purchase occasions for household i.

In our application, f is a discrete distribution that puts all of its mass on the points q_A and q_B with p as the probability of value q_A. To identify the model, $E(\tau_i)$ should be 0, leaving ψ_j as the mean of ψ_{ij}. In other words, because the mean value of the intercept for each brand, ψ_j, is separately estimated, we do not require an additional mean parameter for the distribution of τ_i. Since $E(\tau_i) = q_A p + q_B(1 - p) = 0$, $p = q_B/(q_B - q_A)$. Thus, the probability of $\tau_i = q_A$ (or p) can be implicitly defined as a function of q_A and q_B. In addition, p is constrained to be greater than or equal to 0 and less than or equal to 1 in estimation because p is a probability. This constraint on the probability (p) can be achieved by restricting $q_A > 0$ and $q_B < 0$.

2.   DATA AND ESTIMATION RESULTS

2.1   Data

To estimate the price-sensitivity distribution and the perceived quality level of each brand, scanner panel data from A. C. Nielsen on canned tuna and ketchup were used. To facilitate comparisons across categories and to keep the data analysis manageable, we restrict attention to one "everyday low price" chain in Springfield, Missouri. Although the purchase-history files for each household are complete and accurate, there are problems in constructing competitive prices (see Kim 1992 for details).

In both categories, we restrict attention to households who remain in the sample for at least 100 weeks. This was determined from the shopping-occasion file, which lists all shopping trips for the household regardless of whether or not the household made purchases in the product category. Note that this is a very different sample-selection rule from specifying a minimum number of purchase occasions as is common in the scanner literature. Our sample-inclusion rule is free from the choice-based sampling bias that would afflict samples chosen on the basis of the number of purchase occasions [see Narasimhan and Renken (1991) for more discussion on this point]. It is possible, however, that our sample suffers from attrition bias, as discussed by Winer (1983). Comparison of measured demographic variables of the entire population of households with our sample of households who remained in the panel shows negligible differences.

The tunafish market is complex in the sense that tunafish is available in various forms (e.g., water vs. oil, light meat vs. white, etc.) and different sizes (e.g., 6.5 oz., 3.25 oz., 9.25 oz., etc.). Furthermore, for each form and size there are national brands, private labels, and generics. We restrict attention to "light meat 6.5 oz." brands because this type dominates with more than 90% of the market. We will analyze the top four national brands and one store-specific brand for each chain. One reason for including a store brand in our analysis is to obtain a wide dispersion of perceived product quality, which will reduce the variances of estimates of intercept parameters.

Table 2 shows summary statistics for each UPC of canned tuna analyzed. Three "water" brands, Starkist water (SKW),

Table 2.   Summary Statistics for Tuna

	ADP[a]	WAP[b]	MS[c]
SKW[d]	.75	.69	44.2
COSW	.80	.75	16.3
PW	.63	.63	7.7
SKO	.75	.73	17.8
COSO	.78	.70	14.0

NOTE: The total number of purchases is 13,705. The number of households is 3,093. The distribution of number of purchases for the household has a mean of 4.43 and a median of 3; $Q_1 = 1$, $Q_3 = 5$.
[a] ADP (average daily price) represents the daily average shelf price.
[b] WAP (weighted average price) represents the daily average shelf price weighted by daily sales.
[c] MS represents the market share.
[d] SKW is "Starkist water," COSW is "Chicken-of-the-Sea water," PW is "Private Label water," SKO is "Starkist oil," COSO is "Chicken-of-the-Sea oil."

Chicken-of-the-Sea water (COSW), a store-specific private label, and two "oil" brands, Starkist oil (SKO) and Chicken-of-the-Sea oil (COSO), are included in the analysis. The price measures, average daily price (ADP) and weighted average price (WAP), are computed for each UPC. The average daily price is simply the daily average shelf price, and the weighted average price is the daily average price weighted by daily sales. The weighted average price is computed to determine the percentage of sales for a given UPC that are made during a promotional period. For example, compare the average and weighted average prices of SKO and COSO. The ADP of SKO ($.75) is lower than that of COSO ($.78), but the WAP of SKO ($.73) is higher than that of COSO ($.70). This implies that much of the COSO sales are made during promotional periods.

The total number of panelists is over 3,000, and the total number of purchase records is over 13,000 in all chains for canned tuna. The large number of panelists makes it possible to more accurately estimate the price-sensitivity distribution across panelists. Many other studies of household heterogeneity use samples with a much smaller number of households [for example, Chintagunta et al. (1992) used 135 panelists, Gonul and Srinivasan (1993) used 152 households, and Allenby and Lenk (1994) used 100 households]. Only Kamakura and Russell (1989) with 585 households and Rossi and Allenby (1993) with 777 households used a large number of households. The mean number of purchases for each household is four during the observation period (e.g., 120 weeks from February in 1985 to May in 1987). There are many households with only one or two purchase records. The total sample of panelists is used to estimate the model because we are interested in the behavior of all panelists.

In the choice literature and particularly in those studies that employ the G&L loyalty measure, it is common to eliminate households with short purchase histories. Kim and Rossi (1994) demonstrated that there is a strong bias from restricting the analysis to a sample of households with long purchase histories and/or large volume/frequency. In a random-coefficient approach to modeling heterogeneity, it is not necessary to restrict analysis to households with long purchase histories because even households with only one choice observation add information about the distribution of intercepts and slopes in the population of households.

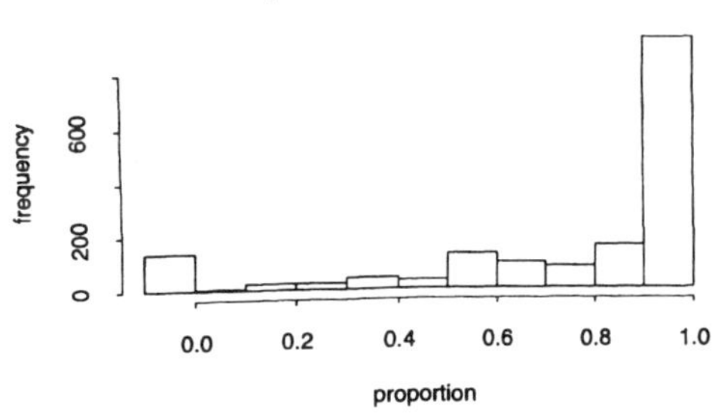

Proportion of Water Purchases in Tuna

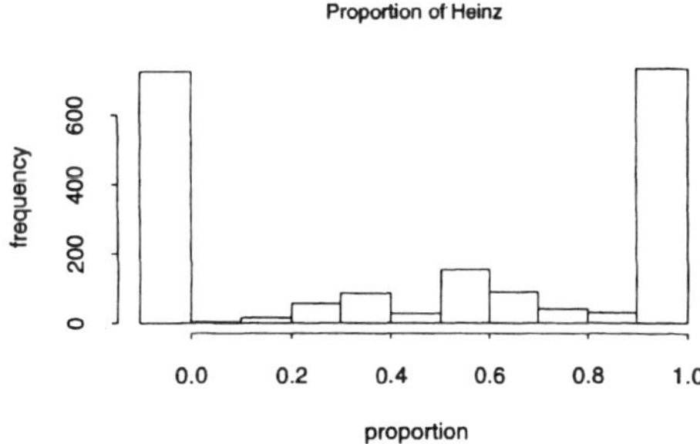

Proportion of Heinz

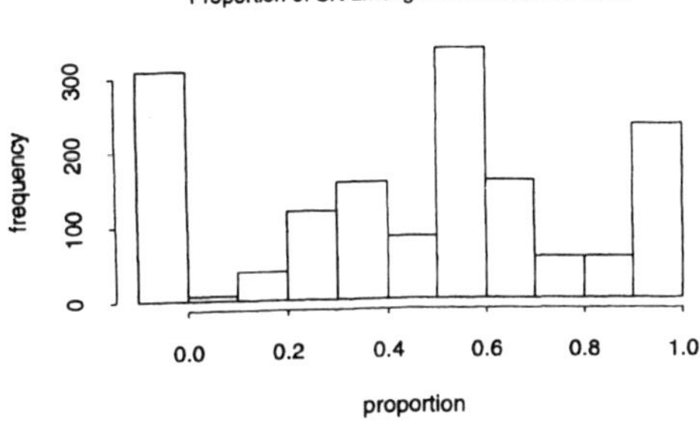

Proportion of SK among Water Tuna Purchases

Proportion of Hunts among Non Heinz Purchases

Figure 1. Form and Brand Loyalty for Tuna.

Figure 2. Brand Loyalty in Ketchup.

The tuna panelists display an interesting pattern of form but not brand loyalty as shown in Figure 1. The top portion of the figure is a histogram of the proportion of water-packed tuna purchases by household. Most households purchase only water-packed tuna, with a small minority buying tuna in oil. The bottom portion of the figure is a histogram of the proportion of purchases of Starkist among water-packed tuna purchases for each household. Very few households are loyal to Starkist. The price of Starkist and Chicken-of-the-Sea are very similar with frequent promotions that cause a great deal of brand switching. Given this pattern of loyalty, it seems most important to capture the differences in tastes for oil- versus water-packed tuna rather than to try to model subpopulations with specific brand loyalty. This justifies our use of an oil/water shifter variable in the specification outlined previously.

Table 3 presents the summary statistics for the ketchup data. Some 2,000 panelists made nearly 5,000 purchases from among four major brands of ketchup. Heinz is by far the market-share leader, with the store brand and Hunts grappling for second place. The differences between WAP and ADP suggest that Heinz is the most promoted brand, whereas the store brand is the least promoted. Due to the low purchase frequency of ketchup, there are very few purchases per household in this category.

Figure 2 is designed to illustrate the key characteristic of ketchup loyalty. We see a significant fraction of households who purchase only Heinz brand ketchup, but there is a good deal of switching among other national brands and the private-label brand. Again, our strategy is to use a Heinz shifter variable to capture heterogeneity in the perceived quality of Heinz. It appears that some fraction of households perceive that Heinz has a significantly higher quality than the other brands.

2.2 Estimation Results

In this section, we discuss the results of fitting our random-coefficient specification to each of the product categories. First, it is useful to document the evidence in the data that supports the assumptions of heterogeneity. As many have noted (see, in particular, Chintagunta et al. 1991), incorporating intercept heterogeneity is very important in improving model fit and explanatory power. It is interesting to ask: What

Table 3. Summary Statistics for Ketchup

Brand	ADP	WAP	MS
Heinz	1.32	1.25	51.0
Hunts	1.36	1.34	20.6
Del Monte	1.43	1.42	5.2
Store brand	.92	.92	23.3

NOTE: All brands are 32 ounces. The total number of purchases is 4,956. The number of households is 1,956. The distribution of the number of purchases for a household has a mean of 2.53 and a median of 2; $Q_1 = 1$, $Q_3 = 3$.

Table 4. Model Selection Criteria

Model	Log-likelihood	Parameters	AIC	BIC
Homogeneous logit	−16,264	5	−16,267	−16,288
Intercept heterogeneity only	−15,201	7	−15,205	−15,234
Slope and intercept heterogeneity	−11,553	8	−11,557	−11,591

is the marginal contribution from accommodating slope heterogeneity as well as intercept heterogeneity?

To address this issue, we fit successive variants of our model to the entire sample of 13,705 tuna purchases. We start with a highly restricted model in which all heterogeneity has been eliminated by restricting all coefficients to be constant across households. We then free up the intercept coefficient by allowing form-loyalty heterogeneity. Finally, we allow both intercept and slope heterogeneity by allowing the variance term in the slope-coefficient distribution to be freely determined by the data. The results are summarized in Table 4. AIC is the Akaike information criterion, AIC = LL − $q/2$, where LL is log-likelihood and q is the number of parameters. BIC is the Bayesian information criterion introduced by Schwarz (1978), BIC = LL − $1/2q \ln(v)$, where v is the degrees of freedom. Unlike the AIC, the BIC is a consistent model-selection criterion. Both the AIC and BIC figures dramatically emphasize the importance of slope heterogeneity. By adding only one parameter to the model, the log-likelihood increases by over 20%. Furthermore, it appears that slope heterogeneity is relatively more important than intercept heterogeneity in this data set because improvement in fit from introducing the slope heterogeneity is approximately four times the improvement from introducing intercept heterogeneity (this finding is robust to the order of introduction of intercept/slope heterogeneity).

The parameter estimates for the tuna category are presented in Table 5. In the tuna specification, the shifter variable is an oil/water indicator variable that takes on two values, q_{oil} and q_{water}. The intercepts are related to this variable as $\psi_{ij} = \psi_j + \tau D_j$, where $D_j = 1$ if the brand is oil packed. The oil constant is estimated at 2.218, and the water constant is set to −.854. Thus, the "oil-loyal" households act as if the intercepts for the oil brands are equal to the estimates +2.218, but the "water-loyal" households add −.854 to the intercepts of oil brands. As mentioned previously, identification restrictions require that the mean of τ be set to 0. This allows us to compute the proportion of oil-loyal households from the values q_{oil} and q_{water}; $p = q_{water}/(q_{water} − q_{oil})$. We can insert the estimates of the oil and water constants into this expression to obtain the maximum likelihood estimate (MLE) of the fraction of oil-loyal households of .28 with a standard error of .013.

The mean and standard deviation of the γ distribution are not particularly interpretable parameters in and of themselves. For this reason, we will use these parameter estimates to compute the implied moments for the price-sensitivity coefficient distributions. The price-sensitivity coefficient $\beta = -\exp(\gamma)$. The mean and standard deviation of the

Table 5. Parameter Estimates for the Tuna Category

	Parameter estimates*
Intercept	
SK water	1.016
	(.019)
COS water	.000
Store water	−1.608
	(.021)
SK oil	−.154
	(.043)
COS oil	−1.125
	(.049)
Gamma distribution	
μ	1.523
	(.026)
σ	.794
	(.027)
Shifter constants	
q_{oil}	2.218
	(.054)
q_{water}	−.854
	(.043)

NOTE: The log-likelihood is −11,326.03, the number of purchases is 11,427, and the number of households is 2,593.
* Standard errors are in parentheses.

distribution of β implied by the estimates of μ and σ are

β (price sensitivity)
Mean   −6.29 (.12)
Std. dev.   5.89 (.14).

The estimated standard deviation of 5.89 shows the dramatic variation from household to household in price sensitivity.

Results for the ketchup category are given in Table 6. In the ketchup specification, we introduce a dummy variable that is a contrast between Heinz and all other brands, $D_j = 1$ if not Heinz, 0 if Heinz. Households who are loyal to Heinz

Table 6. Parameter Estimates for the Ketchup Category

	Parameter estimates*
Intercept	
Heinz	.782
	(.058)
Hunts	.000
Del Monte	−1.139
	(.066)
Private	−2.265
	(.069)
Gamma distribution	
μ	1.715
	(.039)
σ	.618
	(.041)
Shifter constants	
q_{others}	.946
	(.075)
q_{Heinz}	−1.920
	(.146)

NOTE: The log-likelihood is −2,696.29, the number of purchases is 4,956, and the number of households is 1,956.
* Standard errors are in parentheses.

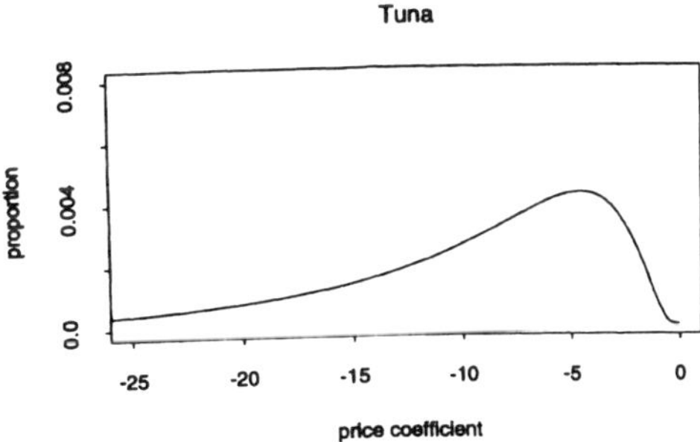

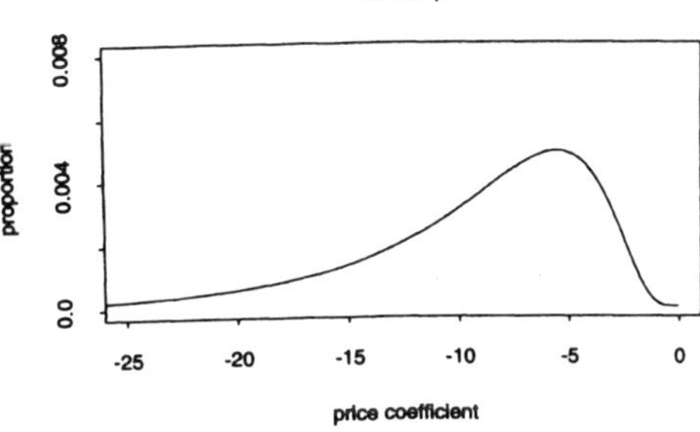

Figure 3.   Price Coefficient Distributions.

subtract an estimated 1.92 from the intercepts of all other brands. The proportion of households who are loyal to Heinz can be inferred from the shifter constants to be .33 with a standard error of .012. Again, we find very substantial price-sensitivity differences across households. The moments of the price-sensitivity distributions are

β (price sensitivity)

Mean	-6.73 (.12)
Std. dev.	4.60 (.22).

Figure 3 shows that the price-sensitivity distributions for the tuna and ketchup categories are quite similar. The high variance of the price-sensitivity distributions is striking, but it remains to be seen if this high degree of heterogeneity affects the outcome of key marketing decisions such as product-category pricing. In the next section, we explore the implications of the heterogeneity distribution for the pricing problem.

2.3 Price Elasticities

One important way of summarizing the effect of price is to compute the price-elasticity matrix. This matrix shows all own- and cross-price elasticities between the set of brands. Note that we define elasticity as the derivative to choice probability with respect to the logarithm of price with all other prices set to their sample averages. Matrices for the homogeneous and heterogeneous logit models are

Homogeneous logit

	skw	cosw	pw	sko	coso
skw	-2.0	.57	.38	.74	.30
cosw	1.8	-3.2	.38	.74	.30
pw	1.8	.57	-3.43	.74	.30
sko	1.8	.57	.38	-3.07	.30
coso	1.8	.57	.38	.74	-3.5

Heterogeneous logit

	skw	cosw	pw	sko	coso
kw	-3.6	.45	.87	1.8	.50
cosw	1.7	-4.2	.55	1.54	.45
pw	2.8	.46	-6.6	2.7	.60
sko	1.7	.38	.79	-3.46	.60
coso	1.5	.36	.58	1.96	-4.44.

Of course, the homogeneous logit elasticities exhibit the well-known proportional-draw property, which implies that the elasticities are proportional to market shares. The heterogeneous logit model displays a richer pattern of cross-elasticities and generally larger own-price elasticities. The implications of these elasticities for the optimal pricing decision are not straightforward. For example, one cannot use a simple elasticity-based markup rule. In Section 3, we pose a stylized version of the category-pricing problem and show how heterogeneity affects the optimal-pricing problem.

3. OPTIMAL RETAIL PRICING

3.1 The Optimal-Pricing Problem Under Heterogeneity

The growing literature on household heterogeneity has focused mainly on the important methodological issues of the form of the heterogeneity distribution and estimation methods. In this section, we demonstrate both the importance of heterogeneity and the usefulness of our random-coefficient model by applying the model to a version of the retailer's optimal pricing problem.

Recently, some researchers have started to examine the retailer problem using models fitted to panel data. In a model without slope heterogeneity, Allenby and Rossi (1991) posed a highly stylized retailer problem as a method of evaluating a nonhomothetic choice model. Vilcassim and Chintagunta (1992) considered pricing problems with household heterogeneity in "intrinsic brand preferences" (intercepts) and in the household consumption rates but not in price sensitivity. Furthermore, the main emphasis of their paper was on promotional issues such as duration and depth of deals rather than on regular shelf pricing, which is our focus. None of the preceding works used actual cost data but, instead, made assumptions about the size of national-brand and private-label margins.

The general problem of determining an optimal retailer strategy must involve many possible policy tools including choice of regular or long-run average prices, choice of promotional depth and frequency, optimal pass-through of manufacturer promotions, feature and display policy, and reaction to policies of competing chains. A full analysis of this problem would require a complex demand model of consumer behavior that would take into account consumer expectations of future promotions, couponing, and inventory decisions coupled with a complex model of the supply side that would include exit and entry of retailers and strategic determination of pricing policies. A fully articulated and reliable model of these complex features of the retailer problems does not exist and would have very formidable data requirements once developed.

To keep the problem of optimal pricing manageable, we have made some simplifying assumptions. We focus on the optimal choice of regular or shelf prices conditional on a given promotional strategy. We assume that promotional policies such as the depth and frequency of deals, as well as feature/display use, remain in place while the level of the various price series is varied to maximize retailer profits. In discussion with major grocery retailers, the retailer conveys some degree of confidence in his promotional strategy but often has little idea of how to set shelf prices for each item within categories. One of the reasons relative pricing within a category has been extremely problematic is that retailers do not know how willing consumers are to pay for brands with higher perceived quality and how to price their private label relative to national brands.

We did not include promotional variables such as display and feature-ad dummies because the principal aim of the article was to address the issue of the substantive importance of heterogeneity for regular or long-run pricing issues. That is, we think of the optimal-regular-pricing problem as holding the promotional timing and discount schedule fixed and varying the long-run price. As such, our estimate of the marginal distribution of the price coefficient is perfectly valid for use in the analysis. In our opinion, there is a good deal of confusion regarding the problem of omitted-variable bias in marketing applications. For example, consider the world with no heterogeneity. There are those who would say that the price coefficient in a model without display/feature is inconsistent because of the omitted and correlated variables. The coefficient consistently estimates the marginal impact of a change in price *given* the joint distribution of price and the other variables. Thus, when the promotional policy is unchanged, this is the appropriate coefficient to use to predict the response to price. If, on the other hand, we were deriving an optimal promotional policy, we would need to add these variables.

The retailer's optimal-pricing problem is posed as a category-management problem in which we focus on determining the prices within only one category at a time. For a given product category, the retailer's problem of finding the optimal set of prices for each brand can be written as

$$\text{maximize}_{\{p_1,\ldots,p_J\}} \quad \pi = \Sigma_j p_j - c_j) D_j (p_s, s = 1, \ldots, J), \quad (3)$$

where p_j is the unit price of brand j $(j = 1, \ldots, J)$, c_j is the retailer's unit buying cost of brand j, and $D_j (p_s, s = 1, \ldots, J)$ is the number of units demanded for brand j, which is a function of the price of all brands in the category.

The solution to the retailer's problem requires cost estimates. Unfortunately, ERIM scanner-panel data does not provide information on the wholesale cost of each brand. Therefore, we have calculated the cost of each brand using the margin data supplied by the University of Chicago/Dominick's Finer Food project. We restrict our attention to the tuna category because cost data are more readily available for that category. All 85 stores of Dominick's carry all four national brands (e.g., Starkist oil and water, Chicken-of-the-Sea oil and water) we are interested in and a private-label brand. The average (percentage) margin for each brand is computed across 85 stores and the 115 weeks of available data. These average percentage margins for five brands are used to compute the cost of each brand in Springfield (Chain 1). In other words, we assume that the percentage margin of each brand in Springfield (Chain 1) is the same as the average percentage margin of each brand in Dominick's.

To completely specify the retailer profit function, we couple the choice-model system with a simple log-linear category-volume model to specify the demand system facing the retailer. We assume that the unit demand of brand j is equal to the category demand, which is a function of prices of all brands times the market share of brand j. That is, $D_j(p) = \text{CD}(p) \, \text{MS}_j(p)$, where CD is the category unit demand and MS_j represents the expected market share of brand j. Both the CD and MS are functions of the price of all brands.

As an alternative to the aggregate category demand function approach just taken, we could have adopted the Chiang (1991) "outside" good model as a starting micro-model and then aggregate. We choose to use an approach that couples the sort of model that can be fit by the retailer using store-level scanner data with our panel-calibrated logit. This is simple to implement and easily interpretable. Moreover, a simple implementation of the Chiang approach assumes that the reason households do not purchase in the category in one week versus the next is that the prices for *all* brands in the category exceed their reservation price for the product. It seems to us that this misses important aspects of the problem, including consumer stockpiling and speculation about the future course of prices. For these reasons, we choose to keep the analysis simple and use an aggregate category-demand model.

To estimate the category demand function, CD, we assume that the unit category demand at week t is a function of the prices of all five brands at week t. Then, we compute the total weekly unit sales of all five brands and the weekly average price of each brand using the purchases by all panelists in Springfield (Chain 1).

The expected market shares, $\text{MS}_j(p)$, are computed by aggregating our random-coefficient logit model. We integrate the choice system over the heterogeneity distribution conditional on our estimates of the heterogeneity-distribution parameters: $\text{MS}_j(p) = \int \text{MS}_j(p \mid \theta) f(\theta \mid \widehat{\eta}) \, d\theta$, where θ is the vector of both the intercept and slope parameters and $\widehat{\eta}$ is the vector of estimated hyperparameters of the heterogeneity distribution.

We can also solve the retailer's problem using a homogeneous or constant-coefficient logit model to compute the expected market shares in the profit function. This provides an important substantive metric with which we can measure the importance of heterogeneity.

3.2 Optimal Pricing in the Tuna Category

We first consider the solution to the optimal pricing exercise for the tuna category. The estimated category-demand (CD) model is given by

$$\ln CD_t = \underset{(.30)}{3.95} - \underset{(.30)}{2.07} \ln p_{SK,t} - \underset{(.31)}{1.70} \ln p_{COS,t}$$
$$- \underset{(.55)}{.35} \ln p_{PW,t}, \quad R^2 = .43; \quad T = 110,$$

(standard errors in parentheses). Notice that in the estimation of the preceding CD function, the price of each of the five brands is not used but instead the share-weighted average prices are used for SK and COS because the correlation between the price of SK oil and SK water (and COS oil and COS water) is very high.

In the profit-maximization problem, optimal prices are determined by the trade-off among the category-demand effect, the own-demand effect, and the cross-demand effect. The price of brand j will influence the category unit demand by the CD function, while it influences the sales of other brands by the function $MS(j)$, which is involved in the logit function. The profit function of the retailer (3) is highly nonlinear and the maximization problem does not have a closed-form solution.

Table 7 shows the results of the optimal-pricing exercise. The left panel of the table shows the average price and the assumed margin (from the Dominick's data). The middle panel shows the optimization results for a homogeneous logit model in which all parameters are constant across households. The column marked "Initial MS" shows the market share of each brand computed by evaluating the choice system at the average prices in the ERIM data. The column labeled "Opt MS" presents the market share computed by evaluating the choice probabilities at the optimal set of prices. The last column gives the new margins assuming that the costs do not change as a result of the pricing exercise. The right panel of the table shows the results of an optimal-pricing solution that assumes that the market-demand system is an aggregated heterogeneous logit model. At the bottom of the table, the expected profit reported in dollars per week for our panel of

households is given under the three sets of prices and provides a measure of the importance of heterogeneity.

The optimal prices computed under the assumption of a heterogeneous model differ markedly from the optimal prices from a homogeneous logit specification. The homogeneous optimal prices are much more extreme and have the retailer dramatically increasing the price of the water brand with the highest intercept (SK) and lowering the COS oil brand price to a level at which there is almost no margin. On the other hand, the heterogeneous-model optimal prices are much more reasonable. We see a lowering of the oil brand prices and a more moderate increase in the SK water price. The difference between the homogeneous and heterogeneous optimal prices is accounted for by underestimation of the price-sensitivity coefficient in models that do not properly account for heterogeneity. The homogeneous logit model-price coefficient estimate is -3.8, which is much lower than the mean of the price-sensitivity distribution in the heterogeneous and model (-6.3). Retailers who fail to take into account heterogeneity will underestimate the extent of switching behavior induced by price changes.

Based on the profit metric, the current prices are far from optimal, primarily because of the insistence on pricing the oil- and water-packed versions of the same brand equally. The optimal prices under the heterogeneous model specification produce a 15% higher level of profits. The prices derived under the misspecified homogeneous model are associated with a 5% lower level of profits than is available from the heterogeneous specification. In the intensely competitive retail environment, a change in profitability of even a few per cent is very valuable. Our results suggest, however, that gross pricing errors that are based on incorrect inferences about the "average" or representative consumer can be more important than a fine tuning based on proper modeling of heterogeneity.

3.3 Optimal Pricing in the Ketchup Category

The estimated CD function for the ketchup category is given by

$$\ln CD_t = \underset{(.25)}{4.60} - \underset{(.37)}{2.77} \ln p_{Heinz,t} - \underset{(.35)}{1.15} \ln p_{Hunts,t}$$
$$- \underset{(.54)}{.02} \ln p_{DelM,t} - \underset{(.37)}{.79} \ln p_{Private,t}, \quad R^2 = .38; \quad T = 110.$$

Table 7.   Optimal Retail Pricing: ERIM Tuna Data

| | Current | | Homogeneous logit | | | | Heterogeneous logit | | | |
| | | | Initial | Opt. | Opt. | | Initial | Opt. | Opt. | |
Brands	Price	Margin	MS	MS	price	Margin	MS	MS	price	Margin
SKW	.75	.27	47.4	35.4	.81	.32	47.3	35.7	.79	.30
COSW	.80	.27	15.0	19.2	.73	.21	12.7	18.2	.77	.26
PW	.63	.26	10.0	9.0	.65	.28	13.3	10.1	.64	.27
COSO	.78	.27	8.1	14.3	.61	.06	6.4	12.7	.71	.23
SKO	.75	.27	19.5	22.2	.70	.21	20.4	23.2	.70	.21
Profits	$31.71			$34.50				$36.37		

Table 8. *Optimal Retail Pricing: ERIM Ketchup Data*

Brands	Current		Homogeneous logit				Heterogeneous logit			
	Price	Margin	Initial MS	Opt. MS	Opt. price	Margin	Initial MS	Opt. MS	Opt. price	Margin
Heinz	1.32	.27	47.0	54.0	1.20	.20	45.0	47.0	1.30	.30
Hunts	1.36	.27	20.0	23.0	1.24	.20	20.0	26.0	1.25	.24
DelM	1.43	.27	5.0	2.0	1.56	.33	5.0	3.0	1.68	.37
Private	.92	.27	28.0	21.0	.91	.26	30.0	24.0	.92	.27
Profits	$11.34			$12.32				$12.59		

Table 8 presents the results of the ketchup optimal-pricing exercise in the same format as Table 7 for the canned-tuna category. Again, we see large differences between the optimal prices computed under a homogeneous versus a heterogeneous logit specification. The heterogeneous optimal price for Heinz is much closer to the actual retail price than the optimal price derived under the assumption of homogeneity.

3.4 Heterogeneity Parameter-Sensitivity Analysis

As discussed previously, the role of the μ and σ parameters in determining the shape of the price-sensitivity distribution is difficult to determine without careful analysis. Furthermore, the translation from changes in the price-sensitivity distribution to changes in the optimal-pricing experiment is complicated. To develop an intuition for the role of shape parameters, we perturb μ and σ away from the estimates for the tuna data, plot the resulting price- and quality-sensitivity distributions, and resolve the optimal-pricing problem for each of the new sets of parameter values. Table 9 presents the results of experiments in which the σ parameter is held fixed at the estimated value and μ is changed. The column of the table labeled "A" has a value of μ that is only 50% of the estimated value, whereas the column labeled "C" has a value of μ that is 50% larger than the estimated value. As μ increases from .766 to 2.288, the price-sensitivity distribution shifts to the left with many more households showing a high price sensitivity as shown in the top panel of Figure 4. As the population distribution of price sensitivity shifts toward households with high sensitivity, we should expect that the retailer will not be able to support large price differentials between low- and high-quality brands.

This intuition is supported by the optimal prices shown in Table 9. With large numbers of price-sensitive households (col. C), the difference between national and private label water-packed prices is markedly smaller than the spread for a situation with many more households that are price insensitive.

The bottom panel of Figure 4 shows the results of experiments in which μ is held fixed while σ is varied. Changes in σ affect primarily the dispersion of the price/quality sensitivity distributions with a small effect on the mean level of sensitivity. Increases in the dispersion of price sensitivity that leave the mean relatively unchanged have a much

Table 9. *Sensitivity to Changes in the Shape of the Price-Sensitivity Distribution: Case I: σ Fixed = .782*

Optimal prices	A $.5\mu = .766$	B $1.0\mu = 1.525$	C $1.5\mu = 2.288$
P_{SKW}	.87	.79	.75
P_{COSW}	.75	.77	.75
P_{PW}	.58	.64	.66
P_{SKO}	.67	.70	.71
P_{COSO}	.67	.71	.72

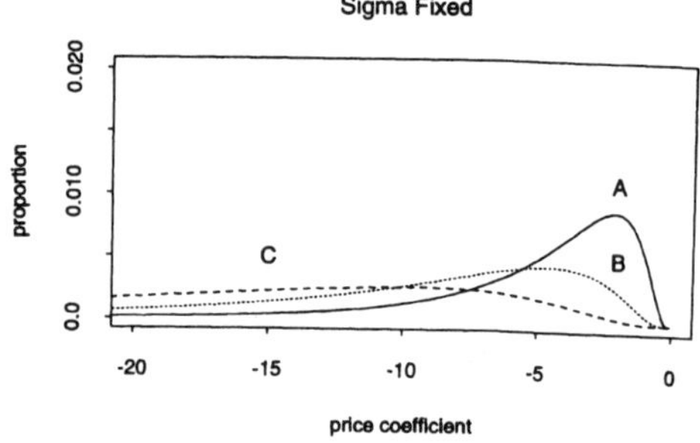

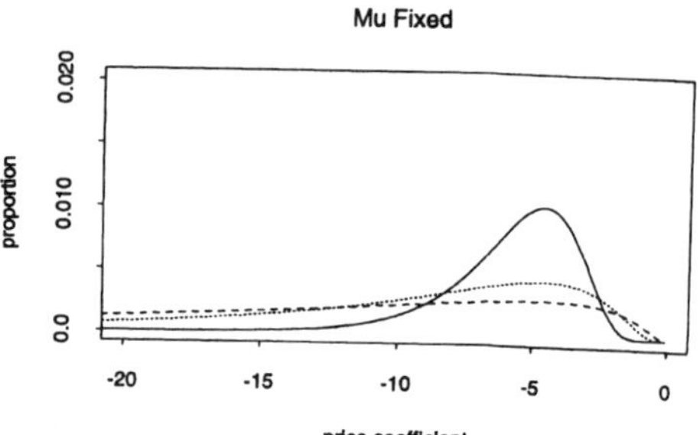

Figure 4. *Effects of Shape Parameters on Price-Sensitivity Distributions.*

Table 10.   *Sensitivity to Changes in the Shape of the Price-Sensitivity Distribution: Case II: μ Fixed = 1.525*

	A $.5\sigma = .391$	B $1.0\sigma = .782$	C $1.5\sigma = 1.173$
P_{SKW}	.79	.79	.78
P_{COSW}	.77	.77	.77
P_{PW}	.63	.64	.65
P_{SKO}	.70	.70	.70
P_{COSO}	.70	.71	.72

smaller effect on the optimal prices than changes in the mean as shown in Table 10. Thus, it appears that the central tendency or location of the price-sensitivity distribution is the key parameter in determining optimal prices. This does not mean that household heterogeneity is not important. As we have shown, models that restrict heterogeneity to the intercepts alone will produce strongly biased estimates of price sensitivity.

Because the parameter estimates used in computing the optimal prices are subject to sampling error, it is very important to assess the role of sampling error in the analysis. If changes in the parameters at the magnitude expected from sampling variation affect the optimal prices, then the results of the optimal-pricing exercise are of little practical use. It is not enough to simply observe that the standard errors are small relative to the parameter estimates. For this reason, we approximated the sampling distribution of the optimal prices by using an approximate simulation method. The vector of optimal prices, p^*, can be viewed as a vector-valued function of the parameters of the choice model, conditional on a given level of prices: $p^* = g(\hat{\theta}; \text{price})$. $g(\,)$ is a function that is only implicitly defined by the optimization problem that produces the optimal prices. Standard asymptotic distribution theory for the MLE allows us to approximate the sampling distribution of the MLE as $\hat{\theta} \sim N(\theta, I_\theta^{-1})$, where I_θ is Fisher's information matrix. We draw from this normal distribution and solve the optimization problem for each draw of $\hat{\theta}$, thereby building up the sampling distribution of p^*. Table 11 summarizes this sampling distribution. We observe that the optimal prices have very small sampling variation and are very insensitive to parameter variation due to sampling error. This insensitivity is undoubtedly due to the high degree of precision of estimation of the random-coefficient distribution parameters that our very large sample of households affords.

Table 11.   *Sampling Distribution of Optimal Prices*

Price	Mean	Std. error
SKW	.785	.0017
COSW	.767	.0012
PW	.641	.0012
SKO	.698	.0021
COSO	.713	.0026

4. METHODOLOGICAL ISSUES AND DIAGNOSTIC CHECKS

4.1 Nonparametric Checks on the Lognormality Assumption

In the analysis reported up to this point, we have assumed that the negative of the price-sensitivity parameter is lognormally distributed across households. We use the lognormal distribution because of its simplicity and flexibility. In addition, the lognormal distribution restricts the price coefficient to be negative. It can be argued, however, that the assumption of normality of $\gamma = \ln(-\beta)$ is arbitrary. It is important to remember that misspecification of the random-mixture distribution is a fundamental problem that can lead to inconsistent parameter estimates and incorrect decisions.

In this section, we check the lognormality assumption using the seminonparametric approach advanced by Gallant and Nychka (1987). They used a series expansion-based estimator to approximate density of γ. They proved that, under very mild regularity conditions, a particular class of series expansion estimators can consistently estimate the unknown density and many functions of the density such as moments, derivatives, and so forth. The difference between the seminonparametric approach (SNP) followed here and the discrete approximations used in the marketing literature (see Chintagunta et al. 1991; Kamakura and Russell 1989) is that we explicitly assume that γ is a continuous random variable with unknown density.

The basic idea of Gallant and Nychka (1987) is to approximate the unknown density by a normal density $\times$ a polynomial, $p(\gamma) \propto \phi(\gamma \mid \mu, \sigma) P_k(\gamma)^2$, where $P_k(\gamma)$ is a kth-order polynomial in γ. The polynomial terms in P_k act to modify the shape of the normal distribution, providing the option of skewness and excess kurtosis. In addition, the SNP density can easily be multimodel, allowing, for example, for the possibility of two groups—one price sensitive and the other price insensitive. The polynomial is squared to enforce positivity of the density. The strategy advocated by Gallant and Nychka (1987) is to keep adding terms to the polynomial part as the sample size increases. The importance of the nonconstant terms in the polynomial part provides a natural method for evaluating the extent of nonnormality in the data.

We implement the following SNP density estimate (We also considered higher-order quartic polynomials in the P_k term of the SNP density estimate and found no evidence of nonnormality.):

$$p(\gamma \mid \mu, \sigma, \delta_0, \delta_1) = k\phi(\gamma \mid \mu, \sigma)$$
$$\times \left[1 + \delta_0((\gamma - \mu)/\sigma) + \delta_1((\gamma - \mu)/\sigma)^2\right]^2,$$

where k is the integrating constant that is a function of σ, δ_0, and δ_1. This specification allows for skewness, excess kurtosis, and bimodality. We insert this new SNP density in the random-coefficient specification outlined in Section 2. That is, we integrate the household likelihood over $p(\gamma \mid \mu, \sigma, \delta_0, \delta_1)$ instead of over the normal density $\phi(\gamma \mid \mu, \sigma)$. One of the advantages of the SNP approximation method is that it lends itself readily to the use of Gauss–Hermite

302   Journal of Business & Economic Statistics, July 1995

Table 12. Comparison to Intercept Finite-Mixture Models

Model: "type"-shifter	Log-likelihood: −11,553	Parameters: 8	AIC: −11,557	BIC: −11,591
Intercept mixture				
2 mass pts.	−11,524	11	−11,530	−11.576
3	−11,510	16	−11,518	−11,586
4	−11,501	21	−11,511	−11,601
5	−11,472	26	−11,485	−11,596
6	−11,468	31	−11,484	−11,615

quadrature methods to perform the integrals necessary to evaluate the likelihood [see Davidian and Gallant (1991) for more on this point].

Using a random subsample of 200 households, we fit both our standard lognormal model and the SNP mixture model. The log-likelihood increases by less than .1%. Conventional likelihood ratio tests for inclusion of the SNP nonnormal terms fail to reject the null hypothesis of normality. Thus, there is no evidence in the data of nonnormality, and we can have a high degree of confidence that the normal assumption for γ is justified.

4.2 Diagnostic Checks on the Form of Intercept Heterogeneity

As discussed in Section 2, we restrict the form of intercept heterogeneity across households to only one key dimension, loyalty to form in the case of tuna and loyalty to one key brand in the case of ketchup. This restriction is based on the observed patterns of loyalty in the data, as depicted in Figures 1–2. As a more formal test of our restricted model of intercept heterogeneity, we compare our model with an unrestricted intercept model in which the distribution over the intercepts is a finite mixture. This unrestricted model is developed from three key assumptions: (1) We retain the assumption that the slope is independent of the intercept, (2) the joint distribution of the $J - 1$ intercepts is approximated by a discrete distribution with a specified number of mass points, and (3) we retain the assumption of lognormality for the quality-sensitivity coefficient. Using the whole sample of 13,705 tuna purchases, our restricted "type"-shifter model is compared to the unrestricted mixture/lognormal model with between two and six mass points for the mixture on the intercepts in Table 12. The less restricted intercept mixture models fit the data slightly better with an .8% higher likelihood value. The intercept mixture models, however, have substantially more parameters. As measured by the BIC criterion, only the two- and three-segment mixture models have a slight edge over our model. It should be emphasized that our "type"-shifter model is not nested in the intercept mixture specification so that it is not possible to perform a standard likelihood ratio test. Our conclusion is that we miss little of importance by using the more restricted specification.

5. CONCLUSIONS

Modeling and measuring consumer heterogeneity alone is not sufficient to help managers price and position their prod-

ucts. We must take a further step by making the estimated models an input into an optimal decision process. In this article, we document a large degree of slope heterogeneity in the panel data and find that this degree of heterogeneity has a material impact on the category pricing decision. We demonstrate how a random-coefficient logit model can be used to derive optimal retail pricing for brands in a product category.

In both product categories considered, there is a great deal of heterogeneity in the price-sensitivity parameter. Previous studies that concentrate on intercept heterogeneity are subject to a large heterogeneity bias in the price-sensitivity parameter. Retailers who fail to take into account heterogeneity in the price-sensitivity parameter will underestimate the extent of switching behavior induced by changes in price and, consequently, obtain suboptimal pricing strategies from the category-profit-maximization problem. We find that the optimal-pricing strategy is more sensitive to movements in the mean of the price-sensitivity distribution than changes in the dispersion of that distribution.

ACKNOWLEDGMENTS

We acknowledge the helpful comments of Greg Allenby, Pradeep Chintagunta, Kris Helsen, and Naufel Vilcassim. We thank Steve Hoch of the Graduate School of Business, University of Chicago, and Dan Nelson of Dominick's Finer Foods for supplying cost data.

[*Received April 1993. Revised January 1995.*]

REFERENCES

Allenby, G. M., and Lenk, P. J. (1994), "Modeling Household Purchase Behavior With Logistic Normal Regression," *Journal of the American Statistical Association*, 89, 1218–1231.

Allenby, G. M., and Rossi, P. E. (1991), "Quality Perception and Asymmetric Switching Between Brands," *Marketing Science*, 10, 185–204.

Blattberg, R. C., and Neslin, S. (1990), *Sales Promotion*, Englewood Cliffs, NJ: Prentice-Hall.

Chintagunta, P. K., Jain, D. C., and Vilcassim, N. J. (1991), "Investigating Heterogeneity in Brand Preferences in Logit Models for Panel Data," *Journal of Marketing Research*, 28, 4, 417–428.

Chiang, J. (1991), "A Simultaneous Approach to the Whether, What and How Much to Buy Questions," *Marketing Science*, 10, 297–315.

Davidian, M., and Gallant, A. R. (1991), "The Nonlinear Mixed Effects Model With a Smooth Random Effects Density," working paper, North Carolina State University, Dept. of Statistics.

Gallant, A. R., and Nychka, D. (1987), "Seminonparametric Maximum Likelihood Estimation," *Econometrica*, 55, 363–390.

Gonul, F., and Srinivasan, K. (1993), "Modeling Unobserved Heterogeneity in Multinominal Logit Models: Methodological and Managerial Issues," *Marketing Science*, 12, 213–229.

Guadagni, P. M., and Little, J. D. C. (1983), "A Logit Model of Brand Choice Calibrated on Scanner Data," *Marketing Science*, 2, 203–238.

Gupta, S. (1993), "A Dynamic Model of Promotional Pricing," working paper, Cornell University, Johnson School of Management.

Heckman, J. (1982), "Statistical Models for the Analysis of Discrete Panel Data," in *Structural Analysis of Discrete Data: With Econometric Applications*, eds. C. Manski and D. McFadden, Cambridge, MA: MIT Press, pp. 114–178.

Kamakura, W. A., and Russell, G. J. (1989), "A Probabilistic Choice Model for Market Segmentation and Elasticity Structure," *Journal of Marketing Research*, 26, 379–390.

Kim, B. (1992), "Household Heterogeneity in the Intensity of Preference for Quality," unpublished Ph.D. dissertation, University of Chicago, Graduate School of Business.

Kim, B., and Rossi, P. E. (1994), "Purchase Frequency, Sample Selection and Price Sensitivity: The Heavy User Bias," *Marketing Letter*, 5, 57–68.

McCulloch, R., and Rossi, P. (1994), "An Exact Likelihood Analysis of the Multinominal Probit Model," *Journal of Econometrics*, 64, 207–240.

McFadden, D. (1973), "Conditional Logit Analysis of Qualitative Choice Behavior," in *Frontiers of Econometrics*, ed. P. Zarembka, New York: Academic Press.

Narasimhan, C., and Renken, T. (1991), "The Representativeness of Panel Members' Purchase Behavior," working paper, Washington University, Olin School of Business.

Rossi, P., and Allenby, G. (1993), "A Bayesian Method of Estimating Household Parameters," *Journal of Marketing Research*, 30, 171–182.

Schwarz, G. (1978), "Estimating the Dimension of a Model," *The Annals of Statistics*, 6, 461–464.

Vilcassim, N., and Chintagunta, P. (1992), "Investigating Retailer Pricing Strategies From Household Scanner Panel Data," working paper, Northwestern University, Dept. of Marketing.

Winer, R. (1983), "Attrition Bias in Econometric Models Estimated With Panel Data," *Journal of Marketing Research*, 20, 177–186.

MARKETING SCIENCE
Vol. 25, No. 5, September–October 2006, pp. 457–476
ISSN 0732-2399 | EISSN 1526-548X | 06 | 2505 | 0457

DOI 10.1287/mksc.1050.0176
©2006 INFORMS

Market Entry and Consumer Behavior: An Investigation of a Wal-Mart Supercenter

Vishal P. Singh

Tepper School of Business, Carnegie Mellon University, 244 Posner Hall, 5000 Forbes Avenue, Pittsburgh, Pennsylvania 15213,
vsingh@andrew.cmu.edu

Karsten T. Hansen, Robert C. Blattberg

Kellogg School of Management, Northwestern University, 2001 Sheridan Road, Evanston, Illinois 60208,
{ karsten-hansen@northwestern.edu, r-blattberg@northwestern.edu}

This paper provides an empirical study of entry by a Wal-Mart supercenter into a local market. Using a unique frequent-shopper database that records transactions for over 10,000 customers, we study the impact of Wal-Mart's entry on consumer purchase behavior. We develop a joint model of interpurchase time and basket size to study the impact of competitor entry on two key household decisions: store visits and in-store expenditures. The model also allows for consumer heterogeneity due to observed and unobserved factors. Results show that the incumbent supermarket lost 17% volume—amounting to a quarter million dollars in monthly revenue—following Wal-Mart's entry. Decomposing the lost sales into components attributed to store visits and in-store expenditures, we find that the majority of these losses were due to fewer store visits with a much smaller impact attributed to basket size. We also find that Wal-Mart lures some of the incumbent's best customers, and that retention of a small number of households can significantly reduce losses at the focal store. Finally, certain observed household characteristics such as distance to store, shopping behavior, and product purchase behavior are found to be useful in profiling the defectors to Wal-Mart. Implications and strategies for supermarket managers to compete with Wal-Mart are discussed.

Key words: entry; retail competition; Wal-Mart supercenter; frequent-shopper data
History: This paper was received March 18, 2004, and was with the authors 9 months for 2 revisions; processed by Michel Wedel.

The time has come, as everyone knew it would. Wal-Mart, which through its four formats had already been selling more groceries than anyone in America, is now the country's biggest supermarket operator...racking up $4 billion more in annual sales than former top dog Kroger. (*Progressive Grocer*, May 2003)

1. Introduction

The role of supermarkets in the grocery retailing industry has undergone dramatic changes over the last decade. Rapid growth of alternative retail formats, in the form of mass discounters, wholesale clubs, and supercenters, has transformed not only the competitive structure of the industry, but also the way in which consumers shop. The biggest threat to the supermarket industry comes from none other than the world's largest retailer: Wal-Mart. In spite of being a relatively new player, Wal-Mart, through its supercenter format, has already become number one in the grocery industry. Patterned after the European hypermarket, a supercenter combines a full-line discount store with a full-line supermarket under one roof. These stores carry both general merchandise and food, including groceries and perishables. They also offer a variety of ancillary services such as pharmacy, dry cleaning, hair salon, and photo development ser-

vices; and gas stations, providing consumers with a true one-stop shopping experience. For an industry already crowded with many players, there are various reasons why Wal-Mart's supercenter format poses an extraordinary challenge. As discussed in §2, Wal-Mart has been able to keep its costs below the industry level, which in turn translates into lower prices for the consumers. Given the razor-thin margins in the grocery industry, Wal-Mart's everyday low prices are difficult, if not impossible, to match. Indeed, as quoted in the *Wall Street Journal* (2003), items at Wal-Mart cost 8%–27% less than at Kroger, Albertsons, or Safeway, even after taking into account discounts from these competitors' loyalty cards and specials. Besides costs, another factor driving the grocery prices down at the supercenter has to do with the main motivation for why Wal-Mart and other discount stores entered the grocery business in the first place: store traffic. A typical supercenter has only 30% of the area devoted to grocery. According to industry analysts, Wal-Mart offers lower prices on food in order to bring traffic into the supercenters with the hope of selling higher-margin general merchandise, and even has the potential of treating the entire food business as a loss leader. National chains and independents alike are feeling the pressure from Wal-Mart. In the past decade, 29

458

Singh, Hansen, and Blattberg: *Market Entry and Consumer Behavior: An Investigation of a Wal-Mart Supercenter*
Marketing Science 25(5), pp. 457–476, © 2006 INFORMS

chains have sought bankruptcy-court protection, with Wal-Mart as a catalyst in 25 of those cases (*Wall Street Journal* 2003). Not surprisingly, Wal-Mart supercenter is seen as a serious menace to the traditional grocery industry, with 80% of supermarket managers citing competition from supercenters as their biggest concern in the coming year (National Grocers Association 2003).

Despite their unprecedented growth and the threat they pose to the traditional grocery industry, relatively little is known about how entry of a supercenter in a market changes consumer purchase behavior or what it does to the bottom line of an incumbent supermarket. Although there have been a number of business press articles covering this new retail format, they provide little information on the issue. Instead, the commentary has ranged from predictions on extinction of traditional grocery to general guidelines on how to compete with this new format. Academic research, on the other hand, has primarily focused on stores that are similar in terms of their product offerings and cost structures (Lal and Matutes 1989, Pesendorfer 2002), or supermarkets that differ only in terms of their pricing formats, that is, every day low pricing (EDLP) versus Hi-Lo (Bell and Lattin 1998, Lal and Rao 1997, Messinger and Narasimhan 1997). With minor exceptions (Fox et al. 2004, Singh 2002), there is limited attention given to alternative retail formats, such as mass merchandisers or supercenters.

This paper provides an empirical study of the impact of a Wal-Mart supercenter entry on sales of a traditional supermarket. We utilize a unique frequent-shopper database that records purchases for over 10,000 households before and after Wal-Mart's entry. The data are drawn from a store located in a small town on the East Coast. The store in question has a well-developed frequent-shopper program, with over 85% of the sales captured on shopper cards. The database records all transactions made in the store, and captures such information as time and date of the transaction, price, promotion, and quantity for every UPC sold. This information was recorded at the individual level for all the customers in the store for a period of 20 months, from November 1999 to June 2001. In August of 2000, a Wal-Mart supercenter entered 2.1 miles from the store. Thus, we observe a reasonably long purchase history both before and after Wal-Mart's entry.

Our primary focus in this paper is on analyzing changes in consumer purchase behavior following the competitor's entry. Entry of a discount store in the market can influence a household's buying behavior in several ways. At the two extremes, some consumers may not change their purchase behavior at all, while others may completely abandon the incumbent and defect to Wal-Mart. Other consumers may shift part of their purchases to Wal-Mart while continuing to patronize the incumbent store. For this group, the lost volume can come from three sources: fewer store visits, smaller baskets, or a combination of the two. Furthermore, these changes in household behavior could be related to factors such as distance to the incumbent and Wal-Mart, household demographics, and other characteristics related to shopping behavior. The primary questions addressed in this paper are

• What is the impact of Wal-Mart's entry on the incumbent supermarket's total sales?

• To what extent are the total observed losses attributed to customer attrition, reduction in store visit frequency, and smaller basket size?

• What are the observed demographic and purchase behavior characteristics of the households that defect to Wal-Mart?

Answers to these questions can be quite important from a managerial perspective. For instance, decomposition of total sales into components attributed to store visits and basket size can be useful in understanding the source of lost volume and in developing store-level marketing policies. Suppose, for example, we find that the lost sales are primarily due to households not visiting the store as frequently as they did prior to Wal-Mart's entry but that, once the shopper is in the store, basket size remains constant. This in turn suggests the need for developing strategies that are primarily geared toward generating store traffic, such as use of deep promotions and feature advertisements. On the other hand, suppose we find that the frequency of store visits remains constant but that the basket size is smaller. In this case, the focus should be on in-store merchandising to increase expenditure once the customers are at the store. Similarly, identifying households based on their observed characteristics can also be quite important because it can allow the retailer not only to target customers with similar characteristics at this store, but also to transfer the findings to other store locations where the retailer comes in competition with Wal-Mart (or other such formats). Store opening information is generally available well in advance, and so preemptive actions can be taken for the households who are at high risk of defection.

To evaluate Wal-Mart's impact on consumer purchase behavior, we develop a joint model of interpurchase time and basket size. Although a popular approach to model interpurchase time used in the marketing literature is the proportional hazard model in continuous time (e.g., Jain and Vilcassim 1991), it has the limitation of only accounting for marketing mix and other covariates when an event occurs (e.g., when a purchase is made). On the other

Singh, Hansen, and Blattberg: *Market Entry and Consumer Behavior: An Investigation of a Wal-Mart Supercenter*
Marketing Science 25(5), pp. 457–476, © 2006 INFORMS

459

hand, a discrete-time approach (Gupta 1991, Wedel et al. 1995) can explicitly account for the covariates in periods during which households do not make a purchase. We take a discrete-time approach and model the household store visit decision using a discrete-choice framework with time-varying coefficients. These time-varying coefficients capture the duration dependence embodied in consumers' choice process. The model, based on an underlying utility-maximizing framework, can be interpreted as a hazard model (Seetharaman and Chintagunta 2003). Besides accounting for the full time path of the covariates, this modeling approach has the advantage of allowing for nonproportional hazards—a feature that is empirically relevant for our data.

Consumers' in-store expenditures are modeled using a semilog specification that has been used extensively in marketing (e.g., Blattberg and Neslin 1990). Both of these household decisions (store visit and in-store expenditure) are modelled jointly, and Wal-Mart's impact on these decisions are captured by allowing for a structural break at the time of competitor entry. The model also allows for consumer heterogeneity, modelled using a hierarchical structure. In particular, the full set of model parameters is allowed to vary across consumers due to both observed (e.g., demographic) and unobserved factors. For inference we use a hierarchical Bayesian approach that, as discussed in Allenby and Rossi (1999), is well suited to making inference at the individual level.

Our results show that the incumbent store lost 17% of its volume—amounting to a quarter million dollars in monthly revenue—following Wal-Mart's entry. The magnitude of the lost sales is quite alarming considering that supermarkets generally operate on a principle of low margins and high volume, with profit margins of only about 1% to 2%. Decomposing the lost volume into store visits and in-store expenditures, we find that the majority of the losses are due to fewer store visits, with little change seen in the basket size once consumers are in the store. This is an important finding, because it suggests that strategies designed to drive store traffic could be an effective way to recover some of the lost volume. We also find that the incumbent loses some of its best customers to Wal-Mart and that a small increase in retention of these customers can significantly mitigate the losses at the incumbent store. For instance, we find that if the retailer is able to retain 5% (10%) of its best customers, it can reduce its total losses by 41% (64%). Finally, in terms of consumer characteristics, we find that Wal-Mart's impact is most pronounced for households living in close proximity to it, which is consistent with the general finding in the retail site-selection literature (e.g., Huff 1964, Brown

1989, Craig et al. 1984). Certain shopping characteristics (e.g., 9–5 weekday shoppers) and purchase behavior characteristics (e.g., store-brand buyers) are found to be more useful than household demographics in profiling defectors to Wal-Mart.

This research makes several contributions to marketing theory and practice. Foremost among these is that we provide an empirical analysis of the impact of Wal-Mart supercenter entry on a traditional retailer. As discussed above, academic research has primarily focused on competition between supermarkets with little attention given to this new retail format. Similarly, past research has studied competition and store choice issues in a static environment, whereas this study considers both the short- and long-run impact of entry in a changing competitive environment, namely, entry by a new competitor. Given the dramatic changes taking place in the retail industry, results from the study should be of interest to both academics and practitioners.

The research is also salient to the growing body of literature focusing on customer management. For instance, our findings that a small proportion of customers account for a large proportion of store losses give credence to the general recommendation in the customer relationship management (CRM) literature on the importance of customer retention. Similarly, our analysis demonstrates how a retailer can exploit the information contained in its frequent-shopper database to understand and respond to its most valuable customers. This is a vital topic because, although the information contained in frequent-shopper databases is commonly assumed to be valuable, many retailers are struggling to leverage this information. The potential difficulty of converting data into valuable marketing strategies is illustrated by the case of Safeway PLC (U.K.), which abandoned its customer card program, citing a potential savings of $80 million per year in administrative costs (*BBC News* 2000). Thus, a secondary objective of this study is to shed some light on the potential uses of the purchase history information, especially in the face of competition.

The rest of this paper is organized as follows. The next section provides a brief overview of the supercenter format, including suggestions made in the business press to counter Wal-Mart. Section 3 presents the data used in the study. Section 4 develops a joint model of interpurchase time and basket size, and §5 presents the empirical results from the model. In §6, we explore various household characteristics that can be useful in identifying potential detectors to Wal-Mart. We conclude in §7 with a discussion on limitations of the current study and directions for future research in this area.

Singh, Hansen, and Blattberg: *Market Entry and Consumer Behavior: An Investigation of a Wal-Mart Supercenter*
Marketing Science 25(5), pp. 457–476, © 2006 INFORMS

460

2.   The Supercenter Format

In this section we provide a brief overview of the supercenter format.[1] We discuss the motivation of discount stores to get into the grocery business, the challenges this format presents to supermarkets, and solutions suggested by some industry analysts. This format has received limited attention in the academic literature, so our discussion is primarily drawn from the business press.

Supercenters, which average 180,000 square feet, are retail stores that combine a discount department store with a full-service supermarket. They offer a wide variety of general merchandise and food items, including meat, produce, deli, and other perishables. In addition, many include ancillary services such as pharmacy, dry cleaning, vision center, Tire and Lube Express, hair salon, income tax preparation (in season), and so forth, providing consumers with a true "one-stop shopping" experience. Meijer and Fred Meyer started this format as early as the 1960s, but it is only with the arrival of Wal-Mart that this format has shown dramatic growth. The first Wal-Mart supercenter was opened in 1988, and in 1993 the company operated only 10 such stores. With 192 supercenters added in 2002, the company currently has over 2,121 supercenters. This unprecedented march by Wal-Mart into the grocery business is taking its toll along the way. According to the 2002 "Channel Blurring" study by ACNielsen, since 1999 consumer visits per year to supermarkets were down 12% while visits to supercenters were up 40%. National chains and independents alike are feeling the pressure from Wal-Mart. In the past decade, 29 chains have sought bankruptcy-court protection, with Wal-Mart as a catalyst in 25 of those cases (*Wall Street Journal* 2003).

Transition to Grocery

What motivated Wal-Mart to enter the grocery business? There are a number of reasons cited for the move, including change in the top management and the arrival of David Glass as the CEO (who had a background in the grocery business). Furthermore, by the late 1980s the discount retail industry was close to saturation, and was highly concentrated with three major players: Wal-Mart, K-Mart, and Target. The supermarket industry, on the other hand, was highly fragmented with small- to medium-size regional chains. Although this industry structure facilitated the transition to grocery, the main motivation for Wal-Mart's venture into the industry was store traffic. Indeed, industry experts believe that Wal-Mart is using food mainly as a traffic driver, with the

hope of spillover to higher-margin general merchandise items, which account for 65%–70% of supercenter sales. The strategy seems to be working, with some reports suggesting that the general merchandise sales are 25%–50% higher at a supercenter than they are at discount stores in the same area (or after conversion of a discount store to supercenter).[2] The supercenter format has been so successful that Wal-Mart has chosen this path for expansion, with plans to add 200 supercenters every year for the next five years (company website). According to Trade Dimensions, with the current growth rate, over three-fourths of Kroger and Albertsons stores will be within 10 miles of a Wal-Mart supercenter within this decade.

Pricing at Wal-Mart

A general consensus in industry reports is that the prices at Wal-Mart supercenter are about 15% lower than traditional supermarkets.[3] Besides the store traffic considerations discussed above, there are several other cost-related factors driving the prices down at Wal-Mart. Foremost, Wal-Mart's size gives the company several advantages over smaller competitors, including bargaining power with the manufacturer and economies of scale in distribution systems. Furthermore, Wal-Mart's large size allows the company to bypass wholesalers with the majority of the merchandise at the supercenters, including perishables, supplied through its distribution centers. This, coupled with an EDLP strategy (which not only helps create a low-price image in a consumer's mind but also offers many operational advantages in demand forecasting) and Wal-Mart's proprietary Retail Link software, gives Wal-Mart a tremendous advantage in logistics and inventory control. According to an independent study by McKinsey & Co., Wal-Mart's efficiency gains were the source of 25% of the entire U.S. economy's productivity improvement from 1995 to 1999. Last but not least, another factor keeping the costs low at Wal-Mart is its nonunionized labor. For the majority of supermarkets, labor, which constitutes approximately 70% of the overhead, is unionized. None of Wal-Mart's employees belong to a union, and industry analysts believe that they get paid significantly less than the industry average.[4]

---

[1] We shall limit our discussion primarily to Wal-Mart. Target and K-Mart each has its own version of a supercenter, but Wal-Mart is by far the biggest player in the industry.

[2] Packaged Facts (1997).

[3] The *Wall Street Journal* (2003) article cited above quotes 8%–27% lower prices at supercenters. A *Time Magazine* (2003) article, "Can Wal-Mart Get Any Bigger?" reports 15% lower prices.

[4] There are a number of lawsuits pending against Wal-Mart due to its labor practices. In one such case in Jacksonville, Texas, the meat-cutters at Wal-Mart voted to form a union in February 2000. Within months, Wal-Mart had decided to close down the meat plant and replace it with case-ready meat packaged by suppliers (*KFPT News* 2002).

Singh, Hansen, and Blattberg: *Market Entry and Consumer Behavior: An Investigation of a Wal-Mart Supercenter*
Marketing Science 25(5), pp. 457–476, © 2006 INFORMS

How to Compete with Wal-Mart?

Competition from Wal-Mart supercenters may be inevitable, but it is not a death sentence.... (Thomas Zaucha, president and CEO of the National Grocers Association)

Given such cost asymmetries, how can supermarkets compete with Wal-Mart? Although there is no one answer, industry experts have given many suggestions. These range from shutting down the store to improving efficiency and cutting costs. In general, the recommendations fall into two broad groups: Become more like Wal-Mart, or differentiate (Rogers 2001). Indeed, there has been a move in the supermarket industry toward consolidation through mergers and acquisitions (e.g., Kroger and Fred Myers, American and Albertson) with the hope of leveraging similar bargaining power and economies of scale as Wal-Mart. Similarly, there has been a drive in the industry toward cost cutting (*Wall Street Journal* 2003). Many stores have also expanded their general merchandise items and other services such as pharmacy and banking in order to provide their own version of one-stop shopping.

Others argue it is not possible to beat Wal-Mart at its own game and recommend differentiation with a focus on the two main weaknesses of supercenters: perishables and convenience. These recommendations include providing a clean friendly store; improving fresh produce and custom-cut meat departments; emphasizing deli, ready-to-eat foods, and salad bars; broadening product assortment; and increasing the focus on understanding customer needs. Another weakness of the supercenters is that they are generally located outside the city limits. However, Wal-Mart has recognized this limitation, and is testing with scaled-down versions of supercenters ranging in size from 40,000 to 50,000 square feet. According to Wal-Mart its Neighborhood Market format will charge the same low price as its supercenters, while providing the same location convenience as supermarkets and convenience stores.

Given the discussion above, it is not surprising that supermarket managers consider Wal-Mart one of their most formidable competitors. Many of the suggestions that industry experts provide on how to tackle Wal-Mart go well beyond the scope of this paper. However, before developing any general principles on the issue, a necessary first step is an understanding of what a Wal-Mart does to a retailer's bottom line, and how it changes consumer purchase behavior. To this extent we present an empirical study that attempts to address some of these issues.

3. Frequent-Shopper Database

The data used in the study come from a single store of a large supermarket chain on the East Coast. The store in question is located in a small suburban town, which provides us with an opportunity to analyze

Table 1 Shopper Card Penetration

	No card	Employee card	Card holder
Sales ($) (%)	12.4	2.0	85.6
Number of transactions (%)	36.0	3.0	61.0
Average basket size ($)	8.00	16.60	33.50

the impact of a Wal-Mart supercenter's entry in a relatively controlled environment.[5] Based on our discussion with the store managers, the store can be classified as typical Hi-Lo format. Besides standard grocery products, the store offers a variety of services such as 24-hour shopping, in-store postal and banking services, video rental, photo developing, pharmacy, and speciality departments such as bakery, deli, salad bar, seafood, and custom-cut meat.

The store also has a well-developed frequent-shopper program. Although the original purpose of such frequent-shopper programs was to create store loyalty by rewarding the best customers, over time the role of these programs has changed to being just another promotional tool. However, they do provide retailers with a wealth of information about their customers. A secondary objective of this study is to demonstrate how retailers can utilize the information contained in their database, especially when faced with competition. The frequent-shopper data that we use are unique, in that they record all transactions made in the store and capture information such as time and date of the transaction, card holder information (if a shopper card is used), and the dollar volume, unit price, quantity, and promotion for *every* UPC sold. At the same time, these data have the drawback (unlike typical scanner panel data) of only making the purchase information available for the store in question. Thus, if a card holder in our sample shops at other stores (including Wal-Mart), those purchases are not recorded.[6] While this may seem like a major shortcoming, one must realize that this is the information typically available to the retailer (unless it purchases data from outside vendors such as Information Resource Inc. (IRI) or ACNielsen).

The data are available for a period of 20 months, from November 1999 to June 2001. In August of 2000 a Wal-Mart supercenter entered 2.1 miles from the focal store. Thus, we observe reasonably long time series both before and after Wal-Mart's entry. Note that our database contains information on all transactions made at the store, but that we can only track purchases for households that are members of the frequent-shopper program. As seen in Table 1, the

---

[5] Over 70% of the households in our database own a house and, on average, have lived at their current residence for 14 years.

[6] Besides Wal-Mart, there is one other major grocery store in the area, as well as several smaller food shops.

462

Singh, Hansen, and Blattberg: *Market Entry and Consumer Behavior: An Investigation of a Wal-Mart Supercenter*
Marketing Science 25(5), pp. 457–476, © 2006 INFORMS

Figure 1   Household Locations

Note. Distance between the focal store and Wal-Mart is 2.1 miles.

usage of the shopper card program for this retailer is quite high, with card holders accounting for over 85% of total store sales. About 2% of the sales are on the employee card and thus cannot be traced back to any individual card holder. Although noncard purchases account for 32% of all transactions, the average order size is significantly lower ($8 compared with $34 for transactions using the shopper card). The non-card purchases often tend to come from the coffee or snack shop, and the pharmacy. For most grocery categories the shopper card penetration rate is well over 90%.

Purchase history information is available for over 22,000 card holders. However, many of these card holders are casual buyers who make few purchases at this store, or who had highly irregular purchase patterns before Wal-Mart entered. The estimation results presented below use data from the top 10,000 customers, who account for 77% of card holder pre-entry sales.

3.1.   Customer Location

A useful piece of information in the database is the mailing addresses for all the card holders. These addresses were geo-coded to compute each household's travel distance from the focal store and from Wal-Mart. Based on the findings in the previous literature (see, for example, research on retail site selection by Huff 1964, Brown 1989, Craig et al. 1989, etc.)

as well as business press (*Progressive Grocer* 2002), we would expect location to play an important role in determining the likelihood of shifting purchases to Wal-Mart. In Figure 1 we plot the locations of the households. The location of the focal store is shown by the large star, and the location of Wal-Mart is shown by the pin. On average, consumers live about 3.5 miles from the focal store and 4.8 miles from Wal-Mart.[7] As is evident from Figure 1, many customers are clustered around the focal store. However, despite the apparent proximity, over one-third of the customers live outside the three-mile radius (considered the trading area of a typical grocery store).[8] In our empirical application, we tried several specifications for incorporating distance, including defining census tract neighborhoods, and linear and quadratic distance terms as suggested in the Hotelling-type theoretical models.

---

[7] These numbers are based on a straight-line distance. While one would prefer to use travel times rather than distance, there is some evidence that straight-line distance is a good proxy for actual travel time. For example, Phibbs and Luft (1995) find a correlation of 0.987 between straight-line distance and travel time, although this correlation drops to 0.826 for distances below 15 miles. Note also that our distance variable is more accurate than that used in previous research that have used the centroid of the zip code in which the household is located to compute distances (e.g., Bell et al. 1998).

[8] Sixty-six percent of the households live within the three-mile radius of the focal store and 78% live within a five-mile radius.

Singh, Hansen, and Blattberg: *Market Entry and Consumer Behavior: An Investigation of a Wal-Mart Supercenter*
Marketing Science 25(5), pp. 457–476, © 2006 INFORMS

463

3.2. Observed Household Characteristics

Besides location, we use a large set of household-specific variables that could be useful in understanding the type of customers that defect to Wal-Mart. These variables are constructed using the census data as well as the transaction history of the households *prior* to Wal-Mart's entry. Table 2 provides the summary statistics on these variables, which fall into three broad categories:

• **Demographics:** The first two demographic variables in Table 2 (INC and HHSIZE) refer to the median income and median household size for the census block group in which the household resides. In general, we find significant variation in household demographics. For instance, the median income level in the block-group ranges from a low of $8,700 to a high of over $105,000. The next two demographic variables (BABY and PET) are dummies, indicating the presence of a baby or a pet, respectively. These were computed from the household purchase history data. For example, if a household is observed to purchase baby products such as diapers or baby food, it indicates the presence of an infant in the family. Similarly, purchase of dog food or cat litter indicates the presence of a pet.

• **Shopping Variables:** We use the time and day of trip information to construct a variable that relates to household shopping behavior: MSHOP (the percent of total visits that were made between 9 A.M. and 5 P.M. on weekdays, excluding holidays). This variable can be treated as proxy for a shopper's search cost. For instance, if a household is observed to make the majority of its purchases between 9 A.M. and 5 P.M. on weekdays, it suggests the presence of a retired or otherwise unemployed member in the household.

• **Product Purchase Behavior:** The last set of variables was created using household purchase behavior in different product types (again created using transactions prior to Wal-Mart's entry). The primary motivation for these variables comes from business press reports that argue that one of the major weaknesses of the Wal-Mart supercenter is the fresh food area. As discussed in §2, Wal-Mart supercenters primarily rely on prepackaged produce and meat from suppliers. Thus households that allocate a large proportion of their expenditures to fresh produce (E-SHOP) and speciality meat and seafood (E-MEAT) are less likely to abandon this store in favor of Wal-Mart. Similarly, large purchases in prepared food departments such as salad bar and deli (E-HMR: proportion of expenditure in home meal replacement) could result in a higher affinity for the store compared with Wal-Mart. Finally, E-PL refers to the proportion of total expenditures on the store brands.[9] The likely impact of this variable in determining whether a household defects to Wal-Mart is not entirely clear. Previous research (Corstjens and Lal 2000) suggests that store brands can create store loyalty. At the same time, researchers have also found store brand buyers to be more value driven and price sensitive (Hoch 1996, Hansen et al. 2006, Pauwels and Srinivasan 2004), and if more price-sensitive households frequent discount stores, we can find the opposite effect.

3.3. Pricing Environment

As discussed above, the database records the price and promotion information for every UPC sold in the store. We expect these marketing mix variables to influence various household decisions such as the decision to visit the store and basket size once in the store. However, creating variables to capture the overall store-pricing environment is a nontrivial task. The store carries over 50,000 unique UPCs that are classified into several hundred categories. Furthermore, several of these products (e.g., in produce and meat departments) do not carry a fixed UPC bar code that remains constant over time. Instead, these products are assigned a temporary code that changes from week to week. This makes the task of creating a price series for these products difficult if not impossible. The matter is further complicated by different price reactions by the incumbent to Wal-Mart's entry in various product categories. Figure 2 shows prices for three products: bananas, spring water, and Italian bread. It is evident that the initial reaction for bananas is to match the $0.39 per pound price of Wal-Mart with occasional $0.25 per pound promotions.[10] Over time

Table 2 Demographic, Shopping, and Product Purchase Variables

Variable	Description	Mean	Std	Min	Max
STDIST	Distance—focal store	3.49	4.70	0.02	49.06
PROXWM	Proximity to Wal-Mart	4.78	4.42	0.18	48.79
INC	Median income in census tract	44,352	16,860	8,713	105,218
HHSIZE	Household size in census tract	2.36	0.31	1.21	3.94
BABY	Indicator for presence of baby	10%			
PET	Indicator for presence of pet	29%			
MSHOP	Fraction of trips between 9 A.M. and 5 P.M. weekdays	0.39	0.24	0.00	1.00
E-SHOP	Fraction expenditure on produce	0.10	0.06	0.00	0.74
E-MEAT	Fraction expenditure on meat	0.14	0.08	0.00	0.77
E-HMR	Fraction expenditure on HMR	0.02	0.05	0.00	0.92
E-PL	Fraction expenditure on store brand	0.14	0.07	0.00	0.59

Note. HMR = home meal replacement.

---

[9] Excludes nonpackaged goods such as items in meat and produce departments.

[10] Price of $0.39 per pound of banana is a heavily promoted item at Wal-Mart supercenters in their advertisements as well as in-store special displays.

Singh, Hansen, and Blattberg: *Market Entry and Consumer Behavior: An Investigation of a Wal-Mart Supercenter*
464
Marketing Science 25(5), pp. 457–476, © 2006 INFORMS

Figure 2   Store Pricing Series for Three UPCs

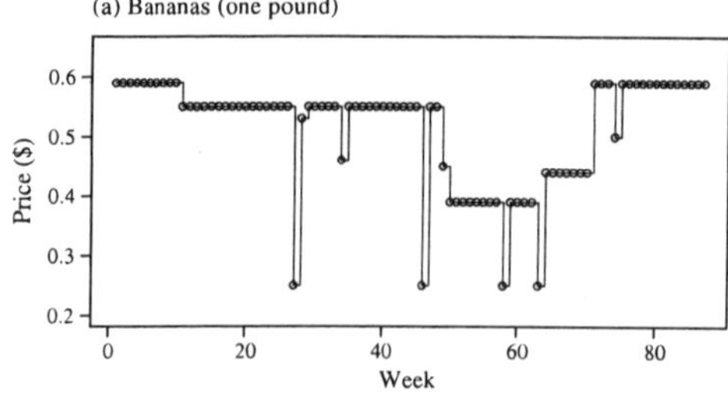

(a) Bananas (one pound)

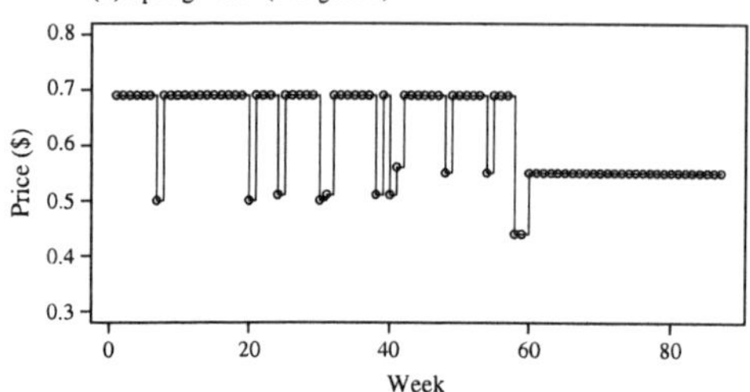

(b) Spring water (one gallon)

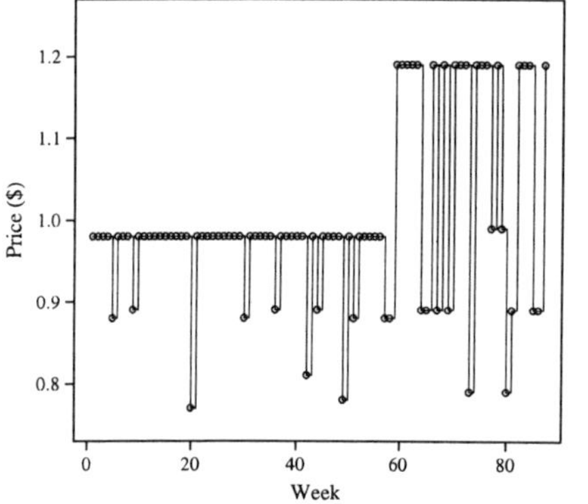

(c) Italian bread (one loaf)

prices went back to \$0.59 per pound. The strategy followed in the other two products is quite different. In spring water the store seems to have moved from a Hi-Lo pricing to an EDLP pricing strategy, while the situation is reversed in Italian bread.[11]

Given the above-mentioned complexities, any measure to capture the overall store price environment would be an approximation at best. Our strategy is

therefore to rely on aggregate measures designed to proxy the weekly price environment at the store. In the empirical application, we experimented with several measures including a basket-price index, a household-specific basket-price index, and overall store- and department-level promotion indices. The basket-price index was created using the share weighted price of the top 100 (250) selling items in the store. For household-specific basket prices, we used the top 100 (250) items for that household prior to Wal-Mart's entry. Finally, promotional indices were created by aggregating the total promotional discount offered on all items falling in that department. For instance, suppose the produce department consists of the following three products with regular and promoted price as: bananas (\$0.55 per pound, \$0.45 per pound), broccoli (\$1.39 per pound, \$1.39 per pound), and red grapes (\$1.00 per pound, \$0.90 per pound). The promotion measure for produce in that week would be \$0.20.

3.4. Store Sales

Figure 3 shows the daily store sales, store traffic (i.e., number of transactions per day), and the average basket size over the sample period. The entry of Wal-Mart is indicated by the vertical line. The spikes early in the data and around Day 400 are the Thanksgiving and Christmas weeks. Two key observations from the figures must be highlighted. First, there appears to be a significant fall in the baseline volume for the incumbent store. Second, looking at the graphs for the store visits and basket size, it seems that a large proportion of the lost revenues at the store level is due to fewer store visits, with little change in the average basket size. To formalize and test this at the household level, we next describe a model that captures these two fundamental household decisions: whether to visit the store, and basket size once at the store.

4. Model

In this section we develop a model to evaluate the impact of Wal-Mart's entry on household purchase behavior. As discussed above, a competing store's entry is likely to result in lost volume for the incumbent store. Suppose we define volume as total expenditure for all households shopping at the store over a period of a certain length, for example, T days. Let V be store volume for this period before Wal-Mart's entry and V^W store volume after entry. A casual method to evaluate the overall impact of Wal-Mart's entry is to estimate the expected value of quantities such as $\Delta_1 \equiv V^W - V$, $\Delta_2 \equiv (V^W - V)/V$, or $\Delta_3 = \log V^W - \log V$. These quantities can be estimated by simply comparing before–after averages of observed store volume. However, there are (at least) three shortcomings to this approach. First, it is important for the incumbent to understand the source of these lost sales in terms of longer interpurchase times and smaller baskets. Second, the impact of Wal-Mart's entry is likely to

---

[11] Our discussions with the store manager did not reveal any particular insight into the matter. It seemed that the store was experimenting with different pricing schemes. However, the store manager did indicate that the focus post–Wal-Mart entry had shifted to emphasizing the fresh produce, seafood, meat, and deli items—a point we return to in §6.

Singh, Hansen, and Blattberg: *Market Entry and Consumer Behavior: An Investigation of a Wal-Mart Supercenter*
Marketing Science 25(5), pp. 457–476, © 2006 INFORMS

Figure 3   **Daily Sales, Store Traffic, and Basket Size, Before and After Entry**

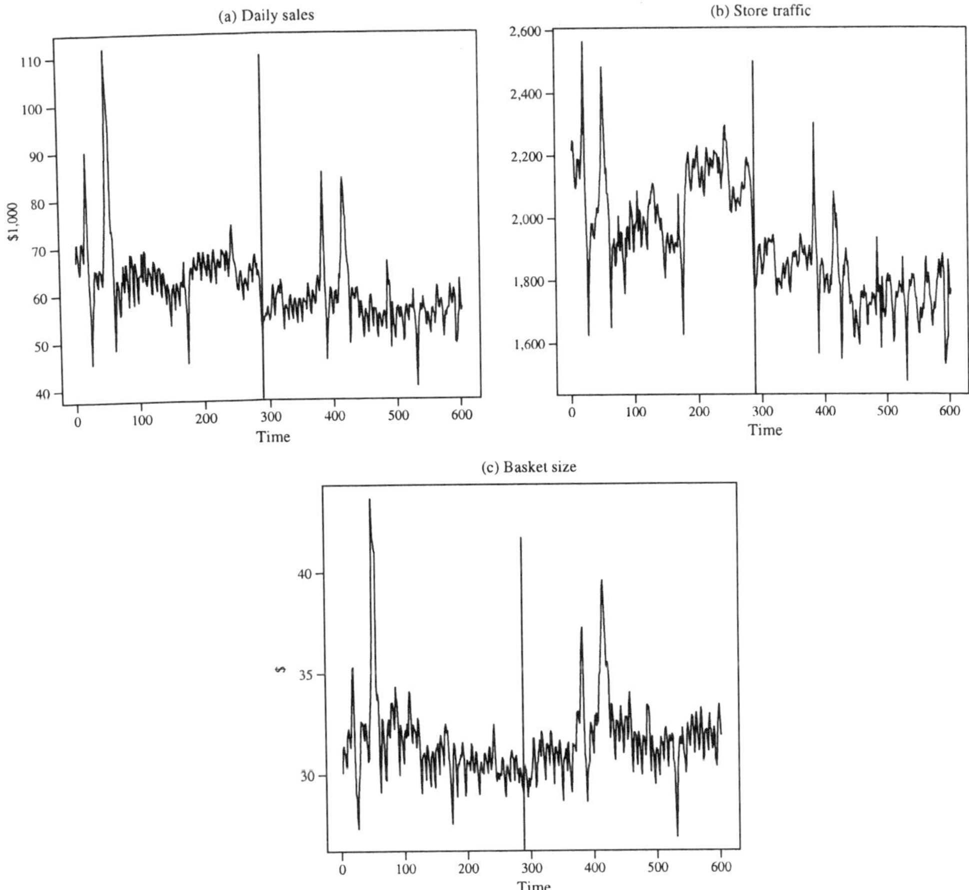

Note. Entry date shown by vertical line.

be different across consumers due to observed (such as demographics) as well as unobserved factors. It is crucial for the store to understand what types of consumers or households display the biggest change in store expenditure and what the causes are of those changes. In other words, if a given household reduces its store expenditure over a certain period after Wal-Mart's entry, is this due to longer interpurchase times (i.e., fewer trips per period), smaller basket size per trip, or a combination of the two? Finally, if the store environment changes after Wal-Mart's entry, for example, if pricing and promotion strategies change, then it is important to control for these changes. For example, if the store promotes more aggressively after Wal-Mart's entry, the promotion effect will be confounded with the pure Wal-Mart effect.

To overcome the shortcomings described above, we start by decomposing overall store volume as

$$V = \sum_{h=1}^{H} e_h, \qquad (1)$$

where e_h is household h's store expenditure over a period of length T. This can in turn be decomposed as

$$e_h = \sum_{t=1}^{T} d_{ht} b_{ht}, \qquad (2)$$

where d_{ht} is equal to one if the store is visited on day t of the period and b_{ht} is the basket size (in dollars) of the trip. The total number of trips over the period for household h is

$$nt_h = \sum_{t=1}^{T} d_{ht}. \qquad (3)$$

466

Singh, Hansen, and Blattberg: *Market Entry and Consumer Behavior: An Investigation of a Wal-Mart Supercenter*
Marketing Science 25(5), pp. 457–476, © 2006 INFORMS

Letting a superscript W denote quantities after Wal-Mart's entry, and letting x_t denote variables describing the store environment (e.g., promotional activity), we can now define "pure" Wal-Mart effects at the individual and aggregate level by holding x_t fixed. For example,

$$E[nt_h^W \mid \{x_t\}_{t=1}^T] - E[nt_h \mid \{x_t\}_{t=1}^T] \quad \text{and}$$
$$E[\log b_{ht}^W \mid x_t] - E[\log b_{ht} \mid x_t] \tag{4}$$

is the expected change in number of trips per period and expected change in log basket size per trip for household h.

4.1. Interpurchase Time and Basket Size

We model the two consumer decisions using a flexible model of interpurchase time (to capture when to visit the store) and semilog regression (to capture basket size once at the store). Both these household decisions are modeled jointly, and heterogeneity across households is captured by using a hierarchical structure where the full vector of model parameters (from both equations) is allowed to vary across consumers due to both observed and unobserved factors. To study the impact of Wal-Mart's entry on household purchase behavior, we allow for a structural break at the time of competitor entry.

Over the past two decades, a number of models have been proposed to capture the purchase-timing decisions of households (see Seetharaman and Chintagunta 2003 for a review). A majority of the empirical studies in marketing have used the proportional hazard model (proposed by Cox 1972) to characterize the purchase-timing behavior of households either in continuous time (e.g., Jain and Vilcassim 1991, Chintagunta and Haldar 1998) or discrete time (Gupta 1991, Helsen and Schmittlein 1993, Wedel et al. 1995). An advantage of the discrete-time approach is that it explicitly accounts for marketing mix and other covariates in periods during which households do not make a visit. For instance, in the current application it may be important to take into account the marketing mix variables on not only the purchase occasions, but also the periods in which households decide not to visit the store.

Our approach in this paper is to employ a discrete-choice framework with time-varying coefficients to capture the duration dependence embodied in consumers' choice processes. An advantage of using this approach is that we can use a flexible specification for duration dependence that allows us to approximate any shape of the household-specific hazard function. In proportional hazard models, such as those typically used in the literature, the impact of any covariate is to shift the baseline hazard up or down proportionately. Our specification is more flexible and allows for nonproportional hazard functions.

Using *days* as the basic time unit,[12] assume that an individual in each time period decides whether to visit the store and make a purchase.[13] Let U_{it} be net benefits for household i of making a purchase from the store in period t. The household will visit the store at t if $U_{it} > 0$. Assume

$$U_{it} = \beta_{i0}' f(\tau_{it}) + \beta_{ip}' p_t + \varepsilon_{it}, \quad t < T_W, \tag{5}$$

where T_W refers to the time periods before Wal-Mart's entry, τ_{it} is time since last purchase, ε_{it} is iid standard normal, and $f(\cdot)$ is some known vector function that can be made as flexible as desired. For instance, we could have $f(\tau_{it}) = (1, \tau_{it}, \tau_{it}^2, \ln \tau_{it}, \ldots)'$. p_t is a vector of time-varying covariates affecting utilities and includes time-varying marketing mix variables such as price and promotion for the incumbent store. The specification in (5) could be extended to include other factors such as expenditures on the previous purchase occasion, weekend, holiday, seasonality, and so forth (see the empirical application below).

Define D_{it} as one when $U_{it} > 0$ and zero otherwise. The probability of purchase at time t conditional on last purchase τ_t days ago is

$$\Pr(D_{it} = 1 \mid \beta_i, \tau_{it}, p_t) = \Phi(\beta_{i0}' f(\tau_{it}) + \beta_{ip}' p_t). \tag{6}$$

This is the hazard rate induced by (5) and captures the notion of individual specific hazard. The model in (5) implies a model for purchase times. Suppose we observe a purchase duration of length t_1, followed by a purchase duration of t_2. Stacking all the right-hand-side parameters and variables as (X_{it}, β_i), these durations then have likelihood

$$\Pr\left(T_{i1} = t_1, T_{i2} = t_2 \mid \beta_i, X_i^{t_1 + t_2}\right)$$
$$= \left\{ \prod_{t=1}^{t_1 - 1} \Pr(D_{it} = 0 \mid X_{it}, \beta_i) \right\} \times \Pr(D_{it_1} = 1 \mid X_{it_1}, \beta_i)$$
$$\times \left\{ \prod_{t=t_1+1}^{t_1+t_2-1} \Pr(D_{it} = 0 \mid X_{it}, \beta_i) \right\}$$
$$\times \Pr(D_{i, t_1+t_2} = 1 \mid X_{i, t_1+t_2}, \beta_i), \tag{7}$$

where $X_i^{t_1 + t_2}$ is the entire path for the covariates: $X_i^{t_1+t_2} = \{X_{it}\}_{t=1}^{t_1+t_2}$.

After Wal-Mart's entry, the utility is assumed to be

$$U_{it} = (\beta_{i0} + \beta_{i0, W})' f(\tau_{it}) + \beta_{ip}' p_{it} + \varepsilon_{it}, \quad t > T_W, \tag{8}$$

where $\beta_{i0, W}$ captures the impact of competitor entry. In the empirical application we separate out the

---

[12] Most marketing applications using discrete hazard models have assumed *week* as the unit of analysis. The primary motivation for the assumption is that the marketing mix variables change on a weekly basis. However, in our sample over one-third of the households visit the store more than once a week.

[13] Like most other marketing data sets, we observe a store visit only if a purchase is made.

Singh, Hansen, and Blattberg: *Market Entry and Consumer Behavior: An Investigation of a Wal-Mart Supercenter*
Marketing Science 25(5), pp. 457–476, © 2006 INFORMS

467

short-run (to capture "curiosity effects") and long-run impact of Wal-Mart and also allow other model parameters (e.g., marketing mix sensitivities) to change after entry.

To model the basket size once the household is in the store, we use a semilog specification that has been used extensively in marketing for modeling sales and expenditures (e.g., Blattberg and Neslin 1990). In particular, let b_{it} be log expenditures for household i in time period t (which is zero unless $U_i(t) > 0$). If a store visit is made at time t, the pre-entry log basket size b_{it} is assumed to be

$$b_{it} = \lambda_{i0} + \lambda_{ip}p_t + \lambda_{i\tau}\tau_{it} + \varepsilon_{b,it}, \quad t < T_W, \quad (9)$$

where p_t is the marketing mix environment on store visit t. The parameter $\lambda_{i\tau}$ captures the impact on basket size due to the recency of the previous visit. In general, we would expect a smaller basket size if the customer had visited the store recently. Finally, we assume $\varepsilon_{e,it} \mid v_i \sim N(0, v_i^{-1})$. After Wal-Mart's entry, the log basket size is modeled as

$$b_{it} = (\lambda_{i0} + \lambda_{iW}) + \lambda_{ip}p_t + \lambda_{i\tau}\tau_{it} + \varepsilon_{b,it}, \quad t \geq T_W, \quad (10)$$

where λ_{iW} captures the impact of Wal-Mart on the basket size.

4.2. Heterogeneity

Because we expect different households to react differently to Wal-Mart's entry, it is important to account for consumer heterogeneity in the model parameters. We also expect household responses to be related to observed characteristics, such as demographics. In this paper we use a parametric approach to model household heterogeneity and let the model parameters vary across households due to both observed and unobserved factors. Let $\theta_i = (\beta_i, \lambda_i)$ be the full vector of coefficients from the purchase timing and expenditure equations discussed above. We assume θ_i follows a multivariate normal distribution with a mean vector ΠZ_i and covariance matrix Ω:

$$\theta_i \mid \Pi, Z_i \sim N(\Pi Z_i, \Omega), \quad (11)$$

where Z_i is a vector containing household characteristics.

For inference we use a hierarchical Bayesian approach. In particular, we use a Markov Chain Monte Carlo (MCMC) procedure to simulate the posterior distribution of the model parameters and to compute household-level estimates of preferences. As discussed in Allenby and Rossi (1999), Bayesian procedures are well suited for these models, especially when one is interested in making inference at the individual level. We use standard conjugate priors on the model parameters. For the parameters in the Π matrix, we use a joint normal prior with mean zero and precision 0.01. We use a Wishart prior for Ω^{-1}

with degrees of freedom equal to $\dim(\theta_i) + 2 = 30$ and set the scale so the prior mean is equal to the identity matrix. Finally, we specify the prior for v_i to be gamma with shape $a_0 = 5$ and inverse scale equal to b. We use a gamma prior for the hyper parameter b with shape parameter equal to 2 and scale parameter equal to 1. The MCMC sampling algorithm was run for a total of 20,000 iterations, and we dropped the first 2,000 iterations to allow for burn-in, leaving us with 18,000 draws on which to base posterior calculations. These procedures have become quite standard in the literature, so we do not discuss the estimation algorithm in detail (a detailed discussion of this is available from the authors).

5. Estimation Results

Model Specification

Before we discuss the results, two important considerations with respect to the model specification are worth mentioning. The first relates to the distance variables discussed in §3.1. As seen from Figure 1, households live in a wide area around the two stores. This dispersion causes a problem if one wants to incorporate distance to the two stores directly as a household-specific covariate. This is because the distances will tend to be highly correlated. The overall correlation between distance to the incumbent and distance to Wal-Mart is 0.96 in our sample, which makes it impossible to estimate two separate distance effects directly. Although one could alleviate this problem to some extent by restricting the sample to households living in a small radius around the two stores, such a restriction will throw away a substantial part of the sample. Instead, we use two approaches that mitigate the problem to a certain extent. For the model presented below, we use the household distance to the incumbent and create an indicator variable for proximity to Wal-Mart (households living within one mile). We also present results for another specification (§6.2) where we use fairly fine grid of region fixed effects (census tracts) that provides us with a clean nonparametric estimate of the distance effects.

The second consideration is with regard to the function f, which, after some experimentation, was specified as

$$f(\tau_{it}) = (1, 0.1\tau_{it}, 0.01\tau_{it}^2, 1/\tau_{it}), \quad (12)$$

where the scaling in the second and third element is to stabilize estimated coefficients. This specification allows for a wide range of different hazard shapes. Recall from above that this function determines the shape of each household's hazard. For example, prior to Wal-Mart's entry, the hazard for household i will be

$$h_i(\tau; p_\tau) = \Phi(\beta_{0i,1} + \beta_{0i,2}(\tau/10) + \beta_{0i,3}(\tau^2/100)$$
$$+ \beta_{i0,4}/\tau + \beta'_{ip}p_\tau),$$

Singh, Hansen, and Blattberg: *Market Entry and Consumer Behavior: An Investigation of a Wal-Mart Supercenter*
Marketing Science 25(5), pp. 457–476, © 2006 INFORMS

where p_τ is the vector of other covariates. We also separate out the impact of Wal-Mart entry in the short- (defined as the first three months after entry) and long-run effects.

Results

In Table 3 we report estimates of the hierarchical coefficients Π and the diagonal elements of Ω in (11) for the coefficients relating to the store trip models (5) and (8). The first column in Table 3 represents the mean numbers followed by the impact of observed characteristics on the parameters. The column labelled "SD" is the standard deviation of the parameter estimates representing the unobserved heterogeneity. Finally, the last column, "DEMO," shows

the fraction of heterogeneity across households that is explained by the observed characteristics. Looking across the rows the first four rows capture the duration dependence prior to Wal-Mart's entry, followed by the short- and long-run effects. The variables *holiday* and *weekend* are indicator variables, while *prom* is the store-level promotion index. Note that all demographic variables except the indicator variables have been mean centered.

The demographic interactions show that several of the household characteristics are significant. However, the parameter variation these observed characteristics explain is not large (ranges from 2%–24%). On the other hand, the large standard deviation terms indicate that most of the heterogeneity across

Table 3   Hierarchical Coefficient Estimates, Duration Model

Attribute	Constant	STDIST	PROXWM	MSHOP	E-PL	E-PROD	E-MEAT	E-HMR	HHSIZE	BABY	PET	INC	SD	DEMO
Constant	**−0.96**	−0.10	−0.23	**−1.17**	**1.17**	−2.97	−2.32	−0.58	**−0.30**	0.07	0.04	0.22	1.79	0.06
	(0.05)	(0.09)	(0.14)	(0.16)	(0.50)	(0.61)	(0.47)	(0.66)	(0.14)	(0.12)	(0.08)	(0.14)	(0.05)	(0.01)
$10^{-1} \times \tau$	**−0.12**	**−0.02**	**−0.04**	0.02	**0.23**	0.14	−0.07	0.11	**0.07**	0.00	**0.17**	0.03	0.44	0.04
	(0.01)	(0.01)	(0.02)	(0.03)	(0.09)	(0.11)	(0.08)	(0.13)	(0.03)	(0.02)	(0.02)	(0.02)	(0.01)	(0.01)
$10^{-2} \times \tau^2$	**0.03**	0.00	0.01	0.00	**−0.06**	−0.03	**0.04**	−0.01	−0.01	0.00	**−0.03**	0.00	0.09	0.03
	(0.00)	(0.00)	(0.01)	(0.01)	(0.02)	(0.03)	(0.02)	(0.03)	(0.01)	(0.01)	(0.00)	(0.01)	(0.00)	(0.01)
τ^{-1}	**−0.82**	**−0.15**	**−0.08**	**−0.60**	**0.63**	−0.35	**0.61**	**−0.47**	**−0.20**	0.03	0.02	0.01	0.56	0.12
	(0.01)	(0.02)	(0.03)	(0.04)	(0.12)	(0.15)	(0.11)	(0.17)	(0.03)	(0.03)	(0.02)	(0.03)	(0.01)	(0.01)
D_{SR}	**−1.13**	−0.09	0.07	**0.68**	**−2.45**	1.23	0.98	0.80	−0.19	−0.12	**−0.23**	**−0.47**	1.85	0.04
	(0.07)	(0.12)	(0.19)	(0.24)	(0.70)	(0.80)	(0.63)	(0.89)	(0.21)	(0.17)	(0.12)	(0.18)	(0.08)	(0.01)
$10^{-1} \times D_{SR} \times \tau$	**−0.05**	−0.02	−0.02	**0.10**	**−0.27**	0.00	**0.27**	0.39	−0.06	−0.01	−0.03	0.02	0.39	0.03
	(0.02)	(0.02)	(0.04)	(0.05)	(0.14)	(0.17)	(0.13)	(0.22)	(0.04)	(0.03)	(0.02)	(0.04)	(0.02)	(0.01)
$10^{-2} \times D_{SR} \times \tau^2$	**0.02**	−0.01	−0.01	0.00	0.01	0.03	−0.02	−0.01	0.01	0.00	**0.02**	0.01	0.10	0.02
	(0.00)	(0.01)	(0.01)	(0.01)	(0.03)	(0.04)	(0.03)	(0.06)	(0.01)	(0.01)	(0.01)	(0.01)	(0.00)	(0.01)
$D_{SR} \times \tau^{-1}$	−0.03	−0.04	−0.08	−0.04	0.08	−0.13	0.07	0.32	−0.07	0.03	−0.01	0.02	0.41	0.02
	(0.02)	(0.04)	(0.05)	(0.06)	(0.18)	(0.23)	(0.17)	(0.25)	(0.05)	(0.04)	(0.03)	(0.05)	(0.02)	(0.01)
D_{LR}	**−1.11**	−0.10	0.03	**0.60**	**−2.76**	1.35	**1.32**	1.19	−0.22	−0.06	**−0.22**	**−0.43**	1.85	0.05
	(0.07)	(0.12)	(0.19)	(0.23)	(0.69)	(0.79)	(0.63)	(0.88)	(0.20)	(0.17)	(0.11)	(0.18)	(0.08)	(0.01)
$10^{-1} \times D_{LR} \times \tau$	**−0.05**	−0.01	0.00	**0.06**	**−0.38**	0.00	0.12	0.13	−0.01	**−0.08**	**−0.07**	0.03	0.29	0.04
	(0.01)	(0.01)	(0.03)	(0.03)	(0.09)	(0.11)	(0.08)	(0.15)	(0.03)	(0.02)	(0.02)	(0.02)	(0.01)	(0.01)
$10^{-2} \times D_{LR} \times \tau^2$	**0.01**	**−0.01**	−0.01	−0.01	**0.06**	0.04	−0.02	0.01	0.00	0.01	**0.02**	0.01	0.08	0.03
	(0.00)	(0.00)	(0.01)	(0.01)	(0.02)	(0.03)	(0.02)	(0.04)	(0.01)	(0.01)	(0.00)	(0.01)	(0.00)	(0.01)
$D_{LR} \times \tau^{-1}$	**−0.05**	−0.04	0.02	**0.12**	0.02	−0.14	**−0.32**	−0.28	0.02	**−0.07**	**−0.04**	−0.02	0.38	0.02
	(0.02)	(0.03)	(0.04)	(0.05)	(0.14)	(0.18)	(0.13)	(0.19)	(0.04)	(0.03)	(0.02)	(0.04)	(0.01)	(0.01)
holiday	**0.12**	**−0.02**	0.00	**−0.34**	0.00	**0.26**	0.08	**−0.18**	**0.05**	−0.01	**0.03**	**0.05**	0.19	0.16
	(0.01)	(0.01)	(0.02)	(0.02)	(0.06)	(0.08)	(0.06)	(0.09)	(0.02)	(0.02)	(0.01)	(0.02)	(0.00)	(0.02)
holiday $* D$	**−0.06**	0.00	0.00	**0.13**	0.06	−0.16	−0.02	0.16	−0.04	0.03	−0.01	−0.03	0.22	0.04
	(0.01)	(0.01)	(0.02)	(0.03)	(0.09)	(0.10)	(0.08)	(0.12)	(0.02)	(0.02)	(0.01)	(0.02)	(0.01)	(0.01)
weekend	**0.03**	**0.04**	0.02	**−0.12**	**0.15**	**0.23**	**0.22**	0.00	**0.04**	**−0.02**	**0.03**	**−0.04**	0.37	0.02
	(0.01)	(0.01)	(0.02)	(0.02)	(0.06)	(0.08)	(0.06)	(0.09)	(0.02)	(0.01)	(0.01)	(0.02)	(0.00)	(0.00)
weekend $* D$	0.00	**−0.08**	−0.01	**−0.73**	**−0.14**	−0.08	0.11	0.07	−0.03	0.01	0.00	0.03	0.32	0.24
	(0.01)	(0.01)	(0.02)	(0.02)	(0.07)	(0.08)	(0.06)	(0.09)	(0.02)	(0.02)	(0.01)	(0.02)	(0.00)	(0.01)
prom	−0.01	−0.01	0.02	**0.22**	−0.06	**0.42**	**0.26**	0.11	0.01	0.00	0.00	**−0.04**	0.26	0.06
	(0.01)	(0.01)	(0.02)	(0.02)	(0.07)	(0.09)	(0.07)	(0.10)	(0.02)	(0.02)	(0.01)	(0.02)	(0.01)	(0.01)
prom $* D$	**0.14**	0.02	−0.01	**−0.07**	**0.27**	−0.17	−0.12	−0.11	0.03	0.01	**0.04**	**0.07**	0.27	0.04
	(0.01)	(0.02)	(0.03)	(0.03)	(0.10)	(0.11)	(0.09)	(0.12)	(0.03)	(0.02)	(0.02)	(0.03)	(0.01)	(0.01)

Note. $D_{SR} = 1$ in the first three months following entry after which $D_{LR} = 1$, and $D = D_{SR} + D_{LR}$. Posterior means with posterior standard deviation are in parentheses.

Singh, Hansen, and Blattberg: *Market Entry and Consumer Behavior: An Investigation of a Wal-Mart Supercenter*
Marketing Science 25(5), pp. 457–476, ©2006 INFORMS   469

Figure 4   Distributions of Inter-Store-Visit Times

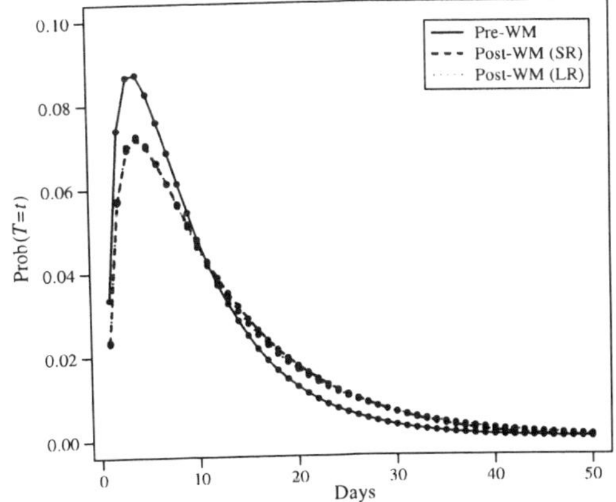

Note. WM = Wal-Mart; SR = short run; LR = long run.

households is due to unobserved factors. Prior to Wal-Mart's entry, consumers derive higher utility shopping on week-ends and during holidays, although the effect of holiday shopping goes down after entry. Interestingly, promotional sensitivity is significantly higher following Wal-Mart's entry. This could be due to changes in consumer base (higher proportion of promotional-sensitive consumer shopping at the store), an inherent change within consumers, or some promotional tactics used by the retailer.

Because it is hard to directly interpret the coefficients of the variables that are functions of τ ("time since last purchase"), we plot the implied distributions of store-visit times. Figure 4 shows the distribution of store-visit times prior to Wal-Mart entry, and the distribution in the short and long run after entry. It is evident that the average inter-store-visit time increases after Wal-Mart's entry (since probability mass shifts from smaller duration times to larger). There does not appear to be a significant difference in the short- and long-run effects.

To indicate the potential impact of customer characteristics on store visits, we plot in Figure 5 the implied distributions of store-visit timing before and after Wal-Mart's entry for three select households. The top graph shows the distribution for household number 1985 in the sample. This household is located very close to the incumbent store. The middle graph shows the visit-time distribution for household number 7202, which is located right next to Wal-Mart. It is apparent from the graphs that the entry of Wal-Mart had very different impacts on these two households, suggesting that household location can be potentially important in explaining impacts across households. Next consider the visit-time distribution for household number

170 (the lower panel in Figure 5). This household is also located close to Wal-Mart and is in fact a neighbor of household number 7202. Surprisingly, we find that entry of Wal-Mart had little impact on household 170. However, a deeper probe into the purchase behavior can explain why we observe these different reactions by these households. Prior to Wal-Mart' entry, household 170 visits the incumbent store twice as frequently and with a significantly smaller basket size compared with household 7202. More importantly, 78% of the total trips for household 170 occur between 9 A.M. and 5 P.M. on (nonholiday) weekdays (compared with only 9% for household 7202). This in turn implies the presence of a retired or otherwise unemployed person in household 170. Thus, besides distance, a number of other household characteristics are important in determining the likely impact of Wal-Mart's entry. We explore these issues further in §6.

Table 4 shows the estimates for the basket-size Equations (9) and (10). The Wal-Mart dummy for the short and long run are negative and significant, indicating that the average basket size goes down after Wal-Mart's entry. The coefficient to τ shows that basket size tends to increase with time since the previous purchase. Basket sizes also tend to be higher during weekends and holidays, although the latter effect is mitigated by Wal-Mart's entry. The promotion parameter has an incorrect sign pre-entry, perhaps due to the aggregate store-level measure that we use. However, similar to the store-visit equation, the promotional sensitivity increases significantly after Wal-Mart. Although not reported here, correlation between the basket size intercept and promotion sensitivity indicates that small basket households are more promotion sensitive, which is consistent with the findings in the previous literature (Bell and Lattin 1998). Looking across the demographic coefficients, we find several of the household characteristics to be significant and the total proportion of the heterogeneity variation explained is a bit higher compared to the store-visit equation. However, there is evidence of substantial unobserved heterogeneity in the coefficients as indicated by the large standard deviation parameters.

Monthly Expenditures
One of the advantages of the Bayesian procedure used for inference is that it provides us with household-level estimates (for example, the posterior mean of θ_i for each household) as a byproduct of the MCMC procedure. These household-level parameters can be used to quantify the combined effect of entry on duration times and basket size by simulating expected monthly expenditure for each household (holding other variables fixed at their mean levels). This amounts to computing the expected value of (2) for $T = 30$ for each household before and after Wal-

Singh, Hansen, and Blattberg: *Market Entry and Consumer Behavior: An Investigation of a Wal-Mart Supercenter*
470
Marketing Science 25(5), pp. 457–476, © 2006 INFORMS

Figure 5   Distributions of Inter-Store-Visit Times for Three Households

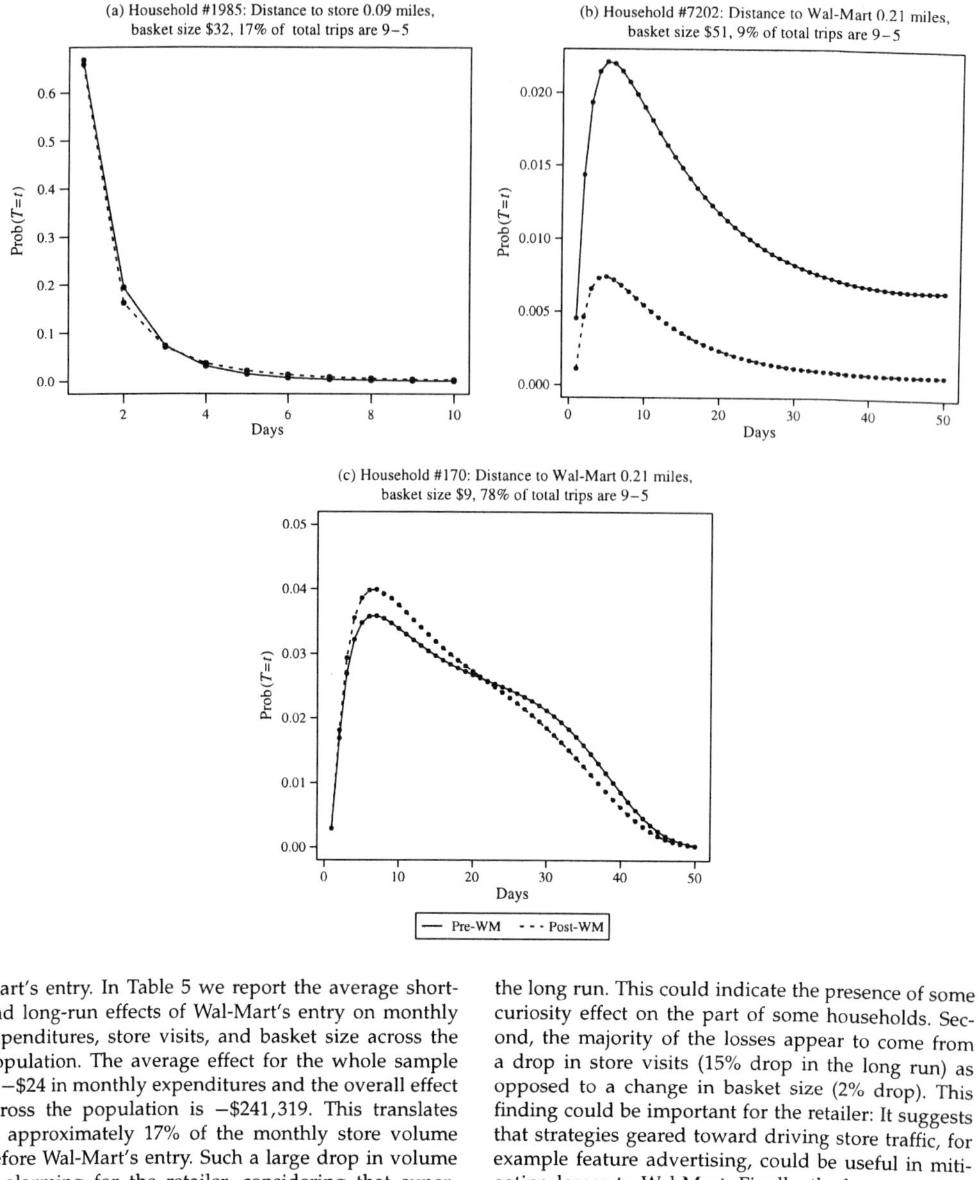

(a) Household #1985: Distance to store 0.09 miles, basket size $32, 17% of total trips are 9–5

(b) Household #7202: Distance to Wal-Mart 0.21 miles, basket size $51, 9% of total trips are 9–5

(c) Household #170: Distance to Wal-Mart 0.21 miles, basket size $9, 78% of total trips are 9–5

Mart's entry. In Table 5 we report the average short- and long-run effects of Wal-Mart's entry on monthly expenditures, store visits, and basket size across the population. The average effect for the whole sample is −$24 in monthly expenditures and the overall effect across the population is −$241,319. This translates to approximately 17% of the monthly store volume before Wal-Mart's entry. Such a large drop in volume is alarming for the retailer, considering that supermarkets operate on the principle of high volume with profit margins only in the range of 1%–2%.

Three observations are notable from the numbers presented in Table 5. First, the effect of Wal-Mart seems a little larger in the short run compared with the long run. This could indicate the presence of some curiosity effect on the part of some households. Second, the majority of the losses appear to come from a drop in store visits (15% drop in the long run) as opposed to a change in basket size (2% drop). This finding could be important for the retailer: It suggests that strategies geared toward driving store traffic, for example feature advertising, could be useful in mitigating losses to Wal-Mart. Finally, the large standard deviations in Table 5 suggest that the impact of Wal-Mart varies dramatically across households. The large standard deviations in turn suggest that characterizing the households that are affected by Wal-Mart's entry the most may be of interest.

Singh, Hansen, and Blattberg: *Market Entry and Consumer Behavior: An Investigation of a Wal-Mart Supercenter*
Marketing Science 25(5), pp. 457–476, ©2006 INFORMS

471

Table 4   Hierarchical Coefficient Estimates, Basket Size Model

Attribute	Constant	STDIST	PROXWM	MSHOP	E-PL	E-PROD	E-MEAT	E-HMR	HHSIZE	BABY	PET	INC	SD	DEMO
Constant	**3.37**	**0.23**	0.01	**−1.08**	**−1.26**	**−1.30**	**−1.08**	−0.11	−0.05	0.21	0.04	−0.19	0.95	0.12
	(0.05)	(0.10)	(0.14)	(0.18)	(0.53)	(0.63)	(0.49)	(0.63)	(0.15)	(0.14)	(0.09)	(0.14)	(0.07)	(0.03)
D_{SR}	**−0.98**	0.08	0.29	**1.11**	**−1.11**	**1.86**	0.43	1.12	0.23	0.05	−0.16	0.28	0.71	0.28
	(0.08)	(0.14)	(0.21)	(0.24)	(0.78)	(0.85)	(0.76)	(0.81)	(0.22)	(0.19)	(0.13)	(0.21)	(0.13)	(0.09)
D_{LR}	**−0.97**	0.08	0.28	**1.13**	**−1.14**	**2.04**	0.45	1.29	0.18	0.08	−0.14	0.29	0.71	0.28
	(0.08)	(0.14)	(0.21)	(0.24)	(0.78)	(0.85)	(0.77)	(0.81)	(0.22)	(0.19)	(0.13)	(0.21)	(0.13)	(0.09)
τ	**0.01**	**−0.01**	0.00	**0.01**	0.00	0.01	0.00	0.01	0.00	0.00	**0.01**	0.00	0.04	0.02
	(0.00)	(0.00)	(0.00)	(0.00)	(0.01)	(0.01)	(0.01)	(0.01)	(0.00)	(0.00)	(0.00)	(0.00)	(0.00)	(0.00)
prom	**−0.04**	**−0.01**	0.02	**0.12**	0.08	**0.21**	0.12	−0.01	**0.06**	0.00	**0.02**	**0.04**	0.15	0.09
	(0.01)	(0.01)	(0.02)	(0.03)	(0.08)	(0.09)	(0.07)	(0.09)	(0.02)	(0.02)	(0.01)	(0.02)	(0.01)	(0.02)
prom $* D$	**0.13**	−0.01	−0.04	**−0.14**	0.11	−0.28	−0.03	−0.13	−0.03	−0.01	0.02	−0.04	0.11	0.21
	(0.01)	(0.02)	(0.03)	(0.03)	(0.11)	(0.12)	(0.11)	(0.12)	(0.03)	(0.03)	(0.02)	(0.03)	(0.02)	(0.07)
weekend	**0.02**	0.01	0.00	**−0.11**	0.11	0.01	0.09	−0.03	−0.02	0.01	**0.04**	−0.03	0.28	0.02
	(0.01)	(0.01)	(0.02)	(0.02)	(0.06)	(0.07)	(0.05)	(0.08)	(0.02)	(0.01)	(0.01)	(0.02)	(0.00)	(0.00)
weekend $* D$	**0.03**	0.01	0.01	**−0.24**	−0.12	0.03	−0.09	−0.02	0.00	0.00	**−0.02**	0.03	0.26	0.05
	(0.01)	(0.01)	(0.02)	(0.02)	(0.07)	(0.09)	(0.07)	(0.09)	(0.02)	(0.02)	(0.01)	(0.02)	(0.01)	(0.01)
holiday	**0.12**	−0.01	−0.03	**−0.07**	−0.02	0.16	**0.18**	**−0.22**	0.01	−0.03	0.00	**0.06**	0.21	0.04
	(0.01)	(0.01)	(0.02)	(0.02)	(0.08)	(0.09)	(0.07)	(0.10)	(0.02)	(0.02)	(0.01)	(0.02)	(0.01)	(0.01)
holiday $* D$	**−0.07**	0.01	0.04	0.01	0.10	0.07	−0.07	0.17	0.00	0.01	0.03	−0.04	0.23	0.02
	(0.01)	(0.02)	(0.03)	(0.03)	(0.11)	(0.13)	(0.10)	(0.12)	(0.03)	(0.03)	(0.02)	(0.03)	(0.01)	(0.01)

Note. $D_{SR} = 1$ in the first three months following entry after which $D_{LR} = 1$, and $D = D_{SR} + D_{LR}$. Posterior means with posterior standard deviation are in parentheses.

To dig deeper into the issue of distribution of entry effects, we assigned households into deciles based on the long-run Wal-Mart effects. In Figure 6 we plot the pre–Wal-Mart monthly expenditures, monthly store visits, and basket size for the households with the largest impact (decile 1) along with the distributions for households in deciles 2 to 10. It is apparent that Wal-Mart has the highest impact on households with large pre-entry expenditures at the incumbent. In particular, the households in the top decile have significantly higher monthly store visits (4.81 versus 3.51) and basket sizes ($63.60 versus $39.71), translating into substantially higher monthly expenditures ($255 versus $113). Aggregating across the households in the top decile, we find that this 10% of the households alone accounts for 64% of the observed losses for the incumbent.[14]

This last finding is troubling for the retailer, because Wal-Mart is stealing some of its best customers. At the same time, it also presents interesting targeting opportunities. As discussed above, traffic generation using feature advertisements could be a useful strategy to pursue. However, feature advertisement represents a communication tool that can rarely be customized to the individual level. On the other hand, customized coupons can readily be used to target the high-value customers that have defected to Wal-Mart. The frequent shopper database already contains useful purchase history and mailing address information, so pursuing such a strategy could be fruitful. By retaining the top 5% of these customers, the retailer can reduce its losses to Wal-Mart by 41%. Thus, understanding the needs and preferences of this handful of customers and the use of targeted mechanisms could be rewarding in the long run.

6. Profiling the Defectors to Wal-Mart

Results in the previous section show that the impact of Wal-Mart varies across households and that a small proportion of customers account for a large proportion of losses at the incumbent store. We now explore the extent to which the households that respond most

---

[14] Another approach to looking at the distribution of entry effects would be to assign households to deciles based on their pre-entry expenditures (most valuable to least) and then analyze Wal-Mart's impact on each decile. Looking at the joint distribution of customer value and Wal-Mart's impact (not reported in the paper), we find that almost 40% of the best customers fall in the top decile of the impact distribution.

Table 5   Before and After Wal-Mart's Entry: Monthly Expenditures, Store Visits, and Basket Size

	Before–Wal-Mart	After–Wal-Mart (SR)	After–Wal-Mart (LR)
Expenditure ($)	127.23	103.64	104.61
	(98.64)	(96.43)	(97.03)
Store visits	3.64	3.14	3.07
	(2.02)	(2.73)	(2.61)
Basket size ($)	42.06	39.79	40.67
	(26.02)	(26.03)	(24.91)

Note. Standard deviation is in parentheses. SR = short run; LR = long run.

Singh, Hansen, and Blattberg: *Market Entry and Consumer Behavior: An Investigation of a Wal-Mart Supercenter*
Marketing Science 25(5), pp. 457–476, © 2006 INFORMS

Figure 6   Pre-entry Monthly Expenditure, Store Visits, and Basket Size by Decile of Impact Distribution

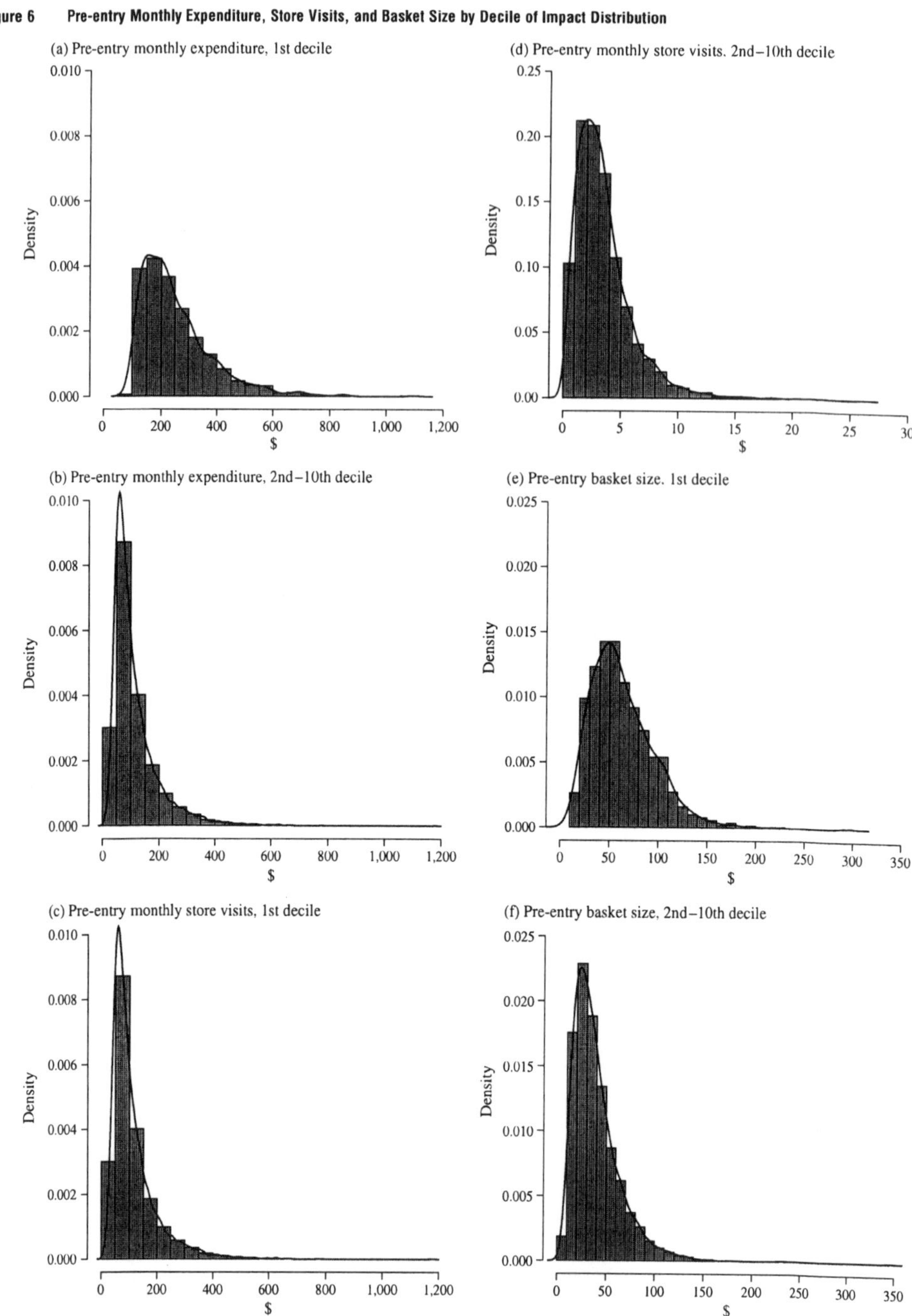

Singh, Hansen, and Blattberg: *Market Entry and Consumer Behavior: An Investigation of a Wal-Mart Supercenter*
Marketing Science 25(5), pp. 457–476, © 2006 INFORMS

to Wal-Mart can be profiled based on their locations and other observed characteristics. Note that from a managerial perspective, such profiling of households that respond to Wal-Mart can be quite important. For instance, it can allow the retailer to not only target customers with similar characteristics at this store, but also transfer the findings to other store locations where the retailer competes with Wal-Mart. To be more specific, consider the problem of identifying the consumers that are at high risk of defection at a different location where a Wal-Mart is scheduled to open in the next few months. To take findings from the experience of this store to the new location, it is important not only to identify the households based on their individual card numbers or the region in which they live, but also to map these households on some actionable demographic or other characteristics. Such mapping then becomes the basis for identifying potential defectors at the new location. Since store opening information is generally available well in advance, it can allow the retailer to take preemptive actions for the households who are at a high risk of defection.

6.1. Marginal Effects for Observed Household Characteristics

In the results presented in Tables 3 and 4, several of the household characteristics were found to be significant. We now compute the marginal effects for the observed household characteristics entering the second stage of the hierarchical model. Note that evaluating the direct impact of the elements of the covariate vector is nontrivial because the covariates affect both store-visit frequencies and basket sizes. We evaluate the overall effect of each covariate on the size of the Wal-Mart effect as follows: Let e_i denote monthly expenditure for a household. The mean pre-entry expenditure at the incumbent for a population with covariate vector $Z = z$ is

$$E[e_i \mid D_{SR} = 0, D_{LR} = 0, Z = z, \theta]$$

$$= \int E[e_i \mid D_{SR} = 0, D_{LR} = 0, Z = z, \theta, \beta_i] \phi(\beta_i \mid z\pi, \Omega)\, d\beta_i,$$

while the mean short- and long-run expenditures after entry are computed analogously with $D_{SR} = 1$ and $D_{LR} = 1$, respectively.

We consider the effect of the covariates on a specific Wal-Mart effect: The change in the log of mean expenditure in the short run and long run, i.e.,

$$\Delta_{SR}(\theta; z) \equiv \log(E[e_i \mid D_{SR} = 1, D_{LR} = 0, Z = z, \theta])$$

$$- \log(E[e_i \mid D_{SR} = 0, D_{LR} = 0, Z = z, \theta]),$$

$$\Delta_{LR}(\theta; z) \equiv \log(E[e_i \mid D_{SR} = 0, D_{LR} = 1, Z = z, \theta])$$

$$- \log(E[e_i \mid D_{SR} = 0, D_{LR} = 0, Z = z, \theta]).$$

$\Delta_{SR}(\theta; z)$ is the change in the log of mean expenditure from pre-entry to post-entry in the short run, while $\Delta_{LR}(\theta; z)$ is the long-run change for a population characterized by covariate vector z.[15] We compute the effects of changing z on $\Delta_{SR}(\theta, z)$ and $\Delta_{LR}(\theta, z)$. In particular, for each covariate z_j we compute

$$\delta_{SR}(\theta, z_{j, \%5}) \equiv \Delta_{SR}(\theta, z_{j, \%5}) - \Delta_{SR}(\theta, \bar{z}),$$

$$\delta_{SR}(\theta, z_{j, \%95}) \equiv \Delta_{SR}(\theta, z_{j, \%95}) - \Delta_{SR}(\theta, \bar{z}),$$

$$\delta_{SR}(\theta, \bar{z}_j + \mathrm{sd}_j) \equiv \Delta_{SR}(\theta, \bar{z} + \mathrm{sd}_j) - \Delta_{SR}(\theta, \bar{z})$$

(and similarly for δ_{LR}), where $\bar{z}$ is the sample average of the covariate vector, $z_{j, 5\%}$ ($z_{j, 95\%}$) is equal to $\bar{z}$ except for covariate j, which is equal to its 5th percentile (95th percentile), while $\bar{z} + z_{j, \mathrm{sd}}$ is equal to $\bar{z}$ except for covariate j, which is equal to $\bar{z}_j$ plus a one standard deviation increase. These effects capture the marginal effect of changing covariate j on the short- and long-run Wal-Mart effect. In Table 6 we report the posterior mean and standard deviation of $\delta_{SR}(\theta; z)$ and $\delta_{LR}(\theta; z)$ for different values of z. For example, for store distance (STDIST) we see that changing the store distance variable from its mean to its 5th percentile (i.e., a population that is very close to the local store) decreases the Wal-Mart effect by 1%, while changing it to the 95th percentile increases the mean Wal-Mart effect by 4%. A one standard deviation increase in distance increases the mean Wal-Mart effect by 2%. In general, the marginal effects of both distance variables are rather small, a point we return to below.

A few covariates do have a substantial impact on the size of the Wal-Mart effect. For example, the measure for shopping costs seems quite important. Recall that the variable MSHOP (percent of trips between 9 A.M.–5 P.M. weekdays) was created as proxy for the presence of a retired or otherwise unemployed member in the household. From the marginal effects we see that the households that do the majority of their shopping between 9 A.M. and 5 P.M. on weekdays are significantly less likely to abandon the incumbent. This finding is not surprising, because these households would tend to have better opportunities to take advantage of the promotions offered at all of the stores in the neighborhood. Similarly, the proportion of expenditures on private label is quite important. In particular, a one standard deviation increase in the private label expenditure ratio (E-PL) increases the size of the Wal-Mart effect by 13% in the short run (16% in long run) compared with the mean effect, thus almost doubling the overall effect for this subpopulation. On the other hand, households with the lowest E-PL have a Wal-Mart effect 14% smaller than the

---

[15] Note that it is not possible to define the effect as the change in the mean of log expenditure, because expenditure has nonzero probability mass at zero (corresponding to moving all expenditures to Wal-Mart).

Singh, Hansen, and Blattberg: *Market Entry and Consumer Behavior: An Investigation of a Wal-Mart Supercenter*
474
Marketing Science 25(5), pp. 457–476, © 2006 INFORMS

Table 6   Effects of Covariates on Mean Wal-Mart Effect

Attribute	Short-run effect: $\Delta_{SR}(\theta; z)$				Long-run effect: $\Delta_{LR}(\theta; z)$			
	$Z = \bar{z}$	$Z = z_{5\%}$	$Z = z_{95\%}$	$Z = \bar{z} + \mathrm{sd}_z$	$Z = \bar{z}$	$Z = z_{5\%}$	$Z = z_{95\%}$	$Z = \bar{z} + \mathrm{sd}_z$
STDIST	−0.22 (0.02)	−0.21 (0.02)	−0.28 0.03	−0.25 (0.02)	−0.22 (0.02)	−0.20 (0.02)	−0.28 0.03	−0.25 (0.02)
PROXWM	−0.22 (0.02)	−0.22 (0.02)	−0.30 0.03	−0.24 (0.02)	−0.22 (0.02)	−0.21 (0.02)	−0.31 0.03	−0.24 (0.02)
MSHOP	−0.22 (0.02)	−0.40 (0.02)	−0.05 (0.02)	−0.12 (0.02)	−0.22 (0.02)	−0.37 (0.02)	−0.06 (0.02)	−0.12 (0.02)
E-PL	−0.22 (0.02)	−0.12 (0.02)	−0.35 (0.02)	−0.30 (0.02)	−0.22 (0.02)	−0.06 (0.02)	−0.39 (0.02)	−0.32 (0.02)
E-PROD	−0.22 (0.02)	−0.22 (0.02)	−0.23 (0.02)	−0.23 (0.02)	−0.22 (0.02)	−0.24 (0.02)	−0.20 (0.02)	−0.21 (0.02)
E-MEAT	−0.22 (0.02)	−0.28 (0.02)	−0.14 (0.02)	−0.18 (0.02)	−0.22 (0.02)	−0.29 (0.02)	−0.11 (0.02)	−0.16 (0.02)
E-HMR	−0.22 (0.02)	−0.24 (0.02)	−0.18 (0.02)	−0.19 (0.02)	−0.22 (0.02)	−0.25 (0.02)	−0.16 (0.02)	−0.17 (0.02)
HHSIZE	−0.22 (0.02)	−0.19 (0.02)	−0.26 (0.02)	−0.25 (0.02)	−0.22 (0.02)	−0.18 (0.02)	−0.27 (0.02)	−0.25 (0.02)
BABY	−0.22 (0.02)	−0.22 (0.02)	−0.26 0.03	−0.23 (0.02)	−0.22 (0.02)	−0.22 (0.02)	−0.24 (0.03)	−0.22 (0.02)
PET	−0.22 (0.02)	−0.25 (0.02)	−0.18 (0.02)	−0.21 (0.02)	−0.22 (0.02)	−0.24 (0.02)	−0.17 (0.02)	−0.21 (0.02)
INC	−0.22 (0.02)	−0.26 (0.02)	−0.18 (0.02)	−0.20 (0.02)	−0.22 (0.02)	−0.27 (0.02)	−0.14 (0.02)	−0.18 (0.02)

Note. Posterior means with posterior standard deviation are in parentheses.

average in the short run (19% in the long run), making the effect virtually zero for this subpopulation. These findings indicate that households who spend a large fraction of their total grocery expenditure on the private label brand are—on average—much more likely to switch to Wal-Mart. Thus, we find that store-brand buyers have a higher likelihood of moving purchases to Wal-Mart, which is in contrast to the findings in the previous literature that suggest that store-brand buyers are also more store loyal (Corstjens and Lal 2000).

Table 6 also shows that households that spend a large proportion on speciality meat and home meal replacement (HMR) items are less likely to defect to Wal-Mart. This seems consistent with the industry reports that these items are better catered at supermarkets rather than at Wal-Mart. Overall, the shopping- and purchase-related variables appear more important than demographic variables. Although the low explanatory power of demographics is a general phenomenon reported in the literature (e.g., see Rossi et al. 1996), we should acknowledge that our demographic variables were computed using census data and may not be as accurate in standard scanner panel data.

6.2. Customer Locations

The discussion above shows that store distances play a relatively minor role in determining the propensity to shift purchases to Wal-Mart. This seems quite in contrast to the findings in the retail site selection literature (Huff 1964, Brown 1989, Craig et al. 1984, and so on) as well as business press (*Progressive Grocer*, 69th annual report, 2002), namely that location is one of the most important factors in determining store choice. Given the importance of location in the retailing world, we re-estimate the model with a different specification that alleviates the high-correlation problem discussed above, to a certain extent. In particular, in the new specification we replace the household characteristics in the second stage of the hierarchical model (11) with $Z_i = \{D_{ji}^r\}_{i=1}^n$, where D_{ji}^r is an indicator variable equal to one if household i is located in census tract region j. This approach has several advantages over the specification that includes distances directly. First, as pointed out, the correlation between distance to the focal store and distance to Wal-Mart is 0.96 in our sample, which makes estimating two separate distance effects difficult. Second, we use a fairly fine grid of regions in our dummy specification that provides us with a clean nonparametric estimate of the distance effects. Finally, the dummy specification allows us to capture other census tract–specific characteristics apart from distance, such as demographics and actions of other retailers in the region. The market has another (independent) supermarket (located in Region 6) as well as several other small convenience or food stores. Thus each dummy coefficient

Singh, Hansen, and Blattberg: *Market Entry and Consumer Behavior: An Investigation of a Wal-Mart Supercenter*
Marketing Science 25(5), pp. 457–476, © 2006 INFORMS

475

Table 7 Average Characteristics for the 19 Census Tract Regions

| Group ID | Frequency | Average distance in miles to | | Percentage change in expenditure after |
		Focal store	Wal-Mart	Wal-Mart (std. dev.)
1	392	6.10	3.70	−25 (48)
2	242	6.88	7.69	−18 (36)
3	1,026	14.11	14.32	−27 (38)
4	241	2.38	1.85	−19 (36)
5	435	1.24	1.57	−16 (34)
6	292	1.33	1.86	−16 (34)
7	345	1.64	2.31	−15 (35)
8	309	2.16	4.51	−17 (34)
9	747	1.65	3.10	−17 (32)
10	1,221	0.64	2.72	−13 (37)
11	249	2.61	4.16	−18 (37)
12	315	5.00	4.63	−18 (40)
13	674	5.10	7.48	−11 (33)
14	626	5.98	7.98	−23 (37)
15	884	0.39	2.35	−15 (38)
16	820	0.71	3.16	−13 (38)
17	963	1.41	3.91	−13 (36)
18	240	2.27	0.82	−38 (34)
19	3,317	1.81	2.42	−18 (40)

will represent the coefficient for a region with a certain composition of distance to Wal-Mart and the local store and other tract-specific information.

The results are presented in Table 7. Note that the regions show considerable variation in distance, ranging from regions very close to the focal store (Regions 15, 10, and 16) to regions close to Wal-Mart (Region 18) to regions far away from both stores (e.g., Region 3). The last column of Table 7 shows the simulated effects and standard deviations by region in the long run (short-run effects are similar). With this specification, we do observe an overall effect of store distance. In particular, the impact is higher in areas close to Wal-Mart (−38% in Region 18) and areas far from both stores (Region 3). The impact of Wal-Mart's entry is lowest in regions close to the incumbent store. However, large standard deviation numbers indicate that even with this specification there is considerable variation across households within a region.

7. Discussion and Future Research

One of the biggest challenges facing the supermarket industry is competition from Wal-Mart. Although a relatively new player, Wal-Mart through its supercenter format has become the nation's largest grocer, and supermarket managers consider it their biggest concern in the coming years. Using a unique frequent-shopper database, we provide an empirical study of the impact of a Wal-Mart supercenter's entry on the sales of a traditional grocery store. We model the two key household decisions of whether to visit the store and in-store expenditure using a flexible model of interpurchase time and basket size. Heterogeneity across households is modeled using a hierarchical

structure that allows the response parameters to vary due to observed and unobserved factors. In order to characterize the potential defectors to Wal-Mart, we use a large set of household-specific variables such as distance to the stores, demographics, and other shopping characteristics.

Results show that the incumbent store lost 17% volume—amounting to a quarter million dollars in monthly revenue—following Wal-Mart's entry. Decomposing the lost sales into components attributed to store visits and in-store expenditures, we find that the majority of these losses were due to fewer store visits with little change seen in basket size. This finding suggests that strategies designed to increase store traffic could be effective in mitigating losses to Wal-Mart. We also find that the retailer loses some of its best customers to Wal-Mart, and that a small increase in retention of these customers can significantly reduce losses attributed to Wal-Mart. Thus the retailer should focus its attention on these select households by understanding their needs and preferences. Finally, we find that certain observed household characteristics—such as distance, shopping behavior, and product purchase behavior—can be useful in profiling the defectors to Wal-Mart.

There are, of course, several caveats to our analysis and potential directions for future research. Foremost, our focus in this paper has been on the two broad household decisions of store visit and basket size, while ignoring the basket-composition aspect. Although a Wal-Mart supercenter carries all products typically found in a supermarket, variation in the quality of products (e.g., in produce and meat), as well as the breadth and depth of assortment, can lead to differential impact across departments and categories. Thus, it is conceivable that while the basket size remains constant, the basket composition changes. Since retailers increasingly employ category management tools where each category is treated as a strategic business unit and pricing, merchandising, promotions, and product mix are determined at the category level (Blattberg and Fox 1995), a category-by-category analysis is important to analyze the differential impact across product groups. In doing so, one can draw upon the extensive literature on developing defensive marketing strategies (e.g., the various strategies suggested in the DEFENDER type models, Hauser and Shugan 1983) to enhance category-level retention. Finally, given the asymmetries across grocery retailers and supercenters in costs and product assortments, it may be useful to study their competition from a game theoretic perspective to analyze the optimal response by incumbents to entry by a dominant retailer (Ailawadi et al. 2005).

There are also several shortcomings related to the data used in the analysis. First, we do not observe consumer purchases outside the store in question. Similarly, our analysis is based on expenditures rather than profitability. It is possible that the defectors to Wal-Mart are not only high-revenue customers, but are also more profitable. Finally, another avenue for future research is based on our finding that the majority of the losses at the store are due to fewer store visits. This suggests that it is important for the retailers to figure out the products that are best suited to drive store traffic. Given that the retailer has to choose a subset of 50 to 100 products from a total of over 50,000 unique UPCs, this can be a nontrivial task. However, with better data and advancements in computing power, we hope some of these issues can be addressed in the future.

References

Ailawadi, Kusum, Praveen Kopalle, Scott Neslin. 2005. Predicting competitive response to a major policy change: Combining game-theoretic and empirical analysis. *Marketing Sci.* **24**(1) 12–24.

Allenby, G., P. Rossi. 1999. Marketing models of consumer heterogeneity. *J. Econometrics* **89**(2) 57–78.

BBC News. 2000. Safeway scraps loyalty card. (May 4).

Bell, D., J. Lattin. 1998. Shopping behavior and consumer preference for store price format: Why large basket shoppers prefer EDLP. *Marketing Sci.* (1) 66–88.

Bell, D., Teck-Hua Ho, Christopher S. Tang. 1998. Determining where to shop: Fixed and variable costs of shopping. *J. Marketing Res.* **35** 352–369.

Blattberg, Robert C., Edward J. Fox. 1995. Category management. Center of Retail Management, Northwestern University, Evanston, IL.

Blattberg, Robert C., Scott A. Neslin. 1990. *Sales Promotions: Concepts, Methods, and Strategies.* Prentice-Hall, Englewood Cliffs, NJ.

Brown, Stephen. 1989. Retail location theory: The legacy of Herald hotelling. *J. Retailing* **65** 450–470.

Chintagunta, P. 1993. Investigating purchase incidence, brand choice and purchase quantity decisions of households. *Marketing Sci.* **12**(2) 184–208.

Chintagunta, P., S. Haldar. 1998. Investigating purchase timing behavior in two related product categories. *J. Marketing Res.* **35**(1) 43–53.

Corstjens, Marcel, Rajiv Lal. 2000. Building store loyalty through store brands. *J. Marketing Res.* **37** 281–291.

Cox, D. R. 1972. Regression models and life tables (with discussion). *J. Roy. Statist. Soc. Ser. B* **34** 187–220.

Craig, Samuel C., Avijit Ghosh, Sara McLafferty. 1984. Models of retail location process: A review. *J. Retailing* **60** 5–36.

Fox, E., A. Montgomery, L. Lodish. 2004. Consumer shopping and spending across retail formats. *J. Bus.* **77**(2) 525–560.

Gupta, S. 1991. Stochastic models of interpurchase time with time-dependent covariates. *J. Marketing Res.* **28** 1–15.

Hansen, Karsten, Vishal Singh, Pradeep Chintagunta. 2006. Understanding store brand purchase behavior across categories. *Marketing Sci.* **25**(1) 75–90.

Hauser, J., S. Shugan. 1983. Defensive marketing strategies. *Marketing Sci.* **2**(4) 319–360.

Helsen, K., David Schmittlein. 1993. Analyzing duration times in marketing: Evidence for the effectiveness of hazard rate models. *Marketing Sci.* **12**(4) 395–414.

Hoch, Stephen. 1996. How should national brands think about private labels? *Sloan Management Rev.* **37**(2) 89–102.

Huff, David. 1964. Defining and estimating a trading area. *J. Marketing* **28** 34–38.

Jain, Dipak, Naufel Vilcassim. 1991. Investigating household purchase timing decisions: A conditional hazard function approach. *Marketing Sci.* 1–23.

KPFT News. 2002. Wal-Mart's Texas union-busting tactics. (November 15).

Lal, R., C. Matutes. 1989. Price competition in multi-market duopolies. *Rand J. Econom.* **30** 516–537.

Lal, R., R. Rao. 1997. Supermarket competition: The case of everyday low-pricing. *Marketing Sci.* **1** 60–80.

Messinger, P., C. Narasimhan. 1997. A model of retail formats based on consumers economizing on shopping time. *Marketing Sci.* **16** 1–23.

National Grocers Association. 2003. NGA Marketing Survey.

Pauwels, Koen, Shuba Srinivasan. 2004. Who benefits from store brand entry? *Marketing Sci.* **23**(3) 364–390.

Pesendorfer, M. 2002. Retail sales: A study of pricing behaviour in supermarkets. *J. Bus.* **75** 33–66.

Phibbs, C. S., H. S. Luft. 1995. Correlation of travel time on roads versus straight line distance. *Medical Care Res. Rev.* **52** 532–542.

Progressive Grocer, various issues.

Supermarket Business News, various issues.

Reichheld, Frederick F., Thomas Teal. 1996. *The Loyalty Effect: The Hidden Force Behind Growth, Profits, and Lasting Value.* Harvard Business School Press, Cambridge, MA.

Rogers. 2001. With Wal-Mart, Look, Don't Listen. *Supermarket Business* (15 January).

Rossi, P., R. McCulloch, G. Allenby. 1996. On the value of household information in target marketing. *Marketing Sci.* **15** 321–340.

Seetharaman, P. B., P. Chintagunta. 2003. The proportional hazards model for purchase timing: A comparison of alternative specifications. *J. Bus. Econom. Statist.* **21**(3) 368–382.

Singh, V. 2002. Consumer behavior and firm strategies in a changing retail environment. Ph.D. thesis, Kellogg School of Management, Northwestern University, Evanston, IL.

Time Magazine. 2003. Can Wal-Mart Get Any Bigger? (January 13).

Wall Street Journal. 2003. "Price War in Aisle 3." (May 27).

Wedel, M., W. A. Kamakura, W. S. Desarbo, F. T. Hofstede. 1995. Implications for asymmetry, nonproportionality and heterogeneity in brand switching from piecewise exponential mixture hazard models. *J. Marketing Res.* **32**(4) 457–462.